41: *Afro-American Poets Since 1955,* edited by Trudier Harris and Thadious M. Davis (1985)

42: *American Writers for Children Before 1900,* edited by Glenn E. Estes (1985)

43: *American Newspaper Journalists, 1690-1872,* edited by Perry J. Ashley (1986)

44: *American Screenwriters,* Second Series, edited by Randall Clark, Robert E. Morsberger, and Stephen O. Lesser (1986)

45: *American Poets, 1880-1945,* First Series, edited by Peter Quartermain (1986)

46: *American Literary Publishing Houses, 1900-1980: Trade and Paperback,* edited by Peter Dzwonkoski (1986)

47: *American Historians, 1866-1912,* edited by Clyde N. Wilson (1986)

48: *American Poets, 1880-1945,* Second Series, edited by Peter Quartermain (1986)

49: *American Literary Publishing Houses, 1638-1899,* 2 parts, edited by Peter Dzwonkoski (1986)

50: *Afro-American Writers Before the Harlem Renaissance,* edited by Trudier Harris (1986)

51: *Afro-American Writers from the Harlem Renaissance to 1940,* edited by Trudier Harris (1987)

52: *American Writers for Children Since 1960: Fiction,* edited by Glenn E. Estes (1986)

53: *Canadian Writers Since 1960,* First Series, edited by W. H. New (1986)

54: *American Poets, 1880-1945,* Third Series, 2 parts, edited by Peter Quartermain (1987)

55: *Victorian Prose Writers Before 1867,* edited by William B. Thesing (1987)

56: *German Fiction Writers, 1914-1945,* edited by James Hardin (1987)

57: *Victorian Prose Writers After 1867,* edited by William B. Thesing (1987)

58: *Jacobean and Caroline Dramatists,* edited by Fredson Bowers (1987)

59: *American Literary Critics and Scholars, 1800-1850,* edited by John W. Rathbun and Monica M. Grecu (1987)

60: *Canadian Writers Since 1960,* Second Series, edited by W. H. New (1987)

61: *American Writers for Children Since 1960: Poets, Illustrators, and Nonfiction Authors,* edited by Glenn E. Estes (1987)

62: *Elizabethan Dramatists,* edited by Fredson Bowers (1987)

63: *Modern American Critics, 1920-1955,* edited by Gregory S. Jay (1988)

64: *American Literary Critics and Scholars, 1850-1880,* edited by John W. Rathbun and Monica M. Grecu (1988)

65: *French Novelists, 1900-1930,* edited by Catharine Savage Brosman (1988)

66: *German Fiction Writers, 1885-1913,* 2 parts, edited by James Hardin (1988)

67: *Modern American Critics Since 1955,* edited by Gregory S. Jay (1988)

68: *Canadian Writers, 1920-1959,* First Series, edited by W. H. New (1988)

69: *Contemporary German Fiction Writers,* First Series, edited by Wolfgang D. Elfe and James Hardin (1988)

70: *British Mystery Writers, 1860-1919,* edited by Bernard Benstock and Thomas F. Staley (1988)

71: *American Literary Critics and Scholars, 1880-1900,* edited by John W. Rathbun and Monica M. Grecu (1988)

72: *French Novelists, 1930-1960,* edited by Catharine Savage Brosman (1988)

73: *American Magazine Journalists, 1741-1850,* edited by Sam G. Riley (1988)

74: *American Short-Story Writers Before 1880,* edited by Bobby Ellen Kimbel, with the assistance of William E. Grant (1988)

75: *Contemporary German Fiction Writers,* Second Series, edited by Wolfgang D. Elfe and James Hardin (1988)

76: *Afro-American Writers, 1940-1955,* edited by Trudier Harris (1988)

77: *British Mystery Writers, 1920-1939,* edited by Bernard Benstock and Thomas F. Staley (1988)

78: *American Short-Story Writers, 1880-1910,* edited by Bobby Ellen Kimbel, with the assistance of William E. Grant (1988)

79: *American Magazine Journalists, 1850-1900,* edited by Sam G. Riley (1988)

(Continued on back endsheets)

American Poets Since World War II
Second Series

Dictionary of Literary Biography • Volume One Hundred Five

American Poets Since World War II
Second Series

Edited by
R. S. Gwynn
Lamar University

A Bruccoli Clark Layman Book
Gale Research Inc.
Detroit, London

Printed in the United States of America

Published simultaneously in the United Kingdom
by Gale Research International Limited
(An affiliated company of Gale Research Inc.)

The paper used in this publication meets the minimum requirements
of American National Standard for Information Sciences—Permanence
Paper for Printed Library Materials, ANSI Z39.48-1984.   ∞™

ISBN 0-8103-4585-4
91-10848 CIP

For Richard Wilbur, on the occasion of his seventieth birthday,
in honor of his distinguished contributions to American letters

Contents

Plan of the Series

The advisory board, the editors, and the publisher of the *Dictionary of Literary Biography* are joined in endorsing Mark Twain's declaration. The literature of a nation provides an inexhaustible resource of permanent worth. We intend to make literature and its creators better understood and more accessible to students and the reading public, while satisfying the standards of teachers and scholars.

To meet these requirements, *literary biography* has been construed in terms of the author's achievement. The most important thing about a writer is his writing. Accordingly, the entries in *DLB* are career biographies, tracing the development of the author's canon and the evolution of his reputation.

The purpose of *DLB* is not only to provide reliable information in a convenient format but also to place the figures in the larger perspective of literary history and to offer appraisals of their accomplishments by qualified scholars.

The publication plan for *DLB* resulted from two years of preparation. The project was proposed to Bruccoli Clark by Frederick G. Ruffner, president of the Gale Research Company, in November 1975. After specimen entries were prepared and typeset, an advisory board was formed to refine the entry format and develop the series rationale. In meetings held during 1976, the publisher, series editors, and advisory board approved the scheme for a comprehensive biographical dictionary of persons who contributed to North American literature. Editorial work on the first volume began in January 1977, and it was published in 1978. In order to make *DLB* more than a reference tool and to compile volumes that individually have claim to status as literary history, it was decided to organize volumes by topic, period, or genre. Each of these freestanding volumes provides a biographical-bibliographical guide and overview for a particular area of literature. We are convinced that this organization—as opposed to a single alphabet method—constitutes a valuable innovation in the presentation of reference material. The volume plan necessarily requires many decisions for the placement and treatment of authors who might properly be included in two or three volumes. In some instances a major figure will be included in separate volumes, but with different entries emphasizing the aspect of his career appropriate to each volume. Ernest Hemingway, for example, is represented in *American Writers in Paris, 1920-1939* by an entry focusing on his expatriate apprenticeship; he is also in *American Novelists, 1910-1945* with an entry surveying his entire career. Each volume includes a cumulative index of subject authors and articles. Comprehensive indexes to the entire series are planned.

With volume ten in 1982 it was decided to enlarge the scope of *DLB*. By the end of 1986 twenty-one volumes treating British literature had been published, and volumes for Commonwealth and Modern European literature were in progress. The series has been further augmented by the *DLB Yearbooks* (since 1981) which update published entries and add new entries to keep the *DLB* current with contemporary activity. There have also been *DLB Documentary Series* volumes which provide biographical and critical source materials for figures whose work is judged to have particular interest for students. One of these companion volumes is entirely devoted to Tennessee Williams.

We define literature as the *intellectual commerce of a nation:* not merely as belles lettres but as that ample and complex process by which ideas are generated, shaped, and transmitted. *DLB* entries are not limited to "creative writers" but extend to other figures who in their time and in their way influenced the mind of a people. Thus the series encompasses historians, journalists, publishers, and screenwriters. By this means readers of *DLB* may be aided to perceive literature not as cult scripture in the keeping of intellectual high priests but firmly positioned at the center of a nation's life.

DLB includes the major writers appropriate to each volume and those standing in the ranks immediately behind them. Scholarly and critical counsel has been sought in deciding which minor figures to include and how full their entries should be. Wherever possible, useful references are made to figures who do not warrant separate entries.

Each *DLB* volume has a volume editor responsible for planning the volume, selecting the figures for inclusion, and assigning the entries. Volume editors are also responsible for preparing, where appropriate, appendices surveying the major periodicals and literary and intellectual movements for their volumes, as well as lists of further readings. Work on the series as a whole is coordinated at the Bruccoli Clark Layman editorial center in Columbia, South Carolina, where the editorial staff is responsible for accuracy of the published volumes.

One feature that distinguishes *DLB* is the illustration policy–its concern with the iconography of literature. Just as an author is influenced by his surroundings, so is the reader's understanding of the author enhanced by a knowledge of his environment. Therefore *DLB* volumes include not only drawings, paintings, and photographs of authors, often depicting them at various stages in their careers, but also illustrations of their families and places where they lived. Title pages are regularly reproduced in facsimile along with dust jackets for modern authors. The dust jackets are a special feature of *DLB* because they often document better than anything else the way in which an author's work was perceived in its own time. Specimens of the writers' manuscripts are included when feasible.

Samuel Johnson rightly decreed that "The chief glory of every people arises from its authors." The purpose of the *Dictionary of Literary Biography* is to compile literary history in the surest way available to us–by accurate and comprehensive treatment of the lives and work of those who contributed to it.

The *DLB* Advisory Board

Foreword

In 1980 *DLB 5: American Poets Since World War II* was published in two parts. Edited by Donald J. Greiner, it contains essays on the careers of over 130 contemporary poets, the eldest of whom was born in 1904, the youngest in 1950. When work on the present volume was begun in 1988, the original intent was to provide essays on approximately 75 other poets, all of whom were born between 1915 and 1960. As the essays arrived, it soon became apparent that there would be too much material for a single volume. Thus, the present book is limited to discussion of the work of thirty poets born before 7 December 1941; a companion volume, dealing with American poets born since the attack on Pearl Harbor, will be published in 1992.

A few general statements should be made about the poets whose work is discussed here. First, several of the older poets who are included, even if their birth dates place them in an earlier generation, came to prominence relatively late in life, which is the case with Amy Clampitt and Ruth Stone; others, such as Miller Williams, Turner Cassity, and Richard Moore, simply have not been treated in earlier volumes of the *DLB;* and, in the case of Fred Chappell, his fiction is discussed in volume 6, but his prizewinning poetry is fully dealt with here for the first time.

With ethnicity and multiculturalism arising as major topics of controversy in American letters, readers may question the absence of black poets here. *DLB 41: Afro-American Poets Since 1955* contains essays on many black poets whose ages fall within the limits of this volume; others who have come to prominence since *DLB 41* was published in 1985, among them Pulitzer Prize winner Rita Dove, will be covered in the volume covering poets born in the 1940s and 1950s. Similarly, because of forthcoming or earlier volumes of the *DLB*, I have not attempted to include a proportional number of Hispanic or Native American poets, despite the frequency with which their poems have recently appeared in anthologies and textbooks. My guiding principle for including a poet has been governed by the likelihood that

readers would wish to know more about his or her literary career.

As American poetry entered the last decade of the twentieth century, serious debates about the literary canon of modernism and postmodernism flourished in the universities. In particular the desire to combine substantial numbers of women and minority writers with the study of established writers caused many English departments to rewrite curricula and design new courses. Two public television series about modern and contemporary poetry seemed to lend approval to these efforts by ranking, in "Voices and Visions" (1987), Elizabeth Bishop and Langston Hughes among the thirteen major poets of the century, and, in "The Power of the Word" (1989), by focusing attention on Native-American and Japanese-American poets. In recent decades the number of women poets, many of them graduates of university writing programs, has increased dramatically. In the 1970s only one woman, Maxine Kumin, won the Pulitzer Prize; four of the winners in the 1980s were women. In 1988 St. Martin's Press published an anthology titled *Gay and Lesbian Poetry of Our Time*—yet one more indication of how recent literary judgments have often followed lines of race, gender, and sexual preference.

Nevertheless, there remains a large measure of uniformity in the backgrounds, educational experiences, and literary careers of many of the leading figures in contemporary poetry. The typical American poet discussed here is male, is now in his fifties or sixties, came from a middle-class childhood, has at least one graduate degree, and currently teaches in a creative-writing program at a major university, where he is a tenured full professor. After a couple of early chapbooks, his first collection was published by a university press, and his most recent book, from a trade publisher, was respectfully (and briefly) critiqued in the *New York Times Book Review* by another poet. If he has not yet published a selected edition of his poems, he will soon do so. He has held fellowships from the N.E.A. and the Guggenheim Foundation, has won numerous awards, and has a new manuscript almost completed, the individual poems of which have appeared in leading quarterlies over the past few years. And so on. . . . Those who doubt the accuracy of this summary are directed to the contributors' notes in almost any anthology of contemporary American poetry.

Such a generalized biographical overview, accurate though it may be in some respects, does not indicate the true degree of diversity in the lives and works of the poets included here. At least two of the poets in this volume have no university degree; several of them have held no academic appointments and have supported themselves by free-lance writing or by following other professions. Several are editors for presses and magazines, and one is an advertising executive. Another is a librarian, and yet another was a nun for many years. One has been physically handicapped since birth, and two were air force pilots. Many of them are distinguished critics or writers of fiction. These poets represent most parts of the country, and there is one foreign-born poet among them. Some are largely identified with the locales, people, and themes of their regions, while others have ties only to the national literary culture. Thus, if there is such a thing as a "typical" poet here, he or she would probably admire Walt Whitman's paradoxical query and response: "Do I contradict myself? Very well, I contradict myself."

The current state of American poetry has become the target recently for several lively assaults. Donald Hall, whose essay "Poetry and Ambition" was widely read and discussed when it first appeared in the *Kenyon Review* in 1983, labeled the standard contemporary poetic product the "McPoem," glumly observing that "every year Ronald McDonald wins the Pulitzer." Hall's essay was reprinted in *Pushcart Prize IX: Best of the Small Presses, 1984-85* and in the February/March 1987 issue of the house organ of the Associated Writing Programs, *AWP Chronicle*, which also reprinted in 1989 "Who Killed Poetry?," an essay from *Commentary* by Joseph Epstein, editor of *The American Scholar*. Epstein notes that "Contemporary poetry is no longer a part of the regular intellectual diet. People of general intellectual interests who feel that they ought to read or at least know about works on modern society or recent history or novels that attempt to convey something about the way we live now, no longer feel the same compunction about contemporary poetry." According to Epstein, the primary culprit is the

"poetry professional" of the writing program, one of many who "published chiefly in journals sheltered by universities; they fly around the country giving readings and workshops at other colleges and universities. They live in jeans yet carry a curriculum vitae." That Epstein's remarks generated enough letters from readers to fill two subsequent issues of *AWP Chronicle* indicates how close to the mark he came. Even Donald Hall, whom most would have expected to agree with Epstein, responded with "Death to the Death of Poetry" in *Harper's*, in which he attempted to prove, largely by citing publishing statistics, that poetry in the United States is in fact flourishing.

The truth of the matter is hard to determine. It is unlikely, on the one hand, that the average man or woman on the street (or for that matter the average English major) could identify a few or, indeed, any living American poets; on the other, the U.S. Congress, that least poetic of institutions, established the position of Poet Laureate of the United States in 1986, and since that year Robert Penn Warren, Richard Wilbur, Howard Nemerov, and Mark Strand have held the office with distinction. Quality may be hard to measure, but no one could dispute that contemporary American poetry is quantitatively impressive. Ronald Wallace's anthology *Vital Signs: Contemporary American Poetry from the University Presses* (1989) contains excellent work by almost all of the major figures on the contemporary scene. *Poet's Market*, edited by Judson Jerome, began to appear on a yearly basis from Writer's Digest Books in 1986, and currently lists almost two thousand publishers of poetry in the United States. In writing "The Year in Poetry" since 1987 for the *DLB Yearbook* I have received an average of two hundred books per year, most of them impressive examples of the printer's, if not the poet's, art. The frequency with which poets give readings on college campuses and elsewhere should also be noted; it may be true that fewer people read poetry today than they did in the past, but it is also undeniable that many more *hear* it than at any period in our literary history. In short, poetry may never become a truly popular art form (those who insist that it was at some time in the past are deluding themselves), but it hardly seems in danger of vanishing.

While it is possible to find almost any type of poetry being written and published in the United States today, from performance poetry that comes perilously close to improvisational comedy to examples of traditional ballads and songs, the three major "movements" of the 1950s and 1960s still find numerous adherents in the present climate. The Academic Poets of the postwar era—Wilbur, Hecht, Nemerov—seem influential still, particularly in the adherence to traditional verse forms, in some of the work of Turner Cassity, Amy Clampitt, Richard Moore, Fred Chappell, Judson Jerome, and Miller Williams— even if the subject matter of these poets is often less rigorously allusive and, thus, more accessible than that of the earlier generation. The Beats, spokespersons for one era's counterculture, undoubtedly influenced many poets who began writing during the protest era of the late 1950s and 1960s. Even though there are few poets writing today whose work resembles Allen Ginsberg's in 1956, many poets share the Beats' distrust of the political establishment and of the icons of American culture. Poets such as Edward Field and Cynthia MacDonald display subtle links to the tradition of outrageousness that began with *Howl*. Also, the mode of confessional poetry is carried on in the work of such poets as Stephen Dunn, Jonathan Holden, and Dabney Stuart, as well as many others who use autobiographical material with a frankness that would have been rare, or even impossible, thirty years ago. The willingness of U.S. poets to talk about their marriages and divorces, their psychological problems, and their childhood traumas mirrors, for better or worse, the increased openness of contemporary society. Indeed, the possibility of a confessional poet's shocking readers has become more remote in recent times; after finding several explicit examples of same-sex erotic poetry in such an ultra-respectable place as *The Norton Anthology of Modern Poetry* one is unlikely to be surprised by any poet's attempt at *épater le bourgeois*.

Generally, one might say that contemporary poetics is thematically and formally conservative. The poems of direct social protest which proliferated in the 1960s are rare, and the type of European-inspired surrealism that was popular in the 1970s and still is prominent in the work of Charles Simic, winner of the 1990 Pulitzer Prize, has been largely replaced by a focus which, for lack of a better term, might be labeled a naturalistic one. The type of postmodernist poem-artifact made popular by the New York Poets of the 1960s and brought to its highest level by John Ashbery provides few younger poets with models. Even the so-called L = A = N = G =U = A= G = E poets remain curiosities whose work is rarely found in journals and is seriously discussed only

in the centers of avant-garde literary theory (though even James Applewhite, a committed regionalist who teaches at Duke, reveals certain influences of deconstructionist poetics). Formally, while free verse predominates in today's poetry, unmetered poems are typically arranged into neat stanzas containing the same number of lines and occasional rhymes. One rarely encounters the types of spatial "splatter painting" so common in the experimental publications in which the Black Mountain Poets used to appear, and even such modest departures as the long-line, intralinear-spaced poems such as James Dickey wrote in the 1960s are seldom seen. Indeed, some poets may be right in claiming that the only legitimate experiments to be made with poetic form lie in returning to the accentual-syllabic tradition of English verse, and Richard Moore, Judson Jerome, and Miller Williams have all addressed the subject in their critical works.

A hundred years ago both English and American poetry occupied a position similar in many respects to that of today. A tumultous century that had begun with the greatest poetic revolution since the Renaissance had almost passed, and, after the florid excesses of Algernon Charles Swinburne, the poets in England must have often asked themselves, "Whither next?" Gerard Manley Hopkins had just died, his major work known but to God and Robert Bridges, and W. B. Yeats, a young man of twenty-five, had published but one slim volume. In America, Walt Whitman had retired to his house on Mickle Street to oversee, in his last two years, the deathbed edition of *Leaves of Grass*; Emily Dickinson's first collection of poems, "corrected" by her well-meaning editors, had just appeared posthumously. Edwin Arlington Robinson had barely attained voting age; Robert Frost, Wallace Stevens, and William Carlos Williams were yet schoolboys; Ezra Pound ran in knee pants through the streets of Philadelphia; and T. S. Eliot, aged two, was the precocious youngest child of a prominent St. Louis family. One world was ending and another had scarcely begun to be conceived.

As one looks back today on the directions that poetry has taken in our own century, tangents that no one could have foreseen at its beginning, one hesitates to make predictions about future directions of American poetry or even about the permanence of the reputations of the poets discussed in this volume. The literary stock market fluctuated wildly, as the current lack of regard for such once-honored poets as Vachel Lindsay, Edgar Lee Masters, and Edna St. Vincent Millay will testify, and it may be true, as some critics have argued, that it is simply not likely for a major poet to emerge from the contemporary scene. On the other hand, it is possible that the poets and readers of some future day will look back on some of their predecessors contained in this volume and feel that sort of kinship whereby great literature has always managed to transcend the years.

I am grateful to the faculty senate of Lamar University for granting a summer development leave to work on this project. Dr. Tim Summerlin, chairman of the Department of English and Foreign Languages, provided help with student assistants, office space, and computer hardware. Dr. John Idoux, former dean of the College of Arts and Sciences and presently executive vice-president for academic affairs, has been consistent in his support for projects of this scope.

Donna Buesing and C. R. Field, both Lamar English majors, lent crucial editorial assistance, much of it of the most unrewarding sort, and Cindy Colichia and Lisa Meshell, departmental secretaries, fielded many a wayward telephone call. As always, my wife, Donna, has been the first audience for the majority of my complaints and doubts. I extend my appreciation to the authors of the essays in this volume, many of whom will be recognized by readers for their prior distinguished contributions to American letters. Finally, I am grateful for the warmth and generosity of the poets whose lives and works are covered here. Not only were they helpful in providing guidance and illustrative material but sixteen of them also sent us essays for use in the appendix, "Poets on Life and Poetry." Thanks to all those involved, this has been an especially pleasant and rewarding project.

—*R. S. Gwynn*

Acknowledgments

This book was produced by Bruccoli Clark Layman, Inc. Karen L. Rood is senior editor for the *Dictionary of Literary Biography* series. Jack Turner was the in-house editor.

Production coordinator is James W. Hipp. Systems manager is Charles D. Brower. Photography editors are Edward Scott and Timothy Lundy. Permissions editor is Jean W. Ross. Layout and graphics supervisor is Penney L. Haughton. Copyediting supervisor is Bill Adams. Typesetting supervisor is Kathleen M. Flanagan. Information systems analyst is George F. Dodge. Charles Lee Egleston is editorial associate. The production staff includes Rowena Betts, Reginald A. Bullock, Teresa Chaney, Patricia Coate, Sarah A. Estes, Robert Fowler, Mary L. Goodwin, Ellen McCracken, Kathy Lawler Merlette, Laura Garren Moore, John Myrick, Pamela D. Norton, Cathy J. Reese, Laurrè Sinckler-Reeder, Maxine K. Smalls, and Betsy L. Weinberg.

Walter W. Ross and Timothy D. Tebalt did the library research at the Thomas Cooper Library of the University of South Carolina with the assistance of the following librarians: Gwen Baxter, Daniel Boice, Faye Chadwell, Jo Cottingham, Cathy Eckman, Rhonda Felder, Gary Geer, David L. Haggard, Jens Holley, Jackie Kinder, Thomas Marcil, Laurie Preston, Jean Rhyne, Carol Tobin, Virginia Weathers, and Connie Widney.

Dictionary of Literary Biography • Volume One Hundred Five

American Poets Since World War II
Second Series

Dictionary of Literary Biography

Betty Adcock

(16 September 1938 -   )

Richard B. Sale
University of North Texas

BOOKS: *Walking Out* (Baton Rouge: Louisiana
State University Press, 1975);
Nettles (Baton Rouge: Louisiana State University
Press, 1983);
Beholdings (Baton Rouge: Louisiana State University Press, 1988).

In an entry for *Contemporary Authors* after
she had published her first collection of poems,
Betty Adcock wrote, "I care about people, our failings, our deaths and the real earth. I have no
program for salvation." The statement quietly
reveals two of the continuing concerns of her poetry: her fascination with the compelling stories
that people tell by living out their lives and her
tough refusal to lean on some transcendent deus
ex machina as a rescue from inescapable suffering. In order to transform those stories into
poems—always written with a luminous economy—Adcock has probed family history and
looked hard back into the Big Thicket area of
southeast Texas, where she was born and spent
her childhood.

Elizabeth Sharp Adcock was born on 16 September 1938 in San Augustine, Texas, the daughter of Ralph L. Sharp, a landowner, and Sylvia
Hudgins Sharp, a teacher of Latin and English.
She graduated from the Hockaday School in Dallas and attended Texas Tech University, Goddard
College (Vermont), and North Carolina State University. She is married to retired music educator
Donald B. Adcock. They live in Raleigh, North
Carolina, and have a daughter, Sylvia Elizabeth,
a journalist.

Betty Adcock, 1988

Adcock has worked as an advertising copywriter and producer and has taught in the Poets-in-the-Schools programs in North Carolina and
Virginia. She has given readings and workshops
in colleges and universities and in 1989 read

Adcock at fifteen with her father, Ralph Sharp

from her work at the Library of Congress. She was visiting writer in residence at Kalamazoo College and has taught creative writing at Duke University. She is Kenan Writer in Residence at Meredith College in Raleigh, an ongoing appointment. For over a decade she served as an editor of *Southern Poetry Review*. In addition to her three major collections, Adcock's poems have been anthologized in collections including the Borestone Mountain Poetry Awards *Best Poems of 1966* and *Best Poems of 1967*; *New Southern Poets* (1975), edited by Guy Owen and Mary C. Williams; *Contemporary Poetry of North Carolina* (1977), edited by Owen and Williams; and *The Made Thing* (1987), edited by Leon Stokesbury. Her poems and stories have also appeared in numerous journals, including *Southern Review*, *Carolina Quarterly*, *Cedar Rock*, *Chicago Review*, *Crazy Horse*, *Georgia Review*, *Kentucky Poetry Review*, *Kenyon Review*, *Mississippi Review*, *Nation*, *New American Review*, *New Virginia Review*, *Poetry Northwest*, *Tennessee Poetry Journal*, and *Tri-Quarterly*.

Adcock's first collection, *Walking Out* (1975), won the Great Lakes Colleges Association New Writers Award, and *Nettles* (1983), her second book, was the recipient of the Roanoke-Chowan Award. She received a 1984 Fellowship in Poetry from the National Endowment for the Arts and in 1985 a North Carolina Individual Artist's Grant. For her third collection, *Beholdings* (1988), Adcock won the 1989 Zoe Kincaid Brockman Memorial Award for the best volume of poetry by a North Carolinian in the preceding year.

The favorable attention *Walking Out* received was well deserved: the collection contains mature poetry in which the themes and images establish the continuing quality of Adcock's work. The anonymous reviewer for *Choice* (March 1976) commented on this maturity: "Unlike many young writers she demonstrates a competent and quiet sense of line and narrative." Her themes include the abandoned child (Adcock was six when her mother died, and the young poet grew up searching for an elusive self among relatives and places that were home-and-yet-not-home); the mystery of time and death in a South where both have a static quality; the beloved widower-father who is mythic in his stature as the inarticulate outdoorsman; and a rapport with the natural world that is more Arnoldian than Wordsworthian. Unlike William Wordsworth, Adcock's relation with nature does not provide a predictable moral or philosophical uplift but an unblinking vision of the "real earth"; she is determinedly unromantic: "Farther than wells go, animals are / whole in the skins of their deaths. / The earliest sea still lurches, giving up roots and teeth" ("Catatonic"). Adcock's fascination with nature is more like that of Matthew Arnold's in "Resignation," where he speaks of nature as the unrelenting "general life" (Adcock's "real earth"). "Not milder," Arnold writes, "is the general lot / Because our spirits have forgot, / In action's dizzying eddy whirl'd, / The something that infects the world."

Yet the overall mood of *Walking Out* is not one of hopelessness. The relief from the barren vision comes from the power of language and the positive power of human relations (although Adcock knows, with W. B. Yeats, that "they too break hearts"). Both of these powers are seen in her "Again Then," as the speaker describes a visit to her aging father:

I have come and I watch
you stroll your dusty townful
of ancestors and upstarts.

You carry a blindman's cane,
the mutter of old age.
. . . .
Words tapped my way here:
I use my own stick,
and I have learned to meet you, father,
dark to dark.

And in "Word-Game" the word *moon* is as potent
as the thing itself: "In a net of sound like the
body's / own singing web, a child / will be rising /
with light for a language."

One of the most memorable poems in *Walking Out* is the title poem. Not only does it capture
the stubborn grittiness of the old fisherman who,
when his boat capsizes, walks across the bottom
of the lake and out to air, it also moves to a metaphorical level found only in the best poems. The
poem takes on nothing of the humorous tall tale,
which such a story might suggest, but becomes a
serious mythic statement of heroic effort: "Starting over, over his head, / he reached for the
earth. / As creatures of water once called on the
future / locked in their bodies, he called on
his past. / He walked. Walked. And there was
enough / time, just enough, and luck." Such description is accomplishment enough, but the
poem pushes further into significant metaphor.
Ever after the experience the old man sees the
world differently: "Things shimmer where he is,
/ His house, his earthcolored wife and sons. /
Every place raises walls around him / the color of
old glass. / Heaven is a high clear skin." The
final image is packed with the universal made possible by the actual: "Beneath the drift of flesh his
bones remember / trying for bottom."

In her *Contemporary Authors* statement, Adcock wrote, "And I care about form. The kind
you *discover*." She usually writes an unrhymed
poem that nonetheless gives the effect of a carefully controlled structure. Yet, on occasion, she
will allow rhyme to help in building toward the climax of a poem. An example is in "Gretel Now."
After a set of near rhymes (*late/safe*, *brothers/
weathers*, *threat/throat*) Adcock moves into a quatrain rhyming *ate*, *bread*, *wait*, *head*, then ends the
poem with the ominous metamorphosis of Gretel
into the witch—in a surprising unrhymed couplet
(*sour/yellow*) to disturb the reader's equilibrium.

The imagery in Adcock's poems goes a long
way to enhance the totality of effect that her
themes—and her treatment of these themes—
have on the reader. Two key images that become
apparent in *Walking Out* through repetition and
variation (but always remaining fresh) are light

*Dust jacket for Adcock's third book (1988), which includes
poems about her native southeast Texas*

and the motion of turning. Not only is the word
light used in its simple form, but there are many
compounds (*snow-light, lightning, moonlight*), many
rhymes with *light*, usually internal, and numerous
contrasting words that denote darkness. Dave Oliphant, in his spring 1984 *Pawn Review* article on
Adcock (and R. G. Vliet), states: "Light, loss, and
memory are constants in Adcock's poetry, even
to the point that they become somewhat predictable, especially the image of light. Nonetheless, the range of revelations the poet achieves
through these three motifs is indeed impressive."

With the word (and concept) *turning*, Adcock conveys a variety of meanings: the passage
of time, the aging of a person, the abrupt shock
a traumatic event can cause, the surprising and terrifying facing of existence. "At the Fair" ends
with these lines: "Behind each fixed look some-

thing quick walked, / jerked at the end of its chain, turned / to cross a face again." And at the end of "News Item" the movie-star-turned-derelict says from his jail cell: "I wait like you / in a small room which seems to be locked. / The lights are on. The last scene flaps in a machine that won't stop turning." Passage of time is stated in a quieter but still ominous way in "Poem from November": "The leaves have fallen, releasing the distances. / This year of my turning moves / in an arc like a preying bird's, / purposeful." More than once there is a clear echo of Theodore Roethke in Adcock's imagery (Adcock mentions Roethke in one poem in the collection), as in the poem "Ripe": "Now a motion has overtaken me, / the turning that happens / at the center of stones."

Paul Ramsey wrote of *Walking Out* that Adcock "often builds her poems on images, but there are sharp variations. When her images tend to the opaquely expressive they stay near to sense and traditional meaning-feelings inherent in them. Thus eyes in closets open blue gifts, hands flood maps with salt. Neither image is literal or metaphorical in usual ways, but each suggests both possibilities. Closed eyes may imagine blueness; hands sweat on maps; the images connote lyric joy and endurance" (*Sewanee Review*, Summer 1976). Guy Owens noted that Adcock's imagery was an indication of her success: "Betty Adcock is a true poet—which means that she is obsessed. The obsessive images in her poetry are water, animals, insects, dreams—and, always, words, the sheer magic of language" (*Columbia* [S.C.] *State*, February 1976). Reviewing the collection in the *Library Journal* (15 January 1976), Joseph Garrison wrote: "the poet shows readers 'how surfaces keep the swimmer up' and how a life of loving the right things is 'long enough.' *Walking Out* is a significant and beautiful book." The anonymous critic for the *Ontario Review* said the collection was "in the running for the best first book of poems published this past year" (Spring-Summer 1976).

Nettles, Adcock's next book, was described by fellow North Carolina poet Fred Chappell as "an enormous advance" upon a good first book, and he said it placed her "in the front rank of younger poets" (*Greensboro News and Record*, 4 March 1984). There are even more of the characteristic Adcock images of light and turning in *Nettles* than in the earlier collection, with the luminosity intensified and the turning more dizzily intense. Death is another repeated theme, but it

Donald Adcock, the poet's husband, in 1990

has now claimed the father ("To My Father, Killed in a Hunting Accident"), has turned the mother's memory to a shining stone ("Mineral"), and is teaching its necessity to the poet, as in "Surviving the Wreck," in which the recovery of a wrecked, submerged automobile is recounted using the imagery of boats, ferries, rivers, and the reappearing "three bay horses."

Balance—of form, idea, and line—is apparent in poem after poem. In "South Woods in October, with the Spiders of Memory," Adcock catches the emotion of running through a spiderweb in the woods, "that silent passage through breaking / unbreathable circles of light / where you were caught quaking and brief / in the fingers of clarity." But she adds the significance, as well: "The world's strung with embraces." The ending toughens such a reference to "embraces": "You go forward by shudder and wreckage . . . brushing the small dead from your face." The subtle internal rhyme and near rhyme of the poem are part of its effectiveness: "and deep as *that water* / from which you could *wake*

Adcock's daughter, Sylvia, with Sweet Thing the cat

Adcock with a pet blue jay

and *wake*. / You can never quite see *what makes* it / to echo and thrum with the *taken*" (emphasis added).

Adcock has the ability to push the poem beyond the reader's expectation, as in "Hand Made," in which a very old family quilt chest, with its imagined contents, becomes the means to imagine a time past. The chest is compared to a "shipwreck / or a child's just-outsized coffin." But then, in a near-miraculous turning, the poet creates an entirely new world, not just of the past but of the spirit:

> green and yellow, whole skies, blue
> herons, lilies, rings, glassware, cows,
> orchards, pistols, red hats, mayhaws,
> the heart's loose change flying.
>
> If you say you would go to that country,
> here is the boat and the river.
> So the way is pure mourning. So we'll weep!
> We'll know everything, weeping for so many,
> hearing the huge, deep-starred tree
> as it answers us, needle after needle,
> with these thick, muddy colors for weather,
> these sharp little stitches holding on
> across the eyes,
> under the breastbone.

Another example of that world-beyond-the-world is in "Repetition," where, after describing a surreal terrain of moon, owl, and fox, the poet asks, "What hound's cry rides our dark like a mane of fever?" The poem takes its title from the mythic cycle of nature and from the *r* sound that ends each of its eighteen lines.

These poems finally reveal that it is the ordinary world that contains such magical turns. In "Roller Rink" a portable rink appears in "McNaughton's field"; none of the country kids can skate, but suddenly "the obscure brother / who was older and came from a nameless far end / of the county" also appears. "He knew, from somewhere, / how to do it, the dance of it turning / faster than music, could bend / and glide smooth as a fish where we fell, / could leap, land and roll on / squatting, backward, one-footed. / We loved him for looking blade-boned and frail, / for being always alone with nothing to tell." That piece of magic is wonderful but does not last; the rink moves on. But while it lasts, "even our shambling, hopeless town / seemed good, just in that turn / before the wheel of the year came down." After growing up, the country children "took any road out we could take; / but none of us with

the sweet-lifting grace / and ease of the promise that farm boy made / who went and stayed." The *made/stayed* rhyme brings a sense of closure.

Most critics agree that central to the *Nettles* volume are "The Elizabeth Poems," six in number, each with its own title. Oliphant writes of these poems: "Her longer sequences are equally effective as a combination of craft and meaning; they also illustrate once more her ability to make of the ordinary an outlet for the emotive thought. 'The Elizabeth Poems' . . . display Adcock's gift for taking such a simple event as a child playing on a bed with pickup sticks and marbles and making these, as she puts it, 'be other, out of her hands. . . .' In section III the child has asthma, and here too the poet finds in the illness a real/mystical quality with which she invests her descriptive/suggestive lines." Chappell also praised *Nettles*, saying Adcock "has an attachment to her material that is more than duty, more even than fondness or love. 'You try to shake that clayey dust. It won't / shake. You'll be back. / Nothing wears out.' There. Her abiding faith in what the blood knows. There is a sadness in that knowledge and a reliable fear: 'What hound's cry rides our dark like a mane of fever?' But for Adcock it is the knowledge most worth knowing, beside which all other knowledge pales. 'Whatever we hoped to say, / it was there all the time'" (*Roanoke Times*, 25 March 1984).

Chappell has also pointed out the distinction between *Beholdings* and the previous volumes: Adcock's third book "is a giant step sideways," Chappell says, because in it "she is experimenting with an almost reckless combination of disparate elements" (*Greensboro News and Record*, 21 May 1988). Those elements are the historic and modern Greek culture and the more familiar Adcock theme of historic episodes of southeast Texas, the Big Thicket country. What holds these separate subjects together, according to Chappell, is that they are part of an "elegiac lament for tribal ways that disappear in durational time but live in history."

It is probably no accident that the title of the opening poem in the volume, "Clearing Out, 1974," is an echo of the title of Adcock's first collection, *Walking Out*, for this new poem's subject is a return to the family home, this time to clear out the desk of the dead father. It is in the dream-memory recollection of the family that Adcock has shown her most characteristic virtues throughout her writing career. In this poem there is that power—the power of detailed invocation—but

Page 4 of a long poem in progress

That tall grandfather with his long blessings
even before breakfast
would drink his coffee from a saucer,
and nothing was stranger than my pallet-bed
at night,   layers of my grandmother's quilts,
whole countries of poverty I'd sleep across.

Look how we grovel here below,
fond of these earthly toys.
On those doomed polar expeditions
the nineteenth century so strenuously blessed,
weren't mammoths found, altogether present
in the ice like great stopped clocks?
I read once of an explorer killed
in a crevasse, *of* how his son,
a quarter of a century gone by ,
came to that place and found the frozen father,
perfect and much younger than himself.
A sliver of cold has never left my heart,
and I come to this weather, this shred
of memory as scared
as if there were a thing to lose.
Look into the blank space
where there was a house:
kettle rim, washtub rib, cotton-fleshed
quilt pattern, cold knuckle of washday,
ax-head, pump handle, the long bones
of the lamplight:
what was laid down stares up through pane
on pane the present's voices turn opaque,
parts of a buried life, some dream unfinished.

What figure can I raise?

                                                            (stanza break)

Betty Adcock

Page from a draft for a poem tentatively titled "Intervale" (by permission of Betty Adcock)

there is something new; the poet must not only invoke but assimilate the past: "I have become rich / with disappearance. I have become this light / pooled now on my father's desk. . . . I have to open it and take the cargo on / myself. There's no one else." But there is another change. At the end of the poem the daughter determines to throw away all the family/father objects she has so meticulously described, setting them all adrift as on a raft: "And the loosed river takes it / toward the turning sawblades of our dawn." Here as in earlier poems the river and the vessel are clear images of death, and, more insistently in this and other poems in *Beholdings*, represent a familiar acceptance of death. The last two lines of the poem are: "A Greek poet said it, Thémelis: / *What would death have been without us?*"

Another poem that combines the power of memory and the image of death is "Remembering Brushing My Grandmother's Hair": "I brushed. She sewed or dozed. The child I was / stood shoulder-deep in dying, in a dress of falling / silver smoothed by silver, a forgetfulness / dimming the trees outside the window like a rain." "The Case for Gravity," with its account of the small child's painful fall from the high porch, suggests a wry bit of theology or at least a gritty endurance:

After the first fall, there are the others:

vertigo's possibilities, the love
like a dropped cup, all hope
spilled so out of reach the world lets go
to bluest distance.
        Always the ground
reels me in to its cruel flowers, nothing ideal,
blue taste of beauty on the bitten tongue.
Say this time too I'll stand
mud-colored, abloom with bruises, vivid with news.

Adcock's work started strong and has grown more compelling with each collection. Reviewer Tom Hawkins (*Southern Poetry Review*, Spring 1989) praised the poem "Pasture Burn-off at Midnight," citing Adcock's ability to visualize a grass fire "in slowed-down animal time" through the eyes of cattle, "the cattle tranced in it": "It is not difficult to be 'tranced' by Adcock's poetry, its intricate and highly personal constraints, its precise imagery, and its visionary reach." Each new volume has illustrated the extension of that reach.

Reference:

Dave Oliphant, "Coming Home to Texas: The Poetry of R. G. Vliet & Betty Adcock," *Pawn Review*, 8 (Spring 1984): 105-121.

James Applewhite

(8 August 1935 -   )

Richard Flynn
Georgia Southern University

BOOKS: *War Summer* (Poquoson, Va.: Back Door, 1972);

Statues of the Grass (Athens: University of Georgia Press, 1975);

Following Gravity (Charlottesville: University Press of Virginia, 1980);

Foreseeing the Journey (Baton Rouge: Louisiana State University Press, 1983);

Seas and Inland Journeys: Landscape and Consciousness from Wordsworth to Roethke (Athens: University of Georgia Press, 1985);

Ode to the Chinaberry Tree and Other Poems (Baton Rouge: Louisiana State University Press, 1986);

River Writing: An Eno Journal (Princeton & Guildford, Surrey: Princeton University Press, 1988);

Lessons in Soaring (Baton Rouge: Louisiana State University Press, 1989).

SELECTED PERIODICAL PUBLICATIONS—
UNCOLLECTED:

"Children in Contemporary Poetry," *South Carolina Review*, 17 (Spring 1985): 66-72;

"Modernism and the Imagination of Ugliness," *Sewanee Review*, 94 (Summer 1986): 418-439;

"Building Confidence in Yourself as a Poet," *Writer* (August 1988): 22-25;

"Postmodernist Allegory and the Denial of Nature," *Kenyon Review*, new series 11 (Winter 1989): 1-17.

James Applewhite's poetry concerns the tension implicit in the relationships between language and landscape, past and present, childhood and maturity, and the rewards and limitations of his love for the narrative and family traditions of the South. Applewhite works within and against these dualities, writing in both traditional meters and free verse. An accomplished critic as well as a poet, he notes that his work is influenced by such diverse figures as William Wordsworth and Jackson Pollock.

Born on 8 August 1935 in Stantonsburg, North Carolina, to James W. and Jane Elizabeth (Mercer) Applewhite, James William Applewhite, Jr., was the elder of two sons in a farming family. At the age of seven he contracted rheumatic fever and spent a year in bed. His family situation has been characterized by his wife, the former Janis Forrest, as one of "overwhelming tension . . . created by the juxtaposition of his father's strong, capable, practical qualities against the fearful, dependent, and emotional qualities of his mother," a dichotomy that recurs often in his poetry. Because of his illness, Applewhite became an avid reader and inventor of stories, encouraged by his mother and her brother Almon, a bachelor uncle Applewhite describes as "his first literary influence" (quoted by V. S. Naipaul in *A Turn in the South*, 1989). Almon told the young Jimmy stories from the *Odyssey*, pretending they were his original inventions.

Although Applewhite's first full-length book was not published until 1975, his apprenticeship as a poet began in college. He received a B.A. from Duke University in 1958, and an M.A. there in 1960. As an undergraduate he was a classmate of Fred Chappell and was significantly influenced by Professor William Blackburn; both were later to become the subjects of poems in which Applewhite meditates on the literary vocation. On 28 January 1956 he married Janis, and they were to have three children—Lisa, Jamey, and Jeff. The family resides in Durham, North Carolina. After earning his M.A., Applewhite became an instructor at the University of North Carolina at Greensboro, where he studied informally with Randall Jarrell at a time when Jarrell was writing *The Lost World* (1965), his last major collection of poems. Applewhite acknowledges his debt to Jarrell's work, as well as to the writings of Allen Tate, Robert Lowell, Theodore Roethke, W. B. Yeats, Wallace Stevens, and Sylvia Plath. But Applewhite's major influence is unquestionably Wordsworth (the subject of his 1969 Duke Ph.D. thesis), as later evidenced in his criticism and in

11

such major poems as "Ode to the Chinaberry Tree." After receiving his Ph.D., Applewhite taught again at Greensboro and held visiting positions at Duke and George Washington University before settling at Duke, where he is now a full professor.

Although Applewhite published some poetry early in his career, including a poem called "The Journey," which won second prize in the 1966 *Virginia Quarterly Review* Emily Clark Balch contest, he did not begin to publish regularly until the 1970s. By the time his first major collection appeared (*Statues of the Grass*, 1975), his work had appeared in *Esquire, Harper's, Poetry,*

Shenandoah, and *American Poetry Review*, among others, and a substantial selection of his work had been anthologized in Paul Carroll's *Young American Poets* (1968).

Statues of the Grass is remarkably mature for a first book, and it announces many of the characteristic subjects Applewhite would return to with greater facility and understanding in later volumes. Poems such as "Looking for a Home in the South" are expressions of the deep ambivalence he feels for the eastern North Carolina tobacco country of his childhood, a place in which "a few houses cling, through camellias and columns, to an illusion / Whose substance of grace

Cover for Applewhite's first full-length collection of poems (1975), which, according to Stanley Kunitz, shows both his "roots in the . . . South" and his "special kind of modern elegance"

never ruled within a South which existed." Alongside these elegies for a vanishing and beloved landscape are poems in which Applewhite confronts deep and often painful memories of his childhood illness and of the sense of loss and triumph he feels about his escape from an enforced invalidism. His concern with family stories, what he later calls "Fictional Family History," is evident in "My Grandfather's Funeral," the first of a series of elegies written for W. H. Applewhite. These poems are courageous, but one senses an overly patriarchal view in them, a limitation the poet becomes aware of and struggles with in later volumes. Since the poet and the speaker in Applewhite's poems are often the same, his devel-

opment as a poet is closely linked to his personal development.

Following Gravity (1980) won the Associated Writing Programs award in poetry and was praised by Donald Justice (in his introduction to the book) as coming "deeply from character." The volume is notable for its increased formal command, greater specificity of memory and description, and most significantly for an identification with the feminine viewpoint that is not present in the earlier volume. The long poem that ends the volume, "The Mary Tapes," is a dramatic monologue supposedly spoken into a tape recorder by a Mary Woods, whose meditations on southern language, religion, and sexuality pro-

First draft for "Clear Winter," published in Applewhite's 1988 collection, River Writing: An Eno Journal *(by permission of James Applewhite)*

who is the clarity of ~~this~~ transparent
~~Metal-ore~~ of the zero for drink.
~~Touch the for zero door.~~

I sniff for the scent ~~of some fire~~,
~~Scent~~ of coffee on wet service or
cigarette. ~~scent~~. All are ~~partly~~
Absent. I turn toward home,
Slow as a pane of ice
This clear sun shines through.
I will kiss my warm wife.
And under the first star,
Gather cedar for a fire.

vide insight into the dilemma faced by the weak or the womanly in the South: "it's what we grew up with, that red-neck / Way of not respecting a woman or kid / Or some little animal because life's been too hard / And men have to work in the sun / Till they hate anything that's weaker than they are." Mary's struggle to understand and forgive men's compulsive drive for power echoes Applewhite's own struggle with his tendency to accept an uncritical view of his father as the practical "saviour" who rescued him from his imaginative but unhealthy mother. The poem presages Applewhite's attempts in subsequent volumes to question the strictures of language and sexuality as they operate on people's awareness of landscape, history, and self.

Foreseeing the Journey (1983) is Applewhite's first fully realized volume of poems. The overarching narrative of a transatlantic plane flight allows the poet to confront the materials of his past in a more coherent and formal fashion. As in the epigraph from John Keats that he chooses for "Returning from the River," Applewhite comes to see that "a Man's life of any worth is a continual allegory." The adult Applewhite still values that Proustian moment or Wordsworthian "spot of time"—in this instance, a moment that, he feels, saved him from illness—the memory of his father mowing the lawn while young Jimmy was bedridden: "The shape of his strength / Would save me from fever, by mowing forever." But darker, less pietistic memories intrude. Applewhite's recollections of selling gold-foil condoms at his father's Esso station and his poems about awakening sexuality prefigure a more disturbing "American Actual" of the present in which "Ills bequeathed as to children / Infect robot and alien." Applewhite's desire to affirm "the incorrigible imagination's pastoral" is severely tested in the volume, though not abandoned:

> Still, we voyage toward Eden.
> Blue planet, Earth-like, hidden
> In coordinates, how beautiful you are,
> Dangled against backgrounds of stars.
> Eyeball seeing no evil,
> We prick you against our will.

Alluding to Jarrell's "seven league crutches," Applewhite holds that poetry may still help one cover great psychic distances, despite infirmities. The poet serves as a guide on a journey through postmodern "jungles" and "the thicket of childhood" alike.

Applewhite's critical study *Seas and Inland Journeys: Landscape and Consciousness from Wordsworth to Roethke* (1985) is notable for his argument that modern and contemporary poetry should be seen more clearly in light of their Romantic precedents, an argument expanded in his recent essays "Modernism and the Imagination of Ugliness" (*Sewanee Review*, 1986) and "Postmodernist Allegory and the Denial of Nature" (*Kenyon Review*, 1989). Applewhite's reformation of his attitude toward Wordsworth and the Romantics in light of contemporary poetry occasions his engagement with current critical theory, serving also as both foil and inspiration for his later poetry. Likewise, his essay "Children in Contemporary Poetry" (*South Carolina Review*, Spring 1985) concerns his thinking about his childhood as a subject for poetry. This subject matter culminates in one of his strongest volumes, *Ode to the Chinaberry Tree and Other Poems* (1986).

The title poem of that volume paradoxically endorses and deconstructs Wordsworth's "Ode: Intimations of Immortality." Although Applewhite retains the Wordsworthian faith that childhood is indeed the site of poetic inspiration, his own ode is distinctively post-Freudian in its recognition of the violence and terrifying sexuality that inhabit the world of the child. He remembers the humiliation of being punished ("And I was a kid little as his body, / Spanked for the sneakiness I did") and the self-conscious guilt about juvenile sex play with his cousin. Despite such humiliation, however, childhood is indeed a "separate country," one that Applewhite believes worth preserving.

Just as his critical engagement enriches Applewhite's autobiographical poetry, it strengthens his landscape poetry as well. *River Writing: An Eno Journal* (1988) grew out of poems Applewhite composed during his daily runs along the Eno River near his home in Durham, North Carolina, but it is not conventional nature poetry. Bearing epigraphs from Jacques Derrida and Paul De Man, the volume is as much concerned with the ways in which language reveals the possibilities of the landscape as it is with the ways the landscape echoes the formal structures of language. As Applewhite says on the dust jacket, the poems are "my repetitive song of belief of the possibility of presence in language." Yet the volume is most interesting when this belief is tested, as in "Constructing the River," in which the presence of the poem itself is "an illusion." Recognizing the insurmountable gulf be-

Dust jacket for the collection of poems that James Dickey praised for their "great dramatic interest, strong interior movement, and . . . true occasions in which the reader can fix and involve himself"

tween sign and material object, Applewhite hopes, nevertheless, to "almost join . . . them":

> Grandsons of Freud, we handle
> The mental toy, make it disappear like mother,
> Fort/da, fort/da. We visit our own funerals with
> Huck Finn. The word-river cherishes time that was,
> That is, that will never again be. Is elegy.

Unlike some of his contemporaries, Applewhite makes his argument for presence in language by confronting the problems of referentiality, not by disavowing them.

Applewhite's most recent volume of poetry, *Lessons in Soaring* (1989), shows him consolidating and refining the insights revealed in *Ode to the Chinaberry Tree* and *River Writing*. In the book, he continues what the jacket blurb calls his "lover's quarrel with the South," but he does so with increased maturity and a renewed sense of himself as the maker of his own family history rather than a passive inheritor. Two poems are remarkable—"A Conversation," addressed to his father, and "A Place and a Voice," addressed to his mother. The latter is a major poem for Applewhite in that he is finally able to view his mother's "emotional claim" on him with a degree of empathy, admitting that "I knew everything / except for you." As in another poem in the collection, "Back Then," a self-indicting, ironic catalogue of male clichés about women—written in heroic couplets—the poet recognizes the reductiveness of his view of his mother as imaginative invalid. "A Place and a Voice" ends wistfully yet affirmatively: "If your voice traveled far enough, / I might inhabit the earth."

In "A Conversation" Applewhite renders the most complex portrait of his relationship with his father. The poem's controlling metaphor is a long-distance phone call over lines crackling with static; despite their "deafness" to one another, the son, at least, is able to hear the father to whom he had often turned a deaf ear. Recognizing their "connection still uncertain as prayer," and recognizing the child alive in his unconscious, the poet understands that what had seemed incalcitrant religious zealotry ("No son can accept a pure / Commandment as in stone") has instead been a necessary and sustaining belief for his father. What the poet gains is a hard-won tolerance for his father's belief:

> How can I feel but elegy
> For the figure of language you've left with me?
> Help me father, I say as in prayer, to hear
> A son's new testament, fairer writ. As the wire's
> Voice, heard last, crackles with the old fire.

James Applewhite's work has received little critical attention. In the era of the literary carnival, his poetry develops a quiet engagement with personal history that must be proclaimed almost tentatively. Yet his remarkable growth as a poet since 1983 and his increasing critical acumen promise him a valued place among contemporary poets. Like his early mentor Jarrell, Applewhite identifies himself with flawed humanity, with what Jarrell calls "something that there's something wrong with—something human" ("The One Who Was Different," *The Complete Poems*, 1969). Like Jarrell's work, Applewhite's poetry finds its sources in what Naipaul calls "his intense contemplation of the physical world of his childhood.... Out of his separation from that first world of his, Jim Applewhite ha[s] gone beyond the religious faith of his father and grandfather and arrived at a feeling for 'the sanctity of the smallest gestures.'" Applewhite's resolute affirmation of these gestures may not call great attention to itself, but it may well be more enduring than the pyrotechnical displays of more fashionable contemporaries.

Reference:
V. S. Naipaul, *A Turn in the South* (New York: Knopf, 1989), pp. 267-307.

Turner Cassity

(12 January 1929 -)

Keith Tuma
Miami University

BOOKS: *Watchboy, What of the Night?* (Middle-
town, Conn.: Wesleyan University Press,
1966);
Silver Out of Shanghai (Atlanta: Planet Mongo,
1973);
Steeplejacks in Babel (Boston: Godine, 1973);
Yellow for Peril, Black for Beautiful (New York:
Braziller, 1975);
The Defense of the Sugar Islands: A Recruiting Poster
(Los Angeles: Symposium, 1979);
Keys to Mayerling (Florence, Ky.: Barth, 1983);
The Book of Alna: A Narrative of the Mormon Wars
(Florence, Ky.: Barth, 1985);
Hurricane Lamp (Chicago & London: University
of Chicago Press, 1986);
Lessons (N.p.: Para, 1987).

SELECTED PERIODICAL PUBLICATIONS—
UNCOLLECTED: "The Airship Boys in Africa,"
Poetry, 116 (July 1970): 211-255;
"Notes from a Conservatory," *Southern Review*, 17
(October 1981): 694-706.

In a *Chicago Review* contributor's note (Summer 1982), Turner Cassity described himself as a
poet who, "in his own sedate way, is perhaps the
wildest of the students of the late Yvor Winters."
The remark is typical Cassity—laconic while simultaneously self-effacing and outrageous. It is also
accurate. While Cassity has never obscured his
debt and allegiance to Winters, there are many
ways in which he does not exactly fit the
"Wintersian" mold; at least the influence of Winters is not so immediately apparent as it is in
much of the work of such diversely talented
poets as Thom Gunn, Edgar Bowers, J. V. Cunningham, Charles Gullans, and Robert Pinsky.
Nevertheless, for better or worse, much of the
praise for Cassity's work has come from sympathetic readers of Winters—Gullans, Donald
Davie, Robert von Hallberg, and Timothy Steele.
But a few poets more indebted to W. H. Auden
than to Winters—Richard Howard, James Merrill, and J. D. McLatchy—have also expressed ad-

miration for Cassity's poetry; and these are poets
who find many of Winters's arguments noxious.
One suspects that these poets may be more recep-
tive to one aspect of Cassity's "wildness," the arch
posturing and camp sensibility evident in some of
the poems, a tone that can seem a departure
from Wintersian earnestness. Formally, Cassity fa-
vors the couplet, that most naked and ostentatious of verse forms. While Winters and most of
his students have experimented with the couplet,
none has done so quite so regularly or so ostenta-
tiously as Cassity, who writes not only heroic couplets but tetrameter and dimeter couplets and
often employs falling rhythms and polysyllabic
and hudibrastic rhymes. Few of the Wintersiand
poets, following their teacher in mining the plain
style, trust the slightly exotic diction of Cassity's
work, where resonant and ceremonious rhetoric
sometimes coexists with vulgar puns and rhymes.
Finally, nobody—not only Winters's students but
no American poet one can think of—resembles
Cassity in his choice of subject matter. Many of
Cassity's poems, both the shorter lyrics and book-
length narrative poems, have British-colonial or
postcolonial settings. While the best of these
poems are alert to historical contingencies and national contexts, viewed as a whole they suggest a
sensibility bordering upon the misanthropic in
their preoccupation with the futility of human ambition and the pervasiveness of evil. Cassity is a
moralist (which fits the Wintersian mold) and an
ironist (which does not necessarily break it), and
his subject matter is human folly at its most grotesque extremes. In this last respect he may
prove himself a southerner, though of the most
cosmopolitan and least provincial variety.

Allen Turner Cassity was born on 12 January 1929 in Jackson, Mississippi, to Allen and
Dorothy Turner Cassity. His family on both sides
was in the sawmill business; he writes in "The
Lumber Baron" (in *Watchboy, What of the Night?*
[1966]) that he "preferred to trees alone / A
smell of sawmill smoke and turpentine, / The saw-
dust pile afire deep in its cone." His mother was

Turner Cassity (photograph by Kerr)

a musician in silent-movie theaters. Raised a Presbyterian, in an environment where one absorbed Calvinism as if by osmosis, he was educated at Millsaps College (B.A., 1951), Stanford (M.A., 1952)—where he studied with Winters—and Columbia (M.S., 1956). His schooling was interrupted by U. S. Army service in the Caribbean during the Korean War (1952-1954); the G.I. Bill paid for his library science degree from Columbia. After graduating, Cassity returned to Jackson to work in the public library, where he was recruited by the Transvaal Provincial Library. From 1959 to 1961 Cassity was a South African civil servant, a member of the Transvaal Provincial Administration. In 1962 he returned to America to work for the R. W. Woodruff Library of Emory University. While one hesitates to offer simplistic explanations based on sketchy biographical knowledge, Cassity's fascination with engineering and technology as well as his highly self-conscious meditations on aesthetics and use-value, on poetic artifice and statement, can probably be traced to an early understanding of his family's work as involving the exploitation of natural resources for human needs. Certainly Cassity's "colonial pastorals"—to use his own phrase—are the result of his years in the army and in South Africa as well as extensive travel around the globe. These poems are "colonial" in their setting and "pastorals" because they sometimes aspire to a mythical representation of that setting—the whole of South Africa shimmers with gold dust in Cassity's poems—though the myth is almost always viewed ironically and treated in the mode of black comedy or farce.

Cassity's first book, *Watchboy, What of the Night?*, is an ambitious effort; the most familiar Cassity technique and subject matter are already largely in place. Many of the poems in the book have appeared in *Poetry* magazine, which has promoted Cassity's work through a series of editors. The collection groups poems by subject matter into sections: life in the tropics, in South Africa, in the Caribbean, and in an American seen as a Hollywood dream or bourgeois farce. There is also a final group of more meditative poems, which includes poems of a personal intimacy and directness found more rarely in Cassity's work after *Watchboy, What of the Night?* For instance, here are the first two stanzas of "Ways of Feeling":

> Here is the opened heart, and here the Calais:
>   You the letters, you the loss.
> The fresh incision you, the drug, the knife.
> Mine is the threatened and surrounding life.
>
> Too radical for more than partial cure,
>   The not unwelcome message, late
> Revealed, at last informs. Not much a lesson
> Then, you teach me now my own discretion.

The lucid exposition with its syntactical balance and careful repetition, the familiar and yet strangely economical metaphysical conceit—all this seems to show the influence of Winters's reverence for English Renaissance poetry. And yet there is a willingness to indulge the sentimental a little that marks the poem ever so slightly as the work of a younger Cassity. That same indulgence is sometimes present in the early poems on political subjects and can result in an outrage that reaches for the tone and resonance of prophetic utterance, as does the ending of "In the Western Province," on apartheid:

> With all compassion numb, with each
> Vain myth inbred beyond renewal,
>
> Apartheid stares in classic pride.
> Youth, knowing what the mirror utters,
> Will not hear now, on either side,
> Time running out in darkened gutters.

That last image is offered without a shade of irony; rhyming "utters" with "gutters" has all the portentousness of a young poet's version of T. S. Eliot. But there is a passionate engagement with his subject that, one sometimes regrets, is missing in more sophisticated and complex poems Cassity would later write on South Africa. The irony and

playfulness that have come to be more typical of Cassity's work are present in this first book in poems such as "Hotel des Indes" and "La Petite Tonkinoise." In the couplets of "Calvin in the Casino" Cassity introduces another mode that will become typical—the philosophical meditation; despite its absurd premise and exotic title, this poem is of the utmost seriousness.

After his first book, Cassity began writing long narrative poems in blank verse. Neither narrative poetry nor blank verse was very much in fashion then, and this fact along with the odd or at least atypical subject matter may explain the neglect these poems have suffered. First, in 1970, Cassity published "The Airship Boys in Africa," a poem that occupied forty-four pages of one issue of *Poetry*. The narrative of the poem concerns a failed effort (in 1917) to fly a dirigible into German Southwest Africa to rescue an isolated fort. But the poem is less interesting for its narrative than for its meditations on German idealism and technology. One character who has escaped a bourgeois existence, the not-so-subtle horror of which is represented by tangled antlers on the walls of hunting lodges, sees the intricate framework of the dirigible's wrecked skeleton and recognizes the image of a similar violence. In the fourth section of the narrative there is a remarkable passage in which the airship is rendered as the image of God:

> The distant hangar shines in morning fog;
> The wide steel doors slide open in the calm.
> Not really visible, the unseen pearl
> Implicit in deep shadow of the shell,
> Forepeak and hull reflect upon the lintel.
> Drilled insects, the mute ground crew emerge.
> As if these parodied the fate they serve,
> They offer, each to each, the weighted rope.
> The handling lines grow taut; the great pearl
>   moves.
> It is the planet and the idol; god,
> And the deceptive image of the god—
> The captive, sympathetic spell of Heaven,
> And the Devourer carried in procession,
> Hive and all-collective energies,
> The idle queen replete with death and honey.

"Death and honey"—such passages in their stately, Stevensian pentameter are ironical, but in the most profound sense. This poem is Cassity's contribution to a short list of narratives of imperial adventure, a list with works by Rudyard Kipling and Joseph Conrad at its head.

Three years after "The Airship Boys in Africa" was published, a small press in Atlanta brought out *Silver Out Of Shanghai* (1973), a book-length poem with illustrations by Steve Fritz. On the title page, Cassity calls *Silver Out of Shanghai* "A Scenario for Josef von Sternberg," and the poem does its best to mimic the expressionistic technique of the filmmaker, who directed *Shanghai Express*. Though the poem is ostensibly concerned with the story of a failed attempt to smuggle silver out of China, its narrative is subordinated to the poem's description of atmosphere and character. No one is as he or she appears to be in this fable; identity is caught in the artificial lighting of Hollywood intrigue. Crooked banking and bankers, drunken nuns, decadent soldiers, and dangerous women provide the surface glitter for yet another of Cassity's examinations of colonial life:

> One clear tone informs the bet is won;
> The red round ash is nourished on the leaf.
> Its smoke, upon the tongue a mother tongue
> Returning, tells, without high barriers
> Of second language, how, past surf and coral,
> Spice re-satisfies the centuries—
> A speech of islands, not as islands are,
> But as the veld knows they must surely be.
> In easy rings, that are the shape of vowels,
> English now, now Afrikaans, the smoke
> Drifts up, an orbit traced; to be in time
> One cosmic smoke: of planets, fan, creation.

The explicit allusion to Wallace Stevens's "Sunday Morning" in the seventh and eighth lines is something more than just an homage to the American master of exotic diction; it means to acknowledge the fact that pleasures have often been dependent on the profits of empire. In Cassity, as occasionally in Stevens, desire is a politicized concept. The "speech of islands" is the speech of political fantasies, which resemble those of certain precursors. Because Cassity is fundamentally a moralist, with a moralist's view of history, there is always a sense in which the "speech of islands" is for him the same no matter what language the current colonizer speaks, and this context gives to this passage as well as the entire narrative a transhistorical, mythic quality of considerable power. As is typical with Cassity, however, *Silver Out of Shanghai* contains more than a few elements of farce.

In the same year that *Silver Out of Shanghai* appeared, Cassity published his second book of shorter poems, *Steeplejacks in Babel*. This volume

has been the most widely reviewed of Cassity's works to date. Richard Howard and Donald Davie have suggested that one of its poems, "In Sydney by the Bridge," can be understood as an *ars poetica*, as Cassity's defense of his poetic:

> Cruise ships are, for the young, all that which varies.
> The aged disembark with dysenteries.
> Always, it is middle age that sees the ferries.
>
> They hold no promise. Forward or reverse
> Impels them to where what occurs,
> Occurs. Such is, at least, the chance of being terse,
>
> And is their grace. . . .

Howard declares this a defense of epigrammatic terseness and grace, and Davie extends Howard's reading to argue that the poem is in fact a defense of "verse," which after all, in the original Latin, means "turning." Howard had already happily noted that this poet was a "turner . . . of the most intricate contours upon the lathe of prosody." Davie, taking note of the poem's ostensible subject matter, ultimately criticizes the poem's "programmatic" nature. What neither critic has sufficiently stressed in his reading is the poem's central conceit. Davie notes that cruise ships suggest the "oceanic feelings" Cassity's terseness disallows. This is true enough, but they also suggest, more broadly, pleasure. Ferries, on the other hand, are boats of some use. Cassity, who has enough of the aesthete's mannerisms to be taken for one, who indeed has a reputation for proudly displaying a mastery of ornate and intricate verse forms, is here defending utility. The ferry boat's "regularity"—a term which may lead one to think about prosody—is only part of the issue; the boat's function is also significant. Cassity believes that the poem's form should be that which most efficiently serves the poem's statement; it should get the human content across, so to speak. In "Notes from a Conservatory" (*Southern Review*, October 1981) Cassity writes that in Winters's "best poems his medium is completely at the disposal of what he has to say. Surely he knew that is what great art is. . . ." One can quarrel with these notions, but there is no doubt that "In Sydney by the Bridge" offers a version of them, as it argues that "the scheduled ferry, not the cruise ship" is "precious."

In many ways *Steeplejacks in Babel* resembles *Watchboy, What of the Night?* in its subject matter and in its grouping of poems: "Bundles for Fascists," "The Thoughtful Islands and the Just Republics," and "Mapping the Lost Continent." The "lost continent" turns out to be Cassity's own, as once again a book of his moves through exotic subject matter to end with more personal poems, the last of which—"Cartography is an Inexact Science"—is a love poem: "Behind us in those bordered lands, does custom, / Growing old, / Map still? Must all who love, / In time, elaborate this unknown edge?" Along with poems about the Huey Long Bridge in New Orleans and several persona poems in which both obscure and famous political figures are made to speak, the volume is distinguished by a poem in three sections of couplets, "In the land of great aunts," in which, like William Faulkner, Cassity explores rituals of the South: making blackberry jelly, visiting the family graveyard. Thinking about an elderly aunt as she surveys the family's gravestones and contemplates the meaning of tradition and continuity, Cassity writes:

> If her stone means to no one, least to him,
> Well-being and the warm continuum,
>
> Do these consanguine join the non-descript?
> The lumber says deny, the shade accept.
>
> Between, the dead are what they were. For what
>   they are,
> The early jonquil glistens in the mason jar.

Whether people value enterprise ("lumber") or pleasure ("shade"), death gives the lie to both. And the moral decisions enforced by its reality preside over this book from its first poem to its last.

Steeplejacks in Babel was followed in 1975 by *Yellow for Peril, Black for Beautiful*, with an introductory note by Richard Howard. The book begins with "Allegory with Lay Figures," which echoes familiar rhythms and rhymes from Eliot's "The Love Song of J. Alfred Prufrock":

> In dark blue suits intently go
> The brisk young men of Tokyo.
>
> They scorn the scooter, purchase cars;
> They meet their girls in coffee bars.
>
> The town they own is haze and tint.
> They, nothing of a woodblock print.
>
> Rather, intelligence, skill, drive—
> High future that does not arrive.

The bulk of *Yellow for Peril, Black for Beautiful* consists of a verse drama, "Men of the Great Man," about the death of Cecil Rhodes (1853-1902), the extraordinarily ambitious and neurotic English imperialist whose gold and diamonds bankroll the prestigious Rhodes scholarships. The play is set at Rhodes's deathbed and reveals the link between the man's mystical imperialism and bizarre ideas about the influence of the natural world. Surrounding Rhodes are the play's main characters, the "men of the great man," a group of homosexual Anglophile males. As is typical of Cassity's poems about life in South Africa (or the history of South Africa), black South Africans remain in the background, to appear at highly significant moments. At the end of the play, after Rhodes is dead and his dependents dispersed, two servants pick up an abandoned bottle of champagne and, "in infinite cynicism," raise a glass to toast Rhodes. The lunacy of the great man, kept carefully out of the press, is no secret to them.

Because it demands knowledge of various colonial histories, opera, early cinema, and kitsch of all varieties, Cassity's poetry is always difficult. But, with a few exceptions where an inventive syntax becomes convoluted, it is rarely obscure. His most recent writing demands more work on the reader's part than many of the earliest poems because the recent poems are less often located in real or historical settings and more often widely allusive and probingly philosophical. *The Defense of the Sugar Islands* (1979) may be an exception; it is a poetic sequence with a narrative about a soldier stationed in Puerto Rico during the Korean War. *Keys to Mayerling* (1983) is a chapbook with a title sequence that extends "Mayerling" to describe lurid and banal life in various locations in America. Mayerling, of course, was the hunting lodge where Rudolf, Archduke and Crown Prince of Austria (1858-1889), enacted half of the Hapsburg court's most sensational double suicide, an event that was "a Chappaquiddick of its time," to use Cassity's own phrase. This is the sort of history that Hollywood and Turner Cassity love to use for working material, but in this particular sequence the history survives only by allusion. Orlando's Disney World becomes, predictably enough, "Viennaworld." Montana becomes a giant hunting lodge. All in all, *Keys to Mayerling* is an engaging but elliptical sequence.

One wonders why Cassity did not reprint the sequence in his most eclectic collection, *Hurricane Lamp* (1986). Despite the volume's diversity, one notes the persistence of characteristic Cassity subject matter. There are poems about the ruined "wonders" among the seven wonders of the world; a German U-boat anchored off New Orleans; Maurice Maeterlinck in Ontario; and leather bars. One poem, "Why Fortune is the Empress of the World," is an updated version of "Calvin in the Casino." The book shows that Cassity has become, if anything, *more* terse as he has aged. And the wit that graces all his books has been mostly freed of the excesses of occasionally gnarled syntax. Donald Davie has compared the poems of the last book to the poems of Charles-Pierre Baudelaire's *Les Fleurs du Mal* (1857), a comparison no doubt a little too generous but one that makes sense if one thinks of Baudelaire as Eliot did, which is to say as a moralist. But Cassity's playfulness, which always gives balance to a moralizing impulse, is also much in evidence, as in the last few couplets of "A Dance Part Way around the Veau d'Or, or, Rich within the Dreams of Avarice":

For gifts in childhood, my backhanded Baal,
Thank you. Your rebate let me countervail;

As in my busy, happy adolescence
You, the silent, stubborn, growing presence,

Sacrificed. I also thank you, center—
Part rather—of my being, for my winter

Each second year vacations. Cross I bear,
How I enjoy your stations! I, sole heir

Of that penurious young scare I was,
Gain now the ruby slippers. Eat cake, Oz.

In a poetry world where self-abuse is often made to pass for transcendence and rapture, such mildly cynical comfort can be quite refreshing. Cassity abuses the world of false idols by offering up his own life as superior fantasy. In Cassity's world, people are never good, but they are usually happy.

Hurricane Lamp is Cassity's best book. If there is a weakness evident in the earlier books, it is that, for all of their polish, the poems too often reflect a speaker proud of his own ingenuity and wit among boorish philistines and ambitious thugs. Cassity has always been clever, and he will not let the reader forget it. One might say in a more pedestrian manner that the poems lack variety of tone. This is not to condemn them; the same can be said of the collected works of many very good poets. Perhaps it cannot be said of great poets. In any case there is evidence in *Hurricane Lamp* that this situation may be changing. There is a new, melancholy note in Cassity's work, and it helps to balance the more familiar irony, as in the last three stanzas of "So Here It Is at Last":

How very long ago, in simple confidence,
One took the day at hand as what would issue
        thence,
        And as the just dessert

Of act and its own past. Vague future, quick to
        come
And sure to disappoint the shape you shadow,
        numb
        Your coming with the sting,

The thrust of change: each hope you monster, year
        abort,
A nothing in our non-response—the drugged re-
        tort,
        The undistinguished thing.

Some of the best ironists and satirists have done their finest work late in life, when they have turned their gaze upon themselves. There is some of this, one hopes, in Turner Cassity's future.

References:

Donald Davie, "On Turner Cassity," *Chicago Review*, 34 (Summer 1983): 22-29;

Charles Gullans, "Turner Cassity: Particulars and Generals," *Southern Review*, 11 (Spring 1975): 487-489;

Robert von Hallberg, *American Poetry and Culture 1945-1980* (Cambridge, Mass.: Harvard University Press, 1985), pp. 83-85, 188-196;

Richard Howard, "Turner Cassity," preface to *Yellow for Peril, Black for Beautiful* (New York: Braziller, 1975), pp. vii-xi.

Fred Chappell

(28 May 1936 -   )

John Lang
Emory & Henry College

See also the Chappell entry in *DLB 6: American Novelists Since World War II*, Second Series.

BOOKS: *It Is Time, Lord* (New York: Atheneum, 1963; London: Dent, 1965);

The Inkling (New York: Harcourt, Brace & World, 1965; London: Chapman & Hall, 1966);

Dagon (New York: Harcourt, Brace & World, 1968);

The World Between the Eyes (Baton Rouge: Louisiana State University Press, 1971);

The Gaudy Place (New York: Harcourt Brace Jovanovich, 1973);

River (Baton Rouge: Louisiana State University Press, 1975);

The Man Twice Married to Fire (Greensboro, N.C.: Unicorn, 1977);

Bloodfire (Baton Rouge: Louisiana State University Press, 1978);

Wind Mountain (Baton Rouge: Louisiana State University Press, 1979);

Awakening to Music (Davidson, N.C.: Briarpatch, 1979);

Earthsleep (Baton Rouge: Louisiana State University Press, 1980);

Moments of Light (Los Angeles: New South, 1980);

Driftlake: A Lieder Cycle (Emory, Va.: Iron Mountain, 1981);

Midquest (Baton Rouge: Louisiana State University Press, 1981);

Castle Tzingal (Baton Rouge: Louisiana State University Press, 1984);

I Am One of You Forever (Baton Rouge: Louisiana State University Press, 1985);

Source (Baton Rouge: Louisiana State University Press, 1985);

The Fred Chappell Reader (New York: St. Martin's Press, 1987);

First and Last Words (Baton Rouge: Louisiana State University Press, 1989);

Brighten the Corner Where You Are (New York: St. Martin's Press, 1989);

The Function of the Poet (Salem, Va.: Roanoke College, 1990).

OTHER: "Welcome to High Culture," in *An Apple for My Teacher: Twelve Authors Tell About Teachers Who Made a Difference*, edited by Louis D. Rubin, Jr. (Chapel Hill, N.C.: Algonquin, 1987), pp. 14-28.

SELECTED PERIODICAL PUBLICATIONS—
UNCOLLECTED: "Six Propositions About Literature and History," *New Literary History*, 1 (Spring 1970): 513-522;

"Unpeaceable Kingdoms: The Novels of Sylvia Wilkinson," *Hollins Critic*, 8 (April 1971): 1-10;

"Towards a Beginning," *Small Farm*, 4-5 (October 1976 / March 1977): 93-99;

"Two Modes: A Plea for Tolerance," *Appalachian Journal*, 5 (Spring 1978): 335-339;

"The Image of the South in Film," *Southern Humanities Review*, 12 (Fall 1978): 303-311;

"Double Language: Three Appalachian Poets," *Appalachian Journal*, 8 (Autumn 1980): 55-59;

"The Seamless Vision of James Still," *Appalachian Journal*, 8 (Spring 1981): 196-202;

"Viable Allegiances," *Abatis One* (1983): 52-65;

"A Pact with Faustus," *Mississippi Quarterly*, 37 (Winter 1983-1984): 9-20;

" 'Menfolks Are Heathens': Cruelty in James Still's Short Stories," *Iron Mountain Review*, 2 (Summer 1984): 11-15;

"What Did Adrian Leverkühn Create?," *Postscript*, 2 (1985): 11-17;

"The Longing to Belong," *Field*, 35 (Fall 1986): 23-29;

"A Detail in a Poem," *Kentucky Poetry Review*, 26 (Fall 1990): 66-75.

A recipient of the 1985 Bollingen Prize, an award he shared that year with John Ashbery, Fred Chappell is one of the most gifted poets to achieve prominence during the 1970s and 1980s. Among the most notable qualities of Chappell's poetry are its variety of forms, superb storytelling and creation of character, humor, celebration of the Appalachian region's traditional val-

Fred Chappell

ues, and serious moral intent. Chappell's poems reveal both erudition and a profound commitment to what he has called folk art, which is grounded in mimesis and in a vital sense of community.

For Chappell, that sense derives most importantly from his boyhood in the Appalachian Mountains of western North Carolina. Chappell was born on 28 May 1936 in Canton, a mill town of roughly five thousand inhabitants some twenty miles west of Asheville, to James and Anne Davis Chappell. His parents were teachers, but his father left that profession to sell furniture and to work the family farm on which the poet was raised. Chappell earned his B.A. in 1961 at Duke University, where he studied fiction writing under William Blackburn, who also taught such authors as William Styron, Reynolds Price, and Anne Tyler. There Chappell formed lasting friendships with Price and with the poet James

Applewhite. On 2 August 1959 Chappell married Susan Nicholls, who had attended Canton High School with him. Their only child, a son named Heath, was born the following year.

Chappell's public life has been relatively uneventful. After completing an M.A. at Duke in 1964, he accepted a position in creative writing at the University of North Carolina at Greensboro. There he has remained—with the exception of a year spent in Italy on a Rockefeller Foundation grant—for more than twenty-five years.

Although Chappell has described poetry as "my first allegiance," his early reputation as a writer was based on the four novels he published between 1963 and 1973. The first of those books, *It Is Time, Lord*, was written at the invitation of Hiram Haydn, then an editor at Atheneum, who had visited Duke and been impressed by one of Chappell's short stories. Both that novel and Chappell's second, *The Inkling* (1965), were written in five-week periods, and both were translated into French, the first one by Maurice-Edgar Coindreau, the translator of works by William Faulkner, Ernest Hemingway, John Steinbeck, and William Styron. Coindreau also translated Chappell's third novel, *Dagon* (1968), which won France's prestigious Prix de Meilleur des Livres Etrangers. All three books are intense psychological studies of characters in extremis. They are novels of ideas that analyze such problems as the nature of time and the conflict between will and desire. As Chappell has commented about this period in his career, "in my early work, my design was as much to harrow my reader as to entertain him." In his fourth novel, *The Gaudy Place* (1973), set in Asheville, Chappell moved toward the comic tone and structures that have become increasingly prominent in much of his later poetry and fiction.

By the time *The Gaudy Place* appeared in print, Chappell had already launched his career as a poet with *The World Between the Eyes* (1971), winner of the Roanoke-Chowan Poetry Cup of the North Carolina Literary and Historical Association. Although this first book of poems lacks the richness of symbolism and implication and the artistry of Chappell's later volumes, it does introduce some of the poet's characteristic themes and techniques. The book opens, for example, with a narrative poem, "February," that focuses upon an almost-archetypal experience in Appalachian literature, a hog killing, and presents that event from the viewpoint of "the boy." As in Chappell's first two novels, a child's perspective is repeatedly invoked, a strategy that foreshadows the autobiographical dimension of much of Chappell's later work. Not that Chappell is writing exclusively autobiographical poems, but his work in this book and later volumes is grounded upon the need to understand and define the self, including the poet's own self. This impulse helps to account for the repeated image of the mirror, and of other reflecting surfaces, in *The World Between the Eyes*. The boy in "February" is thrust into a solid, harsh, yet sustaining physical world, and his response to that world is ambivalence. He is "dismayed / With delight . . . elated-drunk / With the horror." Initiated into the knowledge of death, the boy is at the same time buoyed by the communal nature of the hog killing.

While Chappell's experiences in the Appalachian Mountains provide one crucial source for much of his most successful poetry and fiction, he is also a highly educated man of letters. His po-

etry often reflects themes and concerns that arise as much from his reading as from any particular extraliterary experience. Thus, in *The World Between the Eyes* "February" is followed by the overtly philosophical "A Transcendental Idealist Dreams in Springtime." The juxtaposition of these two poems witnesses not only to the dual sources of Chappell's art but also to the poet's persistent philosophical concerns, especially the relationship between mind and nature, flesh and spirit. The protagonist of *The Inkling* yearns to shape the world to his will and sees desire as his enemy, the body as a traitor, but Chappell's poetry insists upon humanity's dependence on nature. The transcendental idealist of this poem "undresses" the world, stripping away its richness of object and sensation, moving toward a "poverty" that casts no shadow.

Chappell has spoken of this first collection's flawed conception and execution, and he chose to reprint only four of its poems in *The Fred Chappell Reader* (1987). There is indeed no underlying thematic coherence that unifies all the poems; yet, at the center of *The World Between the Eyes*, as the title poem indicates, is the consciousness of the artist as he wrestles with his relationship to nature, to his parents, to the community, and to the objects of his imagination. The poem "The World Between the Eyes" is in part Chappell's *Portrait of the Artist*—but as a child, not the Joycean young man. Isolated, lonely, peopling his world out of his imagination, wandering an autumn landscape both beautiful and decaying, searching for "signs" it is his duty "to read aright, / To know," this child inhabits a world of both menace and promise, a world "of things that bloom and burn," where words, too, "bloom / and burn."

For Chappell, the imagined world that originates between the eyes must not be divorced from the world that stands before the eyes. Though rebellion is one of the book's recurring gestures, *The World Between the Eyes* moves toward a sense of reconciliation, particularly in those poems involving the child's perspective. In "The Mother," for instance, the movement is first away from, then back into the child's home. In "Sunday" the child's initial impatience with "the Lord's goddam day," on which he feels "tight in his clothes as a cork in a bottle," yields to a willingness to listen to "the Voice," to attend to the clear, small ringing of the bells. And in the title poem's closing stanza Chappell declares of the boy, "He's blest in his skins, an old stone /

Chappell in 1978

House, and a sky eaten up with stars"—images that suggest the boy's range of possibilities (he has skins, not a single skin); his past, including his family (the house); and his capacity for transcendence (the sky).

Chappell's greatest poetic achievement is the tetralogy *Midquest* (1981), which consists of four previously published volumes: *River* (1975), *Bloodfire* (1978), *Wind Mountain* (1979), and *Earthsleep* (1980). These interrelated volumes, totaling some five thousand lines, were conceived as a "poetic autobiography" set on the speaker's thirty-fifth birthday, 28 May 1971, a date that coincides with Chappell's own thirty-fifth birthday and with the year he published his first book of poems. Each part of *Midquest* is organized around one of the four elements that pre-Socratic philosophers believed to be the foundation of life. Chappell's choice of these four

elements from the naturalistic phase of Greek philosophy—as opposed to the idealism of Plato— reflects the poet's desire to recover in the contemporary world a greater sensitivity to the creation. As he presents each of these elements, Chappell allows his symbols to resonate as fully as possible, never reducing them to a single meaning. The river of the first part represents the water of Heraclitean flux, an image of time as flowing, of materiality; but it is also a means of physical and spiritual cleansing that promises rebirth. Water can be life-giving rain. It is the instrument of baptism, a means of grace, but it is also a force of destruction in the great flood that demolishes a town's bridge. A similar multiplicity of meanings attaches to the other elements, and Chappell demonstrates considerable ingenuity in their presentation. He does not neatly separate these four elements. Instead they interpenetrate to suggest an ultimate coherence, a distant yet audible harmony of life and death, flesh and spirit. To his wife, Susan, the poet-speaker remarks, "I am swimming your skin / Of touchless fire and earth-salt. Wind drives me forward. . . ."

The eleven poems of each section of *Midquest* trace the same twenty-four-hour period—though by means of wide-ranging memories—and each part opens with the poet-speaker in bed with his wife awaiting a new day. The lyrical voice of these opening poems is one of great beauty of image and elegance of phrase, and it establishes an implicit dialogue, between the speaker and his wife, that underscores Chappell's concern for making connections with people and objects beyond the self. Each section likewise concludes with another lyric celebration of the poet's love for and reunion with Susan at day's end, and the imagery of these closing poems creates a vision of paradise regained.

Similar structural parallels link other poems within individual parts and between two or more parts. In conception and execution, then, *Midquest* is a complex, ambitious work, one that extends the tradition of the long poem in American literature. But Chappell's poem is not like the personal, lyrical, long poems of James Merrill nor the hermetic long poems of Ezra Pound or Charles Olson. The "Fred" of Chappell's poem is a representative figure—though he obviously develops out of Chappell's own experiences, much like the "Walt" of Whitman's "Song of Myself " (in *Leaves of Grass*, 1855). Like Whitman, Chappell aims to write a distinctly American poem, and like Whitman, he is a philosophical poet attuned to the marvels of the physical world and open to a wide range of subjects. Unlike Whitman, however, Chappell chooses to write a carefully structured poem, not a sweeping epic. His pattern he says, in the preface to *Midquest*, is "that elder American art form, the sampler," with its variety of stitches. *Midquest* is thus distinguished both by its formal organization and by its author's mastery of a variety of poetic forms: blank verse and free verse ("the basic 'stitches' ") but also terza rima, rhymed couplets, Yeatsian tetrameter, syllabics, and even alliterative verse. The resulting poems range from dramatic monologues, interior monologues, and verse epistles to elegies, tall tales, and a playlet.

The most important literary antecedent of *Midquest* in terms of structure is not, however, any particular American long poem but Dante's *Divine Comedy*. As in Dante's poem the theme of re-

birth predominates in *Midquest*, with the poet seeking self-transformation in his thirty-fifth year. In Chappell's poem Susan plays the role of Beatrice to the pilgrim-poet, and surely it is no accident that Chappell's essay for the *Contemporary Authors Autobiography Series* (1986) begins not with information about his parents, his boyhood in Canton, or his literary achievements but with a reference to his marriage, "which marked a new life for me." Of *Midquest* itself he has said (in the preface), "it is, after all, in its largest design a love poem." The immediate object of that love is Susan, the poet's muse throughout. Yet the love *Midquest* celebrates is also directed toward nature, the poet's parents, grandparents, friends and neighbors, literature, and the creator (God). In one of his many essays, "Towards a Beginning," Chappell comments on the poet's "traditional role as celebrator of divinity and of the created objects of the universe" (*Small Farm*, October 1976 / March 1977). This traditional role is one he assumes in *Midquest*, and the result is a poetry of affirmation, love, hope, and community. Praise becomes Chappell's instrument of revelation and his response to the beauty the world reveals.

In his preface, Chappell also refers to *Midquest* as a "verse novel." Certainly his skills as a fiction writer are put to good use in the book to create compelling narratives and clearly defined, lively characters. The best developed of these are the poet's parents, his grandparents, and Virgil Campbell, the old shopkeeper "who is supposed," Chappell states, "to give to the whole its specifically regional, its Appalachian, context." As his name suggests, Virgil serves in Dantean fashion as one of the questing poet's guides. Campbell represents, however, not the elegant literary tradition of the author of *The Aeneid* but a homespun oral tradition that sings of whiskey and love, thus reinforcing the poet's commitment to the physical world, yet without leading him to ignore "the Mountains Outside Time." Campbell appears in a poem placed near the center of each of the four sections of *Midquest*, and he thus provides one of the book's unifying structural elements.

Among Chappell's most significant contributions to contemporary American poetry is the humor in the stories his principal characters tell. Campbell is the greatest of those tale spinners, but the poet's grandmother, father, and mother also reveal their skill—that is, *Chappell's* skill—at weaving such stories. Chappell's literary debt to

Cover for the paperback edition of Chappell's "poetic autobiography"

Mark Twain and to the Sut Lovingood of George Washington Harris is evident in these poems, but the continuing oral tradition of his native Appalachia also informs Chappell's comedy. Nor is that humor limited to the voices of his cast of characters, for Chappell himself often creates comedy through his ironic self-portraits and his incongruous juxtapositions of levels of diction and allusion. Standing in a field of Queen Anne's lace, the poet wonders:

> Suppose the world went pure like this all over.
> Would I be a better man? No:
> Just more conspicuous. Still, in this whited
> Sugar-acre I feel purified. . . .
> Am I an angel already? Let me lift
> My wings, let me sing a salving psalm:
>
> *"I'm Popeye the sailor man!"*
>
> Reckon not.

Like Lord Byron, Chappell also creates comic ef-

fects by establishing a tension between subject matter and form, as in "Birthday 35: Diary Entry," or in the terza rima account of his Methodist grandfather's decision to hedge his "final bet" and subject himself to total immersion by a Baptist preacher. Chappell's playfulness and verbal energy are evident throughout *Midquest*.

In addition to the mountain community whose life *Midquest* records, the poem also creates a striking sense of literary community. The varied poetic forms Chappell employs; the countless echoes of and allusions to other authors; the verse epistles to Guy Lillian, James Applewhite, Richard Dillard, and George Garrett; the playlet in which Fred and Reynolds Price discuss the nature and function of literary symbolism—all these features of *Midquest* reflect Chappell's commitment to literature and life as communal activities. Among its many riches, *Midquest* offers Chappell's reflections on the nature of language and literature, reflections that reveal his desire for a poetry and fiction lovingly attached to the physical world ("Surely imagination is sensual"), to "local clarities," and to carefully individualized people and places that nevertheless embody perennial human concerns. It is not the Rimbaudian derangement of the senses he practiced in his youth that an older and wiser Fred seeks to cultivate but the integrated sensibility of Andrew Marvell or John Donne who, he writes, "had senses / alive apart from their egos, and took delight in / every new page of Natural Theology." Yet while "fresh wonders clamor for language," Chappell espouses no easy Emersonian optimism. He rejects, in fact, much of the science-fiction writing that influenced him in his youth because "it counts suffering out," whereas "our faith must be earned from terror."

Although vivid characterization and lively storytelling are among the most prominent characteristics of *Midquest*, meditative poems lay equal claim to the reader's attention. Poems such as "Susan Bathing" and "Firewood"—long, single-sentence, stream-of-consciousness passages—not only articulate fundamental themes but remind the reader that it is, after all, the voice of the poet, of "old Fred," that underlies and unifies all the other voices in the book. Among the fundamental themes are love, the mysterious relationship between matter and spirit, and the quest for emotional and spiritual rebirth. Often, of course, the narrative poems mirror these concerns. The poet's love for Susan, for instance, is paralleled by his grandmother's and mother's accounts of their choices of husbands. But in the meditative poems marriage becomes a crucial metaphor that enables the poet to address the ancient tensions and dualities of the Western philosophical tradition: mind and body, flesh and spirit, life and death, time and eternity. Mocking the spirit of abstraction that has dominated modern philosophy since René Descartes, the poet prefers the company of "Uncle Body," despite the fact that his kinship with Uncle Body eventuates in death. Beyond death, however, Chappell glimpses eternity: "I'll say this about the *Book of Earth*, / The guy who wrote it didn't cheat a jot, / Even the footnotes are brimming over with matter, / Matter aye and spirit too. . . ."

Like Dante the pilgrim, Fred achieves spiritual illumination. He is a dynamic, questing figure. Yet the poem's structure is not linear but symphonic. As with movements of a symphony, *Midquest* operates on the principle of recapitulation. Yet, as with a symphony, there is a sense of

emotional and thematic progression, an intensification of feeling and a sense not only of enlarging insight but of resolution. The poet, who, in the second poem of *River*, laments the disorder of his life and resists waking from sleep, attains a clearer vision of selfhood and is able to "invite the mornings" in the penultimate poem of *Midquest*. In bed once again with Susan, the poet echoes the closing canto of Dante's *Paradiso* in the final poem: "The love that moves the sun and other stars / The love that moves itself in light to loving / Flames up like dew / Here in the earliest morning of the world." The Dantean metaphysical comedy of these lines is balanced, however, by the fleshy Shakespearean comedy of the lines from *Twelfth Night* that Chappell appended to *Midquest*. "Uncle Body" is heard again in the words of Sir Toby and Sir Andrew.

As this final juxtaposition suggests, the voice of the poet in *Midquest* is one of extraordinary range and flexibility, both earthy and visionary, colloquial and lyrical, improvisational and carefully structured. It moves easily from the environs of Greasy Branch and Hogback Ridge to the Mountains Outside Time, from jazz riffs to Bach partitas, from the folk wisdom of Virgil Campbell to the subtleties of metaphysical speculation. It is a voice rich in humor and linguistic exuberance.

Midquest received excellent essay-reviews from Chappell's fellow poets Robert Morgan, Kelly Cherry, and Rodney Jones. Morgan praised Chappell's narrative gifts, "the special talent that can tell stories in measure," and the "great richness of mind and language" evident in the poem. For Morgan, *Midquest* is a "lyric narrative" filled not only with entertaining stories but also with "luminous phrase and detail." Cherry emphasized the poem's journey motif, its celebration of community, and its affirmation of "the resurrection-power of art." Jones praised the book's "extravagant humanity," its "search of what is truly elemental," and its philosophical depth. *Midquest* inspired increased scholarly attention to Chappell's work, as was apparent in the special Chappell issues of *Abatis One*, *Mississippi Quarterly*, and the *Iron Mountain Review*.

In 1980, a year before *Midquest* appeared, Chappell had published *Moments of Light*, a collection of eleven stories that the author has said "may well be my favorite child among my books of fiction." It is a volume that demonstrates Chappell's consistent moral and philosophical concerns and the range of his literary forms; it in-

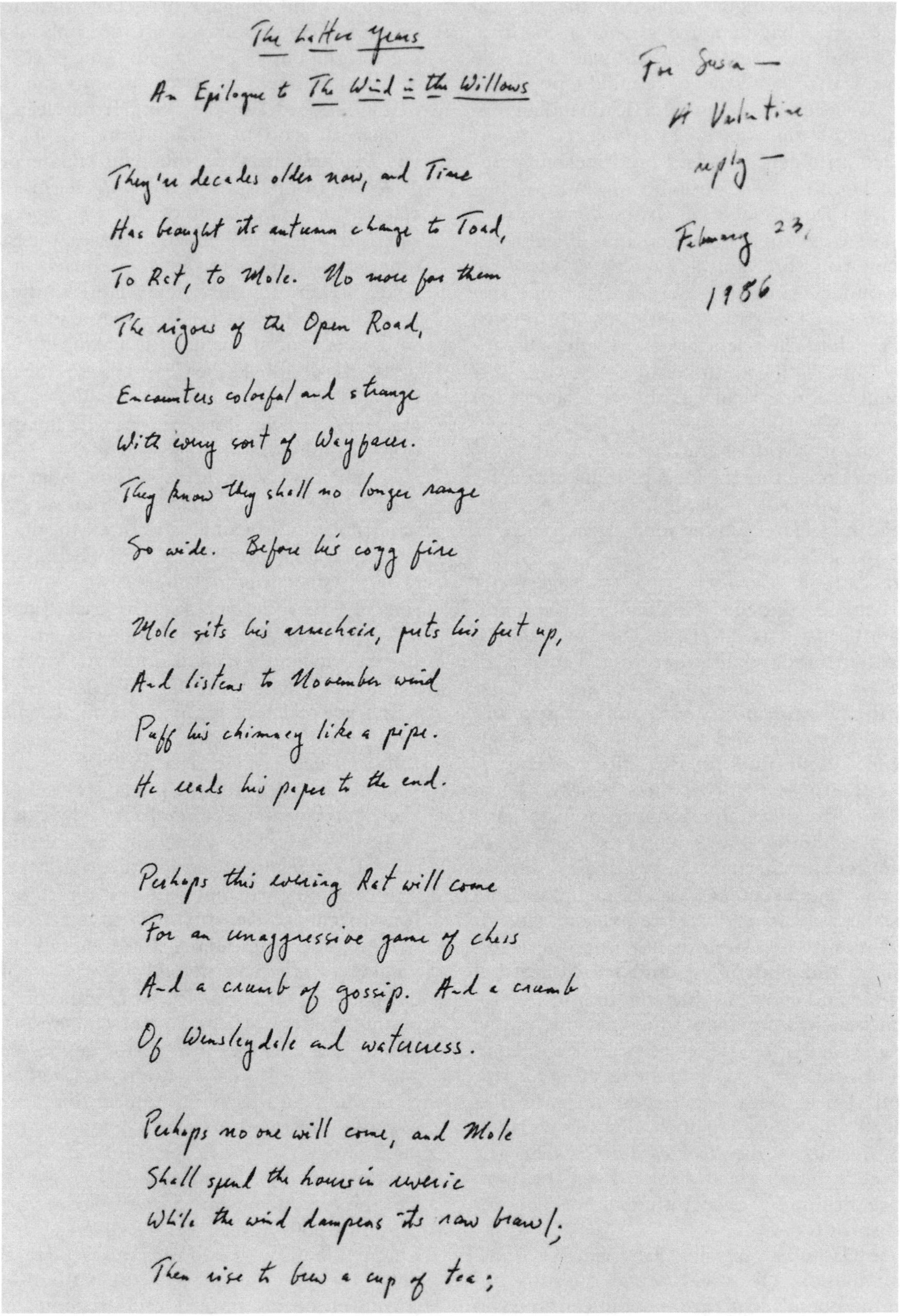

The Latter Years

An Epilogue to _The Wind in the Willows_

For Susa —
A Valentine
reply —

February 23,
1986

They're decades older now, and Time
Has brought its autumn change to Toad,
To Rat, to Mole. No more for them
The rigors of the Open Road,

Encounters colorful and strange
With every sort of Wayfarer.
They know they shall no longer range
So wide. Before his cozy fire

Mole sits his armchair, puts his feet up,
And listens to November wind
Puff his chimney like a pipe.
He reads his paper to the end.

Perhaps this evening Rat will come
For an unaggressive game of chess
And a crumb of gossip. And a crumb
Of Wensleydale and watercress.

Perhaps no one will come, and Mole
Shall spend the hours in reverie
While the wind dampens its raw brawl,
Then rise to brew a cup of tea;

Manuscript for a poem Chappell dedicated to his wife and included in his 1989 book First and Last Words _(by permission of Fred Chappell)_

Then sink into his chair again.

Those days of high empire appear

With the grass blade freshness of spring rain

And paint their pictures in the fire.

So long ago... Now they all slip,

Abstracted, comfortable, and grubby,

Into old age. Though Toad has taken up

Skydiving — as a sort of hobby.

cludes several examples of what Chappell calls "that rare genre, the historical short story," stories that focus on Judas, Benjamin Franklin, Franz Joseph Haydn, and Blackbeard. The principal themes in *Moments of Light* are the loss of innocence and the search for justice in a postlapsarian world. As in *Midquest* one of the dominant motifs is that of pilgrimage, and Chappell structures the book so that it moves toward a sense of transcendence grounded in artistic creation and an exploration of traditional values.

An even more emphatically fallen world appears in Chappell's 1984 collection of poems, *Castle Tzingal*. Chappell has described the book, which consists of twenty-three poems spoken by eight different characters, as "a sort of chamber opera," but the subject matter and form suggest that *Castle Tzingal* also derives from the Elizabethan revenge tragedy and the Gothic tradition so important in southern literature since the time of Edgar Allan Poe. The plot revolves around the murder of the wandering harpist-poet Marco by evil King Tzingal. With the help of the royal astrologer, the king has sought to preserve alive the poet's severed head, only to find Marco's songs unexpectedly haunting the castle.

The world *Castle Tzingal* posits initially is one of violence, avarice, and self-interest, of sycophantic pages and a murderous king. As Queen Frynna remarks, it is "a blackguard time," and this sentiment is reinforced by the events of the poem, its winter setting, and the comments of other characters. Petrus, for example, the envoy to King Reynal, Marco's uncle, reports, "This kingdom lives unclean." The characters most at home in the castle are those most thoroughly corrupt: the king himself; the intriguing homunculus Tweak, a creation of the astrologer's alchemy; and Pollio, the astrologer's page. Tweak and Pollio are both susceptible to Petrus's bribes because the evil of King Tzingal lashes out indiscriminately, even against his confederates. When the king begins to threaten Tweak, the homunculus poisons him and sets fire to the castle. Ironically, Tweak, this "minim man" who opens the book by declaring that he "prefers to flourish by means of fear," learns fear himself, learns that in the Hobbesian world the king creates, no one is safe. Before King Tzingal dies, he has driven both his queen and the admiral of the castle to suicide.

Like *Midquest*, *Castle Tzingal* demonstrates Chappell's skill with narrative and characterization, as he gracefully interweaves the individual voices of the dramatis personae, whose personalities and motives he captures in just a few lines. The plight of Queen Frynna, for example, is aptly rendered in one of her remarks, "I am a captive lullabye in a land / Of battlesong." The corrupt homunculus describes himself as "changeable as cloud, but always, / Of course, a constant Tweak lover." The contrasting nobility of Petrus is manifest in his revulsion against the moral contagion of the castle: "What misery . . . / To have to live in such a state, / And such a state of mind!"

Chappell's diction in this poem is often intentionally archaic (*mammet*, *asterve*, and *assoilment* all appear on a single page) to emphasize the medieval and Renaissance sources of the artistic impulse at work in the book. But *Castle Tzingal* is not simply a literary curiosity, though its form is unique in Chappell's canon. As R. T. Smith notes, the "urgent confrontation of evil" links this book thematically with the moral concerns that pervade Chappell's poetry and fiction. Significantly it is the disembodied voice of the dead poet Marco—an Orpheus-like figure, as Dabney Stuart observed in 1987—that troubles the sleep of the castle's inhabitants, calling them to assess the lives they have led and are leading. Marco would prefer to sing a pastoral song, "promiseful-green and all a-lilt," but "Arcady is fled and gone / Until I rend the guilty sleep / Of Castle Tzingal." That castle also represents the contemporary world, and Chappell's poem thus becomes an allegory that suggests both the immortality of art and its moral import. Yet despite King Tzingal's death, the voice of Marco, with which the book concludes, is not optimistic. Tweak, the king's executioner, is motivated by the principle of self-preservation and by the promise of a duchy, not by the love of goodness. After the visionary affirmations of *Midquest*, *Castle Tzingal* is bleak, its hopefulness muted though hardly extinguished.

In 1985 Chappell published both the novel *I Am One of You Forever* and a new book of poems, *Source*. Chappell has said that the "deliberately episodic" novel grew out of material he had tried to incorporate in *Midquest* but that had failed to fit into the artistic design. *I Am One of You Forever* enabled him to indulge the comic spirit he employs so successfully in *Midquest* and to affirm his ties to the Appalachian region. Chappell has indicated that this novel is meant to be one of four intended to balance the four volumes of *Midquest*, "surrounding that poem with a solid fictional universe."

Source is, at first glance, the most diverse collection of poems Chappell has published since *The World Between the Eyes*. The book's four sections exhibit Chappell's characteristic range of poetic forms and styles; yet *Source* achieves unity and gathers power by revolving around the theme of transformation, an experience fundamental to both life and literature. As in *The World Between the Eyes*, Chappell opens with a poem that recalls a childhood experience. "Child in the Fog" recounts the poet's sense of being abandoned by his mother to "the white fog leopard, / Tree-croucher to eat my bones." That fog appears to dissolve the material world, attesting to the instability of the child's environment. From this encounter the child—and the adult poet—"began to know how / The Hour Without Eyes is gathering in the world."

The remaining poems in the opening section of *Source* reflect the beauty of nature but also reinforce the impression that the poet has lost the world of his childhood, that he lives in a state of exile, haunted by the fact of dissolution. Like generations of poets before him, Chappell finds in works of art one means of combating the decay that time effects.

The second section of *Source*, which bears the same title as the book, opens with an epigraph from the Brothers Grimm, an apt choice since the poems of this section employ a variety of myths, fables, and fairy tales to highlight the story-telling impulse that is central to Chappell's aesthetic. Language and story are the instruments by which human beings define both self and world. Yet Chappell begins section 2 not with a poem that celebrates artistic creation but with "The Evening of the Second Day," a chilling vision of nuclear holocaust and the primitive state to which it reduces humanity. This apocalyptic fable testifies to the terror that stalks the late twentieth century and underscores the need for another species of transformation. What, the poet seems to ask, can the imagination project to prevent such catastrophe?

Implicit throughout the remaining poems in section 2—and explicit at times—is the notion that the artist both records and assuages the losses that human beings suffer. One of the finest poems in the book, "Music as a Woman Imperfectly Perceived," uses lyrical language, the jargon of jazz, and a catechetical question-and-answer format to affirm that music enlivens and humanizes the world. Music is this "azure country" in which one wears "gossamer and armor":

"Can we return alive? / *Alive, but not unchanged.*" Music, as the title of another poem suggests, is a natural resource.

Yet the transformative power of art, for all its consolations, does not exempt the poet from the pain of human existence. In "Transmogrification of the Diva" the singer lies dead. Among the changes "Latencies" envisions is the transformation of a young man from civilian to soldier to rose-covered corpse. In the ingenious "Narcissus and Echo," whose myth of love doomed by self-absorption voices a dominant theme in Chappell's art, Narcissus rejects community and drowns in the embrace of his own waterborne reflection. In the poetic world Chappell creates, no law requires that change be positive. Instead it may yield only death and loss. Chappell's poetry thus stresses the importance of choice and of vision in the shaping of lives. His poems originate in the same impulse to understand human existence that gave rise to the explanatory myths associated with the constellations, "those broken / many heroes we read the mind with"—a phrase whose very awkwardness highlights the difficulty of the attempt. A respect for mystery is central to Chappell's sensibility, as "A Prayer for Truthfulness" indicates. Yet he continues to probe the enigma of time, "the knot too complex to unite," and the tormenting "Pain-of-Children," which he calls "the fire that [gives] no light."

In the seven poems that compose the final section of *Source*, Chappell demonstrates his commitment to change, acceptance of mortality, and hope of transcendence. "I am changing shape again," he declares in the opening line of this section's initial poem, "The Capacity for Pain." Yet the poet offers no easy solutions to the problematic nature of human consciousness, which he had defined in the third section, "The Transformed Twilight," as the "torment torment of being flesh, / Of not being flesh." This duality of human nature pervades the final poems in *Source*. Images of shadow and death, of darkness and stone abound. Chappell finds consolation, however, in the naturalistic tradition represented by the Roman poet-philosopher Lucretius in "Urleid" and in the Christian tradition, which affirms that God shares in human suffering through the Crucifixion. The concluding poem, "Forever Mountain," dedicated to the poet's dead father, is a visionary lyric, a kind of prayer, in which Chappell portrays his father still climbing the mountain of eternity. *Source* thus ends on a note of reconciliation, and its poems confirm

Fred Chappell (photograph by Robert Gingher)

Chappell's ongoing interest in a poetry of ideas, not simply of sensation or of the personal psyche.

The publication of *The Fred Chappell Reader* in 1987 made Chappell's early work, much of it out of print, once again available. *The Reader* includes selections from four of the author's five novels, reprints *Dagon* in its entirety, and offers selections from *The World Between the Eyes*, *Midquest* (sixteen of the forty-four poems), *Castle Tzingal*, and *Source*. Although it contains two previously uncollected short stories, as well as selections from *Moments of Light*, it does not include any new or uncollected poems.

Such poems appeared instead in *First and Last Words* (1989), the title of which reflects Chappell's commitment to exploring what is fundamental to human experience—in this case, language, especially the language of books. The poet's reading and his responses to that reading provide the subject matter for much of this collection, which is dedicated to Reynolds Price The first and third parts of the book are entitled "Prologues" and "Epilogues," each section containing nine poems. Between them stands "Entr'acte," a set of sixteen poems on various subjects. George Garrett has said that Chappell is "the best-read person I know." Certainly this volume attests to the range of Chappell's reading as he meditates on, among other things, biblical texts, *Virgil's Georgics*, Lucretius, Immanuel Kant, Johann Wolfgang von Goethe, Thomas Hardy, Albert Einstein, *The Wind in the Willows* (1908), and Allen Tate's *The Fathers* (1938). Chappell also writes a prologue to Aaron Copland's *Appalachian Spring* (1944) and an epilogue to the film *The Cabinet of Dr. Caligari* (1919).

While such a format takes the risk of reducing the book's audience, limiting it to those familiar with at least some of the works of art that inspired the poems, Chappell often succeeds in creating self-contained psychological studies or philosophical meditations. Moreover, the very structure of the book presupposes a sense of literary community, as do the verse epistles of *Midquest*. That structure insists upon the relevance of the past to the present, on the universality of those concerns that have preoccupied human beings for centuries—love, war, suffering, death, humanity's relationship to nature and to God, personal identity, and the uncertain quest for ultimate truths. The religious dimension of Chappell's imagination, so evident in *Midquest*, is apparent here in the book's opening and closing poems, this volume's own "first and last words," the former a prologue to the Book of Job, the latter an epilogue to the Gospels. Both are among the collection's most powerful poems; yet neither provides a sense of resolution, only a commitment to ongoing spiritual dialogue. In the blank verse of "An Old Mountain Woman Reading The Book of Job," the anguish of the biblical Job is transposed to an Appalachian setting. Like Job, the woman challenges traditional pieties: "Not even Jesus shines clear of Job tonight." And like Job, she refuses to curse God. Yet neither is she resigned. In the poem's final stanza are these lines: "She shuts the Book of Job. She will not suffer / A God Who suffers the suffering of man."

The closing poem in *First and Last Words*, "Scarecrow Colloquy," like "O Sacred Head Now Wounded," the penultimate poem in *Source*, depicts the God who does indeed suffer in the crucified Christ, here depicted somewhat ironically as Ragwisp, a faithful scarecrow whose farmer-creator appears to have forgotten him. Insofar as that farmer figure represents God, the landscape Chappell creates in this poem is still that of the abandoned Job. Insofar as that figure is "the man who nailed me up," the setting is the modern secular world, "this age of snow," which has abandoned God. But the scarecrow is also an image of suffering humanity itself, searching for communion with the divine, ignorant of "the motive of [its] construction." "Scarecrow Colloquy" is among Chappell's most evocative allegorical works, particularly in its balancing of the hard-headed, skeptical voice of the scarecrow's unnamed interlocutor with Ragwisp's profound spiritual longing.

The violence and the cruelty of human history ("Such slaughter, they say, manures the fields of Utopia") preside over many of the poems in Chappell's group of prologues. Death itself appears most notably in "Meanwhile," a prologue to Leo Tolstoy's *Death of Ivan Ilych* (1886). Amidst the chaos of history, Chappell suggests, art offers a sense of order and harmony. Art works toward unity while respecting particularity. Its vision is one of wholeness: "Fragments that might still add up / To compose a figure of the perfected soul." Language, texts of various kinds, link humanity to the past but also energize future transformations. In "The Reader," for example, books open people, not just vice versa. Reconstruction and rebirth are the aim and the hope of Chappell's art, and he insists that such renewal must not neglect the resources of the past.

A volume such as *First and Last Words* reveals the error of any attempt to view Chappell simply as a "regional" writer. What the poet says of Peter Paul Rubens in *First and Last Words* might as easily be said of Chappell himself: he "sinks the piers of vision deep / Into the earth." That earth is most immediately the Appalachian region of his childhood, but Chappell is equally at home in the literary world of what he has called "high culture," as his books demonstrate. Chappell's voice is one of the most inclusive, good-natured, and thoughtful in contemporary American poetry, and his ear is well attuned to the music of words. Replete with the wonders of nature, his poetry also moves toward moral and spiritual truths grounded in something more fundamental than what Wallace Stevens called "the precious portents of our own powers." *Midquest* alone justifies strong claims for Chappell's achievement, but he continues to produce volumes of poems, as well as books of fiction, of unusual artistry and interest.

Interviews:

John Carr, ed., *Kite-Flying and Other Irrational Acts: Conversations with Twelve Southern Writers* (Baton Rouge: Louisiana State University Press, 1972), pp. 216-235;

George Garrett, ed., *Craft So Hard to Learn: Conversations with Poets and Novelists About the Teaching of Writing* (New York: Morrow, 1972), pp. 35-40;

Garrett, ed., *The Writer's Voice: Conversations with Contemporary Writers* (New York: Morrow, 1973), pp. 31-50;

Philip Pierson, "Interview with Fred Chappell," *New River Review*, 2 (Spring 1977): 5-16, 61-73;

Richard Jackson, ed., *Acts of Mind: Conversations with Contemporary Poets* (University: University of Alabama Press, 1983), pp. 153-157;

Paul Ruffin, "Interview with Fred Chappell," *Pembroke*, 17 (1985): 131-135;

Shelby Stephenson, " 'The Way It Is': An Interview with Fred Chappell," *Iron Mountain Review*, 2 (Spring 1985): 7-11;

Tim Tarkington, "An Interview with Fred Chappell," *Chattahoochee Review*, 9 (Winter 1989): 44-48.

Bibliography:

James Everett Kibler, Jr., "A Fred Chappell Bibliography, 1963-1983," *Mississippi Quarterly*, 37 (Winter 1983-1984): 63-88.

References:

Kelly Cherry, "A Writer's Harmonious World," *Parnassus*, 9 (Fall-Winter 1981): 115-129;

Annie Dillard, Foreword to *Moments of Light* (Los Angeles: New South, 1980), pp. ix-xvii;

R. H. W. Dillard, "Letters from a Distant Lover: The Novels of Fred Chappell," *Hollins Critic*, 10 (April 1973): 1-15;

George Garrett, "A Few Things About Fred Chappell," *Mississippi Quarterly*, 37 (Winter 1983-1984): 3-8;

Rodney Jones, "The Large Vision: Fred Chappell's *Midquest*," *Appalachian Journal*, 9 (Fall 1981): 59-65;

John Lang, "Breathing a New Universe: The Poetry of Fred Chappell," *Kentucky Poetry Review*, 26 (Fall 1990): 61-65;

Lang, "Illuminating the Stricken World: Fred Chappell's *Moments of Light*," *South Central Review*, 3 (Winter 1986): 95-103;

Robert Morgan, "*Midquest*," *American Poetry Review*, 11 (July-August 1982): 45-47;

Gail M. Morrison, " 'The Sign of the Arms': Chappell's *It Is Time, Lord*," *Mississippi Quarterly*, 37 (Winter 1983-1984): 45-54;

Charmaine Allmon Mosby, "*The Gaudy Place:* Six Characters in Search of an Illusion," *Mississippi Quarterly*, 37 (Winter 1983-1984): 55-62;

Alan Nadel, "Quest and Midquest: Fred Chappell and the First-Person Personal Epic," *New England Review and Bread Loaf Quarterly*, 6 (Winter 1983): 323-331;

Rita S. Quillen, "Looking for Native Ground: The Poetry of Fred Chappell," *Appalachian Heritage*, 11 (Summer 1983): 14-27;

David Paul Ragan, "At the Grave of Sut Lovingood: Virgil Campbell in the Work of Fred Chappell," *Mississippi Quarterly*, 37 (Winter 1983-1984): 21-30;

Donald Secreast, "Images of Impure Water in Chappell's *River*," *Mississippi Quarterly*, 37 (Winter 1983-1984): 39-44;

R. T. Smith, "Fred Chappell's Rural Virgil and the Fifth Element in *Midquest*," *Mississippi Quarterly*, 37 (Winter 1983-1984): 31-38;

Shelby Stephenson, "*Midquest*: Fred Chappell's Mythical Kingdom," *Iron Mountain Review*, 2 (Spring 1985): 22-26;

Stephenson, "Vision in Fred Chappell's Poetry and Fiction," *Abatis One* (1983): 33-45;

Dabney Stuart, " 'Blue Pee': Fred Chappell's Short Fiction," *Iron Mountain Review*, 2 (Spring 1985): 13-21;

Stuart, "Spiritual Matter in Fred Chappell's Poetry: A Prologue," *Southern Review*, 27 (Winter 1991): 200-220;

Stuart, " 'What's Artichokes?': An Introduction to the Work of Fred Chappell," in *The Fred Chappell Reader* (New York: St. Martin's Press, 1987), pp. xi-xx;

Ellen Tucker, "His Life in Mid-Course," *Chicago Review*, 33 (Summer 1981): 85-91;

James L. W. West III and August J. Nigro, eds., "William Blackburn and His Pupils: A Conversation," *Mississippi Quarterly*, 31 (Fall 1978): 605-614.

Amy Clampitt

(15 June 1920 -   )

Robert E. Hosmer, Jr.
Smith College

BOOKS: *Multitudes, Multitudes* (New York: Washington Street, 1974);

The Isthmus (New York: Coalition of Publishers for Employment, 1981);

The Kingfisher (New York: Knopf, 1983; London: Faber & Faber, 1984);

The Summer Solstice (New York: Sarabande, 1983);

A Homage to John Keats (New York: Sarabande, 1984);

What the Light Was Like (New York: Knopf, 1985; London: Faber & Faber, 1986);

Archaic Figure (New York: Knopf, 1987; London: Faber & Faber, 1988);

Westward (New York: Knopf, 1990).

In 1983 Alfred A. Knopf published a volume of poems by a little-known poet then past sixty years old. Titled *The Kingfisher*, this collection was praised (on the dust jacket) by Richard Wilbur as "extraordinary," by Joel Connaroe (*Washington Post Book World*, 3 April 1983) as "a wonderfully rich and . . . gorgeous book [that] will enrich . . . anyone who opens it," and by Edmund White (*Nation*, 16 April 1983) as "one of the most brilliant debuts in recent American literary history." The author was lauded for "a brilliant aural imagination" and "a quick eye for small, luminous details" (Connaroe), for a "keen mind combined with rich feeling" (May Swenson— on the dust jacket), and for language "used with the conjuring power of an original" (Elizabeth Jennings, *Spectator*, 4 August 1984). Outside the circle of those who read small poetry magazines and poems published in better-known magazines such as the *New Yorker* and the *New Republic*, Amy Clampitt was virtually unknown. Indeed, this poet who shuns the confessional mode so popular with certain modern and contemporary poets treasures her privacy and reveals precious little about herself. In an interview with Judson Brown (*Daily Hampshire Gazette*, 17 June 1987), she said, "I'm very much put off by this whole thing of making human interest stories about someone who published . . . (here there is a significant pause)

. . . late. I don't feel that my own work fits with people whose birthdate mine fits with, because I've been writing lately, and they did most of their work a long time ago." Though her reticence about supplying information, whether autobiographical or artistic, creates some lacunae, a biographical outline of sorts can be constructed.

Amy Clampitt was born on 15 June 1920 in the small farming village of New Providence, Iowa, the daughter of Roy Justin Clampitt and Pauline Felt Clampitt. Amy's father, like his father before him, was a farmer who worked the soil of America's heartland. In a world rather more given to the harsh realities of atmosphere and earth, the family encouraged young Amy's intellectual and artistic pursuits. A poem in *The Kingfisher*, "Imago," offers a glimpse of the poet as a child, "the shirker propped / above her book in a farmhouse parlor / . . . eyeing at a distance the lit pavilions / that seduced her." Her grandfather, a man who loved books and who had written a memoir of his life on the prairie, inspired this diffident child to write. At age nine she began to write poetry, then some fiction. At Grinnell College Clampitt earned a B.A. with honors in English (1941), as well as election to Phi Beta Kappa; then she went on to graduate school at Columbia University on a fellowship. But graduate work, it turned out, was not for her, and within a year she left, eventually taking a job with Oxford University Press, where she became promotion director for college textbooks before leaving in 1951. Europe beckoned: after a five-month trip, she returned to New York City to work as a reference librarian for the National Audubon Society (1952-1959), free-lance editor and researcher (1960-1977)—during which time she resumed writing poetry—and as an editor for E. P. Dutton (1977-1982).

Since 1982 Clampitt has supported herself by writing poetry (*The Kingfisher* has sold more than ten thousand copies) and giving readings, by holding grants (a John Simon Guggenheim Fellowship, 1982; an American Academy and Insti-

Amy Clampitt (photograph by Virginia Schendler)

tute of Arts and Letters Award, 1984), and by teaching (writer in residence, College of William and Mary, 1984-1985; Amherst College, 1986-1987). In 1991 she received a three-year Lila Acheson Wallace Reader's Digest Fellowship.

Clampitt's first published volume of verse, *Multitudes, Multitudes*, appeared in 1974. It is difficult to give a work such as *Multitudes, Multitudes* a fair hearing; the temptation to dismiss it as but a foreshadowing of later work or a mere apprentice piece presents itself. In reality, however, this first collection, while certainly not demonstrating the assurance, poise, and precision of succeeding volumes, need have no apologies made for it. Clampitt's poetry has never been less than interesting, and in *Multitudes, Multitudes*, as she writes on themes to which she has returned in her later work, she gives evidence of a sustained ability to craft remarkable verse. To be sure, some of the poems ("She," "Coronary") never quite seem to catch fire. Awkwardness and hesitation sometimes spoil others a bit. And occasionally the seams show, as in "Time Signatures," where the poet's rhapsody on love reveals some rather hasty stitching of myths into the fabric. Others

have lines that are clotted with thick sounds ("Harlequin Naked") or broken by contracted verb forms ("The Classmates"). Still another, "It Is a Well-Known Fact," suggests that Clampitt has not been able to resist the temptation to force a moral point.

Nonetheless, the majority of the poems are exciting and worthy of being reprinted in a more accessible volume. Several are of particular note: "The Eve of All Souls" is a powerful meditation on death coupled with a plea for deliverance that rises to a conclusion with liturgical force—"for all the souls: / multitudes, multitudes: O Christ, deliver them." "The Christmas Cactus," a three-stanza assertion of the power of nature, is so deftly crafted. And "A.D. 1973," the concluding poem, asserts that the "mystery of the Whole" endures, even in the midst of disorder, as the age of anxiety continues. Though *Multitudes, Multitudes* manifests many of the themes and concerns that have occupied Clampitt ever since—war, the Holocaust, Greece, and mythology (classical, biblical, Romantic, personal)—it does reveal a surprise: love poetry, not just detailing other people's love affairs, as in "Harlequin Naked" and

"A Marriage," but her own, most powerfully in "The Eve of All Souls," "Time Signatures," and "Amagansett":

> But it was you
>
> I found there now, so near, but it was you
> had brought me tranced into a place where still
> some stilled part of me lingers unafraid,
>   though all the messages
>
> are opened, though the news is all invasions
> and all bad.

Clampitt's poetry first came to the attention of a wider reading audience in 1978 when Howard Moss, longtime poetry editor of the *New Yorker*, accepted "The Sun Underfoot Among the Sundews" for publication in that distinguished magazine (14 August 1978). Until his death in 1987, Moss would champion Clampitt's verse and serve as a trusted reader for the poet.

In 1981 the nonprofit coalition of Publishers for Employment invited Clampitt to participate in a workshop project intended mainly to give young people in publishing some experience in book design and production. The result was *The Isthmus*. The fifteen poems gathered there show a poet testing her strengths and exploring the possibilities of language and sound. Some of the poems are evocations of coastal Maine ("The Isthmus," "The Lighthouse," "Vignetting," "Recycling," "Horizontal and Vertical," "Surf" which often interweave subordinate strands of reflection. Others, such as "The Diver," "Agnostic Fragment," and "Saint Audrey's Necklace," are substantially meditations on death and design. Unfair as it may be, the poems in *The Isthmus* inevitably invite comparison with Clampitt's later work, and the comparison finds the earlier poems wanting in some respects. Her eye and ear have not developed to the level she later attained, and her voice is not yet truly distinctive; often the language is simply too prosy.

While her concerns are nearly always greater than mere description, she has not crafted verse with the resonance of significant ideas. Nonetheless, the collection has its pleasures and has greater value than a simple biographical curiosity. The title poem creates a marvelous sense of familiar movement and continuity, as two people are stranded on an isthmus that becomes a tidal island. "Saint Audrey's Necklace" ("tawdry lace" is short for St. Audrey's Necklace) is a memento mori that begins with a dance

and ends with a sobering reflection: "romance, the dancers tell us, / is all ornament, ornament is all, / and Death the mirror, our plaything." And "The Lighthouse" achieves clarity and freshness:

> A dripping sleeve of incandescence
> sweeps the cove, unrolls a corridor
> through caves of starlight
> and steps inside
> the darkened house
> harmlessly winnowing
> the groves of shadow
> like a sleepwalking familiar—
> lightning mollified, a newly
> calibrated force of nature.

Those few readers of Clampitt's first two books of poetry could not have been prepared for the poetry presented in Clampitt's first major collection, *The Kingfisher*. As Helen Vendler has noted, "the advance in this collection over those preceding it is dumbfounding" (*New York Review of Books*, 3 March 1983).

This collection of fifty poems, the majority of which had appeared previously in the *New Yorker*, *Atlantic Monthly*, *Kenyon Review*, or *Christian Science Monitor*, marked an auspicious formal debut for Clampitt, whose verse was lavishly praised by America's foremost poets and critics. Typical are the comments of Frederick Turner as printed on the dust jacket ("this book marks a watershed in American poetry") and Vendler ("an assured and distinguished voice resembling no other has been added to the sum of American poetry").

The Kingfisher is divided into six sections, but it would be inaccurate to attach a rigid structure to this scheme. Rather, recurring themes, generated and sustained by elemental metaphors, direct this collection toward the darkness of the final poem, "The Burning Child," a haunting, reflective exercise that contracts into: "The catwalk shadows of the cave, the whimper / of the burning child, the trapped / reprieve of nightmare between the / tinder and the nurture whose / embrace is drowning."

In his essay "Poetry as Alchemy" Edmund White clarifies Clampitt's method. Responding to his own difficulties in finding plot in her poems, White distinguishes traditional narrative structure with its emphases on linearity, economy, hierarchy, impulsion, and causation from Clampitt's, which is "circular, diffuse, vertiginous, and organized through simultaneity." When he concludes that "her method is the one appropriate to our ex-

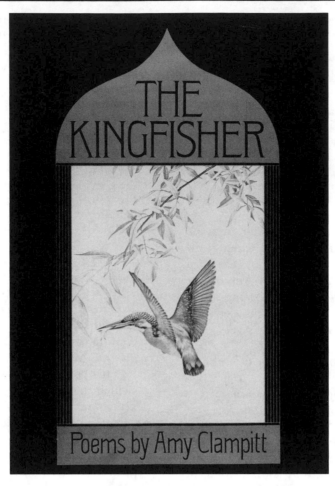

Dust jacket for Clampitt's first full-length collection (1983), which Edmund White called "one of the most brilliant debuts in recent American literary history"

perience," he defends Clampitt against those who might fault her craft, and he underscores the very modernity of her sensibility. This diffuse principle of organization applies not only to individual poems but to the collection as a whole.

The Kingfisher is distinguished by the care with which Clampitt enunciates her aesthetic, which has antecedents and sources as apparently diverse as Gerard Manley Hopkins, Marianne Moore, Elizabeth Bishop, Robert Lowell, Emily Dickinson, Wallace Stevens, and Algernon Charles Swinburne. In seven particularly important poems, Clampitt sets forth, with the strength of informed conviction and integrity, the principles and practices that guide her art.

In the much-praised "Beach Glass," for example, Clampitt writes of the inevitable process of "the ocean [that] goes on shuffling its millenniums / of quartz, granite, and basalt," and she likens that inexorable movement to the process of the intellect: "For the ocean, nothing / is beneath consideration." And so it is for the speaker of the poem, who is collecting shards and spikes of glass washed up on the shore. Clampitt sharpens the distinction between the ocean's flux, which deposits debris on the littoral, and the inexorable process of "an intellect / engaged in the hazardous / redefinition of structures / no one has yet looked at." In "Dancers Exercising" she accepts continuous movement and "the never-to-be-completed" nature of things ("all process and no arrival"), while simultaneously asserting the power of vision to arrange things, if only temporarily, "frame within frame." Such is the power of art, whether poetry or dance. Though the ocean "behaves ... with random impartiality," this poet does not.

Essential to any aesthetic is method, and several poems in *The Kingfisher* afford some understanding of Clampitt's method. "Rain at Bellagio," a sequence of twelve lyrics, each a tessera in a mosaic of memory, illustrates the "all process and no arrival" principle while offering insight into method. At a critical turn, the narrator, on a visit to a friend staying in a villa on Lake Como, gazes out on the water and spies a boat darting back and forth from one shore to another, the trace of its wake lines moving "as though reining / the fragments of experience into one process— / being-and-becoming fused, a single scheme." This is as clear a statement of artistic method and purpose as one might seek.

Further insight into the poet's method can be gleaned from "Balms," a three-stanza poem ostensibly about the narrator's visit to a rare-book room, where she examined an early-nineteenth-century text, *Essay on Colour* (1804), by Mary Gartside. The "watercolor illustration / wet-bright" of "nasturtium hues" elicits immediate synesthetic impressions:

> Sudden as
> on hands and knees
> I felt the smell of them
> suffuse the catacomb
> so much of us lives in—
> horned, pungent, velvet-
> eared succulence, a perfume
> without hokum. . . .

This poem is the result of the process activated by the experience: "Our one / encounter occurred by chance / where pure hue set loose / unearthly gusts of odor / from earthbound nasturtiums."

Often praised for her close observation of objects, particularly those in the natural world, Clampitt is a poet whose senses have been sharpened to remarkable acuity. Observation and immersion are integral to aesthetics. The immersion of which she writes in "Letters from Jerusalem" is not only "inward but also downward." What she calls a "thirst for roots" takes her, in a poem such as "The Sun Underfoot Among the Sundews," down so far that by the end she "start[s] to fall upward," contemplating not depth and darkness but height and light, away from fragmentation and toward a vision of unity.

One of Clampitt's primary strengths, the result of her powers of observation, and achieved through immersion, is her richly detailed poetry of land- and seascape. Though that achievement extends throughout the collection, it is perhaps most evident in the first section, "Fire and Water," which includes a half dozen or so fine examples, often prompted by scenes along the Maine coast, where she often stayed during the

summer. Indeed, that place has exercised considerable power on the poet; she has gone so far as to say that "being by the ocean . . . I sometimes think that's what really got me writing poetry. . . . In a place like Maine, with the tide coming in and going out, you can collect your thoughts and get some perspective" (Fairchild interview, *American Poetry Review*, July/August 1987).

In "The Cove" the narrator and a companion look up to see "a new kind of warbler flirting, all ombré / and fine stitchery," then "down at the grass / we notice a turtle—domed repoussé / leather with an underlip of crimson." In the concluding stanza, the "we" disappears, merging into the natural world in verse that fills the eye with light and the ear with repetition and echo:

> Where at low tide the rocks, like the
> back of an old sheepdog or spaniel, are
> rugg'd with wet seaweed, the cove
> embays a pavement of ocean, at times
> wrinkling like tinfoil, at others
> all isinglass flakes, or sun-pounded
> gritty glitter of mica; or hanging
> intact, a curtain wall just frescoed
> indigo, so immense a hue, a blue
> of such majesty it can't be looked at,
> at whose apex there pulses, even
> in daylight, a lighthouse, light-
> pierced like a needle's eye.

Two other poems, "Fog" and "Gradual Clearing," display the same virtuoso ability to recreate the atmospherics of successive moments at the shore. In "The Edge of the Hurricane" Clampitt infuses descriptive language with a sense of dramatic movement and tension, using the effects of alliteration, assonance, the short line, and the short stanza to whip the verse until the "torn-to-pieces, mud-dark / flounces of Caribbean cumulus keep passing, keep passing" and night falls.

Other forms of nature—animal, vegetable, and mineral—pass under Clampitt's jeweler's eye. In "Camouflage" a killdeer causes the narrator to exclaim "how that brilliant / double-looped necklace could amputate / into invisibility the chevroned / cinnamon of her plumage." A poem about a doe in the woods, "Slow Motion," rises above the commonplace because of the intriguing promise of the opening simile of the first line: "Her liquid look as dark / as antique honey," a promise fulfilled in the caressing hush of succeeding stanzas.

With a botanist's eye and command of nomenclature, Clampitt studies plants, watching "unleafing lindens burn / green-gold a day or two" ("Lindenbloom"); noting "the spent residue of dahlias' / late-summer blood and flame, leached marigolds, / knives of gladioli flailed to ribbons" ("The Dahlia Gardens"); and walking among sundews, "an underfoot / webwork of carnivorous rubies, a star-swarm thick as gnats" ("The Sun Underfoot Among the Sundews").

Clampitt's interest in geology, particularly in how geologists read the history of the earth, surfaces in poems such as "The Quarry" ("Light-years / of ooze foreshortened into limestone / swarm with starfish") and "Imago" ("a chipped flint / would turn up in a furrow, / pink as a peony . . . a nomad's artifact fished from the broth"). A poet of nature, Clampitt has gifts of eye, ear, and imaginative invention that are impressive.

But Clampitt is not simply a nature poet, a versifier capable only of description, even if it be of a high order and polish. Though she shuns the distinction ("I am not a scholar at all," she told interviewer Laura Fairchild), she is a poet to whom the life of the mind is important, for whom ideas and intellectual vigor do matter.

It is quite possible to unravel the skeins of ideas in *The Kingfisher* and delineate serious concerns: Marxist philosophy (in "Marginal Employment"), pacifism and protest (in "The Dahlia Gardens" and "Letters from Jerusalem"), and natural selection (in "The Sun Underfoot Among the Sundews"). Two endeavors seem to engage her most prominently, though: definition/redefinition and aestheticism. In the first area, Clampitt is concerned not only to define concepts and objects; in the process, as in "Beach Glass" and "Rain at Bellagio," she defines herself as a late-twentieth-century woman and poet. And because "nothing is beneath consideration" for her, she writes about an array of subjects, though with definition of one sort or another nearly always in mind. "Fog" is typical in this regard: a short, three-stanza poem of twenty-nine lines, it moves from an opening visual blur ("A vagueness comes over everything") through "a rumor in a mumble of ocean" toward particular definition before culminating in an opacity and aural clarity ("the ticking, linear / filigree of bird voices"). The middle stanza assumes central importance, emphasizing definition by sense:

> Tactile
> definition, however, has not been
> totally banished: hanging

tassel by tassel, panicled
foxtail and needlegrass,
dropseed, furred hawkweed,
and last season's rose-hips
are vested in silenced
chimes of the finest,
clearest sea-crystal.

In "Gradual Clearing" Clampitt examines tactile definition with invention and precision:

> Late in the day the fog
> wrung itself out like a sponge
> in glades of rain,
> sieving the half-invisible
> cove with speartips;
> then in a lifting
> of wisps and scarves, of smoke-rings
> from about the islands, disclosing
> what had been wavering
> fishnet plissé as a smoothness
> of peau-de-soie or just-ironed
> percale, with a tatting
> of foam out where the rocks are. . . .

Several poems attempt hazardous definition: "Sunday Music" attempts to define "the nature of next"; "Camouflage" attempts to define grief, though not in ways as profound as those employed in "A Procession at Candlemas," "Beethoven, Opus 111," and "The Smaller Orchid," which posits a rather touching definition: "Love is a climate / small things find safe to grow in." "Botanical Nomenclature" suggests that tactile definition will be a means of achieving fusion of "being-and-becoming," "as one day everything breathing / will reach out, with just such / bells on its fingers, to touch / without yet quite having seen / the unlikelihood, the ramifying / happenstance, the mirroring / marryings of all likeness." Whether satisfactory or not, these lexical exercises indicate a poet who is concerned to go beyond the merely expressive, beyond the sheerly descriptive or musical, to the plane of significant ideas.

Another idea that occupies Clampitt's attention is the doctrine of art for art's sake, a notion against which she reacts vigorously. Stirred by the possibilities of "pure imagining," Clampitt has realized in *The Kingfisher* more than surface beauties of sound and vision, though she has not yet come (in 1983) to the point at which her verse's technical intricacies enrich the substance of Hopkins, whom she often cites as a major influence on her work. Still, several poems reflect the process of the poet, if not the arrival.

"Marginal Employment," the first poem in "Watersheds," the fifth section of *The Kingfisher* is about conspicuous waste, an exercise involving the Duc de Berry and Karl Marx. It is, at heart, a poem seeking to define both value and cost. The speaker calls the Duc's precious art collection "the scandal / of such squandered ornament," a vulgar display of excess achieved through the labor of countless workers. The precise valuation "escapes mere totting-up." Exactly here, at a significant line break, the poet declares, "The earth's hours / are weightier" (than the Duc's illustrated, treasured *Tres Riches Heures*), and "the burden / of the ocean's robe . . . is more ponderous than greed." That this is meant as a moral of sorts seems clear, but not much more can be understood from the allusive concluding lines. In this enigmatic ending the poet seems to suggest alternative natural sources of far greater value with the implication that they should be the substance of art, and not "any artifice crafted / for an emperor's enjoyment." The world of nature is more ponderous in at least two senses: it has greater weight (substance) and it is more worthy a subject to ponder. But "Marginal Employment" seems to raise more questions than it answers (perhaps that is the function of good poetry), serving as it does as thematic overture for the poems that follow it: "Tepoztlán," "Remembering Greece," "The Reservoirs of Mount Helicon," "Trasimene," and "Rain at Bellagio"— each a meditation on earth's hours and art, set to attempt an answer to the question posed in "Tepoztlán": "who knows what ultimately is, and what's mere invention?" Taken as a sequence, "Watersheds" is an interrogatory exercise that suggests possibilities rather than proclaiming certainties. And that stance, like Clampitt's sense of narrative, is indeed more faithful to contemporary experience.

The utter seriousness of what is a darkening endeavor manifests itself in the last section, "Hydrocarbon," in which the poet contemplates war, destruction, the Holocaust, the self-immolation of a Quaker pacificist during the Vietnam War, and nuclear devastation. This is not art for art's sake, but art for conscience's sake. The shortest poem in the section, "Berceuse," has existential resonance as well as emblematic force; it is nearly a manifesto in shorthand, reading in part:

Listen to Gieseking playing a Berceuse
of Chopin—the mothwing flutter

light as ash, perishable as burnt paper—

and sleep, now the furnaces of Auschwitz
are all out, and tourists go there.
The purest art has slept with turpitude,

we all pay taxes. Sleep. The day of waking
waits, cloned from the phoenix—
a thousand replicas in upright silos,

nurseries of the ultimate enterprise.
Decay will undo what it can, the rotten
fabric of our response connives with doomsday.

Sleep on, scathed felicity. Sleep, rare
and perishable relic. Imagining's no shutter
against the absolute, incorrigible sunrise.

For Clampitt the world of imagination is not an escape, but an entry. Though she does not think of herself as a public poet, she has unwittingly assumed something of that office.

These darker poems give the lie to some critics' comments that Clampitt does not seem much interested in people. Taken with "A Procession at Candlemas," an eloquent elegy on her mother's death; "Beethoven, Opus 111," which fuses images of the composer and the poet's father; and a scattering of other poems such as "A Hairline Fracture" and "Camouflage"—concerned with personal dislocation and grief—the darker poems constitute the journal of a sensitive soul in process.

On a technical level *The Kingfisher* offers a rich and complex vocabulary drawn from a mind steeped in art, archaeology, music, botany, and zoology; a stunning use of the negative particle (*no*) for rhetorical and aural effect (in stanza 7 of "Marine Surfaces, Low Overcast," for example, and stanzas 2 and 3 of "Sunday Music"); and an uncommon ability to use the powers of alliteration and assonance not only for coherence but also for movement (as in "The Edge of the Hurricane").

There are negative aspects to Clampitt's poetry as well: the often-criticized overloading of descriptive detail, particularly with hyphenated adjectives; convoluted syntax (as in "Or Consider Prometheus"); and eccentric line breaks (as in "Exmoor" and "Gradual Clearing"). Moreover, Clampitt is not a poet who handles the sheerly topical well: "Amaranth and Moly," a narrative poem about bailing a woman out of Riker's Island, and "The Dakota," a short poem about John Lennon's death, are disappointing because, unlike "The Dahlia Gardens" or "The Anniversary," they do not rise above quotidian subject matter.

Despite the uneven quality of *The Kingfisher*, it is impressive for its lyric imaginative play, its palpable delight in the world of nature, its engagement with significant ideas, and its sensitivity to the complexities of ear, eye, and heart. Clampitt is a poet whose spirit often transcends her material, not in flights of fancy, but haunting meditations. Acutely aware of the dangers of the undisciplined imagination, Clampitt understands that some poetry should make a considered statement about the world outside the imagination.

In 1983 Clampitt published: *The Summer Solstice*, and in 1984 *A Homage to John Keats*. Both were printed by the Sarabande Press, a small firm run by Joe Marc Freedman and known for its well-designed, carefully produced texts. *The Summer Solstice*, published in a limited edition on handmade paper, with an attention to detail reminiscent of works produced in medieval monastic scriptoria, is a collection of four poems written at Corea, Maine, in four successive summers (1978-1981) around the time of the summer solstice. These painterly attempts to capture land- and seascape, as well as sky, are so successful that they frequently remind the reader of Claude Monet's efforts to capture fugitive light, at particular moments, in one place.

"Observances," the first entry in the sequence, is rather loose and discursive. A poem of six stanzas, with each stanza one sentence, it is often crystalline in its depiction of sky, sand, flora, and fauna. The world of nature moves continuously ("an ocean that's always / the same in being never / the same for a moment"), and it is against this backdrop that the poet comes to the real subject of her reflection: the young woman who

> . . . looked out
> distracted perhaps by the prospect
> from a still larger
> distraction, the soundless
> interior commotion of dying—
> will not be coming back this year
> or the next: unreachable now
> as the far side of the solstice. . . .

Though it suffers from some eccentricities of expression (such as "obsessed susurrus," or "an unlit barque equivocal with fireflies"), an awkward metaphor here and there, and a last stanza that ought to be revised radically or even deleted, this poem has the power of a palpable grief that finds some accommodation with experience.

The other three poems seem less successful. "Midsummer in the Blueberry Barrens," a bittersweet lyric, recalls humankind's inability to heed John the Baptist's call for repentance and simplicity, because "we are still not ready / for such singleness, for so much sorrow." "Arcane Habiliments," a much too proselike description of atmospheric effects on Midsummer Day, seems rather inert for such a subject. Though it begins with a mischievous image—"Midsummer daylight came in rumpled / as a rummage sale, a gypsy ragbag / of fog and fair"—the homely vitality of that promise is not fulfilled in the rest of the poem. And in "The Turning," the last poem, that inability to sustain the effects generated in the first few lines ("The whole world lying ripe / at evening, voluptuous / with light and air—") renders the poem the weakest of the four in *The Solstice*. Though none of the poems in this little book is a developed example of Clampitt at her best, each one—in varying measure—shows a luminescent poetic intelligence at work.

The eight-poem sequence that is *A Homage to John Keats* appears without revision as the centerpiece of Clampitt's second major collection, *What the Light Was Like* (1985). This volume of forty poems is dedicated to the memory of her brother, Richard.

Like *The Kingfisher*, *What the Light Was Like* is a collection of careful design; divided into five parts, it is sustained and directed by metaphors of movement, with the cycle "Voyages" (*A Homage to John Keats*) set as its energizing center. Here again movement is not linear nor plotted on a cause-and-effect grid; rather, ideas hover, then recur with darkening force.

The collection opens with "A Baroque Sunburst," a poem of eclectic descriptive effects expressive of a longing for movement, which is emblematic for the volume and for Clampitt's restless, yearning poetic energies. *What the Light Was Like* demonstrates significant advances for Clampitt: a deepening awareness of the rhythms of life and death, an even more articulate sense of definition, and a greater technical assurance. Poems such as "Cloudberry Summer," with cloudberries described as "pale-jeweled morsels of seed and sweetness"; "Gooseberry Fool," in which "the acerbity of all things green / and adolescent lingers; "Low Tide At Schoodic," wherein "spruces, / turreted above the ledge, / lodge in the downdraft / of their precarious stairwells"; and

Dust jacket for Clampitt's second commercially published book (1985), which is dedicated to the memory of her late brother, Richard, and includes poems occasioned by his death

certainly the title poem itself—all manifest a heightened evocation of place. Land- and seascapes breathe with the vitality of character for this poet who is deeply attached Down East; though not permanently rooted there, this summer visitor, like so many others, has come to feel at home along the coast of Maine. *What the Light Was Like* also contains several poems about animals, especially cats. Both "Bertie Goes Hunting" and "The Spruce Has No Taproot" begin as narrative vignettes before becoming meditations, the former on habit and instinct, the latter on resistance to "one more uprooting." The ostensible subject of both poems, a humble cat, is treated with affection ("Dear beast, luxurious of pelt" opens "Bertie Goes Hunting") and an abiding sense of fellow feeling. Another poem, "Townhouse Interior With Cat," creates a precisely rendered context; the poem is poised and articulate, a virtuoso

performance about something so ordinary that one wonders whether or not it was worth the effort.

In *What the Light Was Like* Clampitt may be even more clearly and comfortably autobiographical than in *The Kingfisher;* certainly a poem such as "Black Buttercups," which calls to mind both Elizabeth Bishop and Marianne Moore, succeeds as an affecting reflection on dislocation, in good measure because of Clampitt's transparently recalled personal experience. Her ability to link resonant imagery with memory enables that experience to become a symbol of the greater dislocation from childhood to adulthood. In a rare occurrence, anger surfaces, as in "Burial In Cypress Hills," which traces a friend's funeral procession ("her case botched by a vandal of a Brooklyn doctor") through East Flatbush to "this motel of the dead." Clampitt's feelings are most palpable in poems about human beings in this collection, which is dominated by themes of death and loss.

"From a Clinic" and "A Curfew" were occasioned by the death of the poet's brother, Richard. Each is an occasional poem in the best sense of the word: an exercise that, though grounded in the experience of a particular event, transcends the quotidian. In the first, the poet, locked in "the denser enclave of the stricken, / eight stories up," juxtaposes her own stasis to the movement of winter geese, "the one thing always on the move," and poses a question that applies not only to them but to her brother and herself as well: "where are they going?" "A Curfew," which bears the notation of "December 13, 1981," the day of her brother's death, juxtaposes several images: her brother ("listening, / head down, eyes impassive, musing, feeling his way"), herself ("my brother dead, I cried over the news"), and "the universe's grand indifference" to both of them. Clampitt's cinematic shifting of perspective sets the hospital-room scene of death within the greater context of a world in unceasing flux, whether physiological, evolutionary, or political. This is the poetry of quest, with Alfred Russel Wallace, Democritus, Clampitt's brother, and the poet herself all linked in a common human process, the search for meaning. One question resonates, posed in "Urn-Burial and the Butterfly," for all of them: "If meaning is a part of any system, / what laws apply?"

The power of these two consecutive poems is enhanced by the placement of a third immediately after them: "Urn Burial and the Butterfly Migration" is a lovely elegy in the English metaphysical tradition, an inquiry that sets in parallel the movement of a butterfly, the dead brother, and the poet, and emphasizes the rigor of becoming. While asserting that "we know nothing / of the universe we move through," Clampitt acknowledges that because "our / home—is motion," there is no rest for the mind in search of meaning. With the vigor of honest clarity, Clampitt avoids the easy, specious answers possible in a poem that yokes movement, death, the butterfly, and the human spirit.

The theme of motion can be seen in the title poem as well as in the "Voyages" sequence. Arguably the finest poem in the collection and perhaps the finest Clampitt has written, "What the Light Was Like" has been described by Christopher Reid (*London Review of Books*, 17 April 1986) as "an elegy of the highest order as complex and as dignified as [John Milton's] 'Lyci-

das.' " Clampitt's memorial to Ernest Woodward, a Maine lobsterman and summer acquaintance of hers, moves with an incremental grandeur. Each stanza has a near-tidal rhythm to it, alternating long and short lines in verse paragraphs of six lines. Like the "iridescent hummingbird" hovering over the lilac bushes in Woodward's front yard, the presence of Walt Whitman and his elegy for the Civil War dead hovers over this poem, cloaking it with a nobility and grandeur born from suffering. Clampitt's description creates a scene reminiscent of paintings by John Frederick Kensett: lustrous and serene, yet lit with quicksilver flashes of life. As Robert B. Shaw (*Nation*, 29 June 1985) has noted, "The poetic imagination which has been able to encompass all the changes of light on the water, all the hum and bustle of the coastal flora and fauna, comes up against the ultimate blankness, the loss of all imagery in contemplating an instant transition from life to death":

> they spotted him, slumped against the kegs. I find
>   it
>   tempting to imagine what,
> when the blood roared, overflowing its cerebral
>   sluiceway,
>   and the iridescence
>
> of his last perception, charring, gave way to
>   unreversed,
>   irrevocable dark,
> the light out there was like. . . .

This is a leap of poetic imagination, a feat of intelligence, empathy, and craft rarely equaled in contemporary poetry. Though the lobsterman's journey has ended, the poet's journey continues from one June to the next: "Among the mourning-cloak-hovered-over lilac peaks, their whites and purples, / when we pass his yard, / poignant to excess with fragrance, this year we haven't / seen the hummingbird."

The metaphor of the journey finds its most developed expression in "Voyages," a series of biographical sequences at the heart of the collection. In her notes to the cycle, Clampitt identifies the source of her inspiration: "The powerful way in which literature can become a link with times and places, and with minds otherwise remote, suggested itself to me as I read W. Jackson Bate's biography, *John Keats* (Harvard University Press, 1963)."

In response Clampitt has fashioned a sequence of poems that trace aspects of Keats's life and career from 1816 to 1818, following him from Margate to Hampstead, Teignmouth, Liverpool, Edinburgh, Chichester, the Isle of Wight, and Winchester. In personal terms, for Keats the period was marked by the death of one brother, Tom, and the departure of another, George, for Kentucky, as well as Keats's acquaintances with Isabella Jones and Fanny Brawne. In artistic terms, the period witnessed agonies of inspiration and composition—"one bookish sonnet: 'Much have / I traveled . . . ' "; an incomplete *Hyperion;* an *Endymion* "stillborn"; and the genesis of *The Eve of St. Agnes.* Reid has aptly described "Voyages" as an effort "to anatomise the development of Keats's imagination at a crucial period of his life." And Reid may well be accurate to deliver a negative verdict on the narrative level of the poems; as other readers have pointed out, "Voyages" is rather bookish, too tied to the documentary mode. Clampitt's lyric mode seems ill wed to such scholarly data.

Yet because it is far more than biographical narrative, "Voyages" may be counted a success. Linked to the journey motif, this series constitutes what J. D. McClatchy has termed "an extraordinary act of self-definition" (*New Republic,* 22 April 1985). Clampitt found points of similarity between Keats and herself: one brother lost, another wandering in a wilderness much like the Midwest she herself left behind—a certain biographical resonance inheres in the data. But far more important are points of aesthetic kinship between the two artists.

In the third poem of the sequence, telling of George Keats's foray into the New World (to Kentucky), Clampitt asks, "what can John Keats / have had to do with a hacked clearing / in the Kentucky underbrush?" It is Clampitt herself who is the answer in this case: she is that point of intersection between the great Romantic mythology and the world of the American landscape.

The kinship is aesthetic: the fondness for myth, high rhetoric, and classical eloquence and images; the delight in sound; the engagement with the literature and culture of the past; the pain of promise unfulfilled, creation stillborn, and the failure of inspiration. Clampitt does not envision herself as another Keats—such presumption is alien to her. Rather, she sees herself as a member of what Alfred Corn (*New York Times Book Review,* 19 May 1985) has termed an "aesthetic community," whose outward embrace includes Homer, Walt Whitman, John Milton, Wallace Stevens, Hart Crane, Marianne Moore,

Elizabeth Bishop, Emily Dickinson—all those poets who hover over Clampitt's verse.

In technical terms *What the Light Was Like* resembles *The Kingfisher*: it is a collection organized according to a plan, here the motif of journeying, from "The Shore" to "The Hinterland" to "Voyages" deep within, out to "The Metropolis" and beyond to "Written in Water." The declaration embedded in the poem "Urn Burial and the Butterfly migration," that "our home is motion," informs the poetry here. According to McClatchy, "sentences take a deep breath and drift through stanzas of development syntactically volute, rhythmically nervous." Clampitt lights on one subject, then others, and spins out the rich possibilities of a flexible, sinuous poetic line. Rarely holding herself to the strict demands of any stanzaic or metrical norm, she creates her own measure. *What the Light Was Like* is distinguished by a somewhat less hurried pace than that of *The Kingfisher*—perhaps showing an even greater delight in pausing to savor the effects of language on the senses and heart—and by a refined ability to handle the long sentence: syntactical patterns are tighter and clearer, as subjects, verbs, and objects are aligned with fewer clauses and phrases intervening. In poems such as "What the Light Was Like," "Black Buttercups," and "A Curfew," Clampitt demonstrates an ability to modulate voice in ways perfectly consistent with and expressive of her poetic concerns. "Low Tide at Schoodic," "Let the Air Circulate," and the title poem indicate valuable attention paid to the arrangement of text on the page: she has carefully shaped the stanzas in "What the Light Was Like" to replicate tidal rhythm; she has playfully set the lines of "Let the Air Circulate" so that words and phrases spin into greater resonance; and she effectively breaks the text of "Low Tide" into verse paragraphs, especially at the point of climax.

If it is consistent in its excellence, *What the Light Was Like* is also consistent in its weaknesses: occasional overloading of descriptive detail (as in "Gooseberry Fool"); strained allusion stitched into the fabric of some poems (such as "A Scaffold"); and a fondness for topical poems that fail to rise to the level of the collection as a whole (for example, "Vacant Lot with Tumbleweed and Pigeons" and "The Godfather Returns to Color TV").

In sum, however, *What the Light Was Like* demonstrates the substantial promise of *The Kingfisher* fulfilled. Though she has a distinctive voice,

Dust jacket for Clampitt's 1987 collection, which includes poems that resulted from her travels in Greece. The marble statue is the Ornithe *by Geneleos (circa 560 B.C.), an important image in the poem "Archaic Figure."*

Clampitt is not a singer but a seer—an authentically American poetic sensibility whose greatest aesthetic affinity lies, not paradoxically, with the most gifted Romantic poet of the English tradition. Like Keats she possesses a heightened sensitivity to the sensuousness of language; an ever-deepening appreciation for the literature and civilizations of the past, particularly Greece; and a longing for light, order, and beauty.

Given the centrality of Keats to *What the Light Was Like*, it seems only natural that Clampitt's next book would dwell upon Greece—and so it does, for the first two sections of *Archaic Figure* (1987), "Hellas" and "The Mirror of the Gorgon," are the results of her travels in Greece. But surprisingly these do not constitute the strongest poetry of the collection.

"Hellas" comprises eight poems of the Greek experience, and while these are often the marvelous evocations of place that Clampitt does so well ("The Olive Groves of Thasos," "Ano Prinios," "Leaving Yannina"), there is far more going on than nostalgic scene painting. In "Archaic Figure," "Tempe in the Rain," and "Dodona: Asked of the Oracle," female experience, whether that of the subject or of the poet, assumes centrality. Clampitt writes of women in myth, whether classical (as in "Dodona," where female deities associated with this most famous shrine of Zeus appear) or religious (as in "Tempe in the Rain," where the poet's search for Daphne yields an icon of the Virgin Mary). "Archaic Figure," a poem of three landscapes—the American Midwest the poet has left behind; East Berlin, where the *Ornithe* of Geneleos rests in the Pergamon Museum; and the world of sixth-century B.C. Greece from which the statue came—condemns cultural relativism and contemporary notions of superiority. This "mere girl" (the Ornithe), who saw "with unexampled clarity to the black core / of what we are, of everything we were to be, / have since become," stands as emblematic figure at the gateway of this collection, speaking with precision, conviction, and not a little disappointment.

Section 2, "The Mirror of the Gorgon," and section 3, "A Gathering of Shades," illustrate Lachlan Mackinnon's understanding of the whole volume as "an exploration of the ways in which women have been perceived and have seen themselves" (*Times Literary Supplement*, 3-9 June 1988). The mythic figure Medusa is central to the first sequence, Clampitt says but it is unclear how Medusa functions other than as a scattered image of "what experience does to the human psyche." Clampitt elaborates by noting that these poems also have to do with "the way experience otherwise scarcely bearable is reflected in the works of art and literature." The seven poems in "The Mirror of the Gorgon" are highly allusive recreations of states of mind and personhood—depression, devastation, exile, and alienation. At some levels, certain poems may become emblematic of whole cultures juxtaposed to heighten similarities ("Seriphos Unvisited," "Perseus Airborne"), or they may underscore what the poet sees as inevitable consequences ("Atlas Immobilized"), but there is so little here that the demanding reader is likely to remain restless, unsatisfied, and more than a little mystified, or even irritated, by references to classical mythology, nineteenth-century travelogues, and autobiographical fragments that do not display the integrating powers of Clampitt's quickened poetic intelligence at its best. "A Gathering of Shades," the most artistically successful section, will be discussed later.

"Attachments, Links, Dependencies," the fourth section of *Archaic Figure*, draws together twelve poems about diverse places and subjects, related by what Clampitt calls "the experience of attachment"—to persons, certainly, but also to places (as in "London Inside and Outside," "Venice Revisited," and "Midsummer in the Blueberry Barrens"), and to varying modes of expression. Sometimes an explicit poetic statement lays matters out, as in "London Inside and Outside":

> The night we took the Underground
> to Covent Garden, we found the foyer
> at the opera a roofed-in waterfall
> of crystal, the staircase we sat on
> at the interval to eat our ices
> carpet-luscious (even to the shod
> sole) as a bed of crimson mosses,

the rose-red lampshades erotic
as hothouse hibiscus.

Other times expression is metaphorically based, as in "A Hermit Thrush," "Continental Drift," and "The Waterfall." Taken as a group, these are not the strongest poems in the collection; they seem to be bound together by the lowest common denominator of the section's title. Though "Venice Revisited" attempts to juxtapose the narrator's second visit to that city with the experience of a homesteader's wife on the American frontier and the astronauts walking on the moon, it simply does not work. "A Hermit Thrush" emerges as the best poem in the section, probably because it weaves readily apprehensible experience into a meditative, poetic fabric that reveals a poet who remains acutely attentive to all her senses, alert to nature, sensitive to others, and honest enough to ask hard questions.

The core of *Archaic Figure* is "A Gathering of Shades," a series of ten poems at whose center lies the volume's finest creation, "An Anatomy of Migraine." This two-hundred-line poem constitutes an inquiry into "what consciousness is made of," and it moves from the historical past to the existential present, as the poet gathers what she calls "an elite / vised by the same splenic coronet"— "Dorothy Wordsworth, George Eliot, Margaret / Fuller, Marx, Freud, Tolstoy, Chopin, Lewis / Carroll, Simone Weil, Virginia Woolf." Within this poem and the nine others that form a "splenic coronet" about it, the women's conditions affect Clampitt the most: Simone Weil, who knew that consciousness pulses with pain; the California woman, Annette Leo, to whom the poem is dedicated; and the poet herself. In the last stanzas of the poem, Clampitt announces the formation of another aesthetic community, this one born of, and oddly sustained by, a liberating pain: "I / live with shades of possibility, / with strangers, friends I never spoke to, with / the voices of the dead, the sunlight like gold / water on the wall— electron-charged, precarious—all tenuously made of consciousness." With "Anatomy of Migraine" as the symbolic center of the section, the preceding poems about women assume their places as voices of a shared consciousness inhabiting a landscape of pain: "George Eliot Country," "Medusa at Broadstairs," and "Highgate Cemetery" follow George Eliot from the Midlands to London, Broadstairs, and Highgate, that famous cemetery where Herbert Spencer and Karl Marx, "his memory red with nosegays ribboned in Chinese," re-

The Prairie

"Tish-ah!" said the grass. . . . . "Tish-ah, tish-ah."
. . . . Never had it said anything else — would it say
anything else.

O. E. Rölvaag, _Giants in the Earth_

The chattering, the whistling, the scratching, the bass, tenor
& treble voices of the steppe — all blend in a continuous
monotonous hum . . . . . You feel a terrible ...
regret, as if the steppe knew how lonely she is, . . .
& through the ... slumber you hear her ... hopeless
cry for a bard, a poet of her own.

Chekhov, _The Steppe_ (trans. ...)

1

That Anton Chekhov, son of a storekeeper,
grandson of a self-emancipated peasant, came
... (among the stillborn ... to do)
into existence at Taganrog, on the Sea of Azov,
a ... of days before my father's birth,
howling too, likewise doomed to strive ...:
the coincidence for a ... , looping ...
electric, for the reason that across the ...
of the childhood of Anton Chekhov (he largely
thought not altogether miserable childhood
it ... but have been), there lay the steppe:
a shimmering cowl of voices, multifarious,
indistinct a ... where everything
... happens : the uncertain ...,
... yearning for a ... a voice, a bard.

Manuscript for a poem published in Clampitt's collection Westward _(by permission of Amy Clampitt)_

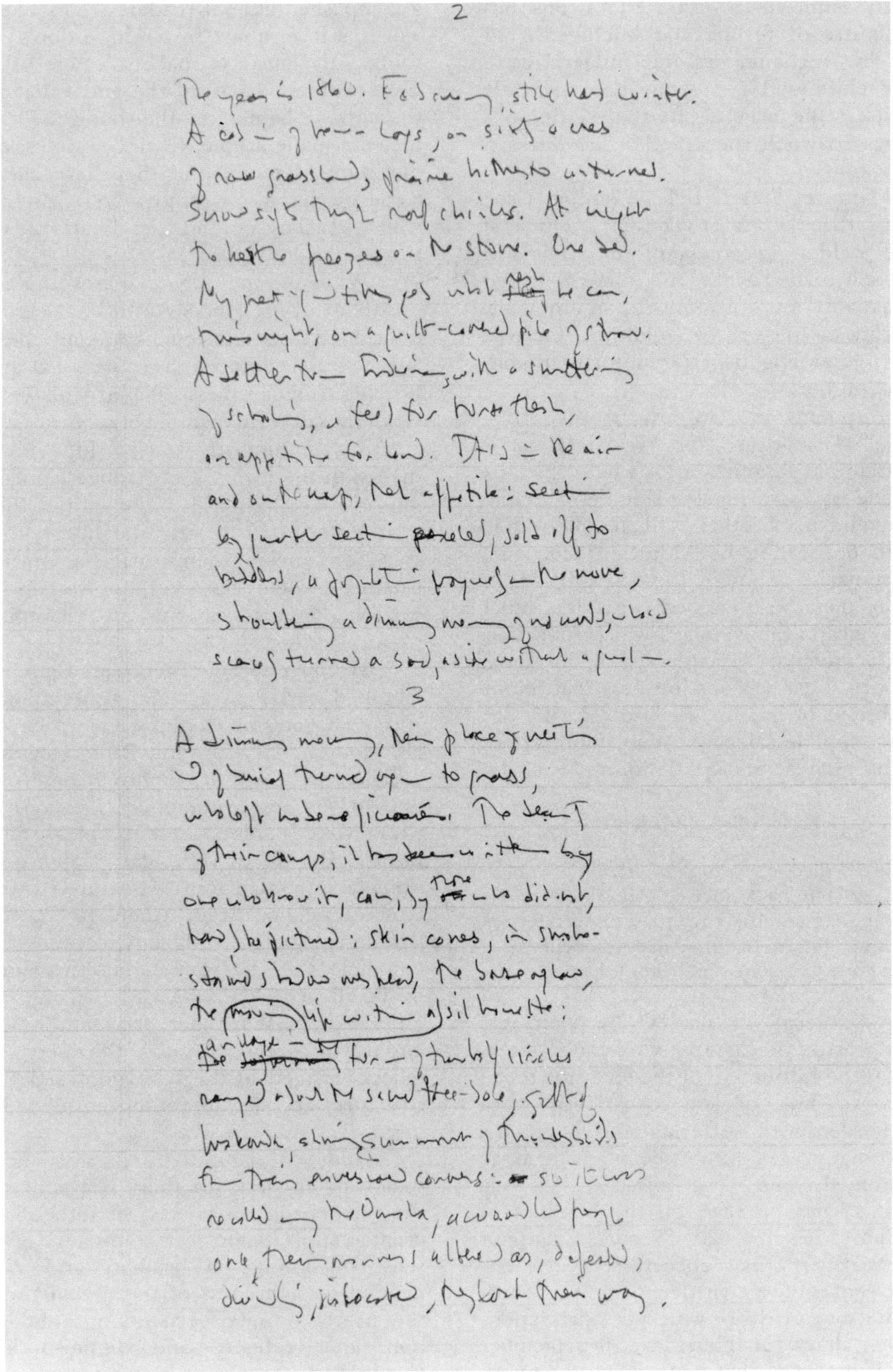

2

The year is 1860. Following still hard winter.
A cold [...] of brave boys, on sixty acres
of new grassland, prairie hitherto unturned.
Snow sifts through roof chinks. At night
the kettle freezes on the stove. One bed.
My poetry [...] the boys, who did what [...] he can,
this night, on a quilt-covered pile of straw.
A settler turned hardier, with a smattering
of schooling, a feel for turned flesh,
an appetite for land. This is the air
and outcrop, not appetite: section
by quarter section parceled, sold off to
bidders, a forgotten purpose—to move,
shouldering a dining room of [...], who
scarcely turned a sod, as he without a purse—

3

A dining room, their place of meeting
of buried turned up—to pass,
who slept in beds [...]. The dream of
their camp, it has been written by
one who knew it, can, by those who did not,
hardly be pictured: skin cones, in smoke-
stained shadow washed, the breeze aglow,
the [...] life within all silhouette;
[...] for—of twenty circles
ranged about the sacred tree-pole, [...]
buckskin, string summer [...]
for their envision canvas:—so it was
recalled [...] the Omaha, a vanished people
only, their memories altered as, defeated,
divided, jostocated, they lost their way.

pose nearby. Somewhere within Eliot's consciousness, a mixture of feeling and intelligence was quickened by "night terrors. The huge claustrophobia of childhood / starting up again: the dried shriek / the claw about the windpipe"—these things spawned the great fictive works of her imagination.

In "Margaret Fuller, 1847" Clampitt traces Fuller's last three years (1847-1850), a time in which the sudden sweetness of an affair with Angelo Ossoli turned bitter, migraines returned, and "an actuality more fraught / than any nightmare: terrors of the sea, of childbirth, the massive, slow / unending heave of human trouble" took its toll on her.

Three poems on Dorothy Wordsworth—"Grasmere," "Coleorton," and "Rydal Mount"—continue Clampitt's inquiry into "what consciousness is made of," weaving the double biography of Dorothy and her brother William; she was afflicted with headaches, he with an "incorrigibly nervous stomach." Though these last poems in the section may be weighted with too much historical/biographical evidence, which sometimes creates a documentary heaviness, they do render vivid, illusory states of consciousness that illuminate dimensions of the creative process while setting up memorable tableaux, none more affecting than this glimpse in "Rydal Mount":

> Her brother, poet laureate
>
> since Southey died, obeys her, sits here
> with her, watching: a doddering pair, like
> gypsies camping out, the way they'd camped
> one night at Tintern, the untended grandeurs
> of a time gone dim gone dim behind them.

In "A Gathering of Shades" the poetry has a purpose worthy of Clampitt's extended attention, for it is the fulfillment of the epigraph to *Archaic Figure*: "The ancient consciousness of women, charged with suffering and sensibility, and for so many ages dumb, seems, in them, to have brimmed and overflowed . . . (Virginia Woolf, *The Common Reader*, on the heroines of George Eliot)." Poetry has become Clampitt's means of access to that ancient consciousness, which she shares in by virtue not only of craft and learning but of deep, wide personal experience. In her diary for Thursday, 30 September 1926, Woolf observed that inquiry "on the mystical side of this solitude" was "frightening and exciting in the midst of my profound gloom, depression, boredom. . . ." For her, the act of writing

accomplished little, if readers are to take her own words at face value ("by writing I don't reach anything. All I mean to make is a note of a curious state of mind. I hazard the guess that it may be the impulse behind another book . . ."). Clampitt, too, has made a note, or rather notes, on a curious state of mind, and they have certainly become the impulse behind a book, *Archaic Figure*, which reaches beyond the limits of Clampitt's first two major collections.

While *Archaic Figure* shares the informing metaphor of the journey with both earlier collections, here the poet deepens and enriches the metaphor as she explores a very personal geography. Probing consciousness, she articulates a necessary, causal relationship between suffering and creativity, finding stronger kinship with the dead than with the living. The strongest poems in this impressive collection deal not with mythology but with history, particularly the history of women able to convert their suffering into writing, whether prose or poetry; those women for whom suffering became catalytic are Clampitt's metaphorical sisters.

Within a period of ten years Clampitt has established herself as a major contemporary poet. Although notes of Hopkins, Frost, Stevens, Lowell, Moore, Whitman, and Bishop shade her expression and color the timbre of her voice, she is one of the few contemporary American poets whose voice is immediately and pleasurably recognizable. Her poetic vocabulary is dense with allusions from myriad sources: nature (from Iowa to Greece), religion (from Athena to Christ), science (from geology to ornithology, oceanography, and entomology), art (from manuscript illumination to Beethoven), and literature (from Homer to Hopkins). In short, her erudition is impressive and never merely decorative; the energy of "an intellect engaged in the hazardous redefinition of structures no one has yet looked at" is invigorating.

And yet Clampitt dwells not solely in the realms of intellect, for there is a palpable life of the emotions in her poetry, an authentic and reverential appreciation for the mystery of nature, a sense of outrage at brutality and violence, a deeply felt awareness of the life of the spirit in the nearly infinite permutations and combinations that enhance and diminish life. Amy Clampitt's poetry, at its best, weaves together the life of the mind and the life of the spirit. Nothing is beneath her consideration; with a singular intensity reminiscent of the Quaker art of "near looking," the very act of observation fuses multiple ways of seeing and reflection into one continuous process. Her intellectual curiosity takes her in many directions as she does what she believes a poet must do: "sort out values, . . . discriminate between the authentic and the phony, preserve what is worth preserving." As Helen Vendler has noted, "to enter a Clampitt poem is to enter a distinguished mind that goes on an unpredictable journey." That journey began some time ago with verses composed by a nine-year-old girl on a farm in Iowa; it has continued with published collections written by an American poet of steadily evolving powers. Clampitt's latest book, *Westward*, was published in 1990.

Interviews:

Judson Brown, "Out of Iowa: A Literary Nomad Encamps Here," *Daily Hampshire Gazette*, 17 June 1987, pp. 25-26;

Laura Fairchild, "Amy Clampitt: An Interview," *American Poetry Review*, 16 (July/August 1987): 17-20.

References:

Richard Howard, "The Hazardous Definition of Structures," *Parnassus*, 11 (Spring/Summer 1983): 271-275;

J. D. McClatchy, "Earthbound and Fired-Up," *New Republic*, 192 (22 April 1985): 38-40;

Patricia Morrisroe, "The Prime of Amy Clampitt," *New York*, 17 (15 October 1984): 44-48;

Robert B. Shaw, "A Fine Excess," *Nation*, 240 (29 June 1985): 803-804;

Helen Vendler, "On the Thread of Language," *New York Review of Books*, 30 (3 March 1983): 19-22;

Edmund White, "Poetry as Alchemy," *Nation*, 236 (16 April 1983): 485-486.

Peter Cooley

(19 November 1940 -   )

Patrick Bizzaro
East Carolina University

BOOKS: *How to Go* (N.p.: G.S.S.C. Publications, 1968);

Voyages to the Inland Sea V, by Cooley and Dennis Trudell (La Crosse, Wis.: Center for Contemporary Poetry, 1975);

The Company of Strangers (Columbia: University of Missouri Press, 1975);

Miracles, Miracles (La Crosse, Wis.: Juniper, 1977);

The Room Where Summer Ends (Pittsburgh: Carnegie-Mellon University Press, 1979);

Nightseasons (Pittsburgh: Carnegie-Mellon University Press, 1983; London: Ferrer & Simons, 1983);

Canticles and Complaintes (Boston: Ford-Brown, 1987);

The Van Gogh Notebook (Pittsburgh: Carnegie-Mellon University Press, 1987).

Peter Cooley writes poetry that possesses the rare quality of being personal without being impenetrably private. Though he draws upon the various elements of his background to write a poetry in which he unavoidably collides with himself, Cooley confesses that he is always "in the company of strangers, myself " (title poem, *The Company of Strangers*, 1975). Cooley's reliance on personal experience for subject matter, or perhaps the self-imposed requirement that he make sense of his life in his writing, has led many critics to view him as a confessional poet. But Cooley has made every effort, especially in recent books, to direct his pursuit of self-knowledge outward, relieving himself of the burden of self-consciousness that makes a poem private and one-dimensional rather than personal and mysterious. He has been more successful in recent years at writing such personal poems than in his early writings.

Peter John Cooley was born 19 November 1940 in Detroit, Michigan, the son of Paul John Cooley, an insurance executive, and Ruth Esther Cooley. Peter received an A.B. in humanities from Shimer College in 1962, spending his se-

nior year in Paris. In 1964 he earned an M.A. from the University of Chicago, where he majored in art and literature and wrote a thesis entitled "e.e. cummings as poet and painter." Cooley married Jacqueline Marks on 12 June 1965, and they were to have three children: Nicole, Alissa, and Joshua. In 1970, after writing a book of original poems, "Vacancies of Sleep," as his dissertation, Cooley received the Ph.D. in English from the University of Iowa, with a concentration on modern literature and creative writing. From 1970 until 1977 Cooley taught at the University of Wisconsin-Green Bay. In 1977 he took a position at Tulane University in New Orleans, where he has continued to teach and is now a professor of English. He has also been poetry editor of *North American Review* since 1970.

Cooley's poetry—which has appeared in over three hundred magazines, including the *New Yorker*, the *Atlantic, Harper's, Esquire, Poetry, Antaeus*, and *Virginia Quarterly Review*—has ignited something of a controversy among critics. There are those who diminish the introspection prevalent in Cooley's poetry by arguing, as Barry Wallenstein does in the *American Book Review* (1980), that "focus on the self is in itself not a liability, but variety and breadth or depth of experience would provide an anodyne to this sort of egocentrism. Cooley's range is a narrow one." By contrast, David Wojahn in *Northeast* (Summer 1981) argues, "Cooley is a solipsistic writer, but he also seeks to be a kind of lightning rod for the suffering of others." Cooley seems to be a writer whose struggle with defining the self, both universal and personal, has signaled to critics a changing aesthetic: what had been characteristic of early confessional poetry has been joined to a sincere concern for the place of all people on this planet, resulting in the kinds of struggles to move away from self-absorption that typify Cooley's writing at its best.

The Company of Strangers, Cooley's first full-length collection of poetry, has been described as having many of the flaws typical of first books, in-

Peter Cooley with his son, Joshua, at their home in New Orleans, October 1989

cluding the juxtaposition of powerful poems with weaker ones. But most critics saw in Cooley's poetry an extraordinary voice, which portrays in sharp and sometimes anguished tones the tension between the poet's public self as a planet dweller and the poet's darker, less understood, private self. But what enables Cooley's poetry to rise above the confessions of others of his generation is the distillation of language, the encapsulation of experience, as in these lines from "The Way Back" with their occasional surrealistic impulses: "The way back is angular, marble, / sunlight turning a frieze to motion, / the horses' hooves, the charioteer, / anticipation of pure ascent." This is the way back to the self that Cooley examines throughout the collection. Most often during such travels he is in the company only of himself, though sometimes in his early volumes he is guided, protected, or inspired by the angels he writes of in generating what Philip Dacey (in *Three Rivers Poetry Journal*, 1978) has termed "a con-

temporary personal angelology." But Cooley always stays close to the planet. These poems, written while Cooley lived in Green Bay, are set in Detroit, in Wisconsin, or, more specifically, in the men's room at the Vic Theater in Green Bay.

Cooley's move south changed the locale of his poems without disturbing his need to focus attention inward and, eventually, outward to note in the behavior of others mirrors of his own motions. *The Room Where Summer Ends* (1979), by narrowing even further the range of Cooley's subjects, offers greater clarity of purpose and integrity of vision than his earlier work. While he continues to search the self in these poems, his new home in New Orleans changes the setting, bringing into his poems bamboo groves and southern flora. "Stranger, north or south, / the trees, the birds, the wind / are your mouth. Speak with them," Cooley instructs himself in "Moving South, He Hears This Colloquy Inside Himself." In "Observances," Cooley shows how the vision

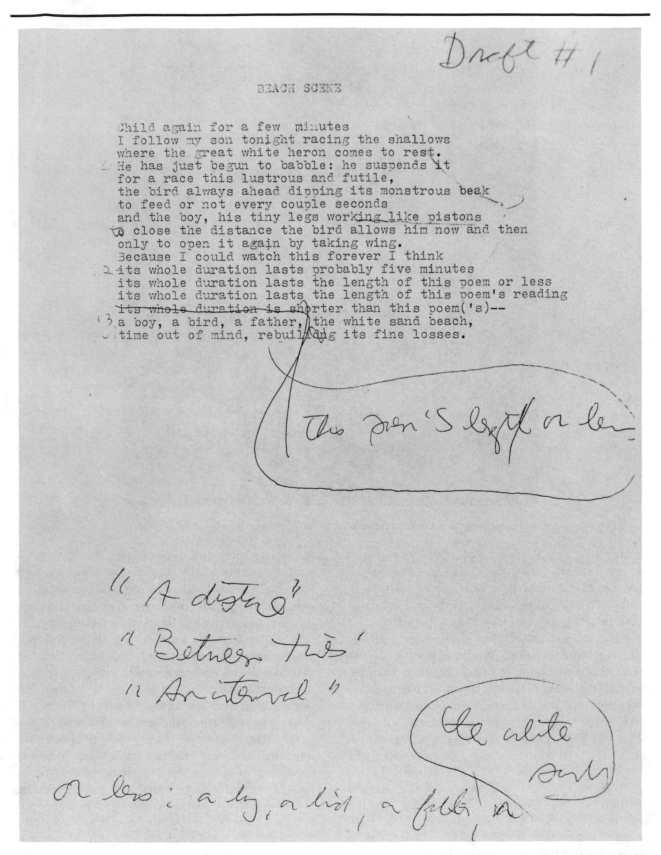

Draft #5

COOLEY - 26

COUNTDOWN

Child again for a few minutes,
I follow my son tonight racing the shallows
where the great white heron comes to rest.
He has just begun to babble; he suspends it
for a race that monotonously fascinates—
first the bird, always ahead, dipping a monstrous beak
to feed or not feed every few seconds,
next the boy, his miniature legs torquing the wind
to close the distance the bird allows him now and then
only to open it again by taking wing.
Because I could watch this forever, I think
its whole duration lasts a poem's length
or less: three shadows one sometimes against the sand and sea
nothing interrupts, rebuilding each one its fine losses.

Final version Appeared in *The Nation*

this poem appears in *The Astonished*
Hours to be published by Carnegie
Mellon in 1992 (January)

Cooley with his wife, Jacqueline, and daughters, Alissa (left) and Nicole (right), at City Park, New Orleans, 1983

has changed to accommodate the new locale, referring to "the bamboo grove" where "gnats fasten on the moon / like a sudden shower in sunlight / Knitting the garden where I lie."

Significantly in this collection Cooley reaches out for new ways to address the recurring dilemma of self and finds portions of his experience not only reflected in nature but also expressed in the experiences of others, including a mute, an idiot, an old man, a hooker, a saint, a madman, an infant, and a hermit. Poems spoken through these characters reveal a way out of the prison house of self-consciousness—the demise and constant burden of confessional poetry—and into the delta of possibilities explored in his more recent work.

In *Nightseasons* (1983) Cooley deals with his mortality, as he contemplates his relationship to his daughters. He writes in "To My Daughter":

> Because you would not let me go.
> Because I could not let you go.
> Because the room stood over us

still dancing and the blue light reeled
at the window and we staggered
until I tore myself from you,
your tiny hands grappling at the air . . .
This is the reason for the poem.

In this collection, Cooley acknowledges his powerlessness, as in "The Secret":

> Because I was too much with myself
> and myself, I went down to the sea this evening.
> The tide was in, and all along the sand
> the dead were waiting. . . .
> . . . .
> The sea looked straight at me—
> it wouldn't flinch, this funny cemetery
> while I stretched out among the tombs
> surrendering the black light in my limbs,
> my head, to drown it.

Cooley admits that little can be done about forces so much greater than he. In "A Coronal" he writes, "He is a small thing being a man / under the azure shadow of heaven / taken back into himself"; in "He," "what a small thing I am still"; and in "To the Stillborn," "The script is too tiny. / I like not being able to read it." In fact he is better able to approach the study of his life objectively when he sees it mirrored in other lives. "Crows Over the Wheatfield," after Vincent van Gogh's painting, prepares one for Cooley's explorations of van Gogh's life and art in the poet's 1987 collection *The Van Gogh Notebook*.

Suzanne Keyworth in the *Hollins Critic* (1989) claims *The Van Gogh Notebook* "offers ways of viewing other works of art and, at the same time, blossoms into moving poems with their own artistic integrity." Clearly this book is biographical—since it highlights van Gogh's life and work—as well as autobiographical, since no doubt Cooley sees in van Gogh many qualities he has seen in himself. Furthermore, critics agree that Cooley seems to see in van Gogh a symbol of all that is most passionate, most alive, and at greatest risk in each human being, and he sings the praises of those human elements as they are expressed in van Gogh's art and life. These lines from "The Loom" are an example: "The loom is a cage. Our bodies are another. / The light falls, a man and woman trade their threads in it. / The light falls and they stumble, fall in it. / They move through each other, they touch and separate. / They find themselves raveled in the expanse of a great cloth." In this collection Cooley focuses upon the relationship between art and poetry, the poet and his subject, and, most important, one person's experience with tragedy in light of another's.

Overall, Peter Cooley has moved through several phases without ever losing sight of his central focus: the journey toward self-awareness and self-understanding. His early works reveal a barebones, almost confessional confrontation with experience, which changes, in later works, to an acceptance of an individual's insignificance, and culminates, in his most recent work, in an investigation of the life and work of an artist whose emotional torment is most like Cooley's own. Cooley has finished a new collection of poems, entitled *The Astonished Hours*, which Carnegie-Mellon University Press will publish in 1992.

Reference:

Philip Dacey, "Coming Apart at the Seams: The Poetry of Peter Cooley," *Three Rivers Poetry Journal*, 11/12 (1978): 7-10.

Philip Dacey

(9 May 1939 -   )

Steven Wilson
Southwest Texas State University

BOOKS: *The Beast with Two Backs* (Milwaukee: Gunrunner, 1969);

Fish, Sweet Giraffe, the Lion, Snake and Owl (Poquoson, Va.: Back Door, 1970);

How I Escaped from the Labyrinth and Other Poems (Pittsburgh: Carnegie-Mellon University Press, 1977);

Men at Table (Wollaston, Mass.: Chowder Chapbooks, 1979);

The London Poems (Marshall, Minn.: Ox Head, 1979);

The Boy Under the Bed (Baltimore & London: Johns Hopkins University Press, 1981);

Gerard Manley Hopkins Meets Walt Whitman in Heaven and Other Poems (Great Barrington, Mass.: Penmaen, 1982);

Fives (Peoria, Ill.: Spoon River Poetry, 1984);

The Man with Red Suspenders (Minneapolis: Milkweed, 1986);

The London Poems II (Peoria, Ill.: Spoon River Poetry, 1989).

OTHER: *I Love You All Day; It Is That Simple*, edited, with an introduction, by Dacey and Gerald M. Knoll (St. Meinrad, Ind.: Abbey, 1970);

Strong Measures: Contemporary American Poetry in Traditional Forms, edited, with an introduction, by Dacey and David Jauss (New York: Harper & Row, 1986).

In *Strong Measures: Contemporary American Poetry in Traditional Forms* (1986) editors Philip Dacey and David Jauss provide an overview of the continuing presence of formal poetry in contemporary writing. *Strong Measures* brought Dacey and his own poetry a wider audience but also led many readers to identify Dacey as a supporter of formalism over free verse, in one of contemporary poetry's most heated critical battles. While Dacey has written poems in traditional forms (some of which appear in *Strong Measures*), he has also continued to compose much of his best work in free verse. A careful study of the range of Dacey's work will show that, rather than being one who dogmatically argues for a return to formalism, he is a poet who explores the variety of methods available to him in order to communicate best the concerns driving him to write.

Philip Dacey was born on 9 May 1939 in St. Louis, Missouri, to Joseph and Teresa McGinn Dacey. Philip's father was an unskilled factory worker for several companies, finally settling at McDonnell Aircraft in St. Louis. When Dacey's parents divorced, Philip, then about ten years old, was raised by his mother, who supported her family by working as a secretary. Dacey describes his background as "working class. Irish and German descent, with a little Polish in there on my mother's side. I had a Catholic education from Incarnate Word nuns and Jesuit priests for sixteen years." He earned a B.S. from St. Louis University in 1961, an M.A. from Stanford in 1967, and a master of fine arts degree in 1970 from the University of Iowa. Dacey served as a Peace Corps volunteer in Nigeria in the mid 1960s and has taught at the University of Missouri in St. Louis, Miles College, and finally Southwest State University in Marshall, Minnesota, where he is a professor of English. In 1985 Dacey was a distinguished poet in residence at Wichita State University. Dacey married Florence Chard on 25 May 1963, and they were to have three children: Emmett, Fay, and Austin.

Critical response to Dacey's poetry has been consistently favorable, as the following list of awards suggests: a Fulbright lectureship in creative writing in Yugoslavia (1988); two National Endowment for the Arts creative writing fellowships (1975, 1980); YM-YWHA's Poetry Center Discovery Award (1974); two Pushcart Prizes for poetry (1977, 1982); first prizes for poems in *Yankee*, *Poet and Critic*, *Prairie Schooner*, and *Kansas Quarterly*; and many regional awards. Poetry by Dacey has appeared in many of the most important journals, including *Poetry*, *Paris Review*, the *Nation*, *North American Review*, *Georgia Review*, *American Poetry Review*, and *Hudson Review*.

Philip Dacey (photograph by W. Patrick Hinely)

Writing of Dacey's first full-length collection, *How I Escaped from the Labyrinth and Other Poems* (1977), Dave Smith calls the author "something of an anachronism among contemporaries" (*Western Humanities Review*, Summer 1978). He goes on to suggest that Dacey's work has a clear connection with Romanticism because of the poet's belief in the ability of the natural world and everything in it to offer insight into human existence. However, this belief is only a suggestion of the larger context into which most of Dacey's work can be placed.

The most common theme in his poems is an exploration of the conflict between the physical and the spiritual. Like Walt Whitman, Dacey argues for the presence of spirit in every physical object—trees, animals, even dinner forks—and his poems explore the ways in which the spirits of these objects are useful to the poet in his search for understanding. Many of the poems, then, examine everyday life by considering as many possible angles of symbolism inherent in everyday things as can be discovered. Dacey might, therefore, be seen as a practitioner of the

conceit poem, because he often extends his comparisons between the physical world and human life to the farthest natural, spiritual, comic, and linguistic possibilities. If Dacey can be called an anachronism, it is because he attempts to explore the metaphorical potential of images rather than experience. Experience is, in fact, merely a catalyst for the analysis of language and symbol, as Dacey noted in a 1979 interview with Jill Field: "My own experiences tend to go underground and get digested in some internal poem-factory. They get chewed up and re-formed in a way that, when they come out, they're no longer recognizable." Dacey is at once Petrarchan (in his use of the conceit), metaphysical, Romantic, imagistic, and mystical, and such apparently differing approaches make him an intriguing poet.

How I Escaped from the Labyrinth and Other Poems offers insight into Dacey's approach. It is revealing that the verb *to translate* turns up in various forms in many of the poems. This "translation" of the physical into metaphor is a consuming passion for Dacey; he seems bent on finding symbolic meaning in everything he sees or all that occurs.

The book begins with the section "Smile A Beast-Smile," a gathering of poems in which Dacey explores the animal world, all the while carefully relating his discoveries to human life. He argues that animals live without the ability to "translate" events into higher meanings, and this lack of ability is both a blessing to them (they live purely and freely by their impulses) and a deficiency (since they cannot come to understand themselves). Animals survive by violence, and Dacey, as he does in his later works, relates this instinctive animal violence to human sexuality. "The Cat" reminds the reader that cats have a long history of stalking prey and hiding gracefully in trees while surveying their territories, but "years later / in the laps of women," they have become domesticated, their claws now "grown short and tucked / like pale fingers / into the folds of a dress." Thus the cat's relation to humans—animals who can see moral implications in actions, and who, therefore, attempt to create acceptable ways of living—has left it without its powers of pure action; it is a sacrifice to the ordering impulses of human intellect, its "head served up on a plate." Dacey explores this issue of the effect of domestication upon men, as well, in later poems. Just as animals are removed from the violent, yet instinctive and pure ways of the wild, so, Dacey suggests, man is reined in by modern life.

The issue of sexuality is considered in "Coming in from Behind," where the narrator explains how one should engage in true animal sex and implies that male dominance is inherent in sexual intercourse performed naturally:

> place your front two legs
> on the back of your mate;
> spread your hind legs wide. . . .
> . . . .
> You see nothing
> of her face.
> Your head is higher than hers.

But readers are reminded that the human ability to impose meaning is both positive and negative: "you would appear proud / were the position not foolish." The feeling of foolishness, no doubt, is created by a social belief that people do not have sex in that way—animals do. It is the same distancing from pure act that one sees in "The Cat."

"An Air a Wound Sings," the second section of the book, deals with the ways in which people may break out of the order imposed upon their lives by society. Violence becomes a way of escape, but within the context of these poems it is

no longer a physical act. If humans are intellectual animals, Dacey's poems imply, then they will commit violence with their intellects. Such acts of violence occur in hospitals, in living rooms, in letters (the mail), and in art. In "After a Fifteenth-Century Miniature Showing King Mark Stabbing Tristan in the Presence of Ysolt," Dacey first describes the orderliness of the scene: "The floor is checkered. / Everything tilts / at wrong angles / just the right way." The murder itself is then described with such terms as "charming" and "sweetness," and the stabbing becomes for the poet a musical "air / the wound sings," a beautiful, natural occurrence in an artificial world.

Even normal events are reshaped to show how humankind looks for ways out of the social trap. "The Obscene Phone Caller" describes how "you" find pleasure in an obscene call—"when he asks you / to take off your clothes, / you do so"—and in the end "you begin / to breathe heavily. / It will be he / who hangs up first." There is, in these poems, a sense that absurdity is useful for escaping a structured, stifling modern existence. These absurd events (or everyday activities that quickly become absurd) often lead to sexual release or discoveries; perhaps Dacey sees in sex the one occasion in which people truly allow themselves to let go.

What readers find in these sections, and in the two remaining ones, are poems that search daily life, art, and the natural world for evidence that man can still set himself free from what tradition has done to him. Dacey clearly argues that such a release is still possible. He shows readers that, in the struggle between physical and spiritual natures, the physical human impulses—or animal instincts—need to triumph. But how will this be accomplished? Dacey's answer appears to be a paradox. His carefully crafted poems, many written in traditional forms, shape the world into complex metaphorical structures, and yet, as he writes in "How I Escaped from the Labyrinth," the escape was simple: "I kept losing my way." But it is only a paradox on the surface, for readers are instructed to use their intellects to learn from the natural world how one goes about "losing his way." These attempts to lose one's way through careful observation—to overcome learned patterns by looking below the surface—make *How I Escaped from the Labyrinth and Other Poems* an engaging, insightful collection of poetry. As reviewer Vernon Young noted (*Hudson Review*, Winter 1977-1978), to read this book by Dacey "is to experience multiple amusements

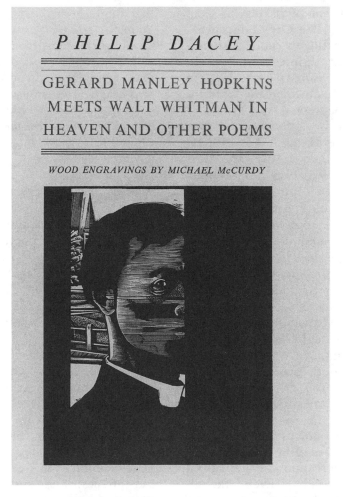

Dust jacket for Dacey's 1982 collection, which the reviewer for Choice *called "a remarkable tour de force"*

and to glimpse some of the finer terrors that lie beyond. . . ."

The Boy Under the Bed (1981) moves further into the poet's consideration of everyday life as material for metaphor. It begins with a series of poems in which the narrator appears to have lost the bravery to take risks—to partake of the many possibilities life can offer. From the first poem of the "Apple-Doors" section, "The Door Prohibited," one senses that the speaker in these poems is aware of, and is saddened by, his hesitancy to try new things—to take the "apple" prohibited him: "the door prohibited, the apple-door, calls, calls or creaks, a smooth / whistle through a crack, a key-hole / where the eye, placed, sees itself, / the secret, trapped, or simply hiding out." In Dacey's first major collection it was the narrator's observation of animals' abilities to act without thought that drove him to open such prohibited doors. In *The Boy Under the Bed* this inspiration has been taken away. "From the Clear-

ing" reminds one of this source of inspiration and reveals the speaker's fear that he has lost it forever. He explains that animals uncover hidden truths by throwing back "the shadow onto themselves. And that / was because the darkness the animals brought / With them was deeper, richer, was black."

In his interview with Field, Dacey discusses his original motivation for writing poetry, a motivation that seems to have become less forceful for him by the time of his second full-length book: "I made a discovery of a private nature that was a shock to me; psychologists use the word trauma. In effect I was wounded and . . . it was through that wound that my first real poetry came. So I associate poetry with the translation of pain into another order." This discovery is somehow related to the concept of violence and animal instinct. By the time of the poems in *The Boy Under the Bed*, this particular impetus for writing poetry has passed, and one senses this lack of direction in the narrator's fear of risking his security, his individuality. In "The Orgy" the speakers worry about participating because such unstructured sex may bring "disintegration" to all: "The God of Orgies / is Disorder / who loves to trample / on a border. / What would we do / without the line / that runs between / your piece and mine?" They decline the invitation because they fear they will lose themselves, but "wept as [they] declined." How can one, then, recover the courage to take chances once it is lost? The "Apple-Doors" section closes with "Rural Fantasia," a poem about children waiting for school buses that never come. The scene soon becomes a static image trapped at the moment when things "almost" happen. The image needs "a key . . . / the thinnest key to ignite / fire" to get the action going again. The narrator is waiting to discover what key will reopen his search for truth.

Section 2, "Spanish Artifacts," provides some evidence of what that key might be. In "Watching a Movie in a Foreign Language Without Subtitles (Cordoba)," the narrator states, "Someone speaks, and you know / You will never understand." But the symbolic meaning comes from what his mind tells him he heard. When a man is shot, it sounds to the narrator as if the gunman said, "We are all dying loaves of bread." Thus the poet finds that his own perception of the natural world offers poetic insight. Even though occurrences seem "inexplicable," they have deeper metaphorical structures the poet can uncover.

In "Nipples Rise to Spirit," section 3, Dacey uses this belief in the metaphorical potential of the everyday as the basis for poems about children, parents, father/son relationships, adultery, marriage, and even the symbols hidden in dinner tables and kitchens. As the title of the section implies, the direction of these poems is from physical to spiritual—or, in literary terms, from object to metaphor. The first poem in the sequence, "Three Anniversaries," illustrates this approach. The speaker examines the tradition that the fifth wedding anniversary is the "wooden" one. He uses this idea to explore how wood can be related to marriage: "We like wood, believe it's / trustworthy. . . . We'll grow into it / like living wood ourselves, / branching out with children. . . ."

Clearly Dacey has found a new motivation for continuing his search for "the secret, trapped, or simply hiding out, as he calls it in "The Door Prohibited." He is often described as one who is optimistic about life—who "believes

that almost everything is for the best," as Vernon Young asserts (*Parnassus*, Fall 1981). Dacey's faith in the world stems from his hope that each event and each object will offer insight into the human condition, and that one can learn from that insight. His "praise of the commonplace and homely," as Robert Phillips has described the poetry in *The Boy Under the Bed* (*Hudson Review*, Autumn 1981), shows a joy for the poetry in everyday life.

Gerard Manley Hopkins Meets Walt Whitman in Heaven and Other Poems (1982) met with much praise for the author's skill in assuming the voices of Hopkins and Whitman, and for recreating Hopkins's poetic techniques and innovations. An anonymous reviewer for *Choice* magazine (October 1981) called the book "a remarkable tour de force." It is a work that pleases because of Dacey's ambition and the light he sheds on Hopkins's poetry. Dacey achieves this triumph through the use of actual biographical information, imagined events and thoughts, and journal entries, letters, and sermon notes composed by Dacey himself. At first such a book might seem a departure from Dacey's earlier emphasis on using objects from everyday life as material for metaphor, but the change is in technique rather than philosophy. Through Hopkins, Dacey continues to examine the tension between the physical and spiritual worlds. He finds, through his understanding of—perhaps even empathy with—Hopkins's battles with desire and love of God, another artist who sought the source of human truths.

The book begins with the poem "Skin" (Hopkins's actual nickname), and readers learn through the voices of the rector of Manresa House (a Jesuit novitiate where Hopkins—the character in the poem—is studying) and Hopkins's master that he seems to be too zealously accepting the idea of physical sacrifice. Hopkins "made a bonfire / At his home in Hempstead the day he left / And burned a stack of poems this thick." The master surmises that Hopkins sees the priesthood as an escape from the physical/spiritual struggle within himself: "I think he thinks in coming here / He's leaving the world behind him and entering / The realm of pure spirit." It is this attempt to discover where pure spirit exists that seems to have drawn Dacey to Hopkins's story, since Dacey himself underwent a similar journey. Readers soon learn, too, that, like Dacey, Hopkins becomes engrossed in careful observation of the world: "I watch too well

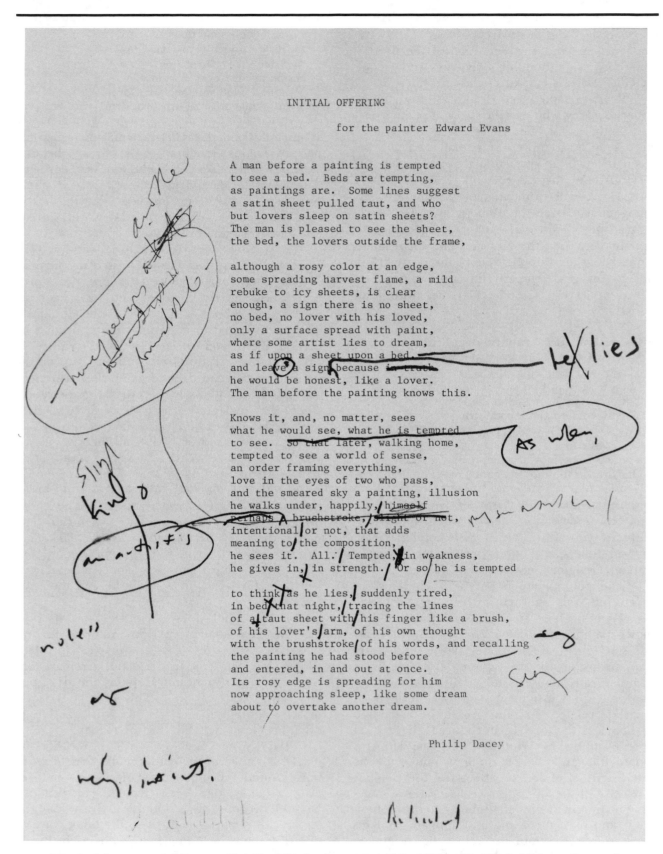

INITIAL OFFERING

for the painter Edward Evans

A man before a painting is tempted
to see a bed. Beds are tempting,
as paintings are. Some lines suggest
a satin sheet pulled taut, and who
but lovers sleep on satin sheets?
The man is pleased to see the sheet,
the bed, the lovers outside the frame,

although a rosy color at an edge,
some spreading harvest flame, a mild
rebuke to icy sheets, is clear
enough, a sign there is no sheet,
no bed, no lover with his loved,
only a surface spread with paint,
where some artist lies to dream,
as if upon a sheet upon a bed,
and leaves a sign because in truth
he would be honest, like a lover.
The man before the painting knows this.

Knows it, and, no matter, sees
what he would see, what he is tempted
to see. So that later, walking home,
tempted to see a world of sense,
an order framing everything,
love in the eyes of two who pass,
and the smeared sky a painting, illusion
he walks under, happily, himself
perhaps a brushstroke, slight or not,
intentional or not, that adds
meaning to the composition,
he sees it. All. Tempted, in weakness,
he gives in, in strength. Or so he is tempted

to think as he lies, suddenly tired,
in bed that night, tracing the lines
of a taut sheet with his finger like a brush,
of his lover's arm, of his own thought
with the brushstroke of his words, and recalling
the painting he had stood before
and entered, in and out at once.
Its rosy edge is spreading for him
now approaching sleep, like some dream
about to overtake another dream.

Philip Dacey

Late draft for a poem that Dacey retitled "Study" before it was accepted for 1991 publication by Midwest Quarterly
(by permission of Philip Dacey)

the wearing, / the mere dress, dross." Does careful, at times tedious, observation of the physical plane turn one's thoughts away from understanding God? Dacey's Hopkins believes it does.

Readers soon meet Hopkins's close friend, Robert Bridges, who sees the spark of poetic greatness in the priest. There are hints, as well, that there may be a repressed sexual attraction between the two, an attraction that only adds fuel to Hopkins's physical turmoil. Late in Dacey's book Hopkins is tormented by dreams in which young men—"Dare / I, Robert, even for laugh, suggest they / Were we?"—enjoy the pleasures of their bodies. Soon these images take on religious connotations, and by the time of the poem "Hopkins to Bridges," Hopkins imagines himself involved in a very sensual encounter with Jesus Christ:

> I was taken aback: saw there the whole
> Man, cock even, Christ-cock, nor nest-
> ed neat and tame on its two eggs
> But aswing, with God sway, God's way
> This way, too, I saw, along the King's
> Thighway, thew and muscle-string.
> . . . .
>   I write to say
> There is a theology of going hard
> Our dreams (but not we, godly) dare.

So, Hopkins discovers, it is in dreams that people come to understand their deepest impulses—truths, if you will. There, spirit combines with physical desires, and one is not confined by intellectual or religious morality.

The penultimate poem finds Hopkins encountering Walt Whitman in heaven, and beside the swimming hole from Thomas Eakins's well-known painting (*Swimming Hole*, 1883), they discuss how poets should undertake to find truth. Hopkins argues for the value of discipline (what Whitman calls "abuse") and sacrifice, while Whitman praises the insights gained by allowing one's desires to rule one's actions. Again the suggestion of homosexual love is introduced, here (and more blatantly) by Whitman, who asks Hopkins to join him and the six nude swimmers in the water. This is, of course, also a call for Hopkins to partake of the joys of physical sensations, something he fought against all his life. After some hesitancy, and playful coaxing by Whitman, Hopkins dives in, races Whitman across the swimming hole, and finally releases himself to the joys (and dangers, Whitman makes clear) of the body. Hopkins says:

> I close my eyes and that's
> My death. I open them, stand up,
> And that's my resurrection. You're the first
> Person my new eyes look on. Let
> My arm around your shoulder, draped
> In my Manley way, signify that.

Whitman asks if the two of them, now a natural part of Eakins's celebration of physical beauty, should "stand / Like two blades, bucks, a certain / Tilt to our heads and jut to our hips / To show our pride in sex?" Hopkins, now believing in the revelatory powers of the physical world, agrees and joins Whitman in the pose.

The book ends with a coda entitled "He Goes to a Costume Party Dressed as Gerard Manley Hopkins," and readers are here presented with Dacey himself, who has "been at work . . . on a book / Of poems about Hopkins." The poet, invited to a costume party, decides to dress as the person who has occupied so much of his thoughts. At the party, Dacey is propositioned by a woman dressed as Marlene Dietrich. Accepting, he follows her up to the guest room, where they make love, the poet all the while describing his lover's body in a way reminiscent of Hopkins's "Windhover." After all, he says, it was Hopkins who asserted that "no one can admire / Beauty of the body more than I do." The poem closes with Dacey asking, "What I / Want to know is, Who's playing Dacey, and Why? / I'll go home tonight and strip down as far / As I can, and maybe meet my part's actor / In the dark. . . ." Readers are left, then, with the implication that only by searching themselves alone, uninhibited, will they discover who is really behind their social masks.

Dacey's book does at times explore its subject too heavy-handedly (for example, in the poem on the sources of art and inspiration, "The Bloomery"), but it is, in the main, a remarkable work that gives insight into Hopkins, the art of poetry, and Dacey, as well. This may be Dacey's most philosophical and abstract work, and it is often his most rewarding for the reader.

Dacey's next book, *Fives* (1984), is, unfortunately, a rather disappointing collection. *Fives* is built around the importance of fives in nature. Dacey's family, one learns from the dedication, has itself become a "five" with the arrival of daughter Fay. In celebration of fives, the book consists of five sections including five poems each. Every poem is a five-stanza, five-lines-per-stanza work. One would assume that a book so carefully structured would have a unity of theme as well, but

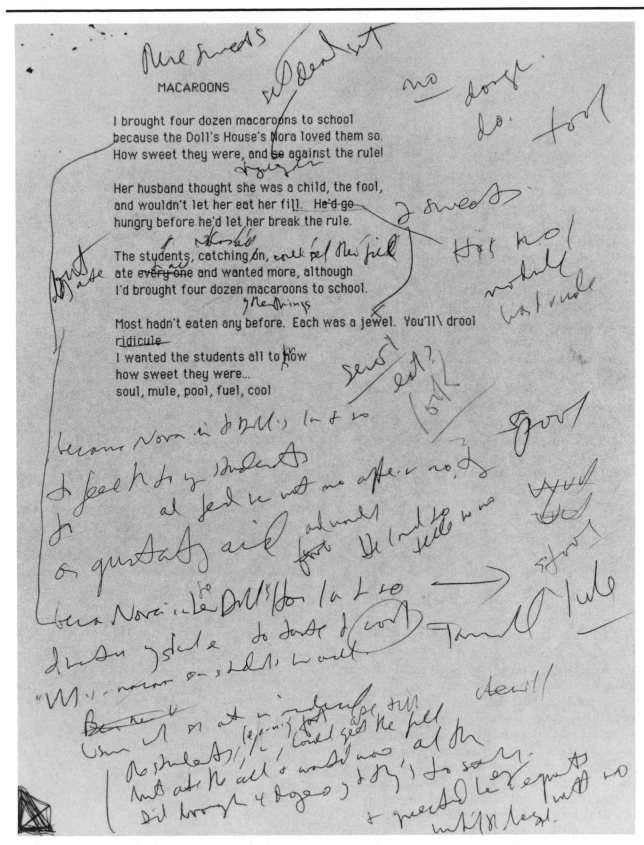

MACAROONS

I brought four dozen macaroons to school
because the Doll's House's Nora loved them so.
How sweet they were, and so against the rule!

Her husband thought she was a child, the fool,
and wouldn't let her eat her fill. He'd go
hungry before he'd let her break the rule.

The students, catching on,
ate every one and wanted more, although
I'd brought four dozen macaroons to school.

Most hadn't eaten any before. Each was a jewel. You'll drool
ridicule
I wanted the students all to know
how sweet they were...
soul, mule, pool, fuel, cool

Early draft for a poem that has been accepted for publication in the Lullwater Review, *Emory University (by permission of Philip Dacey)*

such a unity is never discovered. In general, the sections lack coherence beyond their structural connections. Only section 3, an exploration of women and love of women, fulfills the promise of unity in theme and construction that the organization makes.

More troublesome, however, are poems that suggest Dacey is becoming too comfortable in his established approach. The poems again deal with the symbolism within common events and objects, but here, more often than not, the clever metaphors and surprising connections lose their power through the course of each poem, and endings are disappointing and seem shallow or contrived. It is disturbing to discover, in poems by a poet with a history of revealing wit and insight, that, for example, Dacey advises his audience to read what's "written between the lines" (in "Marginal Existence," a poem about reader/text interaction); or that there are lines that sound like dry information rather than poetry: "Now I want to be Cyaed, / a Welsh verse form" (from "Not Correcting His Name Misspelled on the Mailing Label").

Reviewer Brown Miller suggests that *Fives* is a "gentle, relaxed excursion into metaphoric seeing and knowing" (*San Francisco Review*, January-February 1985). Dacey appears too relaxed here, content to rely on what brought him success in the past rather than take the risks that he argues in earlier books are so crucial in discovering truth.

As noted earlier, Dacey believes poetry to be a "translation of pain into another order," and one learns from the dedication to *The Man with Red Suspenders* (1986) that a painful event, the death of Dacey's sister, Joan, has recently occurred. This fresh tragedy lends many of the poems an emotional force lacking in *Fives* and causes Dacey to put to the test his belief that poetry can reveal meaning and offer solace. In the dedicatory poem, "North Broadway and Grand," Dacey recounts how his only brother, Owen, known for his appearance on the "Candid Camera" television program as "the dancing policeman of St. Louis," supported their sister during her illness—how he was at times "close enough to her / to die himself." When "the most / expensive equipment / couldn't manage" the obstacles and difficulties of the sister's illness and death, it was Owen's "human touch" that "eased / the knot, jam, block, / and everyone got home / safe, everyone." This traumatic experience must have reminded Dacey that it is people who make sense

of the world, who see the spiritual, enduring meaning in the physical plane.

The first section of *The Man with Red Suspenders* explores the obstacles preventing people from connecting with one another and the means by which one can overcome those obstacles. "Ribs in the Holy Desert" includes poems about hitchhikers one cannot help but pick up and who eventually take one's place behind the steering wheel; people who reach others only by dialing wrong numbers; and an office manager who realizes that his quest for order may be destroying his spirit. In many of these poems the external world is cold, cruel, and inhospitable (Dacey may describe it as a "holy desert," but it is a desert, nevertheless). What allows one to break free from this malaise is the unexpected, the uncontrolled. In fact, one may escape by merely maintaining amazement at the variety of lessons to be learned from life—"that when you walk you [will] be amazed / you are not falling" (in "Placating the Gods"). Like Henry David Thoreau, Dacey is putting faith, both spiritual and artistic, in the simple things of the world, for they can remind one of the invigorating presence of spirit that is everywhere. Many of these themes have appeared in the poet's previous work, but in *The Man with Red Suspenders*, the focus is shifted slightly from the search for meaning in the commonplace to a celebration of the ability to break free from crippling modern lives because of the existence of that meaning. Thus these poems are able to be at once darker and more optimistic than much of Dacey's other work, because along with absurdity, dreams, and sexuality as symbols, Dacey now sees great personal tragedy as a means to truth and joy.

Section 2, "Impossible Tail-feathers," is quite often an examination of the role women play in Dacey's search for understanding. In "Someone," a poem that is both social commentary and psychological inquiry, he shows a world where money is related to all things, all feelings:

When I asked him how he was,
he told me about money.
When I asked about his wife,
he said dollars and cents.
When I asked about his children,
he said cash register.

By the end of the poem, a reversal of sorts has occurred. There is an implication that connecting, reaching out to others, can break down dehumanizing social structures: "When I told him my secret, / he whispered what the moon costs. / When I asked him about money, / he said, I'm dying for love."

In section 2 there are more poems about the value of the natural world in a search for meaning. The messages can be difficult to accept, but through these lessons one can be set free. In "Anniversary Poem" Dacey portrays these messages as rocks but closes the poem by arguing that the hard parts of life should not be avoided: "Rocks rise in dreams. / Keep rising. Lift themselves / to heaven. This time / we hold on for the ride."

"Eyes Set Free to Float," the book's final section, is a celebration of nonconformity. Beginning with a poem entitled "The Rules," in which the reader is ordered to "follow rules / Or we go bust you head [*sic*]," Dacey engages in a challenge with the accepted meanings of love, games, art, and *Hamlet*, finding that there are alternative messages and uses of these subjects that work just as well. Then Dacey presents a poem about Wallace Stevens, "In Hartford." Stevens believed that modern authors needed to find new metaphors to translate the human condition into poetry, since the twentieth century is fundamentally different from the periods before it. According to Dacey, the past few decades have made poets more adept at finding new symbols of meaning, rather than relying on the examples of the past. Is the search for new meaning improving because lives are even more superficial and distressing than those Stevens saw around him? If such is the case, Dacey seems to believe that one then has an even greater opportunity to mine the soul-sustaining spirit from an ever-more-mundane, inhuman world.

The Man with Red Suspenders confirms Dacey's place in contemporary poetry as a writer reveling in the wonders of the external world and the spirit they hold. His recent work suggests that, whatever the source of poetic inspiration, Dacey will continue to explore the themes he has examined throughout his career and do so by finding the light of understanding in the most unexpected places:

> The high drama
> at the kitchen stove
> can rock a stage
>
> and burn as if with hot grease
> an audience. Eat well,
> the world advises, and watches, rapt,
> as you get set to do so.

Interviews:

Jill Field, "Interview with Phil Dacey," *Voices* (April-May 1979): 18-23;

Orval A. Lund, Jr., "Philip Dacey: A Study and Interview," M.F.A. thesis, Vermont Community College, 1986.

References:

Philip K. Jason, "Speaking to Us All: New Books by Philip Dacey and Peter Meinke," *Poet Lore*, 76 (Winter 1981): 239-241;

Peter Stitt, "The Necessary Poem," *Ohio Review*, 19 (Spring-Summer 1978): 101-112;

Dabney Stuart, "Sex and Violence," *Tar River Poetry*, 26 (Spring 1987): 46-53;

Vernon Young, "An Irishman and Three Catholics," *Parnassus: Poetry in Review*, 9 (Fall 1981): 164-168.

Madeline DeFrees
(18 November 1919 -   )

Barbara Drake
Linfield College

BOOKS: *The Springs of Silence*, as Sister Mary Gilbert (New York: Prentice Hall, 1953; Kingswood, U.K.: World's Work, 1954);

Later Thoughts from the Springs of Silence, as Gilbert (Indianapolis: Bobbs-Merrill, 1962);

From the Darkroom, as Gilbert (Indianapolis: Bobbs-Merrill, 1964);

When Sky Lets Go (New York: Braziller, 1978);

Imaginary Ancestors (Missoula, Mont.: SmokeRoot, 1978; revised and enlarged edition, Seattle: Broken Moon, 1990);

Magpie on the Gallows (Port Townsend, Wash.: Copper Canyon, 1982);

The Light Station on Tillamook Rock (Lewisburg, Pa.: Appletree Alley, 1989; trade edition, Corvallis, Oreg.: Arrowood, 1991).

SELECTED PERIODICAL PUBLICATIONS—UNCOLLECTED: "The Radical Activity of Writing Poems," *Northwest Review*, 24, no. 2 (1986): 52-63;

"Writing from the Margins," *Writer's N.W.*, 4 (Summer 1989): 1-2.

In a secular age, poetry dealing with religious subjects and employing religious imagery may seem anachronistic, but with Madeline DeFrees's poetry this is not the case. The individual's search for enlightenment, the continual shock to the senses, the ambiguity of good and evil, and the tension between hope and despair are some of DeFrees's themes. Her life as a writer has been relatively quiet, but her interior life is intense. As she has continued to publish books and poems, her reputation has grown steadily, so that her work commands respect and attention from reviewers and readers alike.

Madeline DeFrees, the daughter of Clarence C. and Mary McCoy DeFrees, was born on 18 November 1919 in Ontario, Oregon, in the far eastern part of the state, and moved with her family to Hillsboro, on the western side of the Oregon Cascades, when she was about four. She attended St. Matthew's Grade School in Hillsboro

and went to high school at St. Mary's Academy in Portland. At the age of sixteen, directly upon graduation from high school, she entered the Roman Catholic Congregation of the Sisters of the Holy Names of Jesus and Mary. According to her autobiographical work, *The Springs of Silence* (1953), DeFrees was so reticent about revealing her private life that she did not even mention to her senior-prom date that she intended to enter a convent soon after graduation. DeFrees earned a B.A. in English at Marylhurst College (1948) and an M.A. in journalism at the University of Oregon (1951). After a long career as a teaching nun and as a writer, in December 1973 she was released from her religious vows. Her life as a nun and her subsequent departure from the religious order in her fifties naturally figure as important elements in DeFrees's work.

Remarks of hers in a 1982 interview with Carol Ann Russell suggest that the religious life was a natural choice for one with a sensitive and ecstatic but private nature, and that the vocations of nun and writer are not disconnected. DeFrees's primary models, Gerard Manley Hopkins and Emily Dickinson, exemplify the dedicated life, and DeFrees's work is sometimes compared to that of the metaphysical poet John Donne. On the other hand, the life of a nun was at odds, in many ways, with a writer's work, and DeFrees says there was a great deal of self-censorship in her early writing. Having resumed her baptismal name, she was known as Sister Madeline DeFrees when she began teaching at the University of Montana in 1967; however, during that time she did not wear the habit of the nun. She found that living outside the religious community, even the absence of the religious garb itself, altered the way she thought about her writing and contributed to her creative growth. The conflict between her life as nun and as writer resolved itself only when she asked to be released from her religious vows and was granted that request. Nevertheless, her religious life continues to be a source of imagery and an influence in her work.

Madeline DeFrees in Seattle, which she made her home after retiring from full-time teaching

As Sister Mary Gilbert, DeFrees studied poetry with Karl Shapiro at Portland State University, during the summer of 1959, and with John Berryman and Robert Fitzgerald at the School of Letters, Indiana University, during the summer of 1961. DeFrees taught in Oregon and Washington at all levels, from elementary through high school and college, and later took a teaching job in Massachusetts. Colleges where she taught include Fort Wright College (formerly Holy Names College) in Spokane, Washington (1950-1967); the University of Montana, Missoula (1967-1979); and the University of Massachusetts, Amherst (1979-1985). At the University of Massachusetts she served as director of the M.F.A. program from 1980 to 1983. She also taught at Marylhurst College (summer 1969), the University of Washington (summer 1970), Seattle University (1965-1966 and summer 1972), and the University of

Victoria (fall 1974). Her poetry has appeared in *Best Poems of 1960* and *Best Poems of 1965*. DeFrees has also published fiction, including a story that appeared in *Best American Short Stories, 1962*, and reviews and articles. Her awards and honors include a National Endowment for the Arts fellowship (1982) and a Guggenheim fellowship in poetry (1981-1982). Now retired from full-time teaching, DeFrees lives in Seattle, where she continues to write and publish. She also gives readings of her work and teaches workshops in creative writing.

The self-effacement of the individual in religious life is reflected in DeFrees's first book of poetry, *From the Darkroom* (1964), which is more traditional in form and voice than her later work, though original. In these earlier poems, one rarely finds the individual "I." The landscape of the poems seems fairly unpopulated, and the writ-

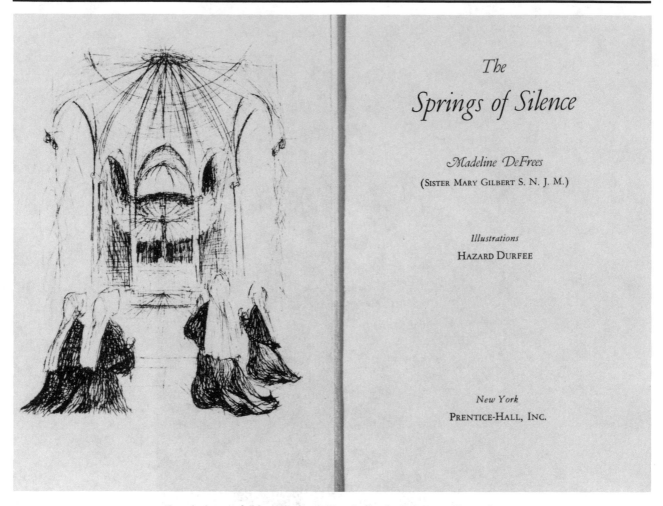

Frontispiece and title page for DeFrees's first book, an autobiography

er's private life does not appear in the confessional or casual sense. As her life changed in relation to the church, so, too, her later poetry changed. The individual self became more apparent and the poems more autobiographical, though never transparent. These later poems are also more open in form and more colloquial.

In her interview with Russell, DeFrees said, "Quite early I developed the habit of pouring my 'real inner life' into some written form—usually poems—and I thought of them as 'off limits' to anyone unless I *chose* to share them. Even then I would watch, as the Little Prince scrutinized adults examining the picture of the boa constrictor who had swallowed an elephant, and if they said, 'That's a nice hat,' I knew I could not trust them." This unwillingness to reveal herself to just anyone and this feeling that the writer's confidence must be won by the reader may have contributed to the difficulty of many of Defrees's poems, a difficulty that caused Valerie Trueblood

to say, of *When Sky Lets Go* (1978), "there are a number of poems in the book that are perplexing after many readings. And she is a poet who makes you *want* to understand; she is worth effort" (*American Poetry Review*, May 1979).

DeFrees's desire to be understood, and yet not to be understood too easily, is never coy, however, but is an expression of tensions, both personal and intellectual, out of which her poetry arises. In the Russell interview, DeFrees explained her reticence in several ways, from "I'm a Scorpio, and they tend to be secretive," to her childhood feelings that her mother was more intrusive than she had a right to be, to the early entrance into the convent itself, where "I lived for a long time in terror of some kind of mental breakdown. The poems were, in a sense, my lifeline because they provided a measure of release for my feelings. At the same time they compounded the problems because I felt guilty about my absolute need for writing." The paradox arising from this conflict between silence and expression is suggested in the titles of her first two books, *The Springs of Silence* and *Later Thoughts from the Springs of Silence* (1962). These, however, are autobiographical prose accounts, the first dealing with her life entering the convent and as a young nun, and the second mainly dealing with the effort of her college, Holy Names, to establish itself in a new location. In her introduction to *The Springs of Silence* DeFrees says that the book is neither autobiography nor fiction but "the essence of a way of life as seen through the eyes of one person who has chosen that vocation." She says she has altered certain events in order to protect the privacy of those concerned and for reasons of craft. Nevertheless the books are commonly considered autobiographies.

From the Darkroom also appeared under the name of Sister Mary Gilbert. While the two books of prose offer pleasant accounts of a life that is mysterious to most readers, they offer little hint of the intensity of her poetry in *From the Darkroom*. The poems fuse religious and secular imagery, as in "Requiem Mass: Convent Cemetery," where an almost medieval religious tone ("The shaft of their Gregorian cuts clean: / through the domed summer" and ". . . crosses where the bones moulder / under the levelling loam") contrasts with images of contemporary life. The drama contained on a tombstone is described as "too big for Broadway and Hollywood / to frame in footlights or celluloid." Poems in this book generally efface the individual. Landscapes are depersonalized, objectified. Where the individual pronoun appears, the speaker seems transformed into a feature of the landscape, as in the "The Undertow": "Pale driftwood demons haunt my shifting coast / cold, in the lunar light, as bones outspread / on windy beaches where the reaching wave / wakes tidal terror in the driven blood." In other instances the speaker is generalized as being part of a group, as in "Nuns in the Quarterlies": "Used in accents in a landscape or seaview, / upright in merciful black on the sand's monotone, / not even the devil's advocate could question / their purely decorative purpose. . . . / Nuns are the fictions / by whom we verify the usual contradictions."

This tone of ironic humor and the objectification of the self into "they" also appears in "Nuns Tour Newspaper Plant," in which DeFrees writes about "a dozen Sisters [who] rove the Fourth Estate. . . . / First told what they will see / then, having seen, / reminded what they saw; politely

moved / to attitudes of disbelief and awe, / they blot up bold statistics, neatly grooved, / revolving at inhuman speed between / a stereotype and iron workings of life's law: / theorems of ancient wickedness reproved."

The tension between repression and expression led, for DeFrees, to the development of a complex poetry that must be read with attention to all the various levels of meaning in language. DeFrees creates complexity in a variety of ways. For example, she often uses words so that they can be read in more than one way, sometimes as puns, sometimes as allusions, sometimes as indications of complex layers of meaning contained in their derivations. In "The Radical Art of Writing Poems," a (1986) essay in the *Northwest Review*, she says, "My most indispensable book is the dictionary—not one, but several, including the *Oxford English Dictionary*. . . . After the dictionary comes the Britannica, with its wealth of information on the most diverse subjects. . . . There are, as well, the standard references: the King James Bible, Bartlett's *Quotations*, Fowler's *Modern English Usage*, Brewer's *Dictionary of Phrase and Fable*, and for myth and folklore, Robert Graves's two-volume work, Fraser's *Golden Bough* and Edith Hamilton's compact *Mythology*. I could cite many others, but these are some of my own standbys." Besides cultivating complexity of language and allusion, DeFrees frequently surprises the reader with a dry, ironic humor. She also suggests multiple readings by enjambment, by breaking lines so as to fracture meaning and send it off in more than one direction, and by making startling, unexpected associations that cause the reader to reassess first impressions.

For example, the first and title poem of *From the Darkroom*, a sonnet divided into octave and sestet, with irregular metrical and rhyme schemes, describes the process of developing a photographic print, an experience probably drawn from the poet's work in journalism, as student, teacher, and college publicist. DeFrees uses language from photography in a deliberately ambiguous way, so that words such as *image, light, positive* (as opposed to *negative*), *fix*, and *wash away* seem to become observations about the creative process itself, the religious life, Christian salvation, and about the transcendence of love. The poem ends with an image of "the instant prized— / Against the lesson all love spurns." If what "love spurns" is the inevitability of death, and the "instant" is "prized" (that is, valued by the observer, and also seized or taken) by the camera, then the photograph transcends time and death, and suggests the transcendence of art, love, and religion as well.

Such possibly excessive interpretation of the poem's language demonstrates the way in which DeFrees's poetry lends itself, particularly in view of her own remarks, to this sort of analysis. Of course complexity is also a result of her love of language and scholarship, and she is frequently playful in the way she builds her associations. Although later poems seem more open in language and more revealing of the author, DeFrees continues to develop complex allusions and imagery. In "The Radical Activity of Writing Poems," she says: "In practice . . . insight may accompany, or even follow, language. Much of the process shares the simultaneity of consciousness, complicated at every instant by memory, sensation and perception." She makes a distinction between poems started from language (more apt to derive from associations in her reading, from found language, and other sources of language that interest and stimulate her imagination) and poems started from experience.

DeFrees's second collection of poetry, *When Sky Lets Go*, was received as a remarkable development following *From the Darkroom*. In the introduction, Richard Howard writes: "How much *more* unusual than the diligently administered, serviceable poems of *From the Darkroom* [of Sister Mary Gilbert] are the extreme and charged ones of Madeline DeFrees." In Trueblood's review of *When Sky Lets Go* she says, "Madeline DeFrees' poems are disquieting. Because of their generality and because the remedies that have failed her are those many of us have saved for later, for last. . . . In leaving behind her past as a nun she performed a clearance, and the poems are her reassembly of life from different and fewer pieces."

Much of DeFrees's book seems to deal with this break, a difficult one but nevertheless a move toward a saving self-definition. In "Driving Home" she moves through a world in which nothing is secure: "The wheels keep pulling / towards that sunny sideroad"; "the highway crew leaves markers / I do not trust"; and "one star is out to get me." Nevertheless, "The gradual curve unwinds / The river again. / Now it is green in the placid / crook of my arm / as the paired hands of those days / I wanted to die."

Several of the poems deal with feelings of isolation and repressed sensuality. The title character in "A Woman Possessed" confronts powerful emotion like a bullfighter facing a bull. Caught up in a desire for release, "she wanted to cast her body on the horns / of that forgetful season." Bullfight images merge with images of the proverbial bull in a china shop to depict the shattering of fragile self-control. But the drama exhausts itself. In a series of volcanic images everything is reduced to "clay of their common drama / and the woman, old." The mood of the poem is one of destructive passion, elevated by a sense of tragic necessity. In "The Odd Woman," DeFrees plays with the language—"At parties I want to get even"—and surprises readers with startling images of the unmatched: "[I] feel awkward / as an upper plate without a partner." Animal images give a sense of strangeness and dislocation: "The cougar jaw yawns on the sofa back," and "the expert hunters / are gutting a deer / for the guest of honor." The party is infused with feelings of predatory violence that arouse discomfort in the speaker and an urge to "get even," either by finding a partner or by retaliating in some way. Waiting for enough time to pass to make a graceful exit, the speaker says, "I pat the head of the beagle / nosing in my crotch and try to appear / grateful. A witch / would mount the nearest broom / and leave by the chimney." Such laconic, unexpected observations distinguish DeFrees's poetry.

In the section of *When Sky Lets Go* entitled "The Blue Nun," DeFrees includes several poems that assert the will to live a full life. In "Orthopedic" there are images of a damaged body and "my salvaged self . . . a lump of deactivated matter, / or black blob on a stick." These make the speaker's sense of damage and loss painfully evident, but there is also a demand: "O lost among women, reclaim / your inheritance of nerve and bone." In "Mexican Crucifix" the writer describes a crucifix, but the description turns into a statement about the difficulty of living in the body and in history: "The body is its own cross," and it is "chained to the dark decades." The "dark decades" may be a reference to the Middle Ages, the dim early periods of history; DeFrees's own life in the convent, wearing black; or the rosary itself, "dark decades" being prayer beads in groups of ten, to which the crucifix may be attached.

"With a Bottle of Blue Nun to All My Friends" ends this section of the book with a playful, surprising twist. What must have been a difficult experience, leaving the convent, is turned into a defiant walk on the wild side: "The Blue Nun has eloped with one / of the Christian Brothers. . . . / The Blue Nun works the late shift / in

Are air we
breathe is success
money.

Compared to

Andrew Carnegie ~~Pro for~~ ~~Compared to~~ the Air We Breathe
(1835–1919)

As a child whose parents believed in pets, Andrew
kept rabbits, his first business venture.
Recruited playmates to gather freely clover and
dandelions. Such a menu, loyally
served for a season, rewarded the friend by
attaching his name to ~~the~~ rabbit. ~~This practice~~ A strategy
that demanded no capital outlay. Years later
on a train, Andrew met a tycoon who confided, I was
one of the rabbit boys.

                    he earned his first wages
            ~~His first wages were paid~~
in Allegheny City: one dollar-twenty a week as
bobbin boy in a cotton factory. The boiler/downstairs
made him anxious. At night he rose up/in bed
turning and twisting gauges. Too little/steam and
workers complained. Too much and the boiler
exploded. Transferred to accounts, he still had to
bathe the bobbins in oil vats. The smell
made him gag.

            That's when he tried a big jump over
~~across~~ the river, hired on as messenger-boy
~~boy~~ for a telegraph company, lifted, he said...into
paradise...with newspapers, pens,
pencils and sunshine about me. Free enterprise,
inhaled from ~~the~~ age ~~of~~ thirteen, brought him
success. Success made him bold.
From bobbin boy to a man of iron and steel, his story
~~story~~ was ~~real~~ Horatio Alger. // ~~The plot~~
                    true

                    The plot quickened
and air grew thick in the Smoky City. He fathered
the Keystone Bridge Works, a rolling mill,
black fumes of a foundry, soot and diesel exhaust
from the Pennsylvania Railway, cost
to be deducted from all that Carnegie Trust. He
bought the Storey Farm with its oil wells
at 40 dollars an acre. Over the ~~whole~~ wide country~~side~~
like de la Renta perfume, the crisp green smell
of money.

He admired Wagner, Herbert, my erstwhile
relative

                    At 30, resigned from the railway, he vowed
~~vowed~~ never again to work for ~~a salary.~~ wages.
He lived ~~simply~~ no master bath like a sports arena.
No indoor sauna. He gave away millions. ~~stalked~~
silent/talent   *for* Libraries sprang up everywhere, their ~~enriched~~ air
deadly as Andrew's writing. Heroes, too,
and music, technology, art.

soporific   his own Gospel of Wealth. ~~His~~ *a simple*
                                                         life

Draft for a poem included in Imaginary Ancestors *(1978 and 1990 editions) and in the 1982 collection* Magpie on the
Gallows *(by permission of Madeline DeFrees)*

Denver. Her pierced ears / drip rubies / like the sixth wound." Readers then see the Blue Nun becoming "Mayor of Missoula"; showing up in "a sleazy dive / outside San Francisco"; being remembered "in Harlem," where "she still carried her needle case"; and, in the last scene, becoming a sky diver—"The parachute / surrounds her like a wimple. / That's what happens when Blue Nuns / bail out. / It's that simple." Using the image of the nun from a brand of wine and putting the character in various lowlife or atypical situations, DeFrees manages both to lighten a serious situation and to suggest something sordid or guilty about the acts of the Blue Nun. At the end of the poem, as the nun descends to the secular life, the line "It's that simple" defies the reader—and "All My Friends"—to make more of a fuss than DeFrees is comfortable with. She uses humor to deflect scrutiny, and, at the same time, she takes charge of the situation by her claims to outrageous behavior.

The final section of the book, "Pictures on the Shifting Wall," focuses on poems of acceptance and resolution, dealing with death, hope, and despair, and—in "The Forgiveness"—DeFrees reconciles herself with her dead mother, the source, she feels, of many of her fears and inhibitions: "Our tears can run together now. I am not afraid / to let you see them."

A chapbook, *Imaginary Ancestors*, was published in 1978, the same year as *When Sky Lets Go*. *Imaginary Ancestors* develops the theme of DeFrees's search for her identity, which she seems to solve by means of the novel fantasy of a liaison in "Emily Dickinson and Gerard Manley Hopkins": "My notebook shows they took a formal cruise, / floated past bridges in the morning light." Emily reveals to Gerard that she carries his image in a locket. In spite of the fact that "he carried Whitman in his greatcoat pocket," Gerard and Emily manage to get together, with the result that "my Grandmother Dickinson, dyed in the clerical woof, / was warped for good. I am the living proof." Besides asserting her literary and spiritual ancestry, DeFrees deals with her real mother's fantasy that she (the mother) was an illegitimate and undiscovered heir to Ulysses S. Grant. In "Burning Questions," DeFrees writes: "She thought / U. S. Grant had left her a fortune, too extravagant / for an orphan." In "Grandmother Grant," DeFrees insists that she herself will settle the question left by her dead mother: "Whoever she was, whatever ties, / here is my claim. I need to come into my own." Other

"Imaginary Ancestors" appear as "Gilbert of Sempringham"—"my saint, if I had you my own, always / in the shadow of the great"—and an earlier Sister Mary Gilbert.

Most of the chapbook, with the omission of one poem and the addition of some others, appears as part of the 1982 collection *Magpie on the Gallows*, which continues to develop earlier themes and to express and reconcile the conflicts of DeFrees's life. Besides the "Imaginary Ancestors" poems, there are two other sections—"Beetle Light" and "Several Lives." She examines death: the death of others ("Slow-Motion Elegy for Kathy King"); the death of animals ("Census of Animal Bodies") and of insects ("Beetle Light"); and the meaning, or lack of it, that death gives to life ("Sifting the Ashes"). The final poem in the book, "Subject Front View, Subject Rear View," begins with an old photo of a house she once owned. Proustian associations remind her of the past: " 'Pull down the blind,' my mother would have said, / throwing a silhouette on the lowered shade. / I hear her admonition nightly as the cold curtain / rings down. Back for unfinished reels, I must / begin as if I would complete them." In dreams she returns to the house and moves through rooms where objects continue their existence "whether we go or stay." Past and present intermingle, and life assumes the character, no longer of a still photo, but of a movie, perhaps a newsreel: "Heroic figures / cloud the silver screen / and news of the ghostly world filters in."

DeFrees has published another book of poetry, *The Light Station on Tillamook Rock* (1989), in a limited edition. It is a long poem in seventeen sections. As explained in the author's preface, DeFrees spent the summer of 1981 living on the Oregon coast, near Tillamook Rock, the site of an early lighthouse. The lighthouse had been purchased by a developer and transformed into a columbarium, a burial place for the ashes of the dead. DeFrees researched the history of the lighthouse and combined historical material, personal narrative, and reflections arising from her readings on memory and perception (she mentions Julian Jaynes's *The Origin of Consciousness in the Breakdown of the Bicameral Mind*, 1976). About the poem, she says, "images of light and water evolve as analogues for human consciousness."

In 1989 she continued to add to the *Imaginary Ancestors* series of poems and has published a new, full-length version with Broken Moon Press of Seattle (1990). In the beginning of the new collection, the author notes that "the poems published earlier should take on an added resonance as they find their place in the more comprehensive picture." The new version of *Imaginary Ancestors* defines the artist's life as she continues to try on various reflections of herself, in such diverse characters as Maria Callas, Andrew Carnegie, Marianne Moore, her own mother, a variety of saints, and others. She also continues to publish poetry, fiction, and nonfiction in magazines, and her publication credits include the *American Poetry Review, American Review, Beloit Poetry Journal, Black Box, Calyx, Good Housekeeping,* the *New York Times, Northwest Review, Paris Review, Prairie Schooner, Saturday Review, Sewanee Review, Poetry Northwest, Iowa Review, New Republic,* the *Nation, Ploughshares, Yankee,* and others. Her work also appears in numerous anthologies.

As an extremely private poet, DeFrees often surprises readers by her worldly insights. With her rich unwinding of language and her mixture of reserve and openness, Madeline DeFrees has contributed an unusual voice and style to American poetry.

Interview:

Carol Ann Russell, "An Interview With Madeline DeFrees," *Massachusetts Review*, 23 (Summer 1982): 265-269.

References:

Robert Holland, "Lost and Found," *Poetry*, 133 (March 1979): 348-349;

Carolyne Wright, "Courage, Honesty, and a Sense of Humor," *Prairie Schooner*, 57 (Summer 1983): 90-94;

Fredrick Zydek, "Smorgasbord or Bread and Water?," *Southwest Review*, 65 (Autumn 1980): 425-430.

Stephen Dunn

(24 June 1939 -   )

SuAnne Doak
Cisco Junior College

BOOKS: *5 Impersonations* (Marshall, Minn.: Ox Head, 1971);

Looking for Holes in the Ceiling (Amherst: University of Massachusetts Press, 1974);

Full of Lust and Good Usage (Pittsburgh: Carnegie-Mellon University Press, 1976);

A Circus of Needs (Pittsburgh: Carnegie-Mellon University Press, 1978);

Work and Love (Pittsburgh: Carnegie-Mellon University Press, 1981);

Not Dancing (Pittsburgh: Carnegie-Mellon University Press / London: Feffer & Simons, 1984);

Local Time (New York: Morrow, 1986);

Between Angels (New York & London: Norton, 1989);

Landscape at the End of the Century (New York & London: Norton, 1991).

SELECTED PERIODICAL PUBLICATIONS—
UNCOLLECTED: "Walking Light: Some Reflections on the Abstract & the Wise," *Crazy Horse*, 28 (Spring 1985): 67-81;

"The Good, the Not So Good," *AWP Newsletter*, 19 (November-December 1986): 1-3;

"Bringing the Strange Home," *AWP Newsletter*, 21 (September 1988): 4-8.

On the back of the book jacket of Stephen Dunn's 1989 collection of poems, *Between Angels*, Philip Booth states, "To read Stephen Dunn . . . is to see the complexities of one's own dailiness brought to light . . . One starts to see the flower on the kitchen table." It is this ability to bring to light both the ordinary, expected, nonthreatening aspects of life and the inexplicable, startling, even subversive elements of human existence that has made Dunn one of the best poetic voices of the late twentieth century.

Stephen Dunn was born on 24 June 1939 in Forest Hills, New York, to a salesman, Charles F. Dunn, and his wife, Ellen Fleishman Dunn. He received a degree in history from Hofstra University (B.A., 1962), played pro basketball for the Williamsport (Pennsylvania) Billies from 1962 to 1963, and afterward worked a few years as an advertising copywriter in New York City. In 1966 Dunn went to Spain, as he says, "to try to change my life and see if I could write poetry, which I had started to write after a failed attempt at a novel." He was encouraged by friend and novelist Sam Toperoff, and two years later he enrolled in the creative-writing program at Syracuse University, studying with Philip Booth, Donald Justice, George P. Elliott, and W. D. Snodgrass.

After graduating from Syracuse (M.A., 1970), Dunn taught fiction at Southwest Minnesota State (1970-1973) and was a visiting lecturer in poetry at Syracuse (1973-1974). Since 1974 he has been a professor of creative writing at Stockton State College in Pomona, New Jersey, while residing in Port Republic with his wife Lois Kelly—a chef he married on 26 September 1964—and their two daughters, Andrea and Susanne.

He has also been adjunct professor of poetry at Columbia University (1983-1987), visiting poet at the University of Washington (1980), and has conducted poetry workshops at Bennington Writers Workshop (1983-1987) and Aspen Writers Conference (1977, 1987), among other places. He has served as director of the Associated Writing Programs' Poetry Series (1980-1982) and has given poetry readings at Yale University, the University of Texas, and the University of Utah, to name a few.

A partial list of Dunn's awards includes the Academy of American Poets Award (Syracuse University, 1970), the Theodore Roethke Prize (*Poetry Northwest*, 1977), a Guggenheim Fellowship (1984-1985), Writing Fellowships to Yaddo (1979-1989), National Endowment for the Arts Creative Writing Fellowships (1973, 1983, 1989), the Helen Bullis Prize (*Poetry Northwest*, 1983), and the Levinson Prize (*Poetry*, 1987). In addition to nine poetry collections (including one chapbook), Dunn has published reviews, essays, and interviews, and his work has appeared in many magazines and anthologies.

Looking for Holes in the Ceiling (1974), his first full-length book, which he considers "poetry that arose from my imagist education," is a strong collection, exhibiting a deft, spare style and evocative imagery. In "The Loss" he writes, "Even the tips of their fingers seem to be retreating," and in "Day and Night Handball" the ball is "hitting and dying like a butterfly / on a windshield."

The speaker in some of the poems is more distant than in Dunn's later work. "An Ambulance is Coming" describes how "a glove is lying on the curb. / There is a hand in it." But other poems have the ability to involve readers more; in them appears his distinctive, conversational voice, his ease of expression that contains depth of meaning. "The Rider" confides, "It is with me, that falling star," asking:

> Who will believe me
> if I insist
> that a large man was riding it,
>
> and the shell of a body
> drove my car home into the vacancies
> of garage and self,
>
> without mishap, or a single regret?

Present in many of the poems is an implied violation of benign-appearing situations that Dunn uses with great effect here and in subsequent books. The title character in "Fat Man, Floating" "would like to follow [the fish] / to the bottom . . . and live without the kind of breath / people shape into knives." Moving from the imagined into the real world, Dunn presages another cachet in his mature work: the ability to offer insights without didacticism.

Full of Lust and Good Usage (1976) manifests his further turn to the personal and the direct, containing sharply drawn imagery and free verse that balances musicality with plain speech. In "In the Room," for example, Dunn writes, "He lets the laugh / bubble up from the webs / of his chest. . . . / He could have lava on his shoulders, / he is that weighted down."

Familial relationships, which Dunn examines with compassion and sensitivity, comprise one motif. Uncloying affection is shown in "Grandfather," in which the title character's "fingers were a cage / and I the bird / he wanted to burst / unharmed into the world." In "Waiting with Two Members of a Motorcycle Gang for My Child to be Born," the gang members shake the speaker's hand, but "it might / have been my head," and he concludes with a wish that his daughter "make men better than they are."

"One Side of the Story" describes a woman who "had the black dress on." The narrator is "thinking of ways to keep the light going." As in succeeding books, Dunn explores in this poem the theme of a relationship's difficult mutuality with eloquent articulation, ending: "The lights go out when we blow them out / or turn them off. It would be lovely, / wouldn't it? to think only what's been felt / remains: that black dress on the floor, / your skin and the drift of my hands."

At times in *Full of Lust* Dunn inserts extraneous images, such as that of "Sophia Loren . . . plac[ing] her / finger on a knot you are tying" ("Small Town: Cracks & Departures"), but most of the metaphors are relevant and incisive without histrionics. "Truck Stop: Minnesota" begins, "The waitress looks at my face / as if it were a small tip," and "For the Sleepless" focuses on "the dead, frozen bird / I stuffed in the garbage / [that] appears before my eyes."

A Circus of Needs (1978) completes what Dunn calls his "preparation for writing poetry." The strength of the collection lies in his increased ability to offer introspections about everyday life without succumbing to banality. "Essay

Dust jacket for Dunn's 1986 collection, which, according to Jonathan Holden, affirms Dunn's "stature as one of the best and most important poets writing in America today"

on Sanity" cogently rejects veneration of the psychotic in poetry, arguing that even if those who are suicidal do "get to the reddest heart of things / it's because they can't see / the world of appearances." Insanity is an intrusion upon "the calm small ordinary / exchanges between people / who know knives / every once in a while are *not* / the silvercoated castrati of their worst dreams."

He injects wry humor into poems such as "Modern Dance Class," where an instructor considers the speaker a "toad among butterflies / he can't bear to look." Dunn returns to erotic discourse with "Scenario," which describes a romantic assignation at "Cafe del Amor," where the speaker says, "when sex intrudes / let no more than a gesture / end the tension." In "Belly Dancer at the Hotel Jerome," Dunn observes that

"Fatima" is "blonde, midwestern," but her skill "danced the mockery out / of [her] wrong name."

By the time of his 1981 collection, *Work and Love*, Dunn was writing what he terms "poems in his own voice," initiating "a continuum on man/ woman relationships," but touching upon other concerns as well. "Late Summer"—with its powerful contrast of "the magnificance, the variety, of animals . . . / "which is a sensible man's proof / that God exists," to Dachau, "a sensible man's proof of the opposite"—is only one instance where he broadens his scope from an inward-looking cosmology.

On occasion he risks glibness, but unlike lesser poets, he is able to pivot from levity to profoundness, first startling, then pleasing readers with his virtuosity. "Poems for People Who Are Understandably too Busy to Read Poetry" opens with this line: "Relax. This won't last long," but ends with "what poetry can do. / Imagine yourself a caterpillar. / *There's an awful shrug and, suddenly, / you're beautiful for as long as you live.*"

At other times Dunn evokes a more poignant mood. In "At the Film Society" a man/ woman interlude occurs after a couple has watched a film in which "Liv Ullman touches . . . with a lust so deepened by grief / the rest of us feel our miseries / are amateurish," and "the best sex rises / like a trapped beast from our vacancies," compelling language that does not need embellishment.

The poem "Essay on the Personal" sets the tone of *Not Dancing* (1984): "finally the personal / is all that matters." In this book, Dunn hones both his subject matter and style, exploring new avenues to familiar topics and, from this point on, relying less on concrete imagery. In "Sick Days" he writes, "To stay at home is to believe too much / in the cycle of the water pump, / the ritual of cleanliness and food," and the abstractions "cycle" and "ritual" form a congruence with his lack of belief in the safety such terms promulgate.

Just when his analysis of everyday life strikes one as restrictive, he turns to universalities, grounding them in experience. Death, in "Wavelengths," is "a music . . . both popular and private," and fear is known by those "who've had experience with the dark / and know how it speaks." Loneliness is contemplated in "Atlantic City" while the narrator watches "the ocean in winter," which is "repetition's secret / link with solace."

"The Routine Things Around the House" describes a twelve-year-old boy's awakening sexuality:

I had asked my mother (I was trembling)
if I could see her breasts
and she took me into her room

without embarrassment or coyness
and I stared at them,
afraid to ask for more.

Jonathan Holden commends Dunn's ability to achieve "aesthetic distance" and find "where the violence within meets, on equal terms, the violence without. . . ." Dunn considers the poem less about an event than "a legacy of limits." Because the boy's mother did not refuse his request or step beyond that disclosure, he is later able "to love women easily." And because Dunn does not cross the line between revelation and exposure, he is able to share that discovery with readers.

Local Time (1986), chosen for the National Poetry Series, exemplifies Dunn's definition of poetry as "an act of coherence amidst the fragmentation of modern life." In "Round Trip," after the speaker is mugged and has "closed the door and [given] whatever in [him] wanted to be alone and pitied / its hard uncomfortable chair," the speaker is once again a sane man grappling with the world's madness, yet still able to hope.

The long, meditative title poem, "Local Time," also ponders outside menaces to a safe domestic world: "The house had double locks / but in the dark a wrong person / would understand: the windows / were made of glass. . . ." Jennifer Krauss comments that it is "between the well-lit front porch and what's 'out there' in the dark that . . . Dunn's poetry dwells."

An element of this apprehension is evident in "Letter Home," in which the narrator admits his inherent, but often inadmissible, fear and need to the woman he addresses: "Last night during a thunderstorm, / awakened and half-awake, / I wanted to climb into bed / on my mother's side, be told / everything's all right—."

In "Parable of the Fictionist" the speaker confesses that he "sometimes longed / for what he'd dare not alter . . . something immutable or so lovely he might be changed by it." Dunn defines the term *fictionist* as "essentially someone who makes things up so that they will be true." This definition is important when applied to his work, because he states: "Though my poems apparently and often do draw from experience, I insist

COMPANIONSHIP

The last time I climbed a mountain
my friend from the west
called it a hill, but it was
a mountain to me,
a few thousand feet, Vermont,
my feet hurting
almost all the way.
Never again, I swore,
would I go against my body
for the sake of companionship,
though maybe I just
should have sworn off mountains,
the tops of them in particular,
those invitations
made to us since childhood,
so hard to refuse.
My friend, a Brooklyn boy,
lived in Colorado
and had learned something like God
lived there too.
I was to climb, he said,
without desire,
one step and then the next.
I was to love the sides
as much as the top,
the wildflowers along the way,
the rocks.
I desired the top to come
down to me. Mid-way
I desired the little parking lot
at the base where my Subaru
waited with its cushions and wings.
At the top, we shook hands
but did not hug. What we'd done
was too small for that,
and there still was the getting down,
a few different ways
I could disappoint him,
as any unequal partner knows,
just by being who I was.

Late draft for a poem that is included in Dunn's 1989 collection, Between Angels *(by permission of Stephen Dunn)*

Dust jacket for the book that gives voice to what Philip Booth calls "one's own dailiness"

for myself that my poems go beyond their original intent. I feel that I'm in a poem with the first moment I startle myself. That moment usually creates an imaginative imperative that I try to extend and be equal to."

Between Angels continues Dunn's evolution into a poet whose concerns, according to Gregory Djanikian, represent a balance "between personal event and a broader historical perspective, between specific emotional upheavals and general categories of feeling and being" (*Philadelphia Inquirer*, 30 July 1989). The title of the poem "Sweetness" is an abstraction Dunn makes tangible by his inclusion of a discussion of the death of a friend's lover: the speaker offers "the one or two words we have for such grief / until we were speaking only in tones."

Tonal shading is what Dunn explores in

"Tenderness": "Oh abstractions are just abstract / until they have an ache in them." He displays both subtlety and explicitness, as in "Clarities," dealing with a Chilean girl tortured to death:

Sometimes there's a pity

only the self can give, amniotic,
   a total curling in.
      I wish
they had killed him, the father,

allowed some end to what he saw.

"Forgiveness" offers initial tolerance for the "terrorist [who] pulls a pin: / Forgive the desperate, the homeless, / the crazed," but the speaker gives way to blunt anger: "No, no more good reasons." Poems such as "To A Terrorist" attempt to reach some understanding of people who perpetrate violence, "knowing there's nothing, / not even revenge, which alleviates / a life like yours," but to whom the narrator finally must say: "I hate the hatefulness that makes you fall / in love with death, your own included."

The title poem, "Between Angels," returns to the complex frustrations of "the bluesy middle ground / of desire and withdrawal . . . among the bittersweet / efforts of people to connect," asking, "The angels out there, / what are they?" The ambiguous boundaries of contemporary life cause Dunn to muse, "Oh, everything's true / at different times / in the capacious day," ruefully admitting the triviality of middle-class vicissitudes compared to those of "half the people in the world / [who] are dispossessed."

It is this duality of internal and exterior considerations that makes Dunn an extraordinary poet. Not only is he capable of investigating the personal without becoming confessional or mundane, he augments his range with external issues. In an age of prosaic diction, he imbues discursive language with lyric intensity, yet does not bombard readers with hyperbole. He maintains an impeccable balance between clarity and concealment, and he remains one of the best practitioners of a realistic and compassionate approach to relationships between men and women. Dunn's latest collection is *Landscape at the End of the Century* (1991).

References:

Jonathan Holden, *Style and Authenticity in Postmodern Poetry* (Columbia: University of Missouri Press, 1986), p. 124;

Jennifer Krauss, "The Home and the World," *New Republic*, 194 (2 June 1986): 39-41.

Dave Etter

(18 March 1928 -   )

James T. Jones
Southwest Missouri State University

BOOKS: *Go Read the River* (Lincoln: University of
Nebraska Press, 1966);
The Last Train to Prophetstown (Lincoln: University
of Nebraska Press, 1968);
Strawberries (La Crosse, Wis.: Juniper, 1970);
Voyages to the Inland Sea, by Etter, John Knoepfle,
and Lisel Mueller (La Crosse, Wis.: Center
for Contemporary Poetry, 1971);
Crabtree's Woman (Shawnee Mission, Kans.: BkMk,
1972);
Well You Needn't: The Thelonious Monk Poems (Inde-
pendence, Mo.: Raindust, 1975);
Bright Mississippi (La Crosse, Wis.: Juniper, 1975);
Central Standard Time: New and Selected Poems (Kan-
sas City, Mo.: BkMk, 1978);
Alliance, Illinois (Ann Arbor, Mich.: Kylix, 1978;
enlarged edition, Peoria, Ill.: Spoon River Po-
etry, 1983);
Open to the Wind (Menomonie, Wis.: Uzzano,
1978);
Riding the Rock Island through Kansas (Iola, Wis.:
Wolfsong, 1979);
Cornfields (Peoria, Ill.: Spoon River Poetry, 1980);
West of Chicago (Peoria, Ill.: Spoon River Poetry,
1981);
Boondocks (Menomonie, Wis.: Uzzano, 1982);
Home State (Peoria, Ill.: Spoon River Poetry,
1985);
Live at the Silver Dollar (Peoria, Ill.: Spoon River Po-
etry, 1986);
Selected Poems (Peoria, Ill.: Spoon River Poetry,
1987);
Midlanders (Peoria, Ill.: Spoon River Poetry,
1988);
Electric Avenue (Peoria, Ill.: Spoon River Poetry,
1988);
Carnival (Granite Falls, Minn.: Spoon River Po-
etry, 1990).

Dave Etter is really two poets—or rather
two sensibilities in one poet. Like the corn he features in his rural Illinois landscapes, Etter is a
hybrid, a cross between Robert Browning and
Emily Dickinson. In this respect he is something

of an anachronism: postmodern poetry, because
of its diversity of form and content, usually
depends on the unified and unifying sensibility
of the poet. Etter's two sensibilities correspond
roughly to the roles of national and regional
poet, and though his consciousness is split, he is
clearly a student and champion of regionalism.

Though his family roots are in northern Illinois, David Pearson Etter was born in Huntington Park, California, on 18 March 1928, to Harold Pearson Etter, the manager of an industrial
gas distributorship, and Judith Goodenow Etter.
He came to the Midwest at the age of eighteen
and attended the University of Iowa, where he
earned a B.A. in history in 1953. After two years
of army service and three years of doing odd
jobs in various parts of the country, Etter settled
down to life as an editor in the Chicago area. He
has worked for Northwestern University Press
and Northern Illinois University Press, as well as
holding an editorial position with *Encyclopaedia Britannica*. Etter now works part-time in a textbook
publisher's warehouse (McDougal, Littell, and
Company) and teaches occasional writing workshops. He married Margaret Ann Cochran on 8
August 1959. With their two children, Emily and
George, the Etters make their home in Elburn, Illinois, a small community west of Chicago. Etter's
poems have appeared in hundreds of small magazines and over sixty anthologies. His first book,
Go Read the River, was published by the University of Nebraska Press in 1966.

A photograph on the back cover of one of
Etter's most recent books, *Electric Avenue* (1988),
shows him seated in a cheap lawn chair before
the stone foundation of his clapboard house. The
paint is peeling from the downspout. In his right
hand, Etter holds a pipe; in his left, a glass of
Jack Daniel's whiskey. (The half-empty bottle sits
on a nearby table.) Etter's short-sleeved shirt is
open down his chest, and under his modified Fu
Manchu mustache, his mouth is open slightly. He
frowns in the sun. If one is from the rural Mid-

Dave Etter

west, this nearly bald man may look like one's father, or maybe grandfather.

As this photograph illustrates, Etter's persona—while it is undeniably suited to his regional subjects—is slightly dated. With the exception of *Home State* (1985), most of his poetry presents a stylized, nostalgic version of his region (Illinois, Wisconsin, Iowa, Minnesota, Kansas, Nebraska), including his mythical town of Alliance, Illinois. This nostalgia springs partly from his 1950s sensibility. One senses that, no matter how comfortable Etter actually feels in Elburn, a town he has settled into as a convert settles into a new religion, his poems are *made* comfortable for readers by the dated view of his midwestern world. A long poem dedicated to one of Etter's regional poetic forebears, Carl Sandburg, ends: "I will be fisherman / Seeker of lost Railroads, / and ambassador to all the forgotten / Kingdoms of Chautauquas and streetcars." In a sense, Etter, like many regional writers, must back into the future. Most rural towns have destroyed what little historic architecture they had in the rush toward development, and television has largely obliterated their culture. What is poetically interesting to Etter does not lie in the present. Alliance, Illi-

nois, boasts no golden arches.

Perhaps that is as it should be, since in Dave Etter's poetry, nostalgia does not imply excessive sentimentality. What he sees, he sees with a cold, clear eye. And what he presents, he presents in images and characters, without editorial comment. He does not sanitize what he sees. Etter's Midwest is a world that includes raw sex, murder, child abuse, misery, squalor—all the waste and detritus of human existence—and trivia. Etter is perhaps the contemporary master of the mundane. It is his unusual gift to be able to give point to the banalities of daily life. But Alliance, unlike Elburn, does not lie in a thicket of nuclear reactors. Etter's mythical landscape, unlike the historical one, is not packed with missile silos from south of Sedalia to the North Dakota border. His homes are filled with drink, not drugs. The earth between his corn rows is inviting enough for lovers to lie down in, not, as in actuality, hard dead minerals, killed by years of chemical herbicide and insecticide applications. He gives little indication of the vicious racism of small-town life and makes scant reference to television.

Etter has always been straightforward about his purposes. His books are invariably introduced

DAVE ETTER

SELECTED POEMS

Dust jacket for the 1987 collection that prompted E. V. Griffith of Poetry Now *to call Etter "one of the best poets in America"*

by epigraphs from his favorite authors and musicians. Most of the authors are midwestern regionalists of the modern period. Etter knows his tradition, and he consciously tries to extend it. In doing so, he joins the Illinois poetic triangle of Edgar Lee Masters, Vachel Lindsay, and Sandburg. Etter exhibits qualities similar to those predecessors. He shares Masters's social insight without the cynicism that inspired it. He shares Lindsay's lightheartedness in the face of insensitivity, and he shares Sandburg's power of imagery. Naturally, he succumbs to the impulse to eulogize his lineage and to remind the reader that some forebears are gone and, therefore, in need of replacement. In "Springfield, Illinois," for instance (in *Go Read the River*), he sees the capital asleep "under a milktoast sky / near Masters's sweet Sangamon." Only a poet in the process of inaugurating his career as an Illinois regionalist could possibly apply the epithet "sweet" to a 150-mile-long slough like the Sangamon. Again, in Etter's second book, *The Last Train to Prophetstown*

(1968), he eulogizes his antecedents: "Lindsay gone. Masters gone. Sandburg gone." But this time he adds a vow, the last line of the poem: "I will begin to move among the living again." Nevertheless, his vision is founded in nostalgia, as the speaker of "The Unfound Door" asserts: "But I know now I know now / it is first love of this place / I want to hang on to."

At the same time, in *The Last Train*, one observes a movement away from the youthful pretense of *Go Read the River* (even the title is pretentious)—with its epigraph from Ross Lockridge's *Raintree County* (1948), the *Gone with the Wind* of the Midwest, and its self-consciously poetic diction (as in a line from "Drought Year": "the high tension wires string up the western sun")—toward a firmer line and a more direct manner of statement. One also finds a deepening of the myth of the regional poet. Now that Etter has anointed himself to succeed Masters, Lindsay, and Sandburg, he must be transmogrified. This event occurs in significant terms. In "Grass"—

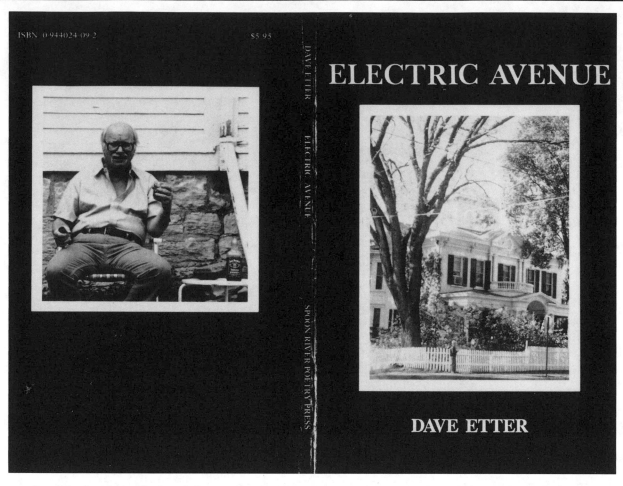

Cover for the 1988 collection of dramatic monologues that continue the story of Etter's mythical "Alliance, Illinois"

redolent of Walt Whitman as well—a poem dedicated to Etter's son, George, the speaker utters this profound wish: "O to be born on prairie grass." Just a few pages later, in "The Poet Dies and is Reborn on the Prairie," Etter associates his own poetic rebirth with the most appropriate myth from Sir James Fraser's *The Golden Bough*: the burial and resurrection of the corn god. As a result of Etter's ritual, "he is a prairie boy again."

Other themes come to light in this second book, not the least of which is the influence of jazz, especially hard bop. Bop, in spirit and as used in the works of other writers—notably Jack Kerouac—signifies both artistic excellence and artistic alienation. Excellence, in the middle-class Middle West as presented by Etter, is as little understood as art. Etter—whose verse has actually been performed to jazz accompaniment on occasion—experiences a double alienation as a poet and as a jazz buff. This alienation serves to defray the nostalgia of his poetic mythology.

By 1968 Etter had founded his career on a

carefully crafted imagism in the lineage of William Carlos Williams, anointed himself as successor to the great Illinois poets with the obvious intention of writing as a regionalist, and embarked on an availing mythography that would both provide a setting for his images and characters and satisfy his desire to follow Masters, Lindsay, and Sandburg.

The poems of Etter's middle period—the 1970s and early 1980s—can be surveyed in his *Selected Poems* (1987). The original books are out of print. Relatively little space in the collection is given to the nine books published between 1970 and 1982 that do not use the dramatic monologue as their controlling form. Remarkable among the poems in these books is "Junkman's Spring" (from *Strawberries*, 1970), which illustrates the synthesis of nature poetry, small-town life, and jazz sensibility in another form Etter uses frequently: a long, narrow poem with from one to five syllables in each line. His poems of this order are usually statements of one sentence or one long breath, and the length of the sentence, contrasted with the brevity of the lines, gives the feeling of a headlong rush. "Well You Needn't," the title poem of Etter's jazz collection (1975), carries an epigraph from Miles Davis that may be taken as a key to Etter's attitude toward his craft: "I'll play it and tell you what it is later." "Bright Mississippi," the title poem of another 1975 collection, anticipates "Leonard Massingail" in *Alliance, Illinois* (1978), in that it is constructed entirely of clichés.

"Barn Dreams" from *Central Standard Time* (1978) captures the surreal element that runs though Etter's poetry. The last dream he recounts—that of a lost lover—is followed by a wish: "May the green winds of chance / blow me always toward / barns." The young boy in Etter's version of the origin of the poetic career, as in Whitman's "Out of the Cradle Endlessly Rocking," is envious (in "Green-Eyed Boy after Reading Whitman and Sandburg"). Despite some apprehensions, the boy joins the poets who "fish for our lost American souls." "Statement," by contrast, gives voice to cynicism and suicidal thoughts, à la Masters. "Boondocks," the title poem of Etter's 1982 collection, sings the pure joy of country life, with corn growing right up to the back porch of the speaker's 1912 frame house. There is, in this same section of the *Selected Poems*, even a modernist poem about poetry. In "That Old-Time Feeling" the speaker rejects his wife's assumption that he wants to buy an old railroad coach so he can use it for a workshop in which "to write those good down-home poems." He insists, rather, that he intends to travel to Wichita in it. This is Etter's twist on Marianne Moore's imaginary garden with real toads: an imaginary railroad with a real trip.

Etter's chef d'oeuvre, *Alliance, Illinois*, has often been compared to Masters's *Spoon River Anthology* (1915). It appeared first in 1978 and then in an expanded edition in 1983; it has been sent by the U.S. government to book fairs in Frankfurt and Madrid, and translated into braille by the Library of Congress. *Alliance* has also been adapted for the musical stage at least three times. The later edition includes poems from *Cornfields* (1980) and *West of Chicago* (1981). Two more-recent books, *Midlanders* (1988) and *Electric Avenue*, consist, like *Alliance*, entirely of poems spoken in the character of various citizens of Etter's mythical town.

The form of the dramatic monologue, which provides the structural unity in *Alliance*, is generally associated with the nineteenth century, although T. S. Eliot updated it in "The Love Song of J. Alfred Prufrock." In general, however, it was already worn when Masters chose it as a way to give speech to the dead residents of Spoon River. Etter uses the form as it has traditionally been used—to give a novelistic quality to the speaker of a poem—but he manages to add a new dimension to it by restricting its length and by making it less rhetorical. Of the 222 poems in the enlarged *Alliance* (1983), only 17 run more than a single page, and none of these is longer than two pages. This concision, further restricted by short line length and colored by the slightly surreal quality of Etter's vision, makes the monologue into an imagistic form.

Whereas *Spoon River* is infamous for its thematic univocality—defeat occupying center-stage for the entire performance—*Alliance*, while not overly complex, has enough thematic tension to reward rereading. Boredom, death, and love provide the coordinates by which one can explore the mythical territory of Alliance. Boredom is, of course, the main quality associated with midwestern life, both by those who live it and by those urbanites and coast dwellers who abhor it. Boredom is a difficult quality to limn, and the dramatic monologue works well for this theme. The inhabitants of Alliance, especially the children, often do not comprehend boredom. They have no objective standard by which to judge their own lives. This situation gives Etter the opportunity to engage in understatement, as when Linda Fulgham, discussing her aunt who is going crazy, says, "It's just too bad the way things go wrong." Susan Sontag once defined boredom as a species of frustration, and the reader sees the connection clearly in *Alliance*. Its citizens do not have the wherewithal to express themselves, so they cannot fully experience the tragedy they witness and suffer.

The frustration and boredom resulting from this inarticulateness is most evident in the love poems in *Alliance*. These are generally not happy poems—happiness being reserved in Etter's mythography for parents who love children—but varieties of frustration. In fact, love, which in literature is generally the only force capable of nullifying, counterbalancing, or justifying the force of death, is hamstrung by boredom in *Alliance*. The culmination comes in the next-to-last poem in the book, when Walter Ingram, drink-

DRINK AND AGRICULTURE

...to die of drink and agriculture.

--Dylan Thomas, Under Milk Wood

Not to die, as in cold-hands dead,
but to die slowly, a slow death,
farming being an old way to die.

Fighting the weeds, cursing the stones.
No cash in pocket, none in bank.
Only pennies turning dark in a jar.

The wife is mostly sick now.
She can hardly wash dirty dishes,
can barely tend the garden plot.

Credit stretched to the last notch.
Stuck with balky tractor, shaky combine,
a barn with a leaky roof.

Booze in the car, booze in the icebox,
booze in the sideboard, booze on the shelf,
booze in the cellar, booze in town.

Lost pigs, sick cows, dead chickens.
The old horse won't eat, won't stand up.
The dog has gone, has hit the road.

There's six townships in this poor man's county,
six gray slabs of flat prairie
under a farmer-breaking sun.

Erosion gives us the nightmares,
the good black loam all washed away,
the land scarred, gullied, turned ugly.

You have a good year, prices go down.
Have a bad year, no one knows your face.
Feast or famine, it hurts the same.

The wife is after me to sell the farm,
to get what we can and get out!
But what's so hot somewhere else?

Sometimes I refuse to sweat this life,
just let my mind drift off like seed
and reach for a bottle of wine.

Dirt farming is for fools like me.
So fool I am, fated to fumble
with a place I can't, won't let go of.

Draft for a poem in Carnival *(by permission of Dave Etter)*

ing gin and sitting in his overstuffed chair, says, "I am fresh out of love." In a town where "One day yawns into the next," a little imagination goes a long way.

Because of the boredom that neutralizes love, death also loses its sting in Alliance. In one of the most poignant poems in the collection, Joe Sprague muses on the relation between rural mailboxes and the gravestones on the other side of the fence from them: "I'm no longer worried about bad news . . . my own fate waits across the fence." Here boredom strives to achieve the heroic status of resignation. Etter, unlike Masters, has found a way to keep death at arm's length through sheer lack of concern, and if Alliance, finally, is not a happy place, neither is it a morbid one.

Alliance comes complete with a verbal map, not unlike its sister city in Minnesota, Garrison Keillor's Lake Wobegone. Carl's Mainline Cafe in Alliance, in fact, is probably on the same railroad as the Sidetrack Tap. The introductory poem in the volume, "George Maxwell: County Seat," gives all the landmarks and many of the local haunts: the Hotel Tall Corn and the "sluggish" Ausagaunaskee River. Alliance, population 6,428, with its dilapidated Victorian homes, its Civil War monument, its railroad tracks dividing Main Street, and its drive-ins, resembles Etter's own Elburn, Illinois. There is only one difference, as George Maxwell points out: "nothing has, nothing could have / really changed." The mythography is complete.

More-recent poems in the *Alliance* mode show distinct progress over the earlier sketches. They are more direct of statement, wider in range of content, and more even in tone. They also show off Etter's sense of humor more effectively. A line that occurs early in *Midlanders* demonstrates the synthesis between Etter's career-long fidelity to imagism and the electricity generated by his interest in surrealism. The character Forrest Day speaks it: "Scarlet windfall apples brighten pale grass." This book also contains aphorisms that apply equally well to the situations of the characters and to Etter's poetry in general. Clark Springstead, for instance, in a poem subtitled "Fender Sitting," opines: "You want to learn, you got to listen." Etter has been listening for thirty years; he has mastered the mimesis of rural midwestern speech. With the terseness of Ernest Hemingway, another character, Todd Lanphere, expresses the purpose of Etter's mastery: "you're never home till you're home." The

poet's mythography has, finally, made him a native.

Electric Avenue continues to develop the myth. The poet himself begins to appear more obviously: in the guise of his characters (the pipe-smoking Gabe Ingels and the hard-bop fan Christopher Moore); in the satirical comment on a local would-be novelist ("Don't know there's much / to write about / in this dull place"); and in person as "Dave," the "visiting writer" in the poem "Sarah Mullen." Beyond these touches, Etter has begun to demand more of the characters. "Victor Tobin: Explanation," for example, captures a real sense of the despair of its speaker. And in this book, for the first time, Etter approaches profound statements in the voice of his mythical townspeople, here in the person of a woman who has lost her bid for election to the school board: "The death of defeat / is the same old verse / the same cold bottom line." The pointed use of poetry as a metaphor merges the fates of writer and character.

A newly expanded version of *Alliance*—over four hundred pages, scheduled for publication by Spoon River Poetry Press in 1992—will likely exceed *Spoon River* in both breadth and depth to stand for the next century as the most insightful poetic version of small-town American life. What remains to be seen is whether an urban culture will recognize the value of such insight.

Despite the justifiable acclaim for *Alliance, Illinois*—acclaim which outreaches the Midwest and transcends the bounds of regionalism—*Home State* is probably a superior book, even in Etter's terms. It is, however, eccentric, in that it consists of one hundred prose poems or sketches. In it the style of Garrison Keillor is crossed with that of Charles Bukowski (for Europeans, the most popular contemporary American poet) to create a hybrid in which humor softens cynicism and cynicism enlivens humor. Etter's sensualist "girl-friend" (a character familiar to Bukowski fans), Doreen, bears a distinct resemblance to Tanya Owens, Alliance's professional female wrestler. With Doreen as a foil, Etter takes his readers on a postmodern tour of Illinois, a tour which, lacking the nostalgic gloss of *Alliance*, finds the incongruities not only amusing, but essential aspects of midwestern life. *Home State* covers the same territory as the rest of Etter's poetry (it includes a section called "Bebop," for instance) and covers it in a way that is more contemporary than modern. The Illinois of *Home State* might actually be recognizable to a punk rocker.

Over forty years ago, in an essay called "The New Provincialism" (*On the Limits of Poetry*, 1948), Allen Tate—one of the New Critics Etter disparages in an epitaph in *The Last Train to Prophetstown*—made some comments that are still pertinent. Without unity of culture, Tate argued, regionalism (which he believed essential to the life and good health of any national literature) would inevitably become provincial, that is, a regional version of nationalism. Instead of communicating universal values, it would limit itself to exclusive ones. This is precisely the danger Etter faces, and some of his poems exhibit just such a regional jingoism. In *Alliance*, for example, Emmylou Oberkfell writes a poem for her fifth-grade class in which the Midwest is the filling of a pie: east and west coasts form the crust. While this sentiment is understandable, justifiable, and perhaps amusing, at least to midwesterners, it does not make a poem. Of the two strains in Etter's poetry, the one represented by *Home State* seems preferable in this respect, since the nostalgic qualities of *Alliance* represent a kind of emotional separatism.

Dave Etter is an impressive poet, knowledgeable and skilled in some major traditions of American poetry: dramatic monologue, imagism, and midwestern regionalism. He is a prolific poet as well: twenty volumes in thirty years of writing. He is intelligent, though slightly anti-intellectual; much useful information may be gained by reading his work. Etter is also a careful craftsman: there are virtually no absolute failures among his published poems. And he is an inventive mythographer: Alliance, Illinois, will succeed Spoon River as a poetic reference point. Further, Etter continues to grow: he is reaching toward profundity in his old age. Unfortunately, Etter's place in American literature is beyond his control, either by talent or force of will. In a culture in which poetry has been completely marginalized, he has chosen a marginal tradition in poetry—regionalism. Without unity of purpose between literature and American culture, the place of poetry remains ambiguous. The function of a regional poet for the entire tradition cannot, finally, be determined. Will Etter's poems be picked up in the twenty-first century like literary arrowheads, or will they become the foundation of a rejuvenated regionalism, the basis for a renovated literary tradition that has worked its way back to the center of American life? Only time will tell. If Etter seems less great than his forebears—Masters, Lindsay, and Sandburg—perhaps it will not always be so. Perhaps he can bear the tradition forward through hard times for poetry, and his reward will come, as it has for many, in being read by future generations.

References:

Norbert Blei, *Door to Door* (Peoria, Ill.: Ellis, 1985), pp. 44-56;

Robert C. Bray, *Rediscoveries: Literature and Place in Illinois* (Champaign: University of Illinois Press, 1982), pp. 156-162;

Robert Killoren, ed., *Late Harvest: Plains and Prairie Poets* (Shawnee Mission, Kans.: BkMk, 1977), pp. 53-70;

David Pichaske, ed., *Spoon River Quarterly*, special Dave Etter issue (Spring 1983).

Edward Field

(7 June 1924 -   )

David Bergman
Towson State University

BOOKS: *Stand Up, Friend, With Me* (New York: Grove, 1963);

Variety Photoplays (New York: Grove, 1967);

Sweet Gwendolyn and the Countess (Gulfport, Fla.: Konglomerati, 1975);

A Full Heart (New York: Sheep Meadow, 1977);

Stars in My Eyes (New York: Sheep Meadow, 1977);

The Potency Clinic, by Field and Neil Derrick, as Bruce Elliot (New York: Bleecker Street, 1978);

Village, by Field and Derrick, as Elliot (New York: Avon, 1982);

The Office, by Field and Derrick, as Elliot (New York: Ballantine, 1987);

New and Selected Poems from the Book of My Life (New York: Sheep Meadow, 1987).

MOTION PICTURE: *To Be Alive*, narration written by Field, Francis Thompson Inc., 1964.

RECORDING: *The Lost, Dancing*, Washington, D.C., Watershed Tapes, 1984.

OTHER: *Songs and Stories of the Netsilik Eskimos*, translated and edited by Field (Cambridge, Mass.: Education Development Center, 1967); enlarged as *Eskimo Songs and Stories* (New York: Delacorte/Lawrence, 1973);

A Geography of Poets: An Anthology of New Poetry, edited by Field (New York: Bantam, 1979).

Looking for a recognized poet who would translate Eskimo songs and legends to teach grade-school children about the Native American traditions, the Education Development Center of Massachusetts selected Edward Field because, as he was told, he was the only poet who could be understood by ten-year-olds. The center's response was typical of many readers who are first drawn to Field's work by the accessibility of his style. Richard Howard notes in *Preferences* (1974) "that mysterious tonality of Edward Field's poetry: a poetry without meter, rhyme, image, without the diet of disciplines and strictures we think of as constituting that shaped share of literature required by *verse*." But as Howard recognizes, jettisoning the normal expectations and conventions of verse does not result, in Field's case, in a poetry that is undisciplined, defective, or merely easy. To the contrary, "by articulating an impulse which usually begins before 'literature,'" Field has created a body of poetry that "vibrates in our minds long after we have put down the book."

In the great modernist tradition, Field has given up the comforts of the literary so that his work might be all the more intense and moving. Field believes he is returning to poetry what has been left out, indeed, not even permitted in the other poetry of his day. He wants to reintroduce humor to poetry, to erase the distinction between light and serious verse. He also wants his work to contain a level of emotion that critics, in earlier stages of his career, condemned as sentimental. He wants to write about all types of sexuality, a particularly daring innovation in the early 1960s, and finally he wants to reintroduce narrative, which for Field means "putting poems in a human context rather than in a world of abstraction." Not all critics have agreed on the success of Field's agenda. Laurence Goldstein complains that Field's practice of "collapsing the conversational into the slovenly" demands from the reader "an indulgence few will grant now that ostentatious displays of sincerity have lost their revolutionary appeal." Clearly Field's style of poetics is risky.

As Field explains, "The whole point of poetry, I thought, was to tell the truth. In poetry you never made anything up. It had nothing to do with fiction. It had to do with, not really confession, but opening up so that everybody would be open. You were supposed to set a good example.... Anything artificial was supposed to be overcome, rejected.... You told the truth, the way you felt it." So single-minded was his desire for absolute honesty and austerity of expression

Edward Field

that at one point in his career he "would only put down what made me cry."

Between his emotions and the language of the poem, Field tries to allow himself no cushion of figurative language, of rhyme or regular meter—all the things that might dress up, falsify, or decorate the truth in a way that would make it more acceptable, agreeable, or pleasant. Such an attitude toward language and art is the subject of two poems, both named "Graffiti," which celebrate spontaneous, unself-conscious, unauthorized truth telling. In the "Graffiti" included in *Variety Photoplays* (1967), he tells the story of an art collector who removed from a men's room a wall "figured over . . . like an oriental temple, / the work of a people, a folk artifact, / the record of lifetimes of secret desires, / the forbidden and real history of man, / and leaving it just as it was, hung it up in his house." Because Field has championed a poetry that is accessible to a large audi-

ence but frequently depicts aspects of real life usually forbidden from high art, Field has gained a loyal and devoted following, encountered a good deal of censorship, and suffered through periods when his work has been overlooked.

Unlike other poets of his generation who favor an aesthetic of personal exposure—poets such as Allen Ginsberg, Sylvia Plath, or John Berryman—Field is not prone to self-laceration or grand gestures of anger, anguish, or angst. Gentleness, modesty, and good humor are the tools by which, in W. H. Auden's words, he gives "suffering its human perspective." Field does not think life's misery has chosen him as its special victim, but rather that pain and suffering are the general lot of all humans, who try to make the best of their estrangement from the world and each other. The palliatives to this human condition of isolation—though never its cure—are acts of kindness and love. In "Sonny Hugg and the Porcu-

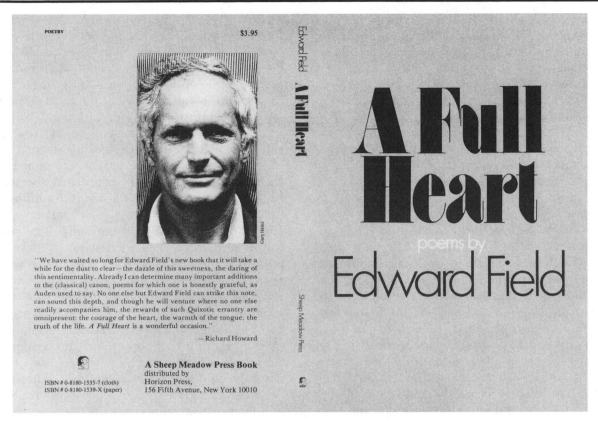

POETRY $3.95

"We have waited so long for Edward Field's new book that it will take a
while for the dust to clear—the dazzle of this sweetness, the daring of
this sentimentality. Already I can determine many important additions
to the (classical) canon, poems for which one is honestly grateful, as
Auden used to say. No one else but Edward Field can strike this note,
can sound this depth, and though he will venture where no one else
readily accompanies him, the rewards of such Quixotic errantry are
omnipresent: the courage of the heart, the warmth of the tongue, the
truth of the life. *A Full Heart* is a wonderful occasion."

—Richard Howard

A Sheep Meadow Press Book
distributed by
Horizon Press,
156 Fifth Avenue, New York 10010

ISBN # 0-8180-1535-7 (cloth)
ISBN # 0-8180-1539-X (paper)

*Cover for one of two collections Field published in 1977, a book that documents Field's search for "a way of expanding out of the
narrow atheism of my father"*

pine" (collected in *Stand Up, Friend, With Me,*
1963), one of Field's early parables involving a
childhood friend, Sonny is determined to find a
way to embrace the porcupine despite its quills.
But even the affectionate and resourceful Sonny
must, in the end, "settle for those creations / Not
quite as darling but with bodies good for hugging." Some expressions of love are impossible.

The porcupine is only one of a series of inap-
propriate objects of affection that inhabit Field's
poetry: Greek goats and donkeys, snow fish, a
baby walrus named Ookie, a giant Pacific octo-
pus, and roaches, particularly "the little ones, expecting like all babies to be adored" ("Roaches,"
in *A Full Heart,* 1977). But the most persistent objects of Field's love are the reluctant and unfortunate monsters that are the central features of
many horror movies—*She, King Kong, The Black
Cat, Island of Lost Souls*—still photographs of
which illustrate Field's *Stars in My Eyes* (1977).
Frankenstein's monster has especially fascinated
Field as the figure who embodies all the cast-off,
unwanted, dispossessed beings of the world and
whose capacity for love is stunted, as well as stimulated, by the rejection, prejudice, and misunder-

standing of those whose affections he hopes to
win. For Field the monster is the ultimate underdog, whose eyes fill with tears "as he thinks of
the stones of the mob, the pleasures of mealtime,
/ the magic new words he has learned / and
above all of the friend he has found" ("Frankenstein," in *Variety Photoplays*).

Field's sympathies for the underdog grow
out of his upbringing. Born in Brooklyn, New
York, on 7 June 1924, he was reared in Lyn-
brook, Long Island, which in the 1930s and early
1940s was a WASP working-class neighborhood
in which Jews were hounded until they left. But
Field's Russian- and Polish-born parents of Jewish ancestry, Louis and Hilda (née Taubman),
stayed, and Field grew up painfully conscious of
his unwanted status, recalling in "The Sleeper"
the time when he "was the sissy of the block who
nobody wanted on their team." In "Unwanted"
he writes of himself, "It is perfectly obvious that
he was not popular at school / No good at baseball, and wet his bed. // His aliases tell his story:
Dumbell, Good-for-nothing, / Jewboy, Fieldinsky,
Skinny, Fierce Face, Greaseball, Sissy." (Both
poems are in *Stand Up, Friend, With Me.*) Field's

97

growing awareness of his homosexuality not only contributed to his sense of alienation, loneliness, and undesirability but also provided some independence.

During World War II Field joined the Army Air Force and served in Europe as a navigator in heavy bombers, flying more than twenty-five missions and surviving one crash into the North Sea. In the poem "World War II" (*Variety Photoplays*) he narrates in harrowing detail how he clung to the side of an overloaded rubber raft until one of the crew exchanged places with him in the freezing water.

During the war Field began to scribble poetry but not until he returned to Europe in 1946 did he really learn to write—by listening to the advice of other expatriate American authors, particularly Robert Friend, whom Field met on a ship to France. In 1948, at the end of this first peacetime trip to Europe, Field traveled to Greece, a visit that resulted in the poems in the first part of *Stand Up, Friend, With Me* and his acquaintance with the work of Constantine Cavafy, the Greek poet whose austere lyrics of homosexual desire, ancient history, and contemporary life, in a language at once demotic, tender, and formal, have been a central and persistent influence on Field.

Returning to America, Field tried to resume his studies at New York University, which he had earlier attended, but he gave up college in despair. Thus began a decade of emotional turmoil in which he took a long succession of jobs in factories, warehouses, and offices and spent years in psychotherapies, which were, according to Field, "more destructive than helpful." In 1956 he began studying acting with Vera Soloviova, a Russian émigré who taught the method-acting techniques of the Moscow Art Theatre. Since the method encourages actors to plumb the depths of their emotion, Field feels it was a factor in his development as a writer. Besides helping him learn to read his poetry to the public—one of the many ways he earned his living in the 1960s and 1970s—the method uses the body as an instrument to reach emotions and was the first of a series of explorations (including gestalt therapy, the Alexander method, yoga, and primal therapy) that led him to a more comprehensive understanding of his problems by encouraging him to act them out.

Stand Up, Friend, With Me, Field's first book, could hardly be described as an apprentice volume. In 1951, with the approval of William Carlos Williams, Random House contracted Field for a book of poems. But he was blocked, unable to finish the poems needed to complete the collection. *Stand Up, Friend, With Me*, published a dozen years later, is an unusually accomplished, mature, and confident debut. After an introductory section of poems about Greece and the Old World, Field turns to "A View of Jersey." New Jersey, for him, is the fantasy child of New York City, which is the place across the river, a place of "dark alleys . . . where rats are the guardians." In many ways New Jersey represents the failure of America to keep faith with its founding impulse to create a society of spiritual, economic, and cultural freedom and harmony. The poems of this section, Field says, represent "a decade of mourning the loss of Europe. They were written at an office desk looking at the Jersey view with Europe impossible," a period when he was "trying to face the reality of working and American life." In "The Statue of Liberty," the concluding poem of the section, Field establishes his critique of American society, which has wasted not only its natural endowment but its cultural inheritance. To Field, the French gave Americans the Statue of Liberty "as a reminder / Of their slogan and our creed / Which hasn't done much good / Because we have turned a perfectly good wilderness / Into a place nice to visit but not to live in."

Field's poems frequently present a sophisticated, happy, or cultured European who is transformed by America into a callous, vulgar, or violent barbarian. In such poems as "Notes from a Slave Ship," "The Ocean Liner," and "What Grandma Knew" (the first of several poems that celebrate the women of earlier generations), Field suggests that the losses of those who immigrated to America were much greater than their gains.

The third part of *Stand Up, Friend, With Me* is harder to characterize. Called "Graffiti," it contains autobiographical poems in which Field discusses himself, usually in the third person. A motif that runs through several of these poems is the need to purge himself of the poisonous anger, self-abasement, and sorrow that afflict him. In "A Journey" he imagines crying "for a long time" until he emerges "a man among men"; in "Nausea" he throws up all the existential angst he has acquired; in "The Half-Wit" he is twisted by seizures in an attempt to accommodate himself to new knowledge about his sexuality.

The final section, which takes its name from its first poem, "A New Cycle," is a happier section than the others. In it Field attempts to reconcile himself with his past and prepare himself for entering a new cycle of life. Literally "the new cycle" refers to a secondhand bicycle Field's father bought him as a child, a bike "which meant more to me than [Father] knew, or could have stood to know," particularly making possible a "paper route, pocket money, // And sexual adventures that would have made [his] hair / Stand up in horror." Especially effective is "Tulips and Addresses," a poem about rescuing tulip bulbs from a dumpster and preserving them all winter so they could be planted in a window box in the spring. The poem concludes with a prayer: "Please God make them come up, so that everyone who passes by / Will know I'm there, at least long enough to catch my breath, / When they see the bright red beautiful flowers in my window." With such tentative moments of repose, the book ends.

The publication of *Stand Up, Friend, With Me* changed Field's life. It won the Lamont Award—at that time one of the most prestigious prizes for a first book of poetry—and in the year of its publication, 1963, Field was granted a Guggenheim Fellowship. Then in 1964 Field was commissioned to write the narration for *To Be Alive*, a film highlighted at the New York World's Fair and a winner of an Academy Award for the best documentary short subject. These changes are reflected in Field's second volume, *Variety Photoplays*, on the surface a happier and lighter book in which he calls "to Ganapati, Hindu God of Auspiciousness" (in the poem of that name) "with his friendly elephant's head, humor in his eyes," to let "the auspicious times continue, . . . / just keep the wolf from my door."

Variety Photoplays is divided into two sections. In the first, Field includes poetic summaries of some popular films (the section includes his poems on Frankenstein) and performs pastiches of certain movie genres, such as the film biography and the tearjerker. These narratives, some quite long, investigate the erotic with a greater freedom than his first book. In recounting the plots, Field reveals their potential, if unrealized, feminism. "Curse of the Cat Woman" and "She" play on the powerful, if bestial, aspects of female sexuality, presenting their heroines as more than the virgin or whore of popular mythology. Though "The Life of Joan Crawford," the longest and wooliest pastiche, paints the feminine as passive and modest—though eminently resourceful—and though "White Jungle Queen"

ends with the title character asserting with a wink, "All I have to do is lie back and wait for Hollywood to call," most of the women Field draws are gutsy, strong, and independent. Still hesitant in the 1960s to deal directly with male homosexuality, Field nevertheless explicitly involves lesbian relationships in two of these poems, "Sweet Gwendolyn and the Countess" and "Nancy."

The second and slightly larger part of *Variety Photoplays* collects the shorter poems Field had written since the time of *Stand Up, Friend, With Me*. These poems are epitomized by "The Tailspin," the concluding poem of the section and the book. Trading on Field's knowledge of aviation from his years in the air corps, the poem gives the excellent advice that the way to get out of a tailspin "as in everything" is to "move the joystick in the direction of the spin . . . to go with the turning willingly / rather than fight." This willing participation in turns of fate, as opposed to a stoic acceptance of them, marks Field's attitude in "Both My Grandmothers," "It," "A Jew on Christmas," and "Three Views of Eden." The penultimate poem, "Prognosis Negative," concludes:

> There really is no preparing for the future
>   (though don't knock money).
> Still one must go on: Life is a struggle to get
>   out of bed, a wise man said,
> and it always seems to be morning again
>   with no maid to bring me juice and coffee
> and the daily masseur still
>   a dream for the future.

Yet there is a kind of modest contentment in the poems and a general hopefulness of future improvement.

Eskimo Songs and Stories (1973—the enlarged version of *Songs and Stories of the Netsilik Eskimos*, 1967) was originally commissioned for school children, but by including some of that material in his *New and Selected Poems* (1987), Field indicated the book's status as a full-fledged part of his poetry. *Eskimo Songs and Stories*, in fact, contains many of the same elements of Field's other work: a concern for folk materials; scatological imagery; a delight in earthy humor; moralistic fables and allegories; and a lyric tenderness toward the lonely, sad, and dispossessed. "Grandma Takes a Foster Child," for example, tells the story of an old woman who befriends a caterpillar. Her children, jealous of the attention she gives it, throw the bug to their sled dogs, "who gobbled the juicy tidbit up." The poem ends with the

EVENING, WITH LEAVES: *The Hague*

There
From tile roofs pigeons in summer rut
are burbling of lust, and a cat
on the toolshed is looking up
Thinks of overhanging branches with yellow eyes,
as blackbirds defend their territory
(if that's what birdsong is) with a trilling
that's ~~fluriladt~~ as nightingales.

In the enclosed garden every bush and tree
loaded with leaf and flower
responds in its individual way *to a wind,*
to a wind that brings ~~its~~ a warm smell of cows *from the polders*
and ~~the golden~~ raintree blossoms ~~fall~~
into the uncut grass with its crop
of new seed, silver in twilight.

Aphids swarm thick on dahlia plants
to drink the sticky sap
and I haul myself with a groan //
out of canvas ~~xxxix~~ sling chair /to hose them off, *rubbing* //
~~rubbing~~ leaf ribs and crisp tips clean, ~~and incidentally~~
~~and incidentally~~ soaking my sneakers,

then ~~fan the~~ *spray* spray idly ~~on the~~ sagging fence
~~and~~ *and* wet down darkening growth and compost heap *in the corner,*
as the last boat gives three long honks,
departing for Norwich.

Two drafts for a poem Field included in his 1987 collection, New and Selected Poems from the Book of My Life *(by permission of Edward Field)*

EVENING, WITH LEAVES

The Hague

From Dutch rooftops, pigeons in summer rut
are burbling of lust, and a cat
crouched on the toolshed ~~is~~ looking up
Through leaves ~~through overhanging branches~~ with yellow eyes //
at the blackbird defending its territory
(if that's what birdsong is), with a whistling
that for me wins the prize from nightingales.

In the enclosed back garden every bush and tree,
loaded with leaf and flower, responds
in its individual way to ~~a fresh~~ wind
that brings a smell of cows from the polders
and shakes the golden raintree blossoms
into uncut grass with its ~~xxxxxxxxxx~~ own crop
of new seed, silver in twilight.

Aphids swarm on the dahlias,
drinking a sticky sap
and I lurch with a groan
out of canvas sling chair
to hose them off, idly rubbing
leaf ribs and crisp tips clean,
soaking my sneakers,

then play the spray on the sagging fence,
to wet down the darkening compost heap,
as the last boat gives three honks from the harbor,
leaving for Norwich.

grandmother, heartbroken by the caterpillar's absence, sitting "down crying by the fire alone." Field treats the Eskimos not as exotics but as ordinary people, almost relatives, with the usual assortment of failings and virtues.

A Full Heart is both more defiant and despairing than *Variety Photoplays*. In "New York" Field celebrates how the people of his city "dare to live their dreams, or nightmares, / and no one bothers to look." And in another poem titled "Both My Grandmothers" (Field has the confusing habit of putting the same title on apparently different poems, although his intention is to indicate that the new poem is an addition to the older one), he thanks his ancestors for giving him strength "even in sorrow, and defeat." This new mood of comic bitterness finds its clearest expression at the end of "Diary: October 11, 1972," which records a day of mishaps and frustration:

> I know what the I Ching would say to all this,
> Get back in tune with the universal order of
>   things,
> stop fighting whatever is happening,
> even this downward negative spiral.
> And if you can't smile, then sigh,
> one of those deep Jewish sighs that say,
> This is how things are going in the universe
>   today, rotten,
> and all is as it should be.

Several events account for this mood of black humor: Field's return to the United States after a revelatory journey to Afghanistan, his entrance into primal therapy, and the blindness of his longtime companion, Neil Derrick, following an operation to remove a brain tumor. Derrick, whom Field met in 1959 and with whom he still lives, is the subject of several poems in *A Full Heart:* "Pasternak: In Memoriam," "Living With an Aries," and the tender "Gone Blind."

But the mood of *A Full Heart*, although seasoned with pain, is leavened by a more relaxed and open response to homosexuality, feminism, and spirituality. "Street Instructions: At the Crotch" and "David's Dream" have a graphic homosexual explicitness that at the time could only be found in the works of Allen Ginsberg and other Beat poets. "The Two Orders of Love" ends with a more assertive claim for gay rights: "Nature needs both [homo- and heterosexuality] to do its work / and humankind, confusing the two separate orders of love, / makes rules allowing only one kind / and defies the universe." Field's feminism is particularly clear in "Being Jew-

ish," his celebration of the struggles of the women in his mother's family who suffered through endless pregnancies and housework, with "never enough money, the beasts their men were to them." But the largest change in *A Full Heart* is the role spiritual issues play. Field has never disguised his Jewish ancestry, but his parents were atheists, rejecting any kind of spiritual authority. As Field says, he had to find not only "what it meant to be a Jew, the inchoate feelings you inherit without the words," but also "a way of expanding out of the narrow atheism of my father who believed the only definition of God was an old man with a long beard in a chair in the sky." Field turned to Gurdjieffian, Sufi, and Buddhist thought, not so much to become an adept or a Buddhist as to find a sense of his own spirit.

Between *A Full Heart* and his *New and Selected Poems*, Field published *Stars in My Eyes* and a few novels coauthored with Derrick, under the joint pen name Bruce Elliot. *Stars in My Eyes* collects, with copious illustrations, all the previously published movie poems into one volume. Field began work on the novels after Derrick, a novelist, lost his sight and needed help composing. The novel writing has brought Field, he says, a much greater sense of discipline, more confidence in handling larger works, and some additional money, since they were written for a mass audience.

The religious themes announced in *A Full Heart* are even more pronounced in "The Crier," the section of recent work in *New and Selected Poems*. One of the most extraordinary of these poems is "Tantra," which combines Field's erotic and religious concerns. He addresses a spiritual master who has become sexually aroused while dancing with Field. The master is not "the least shy about" his erection, and he reaches to grab Field's own penis. But Field has trouble responding sexually. He tells the guru:

> I knew nothing sexual was the least repugnant to
>   you,
> you were willing to get on with it any way I
>   wanted,
> had guessed what I liked, and offered it,
>
> but I was too ashamed in front of the others,
> though my shame came from another time,
> a different world that exists for me
> more than anything in the present.
>
> So I was the one who broke off
> and lost contact.

The poem recounts in homosexual terms the same process George Herbert describes in the 1633 poem "Love (III)," the embarrassment that comes from being accepted unconditionally, despite one's unworthiness, by God. But whereas Herbert's poem ends with triumph, Field's ends in failure, and whereas Herbert concludes his poem strongly with a masculine rhyme, Field allows the sound and rhythm to dribble away.

Field's poem forms a critique of Herbert's poem, as Field brings to light the inappropriateness of Herbert's ending—the male boastfulness of erotic conquest. And unlike Herbert, whose poem moves away from Eros to *caritas* (from love to chastity), Field more forthrightly retains his focus on the difficulty of accepting divine love in its erotic and sensuous form. In so doing, Field suggests his place among the metaphysical poets and reveals a more profound strategy to his self-conscious, "plain" style. Yet who seriously would place this aging homosexual Jew among the likes of John Donne and George Herbert? True, Donne could write about a flea as the incarnation of the Trinity, but such a poem is a far cry from Field's hymn to roaches. Or is it?

His latest poems place Field in such a visionary company. Field's poetry has become stranger and more daring. He combines spiritual meditation, social criticism, and sexual explicitness in a style austerely colloquial and plainly metaphysical. He ends *New and Selected Poems* with "To Poetry," one of his rare exercises in rhyme: "Whatever time is left to offer homage, / there's one important thing I have learned: / No better way than accept your gentle bondage— / my least effort devoted to your service / has been a thousand fold returned."

References:

Laurence Goldstein, "The Spectacles of Edward Field," *Parnassus*, 15, no. 1 (1989): 240-255;

Richard Howard, "Edward Field," in his *Alone with America: Essays in the Art of Poetry in the United States Since 1950*, enlarged edition (New York: Atheneum, 1980), pp. 143-157;

Howard, *Preferences* (New York: Viking, 1974), pp. 73-74.

Robert Hass
(1 March 1941 -   )

Forrest Gander
Providence College

BOOKS: *Field Guide* (New Haven & London: Yale University Press, 1973);
Praise (New York: Ecco, 1979);
Twentieth Century Pleasures: Prose on Poetry (New York: Ecco, 1984);
Human Wishes (New York: Ecco, 1989).

OTHER: Paul Carroll, ed., *The Young American Poets*, includes poems by Hass (Chicago & New York: Follett, 1968);
Five American Poets, includes poems by Hass (Manchester, U.K.: Carcanet, 1979);
Rock and Hawk: A Selection of Shorter Poems by Robinson Jeffers, edited by Hass (New York: Random House, 1987);
Tomas Tranströmer, *Selected Poems 1954-1986*, edited by Hass (New York: Ecco, 1987).

TRANSLATIONS: Czeslaw Milosz, *The Separate Notebooks*, translated by Hass and Robert Pinsky (New York: Ecco, 1984);
Milosz, *Unattainable Earth*, translated by Hass and Milosz (New York: Ecco, 1986);
Milosz, *Collected Poems 1931-1987*, translated by Hass, Milosz, and others (New York: Ecco, 1988).

Though he has translated the work of Nobel Prize-winning poet Czeslaw Milosz and written a critical book (*Twentieth Century Pleasures*) that received the 1984 National Book Critics Circle Award for criticism, it is for his own musical, descriptive, meditative poetry that Robert Hass is primarily recognized. His impressive literary accomplishments—editorial work, translation, poetry, criticism, reviews—derive from his deep-seated conviction, stated in a spring 1981 interview with David Remnick, that "poetry is a way of living ... a human activity like baking bread or playing basketball." Hass's poetic energy has flowed easily into different forms, and likewise it is stimulated by various, and ordinary, situations. He has been known to turn to a friend, out of breath while both were jogging, to instigate a

serious discussion of meter. Identifiable for their heady music, references to nature, art, and literature, and their capacity to disclose the associative, sometimes stumbling-forward quality of human thinking, his poems are less concerned with transcendence than with experience. Rhythmically traditional in the first two books, Hass's poems are active attempts to find form for "dailiness and desire" ("Songs to Survive the Summer," in *Praise*, 1979) in the descriptive and passionate language of a man who identifies the natural world not as "other" but as the medium in which people live, the principal fact of being in the world.

Hass grew up in one of the most dramatic natural landscapes in America, a landscape swarmed by unique flora and fauna—banana slugs, fuchsia, Steller's jays—and marked by sharp mountains sheering steeply off into the algid Pacific. Each of his books of poems, as well as his critical book, is marked by the Bay Area and by San Francisco itself, where Hass was born on 1 March 1941, the son of Fred Hass, a businessman, and Helen Dahling Hass.

Before Robert Hass graduated from St. Mary's College of California (B.A., 1963), he and soon-to-be-psychotherapist Earlene Leif were married (on 1 September 1962). They had three children, Leif, Kristin, and Luke, while Robert continued his education at Stanford (M.A., 1965; Ph.D., 1971), making or renewing important friendships with the poets John Matthias, James McMichael, John Peck, and Robert Pinsky. Hass studied briefly with poet and critic Yvor Winters, the magnetic and magisterial New Critic whose essays are most noted for emphasizing ferociously the moral content of art. Since 1971 Hass has been a professor of English at St. Mary's College of California.

Hass's poetry is less clearly affected by Winters than by William Wordsworth, whose blank-verse music, Romantic imagination (with an emphasis on natural religion, the power of imagination, and the need for spontaneity in thought), and sense for situating the reader in a

Robert Hass

particular place and time can be detected in Hass's earlier work. In the longer poems, such as "In Weather" and "Songs to Survive the Summer," from his first books, there are aspects of Ezra Pound's later cantos: the bolts of rhythmic intensity, the concern for line more than for image, and a historical and metaphorical consciousness. Hass has noted his own affinity for Japanese haiku, and his work similarly attends to the details of quotidian life with remarkable clarity. When he writes, he likes to sink like those Japanese poets into "the place where all that noise stops" (as he told Remnick in the 1981 interview).

With such a compass of influence and interest, Hass has explored distinctive rhythms and forms. Several critics have simplified these distinctions into two styles, short-lined and long-lined poems. In a generally positive review, Ira Sadoff wrote that Hass's short-lined poems do "not seem as substantial" because they "create a strained

and diffuse effect" (*Chicago Review*, Winter 1980). In the *Hollins Critic* Robert Miklitsch went "so far as to say that the shorter line . . . the dominant line of *Field Guide* [1973], inhibits Hass' imagination, which is essentially discursive and meditative, whereas the longer line accommodates it" (February 1980). In fact, Hass's body of work shows a clear movement toward both longer lines and longer poems. And in spite of the occasional dispraises, Hass has had the good fortune of positive and early critical recognition resulting in a Woodrow Wilson Fellowship (1963-1964), Danforth Fellowships (1963-1967), a Guggenheim Fellowship (1980), and a MacArthur Award.

Field Guide was chosen for the Yale Series of Younger Poets Award by Stanley Kunitz, who comments in the book's foreword that "Hass's poetry is permeated with the awareness of his creature self, his affinity with the animal and vegetable kingdoms, with the whole chain of being. . . . Natural universe and moral universe coincide for him,

*Dust jacket for Hass's 1984 collection of essays and reviews, which first appeared in such periodicals
as the* New Republic *and the* New York Review of Books

centered in a nexus of personal affections, his stay against what he describes as 'the wilderness of history and political violence.'" The poems in *Field Guide* are rich with Russian accents, aromas of ferny anise and uncorked wines, and references to plant and animal life: the green whelks and rock crabs, tanagers and Queen Anne's lace, sea spray and pepper trees of the Bay Area. But behind the texture of landscape is the Vietnam War: "They / manufacture napalm / in the fog where Redwood / City sprawls into the bay" ("Black Mountain, Los Altos"). In "Maps"—"The night they bombed Hanoi / we had been drinking red pinot"—and in "Lines on Last Spring," the war also appears. Regarding *Field Guide*, Hass told Remnick, "The whole post-war explosion in America was going on, and my study was a way of holding on, a way of making things that I val-

ued stay put. By getting to know one species of grass from another, one species of bird from another, and by knowing the names, they could stay put. I thought."

In one sense, then, *Field Guide* is an actual field guide charged with the role of naming the world. The poems are full of natural description—muskrat paths and eucalyptus leaves—and the specific names for dozens of flowers and birds. In "Palo Alto: The Marshes" Hass writes, "Walking, I recite the hard / explosive names of birds: / egret, killdeer, bittern, tern. / Dull in the wind and early morning light, / the striped shadows of the cattails / twitch like nerves." The poems connect historical past and present, as well as natural object and human sensation, just as "Palo Alto" contrasts an early spring California day against the legend of Kit Carson. Carson's country, blooming with violence, reenacts itself in contemporary America, in "citizens [who] are rising / to murder in their moral dreams."

Field Guide is divided into three sections. The first, "The Coast," gives the reader a sense of the poet among others: with the dead in "Graveyard at Bolinas," in bookstores with friends, among family, with an intimate, and with a dying poet. The middle section of *Field Guide*, "A Pencil," includes poems on the nineteenth century, poems influenced by or concerned with Anton Chekhov, Yosa Buson, and Robinson Jeffers. Then, in the same section, there is a series of poems called "The Pornographer": the title poem of the series; "The Pornographer, Melancholy"; "The Pornographer at the End of Winter"; and "Politics of a Pornographer." The mind of "the pornographer" is imagined as being formed by intense solitude and by repeated stagings of death in the first poem; by the absence of friends in the second; and by a cold and isolate walk in a landscape filled with blackbirds in the third. In the fourth poem, "Politics of a Pornographer," the pornographer experiences the Oedipal myth, but: "There is no walled city come to. / The sphinx proposes nothing. / There is no plague."

The title poem of the third section, "In Weather," is one of the strongest poems in *Field Guide*; it is a medium-to-short-lined plangent meditation on wreckage and private descendencies of the spirit echoed by February weather. The speaker imagines himself capable of cruelty to women. Later he is startled into joy by his wife's stirring in her sleep, and he considers how to go beyond that momentary happiness through the dim winter, while maintaining alertness. The problem is one of abiding.

Perseverance becomes a major theme in Hass's second book, *Praise*, which was published six years later and gleaned the William Carlos Williams Award along with substantial critical acclaim. In this book Hass persists in emphasizing the importance of details, the dangers that accompany what he calls "the ignorance of particulars," and several poems, such as "Weed," a meditation on horse parsnip, develop from a consciousness of the names of things. Yet in many ways *Praise* addresses the problems implicit in the first book: Can the act of naming the world separate us from the world? How is it possible to bear grief, to accept death, and how can the spirit endure?

In "St. Lucia," a poem whose title recalls not only the folkloric martyr who suffered the loss of her eyes but the West Coast mountain range, the speaker rejects the desire for transcendence: "as if the little song / *transcend, transcend* could get you anywhere." Like Wallace Stevens's narrator in "Sunday Morning," evincing the sad, beautiful mechanism of natural process, imagining worship aimed toward the sun—"not as a god, but as a god might be"—Hass's speaker aches for "a different order of religious awe." He turns his back on the famous paintings at the Louvre and opens himself to "the city in the rain. / Dog shit, traffic accidents." What the speaker desires is not instant transport, but a strength and rhythm for the long haul: "What I want happens / not when the deer freezes in the shade / and looks at you and you hold very still / and meet her gaze but in the moment after / when she flicks her ears & starts to feed again."

One of the most affective poems in *Praise* came, as Hass told Remnick, "out of a sudden realization that the word was not the thing." In "Meditation at Lagunas" Hass apposes the vocabulary and ideas integral to Ferdinand de Saussure's linguistic theories—"the idea, for example, that each particular erases / the luminous clarity of a general idea"—with his own spiritual vocabulary of "longing," "desire," "wonder," "presence," and "thirst." Hass balances formal abstraction—"a word is elegy to what it signifies"—with a colloquial tone:

I felt a violent wonder at her presence
like a thirst for salt, for my childhood river
with its island willows, silly music from the pleasure
   boat,
muddy places where we caught the little orange-
   silver fish
called *pumpkinseed*. It hardly had to do with her.
Longing, we say because desire is full
of endless distances. I must have been the same to
   her.
But I remember so much, the way her hands disman-
   tled bread,
the thing her father said that hurt her, what
she dreamed. There are moments when the body is
   as numinous
as words, days that are the good flesh continuing.
Such tenderness, those afternoons and evenings,
saying *blackberry, blackberry, blackberry.*

While the poem admits an expression of language more complicated than the Adamic one central to *Field Guide*, Hass nevertheless refuses to capitulate to abstraction. In the poem's last line, he disperses the fog of theory by lobbing *"blackberry, blackberry, blackberry"* at the reader.

Getting past the signifier/signified dichotomy is likewise central to "Picking Blackberries with a Friend Who Has Been Reading Jacques Lacan." In this poem two friends are described picking berries, talking "about *L'Histoire de la verité*, / about subject and object / and the mediation of desire." But soon they cannot hear each other; their "ears are stoppered / in the bee-hum." And Charlie's beard is "stained purple / by the word *juice*." The delicious fact of the actual (juice and blackberries) functions in the poem like the slap given by the Zen master to the haplessly logorrheic student to astonish him into immediate awareness of sensual experience. As Hass told Remnick, "Basho says that the trouble with most poetry is that it is either subjective or objective.... It should be neither. It should get past the place where those words have any meaning." In "Picking Blackberries" Hass implies that the solution to abstract intellectual problems "about subject and object / and the mediation of desire" is to go "to get a bigger pot." Such an implication is epistemologically akin to "Mu," the Zen Buddhist response to questions (such as "Do dogs go to heaven?") that are constructed too narrowly for the nature of the answer.

Praise is divided into two sections. The second is the single long poem "Songs to Survive the Summer," which is broken into movements of three-line stanzas. Leitmotifs concerning death, form, naming, Chekhov, haiku, and a recipe for onion soup are worked through nearly obsessively in the context of a father explaining death to his child in the vocative case, reminiscent of Gerard Manley Hopkins's "Spring and Fall." In a sense, the long poem is an iteration and culmination of the book's other poems but in a new form.

In the five years following publication of *Praise*, Hass wrote a series of discrete essays and reviews, primarily for literary magazines such as *Ironwood* and *Salmagundi*. Collected as *Twentieth Century Pleasures: Prose on Poetry*, some of the essays focus on certain American poets (Robert Lowell, James Wright, Stanley Kunitz) and European poets (Tomas Tranströmer, Czeslaw Milosz, Rainer Maria Rilke). Others concentrate on form, prosody, and images (particularly those of the Japanese haiku masters), and one is a memoir titled "Some Notes on the San Francisco Bay Area as a Culture Region." The center of the book is a section of four reviews. In spite of the diversity, *Twen-*

tieth Century Pleasures has remarkable integrity as a collection.

For one thing, all the essays are defined by a common participatory tone, but less avuncular than intimate because of the reverence Hass has for the subject of poetry, which he clearly feels is an essential experience. The tone is also intimate because each of the essays incorporates autobiographical incidents. Hass is generous in allowing the reader more than a glimpse of himself. From tangential commentaries on his family, from conversation overheard in a bar, from travels, and from notes or remarks by Hass's friends, readers may come to believe they know something of the writer; they have an inkling of his worries, his wit, and the associations his mind makes.

In fact, one of the book's central motifs—as seen in the essay "Images"—has to do with how the mind metabolizes images, makes connections, and re-creates form in poetry. Here, as in his own poetry, Hass investigates the relationship between subject and object, between inwardness and death, wonder and imagination. At one point Hass argues that images are not "about" anything so much as they are things themselves, "equal in status with being and the mysteriousness of being."

Twentieth Century Pleasures was widely reviewed and well received, with critics often divided regarding whether "Images" was the best or worst essay of the book. "Images haunt," Hass writes, and "the formality of poetry makes all poems images." Typically Hass's discussion of images and poetry comes to encompass imagination and meaning: "It seems to me that we all live our lives in the light of primary acts of imagination, images or sets of images that get us up in the morning and move us about our days. I do not think anybody can live without one, for very long, without suffering intensely from deadness and futility. And I think that, for most of us, those images are not only essential but dangerous because no one of them feels like the whole truth and they do not last. Either they die of themselves, dry up, are shed; or, if we are lucky, they are invisibly transformed into the next needful thing; or we act on them in a way that exposes both them and us."

In the summer of 1989, five years after *Twentieth Century Pleasures* and ten years after *Praise*, Hass's third book of poems was published. Although it was originally advertised as "The Apple Trees at Olema," Hass retitled the book *Human Wishes* just before it was typeset. "Spring

Hass circa 1984 (photograph copyright by Debra Heimerdinger)

Drawing," the first poem of the four-sectioned book, begins:

> A man thinks *lilacs against white houses*, having seen them in the farm country south of Tacoma in April, and can't find his way to a sentence, a brushstroke carrying the energy of *brush* and *stroke*
>
> —as if he were stranded on the aureole of the memory of a woman's breast,
>
> and she, after the drive from the airport and a chat with her mother and a shower, which is ritual cleansing and a passage through water to mark transition,
>
> had walked up the mountain on a summer evening.

These lines are an announcement. Not only will *Human Wishes* not continue the sorrow-tinged but generally sanguine tone of Hass's first books—since this "man" (no longer "I"), the protagonist

of the initial poem, is already lost at the start, distracted, "as if stranded"—but these poems will embody radically new forms. Hass writes later in the same poem of a need "to reinvent the inner form of wishing." Metonymy pervades this book. The syntax emphasizes an affiliation between materials, events, and thoughts. Hass has been influenced a little by the "Language" poets of the Bay Area. His narrative is frustrated; the images and associations aggregate without transitions.

In "Spring Drawing" Hass works through a series of leaps. He begins with a narrative dominated by an image. Then he makes the narrative reflexive; it suggests the writer writing about the writer trying to write but unable "to find his way to a sentence." By the end of the first stanza, the focus has shifted to the construction of language itself: a sentence is a "brushstroke carrying the energy of *brush* and *stroke*."

In the first section of *Human Wishes*, lines spill over at the right margin; they are not stopped, just as the subject matter, a profusion of

VINTAGE

They had agreed, walking into the delicatessen on
6th Avenue, that their friends' affairs were fo-
cussed and saddened by massive projection.

Movie screens in their childhood were immense and
someone had proposed that need was unlovable.

The delicatessen had a chicken salad with chunks of
cooked chicken and half-braised vegetables in a
creamy basil mayonaisse a shade lighter than the
Coast Range in August. It was grey outside, February;

eating with plastic forks, walking and talking in
the sleety afternoon, they passed a house where
Djuana Barnes was still, reputedly, making sentences.

reputedly

Basho said: avoid adjectives of scale; you will desire
the world less and love it more. *love the world more and...*

Arndt There were other propositions to consider: childhood,
Vistavision, ~~love~~, a pair of wet mobile lips on the
screen at least eight feet long.

On the corner by the liquor store a blind man who had
lost one leg was selling pencils;

he must have received a disability check, but it didn't
feed his hunger for public agony and he sat on the
sidewalk with a tin cup, his face and opaque eyes
turned upward in a look of blind, questing pathos.

Half Job, half mole.

Would a good Christ of Manhattan ~~think charity commended~~ have
~~the restoration of~~ his sight and ~~two-thirds of~~ his
left leg? Or would he have healed his heart and left
him there in a mutilated body? And what would that
peace feel like?

restored.

reaction shot.

Convention calls, at this point, for a quick cut. "The
taxis rivered up 6th Avenue." "A little light touched
the steeple of the First Magyar Reform Church." etc.

The clerk in the liquor store was appalled. "No, no,"
he said. "That cabernet can't be drunk for another
five years."

*ringing the bell
in Mass when the chalice
was lifted. Half asleep,
silvery peal of sound*

sun

— Hass

Draft for a poem in Hass's Human Wishes *(by permission of Robert Hass)*

incidents and images, runs on. In mostly one- , two- , and three-lined stanzas, Hass contours the prose line toward evocation instead of event, toward brilliant moments instead of narration.

More than in any of his earlier work, these poems incorporate multiple levels of diction and rhythm in tense juxtaposition. Another poem from the first section, "Late Spring," begins with the mid-sentence immediacy and the spondaic style of Ezra Pound, but shifts suddenly to an anecdotal, prosaic narrative line, and then shifts again to a lyrical mode: "And then in mid-May the first morning of steady heat, / the morning, Leif says, when you wake up, put on shorts, / and that's it for the day, / when you pour coffee and walk outside, blinking in the sun." As in most of these new poems, the diction in "Late Spring" ranges from the formal—"and because the light will enlarge your days"—to the conversational—"squid so cheap in the fishstores you begin to consult Japanese and Italian cookbooks for the various and ingenious ways of preparing *ika* and *calamari*. . . ."

Throughout the poems in section 1, Hass avoids writing from the perspective of an "I." His characters range from "a man" and "a woman" to "they," "we," and "you." In subsequent sections, Hass does use first person, but the central pronouns are more diversified than in Hass's earlier work, and even in a single poem "I" often alternates with "you" as the dominant pronominal choice.

The multiple pronouns parallel the multiple levels of diction, the juxtaposed rhythms, and the panoply of evoked moments, images, dialogue, and thought that are rapidly and abruptly revealed in the poems. Likewise, one poem can refer to the weather, a snatch of conversation, haiku, a meal, the landscape, and a suicide. The poems are often synchronic experiences, or realizations of the relatedness between disparate elements contained in the function of any moment, memory, or image. In this aspect, they are an applied poetics of new physics; they indicate morphic fields, the connections between all things visible and invisible; they imply, as St. John said, that "We are members of one another."

While the poems in section 1 are marked by a syntax that is mildly refractory to sense, the prose poems of section 2, the longest of the book's sections, retain all the transitions ordinary to spoken stories, but in highly phrased, cadenced lines, not dead blocks of prose. Many of the events connected with these poems take place in Europe, others in California. Some, such as "Conversion" and "Human Wishes," seem to be made up of glances instead of long looks, as though to emphasize the marginal and quotidian at the expense of contemporary taste for the extreme in art, as though to make clear that a poem of details relevant to the movement of thought is as significant, perhaps more significant, than the poem of overt moral statement. These poems are documents of descriptions and impressions carried along by the sensuous pleasure of language. They are striking for their ironic oppositions. In "Museum," for instance, the narrator watches a modern couple as they alternately read the paper, hold their baby, eat fruit, smoke absorbedly, while "all around them are faces Kathe Kollwitz carved in wood of people with no talent or capacity for suffering who are suffering the numbest kinds of pain: hunger, helpless terror."

In "A Story About the Body" a young composer's facile infatuation with an older Japanese painter is extinguished when he learns that she has had a double mastectomy:

> The radiance that he had carried around in his belly and chest cavity—like music—withered very quickly, and he made himself look at her when he said "I'm sorry. I don't think I could." He walked back to his own cabin through the pines, and in the morning he found a small blue bowl on the porch outside his door. It looked to be full of rose petals, but he found when he picked it up that the rose petals were on top; the rest of the bowl—she must have swept them from the corners of her studio—was full of dead bees.

The third and fourth sections of *Human Wishes* are poems of adulthood, of unfulfillment and desire, as "sad or happy," Hass writes in "The Apple Trees at Olema," "as the tide, going out or coming in, at sunset." The poems, medium to long lined and melodic, generally dramatize the evolving relationship between a woman and a man.

"So many prisms to construct a moment!" Hass declares in "Santa Barbara Road," indicating his method. In this, the book's longest poem, a moment of digging in the garden, "trying to marry myself / and my hands to that place," is constructed as a prism of fragments, pieces of relationships between daughter and father and between father and son in the context of home and friends. It is a poem of fatherhood, of wonder at

Dust jacket for Hass's third book of poetry. The painting is The Open Window *by Pierre Bonnard (1921).*

the garden of a family blossoming, each life heliotropic toward a different sun.

The last poem of the third section, "Berkeley Eclogue," is among the oddest and most compelling. Written in whole sentences so terse that often one or two make up a line, the poem is a sort of lover's discourse, although the voices might well be construed to be aspects of one self. "I" and "you" collide in staccato phrases revolving around a complicated falling in love, with the self as narrator and interrogator, wounded and witness, the lost and the lover:

> Then? Then, the truth is, then they fall in love.
> Oh no. *Oh yes.* Big subject. *Big shadow.*
> I saw it slant across the floor, linoleum
> in fact, and very dirty. Sad and dirty.
> *Because it lacked intention?* Well, it did lack art.
> *Let's leave the shadow part alone. They fall in love.*

Elements of both speech patterns merge and depart suddenly in tangents; the relationship between concepts is sometimes more musical than syntactical. Non sequiturs become part of a formula that includes anaphora and an increasing pressure toward a climax. Words recur in different senses, and the lines pound and reverberate with tension ("You bastard, she said, and slammed the door"), humor ("She slammed the door. / He was, of course, forlorn. And lorn and afterlorn. / It made a busy afternoon. The nights were difficult"), and violence ("They beat the child again when they get home"; or, "Your hands are bloody and you do the job"). Language reconstitutes itself in thoughts and in images that influence those thoughts. What narrative there is involves two interlocutors, one who has fallen in love, one who by questions and comments delves into the problem of how such a love came to be. Hass writes in tones ranging from intimate to sarcastic, and he writes of incidents as various as fishing with children and driving a dead man through the rain. He sometimes conjoins passion and bathos: "I would have died for her. *Trala*." And he asserts a poetic form that makes use of repetition, variation, and an absence of connecting clauses. The narrative remains veiled, but the language takes place at great emotional expense to its speakers.

An ars poetica for the entire collection, "Natural Theology" stands out in the fourth section with an initial image—"White daisies against the burnt orange of the windowframe"—that recalls the image, and inverts the color pattern, of "lilacs against white houses" from the first poem, "Spring Drawing."

"Natural Theology" is a tour de force of two sentences, one involving a morning, the plants, "meadow rue and yarrow," and the individual lives that simultaneously open in that morn-

ing light; and the other referring to "the regions of the dark" and the dogs, cats, and human beings alive that night "in postures so various" they can be imagined in sensuous detail.

In *Human Wishes* Hass finds new and adaptive forms. It is a poetry of complex emotional resonances that Hass, coming from a family of relentless optimists, had not explored to such a degree in his earlier books. In *Human Wishes* he picks up the pace of his lines; his concerns are human emotions, including passion and grief.

Interviews:

Sydney Lea and Jay Parini, "An Interview with Robert Hass," *New England Review*, 2, no. 2 (1979): 295-314;

David Remnick, "A Conversation with Robert Hass," *Chicago Review*, 32 (Spring 1981): 17-26.

Reference:

John Matthias, "Reading Old Friends," *Southern Review*, 22 (Spring 1986): 391-406.

Jonathan Holden

(18 July 1941 -)

Thomas F. Dillingham
Stephens College

BOOKS: *Design for a House* (Columbia: University of Missouri Press, 1972);

The Mark to Turn: A Reading of William Stafford's Poetry (Lawrence: University Press of Kansas, 1976);

The Rhetoric of the Contemporary Lyric (Bloomington: Indiana University Press, 1980);

Leverage (Charlottesville: University Press of Virginia, 1983);

Falling from Stardom (Pittsburgh: Carnegie-Mellon University Press / London: Feffer & Simons, 1984);

The Names of the Rapids (Amherst: University of Massachusetts Press, 1985);

Style and Authenticity in Postmodern Poetry (Columbia: University of Missouri Press, 1986);

Landscapes of the Self: The Development of Richard Hugo's Poetry (Milwood, N.Y.: Associated Faculty Press, 1986);

Against Paradise (Salt Lake City: University of Utah Press, 1990);

The Fate of American Poetry (Athens: University of Georgia Press, 1991).

PLAY PRODUCTION: *The Remorseless Daydreams of Mrs. Blanchard*, Columbia, Missouri, Stephens College Warehouse Theater, 13 April 1977.

SELECTED PERIODICAL PUBLICATIONS— UNCOLLECTED: "Non-fiction Prose, the Dramatic Lyric, and the Limits of Genre," *American Poetry Review*, 16 (March/April 1987): 7-12;

"Poetry, Baseball: The Pleasures of the Text," *Antaeus*, 59 (Autumn 1987): 115-126;

"Guns and Boyhood in America," *Georgia Review*, 42 (Summer 1988): 329-339;

"American Male Honor," *TriQuarterly*, 73 (Fall 1988): 155-165;

"The End of Modernism," *Tar River Poetry*, 28 (Fall 1988): 107-114.

Several of Jonathan Holden's books of poetry have won major awards: the Devins Award (1972), the AWP Award (1983), and the Juniper Prize (1985). He has also received two National Endowment for the Arts Creative Writing Fellowships and a Distinguished Graduate Faculty Award at Kansas State University. Both as a poet and as a critic Holden struggles with important questions: the relationship of a poet's past to his poetic vision and vice versa; the potential moral outrage of trivializing real work by treating it as an aesthetic artifact; and the depressed value of poetry in a consumer society. A friend once said of Holden, "He prefers life to art." The best art, Holden would say, serves life by celebrating and illuminating the meaning of the simplest tasks and feelings. In pursuing these goals, Holden counters the influence of the cheapened and empty commodities that dominate the consciousness of a society immersed in mass media or confused by faddish intellectual diversions. His poems do not "imitate" life, for imitations may serve as mere substitutes for reality; rather, with his understanding of the function of rhetorical conventions in human discourse, Holden shows (or attempts to rescue) the power of poetry to analyze and enumerate unexpected relationships between daily experience and rare moments of insight. Part of this aim involves Holden's apparent wish to redeem contention, to affirm the creative aspects of competition while debunking the cultural tendency toward macho aggression.

Jonathan Holden and his twin brother, Stephen, were born in Morristown, New Jersey, on 18 July 1941. Their mother was Janet Conselyea Holden and their father, a physicist and chemist, was Alan Nordby Holden. The boys grew up in New Vernon, a small town close to New York City that, nonetheless, had in Holden's memory the rural charm of "the scenes which Norman Rockwell enshrined on covers of the *Saturday Evening Post* back in the fifties" ("Poetry, Baseball: the Pleasures of the Text," *Antaeus*, Autumn 1987). That background and Holden's mixed feel-

Jonathan Holden

ings about his father's intensely intellectual professional character have been formative influences and recurrent subjects in his mature poetry. He recreates the almost mythic boyhood of the 1950s, filled with the characteristic loneliness and boredom of young boys, the fascination with sports and mildly delinquent behavior, and the exploration of the surrounding countryside and of sexual possibilities that one associates with the literary and popular cultural images of that period.

Although Holden draws many of his poetic subjects from his past experiences, he is not a confessional poet nor even straightforwardly autobiographical. He rarely mentions his mother, for example, and contrary to what many would expect, he never alludes to the experience of being a twin. Except for a recent dedication (in *Style and Authenticity in Postmodern Poetry*, 1986), he has made no overt written reference to his brother, who is now a well-known reviewer of popular art and entertainment for the *New York Times*. Far from asserting the kind of connectedness often as-

sociated with twinship, Holden's poetic persona is independent and isolated. Exclusion of this relationship may be part of the effort evident throughout his work to define himself by differentiation from characteristics that might confirm one of the stereotypes (for example, eastern middle-class intellectual poet) that he particularly wants to avoid. One of the pleasures, however, of Holden's discourse is the discreet, sometimes oblique, revelation of the sophistication embedded in his systematic concealment or overt denial of such qualities. In the linguistic precision and delicacy, for example, of his descriptions of familiar activities such as a pitcher's winding up or a child's learning to ride a bicycle, he may pretend to be naive by hiding behind their subject matter, but the elegance of his language betrays and fulfills his true nature.

Refusal to acknowledge his own intellectuality may be related to the ambivalence he expresses about his father; Holden dislikes desiccated and genteel academicism. On the other

DESIGN FOR A HOUSE / Poems by Jonathan Holden

A Breakthrough Book
University of Missouri Press
$3.50

Cover for Holden's first book (1972), written while he was building his own house in Colorado

hand, he speaks positively of the disciplined empiricism of his father's mind, an inherited characteristic evident in his own meticulous analysis of experience, including the writing and reading of poetry. He has argued, in *Style and Authenticity in Postmodern Poetry*, that poetic language, like mathematics, is valuable because of its "ability to measure, to express subject matter which, without the conventions of this language, would elude us." (One special value of mathematics, for him, is that its expression of its specialized subject matter is truly untranslatable, while poetry is "at least partially translatable.")

After Holden earned his B.A. in English at Oberlin College (1963), he pursued his parallel love of mathematics by teaching that subject in preparatory schools before beginning his graduate work in creative writing and literature. He married Gretchen Weltzheimer on 16 November 1963, and they have two children, Alanna and Zachary. In 1970 Holden received his M.A. from San Francisco State University, and he earned his

Ph.D. at the University of Colorado in 1974. Since then he has taught in and directed creative-writing programs, first at Stephens College and since 1978 at Kansas State University in Manhattan, where he has recently been named University Distinguished Professor and poet in residence. The widely separated locations in which Holden has lived and worked are worthy of mention because they demonstrate the variety he has sought in his effort to distance himself from his eastern background. Both in his poetry and his criticism, his chosen peers are western or, at least, not eastern: Richard Hugo and William Stafford were mentors for Holden in terms of both his criticism and poetry. There is nothing regionally determined about his work, but the values and conventions he espouses separate him from the worlds of John Ashbery and A. R. Ammons, aligning him with poets such as Stephen Dunn, Reg Saner, and Dave Smith.

Design for a House (1972) is a youthful book, written during Holden's years as a young husband, graduate student, and builder of his own house near Nederland, Colorado. He explained in a 1985 interview with Brenda De Martini that he chose "simply to arrange the poems in alphabetic order by title, with few exceptions." The exceptions help frame the book, the first being the title poem, the last a closure poem called "After Building," and about four-fifths of the way through the book a poem titled "Cross Bracing," which includes these lines: "I couldn't understand / why houses stood, until I learned / to cross brace, to notch 2 X 4's / snap in the brace so that the slack / studs tensed together at attention." As happens often in his work, this metaphor on the process of making a solid and dependable thing alludes to poems and to a whole range of human efforts to achieve order and security.

Holden's ability to craft startling and convincing metaphors sets his poems apart from many of his contemporaries. He emphasizes control of rhetorical convention as essential to poetic value, and he certainly has that control, but it emerges more masterfully in his later work. For Holden, the imagination—the maker of artistic value and, not incidentally, of metaphor—is always in a sense an intruder on everyday experience. It is what makes possible the value of experience otherwise only barely perceived or understood. The metaphor is language at the intersection of the physical world and human sentience. Holden's metaphors are not merely language games or verbal tricks. Like many of the objects he describes,

Holden's metaphors evoke intense sensual responses.

In his early poems (in *Design*) the metaphors are often personifications. In "Driving Through Coal Country in Pennsylvania," the ravaged valley is like "someone you know / but can hardly recognize anymore, / scarred up, shaved, sick / from a long operation." Landscapes, buildings, like the house designed in the title poem, and even peaches that "love it [being eaten], they drool, they hurry to help / you undo them"—all these take on human qualities in the realm of Holden's imagination. As with the nubile peaches, the sensory experiences are often based on taste and touch rather than on sight, and the implicit or explicit goal is absorption or consumption. In "How to Understand the Earth," an excavation is like a side of beef to be divided and devoured: "My mattock cut that stuff / like steak. I chewed it / up until I bared the moist, / rare parts, devoured in / shovelfuls the earth's filet." In the second stage of the metaphor, "No meat left," the worker strikes "the earth's thick / skull," shattering his mattock, and is forced in the third stage to try to shatter the "earth's / bones with this crowbar." While the opening section portrays the earth as a steer, the latter sections introduce an uncomfortable ambiguity as the worker tries to "stun him again and again," as in a slaughterhouse, but the image of the steer somehow merges with that of a stubborn human adversary, willfully testing the worker's endurance, with no more promise of nourishment but only, at best, survival.

This kind of transformation, from seeking or pursuing something misperceived as accessible and desirable to a condition of perceiving the thing anew as hostile or immovably resistant, is characteristic of many of Holden's poems: what should be a friendly environment suddenly turns dangerous; tender sensuality shifts to potentially painful manipulation or domination; what is permanent and secure is revealed in all its transience and imperfection. The poet's best hope, then, is to rescue the good from imminent dissolution, or at least to save himself from desolation. This underlying action may sound somber, but in practice it offers opportunities for irony and self-reflexive humor, as in "The Greenness," his contemporary variation on Thomas Wyatt's "They Flee from Me." In Holden's poem a predatory male is finally spurned by his female prey and realizes that his own youth, "slinking past / in a chrome Impala," is lost forever.

Dust jacket for Holden's second collection of poetry (1983), which, according to W. D. Snodgrass, "offers us the ordinary . . . but with the juice flipped on"

Baseball, another of Holden's constant subjects, provides this kind of self-revelation, as in "Hitting Against Mike Cutler," where the naive hitter enters the "shooting gallery" to face a tall, right-handed "gunslinger," who colludes with the catcher to hurl a hissing "hornet" at which the batter swings and misses: "The catcher grins. Good chuck, good chuck, he clucks." The multilayered figurative language of this brief poem may seem to overload it, what with evocations of Hollywood Western gunfighters, the catcher as a dirty-minded "chicken," the pitcher's suggestive preparations ("He spits, / feels up the ball like a small, hard hornet"), and the threatening sexuality of the ball itself. The combination, however, works well to intensify the forced instruction of the lonely batter caught in the line of fire.

Holden's development as a poet becomes apparent in the recurrence of familiar subjects and occasions in his later collections. The second and third, *Leverage* (1983) and *Falling from Stardom* (1984), were put together at roughly the same time from a body of work written during Holden's tenure at Stephens College and his first years in Manhattan, Kansas. He continues to reenact his New Jersey boyhood and adolescent experiences with poems about sexual encounters and killing time. Readers still find powerful poems about work and disturbing poems about driving in the mountains, but new subjects appear as well: fatherhood seen from the father's view of his own children; marriage and infidelity; politics and American culture. The increasing range of subject matter and the complex interaction among the various poems make each book more challenging than the last.

Holden's poems about childhood are really, inevitably, about adulthood as well. Any effort to understand the child's experiences runs up against the mystery and authority of parents, who are always present even when they are not in sight. The drama of childhood is in the realization that parental presence is ineffective when the child evades or ignores their authority or suddenly transcends the need for their support.

The tenderness and sensuality of a father's relation to an infant are evoked in several poems in *Leverage*, especially "Home From Work," "Washing My Son," and "Making Things Grow." Each of these celebrates the simple but exquisite pleasure of physical contact between parent and child and also revives one of Holden's other familiar motifs. In the first, lifting his own son reminds him of his childhood fascination with his father's odors of the outside world and generates a poem reminiscent, in a more positive mode, of Theodore Roethke's "My Papa's Waltz." In "Washing My Son," the act of bathing the infant leads to an extended metaphor:

> Scrubbing
> him is polishing
> this whittled spear
> of wood until
> that new wood shines
> and he's firm,
> sanded down all
> over with my hands,
> healed up
> like a model airplane.

The painstaking act that results in the clean and physically satiated baby, like a perfectly polished model plane, is central to Holden's moral and poetic creed. "Making Things Grow" brings together the vegetable world of the garden, needing weeding and water, with the sensuous interac-

tion of father and daughter, celebrating the satisfaction of "what all unkissed places everywhere / expect."

More problematic, if comical, aspects of father-child relations emerge directly in "Shoe Store," when the father finds the children "foolish" as they evade his values, having been seduced by new shoes: "They are far / away, they've forgotten already / who they are." Indirectly this awareness of the uneasy authority of the father figure is explored in two variations on children's stories, "The Sorrow of Captain Hook" and "Peter Rabbit." Captain Hook, "the only adult in the world," contemplates the hopelessness of distracting the lost boys and Wendy from their euphoric Never-Never Land, though he knows well that the crocodile is not a joke with an alarm clock in its belly but genuine evil (or just temporal reality) that "slides toward you in every shadow, subtly, / without crinkling a single twig, without / breathing."

While one might read "Peter Rabbit" as a poem about childish naughtiness or incipient rebellion fueled by the need for adventure, it is really about "Don't's," and the need to defy them at any age, regardless of the threats that sanction them, since certain psychic profits and forbidden knowledge cannot be gained any other way. Again, the multiple references of Holden's metaphors are apparent as Peter begins to see through or around the simple phenomena he encounters in the garden: "Each wisp of darkness held out the cool / palm of its hand, its hollow of safety, a silk / suit to slip into, try on, cast off. He'd never / noticed such terrain. How its curves console, / its hills reveal."

This poem also provides examples of Holden's control of sound effects—especially onomatopoeia, alliteration, and off rhyme—a skill apparent in many of his poems but displayed here in a manner comparable to some of Wallace Stevens's best effects:

> And a gate was rearing against the sky,
> a rebuke, a giant affront. He squeezed under it,
> his heart twittering. Scritch. Scratch.
> He could hear—a rake, a bee fizz as it rose
> from a daisy, the wind's restless crowds
> in the high reaches of the oak trees behind him.

Peter Rabbit triumphs in his lonely quest through the garden, and at the end he is alive, as well as alone.

In an early poem, "Alone" (in *Design*), Holden uses eating metaphors to evoke the plea-

Dust jacket for Holden's 1985 book of poems, the winner of the annual Juniper Prize from the University of Massachusetts,
an award that includes publication

sures of solitude: "I can lick the clouds off my fingers / and no one can see or care if / I have as much dessert as I want." Other solitary poems evoke the opportunity for enhanced perception that comes from working alone, especially high up in a slightly precarious place. Holden's poetic voice is characteristically isolated. He has written several poems about working alone: "Cutting Beetle-blighted Ponderosa Pine," "On the Roof," and "Cleaning the Flue." The latter (in *Leverage*) echoes "Alone" without the gluttony: while the speaker still revels in solitude ("No one else is up here / and I like it / this way—just me and / my hands, my breath / and my mistakes"), his purpose is to protect his home from fire by cleaning carbon deposits from the flue, and it is an awkward, uncomfortable task that demands some ingenuity. He animates the enemy: "It is crouched in there, / a black spider, / hackles up, ready / to explode at the next / fire." The satisfaction of working on his own, according to his own methods, be-

comes clear when "the flue / gives off a grudging / shine, done right. / Finished." Like many whose daily work is primarily intellectual and seems never to be done, or when done, not to have produced anything tangible, the satisfaction of closure is even greater for him than the sense of exclusive access to the world's pleasures that pervades "Alone."

Isolation is characteristic even of Holden's poems in *Leverage* about working with his father. In "Remembering My Father" and again in "The Swimming Pool," Holden evokes from a distance the backbreaking work his father devoted to constructing and maintaining a swimming pool; while the observer admits using the pool, there is no sense of his having enjoyed or participated in the making. In "With Father, Cleaning Out the Spring," the speaker works closely and in rhythm with his father at the mucky task, a job that is to his liking: "It's loosening us up. / Father grins at me like a troll. / . . . I grin back, I'm in / my element." Implicitly, the father is working well but not really in his own element; nonetheless, at the conclusion "the spring is clear."

There are few simple, single-minded, or one-sided feelings in Holden's poetry; the innocent sensuality of "Washing My Son" and "Making Things Grow" may be the only one. Though individual poems may focus on isolated experiences or specific feelings, almost all his subjects are seen from multiple angles of perception. While William Wordsworth is his most obvious forebear among British Romantics, if only because of Holden's insistence on being a man speaking to men, he understands with William Blake that every impulse and perception has, potentially, many aspects and that even the most precisely bounded vision can be misperceived by those who allow their sight to be distorted by the wrong metaphysic.

The extraordinary title poem, "Leverage," combines isolation, relatedness, work, and the imagination in an effort to resolve the conflict between the creative mind and the ordinary world. Holden finds a clue in a ship metaphor based on a backyard swing that he guides and propels until it takes on the character of the ultimately efficient instrument of work and control, the lever with which to manipulate the whole earth: "I kick at the stars before they set, / strain on both oars, pull the stars / to me again, the mast creaks, / the earth itself rocks as I row, / I have enough leverage now." In the book, this poem follows a detailed account of repair work, "Fixing the Deep-well Jet Pump," a task that concludes with a satisfyingly concrete sense of control: "The jet tensed, the water / firmed, came surging through / the pump, and the evening / was watertight." "Leverage," like other visionary redemptive poems, asserts imaginative mastery comparable to the physical control achieved when the pump works properly. That the final claim of "enough leverage" can be only figuratively, conditionally, and temporarily true is unimportant. In this poem the isolated imagination is both alone and secure in the company of the family, though they are sleeping and unaware of the action.

Falling from Stardom is divided into two nearly equal sections, the first being primarily topical and satirical, while the second section picks up the action of the first poem in the book, "Leaving the Fire," and explores aspects of adultery. Holden has said, in his interview with De Martini, that the persona of the book is "a man who is engaging in some sexually predatory practices

but who is aware there's something the matter with behaving that way.... The whole book is about sexual identity and male narcissism." The early poems in the book, especially "The Secret" and "The Trick," are witty, almost metaphysical in their exploration of the possibilities of their own language and its relationship to the experiences evoked. The savage "Liberace" will survive its own topicality because it is typological and because the satiric target, with or without his historical name, is known to us, as universal as the types of Dale Long, Ed "Whitey" Ford, and the anonymous NFL players of "The Losers." While the book may be about male narcissism, it is given a broad social context by these initial poems. The average male teenager may be just as cynically exploitative and wastefully dismissive as the speaker in "Junk," who realizes in retrospect that the victimized earth is like the humans used and discarded in casual consumption, and that neither, though discarded, can truly be left behind.

The opening poem of the second section, "The Edge," indicates that though the following poems are overtly about adultery, a related subject is various kinds of control and responsibility. In "The Edge," the speaker sets his son free by sustaining him until he can balance his bicycle without parental support—a moment of accomplishment and self-realization known to nearly every child and parent. Interlocking images of boundaries and guidelines, of maps, link several poems in this section as they explore the ways in which being caught in competing relationships, imagined to be secret but plain to smell or taste or see, can lead to ecstasy or remorse. The final poem, "Falling from Stardom," achieves a kind of reconciliation and a formula of renunciation: "Loneliness gives ... freedom to move."

Holden has begun to explore new possibilities in his recent essays and in the poems of *The Names of the Rapids* (1985). Unlike many poets who have written critical essays that serve more to deflect attention from their own poetic practices than to explain them, Holden's essays on postmodern poetic style and conventions inform readers about other contemporary poets but also reveal the philosophical underpinnings of Holden's own works. His emphasis on the role of rhetoric in poetic composition is central to his thinking, as is his view that contemporary poets have abandoned traditional poetic forms in favor of analogues to nonliterary forms of discourse. In *The Names of the Rapids* Holden attempts un-

The Weatherman

> Pray hard to weather, that lone surviving god
>   Richard Hugo
>
> Fostered alike by beauty and by fear
>   —William Wordsworth

1.
He remembered ~~how~~ when a cold front
like a beneficent god
had put to rout a month of fetid air
his mother would proclaim the coming
of "crisp Canadian air," ~~almost~~ smugly, as if she'd
~~had~~ willed such change,
as if the weather were an answered prayer.
The older she became, the more ~~tightly~~ closely
~~enchained~~ her moods were to the clouds.
Her inner weather was exterior.
Long before D. turned professional,
like her he took the weather personally.

He took it personally. He noticed
on the Interstate how driving east
~~is~~ hopeless, ~~how~~ the longer ~~your~~ car
~~keeps~~ trudging towards the dusk the more
decrepit ~~is~~ the light. ~~But~~ heading west
~~is~~ always morning, the edges
of each shadow sharpening the higher
you climb until the light ~~is~~ early
~~even~~ at mid-afternoon. He remembered
one August with his son—driving west
through Kansas, as they approached a cold front—
~~teaching him~~ to see proportionally:
~~how~~ the more severe the weather
the more starkly in relief
the structure of the sky ~~stands out.~~
The lowering ceiling ~~will~~ become an edge,
at fifteen miles away a solid sill,
a window being raised ~~gradually upon~~
some bright nothingness beyond, outdoors.
"Here comes a nasty one," his son would warn,
and together they'd make it disintegrate
into the charred remnants of a circus tent
as they crept under it. ~~But,~~ "Dad, here comes
another one!" Such moments, he loved the boy
so much he thought he couldn't bear it. More
even than himself, though it was dangerous,
~~though~~ the truest love is—oh—dangerous.

                                        (stanza-break)

On this and the following two pages: a working draft for a narrative poem Holden has included in a proposed collection titled
"American Gothic" (by permission of Jonathan Holden)

"The Weatherman," p. 2.

ii.
Though he knew better,
his inner weather seemed exterior.
One day a numbness like a secret front--
a front of nothingness--encroached
from the northwest, all along his left side.
On an illuminated screen, the neurologist
fit a dozen black-and-white transparencies,
the MRI's taken of D's brain.
How like the contact sheets they were
from snapshots of the earth, filmed
from GO-7, the weather satellite he used to map
the coming climate for his audience.
There were the outlines of both hemispheres.
Those white spots, the neurologist explained,
which looked like the radar blips of thunderstorms
were lesions. Except for his numbness
D. did not feel ill. There was no pain.
It was the classic profile of M.S.
Like a frightened child, he kept it to himself.

In Edmund Burke's Enquiry, "The Sublime"
is romantic--a pleasant vertigo
induced by such vertiginous spectacles
as the cliffs of Dover or the Matterhorn
viewed from a secure vantage point--
a park overlook or a museum bench.
As he studied the pictures, taken
from orbit after orbit above his own
inner weather, D. learned
that the modern sublime isn't romantic.
It isn't poetry at all,
but a fear so theoretical
it is as if one were a spectator
to some one else's personal disaster
on t.v. He remembered studying
photographs of the direst kind of cloud--
mammato-cumulus, so named because
of its "nipple-like protuberances"--
and the first time he'd actually beheld
mammato-cumulus how disappointed he had been.
Where was a "nipple?" There was nothing.
Now, thinking back, he knew what he had seen.
In its grey bulges he'd beheld the contours
of a brain. What should he feel?
Here was weather with no vocabulary.

iii.
Terror is a blank. Despair is blank.
How can I speak of this?
If my own son were suddenly to die,

                                      (no break)

Holden, "The Weatherman," p. 3.

```
no vocabulary would suffice.
How D's son, at age ten, died is
is                He'd watched
his father climb.  One morning,
when his Dad was at the station, he decided
to try the ropes.  It was summer again
toward the end of D's time with the boy.
August, Kansas City. (Hell is not,
as the Eskimos believe, a cold place--Hell
is humid.)  A cold front had come through,
the night before, magnificent and final, the sky
gibbering continuously with light,
jumping and answering, signalling
madly to itself:  God who had returned
to save the world again, leaving
the morning sobered up, calm,
chastened as a Monday

though it was a Friday
D's last day with his boy.
He came home from the station early.
He'd ordered a pizza to be delivered.
He was going to take his son to a movie.
Next morning he'd help him pack
drop him at his mother's.
D. felt almost like a boy on his first date.
Pizza for the two of them.  A movie.  It was corny.
But the house was puzzlingly empty.
Where could his son be?  The pizza came.
No one to eat it.

After every possible call to every friend,
after his fury at the boy
for not leaving him a note,
and the fantasies of a kidnapper,
D. literally stumbled on his son
behind the house, lying on his back, face twisted
oddly to one side as if something peculiar
had just caught the child's attention
and he was listening.  The child was clinging
with both hands to a rope.  The rope
had pulled down on top of him a section
of the back-porch gutter.

iy.
If my own son
Wovan man nicht sprechen kann,
wrote Wittgenstein, daruber muB man schweigen.
Whereof one        whereof        if my own
son       No vocabulary would suffice?
unless Time were a word   but not any
kind of word            unless Time were
                              (no break)
```

usual forms, especially more extended narratives and more explicitly analytical and discursive development. Rather than tightening the spring of wit, as he did in *Falling from Stardom*, in this book he recapitulates many of the same kinds of experiences seen in the earlier volumes—learning to ride a bicycle, for example, in "Jim" and "On a Mild October Evening"; working alone at the top of a ladder in "Scraping the House"; and making fine adjustments with the right tools to make sure a machine runs properly in "Tinkering"—but in these new poems he takes time to meditate about significance and about relationships, to make more explicit the larger context, rather than intensively crafting a timeless or suspended object. In these poems he is likely to speculate on the possible meanings of a word or object or experience, rotating the variety for the reader's leisurely inspection.

"The Kite" provides an example of Holden's experimentation with intellectual forms, in this case a verbal equivalent of a figure-ground reversal in a visual image. The opening lines ("This is what the clouds lean / against. The pressure / which makes their lazy edges / fume") focus attention not on the object of the title, but on its context in the physical world. Readers are observers of the ground against which, presumably, the figure of the kite is visible. Holden uses a similar effect in an earlier poem, "Cutting Beetle-blighted Ponderosa Pine" (in *Leverage*), in which he calls attention to the obliteration of "that wonderful colored / map" of the sky because of his cutting down a stand of pines: "With my chain saw I opened / tracts of raw sky," creating a "sky without / a profile," or a ground without a figure to define it, "more sky than anyone / can handle." In "The Kite" he explores the mathematical concepts that would describe the simple physical relationships and shapes created by the ascent of the kite and its subsequent descent, all held together by the image of the kite-string span, as though it were a suspended bridge, not really a metaphor but a mathematical analogue or model to analyze the conflicting and cooperating forces at work. There is no lack of sensory experience, or even of sensuality, in these recent more discursive poems, but they offer, both as technique and as experience, the same kinds of complex and shifting relationships exemplified in "The Kite."

Holden brackets most of the poems in his most recent collection, *Against Paradise* (1990), between two poems on baseball, a familiar theme that deepens as he rethinks it. Memories of his

Caricature of Holden by Fran Worde, a former student of his at Stephens College in Columbia, Missouri

first experience of the curveball are linked to awakening sexuality and to adult loneliness, as the mythical but real curveball, in all its magic, comes "to mean what cannot be and means what is." In the final poem of the book, "Full Circle," which is dedicated to his father, Holden links baseball to the progression of generations as the speaker watches his son pitching his first game. The speaker begins by remembering that there is no politics of pitching, no possible fakery, but the poem evolves to a memory of his relationship as he realizes his links to his son: "If the advice is right / and handed out with style / we never forget the things our fathers say."

The poems of the first and third sections of the book revisit familiar themes in Holden's work—personalized and personified landscapes, ambivalence about the comforts and horrors of home, the security of being in a place one knows perfectly because one has made it oneself, the pleasures and disillusionment of illicit love—and in each case the paradoxical conjunction of isolation and connectedness in Holden's voice deepens the sense of his vision.

At the center of *Against Paradise* is a group of poems of savage, almost Swiftian, irony and anger. Holden has included some of his satiric poems in earlier collections, but this is the most concentrated group to demonstrate his wit and rage against the delusions and hypocrisy inherent in American popular culture and bourgeois private life. These poems, as the book's title tells us, are antipastoral, attacking the comfortable lies that often usurp the very language of poetry in smug assumptions of respectability. The long dramatic monologue "Son of Babbitt" is like a nightmare luncheon. Babbitt's grandson tells of changing his name to protect himself from the ridicule directed at his family, but then in a sudden burst of "honesty," he restores his "real name" and inverts all values, all the while quoting famous passages he learned as an undergraduate English major. The perversion of all language, and of poetry, itself is further explored in "Goodness," where a confrontation with a good Christian lady prompts the speaker to say: "It's no wonder that in every kid's T.V. show / where good and bad have been divided in two / the bad guys get the slick vocabulary." Thinking of the sheriff in the tale of Robin Hood, he continues: "when a grown man licks / the taste of his own language like that / he can't be trusted. He's in politics."

While it is inevitable to link Holden with his British poetic forebears (Blake, Wordsworth, and now Swift), those points of reference should not distract readers from the essentially American quality of Holden's poetics and his voice. While he rejects any connection with the mandarin and academic traditions of American poetry, his elegiac celebrations of boyhood; his exploration of the joys of physical work; his tormented conscience in the face of his sexual encounters; his problematic reconciliation of aestheticism, intellectuality, and rough physicality; and his rage at the duplicity of a culture that is never as good as it pretends to be—all this places him within the mainstream of American poetry, a tradition that has a true passion for the reality of everyday life.

In an essay in *The Rhetoric of the Contemporary Lyric* (1980) Holden uses the phrase "some hard-earned reconciliation" to describe what another poet (Alan Dugan) does *not* offer his readers. The phrase seems to identify precisely what the best of Holden's poems do offer: through successful metaphors that reconcile disparate perceptions, sometimes as the result of extraordinary intellectual or emotional labor, Holden's poems reunite the intellect, the senses, and the world outside that is always recognizable but rarely comprehensible without the intervention of the imagination that produces such metaphors. Holden's creative process is more than a little mathematical, more sympathetic to the scientific method than many poets can manage; he examines each specimen of experience with minute and respectful attention, seeing it on its own terms and within its own actual relationships. When two or more things from disparate contexts are united or merged in his metaphors, they retain their own unique characters within their new identity. In the concluding poem of *The Names of the Rapids*, "Ramanujan," Holden seems to identify himself with the childlike mathematical genius who "could reel off pi's digits to any / decimal place his classmates dared him to." Such a character in one of Holden's typical poems about boyhood would be mercilessly tormented by his schoolmates, but Ramanujan finds his difficult reconciliation among his "cousins," the sparrowlike numbers that keep him company and do his bidding, as one would have daily experience do if only one could control it as he does his intimate numbers. Mathematics and poetry are thus reconciled as friends of experience.

Interviews:
Brenda De Martini, "Interview With Jonathan Holden," *Missouri Review*, 8 (1985): 35-41;
Stan Sanvel Ruben and Earl Ingersoll, "Sensibility on the Edge: A Conversation With Jonathan Holden," *Tar River Poetry*, 26 (Fall 1986): 1-14.

Judson Jerome

(8 February 1927 -   )

Robert Darling
Keuka College

BOOKS: *Light in the West* (Francestown, N.H.: Golden Quill, 1962);

The Poet and the Poem (Cincinnati: Writer's Digest, 1963; revised and enlarged, 1974; revised again, 1979);

The Ocean's Warning to the Skin Diver and Other Love Poems (Point Richmond, Cal.: Crown Point, 1964);

Candle in the Straw (N.p., 1964);

The Fell of Dark (Boston: Houghton Mifflin, 1966);

Serenade (Point Richmond, Cal.: Crown Point, 1968);

Poetry: Premeditated Art (Boston: Houghton Mifflin, 1968);

New Directions in Higher Education (Toledo: Center for the Study of Higher Education, 1969);

Plays for an Imaginary Theatre (Urbana, Ill.: University of Illinois Press, 1970);

Culture Out of Anarchy: The Reconstruction of American Higher Learning (New York: Herder & Herder, 1970);

I Never Saw . . . (Chicago: Whitman, 1974);

Families of Eden: Communes and the New Anarchism (New York: Seabury, 1974; London: Thames & Hudson, 1975);

Myrtle Whimple's Sampler (Hancock, Md.: Trunk, 1976);

The Village and Other Poems (Hancock, Md.: Trunk, 1976);

Publishing Poetry (Hancock, Md.: Trunk, 1977);

Public Domain (Hancock, Md.: Trunk, 1977);

Thirty Years of Poetry: 1949-1979 (New Braunfels, Tex.: Cedar Rock, 1979);

The Poet's Handbook (Cincinnati: Writer's Digest, 1980);

Partita in Nothing Flat (Daleville, Ind.: Barnwood, 1983);

On Being a Poet (Cincinnati: Writer's Digest, 1984);

The Village: New and Selected Poems, edited by James Taylor (Baltimore: Dolphin-Moon, 1987);

Flight from Innocence: A Memoir, 1927-1947 (Fayetteville: University of Arkansas Press, 1990);

Jonah & Job (Santa Barbara, Cal.: Daniel, 1991);

Nude (Long Beach, Cal.: Applezaba, 1991);

The Youthful Look: A Memoir 1947-1952 (Fayetteville: University of Arkansas Press, 1991);

Myrtle Whimple: Selected Poems (Mapplesville, Ala.: Sticks, 1991).

PLAY PRODUCTIONS: *Winter in Eden*, Yellow Springs, Ohio, Antioch College, 1955;

The Wandering Jew, Yellow Springs, Ohio, Antioch College, 1963;

Candle in the Straw, St. Paul, Minnesota, Hamline University, 1963;

The Glass Mountain, St. Thomas, Virgin Islands, College of the Virgin Islands, 1964.

OTHER: *New Campus Writing*, volumes 1 and 2, edited by Jerome and Nolan Miller (New York: Bantam, 1956-1958); volumes 3 and 4 (New York: Grove, 1959-1962);

Poet's Market: Where and How to Publish Your Poetry, edited, with an introduction and notes, by Jerome (Cincinnati: Writer's Digest, 1985, continuing annually).

Judson Jerome's career is a series of paradoxes. While he is clearly liberal, if not radical, in his political and social theories, his poetics have been traditional from the time his work began regularly appearing in print in the 1950s. He is known to many primarily as an innovative educator, yet he has not held a full-time teaching position for over two decades. His name is probably one of the most widely known of any serious poet, but largely for reasons other than his poetry. He has also been consistently ignored by the critical and poetic establishment for the past two decades, despite the quality of his work.

Jerome was born on 8 February 1927 in Tulsa, Oklahoma, to Ralph and Gwen Stewart Jerome. His father was an oil-royalty broker whose heavy drinking led to a divorce when Jerome was

Judson Jerome

nine. Of all his family—and many of his poems deal with domestic situations and family members—it is Jerome's father who has figured most consistently in the poetry from its beginnings to the present. The violent ambiguities in much of Jerome's best early poetry can also be found in his attitude toward his father. He has termed him "the sweetest man alive" when sober, but when drunk "a monster of sarcastic cruelty and obscene crudity." Yet those who loved and would reform the father are not without guilt themselves. Jerome writes in "Alcoholic" (in *The Village*, 1987):

> Years after he was gone I think I saw
> how we insulted him, drove him along:
> His spirit we called nerves, said nerves were raw,
> denied his holy sanction to be wrong.
> The sonofabitch (God bless him) drank and died
> because we understood away his pride.

Jerome attended the University of Oklahoma but was drafted and served in the United States Air Force in 1945. Discharged after a tour of duty on Okinawa, he had intentions of going to New York City to "endure the damnation real writers endure," as he put it, but had only money enough to reach Chicago. He enrolled in an M.A. program in English at the University of Chicago (it was possible at that time to do a three-year master's program without the B.A. at some institutions), and on 20 June 1948 he married Martha-Jane Pierce, the Marty of his poems.

It was in the company of his wife's parents and friends that the young man from Oklahoma first was truly introduced to a broad range of ideas in general and to political and social theory in particular. But it was J. V. Cunningham at the University of Chicago who most directly influenced the formal direction Jerome's poetry was

Jerome in Tulsa, 1928

to take. In an introduction-to-poetry class in which Jerome was enrolled, Cunningham contended simply that "poetry is metrical writing," and he rejected the usual Romantic and mystical pseudodefinitions then popular. Jerome was resistant—his poetry up to this point had been mainly in free verse—but was convinced when Cunningham discussed a poem Jerome had submitted, "My Doubt Ranged Free." From then on, nearly all Jerome's poetry is metered, and much of it is rhymed.

In 1950 having earned his M.A. in Chicago, Jerome was awarded a student assistantship as a Ph.D. candidate at Ohio State University, where he remained until completion of his course work in 1953, when he accepted an appointment as Assistant Professor at Antioch College in Yellow Springs, Ohio. Antioch was not only a smaller institution than those with which Jerome had been associated to this point but was known for its innova-

tive approaches to education. It was at Antioch that Jerome had as a colleague the novelist Nolan Miller, with whom he edited *New Campus Writing,* which gave many young writers in the 1950s their initial exposure in print. Jerome became a father for the first time in 1954 and completed his dissertation, "Rochester and the Generation of Wit," the following year.

It was during this busy period that Jerome began to write more and more poetry. His poem "Deer Hunt," one of his "Kiamichi Sonnets," was published (May 1955; collected in *Light in the West,* 1962) by *Poetry* and widely anthologized. The poem deals with a boy's coming to terms with the expectations of manhood, hunting being a rite of passage in most rural American communities. Jerome catches well the tensions an adolescent male must keep private: "I flinched at every lonely rifle crack, / my knuckles whitening where I gripped the edge / of age and clung, like retching, sinking back, / and then gripped once again the monstrous gun, / since I, to be a man, had taken one."

By 1960 Jerome had published in over thirty of the most respected magazines printing poetry, and he had begun his friendship with John Ciardi, then poetry editor of the *Saturday Review*. Their relationship was as productive as it was irregular. In 1959 Jerome began writing his monthly column on poetry for *Writer's Digest*, which he still does, and was awarded a Huntington Hartford Fellowship; the following year, through Ciardi's influence, he won the Amy Lowell Poetry Travelling Scholarship, on which he lived in England and Spain.

In 1962 Jerome's first book of poems, *Light in the West*, was a selection of the Poetry Book of the Month Club of the Golden Quill Press. It received only one review of note, from John Engels in the September 1963 issue of *Poetry*. Engels found that the strict formalism of the poems was an obstacle to their own realization, that Jerome "often fails through a formal baffling of his vision," and that the poems "do not engage the mind as they should." But Engels adds that Jerome is "a good poet," and the feeling one is left with from Engels's two-paragraph review is that here is a young poet of potential, possibly an important new figure on the poetry scene.

Light in the West is a promising first book, one that escapes many of the common pitfalls of its kind, but by no means all of them. The second section, "Instructions for Acting," is based on a central metaphor both overused in general and overextended in this particular sequence, although there are passages, particularly in "Nightcap," which nearly redeem the poems. The form of many of the poems at times does seem to dictate a certain awkwardness of phrasing, as in "Cages," when the demands of rhyme and meter produce an artificiality of syntax: "of crib we set her free— / gave her a bed with bars / halfway." Yet that same poem is strong overall, as shown in particular by the force of the ending, in which the syllabic stresses and the metrical pattern war in a way consistent with the poem's theme: "no love is sweeter than this hate, / nor hate so hard as age: / Dear child with touching hands, / night, day, age, youth, our veins, / our very ribs are cage." There is a barely suppressed violence in many of the poems that at times is distracting, but when it is controlled, an impressive tension is struck between anger and love. Particularly fine are "Flight by Instruments," "Negative," and "No Such."

"Love, the First Decade" is a celebration of the poet's first ten years of marriage and exhibits a distanced wit with a compassionate warmth rarely found in a first book of poetry. Largely anecdotal, the poem ends with a joyful sadness that Jerome has only been able to recapture with any consistency in his recent poetry. Here the political and the personal are blended more fortunately than one usually finds in poetry:

> Romance, like a party, passed;
> the hangover passed. This year sobriety
> is heavy-bottomed as a bourgeois tree.
> Back then a Wallacite told us in the night,
> his finger wagging, and he too, being tight,
> how liberals tend to fall away in the fight,
> how stodginess conquers love. Love, love me fast
> and witlessly: The serious years fall fast.

In 1964 Crown Point Press published an oversized version of *The Ocean's Warning to the Skin Diver and Other Love Poems* in an edition limited to twenty-five copies. The poems are accompanied by etchings by Kathan Brown and do not present a major advancement over *Light in the West*, as two-thirds of *The Ocean's Warning* is composed of poems reprinted virtually unchanged from the earlier volume. Another limited edition was produced by Crown Point in 1968; entitled *Serenade*, the book consists solely of that title poem of thirty-five lines, again with a series of prints by Brown. Jerome had published *The Poet and the Poem* in 1963—a book dealing with the writing of poetry—which consists largely of material gleaned from his monthly columns for *Writer's Digest*, and in 1968 he published *Poetry: Premeditated Art*, a textbook on poetry appreciation. *The Poet and the Poem* is further evidence of Jerome's practical criticism, very much a "how to" approach, which generally avoids abstract theorizing; while replete with personal anecdotes and in some ways highly idiosyncratic presentation, the book is nevertheless filled with sound and sensible, though unfashionable, advice. In 1966 Jerome published his novel *The Fell of Dark*, a tragic love story, which received a much friendlier reception than did his poetry.

With so many books published in such a relatively brief time, with numerous periodical credits, and with awards starting to arrive, Jerome may have expected continued success, a steady development, and comfortable entrenchment as a professional poet-teacher. This was not to be.

Part of the reason for literary recognition being withheld was the time itself. The poetic fash-

Negative

I have lost the print, but in this negative
you can see her shape, if not much more. That black
is beach. Her hair, here white, was black. That white
is water, laced with black. Its roar and that
of the wind (not pictured here, except as her hair
flies out from her grey shoulders — they were brown)
drowned out our conversation. We lost track
that sun-bleached day (the sun here makes her frown)
of hours, words, kisses, sandwiches and beer —
all used in colorful affirmative.

We left our imprint on the sand. The sea
or wind in another season cleared this away,
and now all black and white in each our minds
remains some blurry dent of how we lay,
some negative of warmth of other lips,
some scrape of sandy thighs, some taste of salt.
I forget now how it was, but how it ends
is negative, the afterglow of a glimpse,
turned inside out, unflushed, with strength for fault,
remembered in the nerves transparently.

Judson Jerome

Manuscript for a poem included in Jerome's The Village: New and Selected Poems *(by permission of Judson Jerome)*

ion that developed through the 1960s was not favorable to work in traditional forms, particularly poems making use of rhyme. Most established poets abandoned form during this time, and few younger poets gained recognition unless they worked in free verse. Jerome not only worked in traditional forms but argued against the basic contentions of free verse in his columns in *Writer's Digest*. Yet neither would Jerome have been easily included with the "academic" poets who continued to write in traditional forms; his subject matter and diction are often too raw for easy inclusion with poets who so highly value smooth polish and irony.

Another factor in the withholding of critical recognition, perhaps even more important than the general spirit of the times, was Jerome himself. He had for years been dissatisfied with the traditional methods of college education and began to pursue other interests besides poetry, interests which would make him far better known as a social critic than as a poet. And the poet who is perceived as primarily something else often receives a chilly reception from the closed, professional poetry world.

In 1963, while on leave from Antioch, Jerome moved with his family to the Virgin Islands to begin, with two associates, the College of the Virgin Islands. It was there, on 21 November 1963, that Jerome's wife, Marty, gave birth to premature twins, one of whom died within a week. The surviving girl, Jenny, was seriously brain damaged, aphasic, epileptic, and suffered slightly from cerebral palsy. Jenny, who would only live to be nineteen, became central in many of Jerome's poems, particularly in "The Village" (in *The Village and Other Poems*, 1976), as well as playing a major role in several of the crucial decisions Jerome would make in the coming decade and a half. The poet has recounted many times that the two family members who recur in many of his dreams, and thereby find their way into his poems, are his father and Jenny.

When Jerome returned to Antioch, he discovered that a revolution, in style if not in substance, had taken place. He had been separated from the campus routine at this point for four years and found Antioch a changed place, full of the sound and fury that was to dominate college life for several years in the 1960s. Jerome embraced the spirit of the times, termed himself professor at large, and gave up classroom teaching, establishing the Inner College, a school-within-a-school at Antioch. Requirements were largely

self-defined by the students, and no grades were given.

Poems were being written by Jerome all during this time, but more and more frequently their themes were primarily social ones. Such concerns, of course, can be proper material for poetry, but they most often result in work that is more polemical than poetic. It is hard to think of English-language poets in the twentieth century, other than W. B. Yeats, W. H. Auden, and Seamus Heaney, who have consistently produced good poetry that was strongly influenced by political events. While Jerome has generally avoided the pitfall of thinly disguised versified propaganda, his personal poetry based on family and childhood is usually his strongest material.

After Jerome's article "The System Really Isn't Working" appeared in *Life* (1 November 1968), he became a speaker much in demand on the lecture circuit and prey to the various temptations with which a celebrity, even an academic one, is so often confronted. He accepted from Ciardi an invitation to the Bread Loaf conferences of 1967-1968, but they resulted in such libertine excesses that Jerome was not invited back, and his friendship with Ciardi cooled for several years. Always Jerome was writing poetry, which was published in various magazines, and giving readings, but he came to be seen more and more as a public figure, a critic of education. This image was strengthened even further when he published *Culture Out of Anarchy: The Reconstruction of American Higher Learning* (1970), based on his visits to various campuses around the country. The book received mixed reviews but solidified the idea that he was an educator who happened to write poetry.

In fact, he wrote little poetry between 1969 and 1973. The year 1970 saw the publication of *Plays for an Imaginary Theatre*, and in 1974 *I Never Saw . . .*, a collection of children's poetry, was published. Neither attracted much attention or enhanced his reputation as a poet.

Shortly before *Culture Out of Anarchy* was published, Jerome became disappointed with the Inner College and moved to an experimental satellite institution connected with Antioch in Columbia, Maryland. Columbia was being developed by the Rouse Corporation as a utopian settlement. It was here that Jerome sensed the real danger to his creative life that his activism was mounting. He has written that he was sick at heart, that his "profession seemed to be taking [him] further and further from the literature that attracted

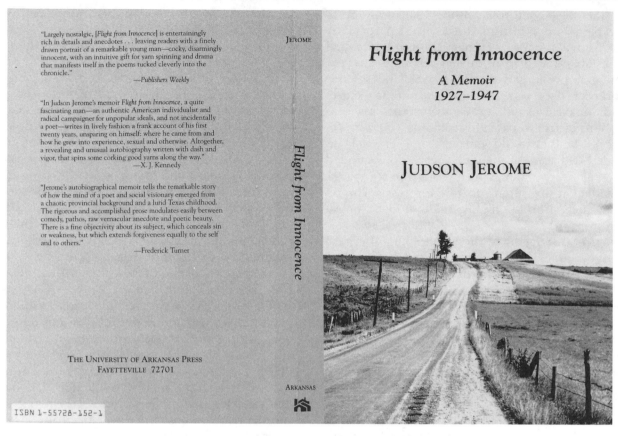

"Largely nostalgic, [*Flight from Innocence*] is entertainingly
rich in details and anecdotes . . . leaving readers with a finely
drawn portrait of a remarkable young man—cocky, disarmingly
innocent, with an intuitive gift for yarn spinning and drama
that manifests itself in the poems tucked cleverly into the
chronicle."
                                                —*Publishers Weekly*

"In Judson Jerome's memoir *Flight from Innocence*, a quite
fascinating man—an authentic American individualist and
radical campaigner for unpopular ideals, and not incidentally
a poet—writes in lively fashion a frank account of his first
twenty years, unsparing on himself: where he came from and
how he grew into experience, sexual and otherwise. Altogether,
a revealing and unusual autobiography written with dash and
vigor, that spins some corking good yarns along the way."
                                                —X. J. Kennedy

"Jerome's autobiographical memoir tells the remarkable story
of how the mind of a poet and social visionary emerged from
a chaotic provincial background and a lurid Texas childhood.
The rigorous and accomplished prose modulates easily between
comedy, pathos, raw vernacular anecdote and poetic beauty.
There is a fine objectivity about its subject, which conceals sin
or weakness, but which extends forgiveness equally to the self
and to others."
                                                —Frederick Turner

THE UNIVERSITY OF ARKANSAS PRESS
FAYETTEVILLE 72701

ISBN 1-55728-152-1

JEROME

Flight from Innocence

Flight from Innocence
A Memoir
1927–1947

JUDSON JEROME

ARKANSAS

Dust jacket for the first volume of Jerome's autobiography (1990)

[him] to it in the first place." Dissatisfied with Columbia, as well as the schooling his children were receiving, Jerome was faced with a further decision: it was becoming obvious that Jenny needed specialized care and would have to be separated from the rest of the family for extended periods of time. Jerome and his wife decided to enroll her at Beaver Run, near Philadelphia, a school following the anthroposophical principles of Rudolf Steiner. Besides creating a haven for Jenny, Beaver Run had a lasting impact on the entire family: it was structured and run as a commune.

Jerome decided he wanted to investigate communes further, and with customary élan applied for and received a grant from the Twentieth Century Fund to do a book on communes. The resultant book, *Families of Eden: Communes and the New Anarchism* (1974), was published in both the United States and Great Britain and received generally favorable reviews. The irony was that the book, in expanding Jerome's focus to the very structure of society as well as society's educational systems, solidified Jerome in the mind of the public as a social critic and pushed what has al-

ways been most central to him, his poetry, further to the background, at least in the popular perception. Some twenty years later, many small colleges as well as nonacademic libraries possess the books on communes and alternative education as part of their collections but do not contain any of Jerome's volumes of verse.

Jerome found that most communes did not have many children, so there was little allowance made for education (it is important to stress that Jerome's interest in communal living comes primarily from his concerns with education). He also wanted to live within a half-day's drive of Jenny. Therefore he decided to found his own commune and did so on a hundred-acre farm near Hancock, Maryland. He named the commune Downhill Farm, saying that life would probably be easier from that point, and also contrasting it to Archibald MacLeish's home, Uphill Farm. Jerome resigned his tenured appointment at Antioch, thereby officially severing what had become a more and more distant professional association. He also wrote what he still considers one of his best poems, "The Village," based on his experience at Beaver Run.

Marty and Judson Jerome surrounded by their family, Christmas 1990

No major magazine would touch it. Jerome at this point was not known primarily as a poet, was working in an unfashionable style, and had furthermore severed all formal academic connections. After his experience with the reception of "The Village," Jerome vowed to play no more "the fame game," as he termed it, and burned the slogan "Put your ego away; you won't need it today" into a wooden plaque at Downhill. Then he stopped sending poetry or other writing to any publisher or magazine that did not request it. Few did. He spent most of his time on the commune, doing chores, making planters and wind chimes, and always writing. His one regular contact with the outside world was his monthly column in *Writer's Digest*, a publication condescended to if acknowledged at all by the literary establishment.

He did some self-publishing under the banner of Trunk Press, the name based on humorous advice he once gave in his column: "Get ahead the way Emily Dickinson did. Try your

trunk." The first chapbook to appear under this imprint, in 1976, was the parody *Myrtle Whimple's Sampler*, a collection of intentionally bad poems in which Jerome aped the style of weekend poets whose work graces the "poet's corner" of weekly newspapers. A more substantial chapbook, *The Village and Other Poems*, appeared the same year. Several of the poems had appeared earlier in *Light in the West*, but the majority had not yet been published in book form. The title poem was, of course, the same poem that had been slighted by the major journals.

In defense of the literary community, it is questionable whether "The Village" is one of Jerome's better poems, despite his favoring of it to the point where it became the title poem of not one but two different collections of his verse. While the poem is a clear statement on a position of fundamental importance to Jerome, it is also one of the few poems concerning his family where his social ideas are so heavily textured over his private concerns that the poem becomes so didactic as to lose much of its emotional force. Certainly one can appreciate "people sharing whatever, / coming / together to work, play, learn, worship, in joy." A few lines later the poet continues: "The point / of life being / nurture, fulfillment, happiness." However, his language is neither nurtured nor happily fulfilled, is indeed nearly lifeless, reading more like a personal essay than a poem. "The Village" is important as an explicit statement of the social philosophy that has come to play such a dominant role in Jerome's life, but it is not a good example of the power of language found in his best poetry. As the language grows more abstract, the force of the verse is weakened; one need only note how well the social and the personal are woven together in "Love: the First Decade" to see the emotional impact of which Jerome is capable when at his best. Probably the strongest section in "The Village" is the fourth and final one, in which Jenny has been left at Beaver Run and the family is forced to deal with both her absence and continuing influence.

The chapbook *Public Domain* was published by Trunk in 1977, consisting mainly of new material, although nearly a third of the poems had appeared in *Light in the West* or in chapbook form. Probably the best of the new poems is "Perhaps an Owl," which evokes the night fear present in the countryside. Despite the natural setting, it is fear of humans that troubles the speaker and his bedmate, but it is the solace of their humanness that sustains them: "Better to sleep, but if you must lie waking, / I'm glad I was there, that we were holding hands." The collection suffered the critical neglect generally accorded to chapbooks. That same year, Cedar Rock Press in New Braunfels, Texas, published Jerome's *Publishing Poetry*—a thirty-two-page guide offering advice for would-be poets who were intent on approaching poetry publishers—the material that provided the germ for Jerome's first *Poet's Market* (1985). It also paved the way for a more substantial involvement with Cedar Rock.

In 1979 David Yates, then editor of Cedar Rock, requested a volume of Jerome's collected poems. This became *Thirty Years of Poetry: 1949-1979*. Jerome refers to the book as "one of the best kept secrets in the literary world." The volume was not reviewed by a single critic. While the physical appearance of the book was marred by Jerome's insistence that he avoid typesetting costs by preparing the copy on his own typewriter, it was one of the more impressive vol-

umes of poetry to be published that year. There is great unevenness, of course, as one almost always finds in a volume of collected poems, and there is a similar unevenness in some of the best poems, but the book taken as a whole certainly deserves consideration. The poems are divided into sections by their dates of composition; thus there is little indication of the structure of the individual volumes of Jerome's poetry that preceded the collection. Earlier violence is greatly softened or eliminated in the later work, and one senses more and more a poet writing to please himself, appreciating an audience but not seeking one, throwing off influences, and usually much more at ease with the form the individual poem takes. There is even conscious archaism in his long, sonnet sequence "Homage to Shakespeare."

In 1983, through Barnwood Press, Jerome published a slim but handsome volume entitled *Partita in Nothing Flat*, which consists of twelve sonnets written to his wife and another woman with whom they were living. The sonnets, some with their form quite disguised, were written in celebration of the poet's somewhat unusual domestic and romantic ménage at Downhill Farm.

The 1983 chapbook also turned out to be something of a farewell to the communal life; soon afterward Downhill Farm was abandoned. The community was founded out of concern for the education of the children, and with all but one of the children having grown up and left, Jerome moved back to Yellow Springs, Ohio, to the "civilization of a photocopy machine, library, gym and swimming pool, art theater and other attractions." While Jerome has not reassumed a full-time position at Antioch, he does regularly take part in summer workshops at the college, as well as writer's workshops elsewhere, and in 1990 he was a visiting professor at the University of Puerto Rico. *On Being a Poet*, a companion to *The Poet and the Poem*, was published in 1984, again making use of some *Writer's Digest* columns, but mostly composed of new writings. Much of the material is personal and disputes the current wisdom of the poetry industry, but the advice is always practical, the theoretical always based on specific instances. Jerome currently works as an associate editor of the *Kettering Review* as well as writing his column for *Writer's Digest* and keeping up a voluminous correspondence.

In his introduction to the final section of *Thirty Years of Poetry*, Jerome wrote: "I have come to think of my poetry as a kind of message in a bottle, which I hope someday drifts ashore." Up

Cover for the collection of biblical poems that, according to Frederick Turner, brings "these marvelous old stories . . . crashing into the twentieth century"

through the mid 1980s there was little evidence of much drifting ashore, though Jerome has experienced an increase in his poetic output during the 1980s. In 1987, however, in celebration of Jerome's sixtieth birthday, Dolphin-Moon Press published *The Village: New and Selected Poems*, a selection of the best work from *Thirty Years of Poetry* combined with poems from the ensuing eight years (1979-1987). It is arranged thematically rather than chronologically, so there is no real sense of development from early to late—indeed, many of the early poems have not been revised as much in successive publications as one might want—but the reader does gain the strongest sense to date of Jerome's strengths and weaknesses as a poet. The family and childhood poems read as the strongest, as usual, but what comes through for the first time is Jerome's considerable ability as an elegist. The number of political poems has been substantially pruned, and the remaining ones read as the weaker works in the selection. "The Village" is once again featured, though the poem does not have the poetic force of much of the rest of the material. Certainly this is the volume on which the reputation of Jerome as a poet to this point in his career will have to be judged.

The Village: New and Selected Poems has yet to be reviewed in major journals, but there is some indication that it will not fall into the same literary vacuum to which *Thirty Years* was consigned. The literary journal *Negative Capability* did mark the appearance of *The Village* and the observance of Jerome's sixtieth birthday by making him the featured writer, his work occupying the first sixty-four pages of volume 7 (1987).

Jerome's standing as a critic and observer of the poetic scene was further enhanced by the publication of *Poet's Market*, a yearly volume serving as an index to publishers of poetry in the English-speaking world. While this makes Jerome's name familiar to younger poets first attempting to publish, as well as the occasional poet, the volumes have also put him back in touch with the publishing community he had shunned in his early days at Downhill Farm. There also seems to be a renewal of interest in Jerome as a critic, due to the slow and halting return to form in poetry. In an edition of *Crosscurrents* devoted to the new formalism and narrative in poetry, Dick Allen writes, "Jerome's deft combination of insight and common sense about form and content is too little noted by serious literary critics, mainly because it appears in a commercial writers' magazine."

Finally, not only should the renewed interest in form gain some attention for Jerome but the increased concern with narrative verse during the 1980s has coincided with Jerome's growing preoccupation with storytelling in poetry. Jerome has written a considerable amount of narrative poetry since the 1960s—"Jonah" (in *The Village: New and Selected Poems*) is probably the most important example of an earlier narrative—and he has recently concentrated more and more on narrative. For the first time in his career, his personal poetic preference may coincide with that of the time.

Jerome has stated that "turning sixty brought me to the happiest and busiest period of my life." Jerome now has several book manuscripts in circulation, one of which consists of twenty short stories in verse. In 1990 he published *Flight from Innocence*, his account of the first two decades of his life. He writes with brutal honesty but also shows warmth and generosity. The volume includes several poems. Hazarding a guess at a writer's eventual standing is always tenuous at best, particularly with a poet who has written so much that has been so little considered critically thus far, but it seems that Judson Jerome may soon get the consideration he deserves as a poet.

Bibliography:

Dick Allen, "A Partially Annotated Partial Bibliography of Judson Jerome," *Crosscurrents*, 8 (January 1989): 174-176.

Papers:

A collection of Jerome's manuscripts is in the Boston University Library.

Ronald Koertge
(22 April 1940 -)

Jane Hoogestraat
Southwest Missouri State University

BOOKS: *The Father-Poems* (Fremont, Mich.: Sumac, 1973);

Meat: Cherry's Market-Diary (Long Beach, Cal.: MAG, 1973);

The Hired Nose (Long Beach, Cal.: MAG, 1974);

My Summer Vacation (Los Angeles: Venice Poetry, 1975);

Sex Object (N.p.: Country Press, 1975; revised edition, Los Angeles: Little Caesar, 1979);

Tarzan and Shane Meet the Toad, by Koertge, Charles Stetler, and Gerald Locklin (Long Beach, Cal.: Haas, 1975);

Cheap Thrills (Stockton, Cal.: Wormwood Review, 1976);

Men Under Fire (Fallon, Nev.: Duck Down, 1976);

12 Photographs of Yellowstone (Los Angeles: Red Hill, 1976);

How to Live on Five Dollars a Week, Etc. (Los Angeles: Venice Poetry, 1977);

The Jockey Poems (Los Angeles: Maelstrom, 1980);

The Boogeyman (New York: Norton, 1980);

Diary Cows (Los Angeles: Little Caesar, 1981);

Fresh Meat (Winter Haven, Fla.: Kenmore, 1981);

Life on the Edge of the Continent: Selected Poems of Ronald Koertge (Fayetteville: University of Arkansas Press, 1982);

Where the Kissing Never Stops (Boston: Atlantic Monthly, 1986; London: Macmillan Children's, 1988);

The Arizona Kid (Boston: Joy Street, 1988);

The Boy in the Moon (Boston: Joy Street, 1990);

Mariposa Blues (Boston: Little, Brown, 1991);

High School Dirty Poems (Los Angeles: Red Wind, 1991).

Between 1973 and 1980 Ronald Koertge published several small books and chapbooks of poems with small independent presses; since then, he has published two longer collections, *Diary Cows* (1981) and the most comprehensive single volume of his poetry available, *Life on the Edge of the Continent: Selected Poems* (1982). Koertge's work falls somewhat outside the mainstream of contemporary American poetry be-cause of his characteristic use of a quirky and unrelenting humor, his selection of down-and-out characters as subjects, and his refusal to take himself or his characters entirely seriously. Koertge provides a slightly askew vision of a more than slightly askew world, ruthlessly ridiculing the cliché, the pretentious, and the ponderous. While the tone of his work is almost always mockingly ironic, it is also, in Koertge's plain, offhand manner, almost always compassionate.

Born on 22 April 1940 in Olney, Illinois, Koertge was the only child of William H. Koertge and Bulis Fiscus Koertge and was reared in Collinsville, Illinois, a town about fifteen miles from St. Louis. He earned a B.A. in English from the University of Illinois in 1962 and an M.A., also in English, from the University of Arizona in 1965. Since 1965 he has taught at Pasadena City College, currently serving as a full professor in the English department there. He is married to the former Cheryl Vasconcellos, also a teacher.

Koertge's first collection, *The Father-Poems* (1973), opens with a sequence of eighteen brief, plain-style poems about a father, imaginary or real, who had apparently been some sort of cowboy in his younger days, before moving on to a rather mediocre life, but who is described sympathetically with a pathos surprisingly not out of place in a sequence of largely sardonic poems. Early in the sequence, readers learn that the father "used to climb trees that were / over a hundred feet high. But not / for fun. He was chasing a squirrel / down so his dog could get it." A few poems later, one reads that "he was looking for work at 47 and the owner of a / new concrete-coring plant down in the valley / finally came out and told him that he was / too old." Here, as elsewhere in Koertge's work, the outrageous and the despairing are presented with the same deadpan tone and in the plainest language, as if some lives or events in the world have claims on people that further embellishment could only detract from. In the remainder of the poems in the volume,

Ronald Koertge (photograph copyright 1990 by John W. Emmons)

Koertge gives attention to a series of marginalized and marginal characters, including the title character in "The Albino Chiropractor," who came on hard luck: "Young men with nerve charts and fancy equipment took away / what little business he had, and the only patients / he could count on were the old scrubwomen who worked / in the shabby buildings around him."

Koertge takes on the dual obligation of, on the one hand, representing in poetry those who are seldom represented there, speaking of a common despair without condescending to the less fortunate, and crucially, on the other hand, refusing to take his own troubles (or even his own sympathies) more seriously than those of others. In the "Interlocutor," a mock-narrative, mock-confessional poem, he deliberately avoids any pretension to nobility in the voice of the speaker:

As I take off my goofy vestments, the real or imaginary problems I have
solved or complicated

sadden me for a moment, but no longer than that.
In fact, the entire period of grief consists of just the time it takes
to lay my head on the pillow and whisper
Boo Hoo.

When Koertge writes in the first person, he frequently represents himself as being somewhat downhearted but coping, often borrowing both metaphor and setting from the world of racing, as when he explains in "Making Do" (in *The Hired Nose*, 1974) that he has moved to the track because "I have had enough of being told and then left / in the lurch like some funky horseplayer." (*Tarzan and Shane Meet the Toad*, published the next year, contains half-a-dozen Koertge poems, mostly also published elsewhere, along with poems by Charles Stetler and Gerald Locklin.)

With *Men Under Fire* (1976) Koertge's work acquired a more serious undercurrent; poem after poem documents a sense of thwarted expec-

Dust jacket for Koertge's 1982 collection, which includes more personal and family poems than most of his previous books

tation, as though nothing in the world of these poems ever turns out as well as the characters might have expected, whether at the racetrack or in the suburban cultures and subcultures of California that are presented. Thus the poem "Men Under Fire" ends with a character who "wants to know / how many more races. / 'Just the nightcap.' / 'Damn,' he says, 'I sure hope we get some more action / in that one'"; and "Newlywed Heiress Takes Own Life" concludes with: "She resembled some rare and plumeless riparian / fowl who had settled by mistake during her / unwilling flight from another country and / had found the atmosphere noxious." A much slimmer book also published in 1976, *12 Photographs of Yellowstone* continues in a relatively serious vein, at times in an almost meditative mode as when, in "The Wind," the speaker awakens in terror at an unknown sound: "Even awake / I could feel the sound wearing / at the edges of my heart." Koertge, who uses the reflective range only rarely, nevertheless

handles it well, particularly when the speaker gazes toward the world beyond himself: "Across the way, beyond the arroyo, I could / see other windows, pipes of light / at whose end people wept or puked."

Ted Simons, in his introduction to Koertge's *How to Live on Five Dollars a Week, Etc.* (1977), aptly comments that "when you see the name *Koertge* on a book cover, you know it's humor. . . . This is a genuinely valuable guide on how *not* to do things . . . from living cheaply, to making it with chicks, for Koertge is a born loser." The book opens with a prose section chronicling a week-long effort to live up to the title, followed by fifteen poems that center primarily on loss at the track, financial loss, or the loss of love, and in some cases all three, with occasional references to the financial plight of the writer in contemporary American culture.

Koertge is not a squeamish poet when he writes about sex, and the revised (1979) version

Koertge circa 1988 (photograph by Bianca Richards)

of his *Sex Object* only narrowly escapes being as offensive as the title seems calculated to promise. Koertge renders both his female and male characters credibly. In "The Women's Movement" he writes: "Because Lucy and Ethel were tired of cooking, they got taken out / to dinner, but too much lip about equality also got them stuck / with their half of the check and a sink full of dirty dishes"; in "Men Watch Football Because They Are Lonely for Other Men," he speculates that men "would like to live / and work with forty other men forever. They would like / to kick ass and get kicked. They would like / to have injuries X-rayed and reported in the papers." Koertge writes often in *Sex Object* and elsewhere about male and female bodies, not always avoiding a sexist perspective. At the same time, he brings an awareness of his own sexism and that of his culture to the poetry.

In *The Jockey Poems* (1980) Koertge uses a short sequence of prose poems to clarify the obses-

sion with the racetrack that runs throughout his work; somewhat predictably he draws analogies between the world of the track and the larger world. The writing here continues to be almost entirely tongue-in-cheek, while displaying a grace that does not require any particular interest in horse racing to be enjoyed: "Each time a jockey balances himself on a bandaged or gimpy horse and bettors look the other way, they establish themselves as metaphysicians in the sense that moral questions can be reduced to chemical laws."

Koertge's largest volumes of poetry, *Diary Cows* and *Life on the Edge of the Continent*, contain well-chosen selections from his earlier work as well as important new poems. However, the arrangement of the poems in these volumes obscures the development of Koertge's work, leveling a chronology that any scholarship on Koertge would need to recover. In general, both books contain more poems about a midwestern child-

Fast Asleep

It is probably the first oxymoron
and begins to unravel at the (edge) — corner
what was til then the blue cashmere
of language.

Tucked into a land of long blonde hair
where foxes think and umbrellas can
do anything, we listen to our parents
keep the kite of the story aloft
with fragrant, boozy breath.

But someone at school said, "Paraguay."
A boy has moved and left a single glove
inside his desk. The tongue of the class
mascot is redder than it used to be.

"Goodnight. Sleep tight," lies crossed
on our lips like the knife and fork
of the good child who is finished.

The door clicks shut. Even (the) — golden
fish settle beside the bubbling diver
while we lie awake, our clean feet
moving a little as we wonder,

How can fast be asleep? How?
And when we wake up, we are older.

Late draft for a recent poem by Koertge (by permission of Ronald Koertge)

hood and more poems of personal history than his earlier books. Koertge has also lessened the distance he keeps between his speakers and expressed emotion, and he has developed a broader cultural vision, including, although not limited to, a more finely tuned appreciation for popular culture.

In the strongest new poems in *Diary Cows*, Koertge tries to revise readers' understanding of popular culture, as when he describes, in "Side-kicks," moviegoers "who could sit in a darkened theatre, listen / to the organ music and watch the best / of ourselves lowered into the ground while / the rest stood up there, tears pouring off / that enormous nose." There is, however, another side to Koertge in this volume, shown in more personal poems, such as "The Chill Factor," in which Koertge writes about his parents: "It [the chill factor] is all my Midwestern parents talk about any more. / I almost said It's No Wonder, We Were Never Very Close, / but I'm not sure even Robert Young & Jane Wyatt are 'close.' "

The presence of the personal and the familial in Koertge's later work is reinforced by the decision to reprint *The Father-Poems* at the center of *Life on the Edge of the Continent*. Further, the section "Excerpts from God's Secret Diary," right before that sequence, exemplifies Koertge's increasing ability to combine his sense of the weirdness and humor of the world he inhabits with the high value he is willing to assign to human emotion and passion. Writing of the moment when God casts Adam and Eve out of the Garden of Eden, Koertge imagines a God who thinks:

> Now they've really done it. Each gets an A for
> contrition, but out they go anyway. I must remember
> to remove the angel with the flaming sword. If
> he stays there until Los Angeles appears, people
> will think this is a car wash.
> . . . .
> I can hear anything in any cosmos and beyond,

yet I choose the sound of their troubled hearts. What a funny God I am.

In addition to poetry, Koertge has worked in other genres, including the open-ended prose form characteristic of *Meat: Cherry's Market-Diary* (1973)—a series of thirty-seven prose fragments under the general heading of "New Butcher from New Jersey"—and of the loosely narrative sequences that make up *My Summer Vacation* (1975). He has also published a novel, *The Boogeyman* (1980), which chronicles a series of unlikely events and relationships among a group of eccentric English teaching assistants. More recently, Koertge has begun to receive much-deserved recognition for three novels intended for the young adult audience: *Where the Kissing Never Stops* (1986), *The Arizona Kid* (1988), and *The Boy in the Moon* (1990). All three are remarkable for the realism with which they present tough and not-so-tough teenage characters coming of age in a world of AIDS and widespread divorce, but often in a world in which tenderness and love are not absent.

Koertge has recently published another novel for young adults (*Mariposa Blues*) and a volume of poetry entitled *High School Dirty Poems* (both in 1991), and he has been awarded an NEA grant in poetry for 1991. He says of his career, "If I knew exactly where my work was headed in the future, I'm not sure I'd want to go along." The development evident in his poetry and the sheer volume of his work suggest that Koertge will continue to be important on the fringes of contemporary American poetry. He has earned a place there through writing a kind of poetry distinguished by its quirkiness, by its uncanny observations about American culture, and—beneath the surface of Koertge's tendency to represent himself as a perennial smart aleck—by its essential seriousness.

Reference:

Ted Simons, Introduction to *How to Live on Five Dollars a Week, Etc.* (Los Angeles: Venice Poetry, 1977).

Ted Kooser
(25 April 1939 -   )

Matthew C. Brennan
Indiana State University

BOOKS: *Official Entry Blank* (Lincoln: University
   of Nebraska Press, 1969);
Grass County (Lincoln: Windflower, 1971);
Twenty Poems (Crete, Nebr.: Best Cellar, 1973);
A Local Habitation and a Name (San Luis Obispo,
   Cal.: Solo, 1974);
Shooting a Farmhouse / So This Is Nebraska (Denver:
   Ally, 1975);
Not Coming to Be Barked at (Milwaukee: Penta-
   gram, 1976);
Old Marriage and New (Austin, Tex.: Cold Moun-
   tain, 1978);
Hatcher (Lincoln: Windflower, 1978);
Sure Signs: New and Selected Poems (Pittsburgh: Uni-
   versity of Pittsburgh Press, 1980);
One World at a Time (Pittsburgh: University of Pitts-
   burgh Press, 1985);
The Blizzard Voices (Minneapolis: Bieler, 1986).

OTHER: *Voyages to the Inland Sea VI: Essays and
   Poems by Harley Elliott and Ted Kooser*, edited
   by John Judson (La Crosse, Wis.: Center for
   Contemporary Poetry, 1976);
Cottonwood County, includes poems by Kooser and
   William Kloefkorn (Lincoln: Windflower,
   1979);
The Windflower Home Almanac of Poetry, edited by
   Kooser (Lincoln: Windflower, 1980);
*On Common Ground: The Poetry of William Kloef-
   korn, Ted Kooser, Greg Kuzma, and Don Welch*,
   edited by Mark Sanders and J. V.
   Brummels, includes poems and notes by
   Kooser (Ord, Nebr.: Sandhills, 1983).

Ted Kooser

The subjects and imagery of Ted Kooser's
poetry unmistakably bear the influence of his
environment, the Great Plains, but Kooser insists
he is not a regionalist writer. However, until the
University of Pittsburgh Press published *Sure
Signs: New and Selected Poems* in 1980, Kooser had
published four of his books with Nebraska
presses and the others with such small houses
as Cold Mountain Press in Texas, Solo Press in
California, and Pentagram Press in Wisconsin.

Hence, Kooser's audience remained narrow and
primarily local. Furthermore, despite a favorable
notice by William Cole in the 2 November 1974
issue of *Saturday Review*, Kooser continued to
write without much critical notice beyond midwestern little magazines, thus reinforcing the notion
of his merely regional appeal. Then, with *Sure
Signs*, critics in national publications began to recognize, as Peter Stitt said in the *Georgia Review*
(Fall 1980), that Kooser is "an authentic poet of
the American people," a poet who wrests a universal resonance from regional subjects.

Theodore J. Kooser, the son of Theodore B. Kooser, a merchant, and Vera Moser Kooser, grew up in Ames, Iowa, where he was born on 25 April 1939 and where he attended college, earning a B.S. in English education from Iowa State University in 1962. Later that year (on 17 November) he married Diana Tressler. He next taught high school in Madrid, Iowa, for one year but then moved to Lincoln, Nebraska, where he has since lived. At first he did full-time graduate study in English at the University of Nebraska; however, when the department failed to renew his graduate appointment for his second year, he launched a successful career in insurance, meanwhile pursuing a master's degree part-time and earning it in 1968. He is now second vice-president of marketing for Lincoln Benefit Life Company. Unlike Wallace Stevens, who kept his careers in insurance and poetry completely separate, Kooser tries his poems out on his colleagues at the office and credits his daily association with them as helping "to keep the language of [his] poems from becoming literary." Mainly, though, he thinks his job in insurance has not been particularly helpful in his literary career; still, as he once facetiously quipped, it has prevented him from giving away good metaphors, as he did when teaching night classes. By giving readings from Berkeley to New York, publishing and editing two magazines—the *Salt Creek Reader* (1967-1975) and the *Blue Hotel* (1980-1981)—and continuing to operate Windflower Press, Kooser has stayed involved in the literary world. Personally, since the 1969 divorce from Diana, by whom he has one son, Jeffrey, Kooser has remarried (in 1977) and lives with his wife, Kathy, outside Lincoln in Garland, Nebraska.

When discussing his biographical roots in the Midwest, Kooser fends off attempts by critics to lump Plains poets together simply because their work shares common literal images of setting: "People have known for years that the best way to involve a reader in what he's reading is to introduce concrete imagery, and when you live in a place you draw your imagery from what's around you" (*On Common Ground*, 1983). Because his poems rely on vivid particular details of ordinary life and present them simply and clearly, some critics, such as Dana Gioia, have cited William Carlos Williams as a major influence—and indeed Kooser studied Williams in graduate school under Karl Shapiro. But what is most impressive and distinctive about Kooser's style, and what gives his work its poetic authenticity, is his own

metaphorical imagination. In poem after poem—nearly all less than one page in both *Sure Signs* and *One World at a Time* (1985)—Kooser first involves his readers through precise particulars and then transforms these images into insightful metaphors. Though Kooser is similar to Robert Bly in his use of midwestern landscapes, Kooser's revelations, unlike Bly's, are rarely sublime. But his technique perfectly illustrates Frost's idea that poetry essentially says one thing in terms of another. Just as Frost used New England for his metaphors, Kooser uses landscapes and portraits of the Plains states and their people as vehicles for expressing experiences and feelings (especially loss, decay, and loneliness) that are universal.

Sure Signs shows an accomplished poet employing distinctive, expressive metaphors, but *Official Entry Blank* (1969), Kooser's first book, unveils a novice experimenting with various forms, subjects, and voices. He tries rhymed quatrains, blank verse, sonnets, haiku, heroic couplets, and even found poems. Several of the more successful formal poems develop a wry, facetious irony that is pleasing, but also slight. For instance, in "Gifted Hands" Kooser writes vividly about his sister's painting horses on coffee cups but then deflates the family pride with an ironic insult in the last line: "We were proud; / we gave her horses to the relatives / until a cousin said they looked like cows." Furthermore, the more serious poems often sound shallow and banal: Kooser writes in another poem about his sister ("To My Sister"), "If I am twenty-seven now, / You must be twenty-three; / It seems impossible, somehow, / That you still follow me." In general, these mostly derivative poems lack the tight syntax and sharp metaphors of his more characteristic later work. He clearly had not yet found his voice. As Gioia points out in *On Common Ground*, "Reading *Official Entry Blank* in 1969, one would have been hard pressed either to predict Kooser's subsequent development or to define his individuality as a poet." Still, occasionally the mature Kooser voice comes through: "Dodo," "Strike," "Suicide," and "Beer Bottle" (a poem also included in *Sure Signs*) anticipate Kooser's technique of transforming precisely described objects into evocative metaphors.

Kooser's next two publications were small-press chapbooks: *Grass County* (1971), a collection of eight poems privately printed by Windflower Press, his own company; and *Twenty Poems* (1973), which Best Cellar Press published. The poems in these books continue the strand in *Offi-*

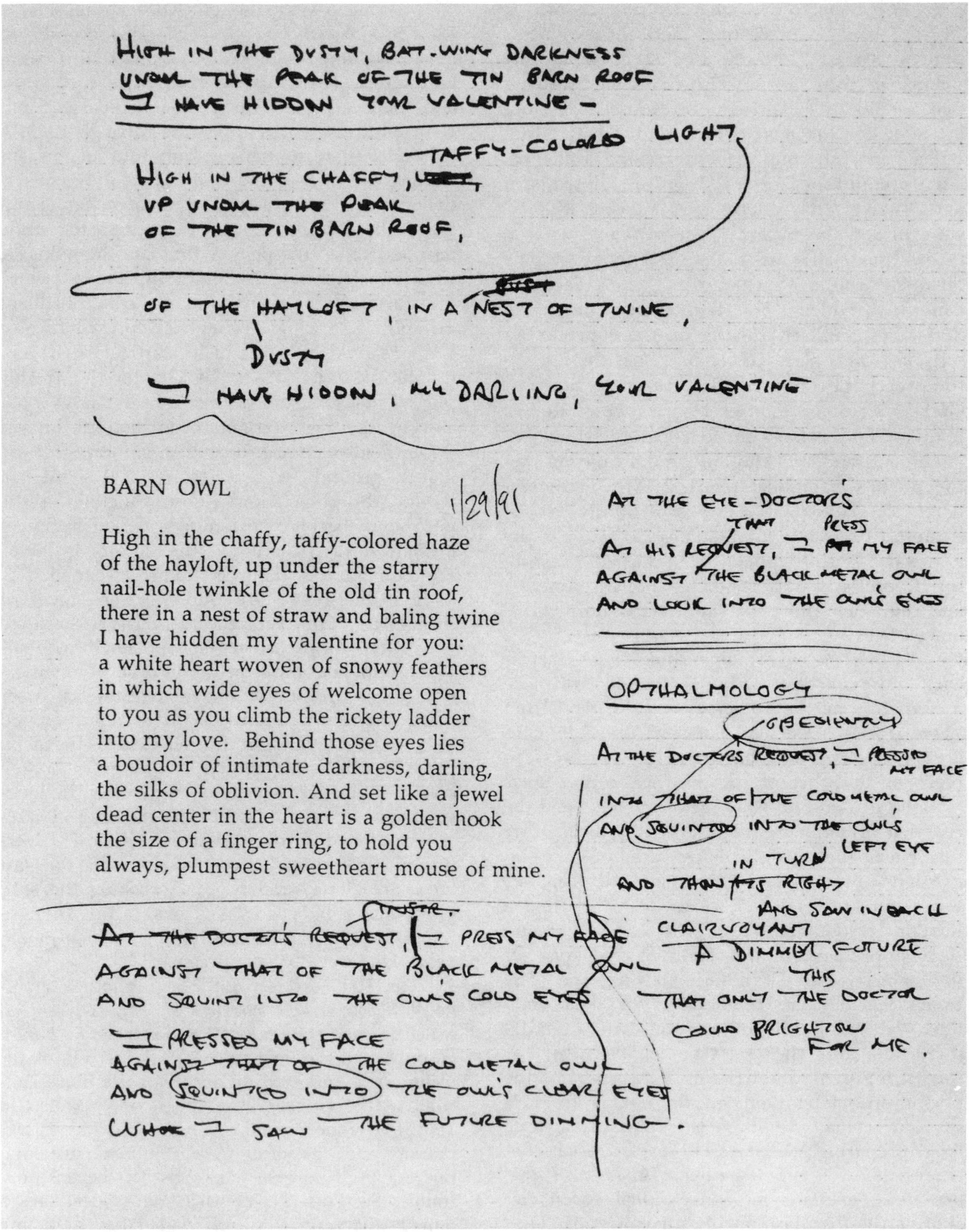

HIGH IN THE DUSTY, BAT-WING DARKNESS
UNDER THE PEAK OF THE TIN BARN ROOF
I HAVE HIDDEN YOUR VALENTINE —

HIGH IN THE CHAFFY, ~~LIGHT~~ TAFFY-COLORED LIGHT,
UP UNDER THE PEAK
OF THE TIN BARN ROOF,

OF THE HAYLOFT, IN A NEST OF ~~BAST~~ TWINE,
DUSTY
I HAVE HIDDEN, MY DARLING, YOUR VALENTINE

BARN OWL

1/29/91

High in the chaffy, taffy-colored haze
of the hayloft, up under the starry
nail-hole twinkle of the old tin roof,
there in a nest of straw and baling twine
I have hidden my valentine for you:
a white heart woven of snowy feathers
in which wide eyes of welcome open
to you as you climb the rickety ladder
into my love. Behind those eyes lies
a boudoir of intimate darkness, darling,
the silks of oblivion. And set like a jewel
dead center in the heart is a golden hook
the size of a finger ring, to hold you
always, plumpest sweetheart mouse of mine.

~~AT THE DOCTOR'S REQUEST,~~ INSTR. I PRESS MY FACE
AGAINST THAT OF THE BLACK METAL OWL
AND SQUINT INTO THE OWL'S COLD EYES

I PRESSED MY FACE
AGAINST THAT OF THE COLD METAL OWL
AND SQUINTED INTO THE OWL'S CLEAR EYES
~~WHERE~~ I SAW THE FUTURE DIMMING.

AT THE EYE-DOCTOR'S
THAT PRESS
AT HIS REQUEST, I AM MY FACE
AGAINST THE BLACK METAL OWL
AND LOOK INTO THE OWL'S EYES

OPTHALMOLOGY

OBEDIENTLY
AT THE DOCTOR'S REQUEST, I PRESSED
MY FACE
INTO THAT OF THE COLD METAL OWL
AND SQUINTED INTO THE OWL'S
LEFT EYE
IN TURN
AND THEN ITS RIGHT
AND SAW IN EACH
CLAIRVOYANT
A DIMMER FUTURE
THIS
THAT ONLY THE DOCTOR
COULD BRIGHTEN
FOR ME.

A late draft for "Barn Owl" and an early draft for "Opthalmology," both works in progress (by permission of Ted Kooser)

cial Entry Blank represented by poems such as "Strike" and "Beer Bottle," and in several instances Kooser's efforts are as good as any poems in *Sure Signs*. Three poems in *Grass County* embody what was to be Kooser's developing style for the next decade and a half. "Tom Ball's Barn," in controlled, restrained, colloquial language, links a farmer's "bare" unpainted barn and "twelve / nail-popping, splintering winters" with his "diabetes and / the swollen leg that threw him / off the silo...." Though it only obliquely refers to characters, "The Sampson Church" (retitled "The Red Wing Church" in *Sure Signs*) similarly focuses on the concrete description of a place partly in ruins, this one in the process of transformation from "the house of God / to Homer Johnson's barn." Here Kooser handles blank verse with such smooth syntax, enjambment, and well-chosen common diction that the poem's traditional metrical form accommodates the colloquial style as naturally as the Sampson Church accommodates "a tractor in the doorway." A third poem, "The Geek," exemplifies Kooser's character poems about the outcast and the alone and their exotic but painfully distanced lives.

Twenty Poems contains some work that is even more impressive, but its results are more mixed. Kooser chose "Selecting a Reader" from *Twenty Poems* as the lead poem in *Sure Signs*, and it expresses well both his desire, in his words, "to reach an audience of people who are not poets or poetry followers" (*On Common Ground*) and the risk that his audience, like the reader in the dirty raincoat in the poem, will "put the book / up on its shelf " and will say, " 'For that kind of money I can get / my raincoat cleaned.' " "Selecting a Reader" recommends itself for its insistence on clear apprehension and realistic acceptance of the ordinary. "My Grandfather Dying" and "The Failed Suicide" are remarkable for their emotional concluding metaphors: the dying grandfather calling out the poet's name, his breath "as sour as an orchard / after the first frost"; and the person who attempted suicide waking from "a four-day coma," his brain the color of "a stone frog" preparing "his leap." However, as Gioia concludes, "most of the new poems [in *Twenty Poems*] are facile exercises in conventional styles," including the then-fashionable surrealism of "They Had Torn Off My Face at the Office," which abandons the realism and feeling of Kooser's more original works.

The next year, though, Kooser published *A Local Habitation and a Name* (1974), his second full-length volume, and again emphasized realism and pathos. He also refined his style, technique, and themes, all of which remained largely unchanged in his works appearing through 1985. *A Local Habitation* contains seventy-four poems, including twenty-four older ones that show, nevertheless, his mature style and themes. For example, "The Widow Lester" is a character study narrated as a first-person dramatic monologue, whereas "Highway 30" and "Spring Plowing" transform common rural scenes through brilliant metaphors. "Spring Plowing" is representative of Kooser's style not only in its particularized geographical setting ("West of Omaha the freshly plowed fields / steam in the night like lakes") but also in the close attention to natural images ("The field mice are moving their nests / to the higher ground of fence rows"). Most of all, though, this poem shows Kooser's method, as the mice subtly become personified, anxious refugees in flight to safer territory: "the old among them" are "crying out to the owls / to take them all. The paths in the grass / are loud with the squeak of their carts. / They keep their lanterns covered."

Even more masterful is "Highway 30," which depends more on simile than personification for its profoundly imaginative effects. After first likening the moon to a car driven away and a star to its sole taillight, Kooser extends his metaphor by comparing motels and cafés to broken crates that have fallen out of the back of the long-gone vehicle. One imagines the motels and cafés as abandoned, broken structures whose "overturned flowerpots," Kooser writes in the last lines, are "lone women ... / crushing the soft, gray petals of old coats." As a vivid picture of highway landscape and as a metaphor evoking loneliness, "Highway 30" is impressive.

In 1975 Kooser published another chapbook, *Shooting a Farmhouse / So This Is Nebraska*, which formed the core of *Not Coming to Be Barked at*, published the next year. In this 1976 book his technique is more adroit and his voice more controlled. In fact, several of the stronger works in *Sure Signs* come from this volume. "So This Is Nebraska" and "Shooting A Farmhouse" are long poems, by Kooser's standards. In seven quatrains, "So This Is Nebraska" deftly describes a Sunday drive on a gravel road. After depicting barns as "dear old ladies" whose "little windows" are "dulled by cataracts of hay and cobwebs," Kooser personifies a pickup truck as kicking "its fenders off and [settling] back to read the clouds." Next he presents the truck "holding a skinny old man" who waits "for someone to wave to." Then, picking up an image in stanza 3 of "a meadowlark waiting on every post" the car passes, Kooser neatly concludes, "You wave / instead and leave your hand out gliding / larklike over the wheat, over the houses." The abundance of run-on lines, as well as the repetition of "you feel" and "you wave" in the last twelve lines, formally approximates the poem's action. "Shooting a Farmhouse" is simpler in design but equally effective. In thirty lines, it catalogues the changes wrought on a farm by reckless hunters: from the first ".22 hole . . . in the mailbox" to the final destruction, when after their "Land Rover / flattens the gate like a tank . . . the newspapers left over from packing / the old woman's dishes / begin to blow back and forth through the rooms."

This desolate image of emptiness recurs in different ways in memorable brief poems also in *Not Coming to Be Barked at*. For instance, in "The Afterlife," Kooser presents a series of aptly chosen literal images that, juxtaposed, evoke the strange, vague atmosphere of a place where "a foreign-language newspaper" rolls "along the dock / in an icy wind," and "the horns of the tugs" turn "our great gray ship / back into the mist." Similarly "North of Alliance" is about the desolation of absence in a house so empty one finds "not even / a newspaper sodden with rain / under a broken window," but finds only marks penciled in a door frame to measure "a child stretching his neck / in a hurry to leave nothing here / but an absence grown tall in a doorway." By ending his concretely descriptive poems on images of emptiness and absence, Kooser generates ambiguous feelings that linger like remnants of dreams.

Despite the assured accomplishment of the poems in *A Local Habitation and a Name* and *Not Coming to Be Barked at*, Kooser veered in a new direction—for him—in the chapbook he published in 1978, *Old Marriage and New*. The pain of his divorce from his first wife, the resulting separation from his only son, and the good fortune of his remarriage all apparently drove Kooser to adopt a confessional style. Gioia has called this volume Kooser's weakest mature collection, one whose poems are sometimes thin and embarrassingly sentimental, though still crisply written. Kooser is clearly more comfortable and more successful with less overtly autobiographical poems, but even some of the more painful poems show his characteristic talent. "Long Ago," for example, moves from the literal scene—an estranged couple all talked out at two in the morning—to a metaphorical ending:

> There is really
> no news, and I feel
> that this night, or the last,
> or last year, a small plane
> has gone down somewhere between us,
> laden with caring.

Old Marriage and New is uneven in quality, but two years later Kooser's *Sure Signs* impressed most critics, even his less enthusiastic ones, with its consistency and unity. Stitt concluded from *Sure Signs* that "Kooser is a good poet . . . a clear and careful writer who deserves . . . attention." In more resounding terms, Gioia announced that the "unified *oeuvre*" presented in *Sure Signs* demonstrates Kooser's status as "the master of the short colloquial imagistic poem. . . . Kooser [has] a genuine poetic style which accommodates the average reader" and exhibits "unexpected moments of illumination from the seemingly threadbare details of everyday life." However, in a *New York Times* review that Kooser calls "nasty" and "sneering," Charles Molesworth objected that Kooser's images, while sometimes "fresh and keen . . . can also be humdrum or clumsy." Molesworth also attacked the consistently brief length of Kooser's poems, which he said makes them risk quaintness. Gioia was also bothered by Kooser's narrow range of technique and his tendency to avoid the risks of failure by changing. This last limitation, revealed in *Sure Signs*, clearly strikes Kooser the hardest, for in comparing himself to Greg Kuzma, another Nebraska poet, he remarked in a 1983 interview (in *On Common Ground*) that whereas Kuzma "keeps experimenting," he himself is "safer" and "more likely to write . . . the Kooser poem."

Unlike some poets who ignore reviews of their books, Kooser reads them and tries to learn from them. Consequently, after *Sure Signs* won Kooser some long-overdue national recognition, including the Society for Midlands Authors Prize for the best book of poetry in 1980, he not only continued to work in the vein of his success (in *One World at a Time*), he also tried a new way of writing in *The Blizzard Voices* (1986), which was originally performed as a play. The poems in *One World at a Time* share the trademark style and themes of *Sure Signs*, but they differ in that the deepening and refinement of Kooser's technique make *One World at a Time* his strongest volume of

THE DOGS

So helpless in his love of you,
Buddy lies just outside the door
to the bedroom crying. ~~[crossed out]~~
~~[crossed out]~~ pitiful Hattie
is less ~~[crossed out]~~. Her claws
~~[crossed out]~~ back and forth across the floor
click ~~[crossed out]~~
       The fool of love
letting me know she's waiting.

Beyond the venetian blinds, the sky
is gooseberry blue.

Shrouded in fog is one of
those metaphors that was
once perfect but whose
life has been depleted
through overuse —

      Suddenly

At the window
You tell me the river
is shrouded in fog
and I ~~[crossed out]~~ say take that shroud
from its slippery table
and snap the wrinkles out of it
and lay it ~~[crossed out]~~ over
the blue breasts
and swollen belly
of those Iowa hills.

At dawn ~~the day~~ the eastern sky
was gooseberry blue. The ~~[crossed out]~~
~~were~~ pale. —   thin
     passed through
Dawn ~~lit~~ the tents and lit them
    [but lit like windows

THE BLACKHAWK WAR

At dawn, the eastern sky was gooseberry
            blue —
    A spider
In the night, a spider had woven a
           web
across the door of Lincoln's tent.

You say the river is shrouded in fog
and I say take the shroud from
that table and lay it over
~~these blue hills~~
    breasts and belly
   of the hills beyond
but why shroud a river. I say
take up the shroud

CRICKET —

You ~~[crossed out]~~ little Singer sewing machine

Whenever I see a cricket
sitting in a corner, I think of
my mother's Singer
sewing machine —

A cricket (sits) in a corner —

ANIMATIONS
    the

I am the poet of animations.
My mind is like Walt Disney's
I see the world as Disney saw it —

A cricket is down on all fours
in a corner, trying to look like
a sewing machine. All night
it sharpened its scissors
the wheel of the grindstone
skidding —

Pages from Kooser's current notebook (by permission of Ted Kooser)

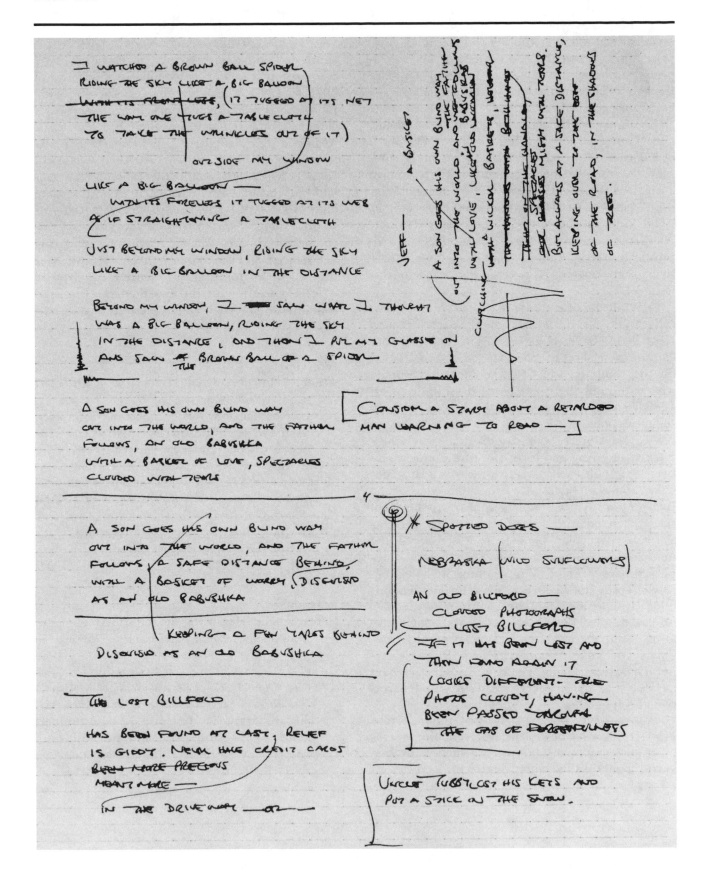

recent work. Many of the best poems again comprise direct presentations of images and metaphors in one or two sentences spanning no more than six syllables a line and less than a half page—as is the case with "Camera," "At the Center," "An August Night," "An Empty Shotgun Shell," and "Laundry," to cite a few. However, *One World at a Time* also contains several fuller, more complex poems: "In the Basement of the Goodwill Store," "A Room in the Past," "The Fan in the Window," and "The Urine Specimen," as well as "The Ride," an elegy for novelist John Gardner. All these poems employ thematic subtlety and a sophisticated style. Indeed, these five poems confirm that Kooser is not simply a regionalist writer.

While in *One World at a Time* Kooser basically built on his earlier success, *The Blizzard Voices* is one of his boldest experiments. In a concluding note, he explains that the book is "based on the reminiscences of those men and women who witnessed the great blizzard of January 12, 1888." In forty-seven pages the book's thirty-six separate poems, titled only "A Man's Voice" or "A Woman's Voice," depict individual experiences during the storm and form a discontinuous narrative. Although each narrative records a different voice, the plain style stays consistent—that of the final "Man's Voice," which appears to be Kooser's. Each poem, however, successfully presents a fresh, particular perspective. In general the monologues are spare and flat, even sometimes repetitive (several end by mentioning limbs or digits lost from frostbite). But one after another sustains the reader's interest through precisely observed, novel details that foster an engaging realism. Still, these poems lack the figurative language and compression typical of Kooser's earlier character poems. Perhaps Kooser will next devise a style and subject that can stress both narrative and metaphor.

Like many poets of the generation before him, Ted Kooser began his career writing poems in traditional forms but then switched to free verse, a mode that better suited his midwestern voice. Through this change Kooser perfected a short, descriptive but strikingly metaphorical type of poem that undergirded all his books from 1971 to 1985. This style enables Kooser to explore the underlying mystery in ordinary rural subjects. Some critics have found his manner of writing distinctive but also limiting. One weakness of it is that, as Gilbert Allen has said, Kooser "writes essentially the same poem over and over again"—or, more accurately, the same kind of poem. Clearly, though it is something of a digression, *The Blizzard Voices* answers this charge and does so without leaving Kooser's earlier subjects and technique entirely behind. As a product of his midwestern environment, Kooser isn't likely to stray far for new themes, even if he continues to graft new techniques onto his accomplished style.

Interviews:

Arnold Hatcher, "An Interview with Ted Kooser," in *Voyages to the Inland Sea VI: Essays and Poems by Harley Elliott and Ted Kooser*, edited by John Judson (La Crosse, Wis.: Center for Contemporary Poetry, 1976), pp. 37-50;

Mark Sanders, "An Interview with Ted Kooser," in *On Common Ground: The Poetry of William Kloefkorn, Ted Kooser, Greg Kuzma, and Don Welch*, edited by Mark Sanders and J. V. Brummels (Ord, Nebr.: Sandhills, 1983), pp. 99-105.

References:

Gilbert Allen, "Measuring the Mainstream—A Review Essay," *Southern Humanities Review*, 17 (Spring 1983): 171-178;

Dana Gioia, "Explaining Ted Kooser," in *On Common Ground: The Poetry of William Kloefkorn, Ted Kooser, Greg Kuzma, and Don Welch*, edited by Mark Sanders and J. V. Brummels (Ord, Nebr.: Sandhills, 1983), pp. 83-99;

Peter Stitt, "The World at Hand," *Georgia Review*, 34 (Fall 1980): 661-670.

Cynthia Macdonald

(2 February 1928 -   )

Charlotte M. Wright
University of North Texas

BOOKS: *Amputations* (New York: Braziller, 1972);
Transplants (New York: Braziller, 1976);
Pruning the Annuals (Hartford, Conn.: Bartholomews Cobble, 1976);
(W)holes (New York: Knopf, 1980);
Alternate Means of Transport (New York: Knopf, 1985);
Living Wills: New and Selected Poems (New York: Knopf, 1991).

PLAY PRODUCTION: *The Rehearsal*, libretto by Macdonald, music by Thomas Benjamin, Evanston, Ill., Northwestern University, 1980.

RECORDING: "This Is the Day," lyrics by Macdonald, music by Judy Collins, Elektra, 1980.

Cynthia Macdonald is best known for the grotesque imagery and sardonic tone in her poems. She is the author of five collections of poetry, as well as a contributor to numerous anthologies of contemporary verse. Both her subject matter and experimental style have attracted critical attention. Her early works have been compared to those of Anne Sexton and Sylvia Plath, but critics of her later books have commented on the development of a more mature style, much of which they attribute to the author's broadened insights into the human psyche. Macdonald began her career as a professional singer, so attempts have been made to describe her work in terms of music. However, if a correlation exists, it is dissonant rather than assonant, cacophonous rather than euphonic.

Born in New York City on 2 February 1928, Cynthia Lee Macdonald is the daughter of Leonard Lee, a screenwriter, and Dorothy Kiam Lee. She received a B.A. from Bennington College in 1950 and began graduate work at Mannes College of Music the following year. In 1954 she married E. C. Macdonald, with whom she had two children, Jennifer and Scott. From 1953 to 1966 she pursued a career as an opera and concert singer

in New York, but by the time she enrolled at Sarah Lawrence College, she had decided on a career of writing and teaching English. After graduating with an M.A. in 1970, she taught at Sarah Lawrence until 1975, the year of her divorce. She then took a position as full professor at Johns Hopkins University, where she remained for four years. In 1979 she moved to Texas to accept an appointment at the University of Houston, where she founded the creative-writing program that she still directs. Her increasing interest in psychoanalysis led to her graduation from the Houston-Galveston Psychoanalytic Institute in 1986.

Macdonald's first book, *Amputations* (1972), initiated the succession of generally favorable reviews she has enjoyed with each subsequent book. Published as the fourth volume in the Braziller Series of Poetry, the collection's display of startling images and techniques attracted immediate attention in trade magazines such as *Kirkus Reviews* and the *Library Journal*. Literary analysis of the book began two years later with Robert Pinsky's review in *Poetry* (January 1974) and R. L. Widmann's Spring 1974 article in *Concerning Poetry* (later reprinted in a 1978 book of feminist criticism). *Amputations* has many of the flaws of a first book—overuse of cliché phrases and obvious puns, and heavy reliance on prosy syntax combined with simple enjambment to make the lines look more like poetry—but it also has what Vickie Karp calls a combination of "wit, rapture, despair, personality, [and] imagination."

The most striking attribute of *Amputations* is Macdonald's matter-of-fact exposition of the grotesque. As the title suggests, nearly every poem revolves around a character who is missing some vital anatomical part. There is, for instance, the former tightrope walker in "Another Attempt at the Trick" who has had his legs cut off just below the knee. There is the son in "Departure" who cuts off both his feet before he is able to leave his mother. There are the anonymous but willing

Cynthia Macdonald (photograph by Gay Block)

victims in "Objets d'Art" whose testicles fill the freezer of the "real ball cutter" female persona:

Preservation
Was at first a problem: pickling worked
But was a lot of trouble. Freezing
Proved to be the answer. I had to buy
A second freezer just last year; the first
Was filled with rows and rows of
Pink and purple lumps encased in Saran wrap.

Most of Macdonald's characters are able to cope with their physical amputations; it is the more subtle one—the severance of the individual from his social environment—that contributes to the book's overriding tone of isolation and anguish. What is surprising is the dearth of the companion emotions of anger and bitterness, a characteristic that sets this book apart from much feminist verse of the 1970s. Instead Macdonald reveals her feminist concerns through startling juxtapositions of nightmarish images, such as a baby at the breast who ultimately ingests its mother

(in "The Insatiable Baby"), or the child whose growth to a height of eleven feet drives its mother crazy (in "Twice Too Long"). Even this technique is seen by some critics as too didactic, too predictable, and, in Pinsky's view, "too directly significant."

All in all *Amputations* was a successful first book of poems, with what Colette Inez, in *Parnassus* (Fall/Winter 1973), called its "wine-dark country of wordplay and pranks." Four years later George Braziller published Macdonald's *Transplants* (1976) as the eleventh volume in his poetry series. This second book received much wider critical attention than the first. Stanley Poss in the *Western Humanities Review* (Autumn 1976) praised it as entertaining, "sprightly," and "classical in [its] polish and wit and distance." Elizabeth Stone of the *Village Voice* (20 December 1976) compared the book to Macdonald's first, noting that in *Transplants* "all [the] people and all [the] voices are more substantial, more complicated—the targets of her wit, yes, but also the recipients of her com-

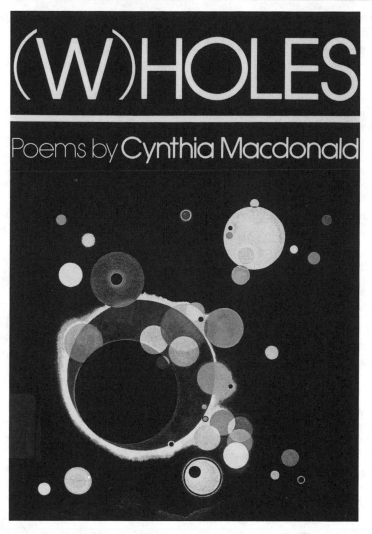

Cover for Macdonald's third full-length collection (1980); the painting is Wassily Kandinsky's Several Circles No. 323 *(1926)*

passion." In *Poetry*, however, a more negative review appeared (in February 1977): Robert Holland commented on Macdonald's "desperate fooling" and her "skewed . . . perspective on human pain" as being "at the base of the major problem in [her] poetry," that is, the emotional distance she maintains from even the most devastating of subjects. Karp, too, with her otherwise positive attitude toward Macdonald, disparages the poet's tendency to remain "numb and inert rather than taut and energized" when confronting "alarming personal grievances."

With Macdonald's portrayal of the lives of grotesque and freakish characters, the poems in *Transplants* are similar to those in *Amputations*, but a crucial difference, implied by the title, soon becomes evident. In her first book Macdonald was content simply to expose the predicament of those "amputated" from society. In her second

she "transplants" them into an alien, and similarly threatening, environment. In "Thanksgiving in Cambridge, N.Y.," for instance, she paints a chilling portrait of a holiday gathering of four women whose lives are consumed by hidden fears. One of the women sees "one fly . . . still alive" in a roomful of dead ones, and she begins to wonder "which one of us / Will crawl alone on the white curtain."

Another important difference that sets *Transplants* apart is the intense anger and bitterness in the collection. The ten "Doctor Dimity Poems" constitute an exposé of the hypocrisy and brutality Macdonald sees as endemic in American family life, which she portrays as especially damaging to women. "A Step Toward Burial," "Stained Glass Woman," and "Looking Into My Father's House" contain comparably violent undertones in their images of divorce, abandonment, incest, and murder. Published just one year after the breakup of Macdonald's marriage, this collection may reflect her personal resentments and anguish. An image from "A Discreet Plot" illustrates a vengeful frame of mind:

> After he had taken off her clothes, leaving her
> Dressed only in her pearls, she lay face down, impaled on him,
> Rotating slowly on the weathervane of his expectations,
> Which in later years she thought of as his folly.

Unfortunately, the result of such feelings is a stridency most critics saw as weakening the effectiveness of the poems.

There are, however, some critics who argue that the anger inherent in the book, and only slightly weakened in (W)holes (1980), Macdonald's third full-length collection, is a source of strength rather than weakness. Feminist critic Elizabeth Stone, for instance (in the Village Voice), writes that she admires poets like Macdonald, "who, without the armor of innocence, forswear Good Manners to tell the truth as they see it." Stone sees the "Doctor Dimity Poems" as "sad and comic" but revelatory of Macdonald's exploration into "richer and more ambiguous emotional terrain." Karp agrees, stating that the passionate anger in Transplants, especially in "The Stained Glass Woman" and "The Stained Glass Man," marks the beginning of Macdonald's success as a poet because it marks her transition from the "false" voice, "arbitrary" line breaks, and "bland" details of the earlier poems to the more mature, "complex," and "accessible" voice of her later work. Karp finds this voice even stronger in (W)holes, especially in "Burying the Babies," a long poem other critics also see as a key poem in Macdonald's oeuvre. Joyce Carol Oates, for instance, cites it as Macdonald's strongest and most ambitious poem, one "which should establish Cynthia Macdonald as one of our most intelligent and provocative poets" (Mademoiselle, June 1980). This thirty-page poem, which has recently been translated into Czech, also attracted the attention of Robert Peters, who calls this complex collage a "vibrant . . . scream" about the role of women in society (Meridian, April 1980).

(W)holes is connected to Macdonald's previous books in its similarity of title, continued fascination with grotesque characters, and reliance on surreal situations, but it also reveals her improved control over her poetic craft. The language contains fewer worn phrases than in Amputations or Transplants; the poems are less likely to sacrifice content to form, as "Francis Bacon (1561-1626; 1910-), The Inventor of Spectacles, Is the Ringmaster" shows:

> The eye is the most courageous organ because,
> in a sense,
> It must always face itself. It lies in its moist
> socket,
> The pot of seeing, and never says that what it
> sees in dream
> Is less than what it sees. Image and imagination,
> Those eyes indivisible.
> In the deep of my eye, I see
> To the edge of self (all those translucent pronouns)
> And beyond into the dark quarter of the circle.

Still, at least two critics thought that Macdonald had not reached her potential with (W)holes. Doug Lang lamented her "flippancy" toward "the world of pain and isolation and grief " she herself creates (Washington Post Book World, 10 February 1980). And Vernon Young stated flatly: "Cynthia Macdonald has long since been taken over by her poems." He labeled her merely "a fairly brilliant coiner and collector of phrases," and he also recommended that the reader "disregard the probability" that Macdonald has anything of value to say (New York Times Book Review, 2 March 1980).

Robert B. Shaw's review of Alternate Means of Transport (1985), although not as harsh, contains faint echoes of Young's sentiments. Shaw says her poems are a "sort of whimsical phantasmagoria, spun out . . . by word-antics." Shaw does find a few poems with a "more substantial art" beneath the "garish verbal surfaces," although he concludes that he was "never once transported" beyond the mundane while reading the collection (Poetry, April 1986).

Young's and Shaw's opinions, however, are overshadowed by the praise from the majority of critics. Karp expressed a representative view when she labeled Macdonald's book "polished," with a "freshness and depth" lacking in the previous collections. She pointed to poems such as "Two Brothers in a Field of Absence" as evidence that Macdonald's talent and persistence have finally born fruit. In this poem, two brothers create a huge woman's form out of fresh hay and lie with it off and on for weeks, using it to enjoy not just "the awe of taking her, / But the awe of having made her." They do not notice when the hay woman begins to smolder, for "wet, green hay /

And Cause his Countenance to Shine Upon (You) ?

The Rabbi & his wife live in the body of Christ:
                                        Corpus Christi
They break bread in it and drink dark red Mogen
                             David
To break the Yom Kippur fast. The ribs of
The city rise around them and it's long watery arms
          + legs
Of the causeway lights in the dusk wrapping the sky's dark fabric as the belt
The pubis of _____ Bluff park gives them around the city
Covering the
                         Shelter   which shelters them
From the Gulf Coast's sexual heat, The city's
                             beard
Seaweed with shrimp, oysters + mussels (bearded,
                   too)
Hangs from the face of the sea with its
                   changeable weathers
Tense as religion, or grammar, calm as beatitude,
                           and or the full moon,
                                 on Fat Tuesday,
Joyous as a dance in the shtetl, or Mardi Gras,
As the mouth's first savour of Aunt Martha's
                   mazoth balls
Swimming in a richer, salty sea of broth.
The eyes of Christ span the gulf of time,
                         looking
At the Passover mazoth. There was as yet
                   no Poland so
The matzoh was still flat as the world was.

Manuscript for a poem in Macdonald's Living Wills *(by permission of Cynthia Macdonald)*

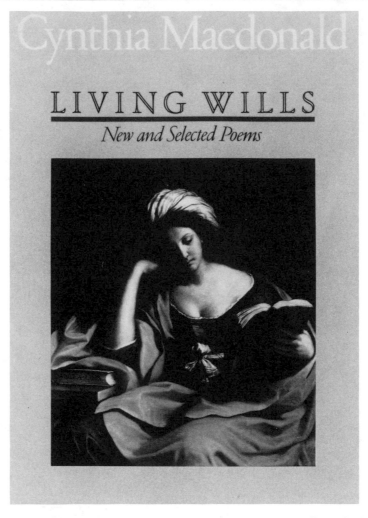

Cover for Macdonald's 1991 collection, which includes poems written since 1985 as well as selections from her earlier books

Can go a long time smoldering before you notice." But the consequences are obvious:

> it flares suddenly
> Like a red head losing her temper, and allows its
> 　　long bright hair
> To tangle in the air, letting you know again
> That what shelters you can turn incendiary in a
> 　　flash.
> And then there is only the space of what has
> 　　been,
> An absence in the field, memory in the shape of
> 　　a woman.

Joseph Patrick Kennedy (*Houston Chronicle*, 17 November 1985), another critic who praised *Alternate Means of Transport*, indicated that the title
poem was evidence of the author's "deep view of
psychic and social phenomena." And Wendy
Lesser wrote in her review for *Book World* (2 February 1986) that this volume reveals Macdonald's
"ability to create compelling visual images woven
magically together, like a Chagall dream-painting
designed by Freud."

That Macdonald's 1985 book bears a title so
different from the others attests to her attempt
to break out of the mold she herself had created
by pursuing similar subjects and themes. Careful
study of the book and the criticism of it, however, reveals a slighter stretching of the boundaries of her familiar poetic territory than was perhaps the intent. *Alternate Means of Transport* continues to rely on surreal situations and characters
set in a dreamlike matrix. However, it does include poems that explore less-familiar territory—
such as the seemingly mundane topics of book-
binding, apartment living, and the wearing of
hats. Her approach to these subjects remains
highly symbolic, and she often elevates the mundane to the level of myth, though with fewer of
the pyrotechnics of her early verse.

What the reader most notices about Macdonald's poetry is her use of the grotesque to comment on the ordinary, along with the utilization of multiple viewpoints within each poem. Although some critics consider this technique a tendency toward what Karp calls "continual chatter about disconnected relationships," most agree that the collagelike dissonance is necessary to Macdonald's purpose. Carol Muske, for instance, asserts that Macdonald's work is a "circus of variety . . . not just verse that will suffice, [but] verse that will alter everything we take for granted about poetry" (*Los Angeles Times*, 29 December 1985). The reader of all her collections notices a marked change from the flippant humor and sensationalism of the first books to the developing poise and integrity of the last ones. Macdonald's 1991 collection, *Living Wills*, includes her best verse from the previous collections (except for "Burying the Babies," which was deemed too long), as well as poems she has been working on since 1985. The new work continues to show the reader what Daniel Bourne has described as "poetry that goes beyond an isolated lyric into a multidimensional narrative of a world that is by turns fascinating and disturbing, a world combining the front pages of our newspapers with the fairy tales of our childhood" (*Artful Dodge*, 1990).

Interview:
Daniel Bourne, "*Artful Dodge* Interviews Cynthia Macdonald," *Artful Dodge*, 18/19 (Fall/Winter 1990): 74-96.

References:
Linda Gregerson, "Unequal Seas," *Parnassus*, 8 (1980): 210-228;
Robert Holland, "Six or Seven Fools," *Poetry*, 129 (February 1977): 285-295;
Colette Inez, "Trio for Saxophone, Harpsichord, and Coloratura," *Parnassus*, 2 (Fall/Winter 1973): 77-86;
Vickie Karp, "Two Poets: Several Worlds Apiece," *Parnassus*, 12 (1985): 407-421;
Robert Pinsky, "Far From Prose," *Poetry*, 123 (January 1974): 241-245;
Stanley Poss, "A Gathering of Poets," *Western Humanities Review*, 30 (Autumn 1976): 353-368;
Alberta T. Turner, *50 Contemporary Poets: The Creative Process* (New York: McKay, 1977), pp. 205-212;
R. L. Widmann, "The Poetry of Cynthia Macdonald," in *Feminist Criticism: Essays on Theory, Poetry and Prose*, edited by Cheryl L. Brown and Karen Olson (Metuchen, N.J.: Scarecrow Press, 1978), pp. 188-197.

Walter McDonald
(18 July 1934 -   )

Charlotte M. Wright
University of North Texas

BOOKS: *Caliban in Blue* (Lubbock: Texas Tech Press, 1976);

One Thing Leads to Another (New Braunfels, Tex.: Cedar Rock, 1978);

Anything, Anything (Seattle: L'Epervier, 1980);

Working Against Time (Walnut Creek, Cal.: Calliope, 1981);

Burning the Fence (Lubbock: Texas Tech Press, 1981);

Witching on Hardscrabble (Peoria, Ill.: Spoon River Poetry, 1985);

The Flying Dutchman (Columbus: Ohio State University Press, 1987);

Splitting Wood for Winter (Denton: University of North Texas Press, 1988);

After the Noise of Saigon (Amherst: University of Massachusetts Press, 1988);

Rafting the Brazos (Denton: University of North Texas Press, 1988);

Night Landings (New York: Harper & Row, 1989);

A Band of Brothers: Stories from Vietnam (Lubbock: Texas Tech University Press, 1989).

OTHER: *A Catch-22 Casebook*, edited by McDonald and Frederick T. Kiley (New York: Crowell, 1973);

Texas Stories & Poems, edited by McDonald and James P. White (Dallas: Texas Center for Writers, 1978).

Walter McDonald is a Texas poet who has written of the dry, harsh landscape of west Texas in such a way as to universalize its rural themes. He is a soldier-poet whose evocations of Vietnam have found ready acceptance among others whose lives were also changed by that war. In his own words (in a 1986 interview with Christopher Woods), he is "more moved by struggle . . . than by flaccid prettiness," so the reader does not find in McDonald's nature verse mere pastoral images, nor in his war poems mere sentimental renderings of buddies and experiences gone by. His style is clean, spare, and masculine, and he is likely to use hunting, fishing, farming, or flying

an airplane as metaphors for existence. If Ernest Hemingway had grown up in west Texas and been a poet instead of a novelist, he might well have written poetry like McDonald's.

Born on 18 July 1934 in Lubbock, Texas, to Vera (Graves) and C. A. McDonald, Walter McDonald grew up on those plains that heavily influence his poetry. His father was a house painter who had fought in World War I. Walter stayed in Lubbock after graduating from high school, attending what was then Texas Technological College (now Texas Tech University), earning a B.A. in 1956 and an M.A. in 1957. It was there, in 1952, that he joined the ROTC and thus began the military involvement that also became an integral part of his poetry. On 28 August 1959 he married artist Carol Ham of Austin. Their three children are Cynthia (now Mrs. Kelly Wright), David, and Charles.

McDonald is an unusual poet in that his early literary efforts were directed toward writing novels. He had written two of them before he went to the University of Iowa in 1962 to begin work on a Ph.D., and he wrote two more before completing his degree requirements in 1966. After a tour of duty in Vietnam from 1969 to 1970, he wrote two more. These novels remain unpublished, except for a short story, "The Prodigal" (*South Dakata Review*, Summer 1972), being based on one, and excerpts from others being incorporated into the stories in *A Band of Brothers* (1989). McDonald did not try writing poetry until one of his colleagues showed him some of his own poetry at the United States Air Force Academy (where McDonald taught from 1960 to 1962 before going to Iowa).

The poems resulting from McDonald's first efforts were published separately between 1971 and 1974 in literary magazines such as *Prairie Schooner* and the *South Dakota Review*, and they were compiled to produce *Caliban in Blue*, published in 1976, five years after his return to Texas Tech University to teach. Winner of the 1976 Texas Institute of Letters Poetry Award,

this small book was reviewed not only in Texas but also in several southwestern publications, and it has continued to be one of his most frequently discussed books. In it are direct and indirect references to Hemingway, James Joyce, and Joseph Conrad, evidence of McDonald's previous interest in the novel. The most frequent comment made by reviewers concerned the intensely sexual imagery used in the poems about war and flying, particularly in the "Caliban" poems. Most reviewers approved of his avoidance of both sentimental and moralistic interpretations in the war poems. Jack Myers (*Southwest Review*, Winter 1977) noticed that McDonald's voice took on "the strong, flat character of the contemporary International Style," and Susan Wood (*Texas Books in Review*, 1977) agreed, saying the book contained "modest poems, not pretending anything or demanding too much."

Three poems from *Caliban in Blue* have continued to be singled out by critics for comment: "Interview With a Guy Named Fawkes, U.S. Army," "Rocket Attack," and "The Jungles of Da Lat." In the third is the especially memorable image of a tiger that has turned man-eater by living off battle carrion: "a most delicate monster / swaying away, its pendant belly / sleek with easy feasts."

Though *Caliban in Blue* was well received, especially for a first book of poetry, McDonald thought his experiment with poetry was completed, since he still considered himself primarily a novelist. However, when poet Donald Justice asked why none of McDonald's poems revealed his Texas roots, McDonald says he "began to feel the call of this wild, semi-arid West Texas" and chose poetry rather than fiction as his method of exploration (1985 interview with Woods). The result was a chapbook published by a small Texas press in 1978, *One Thing Leads to Another*, whose title is ironic in light of McDonald's final turning from the novel to poetry, and of his turning from war-oriented themes to the more ordinary concerns of family and community. He maintains his "spare, tenacious" style of writing in this book, according to Billi M. Rogers (*English in Texas*, Fall 1979), but also incorporates humor, which is largely absent in the previous one.

Anything, Anything (1980) was McDonald's first collection to be published outside of Texas and the first to receive critical attention in nationally distributed magazines. A. J. Backes of the *Library Journal* (15 January 1981) noted McDonald's concern with "family and civilization and the pressures which are threatening both," a continuation of his interests evident in the previous chapbook. McDonald also continued his use of simple language, practicing, according to Backes, "what James Wright called 'the flat poem,' a bare, direct statement about everyday life without rhetorical flourishes." The book's two middle sections contain poems reverberating with hints of evil gnawing at the edges of the everyday experience. In "At the Human Development Center," for instance, luck is for some people "no more than fifteen minutes of crying / in a room with someone who doesn't / beat them." There are several poems in which McDonald returns to combat themes, although the wars are between biblical characters such as David and Goliath, or the devil and human beings, or small boys with BB guns and neighbors trying to raise pigeons, rather than between the United States and Vietnam.

By 1981 McDonald had written enough poetry to develop his own voice. Until then, he says in the 1985 interview with Woods, he had "struggled along under an assumed yoke of too much literary allusion," stemming from the notion he had picked up in college that "T. S. Eliot was THE poet." By 1981 he had read enough of such poets as James Dickey, Richard Hugo, James Wright, Theodore Roethke, and Miller Williams to realize the many interpretive options available to a poet. He began to relax and enjoy the writing process, and editors all over the country responded by publishing the results. *Cimarron Review, New Mexico Humanities Review, Writers' Forum, Kansas Quarterly*, and *Southwest Review* are just a few of the journals that accepted his poetry during this time. He published two books in 1981, one in California and another in west

Cover for McDonald's 1988 collection, which includes some poems based on his experience as an air force pilot in Vietnam

Texas. *Working Against Time*, a chapbook, shows his continued immersion in west Texas family and community life. Its poems are less dramatic than in previous books and deal with subjects such as driving across the parched desert, facing a winter's first chill, or spending time with children. The language continues to be simple: "No trees, few / temptations. Work. Occasional / reproduction: children / who moved on toward the coast" ("Estacado"). Also continuing is McDonald's unsentimental attitude, as evidenced by such poems as "Crossing West Texas," wherein he describes how "spooked jack rabbits / crunch under the tires / like light bulbs."

Burning the Fence (1981) is similar. The anonymous reviewer for *Choice* praised the book as "in-the-grain American poetry" in the tradition of Edgar Lee Masters and William Carlos Williams (December 1981). James Hoggard noted this same wholesomeness and sense of family in "the theme of return to place of origin," in the "conservatism," and in the "plain-speech approach" (*Dal-*

las Times Herald, 3 January 1982). By this time McDonald had largely abandoned the obvious sexual overtones of many of his earlier poems, and he was relying less often on Vietnam for subject matter. Still, most reviewers seemed to overlook the five poems in *Burning the Fence* that mention the war. Two are especially haunting evocations of its effect on individual men who survived. The title character in "Al Croom" lived through the war by "daring the Russian / rockets / to do him in," but he paid a high price for his bravado: "When they shipped him home / it took triple straps / to bind him. / They treated him / for months." And the nameless man in "Veteran," walking to the park on aluminum legs, imagines that "leaves lie in the park / like tiny bombs / ready to explode. Someday / someone raking / will strike a fuse. / We'll all be killed." Regardless of whether or not they deal directly with war, the best poems in *Burning the Fence* "deal with madness, death, and impermanence," as reviewer George Hendrick noted (*Texas Books in Review*, 1982). McDonald himself, in his 1985 interview with Woods, admitted: "In fiction, I had written about Vietnam, and thought I had exorcised the haunting tone through those stories. But when I turned more and more to poetry from 1977 on, I seemed to go through it all over again, but changed from Vietnam to Lubbock, from images of war to surreal images of ordinary situations turned bizarre, the nightmare possibilities of the inevitable."

By 1981 McDonald had published five books in six years. It would be four more years, however, before he published another one. This was not due to writer's block or lack of interest—quite the contrary. Being awarded a faculty development leave from Texas Tech in 1983 and a National Endowment for the Arts Creative Writing Fellowship Grant in 1984, he was able to concentrate full-time on his writing for almost three years. In 1985 he published *Witching on Hardscrabble*, a work in which Hoggard noticed a "maturity and coherence of vision" more obvious than in McDonald's previous efforts (*Dallas Morning News*, 30 March 1986). The book won another Texas Institute of Letters Poetry Award for McDonald and received positive reviews throughout the Southwest. Poems such as "All the Green Summer," "Concorde," "The Norther," "Growing Up Flying," and "Spending the Night Near Matador" were mentioned as examples of McDonald's concern with chronicling what Roger Jones called "his region's psychic influence over its people"

(*Review of Texas Books*, Spring 1986). One short poem that sums up this influence is "Settling the Plains," which ends with these words: "Whatever / they put in the earth they believed / would live if it rained / or the wind blew." This book, more than any other, established McDonald's appeal to a southwestern audience, a regionalism not based just on his images of the land, however. He told Woods in 1986 that region does not always have to mean geography; it can mean "an attitude, or a posture toward certain events."

The Flying Dutchman (1987) also focuses on McDonald's southwestern concerns and attitudes but contains more references to flying and combat than did *Witching on Hardscrabble*. Thomas Zigal of the *Dallas Morning News* remarked: "In no other context is McDonald more convincing than in his poems about war and the flying of fighter planes" (10 April 1988). West Texas, however, is clearly the major concern in *The Flying Dutchman*; Zigal also noted McDonald's reliance on "words elemental to . . . [the] Panhandle world—caliche, hardscrabble, hardpan, [and] stubble." Even so, as B. H. Fairchild (*Texas Books in Review*, Fall 1988) noted, McDonald has "far larger concerns than what is normally called regionalist," evident in such poems as "A Woman Acquainted with the Night" and "Hauling over Wolf Creek Pass in Winter." From the latter, an allegorical poem about a trucker hauling a load of pigs, comes this image:

> Wolves plunge through deep snow
> to the trees, the whole pack starving.
> Revving up, the truck rolls down the highway
> faster, the last flight out of Da Nang.
> I shove into third gear, fourth,
> the herd of pigs screaming, the load
> lurching and banging on every turn,
> almost delivered, almost airborne.

Critical acclaim for this book also came in the form of awards. It received the University of Cincinnati's George Elliston Poetry Award and the Soeurette Diehl Fraser/Natalie Ornish Award of the Texas Institute of Letters.

A chapbook, *Splitting Wood for Winter* (1988), consists of poems McDonald read during the University of North Texas Contemporary Poets Reading Series. It begins with a poem that hints at the instinctively animal nature hidden within a human's heart, and it ends with a poem in which cast-off artifacts are hidden in a trunk in the attic. A more important publication is *After the Noise of Saigon* (also 1988), which won the University of Massa-

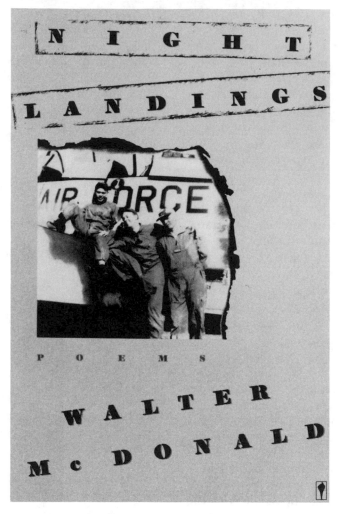

Dust jacket for the collection of poems that James Dickey called "remarkable . . . written from the vision of a man sustained by machinery in terror and exhilaration above the planet"

chusetts Juniper Prize. As the title indicates, this book is a clear return to war themes. "The Food Pickers of Saigon," for instance, describes "those tiny anonymous people who could stick / their hands inside and claw out whatever / remained, scooping it into jars, into their / mouths." In "War Games" a group of men is concentrating on a game played with imaginary dice, while "rockets that crashed down / on the base always killed somebody else." Many of the poems concerning ordinary life also have violent undertones, such as "The Rodeo Fool," "The Guilt of Survivors," and "The Eyes in Joe Hall's Shed."

After the Noise of Saigon is McDonald's most disturbing book, the tone being what Hoggard described as "earthier and more searing than [in] his previous volumes" (*Texas Observer*, 14 October 1988). However, Hoggard also noted that the war poems are "characterized by sympathetic un-

derstanding rather than rage or bewilderment," and Zigal (*Dallas Morning News*, 10 April 1988) wrote that they are "never macho or hawkish, [since] the poet is . . . concerned with ordinary men thrust into nightmarish danger." West Texas themes do play a role in *After the Noise of Saigon*, but the images seem less positive and wholesome than those in previous volumes. Ironically, it is in this book that Hoggard noticed a tendency toward more musical phrasing.

Recently published are *Rafting the Brazos* (1988), from the University of North Texas Press, and *Night Landings* (1989), McDonald's first book from a New York publisher. While *Night Landings* continues to combine poems about Texas with those about Vietnam, its emphasis—despite the title—is on the land and people of Texas. Lines from "Torching Grandfather's Weed Fields," in a section entitled "Things About to Disappear," are indicative of the sense of impending doom that haunts this collection: "starving armadillos / and skunks waddle in at night / by twos, the word gone out / of people up to something." On the other hand, the dominant tone of *Rafting the Brazos* is based on a sense of everything being in its proper place, reminiscent of *Working Against Time* or *Burning the Fence*. Vietnam is mentioned only once or twice. The only weapons in *Rafting the Brazos* are hunters' rifles and fishermen's lures; the only enemies are the elements; and the only blood comes from a castrated calf. Though not sentimental, this collection comes the closest of any of McDonald's works to being a sustained nostalgic view of southwestern rural living.

McDonald has an intense poetic voice. Though he draws on his experiences in Vietnam, Texas, and, to a lesser extent, Colorado, he avoids the confessional mode so prevalent in much of today's poetry. He is adamant in his rejection of biographical criticism of his work, as he told Woods in 1985: "In no way do I feel that poetry—or fiction—is a way of conveying my own facts to a reader so that he or she will say 'Wow, you mean you actually did that?' Experience is valuable for what it is, then the writing takes over: I lie a lot, in poems. I'm not there, frank and undisguised, in a poem or a short story.... I'm trying to write fiction and poems, not autobiography." Though McDonald treats serious subjects, his tone is never ponderous. His poems, as Zigal says, avoid "sterile abstractions or intellectual word-play," instead depicting in a nominalist, straightforward way images of "real life exposed to the bone." With over eleven hundred separately published poems and eleven collections, with numerous awards for both his short fiction and poetry, and with his continued involvement in teaching creative writing, McDonald's influence in contemporary poetics continues to in-

crease. In addition, his publication of *Night Landings* with Harper and Row may indicate a growing audience on a national level. Since 1983 his poems have appeared in such periodicals as the *Atlantic*; *Poetry*; the *Nation*; *Paris Review*; *American Scholar*; *Sewanee Review*; *Kenyon Review*; *American Poetry Review*; *Southern Review*; *Antioch Review*; *TriQuarterly*; *New Criterion*; and *North American Review*. He received an NEA Creative Writing Fellowship Grant in 1989.

It is highly unlikely that he will explore subjects other than those he has already mined, although *A Band of Brothers* (1989), a book of short stories, indicates that future publications will include fiction. Walter McDonald is a poet who balances things: the past and the present; the mountains and the plains; and killing to survive and nurturing to assure life's continuance. Unlike Uncle Bubba in "Honky-Tonk Blues" (in *Night Landings*), who keeps "humming old songs like a scab / he keeps picking at over and over," McDonald has put all his old images, as well as new ones, into the base of a kaleidoscope, and with each new poem he turns it another time, offering the reader a variety of startling reflections.

Interviews:

Christopher Woods, "An Interview: Walter McDonald," *Touchstone*, 10 (1985): 3-12;

Woods, "An Interview with Walter McDonald," *Re: Arte Liberales*, 13 (Fall 1986): 1-6.

References:

W. D. Ehrhart, "Soldier-Poets of the Vietnam War," *Virginia Quarterly Review*, 63 (Spring 1987): 246-265;

Robert Frank, "Walter McDonald: Poet of Sight and Insight," *Poet Lore*, 80 (Winter 1986): 220-226.

Vassar Miller
(19 July 1924 -   )

James T. F. Tanner
University of North Texas

BOOKS: *Adam's Footprint* (New Orleans: New Orleans Poetry Journal, 1956);

Wage War on Silence (Middletown, Conn.: Wesleyan University Press, 1960);

My Bones Being Wiser (Middletown, Conn.: Wesleyan University Press, 1963);

Onions and Roses (Middletown, Conn.: Wesleyan University Press, 1968);

If I Could Sleep Deeply Enough (New York: Liveright, 1974);

Approaching Nada (Houston: Wings, 1976);

Small Change (Houston: Wings, 1977);

Selected and New Poems, 1950-1980, edited by Robert Bonazzi (Austin: Latitudes, 1981);

Struggling to Swim on Concrete (New Orleans: New Orleans Poetry Journal, 1983).

OTHER: "What Is a Poet?," in *Poets on Poetry*, edited by Howard Nemerov (New York: Basic Books, 1966), pp. 114-132;

Despite This Flesh: The Disabled in Stories and Poems, edited by Miller (Austin: University of Texas Press, 1984).

Since 1956, when *Adam's Footprint* was published, Vassar Miller has been considered an accomplished lyric poet. Praised by such colleagues as Denise Levertov, Howard Nemerov, James Wright, and Larry McMurtry, her poems have appeared in nine published collections, in hundreds of periodicals, and in more than fifty anthologies, including Donald Hall's *New Poets of England and America*, Louis Untermeyer's *Modern American Poetry*, and Chad Walsh's *Today's Poets*. On three separate occasions the Texas Institute of Letters has presented her its poetry award, for *Adam's Footprint*, *Wage War on Silence* (1960), and *My Bones Being Wiser* (1963). Leon Stokesbury, himself a Texas poet of considerable reputation, has referred to her (in *Texas Books in Review*, 1988) as "Texas's greatest poet," and this seems to be the general opinion throughout the state; nationally, though not so well known as in her home state,

she is highly respected among connoisseurs of modern poetry.

Vassar Miller was born on 19 July 1924 in Houston, Texas, to Jesse Gustavus Miller, an important Houston real-estate developer, and Vassar Morrison Miller. The young Miller was born with cerebral palsy. Because her mother died when Miller was only a year old, her stepmother became the dominant female influence in her life. Miller began writing at the age of eight when her father brought home a typewriter, a mechanical aid of profound importance for one afflicted with her disorder. In "Subterfuge" she introduces her father, who enters the room carrying the typewriter:

> Bearing it in his arms like an awkward bouquet
> for his spastic child who sits down
> on the floor, one knee on the frame
> of the typewriter, and holding her left wrist
> with her right hand, in that precision known
> to the crippled, pecks at the keys
> with a sparrow's preoccupation.

Since early in life, when a maid took her to evangelistic meetings in a tent, Miller has been deeply religious. Despite her formidable physical handicap, she was fortunate enough—and determined enough—to secure a good education in Houston schools. With the assistance and encouragement of her stepmother, she learned to read, attended junior and senior high school, and earned a B.S. (1947) and an M.A. (1952) from the University of Houston. For the master's degree she wrote, significantly for her later creative work, a thesis on mysticism in the poetry of Edwin Arlington Robinson. She later became an instructor in creative writing (1975-1976) at St. John's School in Houston.

Because of the appreciation for Miller's work in Houston, the Wings Press was founded as a vehicle for the publication and distribution of her work. As well as many poems, she has published several short stories, many book reviews, and an anthology of poems and stories having to

Vassar Miller

do with the disabled (1984). Despite her physical handicap, she has traveled to Europe and elsewhere. A speech impediment associated with her disability has not prevented her from teaching and making public appearances. She continues to live in Houston on Vassar Street, named for her mother, the street and home a legacy from her father's prowess as a real-estate developer. Fortunately, Miller's father left her an ample trust fund. She has never married.

Miller came to the attention of all Texans interested in the literature of the state when, in a 1981 speech at the Fort Worth Art Museum, McMurtry voiced his opinion that she was perhaps the greatest author Texas had produced. Indeed, McMurtry's national reputation has been of considerable assistance to Miller. His clear statement (in the *Texas Observer*, 23 October 1981) that she was the one Texas writer for whom he has "an unequivocal admiration" has had an im-

pact on her reputation in Texas and around the nation.

Miller's themes center on personal concerns: God (sometimes referred to as "Nada," signifying the ineffable, the unknowable); religious faith (involving both belief and doubt—the need to believe and the necessity of doubt); suffering (physical and spiritual); loneliness (brought about by a life isolated from others); acceptance (the need to be accepted by others, to be accepted by God, and—perhaps most important—her own need to accept God); silence (the inexpressible, or that which cannot be absolutely or ultimately articulated); sleep (as the seducer, as death, as reliever of pain, and as restorer); death (as "the dark nurse" that puts one "to bed," and in terms of suicide, nothingness, and eternity); loss (of innocence, of the joys of childhood, and of friends); the erotic (coupled with conventional yearnings for mystical union with God); the role of the religious poet (whose exuberance is associated with youth and childhood); and the barren inadequacy of modern technology. Readers will observe that humor, most often self-deprecating, is rarely absent in Miller's poems, whatever the thematic concerns.

Miller's imagery is emotionally charged, sometimes violent, often erotic, but always appropriate in context. Her father is "ghost, child's god"; her tears of suffering are "orgasmic shivers / along the spine of Midnight Mass"; Christ is a "pioneer in pain"; her diseased body is "this house of gutted portals" and "this ravaged stack"; persons intolerant of her physical disability "would sleep upon the margin of my moans"; sexual frustration is "the jig and jerk / of titillated nerves"; the poet's persona is "the dog-self"; and time is "an angry little beast / clawing inside us, tearing us to shreds."

Miller's prosody is now better understood, thanks to Bruce Kellner's 1988 essay "Blood in the Bone: Vassar Miller's Prosody." Variations on the Japanese *katuata* and haiku, blank verse, open verse, dramatic monologues, villanelles—all these and more can be found in Miller's work. She has always written in traditional forms as well as in experimental modes, and the sonnet has been one of her favorite forms. Miller has said, in her 1983 interview with Karla Hammond, that Gerard Manley Hopkins's "sprung rhythm" has influenced her work, but that it is something that "I sense rather than understand." (Miller's first poem was published in the *Hopkins Review*.)

Other major influences on Miller's poetry are Emily Dickinson, whose stylistic and thematic concerns most closely resemble hers; Edwin Arlington Robinson; the British metaphysicals (John Donne, George Herbert, and Richard Crashaw); and Flannery O'Connor, as Miller's poem "Affinity," in *Struggling to Swim on Concrete* (1983), makes clear. Readers will be occasionally reminded of the American Puritan poet Edward Taylor, though Miller's poetry is not so heavily theological. In the 1960s her work had affinities with the confessionalists Sylvia Plath and Robert Lowell; indeed, the confessional style has, over the years, become more predominant in Miller's work. One may suspect, because of her erotically charged imagery, that Walt Whitman is among her affinities, though there is much in his work that is incompatible with hers. (In the *Houston Chronicle* photograph included in editor Steven Ford Brown's *Heart's Invention: On the Poetry of Vassar Miller* [1988], a copy of *Leaves of Grass* is clearly visible on her bookshelf.)

Three troublesome problems arise in the critical evaluation of Miller's poetic work. First, she has been approached too often as a Texas poet, implying for some that her work is of regional importance only, an inaccurate view considering her record of national publication. Second, Miller is an unusual phenomenon in contemporary literature: a religious poet; some readers, unfortunately, are quick to reject her work on purely subjective grounds, an antipathy to orthodox religious belief. A careful reading of her poetry will demonstrate, however, that she is a poet, first, and a religious mystic, second; religious belief provides her work with substance and texture, much as can be said of the work of T. S. Eliot. Third, her physical disability has entered into discussions of her literary production. No one will deny that cerebral palsy has affected Miller's poetry. Whether her disease has influenced critical evaluation of her work, or whether it ought to do so, is a matter of judgment. The reader and critic must, therefore, be on guard against prejudging Miller's work on provincial, theological, or sympathetic grounds. The poetry speaks for itself, and many critics attest to its power.

A member of the Poetry Society of Texas and affiliated with literary groups in Houston and around the state, Miller was appointed an alternate poet laureate of Texas for the year 1982, an appointment she took seriously. But Miller is not in any sense a propagandist for the Lone Star State. According to Frances Sage, in *Heart's Invention*, Miller is "a Texas poet, though not a poet of Texas. . . . Although she has lived all her life in Texas, nothing in her poetry evokes it. The sources of her poetry are her own religious needs and feelings. She could just as well live any place." In her interview with Hammond, Miller stated, "I would have dealt with the same themes wherever I lived. However, there are some natural events—cicadas, hurricanes, long hot summers, drab unexciting Januarys (no snow storms, few snow storms) that I wouldn't mention if I lived, say, in New England." Still, those qualities regarded as marks of a Texas writer—a strong sense of place and a passion for nature and rural life—are not entirely absent from Miller's work. The "place" she describes is, of course, her inner consciousness, an interesting and terrible "place" indeed; but it is described in images of long, hot summers, drab, unexciting Januarys, hurricanes, and cicadas. And Paul Christensen, a leading authority on Texas poetry, has shown (in *Heart's Invention*) the correlations between Miller's poetic imagery and the southern nostalgia for a long-lost innocence and simplicity. Says Christensen, "her themes are all the losses involved in change, and of how one copes with them." Ironically, though, the tendency is for northern critics to scorn her work because it is regional, and for Texas critics to neglect it because it supposedly lacks regionality. This critical catch-22 will likely be a continuing problem.

Religion is of central importance in the poetry of Miller. Her parents were Presbyterian, and she attended that church for a time; later, the Episcopal faith strongly intrigued her; in recent years she has become affiliated with the Covenant Baptist Church. She told Hammond, "I still love the Episcopal Church ... with its liturgy and its emphasis on the sacraments. I don't know that the change in churches has affected my religious experience so much as the other way around. The change was more for personal than theological reasons." The Covenant Baptist Church is not fundamentalist, at least in Miller's opinion; it has a liberal congregation, one which has adopted some of the features of the Catholic church—for example, the church year. Miller has said that she feels more accepted in this congregation than in any other. Some readers of her poetry simply assume that Miller is Catholic, because of her frequent use of Catholic liturgical imagery. Her poem "Accepting," for example, was composed after she attended Ash Wednesday services in a black Roman Catholic parish. It is true that her paternal grandfather was Catholic and that she often heard her father speak of him.

Occasionally Miller is peeved about reviewers who discount religious poetry or downgrade poets who claim religious faith. "Most critics," she told Hammond, "seem to think that any expression of religious faith is dishonest." A continuation of the Christian mystical tradition can be seen in her work. As Sage puts it, "To examine her poetry is to trace a life, a life marked by her two great spiritual needs: to say the unsayable and to accept a life cut off from others." Kenneth Maclean has pointed out (in *Heart's Invention*) that Miller has over the years remained "an orthodox, Christian religious poet, though not one dependent, except casually, on theology as subject matter. She is also rarely biblical."

Adam's Footprint, now long out of print, marked the appearance of a gifted lyric poet. It contains forty-three brief lyric poems, arranged in alphabetical order according to title (except for the two concluding poems). "Adam's Footprint," the first poem of the collection, describes the nature of humanity, but without the expected Calvinistic context. Adam's footprint is the trace of Adam in the foot of every small child who loves "to hop / On round plump bugs and make them stop." The general theme of the collection is acceptance, in all its variety. Especially powerful is "Reciprocity," a sonnet that attempts to make explicit exactly what mutual acceptance in love entails:

> You who, as though you wished me mere Good
> 　　Morning,
> Would smash your heart upon the hardest stones
> Of my distress as when you once, unscorning,
> Would sleep upon the margin of my moans—
> I yield my want, this house of gutted portals,
> All to your want, I yield this ravaged stack,
> In testimony that between two mortals
> No gift may be except a giving back.
> What present could I make you from what skill
> When your one need is me to need you still?

Miller's second collection, *Wage War on Silence*, received high praise from James Wright, reviewing the book for *Poetry* in 1961: "her formal sense is almost always adequate to the meaning, which in turn is to be found in the intensity of her feeling. Her lyrics, invariably brief, are religious and, sometimes, erotic; though sometimes these two related terrors meet in an embrace which, as [Pablo] Neruda says somewhere, makes a child leap into the bottom of the earth.... As far as traditional form in poetry goes, she has no peer among the younger contemporary writers that I have read. It is just this perfect formal mastery—with a simplicity of diction that is not accidental, and that reveals the concentration of a powerful intellect—which makes especially remarkable Miss Miller's experiments in freer forms...." Miller's concern in *Wage War on Silence* is to celebrate poetry's eternal attempt to utter that which cannot, in any ultimate sense, be articulated.

My Bones Being Wiser, Miller's 1963 collection, is seen by some as having a more pronounced feminist tendency. In her interview with Hammond, Miller answered a pointed question about the feminism that had been ascribed to her in an anonymous review in the *ALA Booklist* (15 March 1964) by saying that "although certainly I am pro-ERA, frankly, as a handicapped individual I have been put down by as many women as

Vassar Miller (photograph copyright 1982 by Nicholas Russell)

men, so somehow I feel a little left out of the concerns of women." Denise Levertov, in the *New York Times Book Review* (21 June 1964), wrote that a few of the poems in the collection were marred by sentimentality but that most were "spare, taut, and exact."

Onions and Roses (1968), Miller's next collection, contains fifty-nine poems and is more confessional and personal in content than earlier volumes. A poignant example is "On Approaching My Birthday": "my mother bore me, as I say, / then died shortly thereafter, no doubt / of her disgust and left me her disease / when I grew up to wither into truth." The title *Onions and Roses* suggests that the collection contains poems of bitterness as well as poems of beauty and gentleness.

In *If I Could Sleep Deeply Enough* (1974) Miller longs for the gift of restorative sleep, forgetfulness, and release from physical pain and exhaustive introspection. Death is never far off

when Miller is speaking of sleep, nor is the symbolic embrace of the lover. In terms of form *If I Could Sleep Deeply Enough* is experimental when compared to earlier collections. As Kellner has pointed out, "only half a dozen of over forty poems employ rhyme in any conventional sense; there are only three sonnets, one of which is unrhymed despite some vocalic echoes. Several poems operate in three-line stanzas, sometimes in parallel syllabification, sometimes drawing tension from contradictions in line length."

Approaching Nada (1976) was composed in Phoenix, Arizona. Ordinarily Miller prefers to work at home, where she can be comfortable with her books and typewriter. In this case the inspiration of the desert landscape elicited a characteristically sensual vision: "Here where these white-headed trees / blanched by the cold desert sun / open on rosy rock / nippled and cocked toward the sky / stabbing my eye with its gaze." *Ap-*

proaching Nada is not really a collection of poems but rather one long poem (in five parts) in chapbook form. Deeply religious in outlook, it reaffirms Miller's religious faith in the sustaining power of God's love. The title concerns her gradual approach to God; this poem is her spiritual autobiography. As she said to Hammond, "the Spanish mystics, St. Teresa, or at least St. John of the Cross, refer to God as Nada, as ineffable. Hindu mystics refer to the Ultimate reality as 'Netti,' 'Not this.' It can be equated with silence. What can you say about the ineffable?" In addition, the poem restates Miller's self-assigned role as a mystic poet with a special relationship to God and to her readers. Death is the central theme of the poem, but death is now presented without a sense of despair.

Death is also a central concern in *Small Change* (1977). One poem in particular is a death vision with highly personal reference, "Memento Mori," in memory of Anne Sexton:

> You think that I am smiling,
> but I'm practicing my death grin.
> I must wear it for a rather long time.
>
> You think that I am sleeping,
> but I'm developing my grave skills
> for when I must do death's motionless ballet.
>
> You think that I am resting,
> but I'm hunched over my decay,
> which makes do for the pretty baby I wasn't.

Selected and New Poems, 1950-1980 (1981) contains what Miller regards as the best of her poems composed over a lifetime. It has received generally favorable notices. The anonymous reviewer for *Library Journal* (15 December 1982) referred to the collection as the year's "best small press book of poetry." McMurtry, reviewing the collection for *Texas Books in Review* (1982), observed that "one of the things writers do is turn pain into honey, for their readers. No pain, no honey." McMurtry applauds Miller's dedication to her art despite her pain and suffering. Two themes of the collection are pointed out by McMurtry: first, "exhaustion of the sort that denies one sleep. Sleep is usually the lover, the seducer, in her poetry. It is the sweetness most often denied." Second, McMurtry observes the theme of "the burden of being misconceived: the failure of the healthy to see the health within the handicap—health of heart, of brain, of feeling. Over the years, she has become less respectful of

this failure." This last concern has led to her editing the poetry and short-story collection *Despite This Flesh: The Disabled in Stories and Poems* (1984), for which she wrote an impassioned introduction. Her credentials being impeccable in this area, she is able to express the truth in powerful prose: "The handicapped . . . too often have been and are being killed with kindness, stifled by overprotection, choked by subtle if sometimes unconscious snubs by genuinely good people who would swear to preferring death over hurting anybody. . . . Some of this slow death is self-inflicted; too many handicapped folk linger, bound by anger, depression, self-pity, or fear in the back bedrooms of their own minds. It is to prevent such pointless dying that this anthology has come into being." This connection is also referred to in the poem "Spastics" in *If I Could Sleep Deeply Enough*.

Of special interest in *Selected and New Poems* is "The Sun Has No History," a poem somewhat reminiscent of Anne Bradstreet's *Contemplations*. Man, unlike the animals and vegetables, has a "history"; he keeps a diary, feels nostalgia, remembers, and leaves fingerprints. Hope does not reside in the dumbness of nature. Only man has the capacity for hope of something beyond a historical nature: "The sun has no history. / Only I, bearing / my Adam and Eve on my back, / dragging under, dragged down, may leap / up to the saddle of hope." Hope is indeed the appropriate mode for the orthodox Christian poet.

Struggling to Swim on Concrete is the ninth book in Miller's poetic canon. Christensen wrote of it in the *Texas Observer* (6 August 1982): "Through craftsmanship, she is beautiful, lithe, eager; one misses her spirit in overlooking this telling surface of her work. Her technique is not merely historical, though it connects with a deep past of religious introspection and quest poetry, but rather archetypal, an economy of the soul, as she longs to perfect the ruined part of herself. These poems harrow hell and also glitter like stained glass windows in their rigor and distillations . . . [and] her vision is singularly this hidden self of beasts and fictions, gods and monsters, which links her to Southern fiction as well as to Central and South American literature of this century. . . ." A sonnet sequence, "Love's Bitten Tongue," which closes the volume, demonstrates Miller's technical brilliance. There are twenty-two English sonnets linked by virtue of the fact that each concluding line serves as an ensuing initial line; in each case, transformations in punctuation, syntax, and rhythm advance the sequence or heighten the significance of it.

Miller has been frequently quoted as speaking of poetry's "trinitarian function: creative, redemptive, and sanctifying." For amplification she told Hammond, "Poetry is creative in that it makes an artifact where none was before, only a mass of thoughts and emotions and sensations; it is redemptive, since it makes art out of non-art, something of beauty and value; it is sanctifying in that it confers order upon chaos. These three functions are one. . . . The poetic challenge of the time is what it has always been, to write with passion and precision." But modern life presents unusual challenges to the poet. According to Miller, contemporary technocrats have a tendency to forget that "Know thyself" remains the essential guide to wisdom. For example, her poem "Report" (in Margaret Royalty Edwards's *Poets Laureate of Texas*, 1966) focuses on technology in space:

> We have orbited in space,
> finding nothing at all except
> planets and stars burbling like
> wounds in sockets of darkness.
>
> We have delved deep into mind
> whose ground is a substance like garbage,
> compost, the seedbed of thought's
> unlikely architecture.
>
> Yet always we whirled
> half-hearing behind us the whisper,
> like a dog chasing his own
> unattainable tail.

Earthly beings grounded in physicality have nothing else but themselves as the final object of knowledge.

McMurtry, in the preface to *Heart's Invention*, notes five characteristics that define both the poetry and the person of Vassar Miller: clarity, precision, intelligence, honesty, and tenacity. Miller continues to demonstrate these qualities.

Interview:

Karla Hammond, "An Interview with Vassar Miller," *Pawn Review*, 7 (1983): 1-18; reprinted in *Heart's Invention: On the Poetry of Vassar Miller*, edited by Steven Ford Brown (Houston: Ford-Brown, 1988), pp. 36-59.

Bibliography:

Steven Ford Brown, "Bibliography," in *Heart's Invention: On the Poetry of Vassar Miller*, edited by Brown (Houston: Ford-Brown, 1988), pp. 160-170.

References:

Robert Bonazzi, "Passionate Scriptures of the Body," in *Heart's Invention: On the Poetry of Vassar Miller*, edited by Steven Ford Brown (Houston: Ford-Brown, 1988), pp. 121-132;

Paul Christensen, "Allowing for Such Talk," in *Heart's Invention: On the Poetry of Vassar Miller*, pp. 60-80;

Christensen, "A Dark Texas of the Soul," *Pawn Review*, 8 (1984): 1-10;

Margaret Royalty Edwards, "Vassar Miller,'" in her *Poets Laureate of Texas: 1932-1966* (San Antonio: Naylor, 1966), pp. 115-116;

Friends of the University of Houston Libraries, *A Tribute to Vassar Miller* [videotape] (Houston: University of Houston, 1983);

Bruce Kellner, "Blood in the Bone: Vassar Miller's Prosody," in *Heart's Invention: On the Poetry of Vassar Miller*, pp. 108-120;

Kenneth Maclean, "Crying Out: Aloneness and Faith in the Poetry of Vassar Miller," in *Heart's Invention: On the Poetry of Vassar Miller*, pp. 81-91;

Larry McMurtry, "Ever a Bridegroom: Reflections on the Failure of Texas Literature," *Texas Observer* (23 October 1981): 1-19; reprinted in *Range Wars: Heated Debates, Sober Reflections, and Other Assessments of Texas Writing*, edited by Craig Clifford and Tom Pilkington (Dallas: Southern Methodist University Press, 1989), pp. 13-41;

McMurtry, Preface to *Heart's Invention: On the Poetry of Vassar Miller*, pp. 11-16;

Sister Bernetta Quinn, O.S.F., "Vassar Miller's Anatomy of Silence," in *Heart's Invention: On the Poetry of Vassar Miller*, pp. 133-152;

Frances Sage, "Vassar Miller: Modern Mystic," in *Heart's Invention: On the Poetry of Vassar Miller*, pp. 19-35;

Thomas Whitbread, "Vassar Miller and Her Peers: A Causerie," in *Heart's Invention: On the Poetry of Vassar Miller*, pp. 92-107.

Papers:

The Vassar Miller Papers are in the University of Houston Special Collections.

Richard Moore
(25 September 1927 -   )

Jane Greer
Plains Poetry Journal

BOOKS: *A Question of Survival* (Athens: University of Georgia Press, 1971);
Word from the Hills: A Sonnet Sequence in Four Movements (Athens: University of Georgia Press, 1972);
Empires (Princeton, N.J.: Ontario Review, 1981);
The Education of a Mouse (Woodstock, Vt.: Countryman, 1983);
The Investigator (Brownsville, Oreg.: Story Line, 1991);
No More Bottom (Alexandria, Va.: Orchises, 1991).

Richard Moore's importance as a writer of intelligently crafted metrical poems is attested to by other well-known contemporary poets and by the frequent and consistent publication of his poetry in the finest literary journals. His versatility is remarkable, ranging from the strict Petrarchan sonnets of *Word from the Hills* (1972), through many inventive lyrical measures, a large group of elegiac-meter poems in journals, the blank verse of the narratives in *Empires* (1981), the rollicking trimeter couplets of *The Education of a Mouse* (1983), and finally the more loosely cadenced, but no less musical poems that he has been publishing recently. Also in recent years his essays on a wide variety of subjects—scientific, mathematical, and musical, as well as literary—have been appearing in distinguished journals.

Moore was born on 25 September 1927 in Stamford, Connecticut, and grew up in Riverside, Connecticut. His father, James Howard Moore, a publisher, was born in New Hampshire of Scots-Irish extraction; his mother, Gertrude Ann Ehrhardt Moore, was of German descent. Richard Moore was educated at Yale (A.B., 1950); Trinity College, Connecticut (M.A., 1956); and at Boston University from 1955 to 1957, when he left its doctoral program. He was a Fulbright Scholar (1958-1959) and a Fannie Hurst Visiting Professor at Brandeis University (1976), and he taught at the New England Conservatory of Music in Boston (1965-1988).

From 1950 to 1953 Moore was a pilot and intelligence officer in the U.S. Air Force, and from 1958 to 1962 he lived in Germany, France, and England. He was married to Vera Rowland (1952-1960) and to Janet Packer (1961-1985). His second marriage produced three daughters: Stephanie, Tania, and Claudia.

In the late 1950s Moore began submitting his poetry to periodicals, achieving success first with the *Saturday Review*. During the 1960s and 1970s his poetry appeared in many well-known literary and trade magazines, including *Harper's*, the *New Yorker*, *Atlantic Monthly*, the *Reporter*, the *Nation*, *Mademoiselle*, *Virginia Quarterly Review*, *Denver Quarterly*, *American Scholar*, *Modern Occasions*, *Poetry*, *Southern Review*, *Sewanee Review*, and *Salmagundi*.

In 1971 the University of Georgia published his first book of poems, *A Question of Survival*. Moore wrote these poems from 1949, when he was still in college, through 1970. Of the forty-eight poems, forty-six had already been published in magazines, representing only a little more than half of the eighty-four poems of his that had appeared in periodicals up to that point. This pattern in his career—of being far more successful (or more diligent) in placing poems in magazines than selling books to publishers—continues to the present day.

A Question of Survival is a 106-page collection of miscellaneous poems organized into six sections, each part being closely knit but contrasting in tone and manner with the others. The poems of the opening section, "Prospects," all have as their locale a hill overlooking a city and, taken together, state or imply the central "question of survival" of an isolated individual vis-à-vis the urban realities seen at a distance below. The next section, "War Wife," chronicling Moore's marriage to Rowland, illustrates several Moore characteristics: high intelligence, deep perception of human foibles, invincible humor, and a love of interesting metrics and rhymes, which may stem from what he calls his "passion for mathematics."

copyright 1983 by Lilian Kemp Photography

The four concluding sections are: "Apparitions," short lyrics about urban and suburban scenes; "Squibs," poems in the epigrammatic, satirical vein; "Creatures," mainly about the animal world; and "Memoir of a Pilot," an extended dramatic monologue spoken by the ghost of a pilot whose jet fighter has crashed into a hospital for retired nuns near Ottawa, Canada.

The echoes between these sections give the book an overall archlike structure: the pilot at the end stands alone, partially free of the socio-historical matrix that still holds him emotionally, much as the observer in the opening "prospect" poems stands alone, temporarily released from the city he inhabits. Similarly the second and second-to-last sections, "War Wife" and "Crea-

tures," share the same marital, domestically centered realm of experience. The first of the "creatures" is a human infant born into a world where all other things and creatures, including the poet himself, seem comically stunted, cut down, or aborted; and the other poems in this section, in their animal imagery—a polar bear performing tricks for his dinner, a scholarly cat, an irrepressible dog "making his mark" in a freshly poured cement sidewalk—reflect the same concerns. The essential difference between the two opening and two closing sections is that the direct and personal in the beginning transforms into metaphor and impersonation at the end: life, as it were, has been reshaped into art. The middle sections seem to show Moore's two basic poetic methods:

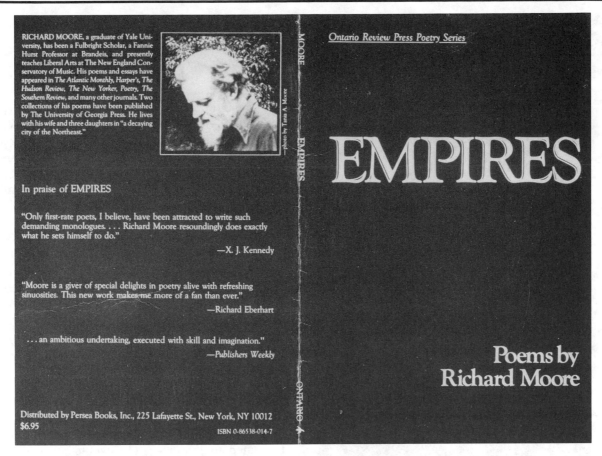

RICHARD MOORE, a graduate of Yale University, has been a Fulbright Scholar, a Fannie Hurst Professor at Brandeis, and presently teaches Liberal Arts at The New England Conservatory of Music. His poems and essays have appeared in *The Atlantic Monthly, Harper's, The Hudson Review, The New Yorker, Poetry, The Southern Review,* and many other journals. Two collections of his poems have been published by The University of Georgia Press. He lives with his wife and three daughters in "a decaying city of the Northeast."

—photo by Tania A. Moore

In praise of EMPIRES

"Only first-rate poets, I believe, have been attracted to write such demanding monologues. . . . Richard Moore resoundingly does exactly what he sets himself to do."

—X. J. Kennedy

"Moore is a giver of special delights in poetry alive with refreshing sinuosities. This new work makes me more of a fan than ever."

—Richard Eberhart

. . . an ambitious undertaking, executed with skill and imagination."

—*Publishers Weekly*

Distributed by Persea Books, Inc., 225 Lafayette St., New York, NY 10012
$6.95
ISBN 0-86538-014-7

Ontario Review Press Poetry Series

MOORE

EMPIRES

ONTARIO

EMPIRES

Poems by
Richard Moore

Cover for Moore's collection of blank-verse historical narratives (1981), which he characterizes as "covertly personal"

in "Apparitions," one sees the sudden lyrical perception of an expressive pattern or metaphor in sensuous daily experience, and in "Squibs" the equally sudden and unexpected sally of wit that leads to a satiric juxtaposition or epigram.

The origin of Moore's style was in the "metaphysical revival" of the late 1940s, which is evident in the sonnet "Struggle," in the "War Wife" section. The finely worked-out metaphor of boarding and piracy to describe an unstable love relationship would likely have pleased a New Critic of the time, though the violence of the action and the ambivalence in the feeling might have made such a critic somewhat uncomfortable.

But Moore's break with the old is clear in the opening poem in the book, "A Way Out":

Was there ever a serious, a devout me?
O, when I think of all the people
with absurd opinions about me,
including myself—reader, I feel
called upon to confess
that I'm essentially pure nothingness
and that this lust I feel to be contained
at bottom may be frivolous and feigned.

The almost flippant tone and the uninhibited relishing of rhyme seem to announce that Moore is a "frivolous" poet. Yet the poem is complex in its irony. The nothingness that the poet claims for himself is like the "hole" on which a wheel turns, and so, in a sense, it is the wheel's most important part. The conclusion has a ring of sadness and is even a little terrifying: the poet, like Odysseus, pretends to be "No One" in order to escape from the Cyclops's cave—which is not just the city below but the night itself.

This central seriousness and drama become evident in the climactic poem of the first section, "The Watch." Written in an elaborate and graceful stanza form that seems to be Moore's own invention (derived, perhaps, from the somewhat similar stanza style of Oliver Wendell Holmes's "The Chambered Nautilus"), it is to some extent a return to the earlier metaphysical style, though the ease and apparently aimless flow of its images place it clearly with the "humorous" Moore. The poet longs to see a fire in the city below and is disgusted with himself for having such a wish. But then the imagined fire, identified with an as-

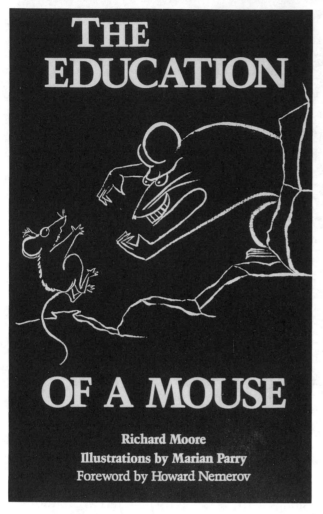

Dust jacket for the first book (1983) of Moore's "mouse epic" trilogy, a project he began in 1958. Excerpts from the second and third parts have appeared in magazines.

pect of the poet's own psyche, begins to acquire an almost mythological significance:

> A fire. It's like a sun—
> unworldly, yet the heart of one.
> A building glows with it, and draws
> crowds, men, faces alight, who pass and pause
> to watch the scarlet claws
> draw earth back into sky,
> as through a black tornado's empty eye.

In the further identifications that follow, one senses the fire as a force in history—the force in man that drives him to creation, destruction, and perhaps ultimately extinction. Yet the poem ends with this quiet stanza:

> And now the light of day
> like a burnt fire sinks away—

and like a melting gauze, has peeled
over the body of the moon, revealed
in a dark starless field,
unterrified and white,
standing out there in nothing but the night.

It is as if Moore were saying that the urge to exist (as the fire exists, by consuming) must eventually destroy humankind, and, therefore, survival lies in being content *not* to exist (in this way)—in standing quietly (and passively) "in nothing but the night." This central paradox permeates all of *A Question of Survival* and gives it unity.

Several of the first reviewers of the book complained of Moore's devotion to rhyme, which in the early 1970s had become highly unfashionable. But now the reader might be more inclined to agree with Pat Seeley, who remarked in her review in the *Denver Quarterly* (Spring 1972), "Noting good poems in this volume rapidly becomes a recounting of the table of contents."

Word from the Hills, a sequence of fifty-eight Petrarchan sonnets "in Four Movements," was written in Huntington, Vermont, between 1962 and 1964, and is Moore's reaction "to America after four years away [in Europe], my family and father, my new family and marriage growing nutty. It seemed all of a piece. The events of my life symbolical of wider themes, the historical moment, the decay of a civilization." The book has a continuous narrative interest from beginning to end, although each of the sonnets could stand alone. It is a long, taut work, its sonnet-sequence form unfamiliar to many contemporary readers, and it must have been much more demanding in the making than the mere selection and arrangement of already published material required to make *A Question of Survival*. Any modern writer of sonnets invites charges of archaism, but two things will keep the reader interested in Moore's sonnets: their surprising rhymes and metrics, which enlarge the possibilities of the Petrarchan sonnet, and their very rightness for his particular purposes in this book.

In the first sequence, or "movement," a son who has moved with his young family into his father's summerhouse—which was once a small northern hill farm—addresses the father in tones of repressed anger and sadness, setting forth the many differences between them. The second movement is more leisurely and lyrical and describes the effect of these strange surroundings on the son's foreign-born wife and on their relationship. The third movement, a literary scherzo, develops the epigrammatic possibilities of the sonnet in a series of satirical vignettes of neighbors, social issues, and contemporary political events, culminating in the son's ironic identification of himself with Lee Harvey Oswald, President John F. Kennedy's assassin. Finally, the fourth section is a kind of ghostly finale in which the spirit of the original primitive inhabitants of the land is invoked in the son's attempt to achieve a sense of union and belonging with his surroundings—historical, inherited, domestic, and personal.

The novelist Dan Wakefield, commenting on Moore's poetry in *Mademoiselle* (November 1964) when *Word from the Hills* was still in manuscript, remarked on Moore's ability to "raise the routine of contemporary life to the level of Myth." There are many examples of this in *Word from the Hills*, none more striking than sonnet 11, in which the sonnet's potentialities for grandeur are brought into full play to identify the father with the cold winter country surrounding him:

> You were so solid, father, cold and raw
> as these north winters, where your angry will
> first hardened, as the earth when the long chill
> deepens—as is this country's cruel law—
> yet under trackless snow, without a flaw
> covering meadow, road, and stubbled hill,
> the springs and muffled streams were running still,
> dark until spring came, and the awful thaw.
>
> In your decay a gentleness appears
> I hadn't guessed. . . .

Two sentences capture the father's tragic life cycle. The father's "decay" is welcome to the son, as is the spring to all, because it ends the long coldness of a rigid life. Yet it is terrible because it is the decay and death of a loved one.

Moore's ability to use the sonnet form to achieve effects of epigrammatic wit and complexity appears in sonnet 49, in the fourth movement, where the ruling tone is one of reconciliation and the resolution of conflicts, as the son asks forgiveness for

> the monstrous things he's said and done,
> which after thirty years he recognizes.
> In spite of all rich fatherhood devises
> to standardize its product, once the fun
> is over, father, see the gamuts run.
> We don't come in convenient shapes and sizes.
>
> Civilization is at fault. Deep dells
> of lofty words entice the young romancer

> from healthy things. But why do loyal cells,
> caught in a dying body, have no answer
> to the corruption when that one rebels
> to save its life and multiplies to cancer?

The octave sounds almost jocular. The son owns up to "the monstrous things he's said and done" and then goes on to sympathize ironically—yet with real feeling—with the father's frustration in his wayward offspring. Even a "rich" father can't "standardize" the "product," the son says, using a metaphor from business, then alludes to the father's sexual pleasure—"fun"—in begetting him, and makes "gamuts" sound like little boys running about a nursery.

But the real complexity comes in the sestet. The blame for the father's frustration lies with civilization, which has taught the son useless games (like writing sonnets), which distract him from "healthy things" (like making money and raising a family). The son is, therefore (the poem concludes with implacable logic), like a cancer cell rebelling in the social body. But the son asks, almost in desperation, why the loyal cells, like his father, have no better arguments for remaining faithful to the body politic and accepting good middle-class values. The son in his newfound empathy with his father is obliged to condemn himself and doubt his own deepest concerns—but it all seems ironic, all in fun, though his words are convincing, and he means them all. It is no wonder that poems this complex, this cruelly questioning, have met with a certain amount of reader resistance; but it may well be that such "defects" will prove to be virtues in the long run. *Word from the Hills* is perhaps the most consistently elegant of Moore's books.

It was nine more years before *Empires* was published, in 1981. In eighty-five pages, Moore's dramatic verse introduces Aaron Burr, Jay Gould, Archimedes, and Cleopatra. Moore wrote the book between 1967 and 1972 and remarks in its "Afterward" that whereas the "personal poems" of *Word from the Hills* had seemed to him "covertly historical," the historical poems of the new book seemed to him "covertly personal."

In the preface X. J. Kennedy says, "Among other aims, Moore sets out to establish a colossal metaphor in setting ancient Rome and expansionist America side by side. . . . It is Moore's art to make these lives impinge on ours. (The vivacity of his Cleopatra has to be read to be believed.) This immense four-part poem (incidentally, cast in fittingly various and flexible blank verse) keeps

Immortality   6/20/90

A nerd remembered for a thousand years
is a nerd still. My father kept recasting
wills in his wild urge to control events
after he died. Ridiculous. And Whitman's
great mausoleum.   I forgive them both.
                then,
Consider, ~~though~~, Ben Jonson. There's no doubt
                                    spellings
about a single word or even how
   ~~of any words~~   all
~~each word is spelled~~ in his great printed volumes.
He saw to everything, the careful man.
Some mocked him for it, even at the time.
(calling those rowdy plays literature!) ~~and~~
and ~~recalled~~ how his friend, Shakespeare, had died
with all his pages flapping in the wind.
It's not for us to care about such things.
I think it is for us, only to find
blessedness, if we can, in what we do,
and G. M. Hopkins tells us there may well have
been ditch diggers and scullery maids more blessed
in this then we, whose words pester the gods.
What happens after our mortality
is their affair and of the mortals after.

and that, after his friend, Shakespeare, had died
remembered how how his friend
              Shakespeare

Early and late drafts for a work in progress (by permission of Richard Moore)

P21   3

stoo

IMMORTALITY

A nerd remembered for a thousand years
is a nerd still. My father kept recasting
wills in his wild urge to control events
after he died. Ridiculous. And Whitman's
great mausoleum. I forgive them both.
Consider, then, Ben Jonson. There's no doubt
about a single word or even spellings
of any words in all his printed volumes.
He saw to everything, the careful man.
Some mocked him for it, even at the time
(calling those rowdy plays literature!)—
and that, after his friend, Shakespeare, had died
with all his pages flapping in the wind.
It's not for us to care about such things.
I think it is for us, only to find
blessedness, if we can, in what we do;
and G. M. Hopkins tells us there may well have
been ditch diggers and scullery maids more blessed
in this than we, whose words pester the gods.
What happens after our mortality
is their affair and of the mortals after.
Poor Ben messed up things for his memory,
made it important now to reproduce
his lines exactly as he had them printed
with that bizarre Elizabethan spelling—
even the u's and v's reversed—which makes them
unreadable to all now but the scholars
(and scholars, we know, can't read anyway).
In blind folly (not sin: there was no sin
in Greek) encroaching on the gods' domain:
hubris it's called and made them fiercely jealous.
And they could punish it so wittily!
Oedipus, trying to subvert the gods'
curse on him, flees on foot to a new city,
and in that very act fulfills the curse;
and with that fine old classicist, Ben Jonson,
similarly. Write for posterity,
draw up your will, perpetuate your folly.

the poet's vow: that he will invent no fact unnecessarily. But where he does invent, as you'll find, he invents spectacularly well."

Two questions naturally arise about *Empires:* what exactly are the implications of the "colossal metaphor" comparing modern America and ancient Rome, and in what sense are these historical poems "covertly personal"? Taking hints from Moore's "Afterward" and relating them to the development of his style thus far, one may arrive at the following account.

"Burr," the first poem to be composed, was a way for Moore to express his sense of the comic in history. But once he sees Burr as a comic figure, calling into question the fundamental values and pretenses on which the American republic was founded, he is bound to see Burr as an image of himself: a kind of rebellious "bad boy," derided and dismissed because his humor is too probing, too destructive.

Remarking in the "Afterward" on his identification with Burr while he was writing the poem, Moore adds ambiguously, "Burr was saying a lot of things I felt ought to be said but were not right for me to say." What things? Things about Thomas Jefferson, Moore goes on to suggest, saying that the procedure of the poem enables him to avoid responsibility for such criticism. But the impersonation also permits him to say other, more crucial things that he obviously feels "ought to be said." His Burr says, for example,

And now, near eighty, I can see at last
I'm a poor judge of character. I think
too well of people, and they don't forgive me.
. . . .
Practical politicians, if you're brilliant,
hide it; and if you cannot hide your brilliance,
comfort the people with the sweet conviction
you've drained it into harmless principles,
empty philosophies, crack-pated theories.
. . . .
How can a Nation gather and be founded
without grand-sounding words? When low men
    lead,
how can they tell the truth? And so the Myth
of the Republic blunders fondly on,
till the compacted lies on which it rolls
crumble to sand and leave us derelict,
obliged to contemplate ourselves at last.

Burr's experience, as presented in the poem, endows utterances like these with an authority that they could not have had otherwise.

The other poems in the book seem simpler in their personal content. Gould, the most ruthless and unprincipled of the robber barons, is seen as a personally gentle, tender person—"I loved my orchids and my formal gardens, / old books, but most the quiet of the night"—whose triumphs seem to emanate from a kind of inner despair:

What could supply me poise to know,
unclouded by my own fears and desires,
what other men would do, so I could trap them?
What but in some bare corner of my mind
to feel a numbness, sense a sick detachment?
Control, perception flourish in detachment.
No one who's desperate to win wins much.

The poem in its very softness and lyricism comes perilously close to being a simple cry of outrage against the ways of wealth.

The blank verse of "Archimedes" returns to the epigrammatic, more strikingly even than in "Burr." The personal content is even clearer (Moore is an amateur mathematician), and the shift of the emphasis to history and the impending collapse of a civilization is more striking—especially in the final pages of the poem, in which the great mathematician foresees his own death in the fall of Syracuse.

But a touch of biographical mystery returns with the last and longest poem in the book, about Cleopatra, who has come to Rome to participate in Julius Caesar's ascent to absolute power, only to learn, at the poem's end, of his murder. Moore's character, like the historical Cleopatra, is pure Greek and has little or nothing to do with either William Shakespeare's aging Egyptian love goddess or with George Bernard Shaw's giggling schoolgirl. For Moore—and probably in the consensus of scholarly opinion as well—Cleopatra was a brilliant and ruthless politician, a gifted linguist and intellectual, who used her sexual attractions, if she used them at all, in connection with her queenly rank in the pursuit of Ptolemaic Egypt's geopolitical aims. Yet one senses a very real physical person in lines like these, complaining about the Roman women:

They think I am too young to be a queen,
too small and frivolous to be so haughty;
dislike my coiled luxuriance of hair
differently tied and shaped each time they see it;
distrust the smile that wholly fills my face,
the eyes that see exactly what they look at,
darkly alight, released from fear and dreams.

Moore in November 1990 (photograph by Virginia Cazort)

The panoramic vista and detail of *Empires* tend to obscure the book's extreme pessimism. In the context of the "colossal metaphor" that Kennedy posits and that Moore surely intends, American and European civilization face a future that will be measured by Archimedes' destruction and Cleopatra's superstitious cynicism and easy violence.

In 1983 the Countryman Press in Woodstock, Vermont, published *The Education of a Mouse*, a sixty-two-page narrative in trimeter couplets, with a foreword by Howard Nemerov. *The Education of a Mouse* is the first part of a planned trilogy; the second and third parts are still unpublished in full (excerpts have appeared in magazines). Moore wrote part 1 in the spring and summer of 1958 and part 2 ("The Marriage of a Mouse") and part 3 ("The Apotheosis of a Mouse") in Paris and London from 1960 to 1961. This makes part 1 of Moore's "mouse epic" his ear-

liest work to be published—aside from a few of the poems in *A Question of Survival*.

In *The Education of a Mouse*, comprising two sections, the mouse-narrator longs to, and finally does, leave his family and the section of sewer they live in, and sets out to find "sunlight and moonlight and stars." "I'd longed," says the mouse in the opening lines, "for a life more pure / than that to be found in a sewer." This need for purity expresses itself primarily in the mouse's distaste for the kind of food available in sewers, but the underlying condition appears to be the mouse's romantic sensitivity:

I was a sensitive soul.
My life in that dark hole
offended my delicate taste.
With a Civilization's waste
I remained unsatisfied;
and "Could there be an outside?"
I wondered, and watched those massed

5 P19 1

after "The Veil"
after "The Literary Life"

6/15/90
held in active
file for notes

THE NAKED SCARECROW

come,
Come, words; ~~and~~ bring   *you too,*   ~~come two,~~ *he* ~~my~~
me solace, ~~with my~~ scarecrow's aid!   ~~and you;~~ ~~bring me~~
Out of old wood and rags I made
and dressed the thing.

ok
gaudily
carefully
They on the wing   ~~wonderfully~~
observed it, ~~properly~~ arrayed,
him *who*
he *he* motionless, save where it flapped, frayed . . .
I heard ~~it~~ sing: *him*

that
O wind, keep up your tearing,
"~~After the long~~ wind's searching, probing,
Soon now: ~~at last~~: definitive disrobing.
No more frills, tricks!

The crows will note me, thus produced,
circle and caw, and come to roost
here, in the sticks."

Gloss:
reaching   *life*
On being ~~recognized in~~ *old age. The original, aim*
bureaucratic, all-befouling
had been to keep those crows of ~~phoniness~~ *away and*
devices
remain an unattended alien. ~~An~~ *Elaborate* ~~art~~ *achieved this*
It was fine, but a little pretentious, a little ~~dead~~ *lifeless*
even. But my experience tore at me, reduced me to my
essential nothingness. Nothing more to fear. Anyone can
roost in me now. ~~be I'm nothing at last~~

Fulfillment is death

Early draft for a recent poem by Moore (by permission of Richard Moore)

and sluggish waters creep past
and gazed in the dismal distance
and dreamed of another existence.

This disposition puts the mouse in conflict with his family: "Whenever I wouldn't eat / some morsel of rancid meat, / they tasted the bitter curse / at the core of the universe." The conflict with the father (who, in the effort to find food for his family, has lost his tail to a vicious rat) is paramount, and the mouse observes:

Those who in a spasm
of hot enthusiasm
thoughtlessly beget us:
how soon do they regret us?
The unseen drop they gave,
the driblet they presented,
a millionfold augmented,
returns, as from the grave.

O father,
what made you turn so pale?
Was it my long new tail?

The family gathers regularly and worships below an opening where light comes into the sewer. The father is skeptical about this, and the mother is pious, but the young mouse is the only one actually to climb up into this "drain," where one day he finds an envelope. The strange new object immediately rekindles his feelings of grandeur:

I surveyed it ecstatically.
Then was it intended for me?
In my small but jubilant brain
as I inched it down the drain
wild thoughts ignited and spun:
Had *I* been ordained by the sun
to accomplish the will of the skies
with this object before my eyes?

What awful responsibilities
fall on those endowed with abilities.

His attempt to use the envelope as a raft and float to the fabled ocean is absurdly catastrophic; but that night he has a dream instructing him how to use it as a canoe, and after a horrendous family argument, he sails off in it, at the end of the first section.

In part 2 the mouse meets "Old Nick," the rat probably responsible for the loss of his father's tail. Nick is also inclined to seduce and eat young mice who are mesmerized by his fast talk

and by his supposed pedagogical interest in their spiritual, emotional, and intellectual well-being.

Moore's narrative is a many-layered and amusing satire on the state of the soul—particularly the sensitive, artistic, and romantically inclined soul—in modern times. Moore's trimeter couplets, poised in slender columns on the pages, carry the reader swiftly through monologues and conversations filled with audacious, effective rhymes. James F. Dorrill named a few in his review "Of Mice—Or Men?" in *Negative Capability* (Spring 1984): "*morsels/doorsills; manikin/satanic in; finicky/been a key; papa/propa* [proper] . . . and the need to find matching rhymes for *sewer* gives such palpable hits as *pure, you're, truer, endure, allure,* and *rue her,* among others."

In view of the book's charm, it is surprising that two thirds of the trilogy—"Marriage" and "Apotheosis" (when the mouse reaches the mystical ocean)—remain unpublished in book form. Nemerov, in his foreword to *The Education of a Mouse,* says of the publishers he tried to interest in Moore's epic: "Were they men, we wondered, or mice." The very uniqueness of the mouse epic—"*sui generis,*" Robert Lowell called it—is probably what militates against it among those used to other kinds of modern poetry. Nemerov remarks that "this mouse had lived a life more essentially critical than my own." It was in his mouse epic that Moore discovered the comic vein that has since informed all his poetry.

Some eighty or ninety poems of Moore's have been published in magazines, and in some instances anthologies, but not as yet in collections of his own. The elegiac-meter poems, a book-length collection Moore completed in the 1970s, deserves particular note. Moore's interest in classical meters dates from the hexameters of "Willy" in his first book, a poem that has been anthologized several times and much admired for its vigor and gusto. Moore uses elegiac meter mainly in a kind of extended verse essay, examples of which are "Poets" and "Pyramids" (*Poetry,* January 1982 and August 1973), "Wife" (*Denver Quarterly,* Spring 1973), "Pygmies" (*Mill Mountain Review,* 1971; reprinted in *Plains Poetry Journal,* April 1988), and "The Abacus: A Rhapsody" (*Modern Occasions Annual,* 1974; reprinted in *Plains Poetry Journal,* October 1988).

The last of these, for example, is a free-ranging improvisation about a Chinese abacus that the speaker has bought and taught himself to use, and the outcome is a deepened perception of what mathematics means or ought to mean to the rest of civilized life. Moore admires the elemental concreteness of the abacus and its charm as a "child's toy," which allows it to combine harmoniously with other human concerns:

> Now for the first time, doing my income tax is a
> pleasure—
>   all those abstract sums
>   something I'm able to touch.
> Also it gives me the pleasant sensation that some-
>   how I'm cheating,
>   adding up medical bills
>   merely by diddling beads.

Moore has published some brief lyrics and even some epigrams in this graceful and difficult meter, but it is in the "talking" elegiac poems that he has most clearly made a contribution to the possibilities of contemporary American poetry.

In the early 1980s, beginning with "Tristram's Attack on Modern Poetry" in the *Georgia Review* (Winter 1981-1982), Moore began publishing a series of forceful, closely reasoned essays on literature and science. In several of these essays, he uses an alter ego, "Tristram Tom Brodie . . . the disgruntled suburbanite . . . of Sweethill, Massachusetts." One senses in this device, again, Moore's urge to indulge in certain comic exaggerations without incurring full responsibility for them. But there may be a more considerable motive as well. The essays, with their wide ranging from field to field in an age when ever-narrower specialization is the norm, constitute a plea for the generalist, unspecialized values of a reader (and writer) uncommitted to specific professional affiliations. As Moore says mockingly in the preface to the first essay, "I am, after all, a modern poet myself and have to be careful of what I say." He seems to be arguing that, in the circumstances of contemporary culture, the cause of truth may be best served if there are some writers who need not be careful of what they say. In a world of marginally comprehensible and often prejudiced experts, he implies, there is a need to set a higher value on untutored judgment.

Thus, Tristram's attack on modern poetry is essentially commonsensical. In the opening pages, Tristram defends the common man's uncritical reliance on customs and stereotypes— "fictions" as Paul Valéry called them—and gives examples to show that poems rely on them to achieve power and complexity. Tristram becomes a kind of Everyman, looking in on the subsociety of modern poetry from the outside and finally calling for a poetry more firmly grounded in common reality and conventions and accessible to ordinary educated readers like himself. The alter ego is thus a vital part of the essay's persuasiveness.

Where will Moore go next? He has published his first novel, *The Investigator*, and *No More Bottom*, a book of satirical and epigrammatic verse (both in 1991). "Tristram's Attack" has recently been republished in *Expansive Poetry: Essays on the New Narrative & the New Formalism*, edited by Frederick Feirstein (1989). Certainly Moore's writings will never be dull; a recent couplet, "The Pause that Refreshes," reads: "Inside, his tomb is alabastered. / Inside his tomb is Al, a bastard." It may well be that the time has come for a wider, fuller appreciation of Moore's comic vision, metrical virtuosity, storytelling skills, and analytical vigor. Having already published over two hundred poems in literary journals, Richard Moore may now be receiving some belated recognition as a valuable, inventive poet and an influential critic.

Lisel Mueller

(8 February 1924 -   )

Judith Kitchen
State University of New York College at Brockport

BOOKS: *Dependencies* (Chapel Hill: University of North Carolina Press, 1965);

Life of a Queen (La Crosse, Wis.: Northeast/ Juniper, 1970);

The Private Life (Baton Rouge: Louisiana State University Press, 1976);

Voices from the Forest (La Crosse, Wis.: Juniper, 1977);

The Need to Hold Still (Baton Rouge: Louisiana State University Press, 1980);

Second Language (Baton Rouge: Louisiana State University Press, 1986);

Waving from Shore (Baton Rouge: Louisiana State University Press, 1989);

Learning to Play by Ear: Essays and Early Poems (La Crosse, Wis.: Juniper, 1990).

TRANSLATIONS: *Selected Later Poems of Marie Luise Kaschnitz* (Princeton, N.J.: Princeton University Press, 1980);

Kaschnitz, *Whether or Not* (La Crosse, Wis.: Juniper, 1984);

W. Anna Migutsch, *Three Daughters* (New York: Harcourt Brace Jovanovich, 1987);

Kaschnitz, *Circe's Mountain* (Minneapolis: Milkweed, 1990).

OTHER: "Midwestern Poetry: Goodbye to All That," in *Voyages to the Inland Sea I*, edited by John Judson (La Crosse, Wis.: Center for Contemporary Poetry, 1971).

In a 1989 interview with Stan Sanvel Rubin and William Heyen, Lisel Mueller stated: "Let me say what countless other displaced persons must have said: I am more at home here [in the United States] than anywhere. At the same time I am not a native; I see the culture and myself in it, through a scrim, with European eyes, and my poetry accommodates a bias toward historical determinism. . . ." Because Mueller's poems are written in English, her second language (her first being German), they reflect an awareness of what words can and cannot do. With her intuitive understanding of the relationship between sign and signified (word and thing), she embodies some of the basic assertions of French theorist Jacques Derrida. She resembles one of her favorite poets, Wallace Stevens, in unearthing imaginative possibilities in the nature of language itself. For Mueller the essential quest is the connection between image and word, between the "thing" and the "idea of the thing." Her poems are, in a sense, metaphysical but rooted deeply in natural images, owing always to the real world.

Mueller's *The Private Life* (1976) was a Lamont Poetry Selection of the Academy of American Poets. *The Need to Hold Still* (1980) was awarded the American Book Award for Poetry in 1981. In 1986, with the publication of *Second Language*, Mueller clearly established herself as an important writer. Her sense of history gives her poems a rare philosophical intensity. Combining the private and the public, Mueller's work demonstrates how each affects the other: no life is unimportant; even loneliness does not take place in isolation.

Born on 8 February 1924 in Hamburg, Germany, Lisel Neumann (later Mueller) came to the United States in 1939. Her father, Fritz C. Neumann, was a political dissident who fled Nazi Germany and settled in Evansville, Indiana. Both he and her mother, Ilse Burmester Neumann, were teachers. Although Lisel spoke German in the home, she soon learned English. She describes this process in a 1980 essay, "Learning to Play by Ear" (in the 1990 collection of that name): "At fifteen you want more than anything to be accepted . . . and though I was never to overcome my natural condition as a loner, the motivation to blend into the prevailing culture was strong, if not entirely conscious." With a strong background in grammar and spelling, she listened to the radio, memorized the words of hit tunes, and became fluent in her new language. Even then, she recalls, metaphor was a puzzle. She could not make a connection between the sky and "a blanket of blue."

Lisel Mueller (photograph by Jenny Mueller)

Lisel spent one year in high school and then attended the University of Evansville, where she graduated in 1944 at the age of twenty. While there she learned to love the poetry of John Keats and studied the work of Conrad Aiken and Robinson Jeffers. She wrote some poetry at this time—flowery, sentimental verse she attributes to adolescence. On 15 June 1943 she married Paul Mueller, an editor. They have two daughters, Lucy and Jenny.

After college Mueller put what she thought of as a phase behind her: she stopped writing. It was only with her mother's death in 1953, when Mueller sensed the need to put her feelings into some order, that she turned again to poetry. This time she decided to become a serious writer, beginning a self-designed course of training, teaching herself to read for instruction as well as pleasure, and setting herself exercises. As she says in "Learning to Play by Ear," "My apprenticeship at this stage was a matter of hit-and-miss, lucky hunches and wild goose chases, a game of hide-and-seek with the masters I was looking for."

Over the next twelve years Mueller honed her craft, learning and practicing traditional forms as well as free verse. She and her husband discovered the New Critics, and together they read T. S. Eliot, Cleanth Brooks, I. A. Richards, William Empson, R. P. Blackmur, and John Crowe Ransom. Mueller's self-imposed education was augmented by yet another kind of education— the birth of her two daughters, four years apart. She was forced to face an essential question: whether it is possible to have a "normal" life and also be an artist. Mueller was determined to have both. A free-lance job reviewing books for a Chicago newspaper kept her in touch with contemporary poetry and forced her to think critically. Her own poems began appearing in magazines in the mid 1950s, but it was not until 1965 that her first book, *Dependencies*, was published. Many of these early poems (now out of print), plus several essays, are collected in *Learning to Play by Ear*.

In many ways the poems in *Dependencies* were part of Mueller's apprenticeship: she describes them as overly decorated and too metaphorical, almost as though she had learned her lessons too well. The book is literary; the poems make reference to other writers and to painting and music. But Mueller's inclination to find some

Dust jacket for Mueller's 1976 book, which Richard Eberhart called "compelling, satisfying"

balance between art and life is evident even in this early work, especially as she reflects on the life of her mother through the perspective of her own new motherhood.

In *The Private Life* Mueller found her characteristic voice and her abiding themes. The poems divide into two equally important strains. One is the domestic—the private, ordinary life of a wife and mother. Such poems chronicle the stages of marriage and the growth of children, showing over and over what is expressed at the end of "Reading the Brothers Grimm to Jenny":

> And what can I, but see
> beyond the world that is
> when, faithful, you insist
> I have the golden key—
> and learn from you once more
> the terror and the bliss,
> the world as it might be?

Folktale unearths metaphor. The old stories contain in them a possibility for understanding the present, and the child demonstrates this with implicit faith. Using this method, Mueller finds a way into her own private material. Such material includes her origins—her parents and grandparents—and she concludes in "My Grandmother's Gold Pin": "I wear it [the pin] / . . . because it is all I have left of an age when people believed the heart was / an organ of goodness, and light was stronger than darkness." She reveals how private and public histories are, in fact, one.

This conclusion leads to the second strain in the book—the political, or public. With the war in Vietnam as a backdrop, several poems demonstrate how events in the news affect Mueller's personal sense of order. Thus she unearths "an interdependency" between the private and public life. She clarified this relationship in her interview with Rubin and Heyen: "There's no way anymore for the individual to escape from History, the public life we all share. Being European-born, I felt this very strongly. That is the story of my parents, who were born shortly before World War I, and their whole life was determined by History. Everything was imposed on them from the outside, because the twentieth century in Germany was catastrophic."

Balance, for Mueller, is essential. It is maintained when the public and private intersect. One poem in *The Private Life*, "Palindrome," imagines a woman's life in reverse, from old age to infancy, a kind of mirror image that will intersect with the self. In "Untitled" the life of an Algerian girl who has been brutally tortured to make her talk is referred to as "my antilife." Mueller does not live in a middle-income, suburban vacuum. Connections are made through an imaginative entry into other lives, coupled with an understanding of how other lives affect her own. In "On Reading an Anthology of Postwar German Poetry," Mueller writes, "I know enough to refuse to say / that life is good," though her stoic good sense leads her to conclude, "but I act as though it were."

In "Naming the Animals" Mueller sees the world as having no meaning until each object has been given a name: "until he named the horse / horse / hoofs left no print on the earth." In contrast, Mueller is also attuned to what cannot be said, or to the possibilities of another "language"—silence. She imagines what dogs can hear that is inaccessible to the human ear. In the title poem, "what happens, happens in silence." Life happens before one names it—in the moment of perception; newspapers reduce the experience to headlines. Poetry, with its charged language and leaps of intuitive understanding, gives voice to what cannot be named—the ineffable space in which hope "is . . . trying to speak" ("Hope").

The Need to Hold Still continues in this vein. Ann Louise Hentz has described the book as an "examination of tangible silence" (*Contemporary Poetry*, 1982). Ironically such examination leads to a book that is inherently about language. "Talking to Helen," for example, is spoken directly to Helen Keller, and the speaker imagines the world growing wet and green in the sudden apprehension of the connection between word and concept.

Mueller had studied folklore and myth as a graduate student at the University of Indiana, and, in *The Need to Hold Still*, she was able to mine the old stories for metaphor. In fact, metaphor becomes the "second language" in this book. She examines fairy tales to see what can be applied to contemporary life; in the process, contemporary life is also examined as the source of new legends. The domestic provides a context in which to test the larger implications of myth. The final poem, "Why We Tell Stories," concludes that the impulse toward narrative is an or-

dering principle—"Because the story of our life / becomes our life." But the individual life is part of something larger, the longer story of the human race, and so every story begins "with the word *and*."

There is a quiet brand of feminism in the poems of *The Need to Hold Still*, a kind of womanly wisdom that comes from raising children and, at the same time, maintaining a distinct sense of self. A long sequence, "The Triumph of Life: Mary Shelley," might seem the most militant. But, although Mueller chronicles the life of a highly independent woman, in Shelley's voice she refuses to romanticize that life. Speaking across centuries, across the two hundred years of medical science that "divide us," the author of *Frankenstein* (1818) talks to today's women:

An idea whose time has come,
you say about your freedom
but you forget the reason

Shall I remind you of history,
of choice and chance, the wish and the world,
of courage and locked doors,
biology and fate?

I wanted what you want,
what you have

If I could have chosen my children
and seen them survive
I might have believed in equality,
written your manifestos.

Seen through the light of history, technology has made feminism possible. She gets tougher: "You don't trust the heart / though you define death / as the absence of heartbeat." The poem recognizes that every age has its own definitions, that science causes people to make new decisions, and that it is impossible to read one age by another. In the end, Shelley says, "I was not your Cassandra." Myth will not provide answers or definitions, only one measure by which to read and interpret the present.

In Mueller's poetry, the woman's body is openly accepted, even celebrated. The opening lines of "Picking Raspberries" are sensuous: "Once the thicket opens / and lets you enter / and the first berry dissolves on your tongue, / you will remember nothing / of your old life." But an old life is assumed—a time before the speaker entered the thicket, an innocent "other" life that carries with it all the child's potential.

THE NEED TO HOLD STILL

POEMS BY LISEL MUELLER

LISEL MUELLER was recently a visiting faculty member in the Goddard College master of fine arts writing program. She is the author of two books of poetry, *Dependencies* and *The Private Life*. The latter volume, also published by LSU Press, was the 1975 Lamont Poetry Selection of the Academy of American Poets. She is translator of the bilingual edition of the *Selected Later Poems of Marie Luise Kaschnitz*.

Louisiana State University Press
Baton Rouge 70803

ISBN 0-8071-0649-0

Dust jacket for the 1980 collection William Stafford praised as "a complete demonstration of a talent early evident and now fully accomplished"

Mueller hints at that self often. Her Venus, for instance, is a far cry from the traditional view. In "Testimony," Mueller not only gives biological history but traces men's attitudes to women, how men would have life be. The truth, her Venus implies, is otherwise: "You forget I was in the sea / a long time, breathing through gills, / before I surfaced on that shell, / the 'glorious moment' you speak of." Mueller goes on to describe how men omit the details in favor of the romance of yellow silk, rose-tipped breasts, and glittering white sand. Her Venus tells it as it was: "No one was there. I was cold and lost. / The scraggly leaves all pointed / in one direction, toward the interior. / I had no other place to go."

The question is not of men versus women, but of individuality. In "The Artist's Model, ca. 1912" the model asks for her "singular name / back" because she wants to be more than an abstraction. The title poem ("The Need to Hold Still") explores this feeling fully. In a stark, barebones language, Mueller describes a field of winter weeds and finds in them a reflection of a woman's aging body. What the colorless weeds reveal is form—the design on which the plant is built, the "shape of the body." In this case, the weeds are a metaphor for the poem itself—the individual's own mark on the world.

Mueller's style makes for a poem that is decidedly rhythmical yet stripped of any excess, allowing her images such visual impact that the accompanying comparison is striking. In "Merce Cunningham and the Birds" she begins to say there are no words to describe the dancers. Then, observing the birds feeding outside her window, she creates a dance of color and movement. The reader easily makes the intended leap without the intrusion of an authorial voice. The comparisons shimmer with association, as in "Poppy," where the petals of the poppy are compared to a child's "crackling crepe paper fever." Often there is an accumulation of metaphor around a single image to demonstrate how one thing is the equivalent of many others. Sometimes this accumulation takes the form of lists or catalogues. Mueller believes that structure is the "most important part of a poem, certainly more than the individual line." The moment of revelation is central,

Cover for the 1986 collection whose title refers to Mueller's second language, English, which she learned after moving from Germany to the United States at age fifteen

and the structure should reflect and strengthen that discovery. In this way, Mueller re-creates the thought process of the poem, making associations seem easy and natural. Noting this style as part of her impulse toward "legend-making," Stephen Corey states that "nothing about her vigorous and sincere working toward minimal subjects, words, and forms is easy" (*Virginia Quarterly Review*, Autumn 1981).

In the 1980s Mueller published translations of the work of German poet Marie Luise Kaschnitz and of a novel by W. Anna Migutsch. Working deeply in both German and English, she came to terms with the metaphorical implications for her own life. Her 1986 book, *Second Language*, invites the reader to look beyond the obvious fact of her two languages into the nature of

metaphor. *Second Language* is a book about memory and recovery, the discovery of one's self in memory, and the melding of past and present in sensibility.

Second Language is constructed in five sections, moving from personal memory through a "trying on" of otherness, to a recognition of the intuitive, and finally to a reclamation of the self. Once again Mueller weds the public and the private to achieve a balanced vision.

In trying to attain some sense of balance, in section 2 Mueller examines characters who are clearly out of balance—a teenage victim of abuse, a clairvoyant, a gospel preacher, a widow, left-handed people, and girls who should have been swans, those "daughters mothers worry about." Watching a pair of identical twins, Mueller discov-

Mueller circa 1988

ers the "lost, illicit other" in the self. If she can understand these lives and their suffering, she may learn to understand herself. The aim is, in this case, the balance of love and grief. The language of grief is a state of mind. In "Metaphor" Mueller writes that "spring" and "fall" may mean nothing to someone in Hawaii, but that loss is universal: "She stares at the prodigal trees, / the bold insistent flowers, / but all she sees is a bitter landscape: / *goldengrove unleaving,* / *bare ruin'd choirs, where late the sweet birds sang*." In the end, the language of poetry becomes a necessity.

In *Second Language* Mueller examines memory and grief; in the opening poem, "Necessities," she discovers yet another language to be learned—"the alphabet of the dead, subtle, undeciphered." In the first section, she comes to terms with her parents' deaths, discovering that they have entered the "history of their photographs." Memory is what keeps them alive; only when she dies will they die. Thus begins the process by which she can contemplate her own death. Oddly enough, as the book unfolds, this turns out to be an optimistic act. The third sec-

tion explores the intuitive, silent communications found in nature, what are referred to as "intimations" or "adjustments." The poems are filled with images of death, but death does not terrify. In "Milkweed Pods in Winter," milkweed releases its seed, and the empty pods reveal the speech of silence: "what we would say to each other / if we could find the heart, / if there were no music / to say it for us / and the appetite of our bodies / did not swallow language clean."

Perhaps the most frighteningly honest moment of the book occurs in "For the Strangers." Looking at the old gods, Mueller calls metaphor a "fiction" that saved humankind from madness, "certainly from the despair / of admitting the broken connection, / that the world resists meaning / not to tease us, but because / there is no meaning / except the one we invent."

The fourth section discovers promise in the work yet to be done. In "Monet Refuses the Operation" Mueller speaks for Claude Monet as he refuses to have his cataracts removed. In his blurred vision, he finally sees a unified world: "I will not return to a universe / of objects that

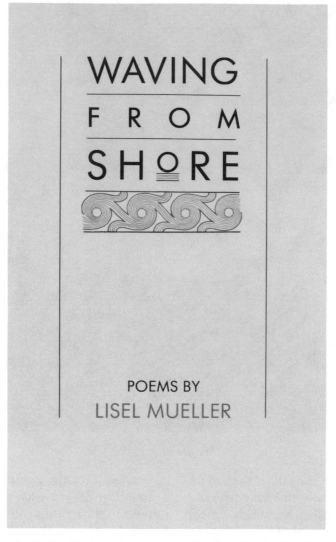

Cover for the 1989 collection whose language Mueller calls "brief and tight-lipped"

don't know each other, / as if islands were not the lost children / of one great continent. The world / is flux, and light becomes what it touches. . . ."

Vision unifies the world and memory unifies the self. In the last section of *Second Language* Mueller reclaims her self. In "What Is Left to Say," the "self" learns that it can "live, after all, / in a world of strangers." "How light we are becoming," she states at the beginning of the final poem. In "Into Space," she looks at the rate of change, the loss of "racial memory," which can strip the self even of personal memory. In the end, memories are scattered like dandelion fluff, falling on strangers. "The Thousand and First Night" is spoken in the voice of Scheherazade, with Mueller recognizing that it is impossible to predict one's life: "I cannot imagine / how this story ends."

Describing *Waving from Shore* (1989), Mueller says, "I've stopped writing catalogs and my language has become as brief and tight-lipped as that of a Norwegian bachelor farmer." With this brevity, however, she demonstrates the power of the lyric. Once again, what cannot normally be said is her territory; that she finds a way to say it is her genius.

In the first section Mueller goes back to her poetic beginnings. The second poem, "When I Am Asked," refers to her mother's death: "I talk about the indifference of nature." Because everything was blooming, because nothing else seemed to be overcome with grief, Mueller placed her grief "in the mouth of language / the only thing that would grieve with me." From there the poems move in slow motion, filled with musical rhythms and sensual language: "Remember how long spring used to take? / And how long from the first locking of fingers / to the first real kiss?" ("Magnolia"). Eventually time slows to a dream, and Mueller perceives herself not as the daring adventurer, the heroine of her dreams, but as the observer who waves from shore.

The second section subtly shifts to the public arena; this section speaks for those who do not or cannot speak—the old, the deaf, the disenfranchised, the autistic, the insane, and the dead. Or rather, in her attempt to understand, Mueller realizes that she cannot speak for them:

> The habit of speech
> is not like riding a bicycle,
> something you never forget;
> it dries up like the habit of tears,
> like playfulness. Nothing in her face
> gives me permission to speak for her,
> even if I could.

Once she has reduced herself to silence, Mueller breaks free in a surprising way. Many of the poems in the final section leap fancifully into speculation. These poems are balanced by an equal number of prose poems, as though the form of poetry, with its felt silences, was not sufficient for the public content of these prose pieces. Their themes are political; they bring the outside world into the home. They read with the easy rhythms of the poetry, but there is usually a place where the rhythm breaks down, where the intensity of the vision overwhelms the structure itself, as in "Triage":

> Bertolt Brecht lamented that he lived in an age when it was almost a crime to talk about trees, because that meant being silent about so much evil. Walking past a stand of tall, still healthy elms along Chicago's lakefront, I think of what Brecht said. I want to celebrate those elms which have been spared by the plague, these survivors of a once flourishing tribe commemorated by all the Elm Streets in America. But to celebrate them is to be silent about the people who sit and sleep underneath them, the homeless poor who are hauled away by the city like trash, except it has no place to dump them. To speak of one thing is to suppress another. When I talk about myself, I cannot talk about you. You know this as you listen to me, disappointment settling in your face.

Mueller not only finds a way out of her self-imposed silence, but she also seems to write herself out of the dilemma facing contemporary poets: how to make a poetry that is germaine to today's society and is, at the same time, not merely polemic. Mueller's sure voice, turned inevitably toward public issues, offers a sense of individual perspective, of vision shaped by years of learning from language itself. So it is, in "Joy," that Mueller discovers the universal in the particular. Remembering a youthful experience of crying at hearing music, she pulls the past tense into the present:

> But it happened again. It happens
> when we make bottomless love—
> there follows a bottomless sadness
> which is not despair
> but its nameless opposite.
> It has nothing to do with the passing of time.
> It's not about loss. It's about
> two seemingly parallel lines
> suddenly coming together
> inside us, in some place
> that is still wilderness.

Waving from Shore has everything to do with the passing of time. Time moves behind these lyrics, adding intensity to the silence and nuance to what is seen or said. In this way, the parallel lines of poet and reader also come together; Mueller shows how the world speaks us.

With this new volume of poetry, Lisel Mueller suggests new directions for her work. One wonders whether she will continue to revive the art of the lyric or whether she will venture into prose. But one can be sure that she will find a delicate balance between public and private, lyric and narrative, and silence and speech. "I have only hindsight," she writes in "Learning to Play by Ear," "which tells me that everything in my life has been grist for the writer's mill. . . . It's enough to make me believe nothing is ever wasted, that there is only gain, accrual, seed lying in wait."

Interviews:
Nancy Bunge, *Finding the Words: Interviews with Poets Who Teach* (Athens, Ohio: Swallow Press, 1985), pp. 96-105;

Stan Sanvel Rubin and William Heyen, "The Steady Interior Hum," in *The Post-Confessionals: Conversations with American Poets of the Eighties*, edited by Earl G. Ingersoll, Judith Kitchen, and Rubin (Cranbury, N.J.: Associated University Presses, 1989), pp. 62-72.

Robert Peters
(20 October 1924 -   )

Charles Hood
Antelope Valley College

BOOKS: *The Crowns of Apollo: Swinburne's Principles of Literature and Art: A Study in Victorian Criticism and Aesthetics* (Detroit: Wayne State University Press, 1965);
Fourteen Poems (Santa Barbara, Cal.: Little Square Review, 1967);
Songs for a Son (New York: Norton, 1967);
The Sow's Head and Other Poems (Detroit: Wayne State University Press, 1968);
Connections: In the English Lake District: A Verse Suite (London: Anvil, 1972);
Byron Exhumed: A Verse Suite (Fort Wayne: Windless Orchard, 1973);
Red Midnight Moon (San Francisco: Empty Elevator Shaft, 1973);
Cool Zebras of Light (Santa Barbara, Cal.: Christopher's, 1974);
Holy Cow: Parable Poems (Los Angeles: Red Hill, 1974);
Bronchial Tangle, Heart System (Hanover, N.H.: Granite, 1975);
The Gift to Be Simple: A Garland for Ann Lee (New York: Liveright, 1975);
The Poet as Ice-Skater (San Francisco: Manroot, 1976);
Gauguin's Chair: Selected Poems, 1967-1974 (Trumansburg, N.Y.: Crossing, 1977);
Hawthorne: Poems Adapted from the American Notebooks (Los Angeles: Red Hill, 1977);
The Drowned Man to the Fish (St. Paul: New Rivers, 1978);
Ikagnak: The North Wind: With Dr. Kane in the Arctic (Pasadena: Kenmore, 1978); revised as *Kane* (Greensboro, N.C.: Unicorn, 1985);
The Great American Poetry Bake-Off, four series (Metuchen, N.J.: Scarecrow, 1979, 1982, 1987, 1991);
Celebrities: In Memory of Margaret Dumont, Dowager of the Marx Brothers Movies (1890-1965) (Berkeley: Sombre Reptiles, 1981);
The Picnic in the Snow: Ludwig of Bavaria (St. Paul: New Rivers, 1982); revised and enlarged as *Ludwig of Bavaria: Poems and a Play*, (Cherry Valley, N.Y.: Cherry Valley, 1987);

What Dillinger Meant to Me (New York: Sea Horse, 1983);
The Peters Black and Blue Guide to Current Literary Journals, first and second series (Cherry Valley, N.Y.: Cherry Valley, 1983, 1985); third series (Paradise, Cal.: Dustbooks, 1987);
Hawker (Greensboro, N.C.: Unicorn, 1984);
The Blood Countess: Elizabeth Bathory of Hungary: Poems and a Play (Cherry Valley, N.Y.: Cherry Valley, 1987);
Shaker Light: Mother Ann Lee in America (Greensboro, N.C.: Unicorn, 1987);
Crunching Gravel (San Francisco: Mercury House, 1988);
Haydon: An Artist's Life (Greensboro, N.C.: Unicorn, 1989);
Hunting the Snark (New York: Paragon House, 1989);
Brueghel's Pig (Los Angeles: Illuminati, 1989).

OTHER: *Victorians on Literature and Art*, edited by Peters (New York: Appleton-Century-Crofts, 1961; London: Owen, 1964);
Pioneers of Modern Poetry, edited by Peters and George Hitchcock (San Francisco: Kayak, 1967);
The Letters of John Addington Symonds, 3 volumes, edited by Peters and Herbert M. Schueller (Detroit: Wayne State University Press, 1967-1969);
Gabriel: A Poem by John Addington Symonds, edited by Peters and Timothy D'Arch Smith (London: Hartington, 1974);
Letters to A Tutor: The Tennyson Family Letters to Henry Graham Dakyns, edited by Peters (Metuchen, N.J.: Scarecrow, 1988).

"We bleat our love in God's pastures," writes Robert Peters in a closing poem in *Shaker Light* (1987), speaking in the voice of Ann Lee, the founder of the Shaker religion. This is a typical Peters move, mixing the physical with the spiritual and contrasting one level (God) with the reality of daily life, which is full of bleats and longings. In-

fluenced by early modernists such as Thomas Hardy and by the frankness of William Burroughs, Hubert Selby, Jr., and the Beats, Peters combines an uncensored vision of human nature with an often baroque vocabulary and a constant awareness of the physical world. His willingness to describe society's viscera has lead some readers to undervalue his contributions; put off by the homosexuality of Ludwig of Bavaria or the brutality of the Blood Countess—to name two historical figures treated in his poetry—they want to dismiss Peters as a deviant or else ignore him completely. In so doing they fail to appreciate the beauty and complexity of his writing and fail, too, to realize the importance of his development of the persona poem.

Much of his imagery comes from his farm background. Born to Sam and Dorothy Keck Peters on 20 October 1924, Robert Louis Peters grew up in a cabin near Eagle River, Wisconsin.

His father was a welder. Robert was the first of four children, and although both parents encouraged his education, he could not escape the realities of rural America in the Depression—homemade clothes, water from the pump, the tending of livestock, and constant worry about money. He describes these experiences in the first volume of his autobiography, *Crunching Gravel* (1988), which is organized according to the four seasons. Peters did well in high school, worked briefly as an insurance clerk, and was drafted into the U.S. Army in 1943. Here he had to confront the stereotypes of a gender role he had uneasily managed to make truce with at home. As an infantryman he was expected to be a good shot and an agile athlete, but he was neither, and felt out of place for not being aggressively heterosexual. Later he would explore these feelings by examining the lives of other nonconformists, including the pious Ann Lee and the pac-

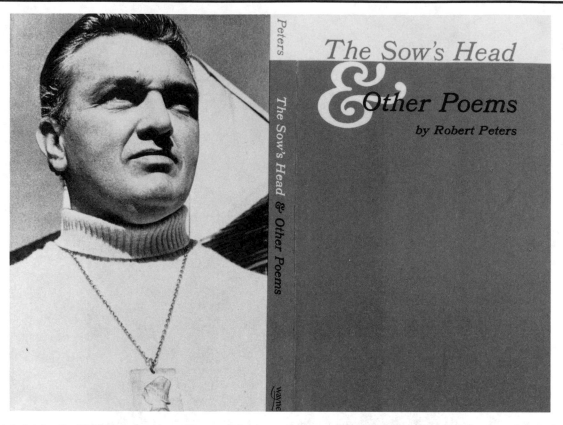

Dust jacket for the 1968 book that shows Peters turning away from conventional verse and toward the surreal and absurd

ifistic King Ludwig. Peters was stationed in South Carolina, England, and Europe, and served until 1946, when he enrolled at the University of Wisconsin, graduating six years later with a doctorate in English. He married Jean Louise Powell, whom he had met in college, on 22 October 1950. Throughout this period, since preschool age in fact, he had been trying to become a writer, but he had not found his creative voice. Duties as a professor further deflected his skill; he began to publish as a Victorianist and to move through the academic ranks. He taught at a succession of campuses—including the University of Idaho, Boston University, and Ohio Wesleyan—before gaining tenure at Wayne State. By Christmas 1959 he and Jean had three children, Robert, Meredith (a daughter), and Richard; later they were to have a third son, Jefferson.

On 10 February 1960 Richard died of one-day meningitis. Peters's grief was immense, and as a way of expiating the loss, he began writing short poems about the boy and his feelings toward him. These became Peters's first major book, the lyrical *Songs for a Son* (1967), published by Norton, on Denise Levertov's recommendation. (*Fourteen Poems*, published the same year,

was a pamphlet he used at readings before *Songs* was released.) *Songs* reveals a writer with a good ear, but as even the title indicates, it was more conventional than anything he was later to produce. The book contains simple diction and short lines so that even a child, it seems, could read it; Peters alternately tries to conjure the dead child into corporeal existence or else alleviate guilt by blaming himself publicly. Peters deals with mortality graphically, as in "Transformation": "I know / that between death's / hot coppery sides / the slime of birth / becomes a chalky / track of bone." As the book progresses, Richard is compared indirectly or directly to fallen birds, fern spoors, and the victims of trolls; these images recur in future work by Peters. While he was revising drafts of this book (1963-1965), he moved to the University of California, Riverside, and he began to make some life-style changes related to the spirit of the 1960s.

The Sow's Head and Other Poems (1968) reflects the changes and, instead of being modeled on the poetry of Theodore Roethke (as *Songs for a Son* was), comes from such promptings as the music of the Rolling Stones. Reading Charles Bukowski, smoking marijuana, exploring homosexuality, and questioning the standards of academia, Peters produced an absurdist, surrealist text that Norton had no interest in. His standing, however, at Wayne State helped him find a publisher there. *The Sow's Head* uses rhymes and natural images in inventive ways, and one poem especially foreshadows later work, a multipage narrative called "Gordon at Khartoum." Referring to the experienced general and Christian mystic Charles Gordon, who was killed during a siege in the 1885 British Sudan campaign, this poem investigates the interstices between fame and fate, using particular details of daily existence. The subject matter recalls Rudyard Kipling and Alfred, Lord Tennyson, but Peters goes beyond them in his groping for psychological understanding. He foregrounds the human qualities of Gordon and questions what he did and felt as he moved through the days before his death.

Connections: In the English Lake District (1972) was also written during the 1960s. A short yet evocative book, it describes walks Peters took in England while on a Guggenheim Fellowship at Cambridge University in 1967; he mixes journal entries with poems about the landscape, William Wordsworth, and contemporary British life, such as the then-famous speedboat racer Donald Campbell. *Holy Cow* (1974) is another book whose publication date belies its earlier, 1960s conception. This collection of fables and bizarre dreams fits in with a time when sex, drugs, and rock'n'roll—so the slogans ran—could save the world. The book's exclamatory title (preserving a dated expression) suits it well. Typical titles include: "the poem as toad," "the little pornographers of power," and "the hangman and his darling."

Writing actively and giving readings, Peters transferred in 1968 to the University of California, Irvine. During the summer of 1968, after many years of difficulties, he and Jean separated permanently (divorcing in 1972), and Peters traveled to Europe with a male lover. *Red Midnight Moon* (1973), *Cool Zebras of Light* (1974), and *Gauguin's Chair* (1977) each present a version of this watershed year. Peters's lack of idealization makes the story of his stormy affair seem gripping; relentlessly, Peters explores the surface of relationships, trying to discover what makes people the way they are—be it sexy, maddening, or confused. Few copies of *Red Midnight Moon* or *Cool Zebras* still exist (stock of the latter having been destroyed in a fire), but *Gauguin's Chair* (which includes a strong title poem and an interview) remained in print for ten years. From the title

poem's opening lines ("The night is a lizard / beneath my shirt") through its five numbered sections, intensity builds almost imperceptibly so that the resolution of the final stanza comes as both a shock and a pleasure. The poem is in the voice of Vincent van Gogh, telling of his supercharged feelings for Paul Gauguin, for art, and for life, as in the closing stanza:

> I love you. I love you.
> And if I had killed you
> as you were dying I would have
> held you, would have lain
> full-length upon you until
> your feet were still.

Love and death, victory and loss—in this poem the terms cross and become redefined, as van Gogh reaches for a unity he cannot obtain.

With Peters's son's death behind him and with a steady companion (the poet Paul Trachtenberg, with whom Peters began living in 1970), Peters's writing shifted away from the strictly autobiographical. The 1973 chapbook *Byron Exhumed* marks the first of his "voice books," the category Peters prefers when talking collectively of his verse biographies. For this book he was led to the subject by a book from the 1930s about exhuming Lord Byron's remains. Writing in a variety of nineteenth-century forms, Peters invents responses from people who have just learned of Byron's death.

In fall 1973 Peters and Trachtenberg drove east together so that Peters could take up residence at the MacDowell Colony in New Hampshire. It was there, in one burst, that he wrote *The Gift to Be Simple*, published in 1975. This text uses the persona of Mother Ann Lee, founder of the Shaker religion. The one hundred poems capture her diction, her sexuality, and her vision—the whole sweep of her life. Peters had found a way to combine history and narrative flow (the usual stock of fiction) with the compression and persuasion of the first person voice, a direction he would follow in seven more books and one he continues to explore. His attention in *The Gift* falls equally on things large and small, from the niter on the walls of a cell, to the tickle of a mouse's whisker, to the full glory of seeing a heavenly vision. For example, an untitled poem, set during Lee's voyage from Liverpool to New York, employs graceful assonance and typifies the movement of the book, as Mother Lee, the speaker, treasures a small object in her hand,

Dust jacket for the 1975 collection of poems in which Peters combines history and narrative, writing from the point of view of Mother Ann Lee, founder of the Shaker religion

then looks into the night sky to see patterns and connections everywhere:

> The leaf is not a leaf.
> What is it?
> Did it whistle down from
> the mizzen,
> dropped by a sailor?
> The leaf is not a leaf.
> The big dipper is wound
> in vines, and a red leaf.
> Is this leaf the spinnaker's?

A companion volume titled *Shaker Light* was published in 1987.

Through the mid and late 1970s Peters was busy with a variety of projects. He was a prolific reviewer and critic, finally collecting his irreverence into the *Great American Poetry Bake-Off* books (1979-1991). As an editor of the Poets Now series for Scarecrow Press, he wrote introductions to books by Edwin Honig, Robin Magowan, Simon Perchick, Charles Plymell, Jerry Ratch, Rochelle Ratner, David Ray, Kathleen Spivack, and Jonathan Williams. His own poetry was equally diverse during this period: *Hawthorne* (1977), a trans-

position of Nathaniel Hawthorne's journal entries into verse, was done at Yaddo; a Carol Yeh painting inspired a lyrical collection—about leaving lovers and leaving children—entitled *The Drowned Man to the Fish* (1978), a book that is less read than some of his others, even though individual moments are quite powerful. The poorly distributed *Bronchial Tangle, Heart System* (1975) is also a love book, trying to untangle Peters's feelings for a Welsh poet. Often parodic, *The Poet as Ice-Skater* (1976) consists of poems about poets, including Goethe, Rimbaud, Whitman, and Tennyson.

The boreal book *Ikagnak* (1978) comes in part from a mental returning to the winters of Peters's Wisconsin boyhood. The first edition was a gorgeous, prize-winning edition of one hundred numbered copies, but it was not until 1985 that a revised version was available in paperback. Elisha Kent Kane is the tale's hero and subject, the Arctic explorer who searched for the lost Sir John Franklin Expedition. Dr. Kane's relief expedition was itself caught in a polar winter and deteriorated into scurvy, jealousy, and death. The text portrays the North well, mixing black humor with black ice. "Diversions," for example, interweaves an ironic ballad by Thomas Hood, about an amputee soldier's loss of his girl, with the grim facts of the ice-bound crew's decline (Hood's ballad is being sung aloud by a delirious sailor). The poems making up the *Ikagnak/Kane* editions appeared first in small-press quarterlies. A list of these periodicals shows the extent of Peters's contacts, with the poems being published in *Bluefish, Kayak, Mid-American Review, New York Quarterly, Poet Lore, Poetry Review, Pulpsmith, Texas Review,* and *Yarrow*. Iconoclastic and always investigating divergent paths, Peters as a contributor, subscriber, and reviewer has always supported "the littles" (thinking of Peters's critical work, one faculty member asked him once during a tenure review, "Why is it you always write about these people nobody's ever heard of?" Peters replied, "That's the point, isn't it?").

After *Ikagnak* other boyhood memories of Peters were focused into *What Dillinger Meant to Me* (1983), as Peters, preparing the prose of *Crunching Gravel*, confronted the iconography of his youth. *Celebrities*, a fold-out chapbook (1981), celebrates Gertrude Stein, Robert Mitchum, Marlene Dietrich, and others. This playful text has echoes of the work of Frank O'Hara.

Started in the mid 1970s, *The Picnic in the Snow* was published in 1982, showing another turn in Peters's style. The first edition, which was sold out by 1984, had been carelessly proofed, yet some readers never noticed, as his rich diction presented a panoply of unusual phrases. This mature work analyzes the important but reluctant ruler King Ludwig, who has his own horse as a dinner guest and muses that "Prussia is as foreign to me as Persia." In its contrasts of beauty and decay, joy and pain, *The Picnic in the Snow* demonstrates central concerns. "Love is a motion in the loins," claims Ludwig, only to grow reflective in the next line: "or, so I've assumed." He must learn to balance head and heart, public and private, and id and ego. Surrounded by blood-and-steel politics, Ludwig negotiates a place in history that suits his own aesthetic vision. Peters began presenting this book in a shortened form as a dramatic reading, ultimately refining it into a one-act monodrama. The shortened version and the corrected poetry text were published together in 1987.

Another individualist, even more eccentric than Ludwig, was Cornwall's Reverend Robert Hawker, Vicar of Morwenstowe; he was a nineteenth-century spiritualist who dressed like a mermaid sometimes at night and who had a fetish for burying drowned sailors. *Hawker* (1984) won the Poetry Society of America's di Castagnola Prize. The book tallies the price of nonconformity. In Hawker's case, although he corresponded with Tennyson and others, his poorly educated parishioners shared no common bond with him or his liberalism, and as a widower Hawker lived a life of virtual exile. Peters sees this isolation of the individualist as almost inevitable; Ludwig, after all, was deposed, and Ann Lee died of injuries inflicted by mobs. Despite this glum prognosis, there is much comedy in *Hawker*. In the poem "A Riddle From the Pulpit" Hawker teases his audience about which is the true right or left bank of a river; in another poem, Hawker appoints himself Pope of the True Church of Opium. Readers may expect this by mid book, since the vicar talks lovingly to his pig, Gyp, cavorts in claret cassock and yellow poncho, and hence seems capable of any surprise.

Haydon: An Artist's Life (1989) is in some senses a companion to both *Hawker* and *The Picnic in the Snow*. As do the others, *Haydon* treats the life of a confused and artistic person, the Romantic painter Benjamin Robert Haydon, and like the others, the book is steeped in period accuracy. *Haydon* questions the risks that art requires. In the final poem, unable to resolve ambition or psychosis, the fictional Haydon—as did the historical one—slits his own throat, finding exit if not solution.

Peters's most deeply disturbing book, which has met the most resistance, is also a dramatic monologue. Having been interested in aestheticism and decadence since graduate school, and having been astounded by the murderous twentieth century, Peters integrated these themes into *The Blood Countess* (1987). Elizabeth Bathory, a Hungarian countess (1560-1614), killed or tortured some seven hundred virgins, bathing in their blood. In her ravings, musings, speeches, and explications, Peters suggests that "violence is the religion of the 20th century" and that God is "the primal mass murderer." Raised in a sadistic, incestuous environment, Bathory states that she did nothing other than what readers, in her place, would have done. This often unsettles audiences experiencing the poem's live performances, especially as some scenes contain graphic descriptions of murder and bestiality. Yet Peters is no exhibitionist; he does this not to thrill, but to educate. If poetry can be about the decline of culture, can it not also be explicit about the elements of that decline? Peters says yes, and he

Robert Peters. Revisions of a page for FOR YOU, LILI MARLENE, a memoir of
WW II. Fall 1990.

Epilogue 3

in this chilly burg."

I lit a cigarette, as we turned towards the car.

"I didn't know you smoked," said Mom.

"Everybody in the Army smokes. The Red Cross used to give
us free Camels with our doughnuts."

"All that good sugar going to waste," said Nell, " while
we lived on rationing."

The old Ford, like most of Dad's cars smelled of recycled
crank case oil, and the upholstery was ripped. Through holes in
the floorboards you watched potholes flash past. A piece of
baling wire secured the back door, right side, which was always
closed. Dad was proud of securing old jalopies for next to
nothing and of making them run. His dream was to find an old
truck he could use for collecting scrap metal and for hauling
trash to the town dump.

As we drove through the Sundstein District, on the outskirts
of Eagle River, the air was fragrant of balsam and pine. The
forest appeared far more cut-over and stunted than I remembered,
Firs reaching a meager eight feet or so. The sandy soil lacked
the nutrients, for spectatularly tall trees. These browned and
withered, their decomposing bark too toxic for later growth. One
could always spot deposits of loam, for there tall healthy trees
clumped together in stands conveying an impression of what the
area was like covered with virgin forests, before the timber
barons whacked everything down.

"Look, Bob." Jane gestured as a pronged buck and a doe

Page from a draft for an autobiography (by permission of Robert Peters)

hopes to prove his point with his art. Just because some aspects of life are unpleasant, he implicitly argues, does not mean that literature should avoid them. In this sense, he carries with him Whitman's spirit, not just in passion and diction, but in a sensibility that refuses to blanch when faced by the indecorous. By looking deeply at violence, Peters makes readers look deeply at poetry's capabilities.

What sets Peters apart from most of his contemporaries is not his theoretical innovation or his leadership of a coterie, but his drive to write about all facets of human experience. His characters sometimes live lives of quiet desperation, sometimes are as public as the sun, and sometimes are no more substantial than a child's last breath. Yet no matter what their glory or depravity, Peters is ready to give them language.

Interviews:

Billy Collins, "Interview with Robert Peters," in *Gauguin's Chair: Selected Poems* (Trumansburg, N.Y.: Crossing, 1977), pp. 124-135;

Don Mark, "Robert Peters: An Interview," *Gay Sunshine Interviews: II* (San Francisco: Gay Sunshine, 1982), pp. 121-141;

William Matthews, "On the Shaker Poems," in *The Great American Poetry Bake-Off*, second series (Metuchen, N.J.: Scarecrow, 1982), pp. 241-250;

Philip Jason, "Robert Peters: An Interview," *Signal*, 1, (Fall 1987): 18-23;

Paul Trachtenberg, "Robert Peters: An Interview," *Paintbrush*, 14, (Fall 1987): 43-49.

References:

James Bertolino, "Robert Peters: An Appreciation," *Bellingham Review*, 10 (Spring 1987): 55-56;

Billy Collins, "Literary Reputation and the Thrown Voice: The Poetry of Robert Peters," in *A Gift of Tongues: Critical Challenges in Contemporary American Poetry*, edited by Marie Harris and Kathleen Aguero (Athens: University of Georgia Press, 1987), pp. 295-306;

Margo von Strohuber, "Menu of Virgins," *Small Press Review*, 20 (December 1988): 10;

Diane Wakowski, "Robert Peters," *American Poetry*, 2 (Winter 1985): 71-78;

Wakowski, "Robert Peters' *Hawker* and *Kane*," *Connecticut Poetry Review*, 6 (Winter 1987): 11-18.

Papers:

All the Robert Peters archives are in the University of Kansas library, Lawrence, Kansas.

Robert Phillips

(2 February 1938 -   )

Robert McPhillips
Iona College

BOOKS: *8 & 8* (Syracuse: Janos, 1960);
Inner Weather (Francestown, N.H.: Golden Quill, 1966);
The Achievement of William Van O'Connor (Syracuse: George Arents Research Library, 1969);
The Land of Lost Content (New York: Vanguard, 1970);
The Confessional Poets (Carbondale: Southern Illinois University Press, 1973);
Denton Welch (New York: Twayne, 1974);
The Pregnant Man (Garden City, N.Y.: Doubleday, 1978);
William Goyen (Boston: Twayne, 1979);
Running on Empty (Garden City, N.Y.: Doubleday, 1981);
Personal Accounts: New & Selected Poems 1966-1986 (Princeton, N.J.: Ontario Review, 1986);
The Wounded Angel (San Diego: Brighton, 1987);
A Public Landing Revisited (Brownsville, Oreg.: Story Line, 1991).

OTHER: *Aspects of Alice: Lewis Carroll's Dreamchild*, edited by Phillips (New York: Vanguard, 1971; London: Gollancz, 1972);
Moonstruck: An Anthology of Lunar Poetry, edited by Phillips (New York: Vanguard, 1974);
Last and Lost Poems of Delmore Schwartz, edited by Phillips (New York: Vanguard, 1979; revised edition, New York: New Directions, 1989);
The Collected Stories of Noël Coward, edited by Phillips (New York: Dutton, 1983); republished as *Star Quality: The Collected Stories of Noël Coward* (New York: Dutton, 1987);
Letters of Delmore Schwartz, edited by Phillips (Princeton, N.J.: Ontario Review, 1984);
The Stories of Denton Welch, edited by Phillips (New York: Dutton, 1985);
Delmore Schwartz, *The Ego is Always at the Wheel: Bagatelles*, edited by Phillips (New York: New Directions, 1986; Manchester, U.K.: Carcanet, 1987);

Triumph of the Night: 20th-Century Ghost Stories, edited by Phillips (New York: Carroll & Graf, 1989);
Delmore Schwartz and James Laughlin: Selected Correspondence, edited by Phillips (New York: Norton, 1991);
Delmore Schwartz, *Shenandoah and Other Verse Plays*, edited by Phillips (Brockport, N.Y.: BOA Editions, 1991)

SELECTED PERIODICAL PUBLICATIONS—UNCOLLECTED: "Abandoned, Not Finished: A Poet Looks at Four of His Poems," *English Record*, 21 (February 1971): 6-20;
" 'Interviewing' Mr. Larkin," *Courier* (Syracuse Library Associates), 24 (Spring 1989): 33-47;
"The Democracy of Universal Vulnerability: The Poetry of Isabella Gardner," *Chelsea*, 48 (Summer 1989): 64-74;
"Visiting the Gregorys," *New Criterion*, 9 (September 1990): 24-34;
"On Painting-Poems," *Pequod*, 28/29/30 (1990): 245-250.

Robert Phillips is a prolific and engaged man of letters—a fiction writer, reviewer, critic, memoirist, editor, anthologist, literary executor, and, most notably, a poet—whose writing has appeared in such prestigious journals as the *Paris Review*, *Ontario Review*, *Hudson Review* and the *New Yorker*. Despite the quantity and diversity of his work, however, and his legion of close friendships over the years with many of America's most prominent writers—among them Delmore Schwartz; James T. Farrell; Horace Gregory and his wife, poet Marya Zaturenska; Karl Shapiro; William Goyen; Elizabeth Spencer; and Joyce Carol Oates—Phillips has never received the level of recognition he deserves. Part of the reason for this is because Phillips was slow to establish himself strongly in any single literary genre. His first two volumes of poetry published in the 1960s were not followed up with a more substantial book of poems for more than a decade. A

Robert Phillips (photograph copyright 1987 by Thomas Victor)

promising collection of stories, albeit also apprentice work, published in 1970 (*The Land of Lost Content*), was not succeeded by a second volume of fiction until over twenty years later. And Phillips's three volumes of literary criticism—including his ground-breaking work *The Confessional Poets* (1973)—were relatively minor due to the constraints of the brief, overview formats in which they were written. But since the publication of *The Pregnant Man* in 1978, Phillips has continued to grow in stature as a poet. The culmination of his development of a wry, vulnerable, humane, and witty poetic voice occurred with the 1986 publication of *Personal Accounts: New & Selected Poems 1966-1986.*

Robert Schaeffer Phillips was born on 2 February 1938 in Milford, Delaware, the son of Katheryn Augusta (Schaeffer) Phillips, a social-column writer and Thomas Allen Phillips, a metallurgical engineer who taught physics and chemistry at the local high school. Much of Robert Phillips's best writing depicts his ambivalent feelings about his boyhood spent in rural Sussex County, Delaware, described by him as "Ninety Miles from Nowhere" in a powerful poetic sequence. As a child, Phillips studied piano while attending grammar school. Early on, his artistic ambitions wavered among music, art, and literature. But to pursue his goals, Phillips recognized the necessity of escaping the narrow confines of Laurel, Delaware, where he attended the public high school. As a youth, Phillips took frequent bus trips to Philadelphia to partake of its cultural life. But his most profound break from Delaware occurred when he left to attend Syracuse University in 1956. He was to remain at Syracuse, first as an undergraduate and then as a graduate student, instructor, and admissions officer, until 1964, when he left, with his wife, the poet Judith Bloomingdale, whom he married on 16 June 1962, to pursue a career in advertising in Manhattan.

Phillips's years at Syracuse were unusually fertile. It was then that his friendship with classmate Joyce Carol Oates began. With Oates, Phillips has maintained a lively correspondence for three decades; her letters to him—along with those from many other significant literary figures—have recently been deposited in the George Arents Research Library for Special Collections at the Bird Library, Syracuse University.

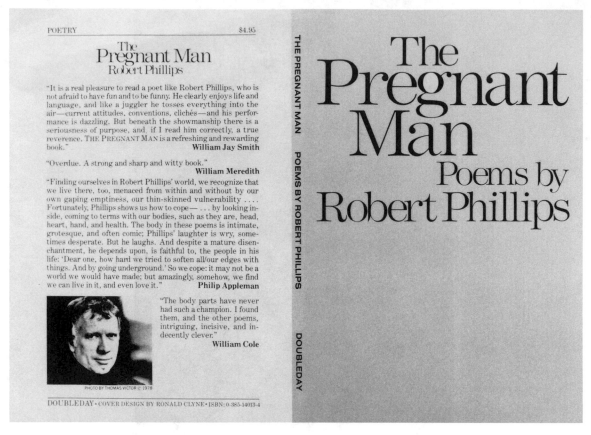

Cover for the 1978 book that Phillips's friend Joyce Carol Oates considered essential reading for all feminists

Oates was to play an important role in Phillips's career: she provided a blurb for the first trade edition of his poems (*Inner Weather*, 1966) and favorably reviewed *The Pregnant Man* in the *New Republic*. Most important, as coeditor of Ontario Review Press with her husband Raymond Smith, she published his *Personal Accounts*.

Phillips also developed his independent literary sensibility and identity at Syracuse. His devotion to such authors as Carson McCullers—on whom he wrote his master's thesis—Denton Welch, and William Goyen, writers who focused on distinctive, isolated rural landscapes and psychologically eccentric or grotesque characters, was encouraged by his professors. These writers, most immediately, influenced the Gothic stories of Phillips's *Land of Lost Content*, set in the imaginary town of Public Landing, Delaware. Many of these stories were written while Phillips was a student at Syracuse. Finally, as the editor of *Syracuse 10*, the college literary magazine—to which he and Oates both contributed—Phillips began to acquire the skills that would help him edit volumes of essays, stories, and poetry, including numerous works by Delmore Schwartz. Now Schwartz's

literary executor, Phillips first came to know him, as well as Shirley Jackson and her husband, Stanley Edgar Hyman, while a graduate student and instructor at Syracuse during the early 1960s.

Phillips's first two collections of poetry, *8 & 8* (1960) and *Inner Weather*, are comprised largely of the poet's undergraduate work and are best thought of as juvenilia. The first book is a limited edition of poems chosen and published by John J. Janos shortly after Phillips received his B.A. *Inner Weather* is a slightly more substantial volume. It shows Phillips's innate linguistic flair, his fluent assonance and consonance, as in these lines from "Sunflowers": "You stand stalking your ground, stiffening in the breeze, / The phoenix of flowers, bright pillars of fire, / Then in umber silence—you burn yourselves out." The volume also announces many of the subjects and types of poems Phillips would focus on in his subsequent work: pastoral poems in the Robert Frost tradition, such as "Sunflowers," "Dandelions," and "Autumn Remnants"; poems on painters, poets, and musicians—Picasso, Aaron Copland, and Amy Lowell; and elegies such as "In Memory of Elizabeth Purnell" and "John Jacobs

Departing." These poems also demonstrate Phillips's grounding in traditional poetic meter, rhyming, and form. Though he would experiment with freer forms in his subsequent work, Phillips never fully turned his back on this early recognition of the centrality of form and meter to poetry. Nevertheless, Phillips himself is, on the whole, dissatisfied with *Inner Weather*, considering it, in retrospect, premature.

It was to be twelve years before Phillips published another volume of poetry. Two years before the publication of *Inner Weather*, he abandoned Syracuse and the academic world for New York City and a career in advertising, which he still pursues. Despite this shift in locale, Phillips remained extremely productive in the literary world during the long hiatus between volumes of poetry. This period saw the publication of *The Land of Lost Content* and his compilation of essays entitled *Aspects of Alice: Lewis Carroll's Dreamchild* (1971), which includes an essay by Phillips's wife. He did much critical writing in Dusseldorf, West Germany, where he spent two years, 1971 and 1972, with his wife and son, Graham Van Buren Phillips (born in 1967), while serving as vice-president and associate creative director of the Gramm and Grey ad agency. There Phillips completed work on his most extensive piece of poetry criticism, *The Confessional Poets*, a seminal examination of Theodore Roethke, Robert Lowell, John Berryman, Sylvia Plath, Anne Sexton, and others. Though Phillips's poetry never quite deals in the psychic extremes connected with these poets, who often verge on suicidal despair, his attraction to the confessional poets would profoundly affect the course of his own poetry, making it more directly autobiographical. This period also saw the publication of *Moonstruck: An Anthology of Lunar Poetry* (1974) and his second critical study, *Denton Welch* (1974), an examination of the hermetic British writer whose stories he would later edit for publication in the United States and whose novels he was to prompt back into print, helping bring Welch a minor cult following in the 1980s.

In 1978 *The Pregnant Man* marked a significant advance for Phillips. Whereas *Inner Weather* was a seemingly random collection of verse, *The Pregnant Man* is divided into three thematically organized sections, which set the pattern for the poet's subsequent collections. The first section, "Body Icons," contains a series of poems dedicated to body parts—hand, foot, head, and penis. The poet examines his physical and psy-

chic makeup in early middle age with a modest and wry sense of humor that is sometimes deeply touching but occasionally overly sentimental. The best of these poems, however, are less about body parts than about states of being. Oates praised the volume for its ability to move beyond sexual stereotypes and considered it required reading for feminists. One sees the theme of androgyny, common to the work of some of Phillips's favorite novelists—McCullers, Welch, and Goyen—in poems such as "A Pregnant Man" and "The Married Man." In the former the poet, after a night of comically grotesque labor, gives "birth / to an eight-pound blue / -eyed bouncing baby / poem," only to see it die "two hours later": "You know / how it is with poems. (My last one had two / heads and no heart.)" "Heart" is Phillips's strength, and sometimes it is needed to compensate for a lack of fully rigorous craft or to carry a perhaps overly stretched conceit like the one above.

"The Married Man" contains a similarly strained conceit, that of a man "cut in two"—one "the sissy side" his mother "dressed like a doll," the other more masculine—looking for someone to unite him. The speaker's wife so causes him to " 'pull [himself] together' " that "it is only when I study hard / the looking glass I see that one / eye is slightly high, one corner / of my mouth twitches—a fish on a hook— / whenever you abandon me." Phillips thus acknowledges the fragility of any state of psychic balance as well as the graceful yet imperfect nature of all human relationships. The third section of *The Pregnant Man*, "The Sacred & the Suburban," establishes another of the poet's major landscapes and themes: the examination of marriage and domestic life in the suburban setting of Westchester County, north of New York City, made part of the permanent literary landscape by John Cheever. This setting reflects Phillips's move to northern Westchester in 1967 from Manhattan. Eventually he would settle into the rural village of Katonah, at whose library he has been in charge of a prestigious series of poetry readings since 1967. The best of the poems in "The Sacred & the Suburban" is "Decks," which playfully likens those expansive wooden constructs typical of the wealthy suburban home to ocean liners. There wives remain while husbands commute to Manhattan in their own "big boats": "Riviera, Continental, Thunderbird!" The poem concludes in a fantasy-vision of these decks becoming unmoored and

Cover for the 1981 collection that prompted James Dickey to call Phillips "likably imaginative"

floating down the local highways—"Saw Mill, / Merritt, Interstate"—to Manhattan:

> You will see
> them by the hundreds, flying flags
> With family crests, boats afloat
>
> on hope. Wives tilt forward, figureheads.
> Children, motley crew, swab the decks.
>   Let the fleet pass down Grand Concourse,
>   make waves on Bruckner Boulevard.
>   Wives acknowledge crowds, lift pets.
>   The armada enters Broadway, continues
>   down to Wall. Docked, the pilgrims
>   search for their captains of industry. When
>   they come, receive them well. They harbor
>   no hostilities. Some have great gifts.

Phillips once again here combines humor with the clever use of extended analogy to yoke two seemingly disparate levels of being: suburban and urban, domestic and occupational.

The appearance of Phillips's third trade volume of poetry, *Running on Empty* (1981), a mere three years after the second attests to his stronger sense of assurance of himself as a poet. *Running on Empty* is even more impressive than its predecessor and develops some of Phillips's previous thematic preoccupations in poems dissecting suburban domestic life; he expands his range, as well, most significantly in a sequence of poems set in the Delaware of his childhood. Somewhat less memorable are the sections of the volume devoted to poets and paintings. The final section in the book, "Survival Songs," becomes stronger in its modified form in *Personal Accounts*. Oddly, however, one of the best poems from this section is omitted from the latter volume. "Lump," dedicated to Phillips's physician, is about a growth the poet imagines to be "the big C that killed Granny, / Uncle, and now wants to kill me." Phillips characteristically draws upon material—illness, operations, fear of death—connected with confessional poets such as Anne Sexton and Sylvia Plath, but treats it more lightly, using puns ("You are an inelegant swell") that make his poetry more appealingly vulnerable and human rather than emotionally extreme and horrifying. Though the lump is ultimately declared " 'perfectly benign,' " only a torn muscle, it nonetheless becomes emblematic for Phillips of "a hard lesson": "Learn to take one's lumps." This conclusion may seem too pat, too much clichéd wordplay—perhaps the reason Phillips chose not to include it among his selected poems—but it also represents risks he is willing to take to communicate painful personal experiences in humane and universal terms. It is a flawed but thematically significant poem.

Many of Phillips's strongest poems on family life—in suburban Westchester and rural Delaware—were first collected in the initial two sections of *Running on Empty*. He has recategorized his suburban poems as "Middle Age Nocturnes" here, representing both his advancing age and his deepening insight into the forces that hold a marriage together. The Delaware sequence, "Ninety Miles from Nowhere," also written from the perspective of the poet's middle years, is a reflection on a harsh childhood dominated by a strong, largely unsympathetic father and a loved but diminished mother. It perhaps constitutes Phillips's most powerful and original achievement as a poet. Both of these sequences have been reorganized, with additions and deletions, in *Personal Accounts*.

In addition to his own poetry, Phillips has made significant contributions to contemporary American poetry in his capacity as Delmore Schwartz's literary executor. In that role he has edited Schwartz's uncollected poems (1979), his letters (1984, 1991), his miscellaneous prose "bagatelles" (1986), and his plays (1991). *Letters of Delmore Schwartz* (1984) was published by Ontario Review Press, run by Joyce Carol Oates and her husband, Raymond Smith. Smith, Phillips's editor, knowing Phillips had another book-length manuscript of poems, expressed interest in publishing it. However, Smith also knew that Phillips's three trade collections were now out of print, and he suggested producing a volume of selected and new poems. This editorial suggestion resulted in Phillips's most thoughtfully organized and resonant volume, the weaker poems from the earlier books deleted, the better of them amplified by being printed with Phillips's most effective recent poems.

In introducing the seven sections of *Personal Accounts*, Phillips explains that his work is not arranged "chronologically but by topic, since I continue to explore certain concerns—preoccupations—from book to book." He also remarks that "the volume's basic unit is the progression not of the poem but of the chapter." This organization of poems into chapters is most effective in the book's first two groupings, which limn the poet's present and past. They describe a movement from a residence in hell to the elegiac pleasures of living in a suburban purgatory that often approaches what Phillips recognizes to be a human impossibility: an earthly paradise. The Westchester poems in "Middle Age Nocturnes" largely focus on how natural and domestic details reflect the condition of a marriage. In the first poem, "Middle Age: A Nocturne," the insomniac speaker takes stock of the sleeping house surrounding him, moving from objects of depleted pleasure—the silver tea service, now tarnished; the grand piano that "bares / yellowed teeth as you / give it the brush off"; and the forbidden liquor cabinet—to a contemplation of his children and wife. The children seem self-sufficient, "bear[ing] new adulthood easily"; the wife appears to be "a gaunt nun of the old order" who "bends to a mystical flame" that excludes her husband. Yet this diminished landscape finally yields a revelation suggesting the resiliency of family life: "But early this morning, / in the upper field— / seven young deer / grazing in the rain!"

Nature can comfort but can also underline the tenuousness of the taken-for-granted stability of a marriage, as in "Autumn Crocuses":

Basketing leaves during earth's
annual leaf-taking, we realize
with a start—something's missing.
The autumn crocuses that would spring

each October by these rocks,
no longer here! We never planted
them, but they implanted themselves
on us. Now, for their lack,

we are poorer. . . .

Yet the very tenuousness that the missing crocuses evoke stimulates the poet's rapt attention, as is emphasized by the delicate play of assonance and consonance with this passage. The poem's

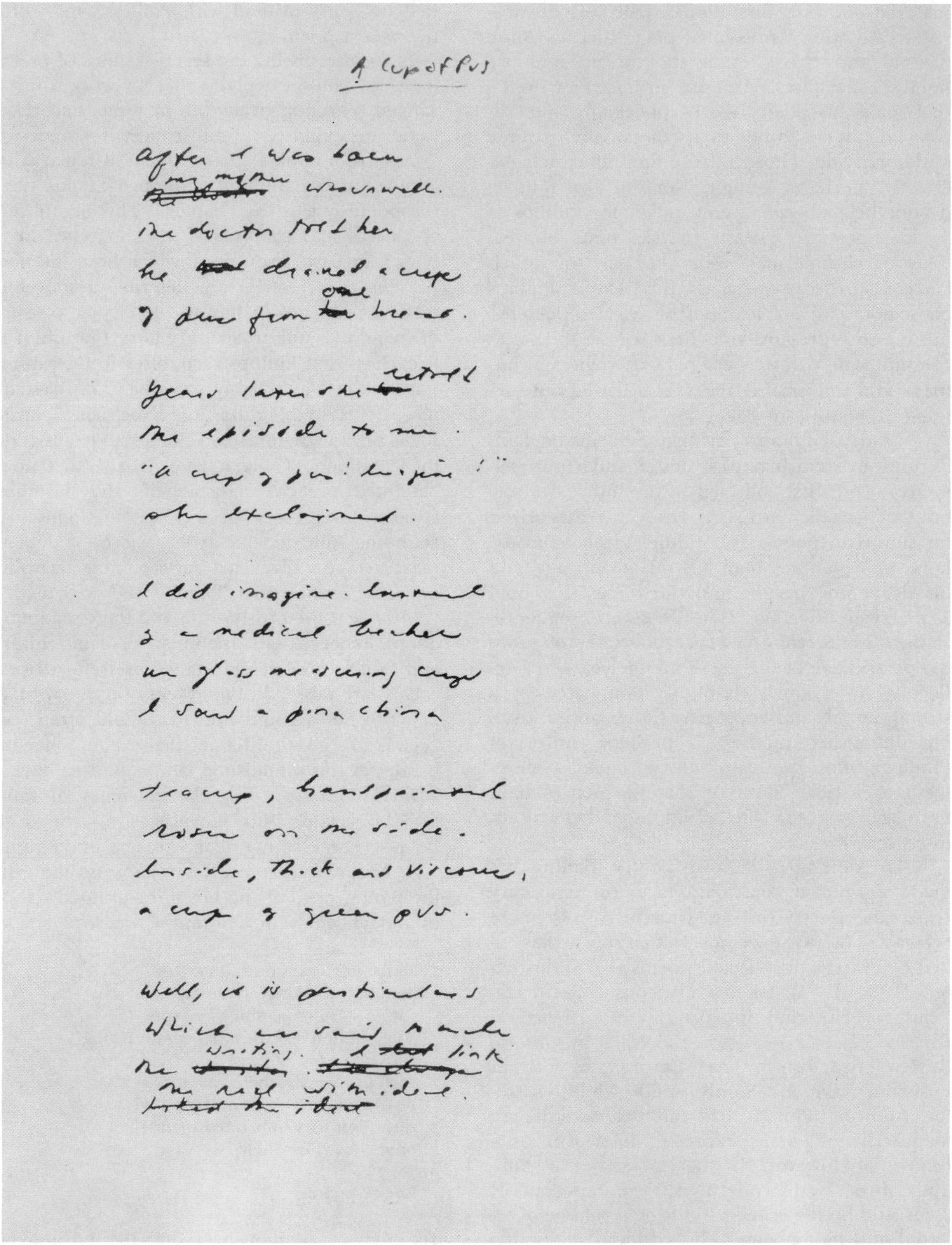
A Cup of Pus

After I was born
my mother was unwell.
The doctor told her
he drained a cup
of pus from one breast.

Years later she retold
the episode to me.
"A cup of pus! Imagine!"
she exclaimed.

I did imagine. Instead
of a medical beaker
or glass measuring cup
I saw a pink china

teacup, handpainted
roses on the side.
Inside, thick and viscous,
a cup of green pus.

Well, it is particulars
which are said to make
the writing. I link
the real with ideal.

Early and late drafts for a poem that Phillips plans to include in a collection titled "The Stone Crab and Other Poems" (by permission of Robert Phillips)

"A CUP OF PUS"

After I was born
~~my~~ Mother couldn't rest.
The doctor drained a cup
of pus from her breast.

Years ~~later~~ she retold
the tale as an aside.
"A cup of pus! Imagine!"
she breathlessly cried.

I imagined. ~~Instead~~ not
~~of~~ measuring cup,
or medical beaker,
but ~~I saw~~ a china teacup--

roses ~~hand~~painted red,
thorns handpainted rust-- _green_
inside, ~~thick~~ and viscous,
a cupful of pus.

D~~o~~ you cringe? ~~Don't~~. Life _is both_
~~is both~~ ideal and real.
~~It is~~ Such particulars
~~which~~ are ~~said to~~ make us feel.

Dust jacket for the collection that was instrumental in earning Phillips a 1987 Award in Literature from the American Academy and Institute of Arts and Letters, whose citation praised his "observational quirkiness, tolerance and rueful intelligence"

music balances the loss of "the unaccountable / we thought we could count on."

Phillips's theme in this section seems to be the consolations of family life, nature, and poetry amidst a sense of middle-age loss and decay, but the solace to be found in his reminiscences of his Delaware youth in "Ninety Miles from Nowhere" is much more limited, achieved through time and distance and almost exclusively represented by the achievement of poetic form. The bleak, "unrelentingly flat" emotional landscape of this sequence is outlined in its initial poem, "Vertical & Horizontal," which portrays the conflict between the speaker's parents. His mother, from the Blue Ridge Mountains, is brought by her husband to live in the horizontal landscape of "the only [Delaware] town he ever knew / or felt comfortable in. . . ." Only once a year, when she returned to visit her native Virginia, "head lifted high," could she escape the fact that, through the dull routine

of her marriage, she was forced to endure an emotionally circumscribed life, pretending in Virginia that "she never had come down in the world."

The severity of the father is emphasized again in "Once," which presents an even rarer escape from claustrophobic routine. It opens with an instance of negative family mythology, the mother explaining to her poet son that Labor Day "is when everybody / else in the country goes to the beach / except us. . . ." It concludes with a limited sense of escape:

One year we went to the beach. A new world,

half an hour away. I never had seen
the ocean. My big toe in the Atlantic!

Mother and the four of us on the beach,
Father on the boardwalk on a bench,

under an umbrella, wearing a ratty straw hat.
Suddenly he was somebody's old aunt!

(Once he'd gotten sun poisoning fishing,
he claimed.) He looked at his wristwatch a lot.

Mother wore an ancient wool bathing suit,
her legs thin as a stork's.

I leapt repeatedly into the muscled sea,
the sea rumbled, my brothers romped,

the sun felt good, the salt smelt good,
Jesus! it was fun, and we never went back.

The tightness of the last four lines, juxtaposing joy and its extreme curtailment, emphasizes the hard-won consolation that is seen again in one of the later poems in the sequence, "Running on Empty." Perhaps Phillips's most controlled and moving poem, it presents the younger poet driving his father's Chevrolet and tempting fate by habitually "running" on an empty tank. This poem's conclusion about survival despite a father's withholding of love embodies the deep core of emotional and formal energy in Phillips's best poetry:

I stranded myself only once, a white
night with no gas station open, ninety miles

from nowhere. Panicked for a while,
at standstill, myself stalled.

At dawn the car and I both refilled.
But Father, I am running on Empty still.

In 1987, a year after the publication of *Personal Accounts*, Robert Phillips won the Award in Literature from the American Academy and Institute of Arts and Letters. The citation noted his "observational quirkiness, tolerance and rueful intelligence" and characterized his poetry as "elegantly open and accessible, his subjects painstakingly explored." As he matures as a poet, as his middle-age advances, Phillips continues to write poems for such quarterlies as *Boulevard*, the *Hudson Review*, *Ontario Review*, and *New Criterion*, poems that glance back at his life in Sussex County, Delaware, and ones that delineate the tangled joys and tribulations of suburban domestic life and the temptations and frustrations of erotic excursions. One of the strongest poems in *Personal Accounts* is "Queen Anne's Lace," an elegy to the poet Isabella Gardner. Phillips continues to excel in this form, as his subsequent elegies to

writers and friends such as Marianne Moore, Howard Moss, Jean Stafford, and art critic John I. H. Baur attest. Remaining poetically engaged with the toll of the seasons, the years, with loves and lives enduring and lost, Phillips is a poet of genuine accomplishment and continued promise. Like Robert Frost, the most profound of his poetic influences, he is a poet from whom one can expect continued richness and wisdom in his later years.

Interview:
Jerome Mazzaro, "Craft Interview with Robert Phillips," *Modern Poetry Studies*, 9 (Autumn 1978): 86-106.

Bibliography:
Tom Baker, "Robert Phillips: A Checklist, 1960-1981," *Bulletin of Bibliography*, 38, (July-September 1981): 139-149.

References:
Darylin Brewer, "Poets in the Corporation," *Coda: Poets & Writers Newsletter*, 13 (November-December 1985): 1-18;
James Finn Cotter, "The Poet's Food is Love and Fame," *America*, 146 (27 February 1982): 156-160;
Cotter, "Public and Private Poetry," *Hudson Review*, 40 (Spring 1987): 149-155;
Dana Gioia, "Business and Poetry," *Hudson Review*, 36 (Spring 1983): 147-171;
David Mason, "Five Poets," *Literary Review* (Spring 1988): 367-374;
Jerome Mazzaro, "Varieties of Poetic Experience," *Sewanee Review*, 95 (Winter 1987): 149-158;
David Sanders, "Divers [*sic*] Crossroads of Earth and Mind," *Tar River Poetry*, 22 (Spring 1983): 38-46;
Robert B. Shaw, "Brief Reviews," *Poetry*, 149 (November 1986): 94-109;
Alan Williamson, "In a Middle Style," *Poetry*, 135 (March 1980): 348-354.

Papers:
The George Arents Research Library for Special Collections, Bird Library, Syracuse University, houses the Robert Phillips Papers. In addition to his own published and unpublished writings, his papers include extensive correspondence with some of the major literary figures of the past four decades.

Pattiann Rogers

(23 March 1940 -   )

Marsha Engelbrecht

BOOKS: *The Expectations of Light* (Princeton, N.J.: Princeton University Press, 1981);
The Only Holy Window (Denton, Tex.: Trilobite, 1984);
The Tattooed Lady in the Garden (Middletown, Conn.: Wesleyan University Press, 1986);
Legendary Performance (Memphis: Ion, 1987);
Splitting and Binding (Middletown, Conn.: Wesleyan University Press, 1989).

If one allows for the advances in scientific knowledge since the time of Ralph Waldo Emerson, it is possible, when reading Pattiann Rogers's poetry, to imagine she received her instruction, in complete spiritual compliance, from Emerson himself, so much is his influence apparent in her work. She has taken to heart the transcendentalist concept, as stated in Emerson's "The Poet" (in *Essays, Second Series*, 1844), that all aspects of the natural world "are symbols of the passage of the world into the soul of man, to suffer there a change, and reappear a new and higher fact." She would be the poet "whose eye can integrate all the parts," the poet "who reattaches things to nature and to the Whole."

Pattiann Tall Rogers was born on 23 March 1940 in Joplin, Missouri. Her early upbringing was traditional Presbyterian; however, when she was thirteen years old, her parents, William Elmer Tall, an inventor, and Irene Keiter Tall, joined a doctrinal sect dedicated to the conversion of nonbelievers. On 3 September 1960 she married John Rogers, a geophysicist, and in 1961 she received from the University of Missouri a B.A. in English literature with a minor in zoology. From 1961 to 1963 she taught high-school English in Missouri. In 1981 she received her M.A. in creative writing from the University of Houston. She and John have two sons, John Ashley and Arthur William. The family currently resides in Castle Rock, Colorado.

The poetry of Pattiann Rogers has appeared in numerous periodicals, including the *American Poetry Review, Carolina Quarterly, Iowa Review, Kenyon Review, New England Review/Breadloaf Quarterly,* the *New Yorker, Poetry, Prairie Schooner, Southern Review,* and the *Yale Review*. In addition to her full-length collections, she is the author of a chapbook entitled *The Only Holy Window* (1984), and her poems are included in several anthologies and textbooks.

Rogers has received numerous awards. From *Poetry Northwest* she was awarded the Young Poet's Prize in 1980 and the Roethke Prize in 1981. The editors of *Poetry* awarded her the Tietjens Prize in 1981 and the Bess Hokin Prize in 1982. Also in 1982 she received the Voertmann Poetry Award from the Texas Institute of Letters for *The Expectations of Light* (1981). She received grants from the National Endowment for the Arts in 1982 and 1988, and a Guggenheim Fellowship for 1984-1985. In 1990 Rogers received the Natalie Ornish/Soeurette Diehl Fraser Award from the Texas Institute of Letters for *Splitting and Binding* (1989).

In 1988 Rogers was the Richard Hugo Poet-in-Residence at the University of Montana. She has been an assistant professor and a senior lecturer at the University of Texas in Austin, a visiting assistant professor at the University of Houston and Southern Methodist University, a faculty member of Vermont College of Norwich University in Montpelier, and she has participated in and conducted several poetry workshops, including the Southwest Writers Conferences in Houston in 1982 and 1986.

Rogers's poetry is solidly constructed around subject matter found in the natural world. This wide array of subjects ranges from the tiny blastula of a frog cell, at one extreme, to exploding galaxies at the other. With this in mind, it is helpful to have a set of Audubon Society Field Guides handy, so varied and often unfamiliar are the things Rogers describes. Emerson said that there are many secrets sleeping in nature, and Rogers awakens some of these by showing the "whistle / Of the red-tailed hawk," the "rush / Of the leaf-nosed bat," and "the soft slip /

Of fog easing through sand" in the poem "Counting What the Cactus Contains," and "the chortle of the Siamese fighting fish" in "Making a History" (both collected in *The Expectations of Light*). Her poems are fascinating bundles of flora, fauna, and scientific fact. It is impossible to ignore the precision of her observations and her commitment to her predominant, transcendentalist theme.

In the first poem of *The Expectations of Light*, "In Order to Perceive," Rogers takes readers into a literal deep darkness, into a sort of sensory deprivation tank; then, through a relentless power of suggestion, causes them to see various manifestations of light—a single candle burning, the lighted helmets of miners, lights on sailboat riggings, star clusters, and so on—and "soon, there is no hesitation to the breadth / Of your discoveries." Readers are then asked to visualize themselves becoming numerous points of fire, rising to blend with the star-filled night sky in the ultimate transcendental experience. In this first poem, Rogers

points to her objective: to compel readers to see themselves as completely at one with the natural world. To this end, she constantly challenges perceptions by providing new perspectives. Readers are taken inside a hatching egg where "a fragile / Break appears, releasing / Light for the first time" ("Containment"). If one is able to achieve the proper perspective, then one may have a response to the question Rogers poses at the end of "Illumination":

> Sitting on a high branch in the cloudy night,
> Can the raccoon see what expectations
> Light has led him to understand?
> When the last leaf of the yellow poplar
> Has been blown away,
> Will the eye of the girl remembering
> Be the only body left there for light?

Rogers commonly uses such evocative questions. One's ability to see from many different angles will impart illumination, the light of understanding. From there it is a small step to the placing of

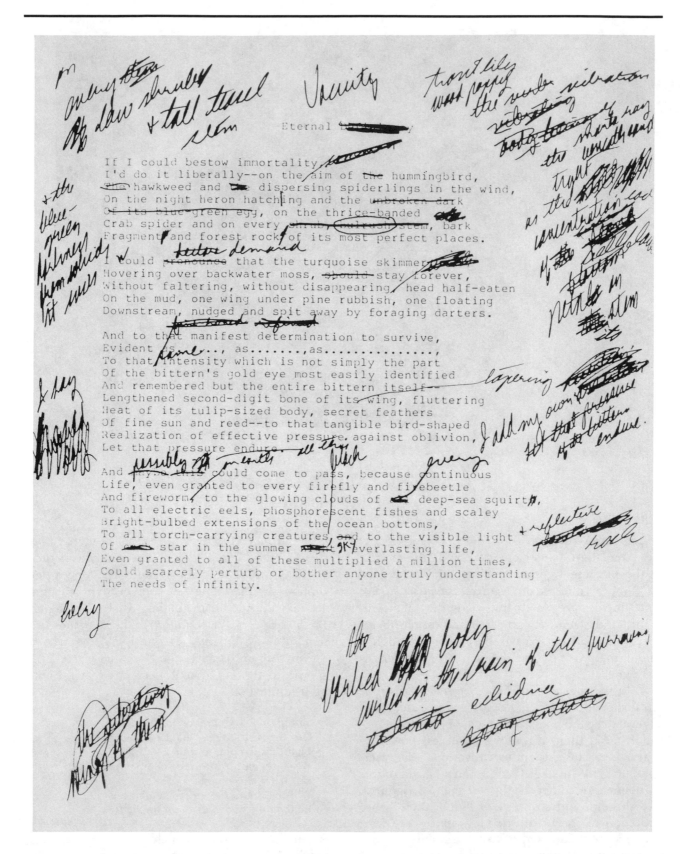

One of approximately twenty drafts for "The Objects of Immortality," published in Splitting *and* Binding *(by permission of Pattiann Rogers)*

oneself squarely into the harmonious realm of nature.

By accepting one's inextricable bond with the natural world, one is able to give meaning to the universe. In a 1987 interview with Richard McCann, Rogers stated that "the meaning we invent is physical, rooted in our bones . . . one with the material of the universe. Our bestowal of meaning is part of the universe." This creation of meaning is all-inclusive and ongoing. As to the affirmation of the human soul, she writes, "I have cherished it. I have named it. / By my own solicitations / I have proof of its existence" ("On the Existence of the Soul").

Rogers bestows lavish attention on the physical nature of the human body as well. In the poem "Being Defined," human touch becomes a way of knowing things that otherwise cannot be verbalized: "What I am now / Is only she who binds space for you. / And your breath, the softest motion / Against my ear, will never understand itself / In any other terms." This sensuality appears in several poems about love and sex. Yet these poems never stray far from Rogers's underlying theme, which is obvious in "Love Song": "It's true. You're no better / Than the determined boar, snorgling and rooting."

There are also poems in Rogers's first book that attach physical significance to abstract ideas, such as praise and persistence, to show that apparently there is need in the universe even for these things: "What if praise and its emanations / Were necessary catalysts to the harmonious / Expansion of the void?" ("Supposition"). In this approach, the subject is recognizable but is newly considered as the poem progresses. Again traditional perspectives are challenged.

Rogers also addresses the creation of art in several poems of this collection, as in "Capturing the Scene." Emerson's "poetic eye" can never be satisfied with mere detail because, no matter how exquisitely the artist has captured the details, as Rogers states, "he must then turn away his face completely / And remember more."

The acts of witnessing and praising the wonders of the natural world continue in *The Tattooed Lady in the Garden*, Rogers's 1986 book. The "synonymy" she proposes in the title poem, "Finding the Tattooed Lady in the Garden," is animated by "the wide blue wing / Of [the lady's] raised hand" and "the crisscrossed thicket, honeysuckle, and fireweed / Of her face," illustrating the omnipresence of this symbolic, transcendental figure. Rogers contrasts this feminine universal being with the concept of a masculine god, which she depicts elsewhere in the book. Her version of Emerson's "choral harmony of the Whole" is called "The Creation of the Inaudible": "His [the god's] exclamations might blend so precisely with the final / Crises of the swallows settling before dark / That no one will be able to say with certainty, / 'That last long cry winging over the rooftop / Came from god.'" Of utmost importance to this poem is the conclusion that "the only unique sound of his being / Is the spoken postulation of his unheard presence." Humans have created the god; creation has become an interaction. The significance of this interdependence is explored again in "The Possible Suffering of a God During Creation," wherein the incomplete god has cried and has not yet had time "to elicit from his creation its invention / Of his own solace."

The darker topics of death and insanity make their first appearances in Rogers's poetry in this same book. Various perspectives are offered by which human beings, as creatures aware of their own mortality, can impart meaning to death. In "The Possible Advantages of the Expendable Multitudes," Rogers notes that individual death may seem odd to a cluster of protozoans, to which humans "might simply appear to be possessed / By an awkward notion of longevity, a peculiar bias / For dying alone." A nest of tadpoles may view death as commonplace and unremarkable, "functioning in a thousand specific places at once, / Always completing the magnitude of its obligations." Rogers points out that death is entirely dependent on the living for its existence. This is in keeping with Emerson's idea that death is part of the order of "the Whole"; as he writes in "Threnody": "My servant death, with solving rite / Pours finite into infinite."

Death and other matters are on the minds of five characters who make their debut in *The Tattooed Lady*. These friends—the dreamer, the artist, the pragmatist, the nurturer, and the sensualist—ponder and speculate. Each represents one aspect of belief. In contrast, knowledge appears in the form of the Indian, Kioka, the natural man, who moves quietly through the poems and to whom profound generalities are attributed: "Kioka / And his ancestors call the infinite and continuous / Record they make of this moment 'The Book / Of the Beginning and The Chronicle of the End'" ("The Definition of Time").

This relativistic approach is carried over into Rogers's *Legendary Performance* (1987). The

Rogers circa 1985 (photograph by John Rogers)

same characters have grown in significance and appear in nearly every poem. Kioka has been incorporated into the circle of friends, although he sets up his tepee on the lawn and remains resolutely in his own world. By transferring her musings to these distinct personalities, Rogers illustrates how each of them discovers truths and meanings according to the limitations of individual perspectives and priorities.

New characters in *Legendary Performance* are "the naked boys"—supernatural alter egos of the main characters—who gallop through on their naked ponies. Imagination is represented by these wild ponies, Emerson's "horses of thought." Just as the boys are dependent upon their steeds, the possibilities the boys represent to each of the main characters depend upon imaginations that are given free rein.

These fanciful characters do not appear in Rogers's next book, *Splitting and Binding*. Instead, she returns to the tangible, personal world she pre-

sented in her first two books. Her emphasis is again the reverent witnessing and praising of all aspects of the natural world. Through her unwavering gaze, readers experience startling images that strike a wide range of sensory chords. Rogers presents many sights and sounds, including eerie phosphorescent creatures of the ocean depths, shrieking blue jays in grief, and hissing geese protecting their nests. Interspersed throughout the book are poems that are pure celebrations of physical sensation. This format is one of Rogers's specialties. Her patient attention to detail effectively helps readers imagine, for example, the delights of rolling in morning dew. However, it is the predominance of vivid visual images that characterizes this collection. Many of these images seem to leap from the page: in the snow, the "wine-red" blood of a white hare; sunlight streaming through the stained glass panels of a cathedral; white birds flying before a dark thundercloud. It is mainly through the skillful and imaginative use of color that Rogers is able to bring these images to life.

The metaphor of light as knowledge and harmony, which she first offered in *The Expectations of Light*, has matured fully in *Splitting and Binding*. Many of the poems function as prisms, splitting white light into its component colors—each color with an attendant physical or spiritual representative—and then binding them back up into the harmonious whole, as in "two yellow wings / Like splinters of morning" ("The Voice of the Precambrian Sea"), and "the white prayer buried in the green catacombs / Of bony coral filled with sea" ("White Prayer"). In "Knot" Rogers writes: "I can unwind sunlight / from the switches of water in the slough / and divide the grey sumac's hazy edge / from the hazy grey of the sky, the red vein / of the hibiscus from its red blossom." A most effective example of this theme of harmony is the poem "For the Wren Trapped in the Cathedral," in which a small bird experiences the transforming powers of the intense colors of stained-glass panels: miraculous greens, somber purples, suffusing scarlets. The bird dreams, in its own fashion, of carrying the secrets of these colors "out into the brilliant white mystery / Of the truthful world."

There are much darker images in these poems, such as the blind and deaf beggar's "enduring darkness of unlimited silence," the "dark sleep" of the inhabitants of "the deep black flow" of the seafloor, and the "dark bones" of feet and hands. Yet, these manifestations of the absence of light, whether it is the light of knowledge, affinity, evolution, or life itself, are all shown to possess at least the possibility of a speck of light. The beggar's darkness is dispelled by his innate understanding of the "sun-split leap of salmon after salmon / Through loop after loop of cascading current." Even the darkest undertones of death are transformed, as in "The Light Inside of Death": "Surely there is a little—maybe like the light / A dark rain carries into the sea on a cold / And broken night or the light held in frozen / Seeds of sumac catching sun along the road. . . ." Then, ever mindful of transcendent origins and destinies, Rogers gathers up her concepts into "Knot," wherein the watcher of the forest discerns dandelion fluff in cobwebs, herons among the reedy lilies, and says, "All afternoon I part, I isolate, I untie, / I undo, while all the

while the oak / shadows, easing forward, slowly ensnare me."

Pattiann Rogers told McCann that she does not want her work to be considered a philosophical system. She deliberately tries to avoid sounding dogmatic or arrogant, and she accords themes of death, insanity, joy, and passion equal attention, free from bias or prejudice. Subtle humor occasionally emerges, as in the personified male toads (in *The Tattooed Lady in the Garden*) who believe that they actually create female toads by their singing. Her long lines are reminiscent of Walt Whitman's, but she takes more delight in the cataloguing of scientific fact. An entire stanza is often a single sentence. Her unmetered and unrhymed lines flow easily and are often enjambed to allow for the full impact of key words. The "I" in Rogers's poems is readily translated into the universal "I" of Whitman. The accurate scientific and sensory observations in her poems describe not only how life is with Rogers but how it is with all of humankind.

Interview:

Richard McCann, "An Interview with Pattiann Rogers," *Iowa Review*, 17 (Spring/Summer 1987): 25-42.

References:

Dick Allen, "Poetry I: Charles Tomlinson, Pattiann Rogers, Geoffrey Hill and Others," *Hudson Review*, 40 (Autumn 1987): 507-516;

Alice Fulton, "Main Things," *Poetry*, 151 (January 1988): 360-377;

R. S. Gwynn, "Second Gear," *New England Review/Breadloaf Quarterly*, 9 (Autumn 1986): 111-121;

Louis L. Martz, "Ammons, Warren, and the Tribe of Walt," *Yale Review*, 72 (Autumn 1982): 63-84;

Christopher Merrill, "Voyages Into the Immediate: Recent Nature Writings," *New England Review/Breadloaf Quarterly*, 10 (Spring 1988): 368-378;

Peter Stitt, "Aestheticians and the Pit of the Self," *Poetry*, 152 (June 1988): 161-173;

Stitt, "The Objective Mode in Contemporary Lyric Poetry," *Georgia Review*, 36 (Summer 1982): 438-444.

Charles Simic
(9 May 1938 -   )

David Kirby
Florida State University

BOOKS: *What the Grass Says* (San Francisco: Kayak, 1967);

Somewhere Among Us a Stone Is Taking Notes (San Francisco: Kayak, 1969);

Dismantling the Silence (New York: Braziller, 1971, London: Cape, 1971);

White (New York: New Rivers, 1972; revised edition, Durango, Colo.: Logbridge-Rhodes, 1980);

Return to a Place Lit by a Glass of Milk (New York: Braziller, 1974);

Biography and a Lament (Hartford: Bartholomew's Cobble, 1976);

Charon's Cosmology (New York: Braziller, 1977);

Classic Ballroom Dances (New York: Braziller, 1980);

Austerities (New York: Braziller, 1982);

Shaving at Night (San Francisco: Meadow, 1982);

The Chicken Without a Head (Portland: Trace, 1983);

Weather Forecast for Utopia & Vicinity, Poems 1967-1982 (Barrytown, N.Y.: Station Hill, 1983);

Selected Poems (New York: Braziller, 1985; revised and enlarged, 1990);

The Uncertain Certainty: Interviews, Essays, and Notes on Poetry (Ann Arbor: University of Michigan Press, 1985);

Unending Blues (San Diego & New York: Harcourt Brace Jovanovich, 1986);

The World Doesn't End (San Diego & New York: Harcourt Brace Jovanovich, 1989);

The Book of Gods and Devils (San Diego & New York: Harcourt Brace Jovanovich, 1990);

Wonderful Words, Silent Truth: Essays on Poetry and a Memoir (Ann Arbor: University of Michigan Press, 1990).

OTHER: *Another Republic: 17 European & South American Writers*, edited by Simic and Mark Strand (New York: Ecco, 1976);

Vasko Popa, *Homage to the Lame Wolf: Selected Poems*, translated, with an introduction, by Simic (Oberlin, Ohio: Oberlin College Press, 1987).

There is a nimble beauty to the poetry of Charles Simic that, given his Eastern European origin, makes many readers think of clever fairy-tale heroes, witty orphans who can charm any ogre with words alone. Yet Simic is vehement about his place in American culture. In a 1984 interview with Sherod Santos, he said, "As for Yugoslavia, I feel like a foreigner there. Everything I love and hate with a passion is over here. I'd die of grief if I left this country for long." Still, Simic's work is like no other American poet's. On the one hand, Sigmund Freud's world of dreams and the surrealism of André Breton are graphically represented; on the other, an abundance of peasants, crones, and woodcutters reminds the reader that, to use an agricultural metaphor, no poetic apple falls far from its tree. (In the Santos interview, Simic said, "I'm not so naive as to pretend that there aren't certain East European elements in my poetry.") While it may be said that Simic is a mythical rather than a historical poet, his role is somewhat more specialized than that of the mythmaker; he is a broker of dreams and images, one who, like those witty youths in the fairy tales, draws on both grim experience and natural playfulness to charm and intoxicate his audience.

Born in Yugoslavia on 9 May 1938, Charles Simic had what Polish-American critic Jan Kott calls "a typical East European education"—in other words, as the poet confided in the Santos interview, "Hitler and Stalin taught us the basics." Simic recalls a joyous early boyhood, undiminished (indeed, enhanced) by the presence of soldiers and tanks in the streets, although the years from 1945 to 1948 were marked by hunger and deprivation. Then, as Simic told Santos with comic urgency, "It became clear to my mother [Helen Matijevic Simic] that if I was ever going to become an American poet, we'd better get moving." The two moved to Chicago in 1949, where Simic's father (George, an engineer) had already found employment with a telephone company. The young Simic discovered jazz as well as Ameri-

can poetry and folklore and underwent the transformation in outlook that made him an international poet and a gifted multicultural spokesman. From 1961 to 1963 he served in the U.S. Army. Educated at New York University, from which he received a B.A. in 1966, Simic worked as an editorial assistant for the photography magazine *Aperture* between 1966 and 1974; he then began teaching at the University of New Hampshire, where he is currently a professor of English. On 25 October 1965 Simic married Helene Dubin, a fashion designer; they have one child, Anna.

Simic's writings have appeared in anthologies and periodicals all over the world; he has published several books of his own work and has edited and translated books by others. Among his numerous awards for poetry and translation are the Edgar Allan Poe Award, the P.E.N. Translation Prize, a Guggenheim Foundation Scholarship, and prizes from the American Academy of Arts and Letters and the Poetry Society of Amer-

ica. Simic received in 1982 a so-called genius award from the MacArthur Foundation, which gives its prizewinners, who are nominated by a secret committee, substantial cash grants with no strings attached. In 1990 Simic was awarded a Pulitzer Prize for his 1989 collection *The World Doesn't End.*

More often than not, Simic's poetry is surrealistic, folkloristic, and Freudian—the stuff of dreams. In an anthology coedited with Mark Strand, *Another Republic: 17 European & South American Writers* (1976), Simic and Strand differentiate between two types of poet, the historical (or poet of social and political awareness) and the mythological (the poet who uses images and archetypes from the unconscious). Within the mythological camp, Simic and Strand make two further classifications: the interrogator and dismantler of archetypes, such as Francis Ponge, and the poet whose poems tell the story of their own creation, such as Vasko Popa, a Yugoslav poet whose writings Simic has translated. Clearly, Simic's work is closer to that of Popa, whose self-creating mythological poems (as collected in *Another Republic*) feature such autonomous protagonists as a number that begins to perform its own calculations, a yawn that becomes bigger than itself, and a math error that leads to possibilities greater than finite truth. Simic, too, deals in alternative worlds; when history appears in his writing, as it does in a poem called "History" in (*Unending Blues*, 1986), it is "arrested and shot" because it "loves to see women cry." Simic is much more interested in self-created worlds devoid of social and political clutter, worlds born out of the nexus of European memory and American experience. It is perhaps to his benefit, then, that Simic's viewpoint is "overdetermined" (as Freud said of dreams), drawing as it does on both wartime memories and the freedoms of American adolescence.

In interviews, Simic has pointed out how his impressions have not so much accumulated as overlapped, how, for example, Theodore Roethke's interest in nursery rhymes, fairy tales, riddles, and magic led Simic to a further knowledge of European folklore and the discovery that many folkloristic beliefs are essentially the same on the two continents. In a 1975 interview with George Starbuck, Simic expressed this simultaneity of viewpoint through empathy with earlier émigrés, the Scandinavians who came to the United States in the nineteenth century: "You find some group of poor Swedes who were out there in the middle of Illinois and at some point they were terrified of that space. Their visions have the quality of all genuine attempts to make a contact with the world through a figure of speech." Simic's rapport with those who are cut off from a greater world, be they in Belgrade or on the midwestern plains, clearly underlies his own "genuine attempts to make a contact with the world through a figure of speech," that is, to make poetic worlds of one's own. As he said in the interview with Santos, "I don't believe in history anymore."

Many young poets are tentative and eclectic, but in *Dismantling the Silence* (1971) Simic writes with assurance. He describes the workaday mortal as being in thrall to unconscious feelings; in "Fear," that tremulous emotion causes one after another person to shake like leaves on a tree until "all at once the whole tree is trembling / And there is no sign of the wind." A sleeping man spins from his dreaming mind a marvelous panorama in "Tapestry," a wondrous picture stretching all the way to heaven and depicting a fox and chicken, a naked couple on their wedding night, an evil crone, and so on. But other people are disturbed by the originality of the sleeping man's artistry and shave off all his hair so he will look like everyone else in this fictional world. In contrast to those unfortunates who seem to be in the grip of others (or, worse, their own unmanageable urges), the poet-speaker in "Pastoral" maintains as much control as he can over his life by humbling himself before such elemental words as *truth*, *gallows*, and *love*. By deliberately invoking such words, the poet is led to insights about the fundamental nature of the world around him and thus escapes the fear and domination spoken of in the two previous poems. Not the least of his insights is this: "There were also many other things / For which there was no word."

These realizations do not come easily, however. There is always "The Inner Man" to reckon with, an entity others claim to know (women say they have held him), even though he remains a stranger to the one in whose body he resides. Simic asserts it may be best simply to let "the body" take over in these poems, as it seems to in a poem entitled "Ax," where it is suggested that the act of chopping wood turns anyone into a primitive being who will grow fur, coarse skin, and long teeth and sleep through the winter like a bear. These transformations are not merely predicted in the poem, however; more than that, "These dark prophecies were gathered, / Unknown to myself, by my body." The body is the "author" of these poems, then. Indeed, the poet who speaks in "Pastoral" seems to be feeling the words *truth*, *gallows*, and *love* (when he whistles for *love*, she answers him in her sleep) rather than thinking them. It is no surprise, then, that so many poems in *Dismantling the Silence* are, as their titles suggest, as elemental as the body that writes them: "Fork," "Spoon," "Knife," "My Shoes," "Stone," and so on.

Simic's *Return to a Place Lit by a Glass of Milk* (1974) both furthers and then departs from his emphasis on the elemental. The book contains several celebrations of the elemental, as, again, the titles themselves indicate: "Watch Repair," "Watermelons," "Breasts." And even more than in the earlier volumes, there is a sense of Simic enjoying a kind of Whitmanian ease, a sense of total bodily centeredness usually associated with singers and athletes in their prime. "Elementary Cosmogony" even posits confidently the requisites

Simic circa 1973 (photograph by David Smith)

for good writing. First, the poet must apprentice himself to the invisible; second, he must bring along his body, "which is my tool box, / Which is my sustenance"; and third, he must adhere to his apprenticeship's most important condition: "The submission to chance." This combination of physical confidence and spiritual humility leads to celebrations of the elemental that are longer and more fully developed than the compact "Fork," "Spoon," and "Stone" in *Dismantling the Silence*. "Brooms," for example, is nearly three pages long and rather thoroughly anatomizes the broom in all its avatars (in dreams, jails, monasteries, and even in the imagined reader's grandmother's kitchen) without ever abandoning its wood-and-straw reality. But Simic's self-assurance in these and other poems, his ability to stretch and to reach what he is stretching toward, should never be taken as a suggestion that the writing is easy. Singers strain their voices, athletes stumble, and poets either have too much or too little to say.

In "Travelling," the speaker turns himself into a sack and is taken out at dawn by an old ragpicker who fills the sack with a tie, an overcoat, some boots; at first the sack is speechless because it is empty, and then it is silent because it is too full to speak.

The language of these newer poems, while handled with Simic's characteristic assurance, is nonetheless more abstract. In "Solving the Riddle," for example, " the same old thing [is] / Telling the same old story / At the kitchen table: // It'll be here tomorrow, / Newly disguised, / hard to recognize" (and, indeed, the riddle never gets solved, since it "keeps changing its answer"). A similar poem called "Two Riddles" describes one riddle lost in an eternal colloquy with itself, and another that cannot even be asked because it spends all its time scurrying around like a rodent. Finally, "Charles Simic" treats the poet's own name as though it were a complete sentence with a subject and several verbs but no object, or at least no object that can be seen.

①   *The Sparrow*

I was stolen by the gypsies. My parents stole me right back. But the gypsies stole me again. One minute I was in the caravan suckling the dark teat of my new mother, the next I sat at a long table eating my breakfast with a silver spoon.

It was spring. My father was singing in the shower; the gypsy was painting a live sparrow the colors of the rainbow.

* This went on for some time. Back and forth. I went in a sack.

Drafts for two of the prose poems in Simic's 1989 book, The World Doesn't End *(by permission of Charles Simic)*

* (4)

"Everybody knows th story about me and Dr. Freud" says my grandfather.

"We ~~were~~ fell in love with th same pair of shoes in th window of a shoe store. The store, unfortunately, was always closed: ~~I would~~ ^one would^ find a sign like "Death in th Family" or 'Back in an Hour', but no matter how long ~~one~~ waited, no one would come to open

Once I met Dr. Freud there admiring th shoes. We glared at each other and went our separate ways."

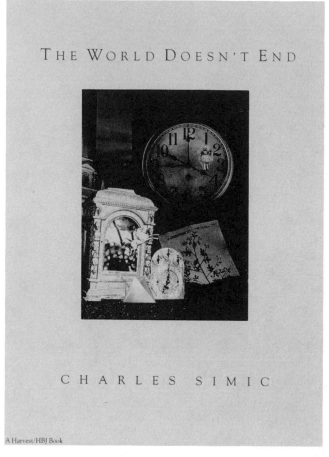

Cover for the book that won the Pulitzer Prize for Poetry in 1990

Writers with sufficient perspective on their careers sometimes have the foresight to establish a line of development in their writing and then, instead of overworking it with too much immediate attention, let it mature while they pursue a tangential concern. Simic does this in a series of linked poems called *White* (1972; revised, 1980). *White* is a deliberate disencumbering, a surrender designed to allow a poet now burdened with his own creations to start over. The first lines read: "Out of poverty / To begin again." In one of the untitled ten-line poems that make up the bulk of the 1980 edition, the speaker describes a scene of poverty in which the only item of value continues to glow over the years like a hard flame; a boy hands the proprietor of a rundown grocery a nickel for a cupcake, and the gleam of the nickel is frozen in the poem for all time. In the interview with Starbuck, Simic recalled this time of poverty in his life and the actual store ("I got more poems out of that place than, than [*sic*] I don't think anything else that ever happened to me in my life"). Poverty, then, is a blank piece of paper

for a poet; it is the white paper on which he writes his first poem, and it is the paper, too, on which he begins again after calling a calculated halt to a career in progress. The last part of the revised edition is called "What the White Had to Say," and here the now-full page guides the reborn poet back to the line of development he dealt with in his first books; it teases the poet for giving names to whiteness and concludes that, as several poems in *Return to a Place Lit by a Glass of Milk* suggest, "the most beautiful riddle has no answer." In the Starbuck interview, Simic noted, "My contemporaries—the younger poets—who have liked my poetry wrote me letters saying 'I hope that *White* is not your new direction.'" He also declares that it is his own favorite book.

Simic turned to a fuller exploration of the self in *Charon's Cosmology* (1977), a collection in which, as Simic told Rod Steier in a 1978 interview, "the poems are much more autobiographical than they used to be." Consequently the poems in this book deal not so much with subjects more or less specific (a fork, a riddle, whiteness) but to a greater extent with the poetic process, the means whereby a subject is discovered or invented. Thus "The Partial Explanation" describes a lonely man in a sparsely furnished, darkening restaurant, a writer desperate not for his meal but for the conversation of the cooks. "The Lesson" deals with a similar-sounding character; this one has been taught that there is a grand design in life and bursts out laughing when he discovers that everything is fluid. This cheerful fellow reappears in "Help Wanted" as a Keatsian vessel waiting to be filled.

Together, these characters in *Charon's Cosmology* define the self as an exploring entity and not an entity to be explored. In the theater that is the setting for "Position Without a Magnitude," a shadow is cast briefly by someone moving between the whiteness of the empty screen and the blinding sunlight, and "you shudder / As you realize it's only you." For a moment, the self is as big as any of the larger-than-life characters of the movie, but, as with them, its evanescence is part of its fulfillment.

Considered in the context established by the earlier books, *Charon's Cosmology* makes it clear that the self Simic describes is better thought of as a verb than a noun; the emphasis is clearly on an entity that *does*. Perhaps Simic's European experience contributes to this formulation of character. It has often been observed that, to Americans, history is something that happens elsewhere, whereas it is a daily reality to Europeans, with their constant reminders of the wars that rolled across the continent almost nonstop for centuries. Right or wrong, most Americans have a stronger sense of being able to better their circumstances than do most Europeans, who seem to have a more restricted sense of personal freedom, as though the best they can do is to slip around one obstacle or another from time to time. Simic's remark about his mother leaving Yugoslavia so he could become an American poet is facetious, but it calls to mind a political-science truism, that the only thing one needs to know about a country is whether people want to get in or get out. In America a transplanted European is an "orphan of history," as Simic described himself to Santos. Cut off from parents (or from the parent culture), the orphan must keep moving or die; one thinks of novelist Jerzy Kosinski, filmmaker Roman Polanski, and other less-celebrated figures who survived postwar Europe precisely by staying on the move and, motherless, managing to survive on their wits.

Vitality is a hallmark of all of Simic's poetry, but the later volumes feature even more active roles for the poems' speakers and other characters. For example, in *Classic Ballroom Dances* (1980), a poem about Christopher Columbus entitled "Navigator" describes the great mariner as a singer above all, yet one whose song disappears into the wind, because it is the singing that is important, not the words or the music. Thus, whereas the early poems often emphasize cutlery, stones, axes, and other objects, the later poetry emphasizes actions performed on or with such objects, often in a transcendental manner. *Weather Forecast for Utopia & Vicinity* (1983) includes a poem entitled "Figuring," in which some orphans find a zero and decorate it and give it gifts until it transcends its ordinariness, if only for a moment; eventually a grown-up gives the hapless cipher a pencil and makes it do homework. ("Figuring" recalls the poems of Vasko Popa translated by Simic in *Another Republic*, poems with numerical protagonists who escape their finite natures.) In "The Writings of the Mystics," a poor scholar skips dinner to read about "a presentiment / Of a higher existence / In things familiar and drab," whereas in an earlier poem he might have concentrated on the dinner or the things he transcends. The speaker of "In Midsummer Quiet" hears a whippoorwill's song, contemplates a stream, a barn, and the first stars of the evening, and ends up "talking to my own conundrums." The earlier riddle poems focus on the conundrums themselves, but this one emphasizes the contemplation that begins with and then transcends earthly sensations.

In the Steier interview, Simic clarified the relation between this active speaker and the objects he speaks about: "A poet's works are kinds of theologies. They really contain the whole view, the entire dogma of that person's existence. I mean everything: from how they feel about plants, certain animals, to how they liked the other sex when they were fourteen. . . . On the other hand, it's not quite a biography. It's a secret. I mean, it's a biography they are not conscious of, and which is not totally identical with the visible person." So whereas other contemporary poets seem to want to dissolve the self (Mark Strand is a notable example), Simic seems almost not to notice it; the self is certainly apparent in his poetry, but it is so busy that it has little time for self-consciousness.

In the later poetry especially, the world is so distracting and contradictory that it seizes the

Dust jacket for Simic's 1990 poetry collection; the illustration is a detail from Saul Steinberg's Eighth Street *(1966)*

self's attention and holds it. "December," a short poem in *Unending Blues*, describes two derelicts with sandwich boards, one proclaiming the end of the world and the other the rates at the barbershop; the self can only wonder. The speaker in "The Marvels of the City" wanders through a pagan metropolis filled with false idols and conflicting philosophies, but he takes his cue from the waiters who, "black hair growing out of their ears / Just took our orders and said nothing."

Inevitably discussions of poetry lead to the question of outlook. Leaving aside tone, technique, and subject matter, one searches for the weltanschauung, the paraphrasable poem part that some readers call the philosophy, message, or theme—the poet's stance toward life and self that is all these things and more. "Dark Farmhouses" in *Unending Blues* is helpful in this regard. In it old people shiver in their kitchens while idling coal trucks on the highway wait for drivers and shovels. An optimism of a certain sort prevails; the drivers will come, says the speaker, who addresses the trucks: "Is it a shovel you need? / Idle on, / A shovel will come by and by / Over the darkening plain. // A shovel, / And a spade." This optimism looks forward to the in-

evitable rather than the miraculous; it recalls Freud's promise regarding the nature of psychoanalysis, that it will not re-create the analysand but merely restore him or her to the world of ordinary unhappiness.

Moreover, like Freud's, it is a language-based optimism rather than a religious or political one. In a 1978 interview with Rick Jackson and Michael Panori, Simic said, "It occurred to me that mythical consciousness, the kind that is still present in our world, is to be found in language," in, for example, such expressions as "counting bats in his belfry" and all that such a metaphor would imply if realized literally, but also the impersonal *it* of the expression "it goes without saying," which is "both minimal and all-inclusive. 'It' can open up to whatever is beyond, can include all other 'its.' This is a mythical situation; you eventually hear the little drama of the expression as its possibilities unfold." The key to optimism, then, is to keep working with the mythic possibilities of language rather than to go beyond it in quest of religious utopia (the Christian model) or to demolish it in order to escape its oppression (Marxism). In *Unending Blues* the title character in "The Fly" is writing "the History of

Charles Simic (photograph copyright 1980 by Thomas Victor)

Optimism / In Time of Madness." His task is not easy, of course: "Some days it's like using a white cane / And seeing mostly shadows / As one gropes for the words that come next!" A commitment to the exploration of the possibilities of language must be of value in itself; if that is true, then every act of writing is inherently optimistic.

That is why "the great God Theory," as Simic defines it in his collection of untitled prose poems called *The World Doesn't End*, is presented as nothing but a chewed pencil stub at the end of a huge scribble. The pencil is worthless and so, one might assume, is the scribble; it certainly has no more prominence in Simic's poem than the pencil has. And besides, it is scribbling, not the scribble, that counts in Simic's world. His work suggests that the struggle with history ("the scribble") will always be a futile one.

The erotics of sheer movement become more and more important as Simic's career progresses. In one of the prose poems in *The World Doesn't End*, for example, a child is stolen by gypsies, is taken right back by his parents, is stolen again by the gypsies, and so on until his head swims and he can no longer tell the difference between his two sets of mothers and fathers. In an-

other, a family is so poor that the child must take the place of the bait in the mousetrap; in a third, the last Napoleonic soldier is still retreating from Moscow two hundred years later and passes German soldiers on their way to the Russian front. None of these poems is joyful, exactly, but each has about it an assurance, even a quiet pleasure in its spatial and linguistic movement.

As Simic says in an essay entitled "Some Thoughts About the Line" (in *The Uncertain Certainty*, 1985), poetry is the "orphan of silence. Maternal silence. . . . The mother's voice calls its name over the roofs of the world." Poetry is an orphan because language never equals the historical experience that gives birth to it; one has the experience, feels the frustration of speechlessness, and then brings the mythic word into the world.

The word that results, though orphaned from history, can nonetheless be miraculous. In the Jackson and Panori interview, Simic explained, "Let's say someone has the experience of walking around in a swamp at night, sees things he wouldn't see in another place or in the daytime, perhaps feels fear, confusion. Now, he would have to be seriously deluded to believe that when he sits down to render all this he can equal its complexity." On the other hand, "let's say he begins to write and arrives at an acceptable equation." The language he ends up using does not convey his experience in the swamp, but "it contains echoes and resonances he never suspected before he began to write about the experience." In this way the poet makes his myths.

Somehow, though, one imagines that Simic would not feel particularly comfortable with the term *mythmaker* or, for that matter, any other noun with its attendant constraints. But if one had to choose, perhaps a word such as *broker* would be best. Simic is a broker of dreams; a cultural orphan, he has learned to survive by trafficking in the dreams everyone needs. One of the prose poems in *The World Doesn't End* describes a father who loves passionately both the writings of André Breton and the country of America, and a son who is going into business with his dad, a boy who thinks "we were going to make a million dollars manufacturing objects we had seen in dreams that night." Since dreams are evanescent, no one owns them, not even the dreamer. But then a broker is only a middleman; he never has title to the property he represents. The great lesson of Charles Simic's poetry is that magic is not inherent in the possession of words but in the pursuit of them.

Interviews:

"An Interview with Charles Simic," *Crazy Horse*, 11 (Summer 1972); reprinted in *The Uncertain Certainty: Interviews, Essays, and Notes on Poetry* (Ann Arbor: University of Michigan Press, 1985), pp. 3-10;

Wayne Dodd and Stanley Plumly, Interview with Simic, *Ohio Review*, 14 (Winter 1973); reprinted in *The Uncertain Certainty*, pp. 11-26;

George Starbuck, Interview with Simic, *Ploughshares*, 2, no. 3 (1975); reprinted in *The Uncertain Certainty*, pp. 27-45;

Rick Jackson and Michael Panori, "The Domain of the Marvelous Prey," *Poetry Miscellany*, no. 8 (1978); reprinted in *The Uncertain Certainty*, pp. 58-67;

Rod Steier, "Moments Worth Preserving and Playing Again," *Manassas Review*, 1 (Winter 1978); reprinted in *The Uncertain Certainty*, pp. 46-50;

Interlochen School students, "An Interview with Charles Simic," *Interlochen Review*, 1, no. 2 (1980); reprinted in *The Uncertain Certainty*, pp. 51-57;

Sherod Santos, Interview with Simic, *Missouri Review*, 7, no. 3 (1984); reprinted in *The Uncertain Certainty*, pp. 68-79.

Bibliography:

Charles Seluzicki, "Charles Simic: A Bibliographical Checklist," *American Book Collector*, 3 (July-August 1982): 34-39.

References:

Victor Contoski, "Charles Simic: Language at the Stone's Heart," *Chicago Review*, 28 (Spring 1977): 145-157;

Richard Jackson, "Charles Simic and Mark Strand: The Presence of Absence," *Contemporary Literature*, 21 (Winter 1980): 136-145;

Peter Schmidt, "*White:* Charles Simic's Thumbnail Epic," *Contemporary Literature*, 23 (Fall 1982): 528-549;

Geoffrey Thurley, "Devices Among Words: Kinnell, Bly, Simic," in his *The American Moment: American Poetry in the Mid-Century* (New York: St. Martin's Press, 1978), pp. 210-228.

Barry Spacks

(21 February 1931 -   )

John W. Crawford
Henderson State University

BOOKS: *The Sophomore* (Englewood Cliffs, N.J.: Prentice-Hall, 1968; London: Collins, 1969);

The Company of Children (New York: Doubleday, 1969);

Orphans (New York: Harper's Magazine, 1972);

Something Human (New York: Harper's Magazine, 1972);

Teaching the Penguins to Fly (Boston: Godine, 1975);

Imagining a Unicorn (Athens: University of Georgia Press, 1978);

Spacks Street: New & Selected Poems (Baltimore & London: Johns Hopkins University Press, 1982);

Brief Sparrow (Los Angeles: Illuminati, 1988).

Barry Spacks's poetry is clear in thought, ungarbled in structure. He avoids obscurity, the abstract, and radical, innovative styles. Some would label his style conservative, but nonetheless he is a poet who understands the true meaning of poetry.

Spacks was born on 21 February 1931, in Philadelphia, to Charles Spacks, a merchant, and Evelyn Schindler Spacks. The young Spacks was educated in the public schools of Philadelphia and at the University of Pennsylvania, where he earned his B.A. in English in 1952. In 1956 he received his M.A. from Indiana University. As a Fulbright Fellow, Spacks did postgraduate work for a short time at Cambridge. From 1957 to 1959 he taught English at the University of Florida. From 1960 to 1981 Spacks served as professor of humanities at the Massachusetts Institute of Technology. Since 1981 he has been a professor of English at the University of Kentucky, then at the University of California at Berkeley and at Santa Barbara. On 10 June 1955 he married Patricia Ann Meyer, a teacher and writer; they have one daughter, Judith.

First a novelist with the well-received book *The Sophomore* (1968), Spacks published his first volume of verse, *The Company of Children*, in 1969.

This book demonstrates vividly Spacks's style of clarity, strong imagery, smooth lyricism, and tight structure. Even in his free verse, he remembers that metrics are important. Miller Williams has called *The Company of Children* one of the best first collections of poetry to come off the presses in a long while, commenting on its universal qualities. In Williams's words, "The poet [Spacks] obviously cares about the world he lives with, and has touched it, and he is not embarrassed to be moved by the world and does not hide from it behind the transparent masks of obscurantism, abstractionism, and new directionism" (*Saturday Review*, 14 June 1969).

Greg Kuzma's criticism of Spacks's first volume runs in the same vein as that of Williams. He, too, comments about the down-to-earth subject matter: students, jury duty, window washing, books, and poetry. The poems, Kuzma further notes, confirm the validity of the poet's common life, never suggesting the forcing of the subject matter into uncomfortable ground. Kuzma compares Spacks's style with that of Robert Frost, with the latter's soundness and optimism, with his graceful structure, avoiding such defects of young poets' work as secret principles of organization, mysterious abstractions, and confusion of meaningful patterns: "The poems in *The Company of Children* are lightly muscled, polite. They have the grace of good swimmers. The ease with which they cover their distances may suggest that the difficult wrestling we admire our larger poets for is not yet part of this poet's commitment. Spacks is conservative; he never strains himself on anything too large for him" (*Prairie Schooner*, Winter 1970).

Spacks's clear imagery is seen in "Freshmen," one of his longer poems from the volume. He identifies universal types of freshman students, including the sulking Achilles, the time-conscious Pascal consulting his watch, and the true "Cordelia—with her just-washed hair / stern-hearted princess, ready to defend / the meticulous garden of truths in her high school note-

Barry Spacks circa 1968 (photograph by James Baker Hall)

book. . . ." Teachers are also included. They arrive as the students "wait bristling, acnéd, glowing like a brand, / or easy, chatting munching, muscles lax, / each in his chosen corner, and in each / a chosen corner." The faculty members are described imagistically:

> green and seasoned, bearers
> of the Word, who differ
> like its letters; there are some
> so wise their eyes
> are birdbites; one,
> a mad, grinning gent with a golden tooth, God
>   knows
> he might be Pan, or the sub-
> custodian; another
> is a walking podium, dense
> with his mystery. . . .

Spacks's lyricism is seen to good advantage in the short poems such as "The Wandering Jew at the Ueno Park Zoo" and "October." In both,

Spacks's sympathy with nature is evident. In the former, the wanderer identifies with the otter, the weasel, and the bear: "The otter swims his pool, my heart; / the weasel furrows in my blood; / and lurching to embrace me comes / the bear whose breast is warm as God." In "October" a wife caught up in Popian pastoral literature does not allow modern society with its violence and obscenities to disturb her quietness:

> Braving the season for the sake of wit,
> she holds each couplet in such close esteem
> no maniac can put a hole in it.
> The year's in tatters, but she makes a seam;
>
> the house is civil, though the wood's insane,
> and man's the missing link who lets the chain-
> of-being shake. It's hanging by a hair.
> My wife sits reading in a garden chair.

The eternal spirit of man to take control of himself and create order and joy in the midst of

228

despair is seen time and again in *The Company of Children*. The fisherman in "Fishing on a Snowy River" appears half-an-inch high against the mountains' treacherous forms, but "the mountains recede; are silk" because his act of fishing is the statement of hope that mankind keeps exhibiting from century to century. In "Robert's Song" the reader is made aware that humankind finds it impossible to leave the "provinces of Doubt," yet the poet asserts, "In the land of good counsel, I am the capital city. / I choose my speed: I am my only hitchhiker. / On fields of rare wishes, I am the wind and sun. . . . / I go / to cast / a shade." And in "To the photographer of a Thorn Tree" the reader comes to understand that humankind brings order to chaos everywhere:

> These thorns were not forged metal till you got
>   there,
> ordering light
> to hold in its passing
> so even the shadows
> of thorns would seem to heal. . . .
>
> Here, you have calmed them to a scheme.
> They rest in their transcendence;
> they cannot alter.
> And you go on, to tulips and to weeds:
> through with them.

In the title poem, a man (humankind) builds his house against all odds, then stands in amazement. The hill he has climbed has grown smaller and he is much taller: "He builds his house, / and then returns / to the company / of children."

Spacks's *Something Human* (1972) is effective because of the continuing simplicity of style and universality of subject matter; this volume also features brief character portraits. In addition to echoes of Frost, one can also hear echoes of Edgar Lee Masters and *Spoon River Anthology* (1915).

In "Child Adam," Spacks apparently presents an autobiographical sketch in which he, like most imaginative children, relives some great scene of the past, in this case God's naming of the various creatures, with the child/speaker as God: "learning the work cut out for me / till all the wilderness was sung, / till lord of all I lived among / I'd set the whole creation right, / *Mother; Father; Day and Night.*"

Being a teacher, Spacks often finds students a suitable subject. In "Students in a Sanctuary" he depicts modern students living daily in a violent, ironic world: "In the nurture of their sleep the students lie, / who soon must wake, to pretensions and praises . . . / to the ever-dwelling in their thought / of Mace, and murder. / But now they sleep." In "Perkins and Plato," Spacks depicts effectively a sophomoric seventeen-year-old student, Perkins, in his egomaniacal attitude, bold enough to title his paper "Perkins and Plato," as if his argumentive dialogue could possibly equal that of Plato: "O Perkins, if only this job could allow me to be / as gracious as Plato! How perfect to have him say, / making your moment a nuclear sub among rowboats / '*Perkins, I can't disagree in any way.*' "

The irony of life is seen well in the brief poem "Sears and Roebuck," where Spacks notes that Roebuck sold his shares early, living for ninety years in modest retirement: "often he must have thought of Sears: / how Sears mucked on, poor cluck; / Sears making millions, millions! on his ashpit; / and Roebuck making . . . Roebuck."

Critic Marie Barroff calls attention to the quiet elegy for Spacks's student Jud Stein, "who suffocated himself in a plastic bag in 'the time of Chicago, the time of Biafra' " (*Yale Review*, Autumn 1972). Barroff points out that the elegy disclaims high elegiacs at the end, while transfixing us with a stroke of somber wit: "And we, we'll invent no comfort, no high Sunk-though- / he-be . . . his little smile has called that bluff, / wrapped for the cold of the journey." As Barroff suggests, the basic mood is hopeful and lighthearted in these poems. They end in easings of tension, outward motions of release.

Spacks's other collections have generally failed to excite critics. Some feel that his poetry has become less concrete, less touching. Roger Dickinson-Brown, for example, finds *Teaching the Penguins to Fly* (1975) a sophisticated book with difficult poetry requiring a special emotional and intellectual comprehension. Dickinson-Brown believes the best aspects of the volume are the unpretentious personifications of animals and plants (*Southern Review*, April 1978). However, Spacks's character poems stand out with intensity in the book. "My Old Professor at the Bar" is one such poem. It produces haunting lines in portraying an intellectual pursuing happiness but finding life most clearly "behind a waterfall," and concluding his search with "a fine regard for black Jack Daniels, / slowly becoming a Mason jar / for homecured liver pickle; making / a Roman grace of solitude." In "My Teacher" the student is succinctly told that the mask he wears with a grin must be shed if he truly becomes what he says he desires to be: a master. The teacher admonishes the student, regarding his mask, "May it melt in the sun."

In a review of *Imagining a Unicorn* (1978), Vernon Young does not condemn Spacks but believes that he is a relatively unresolved poet: "Too many of his poems are those of the witty and not very confident bystander—professor and middle-class householder—alarmed by the state of the world, fearful of an Armageddon which might take place tomorrow" (*Parnassus*, Spring/Summer 1979). Young thinks that such common themes require an uncommon talent for redeeming them. According to Young, in approaching the professor's dilemma or the mother in the nursing home, Spacks fails to touch a nerve and thus leaves the reader unscathed. However, the themes in the volume demonstrate a strong religious spirit. James F. Cotter says, "Spacks shows more religious spirit in his title poem 'Imagining a Unicorn' than in acres of William Everson" (*Hudson Review*, Spring 1979). "Counting the Losses," for example, says better than most Sunday sermons what people may need to hear: the past cannot be relived. The poem alludes to artists who seem entranced with keeping the past alive—Yeats, Rossini, Goya—and ends with an allusion to Heinrich Schliemann, "Digging for Helen's balconies, / For Priam's gate; a lifetime, raising / The other from the dead."

Spacks makes an ironical statement on living in the past in a short poem, "The Ventnor Waterworks." When the speaker's auto coil fails, he recalls, thirty years before, riding his "bike to the Ventnor Waterworks / to drink from the cold of its fountain. I'd enter / as if at a temple; no human sound." In "Elegy" the speaker reflects upon pleasures he and his mother shared years before—stacking fruit of all kinds: dates, oranges, cherries, peaches—as he eyes his mother in the nursing home sleeping her life away, a pathetic end to an active past. Such poems strike a nerve because of the universal themes.

Summarizing Spacks's style is difficult. Richmond Lattimore perhaps expresses it best when he says that Spacks is "easy to read, often delightful, but difficult to review. Think of his repertory of subjects." As Lattimore suggests, that repertory is long: freshmen, crows, cookbooks, clothes, cats, peas, professors, penguins, unicorns, and sparrows, to list a few. But as Lattimore goes on to say, "These subjects lead, of course, beyond themselves: they prove a point or they are accesses to the poet and those who interest him" (*Hudson Review*, Spring 1983).

A few critics do not like Spacks's poetry and regard it paradoxically as either too simple or too sophisticated. Some of his recent verse demands more than casual reading, requiring a keen eye to Emily Dickinson-type ambiguities in what many call "ordinary words and phrases." However, he has not violated the basic commitments of his first two volumes: clarity of expression, concrete images, striking metaphors, and universal themes.

"Brief Sparrow," the title poem of a recent Spacks collection (1988), was published in *Poetry* in October 1986. In it Spacks reminds the reader how insignificant people are: "Think how little depends on us." Just as the Venerable Bede's sparrow flew out from dark back to dark, enjoying one short moment while in the light, so does humankind. It is an old theme, the brevity of life and the experience of truth, but a universal one, and it is renewed by Spacks's metaphor of the bird. Such a poem implies that the stylistic traditions established in Spacks's first two volumes continue in his current poetry.

References:

Greg Kuzma, "The Poet in the Academy," *Prairie Schooner*, 44 (Winter 1970): 358-360;

Richmond Lattimore, "Poetry Chronicle," *Hudson Review* (Spring 1983): 211-212.

Gerald Stern
(22 February 1925 -)

Chard deNiord
Putney School

BOOKS: *The Naming of Beasts, and Other Poems* (West Branch, La.: Cummington, 1973);

Rejoicings (Fredericton, N.B.: Fiddlehead, 1973); republished as *Rejoicings: Poems 1966-1972* (Los Angeles: Metro, 1984);

Lucky Life (Boston: Houghton Mifflin, 1977);

The Red Coal (Boston: Houghton Mifflin, 1981);

Paradise Poems (New York: Random House, 1984);

Lovesick (New York: Perennial Library, 1987);

Leaving Another Kingdom: Selected Poems (New York: Harper & Row, 1990);

Two Long Poems: The Pineys and Father Guzman, edited by Jerry Costanza (Pittsburgh: Carnegie-Mellon University Press, 1990).

OTHER: "Some Secrets," in *In Praise of What Persists*, edited by Stephen Berg (New York: Harper & Row, 1983), pp. 256-266;

"What Is This Poet?," in *What Is a Poet?*, edited by Hank Lazar (Tuscaloosa: University of Alabama Press, 1987), pp. 145-146.

SELECTED PERIODICAL PUBLICATIONS—UNCOLLECTED: "Notes from the River," *American Poetry Review*, 12 (September/October 1983): 36-38;

"What Is the Sabbath?," *American Poetry Review*, 13 (January/February 1984): 17-19;

"Rebuilding the Ruined and Fallen," *American Poetry Review*, 14 (September/October 1985): 9-12;

"A Few Words on Form," *Poetry East*, 20-21 (1986): 146;

"The Bombing of Libya," *American Poetry Review*, 15 (September/October 1986): 21-24;

"Life Is Not a River: Some Thoughts on Teaching Poetry," *AWP Newsletter*, 20, no. 2 (1987): 6-9;

"Caves," *American Poetry Review*, 16 (May/June 1987): 41-46.

Gerald Stern has set out to exorcise sadness and guilt by undertaking large poem after large poem, evoking the ironic power of pathos. He re-

jects decoration as poetic dishonesty. Stern is less concerned with changing from book to book, or even from poem to poem, than he is with continuing to express himself in the only way he knows, by letting his feelings take over. With a sense of mission that obviates art for its own sake, he distinguishes nostalgia from bathos as "not merely something tender and sad but [having] great psychic roots with true and terrifying aspects of rupture and separation" ("Notes from the River," *American Poetry Review*, September/October 1983). This sentiment conjures an image of the biblical fall. Stern continues to plumb the past, maintaining that "we live in grief and ecstasy," that "it is our justice" ("The Goons Are Leaving," in *Rejoicings*, 1973).

Stern educated himself on the city streets, in the public library, and along the river in Pittsburgh. He was born on 22 February 1925 into a second-generation Jewish family, which originally had the Russian name Dogipyat. His Pittsburgh neighborhood was rife with gangs and anti-Semitism, prompting him into brutal fights. His maternal grandfather, perhaps his strongest childhood influence, was a rabbi and *shachat* (a kosher butcher or "chicken killer") in Byalostok, Poland, and in Pittsburgh. Stern's father, Harry, the son of a Ukrainian immigrant, was a clothing retailer; Stern's mother was Ida Barach Stern. Clearly, the chances for the young Stern to develop into a renowned American poet seemed slim. The only Jewish poets of any repute during his youth were Delmore Schwartz and Karl Shapiro. Many American universities, including Ivy League schools, were still blacklisting Jews from both their undergraduate and graduate programs. Despite his dim prospects for a literary career, Stern spent his college years at the University of Pittsburgh studying literature. Although he had begun to write poetry at this time, he had no friends who were poets, much less mentors. He carried around Louis Untermeyer's *Modern American Poetry* (1942), wrote some poetry, and

Gerald Stern (photograph copyright by Star Black)

began reading Thomas Wolfe's novels, but that was the extent of his literary pursuits.

After graduating with a B.A. in English in 1947 from the University of Pittsburgh, Stern took a year off to read. He had spent a year in the army from 1946 to early 1947, specializing in counterintelligence, and thus had some savings from the GI Bill.

The notion of going to school to study poetry never occurred to him. He was consuming literature in his own way without the self-consciousness of academia. Recalling these early days, Stern wrote in any essay entitled "Some Secrets" (1983): "I'm a little proud of my terrible isolation, and even delight a little in its mystery, as if it were the result of some master plan, and certainly my poetry has resulted from it." Yet he also wishes he had had a little "nourishment somewhere." He read *Poetry*, along with the other little magazines in the University of Pittsburgh library. Ezra Pound and W. B. Yeats were his favorite con-

temporary poets. His classical favorites included Christopher Marlowe, John Donne, John Keats, Samuel Taylor Coleridge, and Robert Browning.

Stern entered Columbia's graduate school of English in 1949 and earned an M.A. the following year. After a year in Europe with two college friends, Jack Gilbert and Dick Hazley, Stern returned to Columbia to earn a Ph.D. in literature. He studied for a year with Lionel Trilling, but then dropped out of the program, having grown impatient with the unemotional rigors of academia. During his last year at Columbia, Stern supported himself by teaching English and serving as interim headmaster at the Lake Grove School in Long Island.

Stern married Patricia Miller on 12 September 1952. (They were later to have a son, David, and a daughter, Rachel, but eventually, in the late 1980s, were divorced.) With his bride, Stern went back to Europe in 1953 and remained for three years, traveling around but settling in Glasgow for a year to teach high-school English. This period in Europe was a frustrating but romantic interlude for Stern. He wrote an epic entitled "Ishmael's Dream" while staying in a fifth-floor Parisian walk-up on Rue Boucherie. He had prepared for this ambitious poem by reading Hart Crane's *The Bridge* (1930), John Milton's *Paradise Lost* (1667), and the biblical Book of Isaiah. Stern later sent his poem to W. H. Auden, who responded by inviting the young poet to his Manhattan apartment for tea, but Stern never managed to arrange for the poem's publication.

Upon his return from Europe, Stern secured his first college teaching job, at Temple University in 1956. For the next twenty years (until the publication of *Lucky Life* in 1977) he balanced a virtually unrecognized writing career with teaching English at various colleges and universities, including the University of Pittsburgh, Sarah Lawrence College, Columbia University, and Somerset Community College. From 1982 to the present, he has held a tenured position at the University of Iowa Writers' Workshop, teaching poetry. In 1990 Stern returned briefly to the New York area as a visiting professor at Princeton and New York University.

Slowly, throughout the 1950s and early 1960s, he shifted from tendentious emulation to self-discovery. Allen Ginsberg's *Howl* (1956) had been written, deafening the New Critics. Stern would work on one last ambitious, long poem, "The Pineys" (1969; collected in *Two Long Poems*, 1990), before breaking into his mature pace. Although "The Pineys" contains the same style as his later poems, it is, he says in the essay "Some Secrets," "indulgent and tedious." From this nadir, his real voice arose. He began writing shorter poems that unleashed his pent-up feelings of loss and failure. His poetic ambition had diminished enough, perhaps out of exhaustion, to allow for a relaxed embrace of his own kind of joyous grief. He speculates that it might have been something as trivial and banal as a trip to the doctor—and hearing he was overweight—that triggered his slight change in perspective, permitting him "to tap into material that was formerly warded off or ignored. . . . Was it my lot to speak for the second half of life and not the first?" ("Some Secrets").

Rejoicings marked the beginning of his mature voice. As the title indicates, he adopted an ecstatic spoken style that forsook epic ambition for desultory utterance, as in "This Is Lord Herbert Moaning": "My whole life is centered now in my lips / and their irruptions." These irruptions dictated their own poetic form, an associative flexibility that contains sinuous lines with natural pauses for end-stops. Stern's abrupt shift in outlook and poetic purpose seemed to result from a revelation; he suddenly realized that he had been treating poetry like a parlor game, despite his dedication to it, as he claims in "The Bite":

> I didn't start taking myself seriously as a poet
> until the white began to appear in my cheek.
> All before was amusement and affection—
> now, like a hare, like a hare, like a hare,
> I watch the turtle lift one horrible leg
> over the last remaining stile and head
> for home, practically roaring with virtue.
> Everything, suddenly everything is up there in the
>   mind
> all beauty of the race gone
> and my life merely an allegory.

Like Walt Whitman, Stern made the rather late discovery that he could not write about himself without some notion of persona overriding his lyricized experience. This realization—which continued full force into *Lucky Life* (the 1977 Lamont Poetry Selection)—hinged on Stern's awareness that his personal experiences were only glorious when depicted in a larger glory, and unveiled as a series of oxymorons. Earthly paradise, beautiful weeds, and compassionate animals fill his poems, transporting the banality of his urban background into a wild landscape. Stern embraced his ordinary surroundings and nostalgic past with clear yet secular devotion. It is unsurprising, then, that he would, in this worldly mind-set, choose luck over grace. He writes in "Lucky Life": "Lucky you can be purified again. / Lucky there is the same cleanliness for everyone. / Lucky life is like that. Lucky life. Oh lucky life. / Oh lucky lucky life. Lucky life."

Stern wrote now out of a personal need that adopted poetry for its emotional shorthand; that is, he was no longer trying to write poetry: he was trusting implicitly in his passions. He was ending poems roughly, with emotionally logical conclusions. With this new license, a confident solitary voice, Stern recognized an irony in T. S. Eliot's famous antiromantic criterion for the poet as stated in "Tradition and the Individual Talent": by subverting the exigencies of Stern's own personality with universal images, thus creating a mythology of the self, Stern could also succeed at "seizing and storing up numberless feelings, phrases, images, which remain there until parti-

Cover for Stern's 1984 collection, which includes poems on private and public loss and on mythical and ordinary topics

cles which can unite to form a new compound are present together."

Stern attacked the page with romantic fervor, as in "Rejoicings": "I have come back one more time to the shore, / like an old prisoner— like a believer— / to squeeze the last poetry out of the rubbish." An authority had settled into his poetry, banishing conventionalism and awe of goyish and Ivy League criteria. Stern felt suddenly compelled to create his own ecstatic cabala, as seen in "Burst of Wind Between Broadway and the River" (in *Rejoicings*):

> There at the little chairs and the round tables
> the rebbes read and eat.
> I walk between them like a learned soul,
> nodding my head and smiling,
> doing the secret steps and making the signs,
> following the path of authority and silence,
> I and the dust, in the black soup and the herring.

The poems in *Rejoicings* and *Lucky Life* seem both native and foreign, free of the academy's auspices. They have similarities to the work of Whitman, Vladimir Mayakovski, Nazim Hikmet, and Pablo Neruda. The poems are expansive, democratic, and lyrical—an immigrant's revenge on crusty eloquence, a bohemian celebration. This new voice was proudly shameless, for its heritage of persecution and displacement was too deep for reticence. Stern was transforming the American landscape into his own dioramas, as in "Psalms" (in *Lucky Life*):

> When I drove through the little bald hills of Tennessee
> I thought of the rabbis of Brooklyn bent over their psalms
> I thought of the tufts of hair and the bones and ridges
> and the small cows eating peacefully
> out on the open slope or the shadows
> while the forehead wrinkled and the gigantic lips moved
> through the five books of ecstasy, grief and anger.

Abraham Heschel writes in *The Prophets* (1962), "Authentic utterance derives from a moment of identification of a person and a word; its significance depends upon the urgency and magnitude of its theme. . . . This is the secret of the prophet's style: his life and soul are at stake in what he says. It is an involvement that echoes." The passion that continues to rage through Stern's poems with prophetic urgency seems largely inherent. But Stern is careful to underscore the impetus of his harsh experiences. A key event to which he returns often in discussing the provenance of his inspiration is the early death of his only sibling, Sylvia, who died at the age of nine of spinal meningitis. Stern was eight at the time. When his mother refused to accept her daughter's death after a prolonged period of grieving, Stern became the outlet for her transferred affection. He recounts his mother's taking him to bed with her while she wept, crying "Sylvia, Sylvia, Sylvia." As painful as this role must have been for him as a child, Stern did not ultimately reject it. Rather, he embraced it, assuming the embodiment of her loss, while finding a way to grieve himself. He writes in "Joseph's Pockets" (*The Red Coal*, 1981):

I borrow a book from the bleak office and open
to the page to be read at the graveside of a sister.
I ask her first to remember her shocking death
and all the clumsiness and sadness of her leaving.
I ask her to describe—as she remembers it—
how I stood in front of her white coffin
and stared at the mourners in our small living room.
I ask her to think again about the two peach trees,
how close together they were, how tiny their fruit was,
forty years ago in the light rain,
wherever she is, whatever sweet wing she's under.

This death planted in Stern's childhood the fact of a sacred synergism between all things, especially those things that stay in one's memory. Two peach trees become universal, not by virtue of Stern's lyricized experience but because he invites readers into a world of loss where particular trees, perhaps Sylvia's favorites, are chosen as natural metaphors; the peach trees suddenly become poles for all grief. From this one experience of critical loss, Stern has extended his empathy beyond familial boundaries to the afflicted family at large, whether they be Holocaust victims, dead possums, or weeds. "I think I have a bone somewhere in my spine," he confesses, "or a wire somewhere in my system, or a feather, that attracts me endlessly to the ruined and fallen" ("Rebuilding the Ruined and Fallen," *American Poetry Review*, September/October 1985).

Because of his accurate empathy, Stern is frequently compared to Keats. Interestingly, both poets lost beloved siblings early in life. For both, the spirit of the lost loved one assumes the identity of foreign objects—urns, squirrels, trees—allowing for negative capability. Both poets had the courage to accept the onus of loss, to become its voice, to resist the temptation of opiates, decoration, and distraction when melancholy descended upon them. Stern's only fear is that he will turn his subjects into symbols, thus losing their real identity. He wrote in "Notes from the River": "when I allow my own prejudice and my own sentimentality to enter; when . . . I forget I am converting a real person, I find myself in a slippery place. Not only do I dehumanize the woman, not only do I not allow her her humanity, but I do the same thing to the man, wherever he is. It is as if, by concentrating so much on the symbol, it is as if, by forcing the real man to become a symbol, and remain only that, that I also do an injustice to him, that I don't ever allow him tears, or regret, or change of heart, that I don't let him break away, and that I don't make distinctions between one man and another, any more than I did between one woman and another, and this has too much to do with Hegel, and too little to do with Keats. I do it for both reasons, but I deny them both life."

Such worry is a healthy sign of sympathy. But it is important to remember that Stern most often begins his poems with himself rather than with another, proceeding from the convex borders of his own experience into the "rough zone" of vulnerability. He believes that his thought process and feelings are a kind of metaphysical key for understanding the nature of things. Stern aspires to a close relationship with the inanimate, plant, and animal world. Immediate examples of such Taoist and Aristotelian devotion leap off his pages: "Today it was just a dry leaf that told me / I should live for love" ("Today a Leaf," in *Paradise Poems*, 1984); "Dear mole I have forgotten you!" ("Dear Mole," in *The Red Coal*). These lines show a deep belief in the distinct sovereignty of objects. Stern claims that people have the unique attribute of vivifying the world, but not for the sake of making it universally human. Rather, people are most human, his poems argue, when they are least self-referential. Stern's persona is thus a

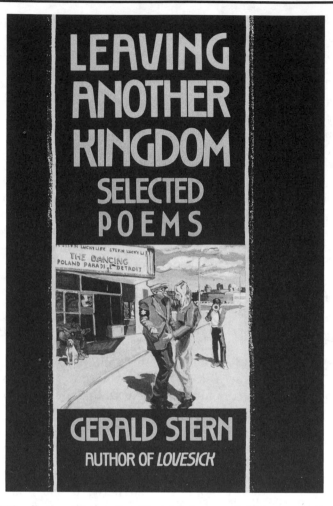

Dust jacket for Stern's 1990 collection of poems that Muriel Rukeyser called "the poetry of a profoundly realized life"

poetic vehicle for demonstrating the irony that the more passive one's creative aggression is, the more real the world becomes. This scheme does not de-emphasize the individual in an Eastern way. On the contrary, Stern's individuality remains firmly intact within his personality. He forces readers to see that they have made too automatic a connection between national identity and the natural majesty of the land, that they are, in reality, all too often ugly Americans. For the reader to believe this message, Stern must write with authority, being careful not to preach. So he lets the world speak through him.

In each book following *Lucky Life*, Stern has expanded his voice in both volume and length. In *The Red Coal* he hearkens to Isaiah's calling, a transforming personal event that spawns exhortation out of self-effacement. The biblical passage from which Stern chose his title reads: "Then one of the seraphim flew to me carrying in his hand a glowing coal which he had taken from

the altar with a pair of tongs" (Isaiah 6:9). After Isaiah has volunteered to deliver the divine message, whatever it may be, Yahweh entrusts him with the dark irony. "Go and tell this people," he says. "You may listen and listen, but you will never understand. / You may look and look again, but you will never understand."

Despite this vain tradition of uttering truth to deaf ears, Stern has willfully chosen to follow it. In so doing, he preserves the integrity of the entire scripture, bridging any canonical distinction between old and new. He reiterates with abandon from his wilderness post the importance of immediacy, the ambiguity of the present, and the terror of hesitating. Like a prophet, old or new, Stern understands grief. His implosive litanies announce that agape, justice, and authority transcend ecclesiastical boundaries with fundamental human precepts, that the Sabbath, for instance, as a day for man, is a "dream . . . a work of art . . . a poem" ("What Is the Sabbath?," *Ameri-*

can Poetry Review, January/February 1984). This human inclination has compelled him to be devoutly irreverent, as in "Good Friday, 1977" (in Lucky Life):

> Suddenly there are hundreds of fishermen on the road,
> wearing hats and waders and thick shirts and badges.
> Their cars and trucks are lined up on the lawns and ditches.
> Dozens are in the water already,
> side by side, casting and reeling in the foam,
> ending Christianity once and for all on this small river.

Although Stern views his declarations mythologically, he does so with ironic savvy, parodying narcissism: "Everyone is into my myth! / The whole countryside / is studying weeds, collecting sadness, dreaming / of odd connections . . ." ("This Is It," in Lucky Life). But he ultimately holds firm to his mission of witnessing, using humor in its most responsible role as criticism. This is his Judaic compulsion, to write amusingly, rhapsodically, apocryphally, like a Hassidic storyteller. Stern takes his wildness from nature. But he is not as wild as what he reveals. Otherwise he would merely be sensational, and he is not that.

Stern uses continuous clarification: neither ecstasy, nor grief, nor anger are ever static. He recalls the past with fastidious reverence, zeroing in on events, emotions, and thoughts, in telescopic fashion, until they appear in vivid detail on the page. These constitute the quotidian data, as well as historical horrors and contemporary injustices, substantiating his emotions, allowing, as Theodore Roethke once wrote, "the nobility of the soul to be at odds with circumstance" ("In a Dark Time," in The Far Field, 1964). Although sane, Stern often employs the reverie and rhetoric of madness before concluding clearly, marshaling a beguiling ambiguity between the burning insight of craziness and cool objectivity. Themes of persecution, mystery, biography, and law emerge in all his books on a common ground. Animals abound throughout his poems—monkeys, possums, apes, dogs, cows, and squirrels—along with numerous plants. Stern's landscape is a burgeoning one, a wild garden.

Paradise Poems marked a significant increase in Stern's ambition as he risked turning directly toward charged themes of personal and public loss, as opposed to his more random subjects of everyday minutiae. In such poems as "The Expulsion,"

"Kissing Stieglitz Goodbye," "Groundhog Lock," "One Bird to Love Forever," John's Mysteries," "The Same Moon Above Us," and "Sycamore," Stern carries on elegiac monologues with a largeness of spirit and metaphoric craze: "I lie alone / waiting for sweetness and light. . . . / I am a drop of white paint, I am a prow of a ship. / I am the timbers, I am the earthquake— / in eighty or ninety years / someone will dream of Crete again and see me / sitting under this tree" ("John's Mysteries"). In "The Expulsion" and "Kissing Stieglitz Goodbye," Stern confronts, respectively, the loss of his father and his beloved city (New York) in a style that adds mythical allusion, narrative, and sustained emotional honesty to his already established lyricism. These poems announce the poet's mature readiness to effect full catharsis in both the reader and himself. Although Stern had already successfully done this in "Joseph's Pockets," one must recall that the origin of that poem's grief—his sister's death—preceded the death of his father and his move to the Midwest by up to fifty years. No longer content to cast his sorrow in primarily short lyrics, Stern extends himself narratively, in concert with his imaginative flights and extended metaphors, to write consistently beyond minutiae, chronicling the adult "sadness" and "secrets" he had known would take time to discover: "It will take us time / to remember each other's secrets. . . . It will take us time to find our sadness" ("I Am So Exhausted," in Lucky Life). Stern finds this sadness in Paradise Poems by writing empathic litanies: "Lament, lament for the underlayer / of wallpaper, circa 1935. / Lament for the Cretans. . . . Lament for Hannibal" ("The Expulsion").

In the public poems of this volume, Stern writes of the suffering of the Jews in the Holocaust ("Soap"), the Jewish actor Adler ("Adler"), the dear poets of Perigord ("Near Perigord"), and the homeless ("The Same Moon Above Us"). These poems show deep affection, anger, and startling empathy: "I write this poem, for my little brother, if I / should call him that—maybe he is the ghost that lives in the place I have forgotten, that dear one / that died instead of me—oh ghost, forgive me!" ("Soap"); "I see him lying there watching, the wind cleaning / the blue sky, pulling a piece of sock / over his raw ankle, asking himself / what he was punished for" ("The Same Moon Above Use"); "They will look at him / with hatred reminiscent of the Plains / of Auschwitz—Buchenwald—and drive him mad / an inch at a time" ("Adler").

Pages from a work in progress that Stern calls "Someone Will Do It for Me" (by permission of Gerald Stern)

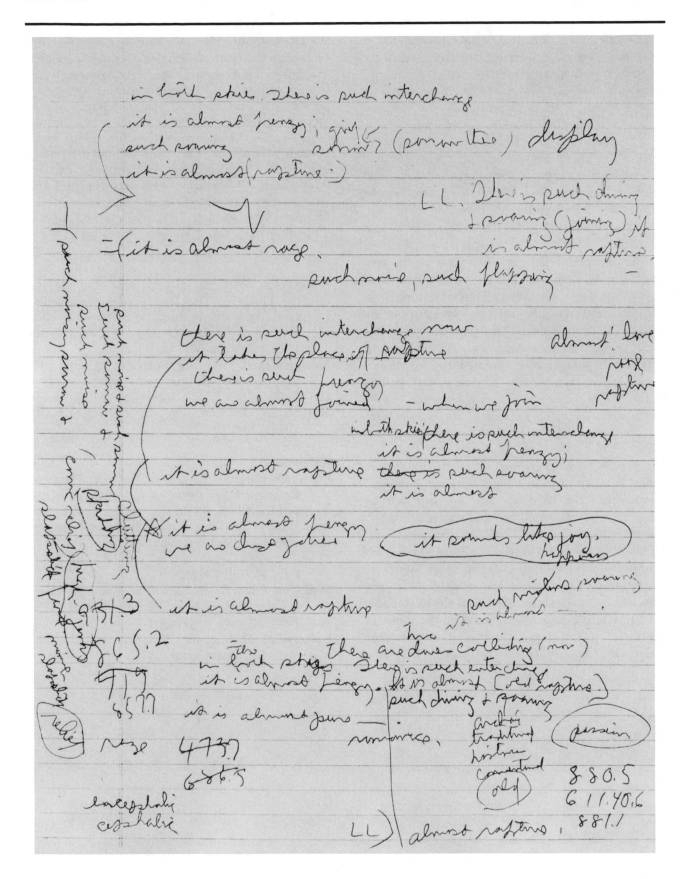

While Stern does not forsake shorter forms in *Paradise Poems*, continuing to evoke signature scenes of pathos and ecstasy (as in "Singing," "Huzza," "Moses," "May 15," "Moscow," and "The Dancing"), he does undertake the welcome new step of opening doors to secret rooms.

In *Lovesick* (1987), with the awareness that silence is the poet's last choice, Stern writes instead with elaborate urgency, focusing unblinkingly on death in such poems as "The Dog," "No Longer the Terror," "Bob Summer's Body," "Neither English Nor Spanish," "The Blink of an Eye," and "It Was a Rising." There are a few outright celebratory poems in *Lovesick*, such as "Grapefruit" and "A Garden," but they are harder won, set as they are amid Stern's Orphean impulse to descend into the underworld and gaze back in defiance. The numerous extended narratives in this book rebuke both silence and the specter of death with imaginative forays into the underworld, where spirits are "nodding and smiling in the plush darkness" ("Bob Summers' Body"). Stern walks despair's edge in these poems, writing "between one long-faced birthday and another" ("The Blink of an Eye"), surviving another year with oblivious glee: "I don't have birthdays anymore . . . / I just go on, although I hardly feel / the sadness, / there is so much joy being there on the small bench, / watching the sycamores, / looking for birds in the snow . . ." ("This Was a Wonderful Night"). Stern's broad recognition of beatitude in creation saves him from morbidity, but *Lovesick* is less overtly about love than death. Lovesickness, as Stern shows in poem after poem, is a dance with death to the music of paradise. In this tension between erosive time and earthly beauty, Stern concludes: "I look at the clock again, I chew my flower" ("Steps").

John Keats wrote that the poet has scant personality of his own since he must constantly assume the identity of other things, but the poet's personality can also be transcendent. Gerald Stern preserves and sharpens his identity, continuing to make the discovery that the self is large enough to embrace the world without becoming awash in it. He ascends into the light of his own ecstatic vision. This journey embraces a proud atavism, "so we can watch the stars together, / like the good souls we are, / a hairy man and a beast / hugging each other in the white grass" ("For Night to Come," in *The Red Coal*).

Interviews:

Sanford Pinsker, "The Poetry of Constant Renewal and Celebration, an Afternoon Chat with Gerald Stern," *Missouri Review* (Winter 1981/1982): 53-60;

Mark Hillringhouse, "An Interview," *American Poetry Review*, 13 (March/April 1984): 19-31;

David Hamilton, "An Interview with Gerald Stern," *Iowa Review*, 19 (Spring/Summer 1989): 33-65.

References:

Frederick Garber, "Pockets of Secrecy, Places of Occasion," *American Poetry Review*, 15 (July/August 1986): 38-48;

Jane Miller, "Working Time," *American Poetry Review*, 17 (May/June 1988): 14-16;

"The Poetry of Gerald Stern," special issue, *Poetry East*, 26 (Fall 1988);

Jane Somerville, *Gerald Stern: The Speaker as Meaning* (Detroit: Wayne State University Press, 1988);

Somerville, *Making the Light* (Detroit: Wayne State University Press, 1990).

Ruth Stone
(8 June 1915 -   )

Wendy Barker
University of Texas at San Antonio

BOOKS: *In an Iridescent Time* (New York: Harcourt, Brace, 1959);

Topography, and Other Poems (New York: Harcourt Brace Jovanovich, 1971);

Unknown Messages (Urbana, Ill.: Nemesis, 1973);

Cheap (New York: Harcourt Brace Jovanovich, 1975);

American Milk (Fanwood, N.J.: From Here, 1986);

Second-Hand Coat: Poems New and Selected (Boston: Godine, 1987);

The Solution (Baltimore: Alembic, 1989).

Tillie Olson, in the *Iowa Review* collection *Extended Outlooks* (1982), calls Ruth Stone "one of the major poets" of the latter twentieth century, describing her poetic voice as "clear, pure, fierce." Olson is not alone in her high praise for this poet. Patricia Blake in *Time* (22 December 1980) singles out Stone as one of the most powerful and sensuous of woman poets writing since Sappho. Sandra M. Gilbert (in *Extended Outlooks*) praises the "terrible clarity of her vision," and Julie Fay in the *Women's Review of Books* (July 1989) insists that a place be made for Stone "among the better-known poets of [her] generation." Frances Mayes, reviewing Stone's 1987 book, *Second-Hand Coat*, in the *San Jose Mercury News* (10 July 1988), observes that Stone is not only "wise and abundantly gifted," but that, in addition, her poetry is "stunning work" that spans a "superb range of evocative experience."

Perhaps it is this wide range, one of Stone's best characteristics, that, paradoxically, has caused the work of this poet only recently to be given the attention it deserves. For the work of Stone is as difficult to categorize as the poetry of Emily Dickinson. Lush, lyrical, even at times Tennysonian in its music and meter, Stone's poetry is also, as Donald Hall has said in *Hungry Mind Review* (Spring 1988), "relentless as a Russian's."

Born on 8 June 1915 in Roanoke, Virginia, in her grandparents' house, Ruth Perkins Stone was surrounded by relatives who wrote poetry, painted, practiced law, and taught school. Intrigued by the large collection of books in her grandparents' library, Stone began reading at three. She attended kindergarten and first grade in Roanoke, but then moved to Indianapolis where she lived with her father's parents. Living at that time in her paternal grandparents' home in Indianapolis was Stone's aunt, Harriet, who played writing and drawing games with her niece. Together they wrote poems and drew comical cartoons: Stone refers to Aunt Harriet as "the best playmate I ever had." The poet's mother, Ruth Ferguson Perkins, encouraged her daughter's "play." This was a mother to whom poetry was an essential part of life: while nursing Ruth as a baby, she read the works of Alfred, Lord Tennyson aloud. As her child grew, she openly delighted in Ruth's irrepressible creativity.

Writing, poetry, drawing, and music also surrounded Ruth Stone during her childhood in Indianapolis. Her father, Roger McDowell Perkins, was a musician, a drummer who often practiced at home. As Stone tells it, on the nights he was not gambling, he would bring home an elegant box of the best chocolates and some new classical records. There would be music and candy while he read out loud to them, sometimes from the Bible, sometimes from humorous pieces by Bill Nye. He was "crazy about funny stuff," says Stone. Humor was, in fact, a large part of the pattern of family life in Indianapolis. At dinner parties, the poet remembers, her uncles told one funny, fascinating story after another. Every member of her father's family had an extraordinary sense of the ridiculous, an ability to see through the superficial.

And yet this family of English descent also played its part in polite Indianapolis society. Stone's paternal grandfather was a senator, and in keeping with the familial social position, his wife gave frequent formal tea parties. Stone remembers pouring tea, learning to be a lady, something she says she later "had to learn to forget."

Ruth Stone (photograph courtesy of AWP Publications, Old Dominion University, Norfolk, Virginia)

Perhaps part of the fascination of Stone's poetry has to do with the counterpoint between a lyrical, ladylike gentility and a sharp, blunt, often bawdy ability to see into the core of experience. Indeed, the poetry of Stone is as informed by a knowledge of the sciences as it is by a novelist's eye for character, an artist's eye for color, and a musician's ear for sound. At the age of eight Stone read about meteors. Out in the grassy yard at night, she would lie on her back and study the stars. Once she found in the library a photograph of a galaxy that, as she puts it, "changed me terribly." When she read, in the *Phi Beta Kappa* magazine, an article about the new theory of the expanding universe, she became inquisitive about physics. She was also passionate about botany: "I wanted to absorb everything about the real world." When not intensely observing "real" phenomena, she read everything she could find; frequently she took encyclopedias and dictionaries to bed with her. She was, as she puts it, "obsessive about language."

It is no wonder then, with such passionate and diverse interests, that this poet's complex work has defied categorization. Diane Wakoski, in a paper delivered at the 1988 Modern Language Association convention, recognized Stone's poetry as embodying the comedic tradition of Dante, with its enormous range of human experience. As Wakoski put it, Stone is "opening the door to an American comedic verse." Stone's work could also be compared to William Shakespeare's plays, in that, immersed in the world of her poems, readers may find themselves moving inexplicably from laughter to tears and back to laughter again.

In an Iridescent Time (1959), Stone's first collection, includes poems written primarily while her husband, novelist and poet Walter B. Stone, was teaching at Vassar College. By that time the Stones had three children: Marcia, born in 1942; Phoebe, born in 1949; and Abigail, born in 1953. By 1959 Stone's reputation was established: in 1955 she won the Kenyon Review Fellowship in Poetry, received the Bess Hokin prize from *Poetry*, and recorded her poems at the Library of Congress. Individual poems had been published in the best magazines, including *Kenyon Review, Poetry*, the *New Yorker*, and *Partisan Review*.

Stone's first collection is aptly named: the poems are "iridescent," shimmering with music and echoes of Tennyson and the Romantics. These poems focus on youthful, exuberant family life, as in the title poem, in which the speaker remembers her mother, washing and hanging out to dry the brilliantly colored "fluttering intimacies of life." The laundry in this poem shines in memory and gleams with the energy of the daughters who hone "their knuckles" on the washboard. The title poem is also characteristic of this collection in its formal qualities: "tub" rhymes with "rub-a-dub," and the girls shake the clothes "from the baskets two by two," draping them "Between the lilac bushes and the yew: / Brown gingham, pink, and skirts of Alice blue." The vitality and whimsy characteristic of this collection also spring from the opening poem, "When Wishes Were Fishes," in which the rhythm and meter gallop: "All that clapping and smacking of gulls, / And that slapping of tide on rock"; "Our senses twanged on the sea's gut string, / . . . and the young ladies in a flock / . . . ran the soprano scale and jumped the waves in a ring." The air is "suncharged" over the "kelp-smelling sea," at "the edge of the world and free."

Yet this shimmering world is not entirely free, not simply youthful and buoyant. The "Sunday wish" of the girls in "When Wishes Were Fishes" is "to bottle a dredged-up jellyfish"; though innocents, they are also becoming aware of the "Seaweed and dead fish" strewed on the sand. The sense of youthful vitality is underscored by a sense that all this lushness and youth cannot last, that something ominous is lurking close at hand.

In Stone's second volume of poetry, *Topography* (1971), such ominousness occupies the center of the collection, for this volume maps the territory of grief at its most acute. Written after the death of her husband, Walter, which occurred while the family was in England, *Topography* was published twelve years after her first book. In this second volume, music is still present, but rhyme is less frequent. Forms are less closed in this collection, as if to emphasize that nothing, not even the striking images of these poems, can contain the grief.

The poems that comprise *Topography* were, for the most part, written from 1963 to 1965,

when the poet was a fellow of the Radcliffe Institute. The book opens with a short poem reflecting on marriage, "Dream of Light in the Shade": "Now that I am married I spend / My hours thinking about my husband. / I wind myself about his shelter." As if an echo from *In an Iridescent Time*, this poem, with its light touch and its wry attitude toward a wife's life, causes the rest of the volume to be read even more tragically, since the central fact underlying the book is that there is no longer anything to wind around, no longer any center, or any firm ground.

The second poem of *Topography* is "Arrivals and Departures," in which "the terminal echoes in the ears of a single traveler, / Meaningless as the rumble of the universe." *Topography* maps the journey from that arrival at the place of death, that departure from "normal" life initiated by the death of the mate. The speaker has been dropped off in this meaningless, rumbling "terminal," and must now map out alone both her destination and her itinerary. Imagery is stark: the counter in the terminal is wiped with a "grey rag," and the coffee bar is dirty. Everything has been spoiled, dirtied, and decayed. In "The Excuse," Stone writes: "It is so difficult to look at the deprived, or smell their decay, / But now I am among them. I too, am a leper, a warning." Poems in this collection contain images of "sucked-down refuse" ("Memory of Knowledge and Death at the Mother of Scholars"), "dead still fog" ("Fog: Cambridge"), and "repelling flesh" ("Being Human").

Yet, under the decay, under the almost devastating shock, the poems also trace the way out of this "terminal." One way is through the brutal honesty of many of these poems. "Denouement," for instance, maps the territory of anger following the death of a husband who took his own life: "After many years I knew who it was who had died. / Murderer, I whispered, you tricked me." But it is not only anger that is so powerfully mapped in these poems. In "Stasis" the poet says, "I wait for the touch of a miracle," and gradually, through the pages of *Topography*, small miracles do occur. Slow healing is the subject of poems such as "Reaching Out": "We hear the sound of a hammer in the pony shed, / And the clean slap of linens drying in the sun; / Climbing the grass path, / Reaching out before we are there / To know, nothing is changed." Old memories begin to surface, to shine into the present time, as in *In an Iridescent Time*; in "Green Apples" Stone writes: "In August we carried the old horsehair mattress / To the back porch / And slept with our children in a row. . . ."

But for all its moments of stasis, of acceptance, even at times of brief happiness beyond the grief, *Topography* maps no simple country. Section 4, for instance, shows Stone's skill as a naturalist. In poems such as the comic "Pig Game," in which pigs, like poets, "live within / And scan without," and the determined "Habitat," in which the wolverine "is built for endurance," Stone moves beyond the shock and anger of early grief to a wide perspective and rich connections. There is also much humor here, especially in the nursery-rhyme-like poems such as "I Have Three Daughters." The title poem, "Topography," concludes the volume. Wry, wise, funny, and redolent with a sense of the possibilities that exist beyond the lost and mourned husband, the poem ends, "Yes, I remember the turning and holding, / The heavy geography; but map me again, Columbus."

Stone's 1975 book, *Cheap*, is characterized by a movement beyond "the terminal," beyond the paralysis that underlies much of *Topography*. These poems were written while Stone was slowly migrating across the country, from university to university. She taught at the University of Illinois (1971-1973), at Indiana University (1973-1974), and at Center College in Kentucky (1975). The changes since *In an Iridescent Time* are clear from the titles of poems. In Stone's first book, poems are titled "Snow," "Ballet," "Collage," "Swans"; in *Cheap*, poems are titled "Cocks and Mares," "Who's Out," "The Nose," "Bazook," "Bored on a Greyhound," and the much-anthologized "The Song of Absinthe Granny."

In *Cheap* Stone's humor comes into its own. *Topography* was less mannered, less lyrical than *In an Iridescent Time*; *Cheap* is even less so. The poet has moved through the country of grief and has emerged, seeing everything, right down to its frightening, funny core. Connections between human and nonhuman life are made even clearer—in "Vegetables I" eggplants are compared to decapitated human heads, "utterly drained of blood." In the market, they seem "to be smiling / In a shy embarrassed manner, / jostling among themselves." In "Vegetables II" Stone writes:

It is the cutting room, the kitchen,
Where I go like an addict
To eat of death.
The eggplant is silent.
We put our heads together.

You are so smooth and cool and purple,
I say. Which of us will it be?

Such wryness and pithiness characterize this collection, which is tighter, more ironic, and wiser than either of the first two collections.

Styles and themes begun in the earlier volumes do continue. In the title poem, "Cheap," young love is the subject of fond scorn: "He was young and cheap . . . I was easy in my sleep"; the boy and girl are "braying, galloping / Like a pair of mules," running "blind as moles." Marriage and betrayal continue as themes. In "Codicil" Stone writes of a widowed landlady who keeps all the eggs her ornithologist husband collected, comparing all the "secret muted shapes" of "unborn wisened eggs" to the stillborn possibilities for her own marriage. Stone continues to examine her widowhood in poems such as "Loss" ("I hid sometimes in the closet among my own clothes"), "Habit" ("Every day I dig you up . . . I show you my old shy breasts"), and "The Innocent" ("I remember you / in the sound of an oak stake / Hammered into the frozen heart of the ground"). Other poems are lighter: "Tic Tac Toe" makes fun of all good intentions, of people "pulling in their stomachs and promising / To exercise more, drink less, grow brilliant."

Some poems in *Cheap* use the nursery-rhyme style of earlier poems. "Bargain," "The Tree," and "The Song of Absinthe Granny" all incorporate sing-song rhythms. Diana O'Hehir (in a paper delivered at the Modern Language Association convention, December 1988) observed that Stone's use of rhythms and comical word patterns, often coupled with terrifying subject matter, accounts for much of the poems' power. As O'Hehir put it, Stone "lures the reader in with the familiar rhythms of childhood, promises a pattern which the reader can join in on and follow along with, then yanks the entire structure out from under the feet," so that the reader is "surprised, startled, and made to follow gasping."

Surprising, startling, *Cheap* was the most direct, the most piercing of Stone's collections, until her *Second-Hand Coat: Poems New and Selected* was published in 1987. Here one finds a poet writing in her fullest power, relying upon craft, music, wisdom, and humor. "Orange Poem Praising Brown" captures the anxieties of the writer with admirable wit: "The quick poem jumped over the lazy woman. / There it goes flapping like an orange with peeling wings." A dialogue continues between the woman and the brown poem: "Watch it, the poem cried. You aren't wearing any pants.... / Praise my loose hung dangle, he said. Tell me about myself in oral fragments...." "Some Things You'll Need to Know Before You Join the Union" is another comic poem for poets:

> At the poetry factory
> body poems are writhing and bleeding.
> . . . .
> The antiwar and human rights poems
> are processed in the white room.
> Everyone in there wears sterile gauze.
> These poems go for a lot.
> No one wants to mess up.
> There's expensive equipment involved.
> The workers have to be heavy,
> very heavy.
> These poems are packaged in cement.
> You frequently hear them drop with a dull thud.

Part of Stone's humor is based on the characters who populate this volume, characters who may remind readers of Fred and Ida of "Bazook" in *Cheap*. Stone's characters are outrageously funny, and very real, similar to those of Charles Dickens and Mark Twain. As Kevin Clark observed (in a paper delivered at the 1988 Modern Language Association convention), they are often grotesques, in which readers may recognize themselves. As in the poem "Bazook," many of the characters in *Second-Hand Coat* have gone "beserk" [*sic*]; but the poems question what is meant by "sanity" and "insanity." Mrs. Dubosky in "What Can You Do?"; Aunt Virginia in "Curtains"; Uncle, Little Ivan, and Aunt Bess in "The Miracle"; the Masons in "Sunday"—all are a little daft, yet, as Clark noted, they show readers the truth of who *they* are.

The humor of *Second-Hand Coat* also extends to the poems that show Stone as an avid student of contemporary science. Just as the young Stone took encyclopedias to bed with her, the mature Stone reads everything she can about astronomy, the new physics, the natural world, the galaxy, neurons, and protons. Much of the effect of these poems has to do with Stone's immense knowledge of the way the world actually works, and in many of these poems, she fuses the wacky humor and drummer's rhythms of her father, the lyricism of her mother's reading of Tennyson, and her own relentless curiosity, wit, and wisdom. "The bunya-bunya is a great louse that sucks," Stone begins in "From the Arboretum," a poem that goes on to show the intricacy of relatedness: "Rings of ants, bark beetles, sponge molds, / even cockroaches communicate in its armpits. / But it protests only with the voices of starlings, / their colony at its top in the forward brush. / To them it is only an old armchair, a brothel, the front porch." Other poems are even more obviously based on Stone's scientific knowledge. "Moving Right Along" begins, "At the molecular level, / in another dimension, oy, are you different! / That's where it all shreds / like Watergate." Like the new physicists who have come to the conclusion that there is no such thing as objectivity, that all depends on point of view, Stone questions the possibilities for clear answers in "At the Center": "The center is simple, they say. / They say at the Fermi accelerator, / 'Rejoice. A clear and clean / explanation of matter is possible....' " The poem continues with the speaker's questioning: "Where is this place, / the center they speak of ? Currants, / red as faraway suns, burn on the currant bush." The eyes of the beloved, now long dead, are "far underground," where they "fall apart, / while their particles still shoot like meteors / through space making their own isolated trajectories."

In *Second-Hand Coat* the grief of the widow is softened, muted. In "Curtains," another tragicomic poem, the speaker asks at the end, "See what you miss by being dead?" In "Winter" she asks, "Am I going toward you or away from you on this train?" "Message from Your Toes" begins, "Even in the absence of light / there is light. Even in the least electron / there are photons. / So in a larger sense you must consider your own toes...." Stone connects electron, photon, and toes in a poem that elicits laughter in the beginning and a deep sense of poignancy at the conclusion: "And your toes, passengers of the extreme / clustered on your dough-white body, / say how they miss his feet, the thin elegance of his ankles."

Often poignant, as in "Liebeslied," some of these poems are as lyrical as any in *In an Iridescent Time*. In "Names" the internal rhymes offer the reader as rich an inheritance as all the "plants on the mountain," with their names like "pennyroyal, boneset, / bedstraw, toadflax—from whom I did descend in perpetuity." The music in *Second-Hand Coat* is far more intricate than that of previous collections; sound in Stone's poetry deserves more study.

Second-Hand Coat is a book that, like the speaker's mother in the poem "Pokeberries" (as Donald Hall has observed), splits language in two. The next-to-last poem in the section of new poems in *Second-Hand Coat*, "Translations," may well be Stone's best poem to date. In it one sees the most powerful characteristics of the collection: a tone of forgiveness and understanding, and, through anger and aversion, a deep forgiving love.

There is also laughter. "Women Laughing," for instance, incorporates all the lyricism of *In an Iridescent Time*, with a new complexity, a richer, maturer vision:

> Laughter from women gathers like reeds in the river.
> A silence of light below their rhythm glazes the water.
> They are on a rim of silence looking into the river.
> Their laughter traces the water as kingfishers dipping
> circles within circles set the reeds clicking;
> and an upward rush of herons lifts out of the nests of laughter,
> their long stick-legs dangling, herons, rising out of the river.

Ruth Stone's poems are indeed "nests of laughter," of wisdom and humor. With *Second-Hand Coat* Stone's poems have not only moved far beyond personal grief but have also risen to the stature of perhaps the finest poetry being written today.

Interviews:

Sandra M. Gilbert, "Interview: Ruth Stone," *California Quarterly*, 10 (Autumn 1975): 55-70;

"A *Concourse* Interview with Ruth Stone, Jackson Maclow, and Agha Shahid Ali," *Concourse: The New Periodical of Literature and Arts*, 1 (April 1989): 1-8;

Robert Bradley, "An Interview with Ruth Stone," *AWP Chronicle*, 23 (October/November 1990): 1-5.

References:

Leslie Fiedler, *Waiting for the End* (New York: Stein & Day, 1964), p. 221;

Sandra M. Gilbert, Wendy Barker, Dorothy Gilbert, Diana O'Hehir, Josephine Miles, Tillie Olsen, Charlotte Painter, Susan Gubar, "On Ruth Stone," in *Extended Outlooks: The Iowa Review Collection of Contemporary Women Writers*, edited by Jane Cooper, Gwen Head, Adalaide Morris, and Marcia Southwick (New York: Collier, 1982), pp. 323-330;

Harvey Gross, "On the Poetry of Ruth Stone: Selections and Commentary," *Iowa Review*, 3 (1972): 94-106;

Geoffrey H. Hartman, "Six Women Poets," in his *Easy Pieces* (New York: Columbia University Press, 1985), pp. 113-117.

Dabney Stuart

(4 November 1937 -   )

R. S. Gwynn
Lamar University

BOOKS: *The Diving Bell* (New York: Knopf, 1966);

A Particular Place (New York: Knopf, 1969);

The Other Hand (Baton Rouge: Louisiana State University Press, 1974);

Friends of Yours, Friends of Mine (Richmond, Va.: Rainmaker, 1974);

Round and Round: A Triptych (Baton Rouge: Louisiana State University Press, 1977);

Nabokov: The Dimensions of Parody (Baton Rouge: Louisiana State University Press, 1978);

Rockbridge Poems (Emory, Va.: Iron Mountain, 1981);

Common Ground (Baton Rouge: Louisiana State University Press, 1982);

Don't Look Back (Baton Rouge: Louisiana State University Press, 1987);

Narcissus Dreaming (Baton Rouge: Louisiana State University Press, 1990).

OTHER: *Corgi Modern Poets in Focus: 3*, edited by Dannie Abse, includes poems by Stuart (London: Corgi, 1971), pp. 135-157;

"Dabney Stuart, A Selection" (includes "Knots into Webs: Some Autobiographical Sources"), *Poets in the South*, 2, no. 2 (1980-1984): 3-34.

As a poet of the third generation of modernists, Dabney Stuart has produced a body of work that reveals a rich texture of influences. Beginning as a careful formalist in the accepted manner of the 1950s academic poets, Stuart has worked through a variety of styles to achieve, in his most recent books, a voice that sounds like no other contemporary's. Yet his stylistic variety and use of several formal strategies do not overshadow the concerns of his poetry, which have changed little in twenty-five years. He himself has said, "I have been consistently involved with certain themes, themselves less fragmented and wandering than my voice: son/father and father/son, levels of consciousness, the unforeseen and ubiquitous past, the aloof self-regard of women, the illusion of solidity and perspective, death and

punning" ("Knots into Webs: Some Autobiographical Sources," *Poets in the South*, 1980-1984). Stuart, like many poets of this third generation, has chosen autobiography, rather than any external system of values, for the mythos that underlies his work. A serious student of post-Freudian psychology, he often elevates parents, lovers, and children to the level of archetypes; and the poet's pursuit of these subjects, from his first book to his most recent, has the force of a recurring dream, the full meaning of which he is still in the process of interpreting.

Stuart was born on 4 November 1937 in Richmond, Virginia, into comfortable middle-class circumstances. His mother, Martha von Schilling Stuart, was the daughter of a German immigrant, Leopold Marshall von Schilling, a banker and auto dealer in the Tidewater town of Hampton, where Stuart spent summers during his boyhood. His Stuart forebears originally farmed in King William County on the middle Virginia peninsula. His father, Walker Dabney Stuart, Jr., was a hardware wholesaler, and several of the young Stuart's early poems indicate his distaste for the world of business: they hint at a conflict between father and son over choice of profession. Like many other southern writers, Stuart returns time and again to these family relationships and legends for the subjects of his poems.

Stuart attended Thomas Jefferson High School in Richmond, where he was an outstanding athlete, earning letters in football, baseball, and basketball. After graduating first in his class, he attended Davidson College in North Carolina, where he played baseball two years, won election to Omicron Delta Kappa and Phi Beta Kappa, and served as salutatorian at his 1960 graduation. He attended Harvard as a Woodrow Wilson fellow, receiving his M.A. in 1962. His academic career has included faculty positions at the College of William and Mary, Middlebury College, Ohio University, Trinity College, the University of Virginia, and Washington and Lee University, where he has taught since 1965. From 1966 to

Dabney Stuart (photograph by W. Patrick Hinely, Washington and Lee University)

1976 he was poetry and review editor of *Shenandoah*, a prestigious literary quarterly of which he became editor in chief in 1988. Among his awards are two fellowships from the National Endowment for the Arts, the Governor's Award for contributions to the creative arts in Virginia, the Dylan Thomas Award of the Poetry Society of America, and a Guggenheim Fellowship. *Don't Look Back* (1987) and *Narcissus Dreaming* (1990) were both nominated for the Pulitzer Prize.

Stuart is emphatically not a confessionalist, if, by that overworked term, we mean one who directly uses the materials of his or her most personal moments for poems—the method, say, of Sharon Olds. In Stuart's poetry a qualifying distance, a third-person point of view, a surrealistic texture, or the use of the past tense makes even recent events appear through the screen of memory or reverie. As James H. Justus notes, Stuart "typically withholds from the chosen poetic object . . . distinctness of form, and consciously in-

fuses the object with the swirling impressions of dream and fantasy"; in doing so, he makes "the language of dream as comprehensible as the language of consciousness." Nevertheless, the real tensions of family life have played prominent parts in Stuart's poetry, with ex-wives' and children's names even appearing acrostically in his poems (his first three marriages ended in divorce). From 1960 to 1962 he was married to Suzanne Bailey, the mother of his daughter, Martha. After a childless marriage to Betty Kantor (1963-1964), Stuart wed Martha Varney on 14 August 1965. The marriage lasted until 1977, and two sons, Nathan von Schilling and Darren Wynne, were born of the union. As Stuart has said (in "Knots into Webs"), "My responses to my own children—a daughter and two sons—my difficulties with marriage and family life, my belated consciousness that Adam's curse is mine too, and so on, echo the experience of millions, and are unremarkable. Though they are fit material for poems, they don't seem necessarily connected to the primary activities from which the impulse toward poetry derives." Since 20 January 1983 he has been married to Sandra Westcott, an editorial assistant for *Shenandoah*.

This "impulse toward poetry," according to Stuart, first found focus when he was fourteen years old and began to write poetry echoing Edgar Allan Poe, whose "The Raven" was often recited at bedtime by Stuart's mother during his infancy. Two earlier incidents, however, seem to have had a significance unknown to him as a child, and he has explored these memories in both prose and verse. "When I was five years old, the summer before I entered public school, I almost drowned," says Stuart in his autobiographical essay "Knots into Webs" (in "Dabney Stuart, A Selection," *Poets in the South*, 1980-1984). He recalls how he fell into Hampton Creek and was pulled out by his grandfather: "But I can still see my arms breaststroking through the thick green water, feel my legs frogging behind. Like I was born there. My breath spills out of my mouth and nose in a chain of endless bright bubbles. I am aiming at a barnacled support post. I never try to surface." In "Rescue," a poem in *The Diving Bell* (1966), Stuart remembers the same event: "I am no better swimmer / Now than I was at five / And the past is more treacherous water / Than the creek you fished me from / Then, finding me by the bubbles / That were the chain of my breath." Over twenty years later, in *Don't Look Back*, Stuart returns to the scene in "Taking the Wheel":

> The first time I tried
> to be fish
> —finning wide-eyed through the drowning water,
> happy to change my nature—
> I never wanted to come back, give up that warm
> release from everything, being all over.
> But you pulled me out anyway, set me adrift
> on the ground again, kicking and crying,
> as if to say, *Shove off, it's not that easy.*

Another of what Stuart terms, in a phrase reminiscent of William Wordsworth, "knots of memory" took place when he was a child in his father's hardware warehouse, which served as a playhouse: "an indecipherable warren of enormous storage rooms and tiny cubbies, connected by mysterious passageways." Stuart's poem "The Warehouse Chute" (in *The Diving Bell*) provides a further example of how childhood experience, transformed in the poem, begins to "spread, as if

into webs, so that what once was hidden and undifferentiated might become more open" ("Knots into Webs"). The description of the long, exhilarating slide down the multistory delivery chute ends with a sober epiphany:

> Now in my dreams the spiral
> Spirals without end.
> I see myself on every level
> Smiled at by a carton,
> Never [Dante's] Beatrice, smiled at
> By this past that hands me on,
> Guideless, always going down.

Justus notes that "poems of descent" are encountered many times in Stuart's work: "A typical movement is the felt need to plunge beneath or behind surfaces," and this is often expressed symbolically, as even the title of Stuart's first book indicates. *The Diving Bell* includes poems that first appeared in important literary magazines, the *New Yorker* and *Poetry* among them. The book's title comes from a passage in Thomas Mann's *Magic Mountain* (1924; translated, 1927): "He searched the past for a pattern into which he might slip as into a diving bell, and being thus at once disguised and protected might rush upon his present problem." Robert Lowell's *Life Studies* (1959), with its tangle of family history and love-hate relationships, was an influential book, and there are echoes of Lowell's formal and rhetorical practices in Stuart's poetry, as in "Canned Goods":

> My belly full of this domestic life
> I stalk the kitchen, hungry for sharp knives.
> Or poison. My cat, content with all nine lives,
> Gets in his licks. I want to leave my wife,
>
> To hit the alleys with him where he howls
> The stupid moon, claws over garbage cans,
> Toms every Tabby. The shrivel's in my glands:
> I'm fixed. He goes alone. I move my bowels.

Many of the poems in the book's three sections— "Paternal," "Maternal," and "Others, Up to Now"—are what might be termed "poems of the tribe," concerned with family backgrounds, childhood memories, and rites of adolescent initiation. "The Soup Jar," for example, has been frequently anthologized and remains one of the best examples of Stuart's work in formal stanzas. The poet recalls how he and his father once experimented in the kitchen with a "tricky gadget guaranteed / To open anything"; their attempt to open a jar results in a bloody accident:

Someone else tied my tourniquet. He paled
And had to sit down. Seven stitches later
We cleaned the floor and had another dish for sup-
     per.
Alone, he got nothing. It took us both to fail.

Weeks after, my world spun around that jar
And I saw it, and him, through angry tears.
Now it seems, recalled through these shattered
     years,
So small a thing—some broken glass, a scar.

Stuart's sporting experiences—football, baseball, fishing—have provided him with material
for many poems; in "Fall Practice," memories of
football drills and adolescents boasting about
their sexual exploits are conflated: "I couldn't believe their talk. They'd cat all night / Yet next day
hit the dummies, digging the turf, / Sweating, driving themselves for all they were worth / Into
each other like bulls, brute against brute. / Whatever they got, girls, drunk, it wasn't enough."
Though the poet calls himself "the quarterback,
the thinker," he ironically adds that he "worked
at the center's butt." In another vein, a short narrative lyric, punningly called "Ties," attempts to
"untie" another "knot of memory":

When I faded back to pass
Late in the game . . .
. . . .
My father, who had been nodding
At home by the radio,
Would wake, asking
My mother, who had not
Been listening, "What's the score?"
And she would answer, "Tied,"
While the pass I threw
Hung high in the brilliant air
Beneath the dark, like a star.

A contact sport is the vehicle Stuart chooses in
writing both about an adolescent's attempts to understand sex and about his quest for parental attention and approval.

The Diving Bell received wide attention for
a first collection. William Meredith noted (as
quoted on the dust jacket) that Stuart "confronts
his young life with an imagination that's like a scal-
pel and it is full of astonishing recuperations. Theodore Roethke said somewhere that a book
should reveal as many sides of a writer as is de-
cent for him to show. *The Diving Bell* has that
kind of reticence, not common among us." Conrad Aiken praised the way poetic skill was subordinated to a concern for accuracy: "The poems

have that quiet sort of veracity, of sounding absolutely true to the essence of experience, that ends
by establishing a *poetic* medium by the simple process of truth-telling" (dust jacket). While most of
the reviews of *The Diving Bell* were favorable, Richard Tillinghast, writing in *Poetry* (July 1967), tempered his praise with some criticism of Stuart's tendency to dwell on his family background: "As a
traditionalist, he needs not only to accept the
past, but as it were to be accepted by the past. . . .
Many of the poems about his father, for example, indicate less an actual closeness than an underlying need for closeness." According to
Tillinghast, "Stuart has not put his personal
stamp on the craft of poetry. He is still ill at ease
with it, and it prevents him from fully dealing
with his world."

Only three years passed before Stuart's second collection, *A Particular Place* (1969), was published. Unlike the poems in the first book, the
work collected here is looser in construction;
there are still rhymed, metrical poems, but open
forms predominate. At the time, Stuart commented, "I feel I have done as much as I am capable of doing in the traditional verse forms of
lyric poetry, and that now the essential task is to
find or more properly invent forms of my own.
Which is to say that in terms of my life as a poet
I am just the other side of apprenticeship."

The first poems in *A Particular Place* do
have a different look and sound. "His Third Decade" opens with a sentence fragment which
spills, with no punctuation, into a grammatical
"squint" in the third line; the beginning of the
third stanza is similarly disconnected, and its grammatical relationship to the other lines is not made
clear until the first line of the poem's final
stanza:

Ends in a house
Collapsing into itself

Whatever direction the wind takes
There is a wall to receive it

Caught inside
At the last moment

The moment where four winds meet
And the walls give in
To what is beyond them

He finds himself
Unsafe anywhere

Stuart circa 1973 (photograph by Robert Lockhart)

But tries the basement stairs, going
Down.

Another "poem of descent," this one attempts to move into the subterranean realm of the unconscious and, thus, into tribal memory ("Meets all his fathers / In the taproot of an oak"). The persona's motive is self-preservation, and images of hunter, prey, and physical and spiritual entrapment appear several times in the book's first section, even in a poem called "Love Letter": "He found / A single feather in the sprung trap / He took it home / And with it / Wrote to his wife." The general tone of the poems bespeaks an impending emotional crisis, the exact causes of which are never revealed.

Stuart uses more traditional modes in the book's second section, and the love lyrics that open it seem an attempt to balance the earlier melancholy. In "Anniversary" he wittily plays on the preposterous conceits of metaphysical love poetry:

Our first year turns. Were this another age
I'd have figures ready made
And wouldn't have to think up how to say
The sun could warm the world by circling us,

The bands upon our fingers tune the spheres,
Two Adams treat us with a single tree
Whose apple falls through darkness into light.

In other poems in this section there are echoes of the then-fashionable confessionalists. "Lines," a poem addressed to the Stuart's estranged young daughter, betrays in its apostrophes and formal music the influence of W. D. Snodgrass's *Heart's Needle* (1960). Stuart writes: "I saw you every day / Once, before you and your mother / Went your own way. / Though your other / Weaning was slower, you left my breast / And eat in the diner now, my guest." Dannie Abse, in a 1971 essay introducing a selection of Stuart's work (in *Corgi Modern Poets in Focus: 3*), observes that Stuart's attempts to break away from such "tight corseted forms" and to establish his own voice led him away from explicit statements and toward a style "even more abstracted from prose reality"—in other words, the manner of the book's opening section, which, Abse notes, "chronologically was written last." Throughout *A Particular Place* traditional symbolist lyrics such as "The Fisherman" ("These waters might yield / A catch so rich and strange that I could wield / It no better than my dreams") coexist with poems such as

"Bridge" that seem indebted to surrealism: "He held one suit; it was black. / To himself he called it what it was. / All its edges were sharp / Even at arm's length. / It repeated itself one end to the other."

In keeping with its title, the book's final two sections concentrate on places important to Stuart: section 3, "The Charles River," is a long meditative poem drawing on his Harvard years, and section 4, a sequence called "Rockbridge Poems," focuses on locations in the Shenandoah Valley near Lexington, which include Natural Bridge and Goshen Pass. Many of the poems illustrate how the intrusions of civilization ("Three of them split the Valley now: Parkway, / Eleven, Interstate") have modified but not completely erased the landscape of the past. In "Jump Mountain," about a place so named because of "the sharp drop / To stone on the other side / Which an Indian prince and his bride / Made their marriage bed," Stuart says the mountain retains an aura that distracts local fishermen and hunters and keeps "the barbed hook from the bass / or lead from the quail." In "Rockbridge Baths" a once-fashionable spa is forgotten, while its springs "have been channeled to the Maury [River] / Or have run off underground, as if to say / *What has been forgotten will be served.*" In 1981 "Rockbridge Poems" was republished as a chapbook by a small Virginia press, and the edition quickly sold out.

In a comprehensive review of *A Particular Place*, John Unterecker observed that it is "through a fusion of place and self that the book most conspicuously succeeds. Its dominant subject matter—overt subject matter—is time: the various human seasons in which one man puts down roots (by way of ancestors, wife, children) and the sometimes shifting places in which those roots descend (places in which he grew up, was educated, and—a changed man—to which he returned). But beneath that overt subject matter, almost obsessively, runs a preoccupation with the more intimate places ... [that] help define the dark subterranean self who searches the nature of identity, the meaning of existence, the validity, indeed, of the world" (*Shenandoah*, 1969).

The increased combination of traditional and innovative elements in Stuart's poetry, already hinted at in *A Particular Place*, becomes even more apparent in his next two books: in the first, the poet attempts to free himself from the poetic past; in the second he openly acknowledges his reliance on it. *The Other Hand* (1974), Stuart's first book from Louisiana State University Press,

represents his most serious attempt to break both with tradition and with his own earlier practices. Almost without exception, the poems are short-line, free-verse lyrics that use intralinear spacing and very little punctuation (only one poem uses commas and periods; perhaps significantly, the only article of punctuation used repeatedly is the question mark). The opening stanzas of "Draft Exile in Canada," one of the few poems in the book with an identifiable dramatic persona, reveal these techniques:

> The prints from the book club swelled
> Cracking their frames
> Fear ran in the walls
> Like mice
> All the words of the household stumbled
>
> Monks on the tube shed
> The only light   orient
> I could hear history groping
> Like a blind man in a strange room
>
> Feature by feature
> My father swept his face under the rug.

A mordant surrealism is apparent in the poem, especially in the punning references to Buddhist self-immolations in Vietnam and to the speaker's father's attempts to "save face." Other images, though, remain obscure: "prints from the book club" may simply indicate a middle-class milieu, but it is unclear why they swell and crack. Later, the speaker's final question appears to betray Stuart's impatience with those who would use escape as a means of protest: "But what will I do / When there are no more borders / Pull the fire up to my chin?" An implicit conservatism underlines much of Stuart's poetry, but he is not a poet to make outspoken comments on issues. Indeed, the public poem is rare in his work, though several pieces in *The Other Hand* evoke, like "Draft Exile in Canada," the tensions of American culture in the late 1960s and early 1970s; others, such as "The Broken City," impart a mood of general social collapse. In "Sulla Writing His Memoirs," Stuart has the Roman general and dictator remark, "The distances of war / March toward me from every direction." "Morning After a Storm" features an unidentified king who says, "Wars do not necessarily mean / The ruin of the regions in which they rage."

Like W. S. Merwin, who uses in *The Lice* (1967) a similar method to warn of imminent ecological disaster ("The Last One") or to denounce

Whatever his next death is
he knows it will be
undone the week after;
he'll be back here raising
his glass in the long mirror *saturday's here*

SERIALS, 1947

~~Indiana Jones~~ finds it
easy/to manage waking
each morning/with the sear
of blue steel in his gut,/
a dizzy rod of white *neon*
~~neon running~~
running from temple to temple ~~behind~~
behind his eyes, easy
to burn with July in February
when the thick fold of green
blooms in his pocket and nylon
tricot amulets dry lazily
on the shower rod. Desire
is one thing he thinks, lying
in bed under the slow ceiling
fan or waxing his *mahogany*
~~mahogany propellor before~~
propellor before takeoff. My desire   *& my*
another. It lifts me beyond
the cockpit, the sponsor's *word,*
~~word,~~ whatever my body does
while it dies, while its dying
lives. ^He rescues   *restores*
the semimaculate woman
bound ~~roped~~ in her last ditch, takes ~~off~~
~~off~~ again under the twined ~~footholds~~ *sag*
of a swinging bridge, makes
his slipstream tremble in the wild
blue, yonder; he's heading
home for the smoky *gambit,*
~~gambit,~~ the ~~next~~ husky
voice at the bar/seeking
to slip into the tableau./ ~~He's one~~
~~of a kind,~~/dusting the treetops?
with his shadow/under
radar, avoiding mirrors,/ ~~never~~ *always*
gearing ~~waking~~ up
for more/~~until~~ it's over.
before

Draft for a poem in Narcissus Dreaming *(by permission of Dabney Stuart)*

imperialism ("The Asians Dying"), Stuart in his early period wrote a portentous poetry of unrelieved solemnity. Even though some of the poems in the final section of *The Other Hand*, "The Real World," are love poems, they offer little comfort. In "Making Love," Stuart writes:

> Often when the evening
> Forgets its hour and the day turns
> Into itself my wife
> Remembers
> The years before me
> She keeps her
> Distances
>
> I would have it no other way.

This chilly resolution is far indeed from Matthew Arnold's "Dover Beach," which offers, if not easy solutions to the problems of living in a confused, threatening world, at least some measure of comfort in physical love and emotional fidelity. The situation in "Making Love" only inspires the speaker to ask a series of bitter rhetorical questions:

> Was it to come here
> I scrapped the billboards?
> Tunneled beneath textbooks?
> Was it to lose my head
> This way
> I starved my clichés?
> Is this no different
> From that other boneyard?

In a review in *Poetry* (July 1975) Joseph Parisi observed that, while "the themes are important" in *The Other Hand*, "the tone is curiously detached; the speaker, having already gone through it all, seems disinterested. . . . Many lines speak out against alienation, but the speaker's disengagement and control and distancing leave the reader untouched." According to Parisi, the love poems reveal a "heavy and constricting compromise . . . , nebulous glimmerings of (perhaps) messages too personal for our general comprehension." More positive was D. E. Richardson in the *Southern Review* (1976), who said, "Stuart's words are achieved with the greatest difficulty; to read them with the care they deserve is well-nigh to break one's heart, they are hedged about with such a void." Richardson nevertheless begged some relief from the book's grimness of tone and obliquity of subject: "one wishes that Bottom the Weaver or even the Bourgeois Gentilhomme would walk in and speak prose. As beautiful as

these poems are, and they are very beautiful, the reader yearns for some prose to complete them, to suggest the possible harmony of the poet's uncommon mind and the common life." Although Stuart referred in 1978 to *The Other Hand* as "so far my most honest performance," this honesty is reached only through a stubborn inaccessibility that makes it the poet's most troubling and difficult book.

In the same year *The Other Hand* was published, a collection of children's verse, *Friends of Yours, Friends of Mine* (1974), also came out. This comic bestiary displays Stuart's delight in his two young sons, Nathan and Darren, to whom the volume is dedicated. The title character in "The Electric Eel" despairs at being too long and has "one big wish: / To swim around like other fish"; she receives wise words from a philosophical fellow-creature:

> "Next thing, you'll want to sing a song,"
> The clam said. "Listen, you've got style.
> What other fish can make a smile
> Out of herself by curving? Cripes,
> You were *made* to sneak through pipes,
> The deep-sea slalom's your event.
> When God said, 'Here's my filament'
> You're the creature that He meant—
> A lamppost moving through the dark,
> Your grandpa guided Noah's ark.
> If we had bridges in the sea
> You'd be the only one for me.
> So stretch it out and love it, sport.
> It's ordinary being short."

Round and Round: A Triptych was published in 1977, and aside from a few fugitive pieces of light verse and sections of long poems in *Common Ground* (1982) and *Don't Look Back* (1987), it contains Stuart's most recent extended work in traditional forms. In a note to the book he warns, "It seems needful, in light of some early response to the ballads and songs in this volume, to say that, though many unconscious and mysterious turns constitute the essential career of a poem, the echoes of Yeats (and Edwin Muir and others in whose tradition the poems in Panel One are composed) are intentional." The first part, or "panel," of the triptych, "Ground Speed," consists of twenty-eight poems; many of them are songs in the voices of several recurring personae—the Fool, the Poet, and the Slut—while others narrate the exploits of a wide cast of other characters. One of these is the allegorical-sounding Bobby Cross, whose pyrrhic victories in battle with a Satanic stand-in call to mind John Crowe Ransom's "Captain Carpenter." Stuart writes:

> They fell on the ground together
> Tangled to the last,
> The adversary disappeared
> Though Bobby got up first.
>
> Dust crusted on his eyelids
> And in his nostrils dust,
> Insofar as Bobby thought
> He thought of dust.
>
> *Bobby Cross O Bobby Cross*
> *Round and round he goes*
> *And whether he won or whether he lost*
> *No man knows.*

The book's title is echoed in the poem, as it is in "The Slut's Second Song," which similarly focuses on the ambiguity that exists in trying to determine victor and vanquished:

> Neither the wise one
> Nor the dunce
> Can keep both heads up
> At once;
>
> When the fit's on
> Alike the bold
> And the sniveling
> Bow down.
>
> Though they lay me
> Flat on the ground
> I circle them
> Around and round;
>
> Though they depart
> To do and do,
> I am the ending
> They come to.

Stuart's handling of a variety of song-related stanza patterns constitutes a major tour de force, but the poems perhaps succeed best when the form is stretched to the point at which only a few hints of the original shape are retained. "The Ballad of the Frozen Field," which explores a "mind of winter" sensibility, reminiscent of Wallace Stevens's "The Snow Man," contains only one pair of true rhymes and one line of regular iambic feet:

> This is the true end of desire:
> The closed ground deflecting sleet;

> All seasons tend to this season
> And the world is flat.
>
> This is the true end of exploration
> Over the low and the high seas;
> Whoever fares may try lightly
> All edges but these.
>
> This is the true end of language,
> That Way of ways:
> All sound shaped to the one sound,
> Ice echoing ice.

The other two panels of *Round and Round* are "Fair," a sequence largely made up of character sketches of sideshow performers, as in "The Hermaphrodite" and "The Snake Charmer"; and "Data Processing," a group of poems of mild social satire. "Mirrors," in panel 2, shows how Stuart uses the people and attractions of the fairground to express, through the method of allegory, several of his characteristic themes, in this case the unpleasant rewards of self-discovery: "Everywhere / I turn / The hall of mirrors / Brings me / To myself," a state of affairs that the speaker concludes is probably "a lot better / Than looking back / Over my shoulder." The poems from the book's final section are more difficult to characterize, but they again display many of Stuart's familiar gestures. "An American Legend" includes a catalogue of flatly stated facts about sex ("Unless a man and a woman practice mutual control / Of the man's tendency to climax before the woman / It is doubtful they will satisfy each other"). The poem asserts that what passes for love in American society is often no more than narcissism: "Darling, I love you. Darling, I love myself." "A Lesson in Oblivion" is addressed to the narrator's "keeper, / Goaltender, hardy watchdog of the lone / Prayree, immaculate conception," and consists of a comic series of absurd questions: "Would you cross / An eagle with a rattlesnake and kneel / before their issue, or print its likeness / on your currency?" Yet the poem's final question and the alter ego's response to it are anything but humorous:

> If you had the chance
> Would you do it the same way
> All over again
> Without changing a thing?
>   And he said
>
> Yes. Except I'd have your tongue cut out.

J. D. McClatchy, reviewing *Round and Round* in *Poetry* (August 1978), complained that the

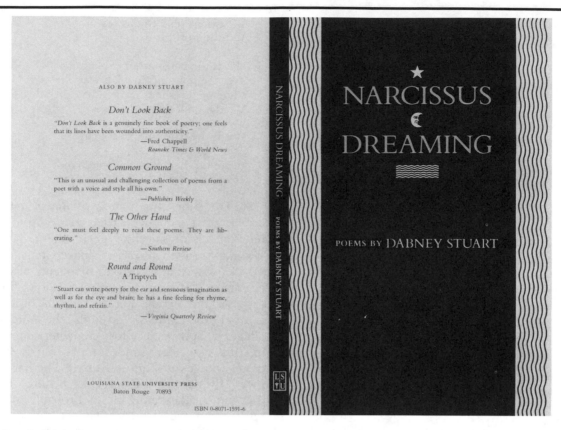

Dust jacket for the 1990 collection of poems that Daniel Hoffman calls "reports from deep in the Zone of Interior"

book's triptych structure is no more than "a poet's afterthought, an unnecessary 'structure' to link the poems and so brace or substantiate the book. The third 'panel' is merely a set of miscellaneous poems equipped with all the modern conveniences they satirize, too familiarly." Indeed, the divisions in the book, according to both formal strategy and subject matter, are not easily reconciled and could well be discussed in the light of almost any tripartite divisions: a Freudian might assign the id to the ballads (with their focus on the appetites, particularly sexual), the ego to the "Fair" poems (with their themes of self-discovery and deceptive appearances), and the superego to the final section (with their social consciousness). On the other hand, the term *triptych* has built-in religious associations, one of which brings to mind the allegorical three-part medieval altar piece. But McClatchy is ultimately right; the individual poems are not strong enough to stimulate much serious inquiry about larger structures. McClatchy concludes by wishing that "Stuart, a poet who knows what he can do and what others have done, would not bury his talent in such common ground."

The last two words of McClatchy's review, by an odd coincidence, match the title of Stuart's next collection, *Common Ground*. This and Stuart's two subsequent books possess a consistency of technique and voice lacking in the earlier volumes, and, taken together, they constitute a trilogy. *Common Ground* is, above all, a book in which the mature poet lays to rest some of the demons from his past—his relationships with his father and an ex-wife being the most prominent—and modifies his view of the earlier versions of himself with an affectionate irony. He notes in "Cut Off at the Pass," the book's opening poem, "My own rare distances / have become closed baggage / trailing a shred, a loose ribbon, / a tatter of my former self." In the penultimate poem, he describes "a fading version of myself, / A suitcase in each hand, shuffling / Out the door, Old Baggy Pants, not quite / Chaplin, not quite my father." Indeed, fatherhood is a major concern in the book, particularly in two elegiac poems about Stuart's father, who died in 1971, and in several other poems that deal with—and at times directly address—the poet's sons.

"Mining in Killdeer Alley," which originally appeared in the *New Yorker* and has been collected in *The Made Thing: An Anthology of Contemporary Southern Poetry* (edited by Leon Stokesbury, 1987), is dedicated to the poet's older son, Nathan, and describes a generational laying on of hands. The poem gives an account of how a flock of killdeer settled outside the poet's home "every day the last seven months before the gift" (the original meaning of *Nathan* in Hebrew), the child's birth:

> So that my father, who we thought was dying,
> Could see him, we carried his newborn grandson
> Up the back stairs of the hospital. The light was broken
> All over the blanket, and our child swam in his glasses
> With pieces of that broken light.
>   Their russet throats,
> The sun shattered in the gravel,
>   the gray veins
> Of his impeccable wrist,
>   Lord, for the life of me.
> When we brought him home they had flown away.

Stuart is consciously ambiguous in his use of personal pronouns in this passage; "his" and "him" connect the just-born with the about-to-die in the word *impeccable*, literally "without sin," which could refer to either father or son. The poem's concluding line is rich with traditional symbolic associations to the passage of the seasons and the brevity of human existence. "Mining in Killdeer Alley," despite its curious title (the poem makes no literal reference to mining), remains one of Stuart's most touching poems.

A narrative poem about Nathan, "Snorkeling in the Caribbean," displays Stuart's talent for finding appropriate metaphors in the "common ground" of an anecdote from a family vacation. His son being badly stung in the foot by a sea urchin, the poet-father receives a lesson in folk medicine: "The beach people told me I had my choice / Of going down on my knees before him and pissing on his wounds / Or binding him up and seeking out the amputator. / It wasn't prayer but it worked." The poem concludes with the speaker directly addressing the son: "brave child who refused to cry, / Whose pain my urine eased, who learns to swim / Behind a mask like mine."

That fathers and sons are fated to play the same roles over and over again, from generation to generation, is implicit in many of Stuart's poems, though many of these later poems hint that the "mask like mine" does not necessarily have to be a tragic one. Laius and Oedipus present only one of many models for this relationship; Aesculapius, the archetypal healer, was after all the son of Apollo, the god of lyric poetry. In the poem "Common Ground" Stuart speaks of times when "everybody had trouble sleeping, the children / Were feverish for no apparent reason, birthday parties / Were canceled, pets of all kinds / Were still and silent," but it is clear that these events are now in the past, and his most trying memories are subsumed in a general air of reconciliation. Some of the most memorable lines in *Common Ground* occur in a poem with the significant title "Histories": "There was a wound who loved its knife / And Kept calling *Come back, come back*, / I am not deep enough, / And when it began to heal cried / *Save me, I disappear*." Even if the book's title speaks of shared space that is often constricted and as precarious as an aerialist's high wire—as in "At the Circus, or Thereabouts": "the two of them make a sort of love / Up there, trusting each other, equally lit, / Having only one common ground, and one way / To go, back and forth"—at least it does not describe another emotional battlefield like those Stuart has previously visited. This sense of hardearned truce led Fred Chappell to remark, "There is a happy goodheartedness in this book that transfigures even the saddest subjects. . . . The sensibility that comes across here is a peaceful and happy one, endowed with a language capable of handling almost anything" (*Roanoke Times & World-News*, 27 March 1983).

An issue of *Poets in the South* (1980-1984) was devoted to Stuart's work. A retrospective essay by Barbara Fialkowski compares Stuart's method with Stevens's. According to Fialkowski, Stuart's earlier poems "engage biography in a tentative and despairing way [in which] the past is painfully recognized for its emptiness and self-realizing solitude." On the other hand, Stuart's later poems "provide an artistic resolution by celebrating the solidity of the Word and the organic and real processes by which it achieves its ability to inform." Cut off from the religious beliefs of the past, Stevens, the prototypical high modernist, "had to wrestle poetry from the visionaries, the transcendentalists." Stuart, writing over half a century later in what Fialkowski labels a "post-confessionalist" mode, has set himself the task of wrestling it from the verse-autobiographers, the humdrum chroniclers of the quotidian: "Stuart's poems struggle against imminent solitude, solipsism, and loneliness in an heroic effort to make human contact. The poem becomes a common

Manuscript for "Grubbing Thistle," a poem accepted for publication by TriQuarterly *and included in a proposed collection titled "Long Gone" (by permission of Dabney Stuart)*

ground for such an effort."

Don't Look Back, Stuart's 1987 collection, is ironically titled, since many of the poems return to Stuart's early life for their subjects. But this time the mode is comic, another sign perhaps of the poet's acceptance of the past. The child's search for selfhood in "Finding My Face" is enacted in a bizarre setting, like an episode from a surrealistic situation comedy: " 'What have you done with it this time?' / my mother asks at breakfast. / 'How can I carry on with my holy work if you're not watching?' " Later, the speaker finds himself a misfit in his father's business world:

> In the warehouse we discover my nose
> deep in a hogshead of curing tobacco.
> At first my father mistakes it for a raisin.
> He hands it to me, tells me I'm lazy.
> "You'll never make any money that way," he says,
> but I sense a grudging admiration for something—
> my shrewd choice of environment?
> He pokes me in the ribs and gives me a wink
> before vanishing behind an inventory graph.

The poetic quest for the perfect soul mate ends in the absurd nightmare of "The Girl of My Dreams Is Dying," in which the romantic ideal is cruelly confronted after a radical double mastectomy: *Lose / something?* I ask. / *Your future* she says and spits / five or six teeth at me." When the speaker tries to embrace his dream, he grasps only synesthesia and paradox, "a hint / of eucalyptus and mint, the sweetest / echo of nothing I've ever heard."

A desire for what Chappell calls being "wounded into authenticity" (*Roanoke Times & World-News*, 30 August 1987) runs through *Don't Look Back*; it is apparent in titles such as "This Is No Dream, This Is My Life" and seriocomic self-portraits, as in "Snapshots of the Writer Entering Middle Age": "He was caught often with his mouth open / but this time his astonishment seems / drier than usual, less rehearsed...." While there are echoes of formal patterns in many of the poems in both *Don't Look Back* and *Narcissus Dreaming*, one is left with a general sense of spontaneity in their "less rehearsed" manner. Nevertheless, in these two books, Stuart has written numerous acrostics, one of the most limiting of all poetic forms. The "discovered" name spelled by the first lines' initial letters proves the perfect vehicle by which Stuart, in "Discovering My Daughter" (*Don't Look Back*) can speak of reestablishing a relationship with the long-estranged child of his first marriage:

> Most of your life we have kept our separate places:
> After I left your mother you knew an island,
> Rented rooms, a slow coastal slide northward
> To Boston, and, in summer, another island
> Hung at the country's tip. Would you have kept going
> All the way off the map, an absolute alien?

> Sometimes I shiver, being almost forgetful enough
> To have let that happen. We've come the longer way
> Under such pressure, from one person to
> Another. Our trip proves again the world is
> Round, a singular island where people may come
> Together, as we have, making a singular place.

One sees many paradoxes in Stuart's work, not the least of which is that his syntax and meaning are often most straightforward when he is working under the tightest formal restraints. Taking its cue from passages like these, the *Virginia Quarterly Review* (August 1987) noted that Stuart "seems more relaxed and comfortably at home with a variety of approaches than he has been in his previous collections." Stuart's discreet handling of sometimes-tortured autobiography is better understood if one heeds what the same issue of the quarterly had to say about confessionalist Sharon Olds: "her preoccupation with suffering goes beyond an effort by an honest artist to come to grips with a gruesome century and becomes an indulgence of morbid private obsession. A catalogue of dismemberment and sickness lovingly described finally amounts to a drearily conventional exercise in modernist aesthetics, which the poet's equally conventional 'affirmations,' also part of the exercise, cannot redeem. We mock the 19th-century critics who would have called such a book unhealthy, but I suspect that many readers might now be willing to admit they may have been right." Too many contemporary poets have become exhibitionists; compared to them, Stuart is the model of decorum, always managing to distance himself and the reader from the mere *facts* that may or may not lie behind the poems. Paul Ramsey cites Stuart for providing excellent examples of the "deconstructive lyric" that has become an important genre in contemporary poetry, a type of poem marked by "uncertainty; the sense of being interlocked within a lock to which the key is also locked, therein or elsewhere; the vivid near-solipsism in the presence of a world that dazzles rather than enlightens" (*Chronicles*, March 1989).

"Ex-Wife," one of the most powerful poems in *Don't Look Back*, imagines the poet as voyeur, looking in on his ex-wife's bath while she reads an unidentified book, perhaps one of his own. But Stuart is not interested in revealing intimacies; his purpose is to explore the timelessness of the emotions, how the memory of past love can exist independent of the memory of the unhappy events that eventually ended it:

> I lay the binoculars on the windowsill,
> tip my head toward the bricks.
> I don't know she will be dead in five years
> but I wish I could help her. Hand her
> the soap, take her riding in my tan car
> by the river, meet her again coming
> across the bridge on fire in her red scarf.

Stuart is committed to giving himself, and his readers as well, no easy answers to the questions his poems raise. He is resigned "to scour the world for the book with two texts, / one lying transparently on the other / as if whispering to it, / opening secrets, filling the gaps" (Ex-Wife").

In his recent collection *Narcissus Dreaming*, even the title reveals two of Stuart's persistent themes: observation of the external self, matched with simultaneous investigation of the unconscious level of existence. Daniel Hoffman, as quoted on the dust jacket, calls these poems "reports from deep in the Zone of Interior [that] are darkly haunting, at once strange and familiar as are bent mirrors' truths, and tinged with humor." In the book's title poem, Stuart draws his trope from one of his characteristic sources, fishing, and explores the archetypal character's (and perhaps the poet's) desire to free himself finally from the demands of self-scrutiny and inhabit a world where everything is not overlaid with his own image. But the method is not escapist ("He might be getting ready / to step out over / the side, but there's nowhere / to go"); self-acceptance (the "perfectly imperfect fit" of one's own skin) can come only at the end of a long struggle to "land" the prey:

> Bob, line,
> sinker, hook return
> to him, bringing
> his reflection off the water
> as if it were a laid-out suit
> of clothes lifted
> by its center. He lowers
> it into the boat, takes
> it upon himself,
> drenched, obscene,

> a perfectly imperfect fit,
> leaving the water
> imageless, opaque,
> other.

In keeping with the focus of the title poem, the poems in *Narcissus Dreaming* for the most part move away from autobiography toward encounters with others, with "the Other." Many of the poems are descriptive pieces in the third person, and satire appears more frequently than in any of Stuart's earlier collections, except perhaps *Round and Round*. In "Surface Tension," he depicts a drowsy poolside beauty, a female version of Narcissus, as one whom life spares "the grit and pollen of normal air, / letting her sleep through everything / with her eyes open." "Gospel Singer" is another memorable piece of visual reportage:

> Everything
> rides on his bringing
> his mouth down to the mike,
> almost into it. It is more
> than intimate. He delivers
> his part
> with such control
> you hear nothing
> but music, as if
> he were breathing
> song.

"Umpire" unexpectedly explores the tactile, as well as visual, sensations of baseball:

> Crouching, he rests
> his hand absently
> on the catcher's ribs,
> feels the tender
> vibrations of the ball hitting
> the mitt, sensing
> the red seams' rapt
> nestle into the leather.

In recent years, in spite of the loss of central vision in his left eye, Stuart has worked seriously as a painter, a hobby that dates to his college days. The strength of his visual imagery has not often been cited by critics but nevertheless should occupy an important place in any estimation of his achievement.

Similarly undervalued is Stuart's position as a satirist. The occasional satirical poem appears in most of his collections, but *Narcissus Dreaming* contains several witty examples of Stuart's insider's knowledge of the literary wars. In "Franz

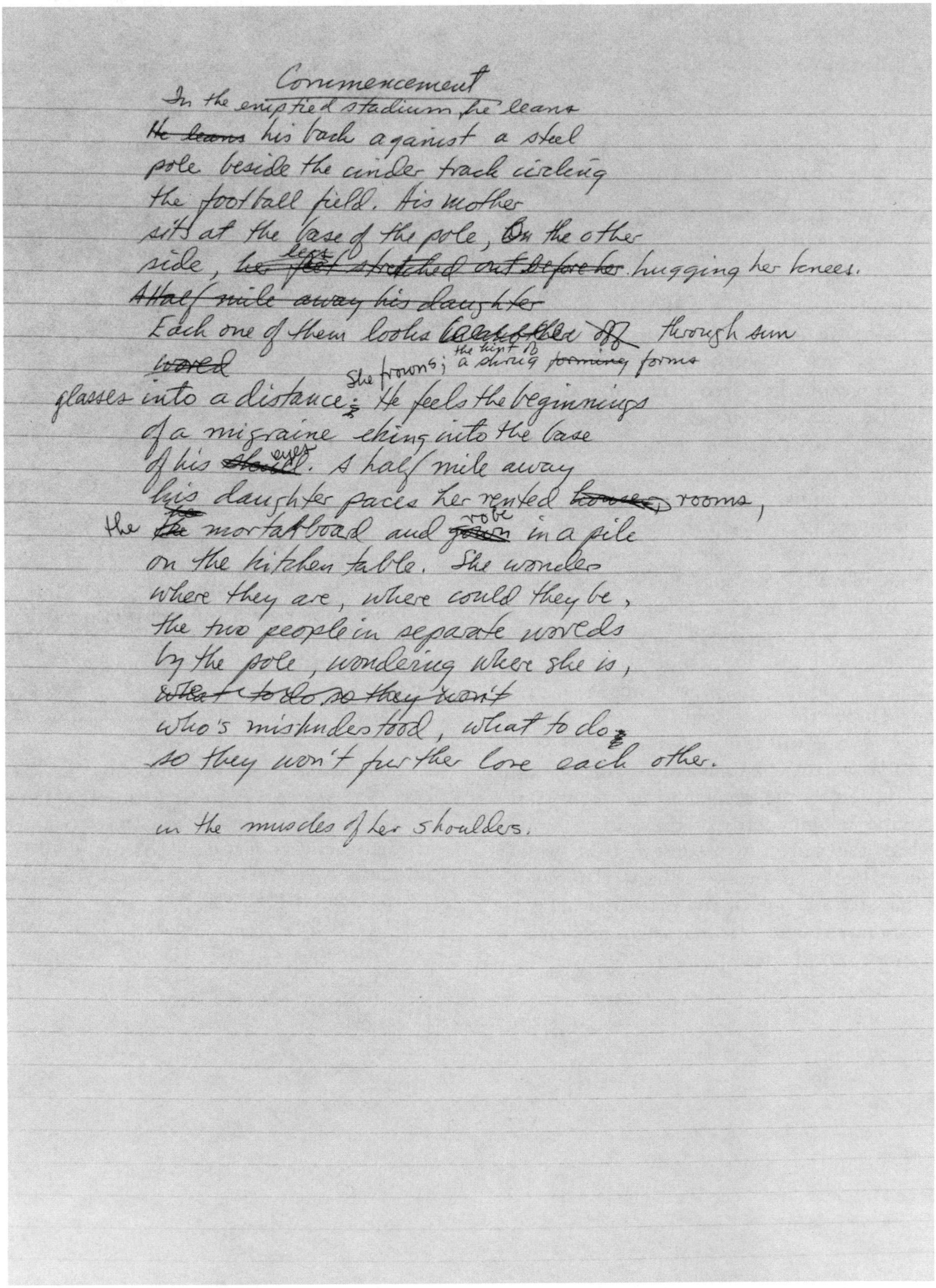

Commencement

In the emptied stadium, he leans
~~He leans~~ his back against a steel
pole beside the cinder track circling
the football field. His mother
sits at the base of the pole, ~~On the other~~
side, ~~his feet stretched out before her~~ hugging her knees.
~~A half mile away his daughter~~
Each one of them looks ~~(illegible)~~ off   through sun
~~word~~   She frowns; the tiny to a string forming forms
glasses into a distance. He feels the beginnings
of a migraine eking into the base
of his ~~eyes~~. A half mile away
his daughter paces her rented ~~house~~ rooms,
the ~~the~~ mortarboard and ~~gown~~ robe in a pile
on the kitchen table. She wonders
where they are, where could they be,
the two people in separate worlds
by the pole, wondering where she is,
~~what to do so they won't~~
who's misunderstood, what to do,
~~so they won't further love each other.~~

in the muscles of her shoulders.

Manuscript for a work in progress (by permission of Dabney Stuart)

Kafka Applies for a Literary Fellowship," the Austrian writer fills in the blanks with a candor that is rare indeed in applications:

> If awarded this grant
> I will burn the money
> to write by. The light
> will cast the shadow
> of my pen on the wall
> behind my head. I will call
> the work, tentatively,
> *The Foundation.*

The title character in "The Blurb Writer," confronted with the dishonesty of having his name appear in "one year on the back / of 26 books ... / under paragraphs he rarely / remembered writing," begins to see himself as a literary Robert Oppenheimer: "*This is death* he thought. *I have / created death*, and he saw / his blurbs rising like mushroom / clouds, carrying their sickness / into the atmosphere forever." In addition to these literary pieces, some poems allude to movies ("The Long Goodbye," "Moving Pictures," "Serials, 1947") and television ("... like an episode / of Phil Donahue in pantomime, / tuned to itself, articulating nothing / beyond the only word that matters, *Watch*" ["On the Air"]), with varying degrees of irony. One of the most original poems in *Narcissus Dreaming*, one which manages to be both satirical and serious, is "The Cabbage in History," a soliloquy spoken by the vegetable who "can wrap / the ground imagination / of the Middle East in one / leaf, a gesture / as modest as God / riding into Jerusalem / on an ass." The wry humor of these lines reveals one of the most appealing aspects of Stuart's talent, one that seems more in evidence in his recent work.

Stuart and his wife, Sandra, spent the 1987-1988 academic year in New Zealand on a grant from the Guggenheim Foundation. Other than in *Rockbridge Poems* Stuart has only occasionally written about places. "Tane Mahuta," a poem about one of the few large kauri trees remaining in New Zealand, appeared in *Tar River Poetry* (Fall 1988) after the poet's return, and other poems written in and about New Zealand will be collected in "Long Gone," a work in progress. A selected edition of Stuart's work is long overdue, and when such a retrospective collection is published, it will doubtless occasion new assessments of his "particular place" among the leading poets of his generation.

References:

Dannie Abse, Introduction to Stuart's poems in *Corgi Modern Poets in Focus: 3*, edited by Abse (London: Corgi, 1971), p. 135;

Gilbert Allen, "Dabney Stuart," in *Contemporary Southern Writers*, edited by Joseph M. Flora and Robert Bain (Westport, Conn.: Greenwood, 1991);

Barbara Fialkowski, " 'Ghostlier Demarcations, Keener Sounds': A Reading of Dabney Stuart's Poems," *Poets in the South*, 2, no. 2 (1980-1984): 35-42;

James H. Justus, "The Recent South," in *The History of Southern Literature*, edited by Louis D. Rubin and others (Baton Rouge: Louisiana State University Press, 1985), pp. 540-543;

Paul Ramsey, "The Deconstructive Lyric," *Chronicles* (March 1989): 28-30;

John Unterecker, "The Validity of the World," *Shenandoah*, 21, no. 1 (1969): 70-76.

Miller Williams
(8 April 1930 -)

Leon Stokesbury
Georgia State University

BOOKS: *A Circle of Stone* (Baton Rouge: Louisiana State University Press, 1964);

So Long at the Fair (New York: Dutton, 1968);

The Achievement of John Ciardi (Glenview, Ill.: Scott, Foresman, 1969);

The Only World There Is (New York: Dutton, 1971);

The Poetry of John Crowe Ransom (New Brunswick, N.J.: Rutgers University Press, 1972);

Halfway from Hoxie: New and Selected Poems (New York: Dutton, 1973);

How Does a Poem Mean?, by Williams and John Ciardi (Boston: Houghton Mifflin, 1975);

Why God Permits Evil (Baton Rouge & London: Louisiana State University Press, 1977);

Distractions (Baton Rouge & London: Louisiana State University Press, 1981);

The Boys on Their Bony Mules (Baton Rouge: Louisiana State University Press, 1983);

Patterns of Poetry: An Encyclopedia of Forms (Baton Rouge: Louisiana State University Press, 1986);

Imperfect Love (Baton Rouge: Louisiana State University Press, 1986);

Living on the Surface: New and Selected Poems (Baton Rouge: Louisiana State University Press, 1989).

OTHER: *19 poetas de hoy en los Estados Unidos*, edited by Williams (Santiago, Chile: USIS, 1966);

Southern Writing in the Sixties: Fiction, edited by Williams and John William Corrington (Baton Rouge: Louisiana State University Press, 1966);

Southern Writing in the Sixties: Poetry, edited by Williams and Corrington (Baton Rouge: Louisiana State University Press, 1967);

Nicanor Parra, *Poems and Antipoems*, edited and translated by Williams and others (New York: New Directions, 1967; London: Cape 1968);

Chile: An Anthology of New Writing, edited by Williams (Kent, Ohio: Kent State University Press, 1968);

Parra, *Emergency Poems*, edited and translated by Williams (New York: New Directions, 1972; London: Boyars, 1977);

Contemporary Poetry in America, edited by Williams (New York: Random House, 1973);

Railroad: Trains and Train People in American Culture, edited by Williams and James Alan McPherson (New York: Random House, 1976);

A Roman Collection, edited by Williams (Columbia: University of Missouri Press, 1980);

Sonnets of Giuseppe Belli, translated by Williams (Baton Rouge & London: Louisiana State University Press, 1981);

Ozark, Ozark: A Hillside Reader, edited by Williams (Columbia & London: University of Missouri Press, 1981).

RECORDINGS: *The Poetry of Miller Williams*, New York, Norton 23237, 1974;

Poems of Miller Williams, New Rochelle, N.Y., Spoken Arts, SAC 1160, 1982.

Among those poets of the American South whose careers began in the 1960s and who achieved national recognition in the 1970s and 1980s, Miller Williams is the most gifted and has compiled the most significant body of work. His prodigious literary output has resulted not only in nine collections of poetry but in fifteen additional books he has authored, edited, or translated. Williams's poetry exhibits a remarkable consistency of vision and voice throughout his career. Unlike the majority of poets of his generation, who seem to have written their strongest and most memorable work before the age of forty-five, Williams has grown from book to book. The result of this long and steady artistic development is a mature and informed art that is being written by a major poet only now reaching the height of his powers.

Miller Williams

Miller Williams was born on 8 April 1930 in Hoxie, Arkansas, and was the son of Ernest B. Williams, a Methodist minister, and Ann Jeanette Miller Williams. Because the Reverend Mr. Williams was assigned to various congregations during his son's youth, the family did not settle for any extended period in one town. The young Williams lived in Arkansas until he was twenty-two, and he has always considered the state his home, having resided there for the last twenty years as well. His being an Arkansan and a southerner has helped to form his sense of identity and poetic voice. Although he can be considered a regional writer in only the best and most general sense of that phrase, being from the South has always been important to Williams. He once told bibliographer Lymon B. Hagen, "I don't love the South because it is good. I love it because it is whatever I am. I also have a real affection for the United State of America, but not because it's good. I have a deep love for my grandfather. You might not have called him good, but whatever he was I am. There's a kind of sham, a kind of smugness, in cutting yourself off from whatever you are. I either write out of my roots or I

don't write. And these are my roots."

Williams graduated from Arkansas State University in 1950 with a bachelor's degree in biology, and from the University of Arkansas at Fayetteville in 1952 with a master's degree in zoology and anthropology. After serving as an instructor of biology in various colleges for a few years, Williams gave up teaching and spent the late 1950s and early 1960s working at a variety of jobs. These included working in a popsicle factory and as a projectionist in a movie house, traveling as a field man with a New York publishing house, running a Sears furniture department, and selling tires for Montgomery Ward. On 29 December 1951 Williams married Lucille Day, a pianist. The couple had three children: Lucinda (born in 1953), a well-known professional singer; Robert (born in 1955); and Karyn (born in 1957). The marriage ended in divorce after fifteen years.

In 1961 Williams met the poet John Ciardi, who, along with Howard Nemerov, helped Williams's early career as a poet and teacher of literature. Although he had no degrees in the field, with the encouragement of these two and on the basis of his growing credentials as a poet, he was able to secure a teaching position in the English department of Louisiana State University in 1962.

After several years there, followed by several more at Loyola University in New Orleans, where in 1968 he founded the *New Orleans Review*, Williams joined the graduate creative-writing faculty of the University of Arkansas in 1971. Since then he has resided in Fayetteville with his second wife, Rebecca Jordan Hall Williams, whom he married in 1966. He served at various times as director of the creative-writing program and chair of the translation program and the comparative literature program, then took the reins of the University of Arkansas Press as its founding director in 1980. Williams's writings have appeared in many anthologies and textbooks, and his poetry has received numerous honors, including the Bread Loaf Fellowship in Poetry (1961), the Amy Lowell Travelling Scholarship in Poetry (1963-1964), a Fulbright Lectureship in United States Literature at the National University of Mexico (1970), the New York Arts Fund Award for Distinguished Contribution to American Letters (1970), and the Prix de Rome of the American Academy of Arts and Letters (1976).

Williams's first book, *A Circle of Stone* (1964), inaugurated the poetry series of Louisiana State University Press. Like most first collections, *A Circle of Stone* is uneven in its ambitions and accomplishments. But, as is the case with each of Williams's collections, the volume contains works of true brilliance. The poem that stands apart and above the others as the first of his seminal poems is "The Associate Professor Delivers an Exhortation to His Failing Students." One of the most remarkable things about Williams's work as a whole lies in how the majority of the poems support a single consistent vision; the poems inform each other. The vision of the world Williams sets forth, which finds its first embodiment in "The Associate Professor Delivers an Exhortation to His Failing Students," is one of skepticism. Williams's education in the sciences, particularly biology, has reinforced for him the importance of the phenomenological over the abstract, an awareness handed down to him by his parents. So Williams's poems are centered in material things, or, as a later title states, *The Only World There Is* (1971). But all the things become emblems, tools, and frustrations of the spirit, which is faced with a central paradox: humankind is compelled to seek what is true and meaningful about existence and the universe, yet has only observation and reason as aids. At the same time, one becomes aware that the more one tries to learn the truth of the world, the less one can actually be sure of anything. This abiding irony, reaching from the cosmic level to the most mundane and permutated a hundred different ways in a hundred different subject matters and themes, is the eye around which the storm of Williams's poetry revolves.

"The Associate Professor Delivers an Exhortation to His Failing Students" is the last poem in *A Circle of Stone*. This is significant, as is its placement as the first of his recent new and selected poems (*Living on the Surface*, 1989). The poem is a dramatic monologue, and it is clear that the real speaker is Williams himself, wearing a mask that reappears in several later poems. Among the various ironies in the poem is the fact that the associate professor does not exhort his failing students to try to pass biology, the course he has tried to teach them, but rather to recognize within themselves that failing is the central activity of human life: "failing is an act of love / because / like sin / it is the commonality within." The poem makes clear how much Williams has inherited from his Methodist father. The evangelical nature of the poem, and indeed many later poems as well, gives an unusual tone to a common theme in twentieth-century literature. After admitting that he has failed as well, the associate professor tells his students:

> how, after hope, it sometimes happens
> a girl, anonymous as beer,
> telling forgotten things in a cheap bar
>
> how she could have taught here as well as I.
> Better.
>
> The day I talked about the conduction of currents
> I meant to say
> be careful about getting hung up in the brain's
>   things
> that send you screaming like madmen through the
>   town
> or make you
> like the man in front of the Safeway store
> that preaches on Saturday afternoons
> a clown.
>
> The day I lectured on adrenalin
> I meant to tell you
> as you were coming down
> slowly out of the hills of certainty
> empty your mind of the hopes that held you there.

Cover for the special Williams issue of the Dickinson State College literary journal (drawing by Den Navrat)

All one can be sure of, then, is that one is alive, alone, and often afraid. People have no sure answers to the only questions that matter: where they came from, why they are here, and where they are going.

The associate professor finally tells his students that if they can learn this lesson, and carry it on to others, they will have done as much as human beings can do in this life:

> how failing together we shall finally pass
> how to pomp and circumstance all of a class
> noble of eye, blind mares between our knees,
> lances ready, we ride to Hercules.

> The day I said this had I meant to hope
> some impossible punk on a cold slope
> stupidly alone
> would build himself a fire
> to make of me an idiot
>
> and a liar[?]

The ending states an irony that is almost comic: because one cannot be certain of anything, one cannot even be certain of what one does not know. Against all logic, even the logic that Williams turns against scientific epistemology itself, there occasionally does come a Promethean hope for an inspired figure who might manage to build a fire out of nothing. Neither the associate professor nor Williams can tell from where such a revelation might come. It is the unending, dark joke of life.

Critical reception of Williams's first book was generally positive. The *Virginia Quarterly Review* (Spring 1965) was typical: "Much of Williams's success . . . [his] fusion of the simple and the complex, his ability to have his words and images carry a weight of implication that seems alien to the bulk of what we consider contemporary poetry . . . is a direct result of his interest in the essentials of poetry, the refreshening of universal themes by the creative and imaginative use of language and image. The poems in this book . . . are those of a poet, true in the richest sense, classical in their careful construction, romantic in the person of their imaginative spirit."

Williams's *So Long at the Fair* (1968), is probably his least successful collection. Although the paradoxical vision of his first book is exhibited in this second one, too many of the poems fall into either a simple game, playing with words, or an almost morbidly bleak and humorless picture of human existence. One strong poem is "And When in Scenes of Glory," in which Williams tells of the day he was baptized or born again: "A woman so skinny I could smell her bones / hugged me because I'd turned away from sin." Just as Williams turns his skeptical eye on science, he is likewise skeptical about the faith of his father and finds nothing there. The speaker in the poem is baptized on Sunday, and the poem concludes, "Monday morning we had oatmeal for breakfast / After school Ward West kicked the piss out of me / Tuesday it snowed," implying that none of these events has more significance to the boy than another.

Clearly the most outstanding poem in *So Long at the Fair* is "The Caterpillar," a brief narrative in which the speaker and his daughter notice a caterpillar on the lip of a bowl left in the grass in their backyard. After watching the caterpillar circle the bowl half-a-dozen times, the father and daughter go inside to supper. Later, before bed, they check again and find it still going around the lip of the bowl. Williams then tells how, in the middle of the night, the speaker follows his daughter out to the backyard again, where they discover that the caterpillar has died. The father tries to console the child with the words, "honey they don't live very long," and the man and girl return to their beds. The poem closes with a quiet yet powerful metaphoric leap: "Stumbling drunk

around the rim / I hold / the words she said to me across the dark // *I think he thought he was / going in a straight line.*" Thus Williams has found another metaphor in his landscape to mirror the paradox of human life: people may think they know where they are going, but they do not; they act as though they are headed to some conclusion or accomplishment but may in truth be going nowhere.

The publication of Williams's *The Only World There Is* corresponded with his move in 1971 to Fayetteville, Arkansas, and with his increasing concern about the tangible things of this world. An original way of seeing continues to give the best of these poems his individual stamp. One example of his style of perception is found in "Plain," in which the speaker describes the decals on a teenager's old car, "the first thing ever / he has called his own":

> Between two Bardahls
> above the STP
> the flag flies backward
> Go To Church This Sunday
> Support Your Local Police
> Post 83
> They say the same thing
> They say
> *I am not alone.*

Here Williams confronts the central facts of human consciousness: the loneliness and fear that come from awareness of isolation. Meaning must be grounded in the tangibles of this world.

The poem "Let Me Tell You" is a course in the writing of poetry, warning the reader of the essentially dissimulating and exploitative nature of the act. The speaker says to notice everything: "The stain on the wall paper / of the vacant house, / the mothball smell of a / Greyhound toilet. / Miss nothing. Memorize it. / You cannot twist the fact you do not know." This preoccupation with remembering and manipulating this "only world there is" ends with a striking concentration on the physical:

> When your father lies
> in the last light
> and your mother cries for him,
> listen to the sound of her crying.
> When your father dies
> take notes
> somewhere inside.
>
> If there is a heaven
> he will forgive you

if the line you found was a good line.

It does not have to be worth the dying.

In 1973 Williams published *Halfway from Hoxie: New and Selected Poems*, which met with generally favorable critical response. As *Library Journal* reported, "The humorously mordant homespun of [the] earlier poems has given way, in the new poems closing the book, to a profound difference. The difference is one of depth: Williams's roots plumb a darker ground, discover a harsher reality, a more sardonic voice riven with compassion." The difference is actually a matter of degree rather than a breaking of new ground: the dark, the harsh, and the sardonic are encountered more frequently. Typical of the new poems is "A Toast to Floyd Collins," referring to the man who, while trapped in Mammoth Cave in the 1920s, inspired a media circus that surrounded futile attempts to rescue him. The litany of toasts in the poem begins with one "To Mitzi Mayfair," an obscure 1940s starlet who appeared in a movie Williams saw in his early teens entitled *Four Jills in a Jeep* (1944). The starlet's name appears in several of Williams's poems as a personal symbol for the fondly remembered idealism of youthful love. The poem continues toasting a list of people dead and alive, and parts of the inanimate world. It concludes:

> To the sound of a car crossing a wooden bridge
> To the Unified Field Theory
> To the Key of F
>
> And while I'm at it
> A toast to Jim Beam
> To all the ice cubes thereunto appertaining
> To Jordan knitting
> A silver cat asleep in her lab
> and the sun going down
>
> Which is the explanation for everything.

This catalogue of the sensual, a celebration of the odds and ends of life, is at least a temporary stay against fear and loneliness.

Why God Permits Evil (1977) represents a leap forward for Williams. The depth that *Library Journal* referred to when praising the previous volume is more notable. The majority of the poems resonate with a rich timbre. The book contains Williams's longest poem, the tour-de-force manifesto "Notes from the Agent on Earth: How to be Human," a sort of epistolary monologue consisting of messages from a hidden advance scout to a civilization on another planet on how to pass oneself off as a member of the human race. The message is a bleak one, labeling the major human attributes once again as fear and isolation, and its principal advice is to be careful—of almost everything. The implication is clear that something about the human condition will never be satisfied. Reminiscent of George Herbert's "The Pulley," Williams's vision of man is of a purely secular entity who will always want what he does not have: "Think of this: running around the planet, / along the equator exactly, an iron fence; / half the population of the planet / stands on either side and shakes the bars / screaming to be let out, to be let in."

The crowning achievement of the book, however, and perhaps of all Williams's poetry, is the title poem, based on an ad on a matchbook cover, "Why God Permits Evil: For Answer to This Question of Interest to Many Write Bible Answers Dept. E-7." The poem begins with a catalogue of people in the past who found this question of interest, such as John Calvin, Thomas Aquinas, and Job. If they did not get an answer, the chances are slim that "Dept. E-7" will do any better. In a mocking allusion to William Wordsworth's cry for John Milton's return (in the sonnet "London: 1802"), Williams calls to those well-known people from the past, "You should all be living at this hour." Then the poem takes readers to "Dept. E-7":

> Some place on the south side of Chicago
> a lady with wrinkled hose and a small gray
>
> bun of hair sits straight with her knees together
> behind a teacher's desk on the third floor
>
> of an old shirt factory, bankrupt and abandoned
> except for this just cause, and on the door:
>
> Dept. E-7. She opens the letters
> asking why God permits it and sends a brown
>
> plain envelope to each return address.

Then the poem takes an even starker direction. The woman is not alone. There are other doors with other desks, departments E-6, E-5, and so on, each with answers for other unanswerable questions: "how we rise / blown up and burned, for how the will is free, / for when is Armageddon, for whether dogs / have souls or not and on

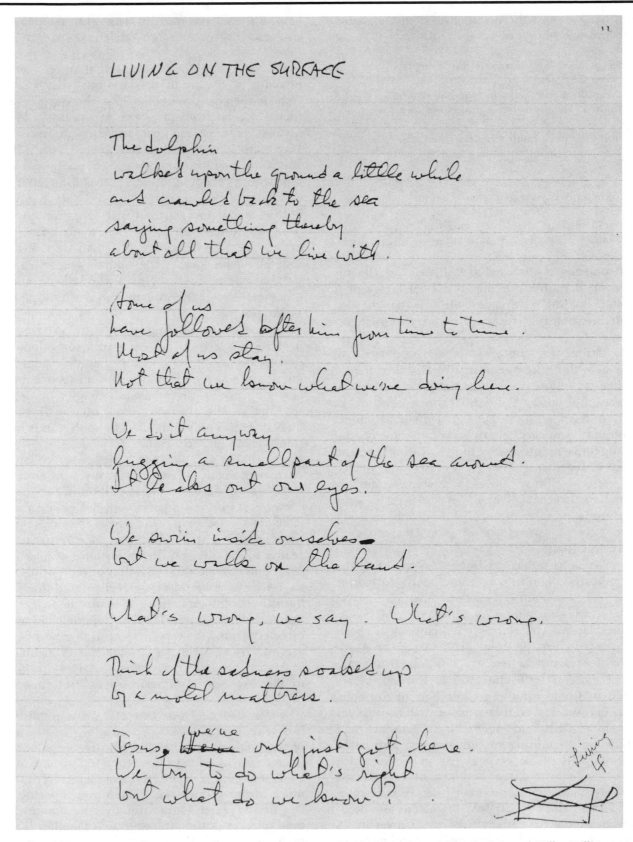

LIVING ON THE SURFACE

The dolphin
walked upon the ground a little while
and crawled back to the sea
saying something thereby
about all that we live with.

Some of us
have followed after him from time to time.
Most of us stay.
Not that we know what we're doing here.

We do it anyway
lugging a small part of the sea around.
It leaks out our eyes.

We swim inside ourselves
but we walk on the land.

What's wrong, we say. What's wrong.

Think of the sadness soaked up
by a motel mattress.

Jesus, we've only just got here.
We try to do what's right
but what do we know?

Manuscript for the title poem in Williams's 1989 collection of new and selected poems (by permission of Miller Williams)

and on," beyond the possibilities of the alphabet and possible numbers, off into infinity:

> where cross-legged, naked and alone,
>
> there sits a pale, tall and long-haired woman
> upon a cushion of fleece and eiderdown
>
> holding in one hand a hand-written answer,
> holding in the other hand a brown
>
> plain envelope. On either side, cobwebbed
> and empty baskets sitting on the floor
>
> say *in* and *out*. There is no sound in the room.
> There is no knob on the door. Or there is no door.

For someone as absorbed as Williams with the unsolvable paradoxes of life, this final image of a woman holding the unattainable answer to the ultimate question is a vision of heaven, also unattainable.

Critics, for the most part, recognized the new growth in the poems in *Why God Permits Evil*. Williams's fellow poets were particularly ready to praise the book. William Stafford said of it, "There is a long look that signals helpless understanding; you are sharing knowledge of the strangeness in inevitable things. Ultimately, the voice is reassuring, though: it can't save you or be heroic or brave, but you do have company. You have overheard someone you need in your life, someone who can see who you are and not turn away" (*Quarterly Journal of the Library of Congress*, Fall 1979).

Williams published *Distractions* in 1981. It is his shortest book, containing only forty-four pages of new poetry. The last fourth of the volume consists of Williams's translations of poems from various languages. Williams had been awarded the Prix de Rome of the American Academy of Arts and Letters in 1976 and, as a result, spent most of 1976 and 1977 in Europe; he resided in Rome for the greater part of the time, working on his translations of the sonnets of Giuseppe Belli and poems from German and French, thus adding to the body of translation growing out of an earlier year in Chile, which had resulted in three volumes of translations from Nicanor Parra and other poets of that country. During the late 1970s Williams was also occupied with the development of the University of Arkansas Program in Translation, a concern possibly contributing to a smaller output of poetry over the period represented by *Distractions*. The

book was well received by critics, but it is not as strong as *Why God Permits Evil* or the books that follow.

Even though *Distractions* might be seen as an intaking of breath to prepare for what was to come in the next three collections, there are nevertheless several brilliant poems in the book. Most notable, perhaps, is "Love and How It Becomes Important in Our Day to Day Lives." This ironic and comic title introduces a surreal poem that begins with a catalogue of what seem to be characters from television commercials, people involved in the meaningless activities that American advertising would have the public believe constitute average American behavior: "the man who sings a song about his socks, / the woman who tells how well her napkin fits, / the man who sells the four-way slicer-dicer, / the woman who crosses tape between her tits, / and scores besides trample my yard, a mob / demanding to be let in." These figures from television are compared to Sodomites demanding to be let in to get at the speaker's guests (in a straightforward allusion to that mob besieging Lot in the nineteenth chapter of Genesis), but as the speaker points out, he has no guests; he has only himself. The mob stands outside demanding to come in while the whole house shakes and the porch begins to collapse. At that moment: "Then comes my wife as if to wake me up, / a case of ammunition in her arms. / She settles herself against the wall beside me. / 'The towns are gone,' she says. 'They're taking the farms.'" The wife's appearance returns the reader to the title and the importance of love.

This volume also was well received by the critics. *Choice* (October 1981) correctly stated that *Distractions* "firmly establishes Williams as a poet of the American idiom. That his language is most often colloquial, however, is not to say the poems are nonlyrical. Williams has the practiced ability to continually rediscover what is vital and musical in the language Americans speak and imagine by."

The Boys on Their Bony Mules was published two years later, in 1983. Because of the strength of the book as a whole, and because some of the poems clearly refer to the year 1977, which Williams spent in Europe, it can be inferred that much of this volume was written over a period of five or six years. The unusually long amount of time spent in putting the collection together is apparent in its overall success.

The same themes pervade the poems. Humanity continues to be hopelessly in the dark

Dust jacket for Williams's 1989 book, for which he was awarded the Poets' Prize in 1990

about the meaning of life and death, and left with little hope but survival by holding onto one another, itself the source of much pain. In the gnomic "Trying," this quiet desperation is made manifest: "The husband and wife had planned it for a long time. / The message was folded into a paper boat. / The children were all asleep. In the backyard / they put the boat in the pool. *We are here. Save us*." The people in Williams's world are compelled to survive as best they can and try to make sense of the meaningless. "Living on the Surface," which would eventually become the title poem of his 1989 volume, captures Williams's view of this plight as well as any poem he has written. Williams's background in the sciences again defines his perspective and the data from which he draws:

> The dolphin
> walked upon the land a little while
> and crawled back to the sea

> saying something thereby
> about all that we live with.

> Some of us
> have followed him from time to time.
> Most of us stay.
> Not that we know what we're doing here.

> We do it anyway
> lugging a small part of the sea around.
> It leaks out our eyes.

> We swim inside ourselves
> but we walk on the land.
> What's wrong, we say, what's wrong?

> Think how sadness soaks into
> the beds we lie on.

> Jesus, we've only just got here.
> We try to do what's right
> but what do we know?

Williams has more powerful poems, but none that more succinctly sets forth his basic vision.

Imperfect Love, published in 1986, was Williams's finest single volume to date. The same quirky and individual attitude toward the world continues to be present, but there is more. Continuing to explore deeper places, Williams has come into a richer understanding of himself as a man and artist. The irony and skepticism of the past are still present, but they are tempered with a tenderness rarely seen before. "On a Photograph of My Mother at Seventeen" begins with a description of the photograph, then moves quickly to the real subject, the speaker's mother at the present moment—old and taken by some disease of senility such as Alzheimer's; she is tied to a chair and trying to pull free of it and the world. The speaker then moves through a series of metaphors to help him try to understand the fact before him: bones seem as hollow as a bird's bones; they could be kite sticks and she could be a kite, with her paper skin. Then he thinks he sees some spark of recognition in her face: "Maybe a door opened, where other men / and women come and go, and closed again. / How much we need the metaphors we make / to say and still not say, for pity's sake."

Williams brings this tenderness and love even closer to the surface in a poem on the birth of a grandchild, "A Poem for Emily." It is a sign of rare skill that a poet who has spent his career steeped in the satiric and the darkly ironic can turn about with such obvious success to write a poem as compelling as this one. This poem is a good example, also, of Williams's growing penchant for traditional forms. In the first of four rhyming quatrains, the speaker addresses the child directly: "Small face and fingers and farthest one from me, / a hand's width and two generations away, / in this still present I am fifty-three. / You are not yet a full day." The apostrophe continues with the realization that, when the speaker is sixty-three and the child is ten, she will be filled with other things besides the thought of him. But when he "by blood and luck" is eighty-six and she is thirty-three and has children of her own, he knows that she will have read them the very poem that he is now both writing and saying to the child, and that then the children, his great-grandchildren, will know that he loves them, too, and loves their mother as well. Here the poem takes a surprising turn. Williams has always been interested in the space-time continuum. More than one of his poems has to do

with the possibilities and paradoxes of time travel. So the poem suddenly becomes a sort of time machine to keep love alive beyond the life of the person feeling the love:

> Long ago,
>
> a day I watched awhile beside your bed,
> I wrote this down, a thing that might be kept
> awhile, to tell you what I would have said
> when you were who knows what and I was dead
> which is I stood and loved you while you slept.

The penultimate line is technically a formal intrusion into the quatrain form that Williams has set up. But it is the stroke that carries the poem to its height of achievement. Williams has found the perfect formal means to convey his idea, spirit, and intent.

The second half of *Imperfect Love* consists entirely of monologues, dramatic and otherwise. He takes his vision of the world and puts it into the mouths of others after having reiterated his themes in so many different ways himself. The voices are as various as the world: a senator, composer Robert Schumann, a businessman, a waitress, a prisoner on death row. One of the best monologues is "The Aging Actress Sees Herself a Starlet on the Late Show," because it allows Williams to develop further the idea concerning time and art that he introduced in "A Poem for Emily": "How would you like / your first time doing something to keep repeating / for everyone to look at all your life?" Although the actress at first sees only the negative side of this endless series of confrontations with her own past, there is compensation: "How would you like never being able / completely, really, to die? I love that."

The strongest and most memorable of the dozen monologues in *Imperfect Love* is "Ruby Tells All." Ruby, a middle-aged waitress who has spent her life working at a truck stop, speaks this poem to someone, perhaps a customer at 2 A.M., going over her life and what little she has been able to discover about what it all has meant. With the exception of the thinly disguised associate-professor poems and the "Agent on Earth" manifesto, Williams made little use of the monologue/persona device before its use in *Imperfect Love*. But in this collection he expands his range to a group of speakers who have little in common with each other except their humanity—and that is the point. They speak for him, and do so convincingly, of the "only world there is," where one is compelled to exist, "living on the surface."

Miller Williams (photograph by Constantine Christofides)

Ruby the waitress may know little about poetry, but she knows a great deal about life and surviving. When she comes to such conclusions as "I wouldn't take crap off anybody / if I just knew that I was getting crap / in time not to take it," the reader feels the same shock of recognition that a reader of one of Robert Browning's or Robert Frost's dramatic poems might feel. Ruby knows nothing about the space-time continuum and probably does not conceptualize the paradoxes of existence. But she does know this:

> Everything has its time. For thirty years
> I never had a thought about time.
> Now, turning through newspapers, I pause
> to see if anyone who passed away
> was younger than I am. If one was
> I feel hollow for a little while
> but then it passes. Nothing matters enough
> to stay bent down about.

Ruby is a survivor, like Williams, and he says through her, as elsewhere in *Imperfect Love*, with more conviction than in any earlier work, that strange as it may seem and in spite of everything, "against appearances / there is love, constancy, and kindness."

Critics have noted that Williams seems to have found in *Imperfect Love* the comfortable blending of the colloquial and formal that he has always strived for and on occasion in the past was able to achieve. Sydney Burris, writing in *Contemporary Literary Criticism* (volume 44), said: "He is a formalist very much in the American grain who makes the popular migration toward 'traditional form' seem stuffy and ill-informed, yet he has an imagination of such diversity that his work makes less formal, ostensibly unfettered poems seem pale and anemic."

At the end of the 1980s Williams found himself in what must have seemed an enviable position for a poet. After spending his fifties writing and publishing his two strongest volumes, he was ready to publish a second "new and selected" volume, which would serve as a retrospective of the more than three decades of verse he had written. *Living on the Surface* appeared in 1989 with a generous and wise selection of poems from his first eight collections and fifteen new poems as well. The new poems continue in the vein that Williams had found in *Imperfect Love*. In the dramatic monologue "Rituals," the speaker is a moonshiner who has just returned from his brother's funeral. His brother was a suicide victim and a preacher—an ironic situation that Williams makes the most of. The moonshiner gives instructions on how to make what he and others use to blunt the pain of existence, his mash liquor. The poem takes place in the woods somewhere, at the speaker's still, and closes with his instructions to his guest on how to get back to town, not to look for the signs used for markers coming out to the still. He would not be able to see those. The way is to look first for a sign that says "*Baitshop and Christian Bookstore*," and then two miles later a barn roof will say: "*See Rock City. Jesus Christ is King*." Then, he is to turn left two miles further where "*a rock will say / An Isolated Virtue Is a Terrible Thing*." Though there is no bait and bookshop anymore, "We use the sign to give directions by. / Something like the light of a dead star. / If you've never been here before / it's still one way of knowing where you are." The last lines are an example of Williams's unmistakable touch. While the talk seems to be of the baitshop-and-bookstore sign, Williams means, in fact, ritual itself, which is an agreement to honor signs behind which there may no longer be any substance.

Miller Williams remains an arguer to the end; the penultimate poem in *Living on The Surface* is "He Speaks to His Arguing Friends and to Himself." As people will do, the friends have been arguing over the big questions: free will, the soul, the afterlife, honor, works, faith, greed, and so on. But Williams tells them, and tells himself, that the question of final cause is the only one that matters. The idea of an eternal entity that was here before humankind and was always here is so far beyond human ability to imagine that it does no good to try. And if one cannot believe one came from such a being, it is just as impossible to believe one did not. People are better off not perplexing themselves with what cannot be known: "We have enough to fret about. / Almost all of us concur, / we'll live with the holidays we have / and the grace of God as if it were."

This is not Williams's final statement on the issue in *Living on the Surface*; he includes one last poem. It is entitled "A Glass Darkly," and the reason for placing it at the end of his book is clear: as the poet has repeatedly shown, people do see as through a glass darkly, but as the title of the poem and its place in the book suggest, there may come a time when they see things, perhaps even some God, face to face. The closing irony, though, is that the poem is about sitting in a bar enjoying a glass of beer, about the here and now, about the rituals people use to keep themselves going until the end.

Miller Williams was selected as the recipient of the 1990 Poets' Prize for *Living on the Surface*. This prestigious award, honoring the best American book of poetry published in a given year, was established in 1988 after the National Book Award dropped its category in poetry. In 1991 Williams saw the publication by the University of Missouri Press of *A Habitation and a Name: Essays on the Poetry of Miller Williams*. These events clearly place Miller Williams among the ranks of the major contemporary American poets.

Bibliography:
Lymon B. Hagen, "Miller Williams: A Bibliography," *Bulletin of Bibliography*, 44 (December 1987).

Interviews:
Ray Wheeler, " 'A Beer-Drinking Soul': An Interview with Miller Williams," *Dickinson Review*, 3 (Spring 1973): 5-20;
Richard Jackson, "The Sanctioned Babel," in his *Acts of Mind: Conversations with Contemporary Poets* (Tuscaloosa: University of Alabama Press, 1983), pp. 7-12;
Irv Broughton, *The Writer's Mind* (Fayetteville: University of Arkansas Press, 1990), pp. 339-360.

References:
Michael Burns, ed., *A Habitation and a Name: Essays on the Poetry of Miller Williams* (Columbia: University of Missouri Press, 1991);
James Whitehead, "About Miller Williams," *Dickinson Review*, 3 (Spring 1973): 26-40.

Appendix

Poets on Life and Poetry

Betty Adcock
Certain Gifts

From American Arts, *11 (May 1980): 8-9.*

I grew up in a small town in rural East Texas. There it was assumed that even if things weren't as they had always been, they were at least *connected* to what had always been. Events had time to happen large. Any wedding or murder, election or birth took place slowly, bringing with it a store of related happenings from another decade or another century. These clusters of ghosts and likenesses were dragged in and set up in as much state as the current bride, corpse, candidate, or baby.

I don't remember having been officially taught much, except in school, where it was partial and inevitable. There were some piano lessons at home, and a brief study of "ballet" with Mrs. B., whose chief qualification was that she had once been a baton twirler and could still do the split. Church was a kind of instruction, the Sunday School requiring considerable memorizing of the Bible, but that was fine, royal and resonant, and full of serious mysteries: Psalms, Job, Ecclesiastes. We were mostly unimproved and free.

An only child, I liked wandering over our own acres alone or with my grandfather, through the garden and along increasingly narrow paths to a deep wood where there was a brick pool full of scum and frogs. Brick steps led mysteriously straight into black water. Later I learned that the great uncle who had built our house had made this pool. In cleared spaces around it he had cultivated a reputedly spectacular rose garden, long since reclaimed by the forest. He had liked to come to this wood, the pool fresh, the roses blooming, to read and bathe. In his place, my grandfather and I built fires, roasted sausages on a stick, and noticed birds and animals. He showed me how to make the mourning dove's cry and how to answer the horned owl at dusk.

Sometimes, awake at night, I would hear the unanswerable cry of a cougar not far from the house.

Death was a part of our living. Family members usually died at home with a host of relatives and a more or less seamless past to see them off. Small deaths of animals were simply necessary: chickens beheaded for dinner, hogs slaughtered in November, the bodies of deer and squirrel and quail broken for our table. It was not imagined that things could be otherwise, as indeed they are not otherwise, anywhere, though the form may be different and the substance hidden or dressed up.

The town itself was a knot among fields and woods. It was a selvage we lived upon, an edge always in danger of raveling. In the violence people sometimes committed, in the poverty of many families, in the extremes of weather and of human power, something half-known seemed about to take over. Even the churches shed strips of paint in the fiery, humid summers. Even the arrangements of sensible merchandise in the stores seemed fragile, likely to topple.

Behind my uncle's store, a high ceilinged room held tall stacks of flour and feed in cloth sacks. My friends and I spent whole afternoons building castles of these. We hefted walls of our future bread, dreaming warfare and rescue, dragons and movie stars in a thick haze of flour dust.

I read what came to hand, Grimm and Anderson early, and later on, books with rotting bindings, Shakespeare among them. I remember reading all of Keats in a summer porch swing, not understanding a bit of it, along with the unexpurgated *Gulliver* and a book about galleons. I read, ready or not.

We were lucky enough not to have television until very late. Unluckily, the town had no library. But we had a movie theater. On Saturdays, when the stores were festively open until 10 p.m., there were double-features. I loved the movies, but I have forgotten them all. I have not forgotten how, afterward, down the still lightsome Saturday street, we could go into the glassbrick and blue neon City Cafe and watch the big men flirt with the waitresses, nickels in the jukebox for Hank Williams and "Slow Boat to China." With stately turn and counter-turn, the mean talk moved between truckers and farmers and the girls dishing up in cavernous blue light. I always ordered, with prolonged pleasure, a Doodle Burger, so named because the french fries which came with it were long, tight corkscrews. Were they cut by machine? More likely someone in the kitchen labored unquestioningly at a Sisyphean curl of potato.

My generation questioned much. Some beat at the town with everything they had until they knocked a way out. Some went away to learn and came back to change things. Some stayed and lived their parents' lives. Some of us moved far away and tried to become wiser than we had been, but we who left took with us certain gifts:

how time can flow more ways than one; how events in human affairs *mean*; how intricate and sometimes violent is the pattern that the shadows of wilderness trace upon our lives, and how the dying of wilderness will pattern our futures; how fragile the edges are upon which human beings live. And we took with us the sounds of the rich languages of poverty and faith, however far we were from either.

These are deeply ambiguous gifts. I cannot guess how others may have used them or been used by them. When I left the town for good at eighteen, I was already writing poems.

Fred Chappell
A Detail in a Poem

An article first published in the Fred Chappell issue of Kentucky Poetry Review, *26 (Fall 1990): 66-75.*

The case of the fellow with three afflictions may be instructive. He was agnostic, insomniac, and dyslexic; and so he stayed awake all night wondering if there really was a Dog. In the same way, writers often wonder if interviewers and the genuinely curious have hit upon the best query when they ask: "Where do you get your ideas?" To a writer this is like asking a dentist: "Where do you find all those teeth?" Or asking a major league shortstop: "Where do all those baseballs come from?" Or asking a real estate dealer: "Where do you get your reality?"

The writer, who has an urge to seek the literal image behind metaphorical language, will imagine that there really is a place he could travel to and when he arrived there would find Ideas dangling from tree branches or lying on the ground or offered for sale in Idea Boutiques. But he knows that there is no such place; if there were, the politicians would have discovered it long ago and surrounded it with a monstrous defensive installation and pillaged the Ideas and watered them down and dealt them out expensively

to you and me ounce by fluid ounce, drop by starveling drop. The fact that our politicians have no fresh ideas would seem to argue that no such place exists. Or that they passed through it without a flicker of recognition.

And anyhow, the writer is ambivalent in his regard for ideas. He is not exactly certain in the first place what a literary idea might be and, if he is wise, tends to distrust ideas as subject matter for his writing. Let us say that the impulse to write a novel has struck me, poor ole Fred, once again. I have decided to write about an overheated woman who proves unfaithful to her stodgy husband and so brings misery to them both and to others as well. Can we call this narrative germ an Idea? How well will it show up in the company of other ideas, those of Schopenhauer, say, or of Hegel or William James?

Well, in that high-powered company my idea is going to look awfully scrawny, and yet *Madame Bovary*, Flaubert's novel that tells this grimy little tale with such ferocious precision, is a seminal masterpiece of modern literature.

Perhaps, though, the plot of his story is not what we should identify as Flaubert's idea. After all, it was only a banal little episode, sordid and flimsy, that he pursued in the spirit of a wager. Perhaps his idea was in his treatment, his relentless focus upon the telling detail, his rigorous pursuit of psychological logic, his literally agonizing search for the mot juste. The facts of his biography as evinced in his correspondence suggest that this was indeed the case, that method and manner of treatment were foremost in his mind and the broad circumstances of his plot almost a pretext for the exercise of his treatment.

But can his noble determination in this regard justly be called an idea? Surely it is no more than an intensification of vocational skills of the sort we hope that the physician, the priest, and the automobile mechanic will habitually practice. Flaubert has only made the exercise of his craft a matter of conscience; he has added the imperatives of moral duty to the task of describing the sound of a fly buzzing in a dusty attic room, the excitement of a flighty woman preparing to attend a ball, the vision of a young man's deformed foot further tortured and mutilated.

I will make bold to opine that what possessed Flaubert was not an idea. If it had been a mere idea it could not have so thoroughly engaged his intelligence and allegiance for so long a period of time. Literary ideas tend to be thin and ghostly little entities, mewling in the late hours of the night for expression—like a cat asking to be let out—but soon proving exhausted and infertile.

It is a perverse kind of fun to point to literary triumphs which are not fine ideas: *Napoleon attacks Russia but is defeated by the determination of the populace and inclement weather.* How can that be an idea? Didn't this episode, or something very much like it, actually take place? So that Tolstoy found his "idea" in the same place that dentists find the teeth they drill; ideas and teeth are out there in the world to be found.

Here's another: *The day after a wild party in the woods a young faun tries to recall a nymph's name and telephone number....* Maybe there is the shadow of an idea over that poem; my précis here does give off an odor of the excessively literary. And yet it was Stephane Mallarmé, was it not, who warned us about the use of ideas in poetry? His remark to his friend, the painter Edgar Dégas, is perhaps too famous. "Poems are made of words," he is reported to have said. "Not ideas."

Please understand that I am not complaining. A writer shouldn't resent being asked where he gets his ideas. He probably does not resent any questions about his vocation except those from the Internal Revenue Service. But this particular question baffles him because he is not sure that he has any ideas or has ever had any. When my wife asks me how to repair her steam iron or dishwasher my almost invariable reply is, "I have no idea." When she asks how we are to raise some cash to get the car fixed, again I make the same reply. Or more succinctly: *"Oh God."*

The same with stories and poems.

I suspect that most writers believe that ideas come in solid shapes with firm outlines, that they are clear, immediately recognizable for what they are, and—after proper study, of course—perfectly comprehensible. I think that they think of ideas as being the sort of things that physicists have, and mathematicians and engineers. What writers have must be something else.

If we abstract a justly famous idea from its historical context, it should be in its largest applications still valid if ever it was valid. Newton's inverse square law of universal gravitation should hold true on the moon and on Mars as well as upon our own planet; those alive in the year 1800 B.C. should have found it to be as correct as those in the year 1990 A.D. do. Euclid, Leibnitz, Einstein, Mach, Aristotle, Galileo, and many other grand figures discovered or formulated ideas whose truth or at least whose self-sufficiency cannot be changed by time, place, or circumstance. Not all the ideas of these thinkers are equally valid, and when some of them are shifted in time and space they begin to show the strain of being wrenched from their origin. Yet Plato's idea of ideal forms, if it is ever true at all, is just as true in modern Afghanistan as it was in ancient Greece.

But if we lift poor Emma Bovary from the context of provincial France in the nineteenth century, she will not transplant. Removed to the context of present-day French society, she will suffer agonies much less dire for her indiscretions, and it might be surprising to find that she had to suffer at all. Nor could she retain those outlines of character by which we recognize her if she were transplanted to earlier centuries, to the fifteenth or even the eighteenth, because her class, station, temperament, ambitions, fancies, weaknesses, whims, and powers of observation are partly, and sometimes largely, produced by the historical, sociological, and *literary* type that she is: a petite bourgeoise in the century when the bourgeois first came, like a cabbage rose, to its beautiful vulgar glory.

Emma is of course much more than a stereotype. If we could describe all the qualities the average bourgeois woman of that time and place had with an accuracy amounting even to certainty, we still should not have described Emma Bovary. Too much is left over, too much that can only be presented or implied by the small, the tiny, even the minute detail, by those fleeting particulars that impress her mind and spirit and with which she impresses others.

Emma will not come away from her large background, her broad setting or even the microscopic details of her circumstance. She is not an idea. Without Emma, without this one Emma and no other Emma in the world and in the history of the world, there is no story. The story is not an idea. It has all the complexity of a philosophical system, and it marshalls data for its support in the way that a philosophy will support itself with mathematical formulae and logical demonstrations, but *Madame Bovary* is not an idea because Emma is so superbly an individual. No matter how many other stories like hers we hear about, no matter how strongly she may remind us of a living person with whom we are acquainted, we always recognize that she is she and no one else, and that if she were not, if she became a representative type, merely an Idea, the brilliance of the novel would dim and its tragic power would weaken and lose its grip.

What, then, can the writer do? Someone approaches him at a party or in some less appropriate setting and says, "I have a great idea for a story. All I need is for someone to write it down." Why does he not immediately accept one of these generous offers? "Good Lord," he might say. "Just in the nick of time! I haven't had an idea in days. Let's sit down and go over it, you and I."

I have actually heard of this exchange taking place a few times, and once it even worked out pretty well. But usually the writer mumbles some vague encouragement to his new acquaintance, something to the effect that since this idea belongs to its originator there might be legal complications about lending his own labor to it. He will undoubtedly add some remarks about how crowded his writing schedule already is with promises, commitments, and deadlines. In short, he tries to find some socially acceptable way to run for his life. For me, being offered an opportunity to treat in writing someone else's "idea" is like being invited to wear his clothes, sleep in his bed, and use his toothbrush.

Thanks.

But no thanks.

It is interesting to observe that never in my experience has anyone said to me: "Say, I have a really great idea for a poem. All I need is for someone to write it down."

One reason no one has tempted me in this fashion is quite simple. People realize that there is no money in poetry, that when you share an idea for a poem with someone it has all the financial advantage of telling them about a dream you had last night. (In fact, an idea for a poem shares some of the qualities of a dream.)

Another reason is related to this lack of monetary incentive. A person who has an idea for a poem invariably desires the pleasure of composing his poem. He recognizes instinctively— whether or not poetry is his vocation—that the best reward he can possibly get for his poem is in finding language for it. If he is unaccustomed to composition, he may imagine that the task is easier than it is, that power and precision and resonance of utterance shall come to him in an explosion of candescent inspiration. Maybe this is exactly what does happen to him; such revelations are not unknown. But if he is afflicted with the usual bad luck of a writer, he will find the process more laborious than he had thought—and for that very reason more rewarding, perhaps even more joyful.

It is obvious that the person who possesses the idea that is searching for a writer has no conception that the writing of prose has any affinity with the writing of poetry. If he thought about it he might be willing to acknowledge that for some people at least the composition of verse can afford real pleasure. ("Why the hell else would they do it?") But prose writing appears to him as a type of specialized carpentry. It is the duty of his captive writer—when at last he succeeds in capturing one—to build him a word-box to put his Idea in. He conceives of the *craft* of fiction as a process of packaging; of the *art* of fiction he has no conception at all.

But I have found some real pleasures in writing fiction, and I cannot imagine that I am the only person who has done so. It is true that writers, fictionists and poets alike, usually dwell upon the difficulties of the job, upon the painful soul-searching they find that it requires, upon the scrupulousness of attention, the burden of research, the quandaries of moral justification, the crushing necessity for verisimilitude. But they talk about these matters in such tortured terms mostly in order to make themselves look good. They have it in them to preen a little bit as martyrs. A writer might be described as someone who is born to be improperly appreciated. By his own estimation, anyhow.

Yet genuine pleasures are to be encountered in the writing of fiction. They are often, but not always, the same as those found in writing poetry. The satisfaction of finding just the right word or phrase, the final best sentence arrangement, the absolutely telling colloquialism for a line of dialogue, the verbal tag that implies a whole past and future history for a character. These satisfactions come almost always as surprises, even after a process of long labor, and sometimes after the writer has despaired of ever finding a way to convey his intention with the necessary precision. There are dissimilarities between these particular satisfactions; the different rhythmic demands of prose and poetry require different methods and give rise to emotions finely divergent. Still, these tiny triumphs on the whole resound alike in the writer's psyche. . . .

Poetry sometimes demands the same kind of pointed, necessary, and inevitable detail that fiction does. It is obvious that narrative poetry bears many close resemblances to fiction, even though poets usually more enjoy remarking on the differences than the likenesses. I will confess that I do remember with some pride one instance of finding for a poem I was composing a detail that I thought was exactly the one I needed in order to make the character, her story, and the poem unique.

The poem I refer to is called "My Grandmother Washes Her Vessels" and contains only the thinnest thread of narrative line. A boy about thirteen years old is helping his grandmother clean the big steel milk cans which hold the milk their dairy farm sells to distributors. As they go about this task, the lad questions the old lady about her own youth. She falls to reminiscing first about her courting days and then about her wedding day.

The purpose of the poem is primarily to draw a portrait of the grandmother and to imply the effect of historical revelation upon the boy. She remembers how her Frank courted her and what an attractive man he was. Clearly she loved him, and she judges that she made a good choice in marriage. Yet she cannot help thinking how it was before the courtship and how inviting a life of independence would always be.

> But getting married to Frank
> Wasn't the beginning of my life.
> I'd taught school up Greasy Branch since I
> Was seventeen. And I took the first census
> Ever in Madison County. You can't see
> It now, but there was a flock of young men come
> Knocking on my door. If I'd a mind
> I could have danced six nights of the week.

But she did marry, and now recalls the decision she made on her wedding day. She traveled alone, a party of one, to the ceremony, driving a horse and buggy, but still not finally committed to her choice.

> I came to where we used to ford
> Laurel River a little above Coleman's mill,
> And I stopped the horse and I thought and
>   thought.
> *If I cross this river I won't turn back.* I'll join
> To that blue-eyed man as long as I've got breath.

Her decision is a momentous one: whether to give up a large measure of her personal freedom and some measure of her independence to live in marriage in traditional subordination (but *not* subjection) to her husband—or whether to turn around and go home, accepting the life of a spinster.

Then she hears the song of a bird, a yellow-hammer. This music makes her aware of the natural world around her, the trees, the river, and the cool June day. She feels, too, the force of the springtime in her blood and makes her eternal election.

> And then my tears stopped dropping down, and I
>   touched
> Nellie with the whip, and we crossed over.

These lines conclude the poem. I make no special claims for this poem nor for anything else I have written. I employ it here as an illustration of a certain kind of usage of detail.

It would be inelegant and even obtuse to title a poem "Sex Life of My Grandmother." Yet a large part of the subject of this poem is indiscretion. The boy—and we readers—chance upon the old lady when the mood to talk is upon her. What I needed, it seemed to me, was a detail that would alert us to the usual character of the woman as well as to the unusual nature of this moment when she is going to reveal more about herself than she ordinarily would do. I needed, I thought, a gesture that would seem a little coy, a little self-conscious, slightly embarrassed. Yet it should hint, too, at her humor and her affectionate teasing and her love not only of life but of the memory of life.

Then when the boy asked one of his naive questions, I felt that I saw my opportunity. The grandmother has complained about her hired help, saying that the quality of their labor is hardly worth the feeding of them. The boys asks, "Don't you like men?"

> Her hand hid the corner of her childlike grin
> Where she'd dropped her upper plate and left a
>   gap.
> "Depends on the use you want them for," she said.
> "Some things they're good at, some they oughtn't
>   touch."

It is clear that she is making a small joking comment about the romantic shortcomings of men and about their sexual clumsiness. But for me the larger interest lay in her gesture, pressing her hand over her mouth to hide her broken denture. It is a gesture coquettish as well as modest, teasing as well as serious. Under the guise of relating family history she is willing—this one time, at least—to make an uncharacteristically personal confession. He is too young to realize it, of course, but she is beguiling her grandson into a humorous, affectionate conspiracy regarding the memory of his grandfather. To some small but supremely important degree her courting days have never ceased.

Peter Cooley
Into the Mirror

A previously unpublished article.

My poetry begins as a silence I am listening to inside myself. To make that silence speak I call on images, rhythms, sound. They become the embodiment of the silence, the silence voiced.

***

Sometimes a rhythm itself will lead me into a poem. I don't mean a regular metrical pattern. It's a rhythm I feel inside my body with no physical sensation. Then I try to find sounds corresponding to the rhythm, then words. This is all part of the imagination at work, a process partly conscious, partly unconscious. I know very little about music, so the rhythm is not derived from any analogues in musical notation.

***

When I first became interested in poetry I thought it was memorable phrases, not morals but rich clusters like Hart Crane's "adagios of islands" or Emily Dickinson's death fly with "blue—

uncertain stumbling Buzz—." Even though I think now of constructing a total poem and work to give the reader an experience, I'm still addicted to this sort of language. I try to write by the stanza, the line, or the phrase, yet I still write word by word by word.

***

I know my poems are very circumscribed; they move in, not out. I want the reader pulled toward them face to face as if he or she were drawn into a mirror. While the reader reads, he or she is in that mirror: I control the associations. This has delimited my vocabulary in poems, though I've tried not to narrow my context by writing too much on particular subjects or using predetermined forms.

***

I'd like to think of the act of reading as ritualistic eucharistic, to assume that my poems have a sacramental function. I'd reach out to save the reader if I could, my words wafers and wine. But

I tend to back off from this old poet-as-priest business and try to find something more modest to claim.

***

If nothing else, my poetry does hold onto moments of perception and feeling which most people let go of through indifference, fear, or lack of energy. When it's successful, I think my work takes such moments and opens them up so the reader can experience them in their small but poetically extended time frame. And if he or she finds a self there, empathizing with the emotions, he or she shares perhaps this privileged moment with me and enters a kind of state of grace.

***

Am I escaping from the world around us? Are these the poetics of the indifferent 1970s? I hope not. I am very much aware that we all exist in an environment increasingly depersonalized by technology; our emotions are cut to size for us and wrapped in Saran Wrap. We've all heard this a hundred times: it's still true. Even in New Orleans, where I'm living now—and this city is one, surely, of the few places in the U.S. where a distinctive culture centuries old continues to thrive—there are signs that the world is gradually becoming Los Angeles. All you have to do is visit a commercial bookstore in any town or city to know what I mean. Someone has decided that we've lost interest in imagination; we're supposed to be gobbling up confessions, how-to's on everything from sex to macramé, the histories of last week's scandal. People have little contact with imagination. A recent article in the *Chronicle of Higher Education* stated that college does not significantly change students' reading tastes. I don't think the students are to blame for this. . . .

***

I would like to think that my poetry, all poetry—because by writing I am a part of all poetry ever written and ever to be written—opposes this sterile culture. It forces the reader to experience minute particulars which he or she must read carefully, rhythmically, to deal with a particular world as concrete but more ordered than our own.

I struggle for particularity and precision, not to number the streaks of the tulip or to insist on "no ideas but in things" but because I know that paradoxically only by the utmost concreteness can the general be named and saved. Remember Mallarmé's maxim about the absent flower? I am after that ideal flower, too, but I think my poems, more pedestrian, more accessible than his, will get the reader to it faster. Yet given the state of culture, few people will ever see them.

***

Finally, then, I'd have to say that my poetry has a very moral purpose. As an expression of imagination, it demands that you stretch your sympathies to experience it. And in that stretching you extend yourself as I did in constructing it so I could speak to you. That stretching, that taking on of another's experience, is exactly what we need nowadays in a world made geographically smaller but hardly more compassionate toward human differences. There, in my poem, for a few minutes we share a common life. Who can deny that even when the poem is tossed aside or forgotten we have somehow moved closer to each other's feelings?

Philip Dacey
Eyes Across Centuries: Contemporary Poetry and "That Vision Thing"

Excerpted from a forthcoming article in the Mississippi Review.

Does contemporary poetry lack vision? Let me give you a curmudgeon's answer: there is no such thing as contemporary poetry. Perhaps turning fifty, as I did last year [in 1989], "concentrates the mind wonderfully," as Dr. Johnson said of an imminent hanging, or maybe aging simply unbalances the mind; in any case, I am convinced that the emphasis in recent decades upon what is "contemporary" in poetry is a function of the modern humanist's envy of the physical scientist, who for well over a century now has gotten the glory and the money. Such envy, given human nature, is no surprise, but the emphasis is nevertheless misguised and distorting.

In the sciences new information regularly supplants the old—science is by definition all avant-garde, and the scientist must keep up with the Joneses and the Keplers and the Bohrs—whereas the new in poetry extends rather than replaces the old. An analogy might be as follows: dead leaves giving way to new leaves on a tree equals science; rings added to rings on the tree equals poetry. All of poetry's surviving voices are always present—and they are strengthened, not weakened, by the passage of years.

From this point of view, the latest poetry is therefore not that which is of most interest, a la science, but only that which is least tried, a kind of fledgling literature, to be given its due, for sure, but not afforded a central place in the total existent corpus. Time will do that where it will, and time's will is beyond prediction. Thus the successful fight to get contemporary poetry taught in the schools may after all have resulted in a Pyrrhic victory.

Likewise, the "lack of vision" at issue may be merely a case of expecting too much too soon, anatomizing what cannot yet bear such scrutiny, and may never. Time reveals vision—we know it's there if a work looks us in the eye across the span of hundreds of years. Eyeball to eyeball with our contemporaries, however, we cannot recognize vision because it has no room to prove itself. Anyway, if we could, we would probably not be impressed, as it is most likely our own.

During a recent sabbatical, I spent a large part of the year reading, for the first time, Lucretius, and then, amazed at his freshness and power, re-reading him. A few years before that I had discovered that Virgil is alive and well in his *Georgics*. But my personal reading habits are not the point here; the point is that Lucretius and Virgil are contemporary poets; i.e., they are speaking now to us.

I think we should leave contemporary poets alone—"alone" as in "don't bother them," but also as in "solitary." How can they create a long-distance vision with us crowding them?

The poetry workshop as we know it is an incestuous anomaly that will fade as its practice weakens the tribe. A second life is possible for our beloved Iowa Program in Creative Writing and its children and grandchildren only if they shift from the Engle model to the Auden model—memorizing; taking care of cows; studying science; practicing poetic forms; and reading fewer living poets than dead ones. There is not enough time to read our calendar-contemporaries, and they don't need us anyway; they have the long future. The dead are our contemporaries and need us, for we are their future.

Madeline DeFrees
The Poet's Kaleidoscope: The Element of
Surprise in the Making of the Poem

An article first published in the Seattle Review, *10 (Fall 1987): 36-44.*

My mind and imagination have always worked like a cement mixer. For years I've referred to my poetic process in those terms, throwing everything into the hopper where it churns around for awhile and comes out fused. When I retired from teaching in 1985, my colleagues in the University of Massachusetts Writing Program made me a gift of a shiny new metaphor. Instead of the usual engraved gold watch, they chose an acid-etched brass kaleidoscope by the noted artist Stephen Auger. In making the presentation, James Tate said that it was time to change my metaphor to one that more accurately reflects the making of my poems.

During the past few weeks I've examined the process more closely, with special attention to the part craft plays in shaping experience into poems. Let me begin by quoting the inventor of the kaleidoscope, Dr. David Brewster, who explains that the name comes from three Greek words meaning *to see beautiful forms*. In his 1819 *Treatise on the Kaleidoscope*, Brewster writes:

> . . . The Fundamental principle, therefore, of the kaleidoscope, is that *it produces symmetrical and beautiful pictures by successive reflections, into one perfect whole.*

> . . . *There are few machines indeed which rise higher above the operations of human skill.* It will create in a single hour, what a thousand artists could not invent in the course of a year; and *while it works with such unexampled rapidity, it works also with a corresponding beauty and precision.*

> (Emphasis added)

Setting aside for the moment the unexampled rapidity and the high rise beyond human skill, allow me to fling against the skyline one of those castles the poet repeatedly builds from airy nothings. The names of such local habitations follow the poet everywhere, collect chaotically in his enclosed world like semiprecious stones inside the kaleidoscope.

Most poets would agree that craft, like money, is not the first consideration in art, but it's far ahead of whatever comes second. It seems natural, then, that among themselves and in the classroom, poets should talk about their craft. Whether the exchange be oral or written, they may later feel a nagging uneasiness about such shoptalk. I confess to sharing this divided eagerness and reluctance, so perhaps the initial task is to identify the sources of anxiety.

Let me call the first the *Echo Effect*. When my ego is weak, it's harder to write the morning after I work on a craft essay or conduct a graduate workshop. I sit down at my desk, and a pen-activated playback of the previous day's comments comes on to challenge me, closely followed by: *Aren't you that hotshot poet who was telling the world how to do it?*

This kind of self-talk is just what a flagging ego needs to shut off the water main before the intake valve has admitted so much as a trickle. Premature evaluation is the writer's No. 1 Enemy, and, as Pogo observes, *Not only may we be him, he may be us.*

A second misgiving has to do with the way theory is sometimes applied. Readers or listeners may do such appalling things with the techniques you suggest that you want to take a vow of perpetual illiteracy. Or they may use against you the strategies you recommend, dissecting your poems in such flatfooted and gruesome detail that you wish you had written in Urdu.

Still another source of concern may be the *Self-consciousness* brought on by directing too much attention to one's own creative process. I'm tempted to say that the more intuitive the poet, the more dangerous such analysis may be. If we could be perfectly sure *how a poem happens*, we might duplicate the product at will, much as the chemist in the laboratory formulates the perfume of gardenias or the odor of skunk.

Stephen Auger's brochure refers to his creation as "a unique series of one-of-a-kind . . . kaleidoscopes." Every poem should be one-of-a-kind. Imitation of self or others (writing "fashionably") destroys that uniqueness, substitutes the *Factory Approach* for the handmade. Imitation may be a valid way of learning to write, but it has limited place in mature work except as a special effect.

To refer to a poem as a *product* (as I did a few sentences ago) is already a mistake, suggesting a mechanical process assured of identical results each time it is followed. The activity is really closer to taking a series of steps in the dark, emerging finally in unknown territory and claiming it as home. The poet walks a tightrope between familiarity and surprise, maintaining the delicate balance between recognition and discovery. Because the poem must surprise the poet as well as the reader, must be a kind of self re-formation that makes sense of experience, it satisfies some deep need of the human spirit.

Thus far, I have spoken of theory as a danger better left to the critic. Now it is time to say that the danger is one most poets should confront. Because it is the nature of the mind to know, if we are at all curious about poetic process, the questions must be pursued.

Until the poet has *some* understanding of the difference between his better poems and his discards, writing will be mostly a matter of accident and luck. Still, there are grounds for asking whether forgiveness exists after such knowledge.

If poets have little choice about playing critic, at least in private, a more important question may be: How does a poet keep his critical shadow-self out of the poems? First, by not taking himself too seriously. It's easy to be hypnotized by the sound of my own voice, entranced by the smooth contours of a sentence or a paragraph. We catch ourselves in action, then turn practice into precept and repeat ourselves until we become glib and boring.

***

Because poems, unlike paintings, belong to a class known as linear art, the reader cannot take in the whole poem at once; its designs appear in rapid succession, in shifting perspectives, in changing light. If we insist on knowing *how* a poem works, we may do what any child might do with a crude kaleidoscope: take apart the flimsy cardboard tube, extract the cheap mirrors, spill the bits of colored glass, perhaps count them like hoarded coins. Once we disassemble the kaleidoscope, we learn a hard truth: to disclose the secret is to lose sight of the mystery.

Language, the poet's medium, may be as limited as Basic English or as extensive as the collection of words in the *Oxford English Dictionary*. It may even extend to words and phrases borrowed from other languages. The number of word combinations must approach infinity. In this respect, too, the poem resembles the kaleidoscope:

> The combination of hand-selected gems and glass objects, mirror assembly and lenses allows for the creation of more than 1/2 million different images. . . .

Theoretically, it would be possible for two poets using a strictly limited word pool to write two very different poems. Even a slight change sometimes makes a vast difference in total effect. Take the anonymous 15th-century lyric:

> Western wind, when will thou blow,
> 　　The small rain down can rain?
> Christ, if my love were in my arms
> 　　And I in my bed again!

When some printer or prude (perhaps the two-in-one) changed a single syllable, without a hitch in the rhythm, a major shift occurred:

> Christ, if my love were in my arms
> 　　*Or* I in my bed again!
> 　　　　　　　(Emphasis added)

At this point you will note that attention has gradually shifted—one might almost say inevitably—from the whole to the parts. This is a natural movement because *the poem is no less a linear art for the poet than for the reader*. That unexampled rapidity earlier claimed for the kaleidoscope *is* "above the operations of human skill," but occasionally it may be experienced as a dividend from years of hard work. The "given poem" surfaces from some deep well in the unconscious, a surprise bonus to the diligent poet. It seems to write itself in a way that amazes him even more than it does the reader. The general public, preferring inspiration to perspiration, continues to believe that all poems are automatic writing.

Once a complete draft of the poem is on the page, the task is to strengthen the weakest links in the verse-chain. When I reach this stage, I find it useful to adopt a version of Matthew Arnold's "Touchstone Theory." To avoid paralyzing myself, I compete not against Shakespeare, Yeats, and Donne but against my own best lines in the poem I am working on.

Such attention to detail and insistence on quality requires great patience on the poet's part because most of us are too eager to abandon a poem for the next one down the road. If you want to *finish* a poem, better to think of the *fine finish* required for restoring old masterpieces. Or you might try Bill Stafford's maverick procedure: "I try to keep from closing out the poem as long as I can."

***

After all that, it's time to turn to the list I've been compiling since I began. I offer it as indicative merely: a random assortment of colored glass and stones that may be drawn into loops and spirals. The lenses of other eyes, the mirrors of corollary experience, and your own successive reflections may turn the pieces into the perfect whole.

1) *Clichés:* Every writer needs a cliché detector. Maybe it takes years to acquire a cupboard full of outworn phrases in much the way an infant develops immunities to cold viruses. Although I try to recognize and eliminate clichés in early drafts, I sometimes use a "cliché module" to plug a gap, underlining it for a later substitution. Or I may see whether it's possible to give the phrase a new twist. In "Hagios Panaghiotes: The Church in Tolon" I first wrote:

> . . . Demented chandeliers: crystal
> and gold in clouds of plastic. The bearded
> saints look down—martyr and mystic—bald,
>   severely
> drawn. All of us are old. The operation
> was successful, *but the patient*
> *died.* . . .
>
> (Emphasis added)

One opportunity the line break provides is that of increasing surprise. In the underlined passage above, the word *died* is utterly predictable: an opportunity wasted. When a graduate student confirmed my uneasiness about the word, I revised the passage:

> . . . All of us are old. The operation
> was successful, but the patient
> stars flicker to a halo in the dome. . . .

The variation on the cliché is accurate because it evokes paintings on the ceilings of Greek churches at the same time that it implies death—the dome serving as stand-in for the life of the mind.

2) *Line-breaks:* Because my personal computer is programmed for complexity I spend a lot of time trying to simplify: whittling five-syllable words down to one, cutting out qualifiers, cleaning up sentences, letting go the weakest of seven types of ambiguity. Gradually seven other demons tie my lines in knots. It's time to sweep and garnish again.

When I first changed the lining in my poems to help the reader with their density, I found myself exploiting the possibilities of line breaks to introduce multiple meanings. In this device, I am able to play the integrity of the line—the slight pause it signals—against the sentence which pushes grammatically towards closure. The resulting tension gives the poem a dynamic quality, a feeling of energy trying to escape the cage of form. An example of the way multiple meanings emerge will help to clarify:

> the blue-collar parade passes through
> my kitchen, *pitches its tense*
> *holsters of wrenches & hammers on top of the organ,*
> camps in my bathroom. . . .
>
> "The Joy of Remodelling"
> (Emphasis added)

In my judgment, this strategy works best when there are two successive lines, each with its distinct "meaning" and a third sense arising from the combination. In the example, *pitches its tense* (an obvious pun on *tents*) gives a sense of completion and is supported by *camps in my bathroom.* The next line functions grammatically as an absolute phrase if we read it as an independent unit. The effect is that of placing it in parentheses or between dashes or commas. In this way, we have three images for the price of one: 1) a kind of gypsy encampment of workmen inside the speaker's home; 2) an assortment of serious hardware in leather sheaths, strapped to the workmen's hips; and 3) the primary image, that of hammers, pliers, etc., tossed on the Wurlitzer. In a way, we have the kaleidoscope's unexampled rapidity. At least one other image occurs to me, but enough is enough.

3) *Compound words:* These words, whether nouns or verbs, present interesting opportunities to pursue a buried metaphor or restore the vanishing life in language. Because living languages are

constantly changing, one function of the poet is to restore archaic and obsolete senses of words or make use of word derivations to surprise the reader into taking a new look at the words he uses so carelessly. Earlier on, I spoke of "a vow of perpetual illiteracy." I found that phrase mildly amusing—paradoxical because one doesn't *unlearn* the ability to read and write. At another level, I was extending one rare meaning of *illiterate* (*not written*) to *the state of being not written*. Thus, I was saying that mangled quotes or their muddled application made me consider elected silence.

One discovery of the life buried in language occurs in a poem in Sandra McPherson's *Elegies for the Hot Season*: In "Selling the House," she writes:

> . . . The roof
> Will have no more temptation to eavesdrop.

Reading that, I've always pictured the eaves as a pair of elephant ears, hanging out from the house to pick up juicy conversations, but recently I learned that the word originates with the practice of early peeping Toms and private eyes standing "within the 'eavesdrop' of a house in order to listen to secrets" (*Oxford English Dictionary*, Compact Edition, Volume I, p. 829). Earlier in the same poem, McPherson speaks of "the dumbwaiter, / Trapped in the basement, a damned soul. . . ."

Another advantage of compounds is that one may pursue either of the terms, as in this example from my poem "Sanding the Chairs":

> Every layer of paint, a country of wishes: the days
> of *townships lying in harbor*
> *riding at anchor*
> *follow the stars.*
>
> 　　　　　　　　　　　(Emphasis added)

Here, the credibility of the lines is established by easing into the metaphor with a transitional statement that applies to both towns and ships. Once that claim is made, the poet follows the ships.

4) *Metaphoric Trust:* All poets need a Trust Fund to see them through hard times. James Wright had a huge one. He'd simply say, *You will believe this*, and most of the time we did. A metaphor can sometimes be kept aloft by sheer nerve of the poet. Instead of precise elaboration, the poet substitutes "acting out":

> . . . a spider
> big and black as a taxi stalled at the corner.

> *Let's go for a spin.*
> 　　"The Basement Shower"
> 　　(Emphasis added)

Later in the same poem, the reader encounters: "Hum of the motor / loud in my ear, meter ticking away / towards reckoning." In this instance, the transition is effected through the word *stalled*, which evokes the taxi and the shower stall.

5) *Repetition:* All writers are familiar with the uses of repetition, and all English teachers place it on the Ten Most Wanted List. One sign of an incipient poet may be the willingness to make the teacher eat her words by serving triumphant menus of the rules turned to mincemeat. We learned as children to value repetition, and our attachment to it is manifest in the chorus and the refrain. Some of this has to do with the pleasure of recognition, of the familiar, and of our ability to take part in a poem or song by anticipating the next move. In contemporary poems, the poet often varies the line to add the bonus of surprise.

6) *Visual Adverbs:* Because linking verbs in English set up the expectation of predicate nouns or adjectives, the poet is free to surprise the reader by deliberately confusing adjectives and adverbs:

> 　　. . . and Grandma
> shipped crates of *oranges*
> *that grow largely in California.* . . .
> 　　"Honesty," *Magpie on the Gallows*, p. 31
> 　　(Emphasis added)

7) *The Eerie Approach:* Poets of my generation are more strongly influenced by the *sound* of language than most younger poets are. Whether you consider this fortunate or not, it does serve to enhance the element of surprise, as *the poet follows his ear outside the predictable "language matrix."* At times I may accept words because their sound pleases me, then look for others with similar sounds but more appropriate meanings. An example:

> . . . Your breath in a broken flute
> might resurrect its note. I am learning to follow
> slow birds to raucous pickings. . . .

I didn't like that too-literary flute, which got into the poem because it was part of an actual scene, so I searched among the flotsam and jetsam of my prevailing water imagery and came up with:

> . . . Your breath in a globed float
> might resurrect its net. I am learning to follow
> slow birds to raucous pickings. . . .

Eerie approaches. That's a cheap shot, but I couldn't resist the pun. It gives me an opening to distinguish between *shock* and *surprise*. As a young poet, I was so concerned about not sounding like a three-name lady poet or a pious nun that I kept my shock gun handy. Since then I've come to believe that surprise is a far more durable quality.

***

What I began with such reluctance has generated its own momentum. Writing this essay has been a little like writing a poem, only more chaotic because the essay is longer. Because form emerges from the writing process, once I begin to see the dim outlines of a unity or a controlling metaphor, it's like putting a foundation under a house that's already built. The most difficult part is dealing with the chaos of shifting ideas and the stack of pages that record them.

Some interior sensor must know when a poem, a story, or an essay is coming on. It makes me tidy up my work space and the whole house. I call it "Clearing the Decks." After everything is neat on the outside, it's slightly easier to sustain the inner chaos. By the time I finish the piece, I've moved the chaos outside again.

The truth is, the poet's kaleidoscope *does* sometimes work with *unexampled rapidity* . . . with a corresponding *beauty* and *precision*. More often, it works with agonizing slowness to create order (symmetry, pattern) from the random, the accidental, the chaotic. Day after day, the writer must be willing to confront that chaos to bring the poem to completion. Words mirror objects already viewed through the lens of the poet's eye, and the language corresponds in some way to Plato's Ideal Forms, so that it becomes available to the reader, who is surprised into recognizing what he already saw or knew without knowing that he knew it. The kaleidoscope works, too, with beauty and precision. Those qualities, especially precision, are the function of the poet's craft.

Stephen Dunn
The Good, The Not So Good

From the AWP Newsletter, *19 (November/December 1986): 1-3.*

The good poem may be political, but is more interested in understanding the dynamics of any human situation than it is in effecting change. Nevertheless it is a desirable, subversive act to replace what passes for truth with a more accurate/deep approximation, whether the subject is a dinner party or poverty. Precision, therefore, is more radical than passion, though precision without passion might be still another definition of a not so good poem.

The poet distracted by the possibility of effecting change is looking too far ahead to be a trustworthy witness of what's in front of him/her. It has long been said that a poet must have vision. The good poet's vision is of the here and now. The world, properly seen, becomes the future.

*

The good poem is implicitly philosophical. The not so good poem, conversely, may exquisitely describe a tree or loneliness, but if the description does not suggest an attitude toward nature, or human nature, we are left with a kind of dentist office art—devoted to decoration and the status quo.

*

The good poem is elitist, if by elitist we mean pandering to no taste lower than our own. It is not elitist in the pejorative, political sense. It does not aim to exclude. It aims to find and set a standard of truth and excellence and beauty toward which anyone can aspire.

Often the not so good poem suffers from what may be called the egalitarian error; in its desire to be compassionate and fair it becomes merely correct.

*

Poets must be both cocky and humble. They must trust their own assertions and observations in the face of overwhelming uncertainties. They must know their job is not to offer The Truth, but to be persuasive about their version of it. The key is in the voice. In the good poem, the voice informs us that the poet embodies what the poem asserts.

In the not so good poem, there is sometimes a discrepancy between voice and that which is said. It is the sound of tin when someone is telling us about gold.

*

The good poem maintains a delicate balance between strangeness and familiarity. The author must make the familiar strange enough to be re-seen or re-felt by the reader. The truth always is a little strange because the conventional world has little interest in the truth, and regularly accepts packaged versions of it. But a poet should never be strange for the sake of being strange; the purveyor of such poems is at heart a sensationalist and is insufficiently interested in the human condition.

The not so good poem may err by leaning slightly toward strangeness or toward familiarity, thus giving us a slightly false sense of the real.

*

The good poem informs us in ways we couldn't have been informed if the poem had not existed. It has surprises throughout, and its words and rhythms convince us they are the inevitable words and rhythms for the feelings and thoughts that the poem explores.

The not so good poem is a well-made version of these feelings and thoughts, to which we accede without astonishment.

The good poem illuminates its subject so that we can see it as the poet wished *and* in ways the poet could not have anticipated. It follows that such illumination is two-fold: the light of the mind, which the poet employs like a miner's beam and that other light which emanates from the words on the page in conjunction with themselves, a radiance the poet caused but does not control.

*

The absence of wit or humor in an individual poem is, of course, understandable. It is somewhat less understandable in a body of work. The ideal body of work should reflect that the world is, in part, comic.

One characteristic of certain not so good poems is a kind of unredeemed earnestness, the language suffering because the poet was suffering.

*

The good poem alters us a little bit, or is capable of doing so. At the least, it moves us closer to what can be known and believed about the world, and our second selves (those parts of us which always know better) store such information in the vague repository which is consciousness. We may continue to behave badly after absorbing a good poem, but it might be slightly harder to forgive ourselves.

The not so good poem often allows us to make of it what we will. It doesn't fundamentally enough confront our sense of the world or of ourselves. Once again, we are given permission not to change our lives.

*

The good poem arises out of necessity or discovers its necessity in the act of composition. Necessity is linked to rhythm. When a poem's rhythm is off, usually it's because the poet has not yet located what is central in his/her subject. Therefore, the most fundamental act of revision is for the poet to locate the poem's informing principle, its locus of concern.

With the not so good poem revision is mostly a cosmetic issue; this word instead of that, the poet becoming willful because what was felt or thought has no fulcrum—almost anything can be substituted for anything else.

*

The good poem allows us to believe we have a soul. In the presence of a good poem we remember/discover the soul has an appetite, and that appetite is for emotional veracity and for the unsayable. The general condition of the soul, therefore, is stoic hunger, stoic loneliness.

Paul Eluard wrote "There is another world, and it is in this one." The not so good poem isn't able to startle us into consideration of that world. The soul is never pricked into wakefulness.

*

In a not so good poem we may be aware of the author's intelligence, imagination, skill with language, etc., but we may not feel the presence of a superior intelligence, superior imagination, a superior skill for language. In the good poem we find ourselves yielding to such a presence, to that which is larger than we are.

*

The good poem simultaneously reveals and conceals. It is in this sense that it is mysterious.

The not so good poem is often mysterious only by virtue of its concealments. Or it wears exotic clothing to hide its essential plainness.

*

All poems are formal in one way or another, but the good poem demonstrates its form in a series of satisfactions. It makes both overt and subtle promises in diction, content, structure, rhythm, tone, texture, etc. The subtle promises, when fulfilled, satisfy us most, often long before we know what they are. For example, one of the formal promises a poem makes resides in what it won't do; what can be called the poem's hidden manners. Equally pleasing is the violation of a poem's manners at intervals regular enough to suggest method.

Perhaps one aspect of a not so good poem is that it neatly fulfills its overt promises, leaving us oddly dissatisfied.

*

The good poet "lets in" the unruly, the difficult, the unformed—in a sense, the unmanageable—and is able to make a livable environment for them. The more the imagination can accommodate, the more chaos the poet is equal to, obviously the richer the poem.

The not so good poem may try to let in the very same elements, but is overwhelmed by them. The poem, then, is too much like one's unreconstructed life; we can learn little or nothing from it.

*

A cliché is not only tired or dead language. For the poet it is all unevaluated language. It is language that hasn't passed through the poet's resistance mechanism. Resistance leads to discovery. No, no, no, no, and then yes. The good poem offers us a small, vibrant replacement for the available world which the poet wouldn't accept.

The not so good poem sometimes too easily reflects or accommodates the available world. Its author said yes too soon.

*

There's no reason why an abstract poem cannot be a good poem. Though no poem purely does one or the other, the poem that appeals to the mind can be as passionate or as convincing as the poem that appeals to the senses; it simply must find ways to get around the tendency of the mind to be argumentative. In the right frame, with the right focus, the right tone, bare branches can be exciting, seductive. Even ideas about bare branches.

The not so good abstract poem does not sufficiently distract the mind—with rhythm, wit, irony, form, etc.—from thinking of contraries. The mind says this poem is too spare. Why aren't there leaves?

*

For a personal poem written in the first person to be good the poet must work against the dangerous tendencies of the "I"—self-congratulation, solipsism, untransformed confession. To the extent the poet believes that the experience rendered in the poem is peculiar to him/herself, the poem will be tainted with narcissism. Details often will be chosen because they "happened," rather than because they arise out of the imperatives of the material. This is to say that the good personal poem is always to some degree fictive.

The not so good personal poem makes us feel uncomfortable the way the problems of strang-

ers do. We're not quite sure why they're telling us what they're telling us. At best, the problem is interesting, but we feel more like voyeurs than listeners who have some stake in what we're being told.

*

There are many types of good poems, but two broad types might be worth isolating: 1) The poem in which the poet is still involved in the struggle that the poem explores, which gives us the experience of the struggle. 2) The poem in which the poet has passed through and gotten beyond his/her subject matter, the poem of maximum perspective.

In the first, the poet suggests no way out, but rather reports, registers, evaluates, thus "making" the conditions of a recognizable world so that we can better feel and see them. This is the poem we often feel most close to, as if written by a profound comrade. Generally it is more interested in what living in the world truly feels like than in what it means, though the former goes a long way toward articulating the latter.

The second might be equivalent to the stance of the Buddha who had to go into the city of temptation and sin before he could be fit to be the Buddha. True simplicity, in this case, suggests a passage through something onto higher ground. This is the wise poem, convincing only if we sense everything in the poem feels like it's been discovered, not delivered from on high.

The not so good poem is written, perhaps on the same subject, by a person of different stature. Somebody's disciple, perhaps. Or a sensitive comrade instead of a profound one.

*

All poems are moral to the extent that they are evidence in content and form of an attentiveness to the details and circumstances of our lives. They get right the things they pay attention to, which always implies a correction of some sort. The issue is not right versus wrong. It's right versus off (the imprecise, the superficial, etc.).

The morality of the poet is to keep his/her tools sharp, always to be ready for the convergence of deep concern with subject matter. In this sense, craft and care for the integrity of language are the only things that separate the poet from the obvious moralist.

The not so good moral poem often works against some abuse or injustice and in its zeal gives content more attention than composition. This is the gift that falls apart, the one years later you can't seem to find when the giver comes to visit.

*

It is often tempting to conclude that in a good poem the poet has taken large risks. But risk is rarely the right word. Ambition is more precise. Some poets, formally or otherwise, are more ambitious with their material than others are, but they are more likely thinking about how to do justice to that material than about going out on a limb. The success of a good poem is linked to its necessity, to a subject that presents itself to the poet with a particular urgency. And the methods and devices employed by the poet arise out of the same necessity: the gestalt of subject and craft. (Of course in politically sensitive or totalitarian countries certain subject matter involves true risk, the risk of publishing the necessary poem.)

Interestingly, the not so good poet in Western countries often takes more risks than the good poet. Superior craft and talent lessen the likelihood of falling on your face. In basketball, for example, it's common to hear that the very good player wants the ball at the end of the game, wants to take the crucial shot. This is not bravery, but confidence, and a kind of obligation. The not so good player is likely to shoot too hard or soft, or just inaccurately. Nevertheless, it is sometimes necessary for the not so good player to take the big shot. This should be applauded at the time, regardless of the result. In the long run, though, all that matters is true accomplishment, not one very good shot but many, some of them memorable.

Edward Field
The Poetry File

Excerpted from an essay in Field's poetry collection Laughing Lips, *forthcoming from Black Sparrow Press.*

> With a talent for speech,
> I had no language.

Poetry for me, as for many American poets, is a rescue from incoherence. We don't have the language at our fingertips. We are pre-literate.

Why do I write the way I do? Much of my life has been spent in a state of fear and confusion. Clarity, therefore, has been my goal. My poems are moments of hard-won clarity. So, aiming for obscurity makes no sense for me.

Though I don't speak Yiddish (a language my parents kept for their private life), in my poetry I try to leave in any Yiddish word order or turn of phrase or intonation surviving from childhood. Locked into them are layers of old feeling, some of which I am barely in touch with and have to discover. I once wrote:

> The reason I need to write poetry is
> I keep forgetting important things—
>
> like my feelings.

Without undervaluing elaborate syntax and elegant language, I prefer to explore the poetry of ordinary, everyday speech. And the language of feeling is mostly simple. Today, you are almost made to feel you don't have a right to be a poet if you are not reticent.

Another paradox: I write in the language inside my head, the language I think in, but then, oddly, it gets judged by the language, and standards, of the outside world. Like my dreams of being naked when everybody around me is dressed. My poems expose me to the world, but I can't help it. Maybe one of the reasons I write is to expose myself, but I envy poets who keep buttoned up.

Actual censorship may not exist, but if you write the words inside your head, it often won't be publishable. Every poem I write seems to have something, one word, that makes it impossible to publish: what's so terrible about the word "hard-on," for instance?

I never wanted to write poetry that sounded like poetry. And I still don't want the language of my poems to be noticeable or distracting, so that the poem can talk straight to the heart and the mind. But the critics, fashionably, concentrate on the language. Even the editors are first looking for language (fancy, self-conscious, odd, willed), language that stands out—or it's not poetry for them. I use unadorned language, which is criticized as cliché. But Auden and Cavafy, my models, were both plain-spoken poets.

> I'm suspicious of fancy language.
> I always imagine the most elegant poets
> have shitty toilets, dirty asses.
> In their lives they're dirty,
> and like everyone, do dirty things.
>
> Even Stevens, too pure ever to use the words,
> I like to think of holding his cock
> and farting with gusto.

Poetry-as-language vs. poetry-as-voice. Or poetry for the voice. Wallace Stevens said, "Music is feeling then, not sound."

Poetry is not far from my daily speech, my everyday emotions—so writing it can be as simple as making a shopping list. But the trouble is that what I think about seems so ordinary that I don't bother:

> The great leap   over the gap
> between getting an idea   and writing it down.

When the words of a poem come into my head, maybe while I'm shaving or lying in bed, it hardly seems worth it, and I have to force myself

294

to go jot them into my notebook. But when I look again later, it's not ordinary at all.

I do try to say things in a minimum of words, the words that say something neatly—which is my definition, not of poetry, but of poetic language. For me, poetry aims for the simplest possible language (though not always possible). Prose needs florid passages for variety, effect. Continual simple language is monotonous in prose. I always liked the dictum (by whom?) that poetry should be at least as well-written as prose.

Poetry and prose draw closer together on the West Coast, draw further apart on the East Coast, where poetry becomes more literary, moves toward artifice. I tell myself:

> Mannerisms
> do not make it poetry
> —yet, sometimes, they succeed.

Vendler writes approvingly of: "The visible estrangement of poetry from prose" (*New Yorker*, April 4, 1988).

If one way of poetry is to be superior, elitist, snobbish, the other is to rescue the clichés, the banal, and use what is vigorous in the popular language and culture, rescue it, as it were.

Part of poetry for me is saying interesting things—interesting and inspiring things, that in the saying, the way they are said, help people, point to a better life. My favorite poem is the 23rd psalm, which I see as a useful one. STAND UP, FRIEND, WITH ME: that's what I see poetry as doing/meaning. Though I no longer expect it to be emblazoned on the banner of the revolution. I did hear that it was on a placard during a Gay Pride march, several years ago.

Recently in England at a friend's house, unable to sleep I turned to the bedside books, tried to read the *Collected Poems* of Keats. But only the famous poems were at all successful, and in fact stood out like diamonds in a mass of versifying sludge. Then I turned to an old Oxford book of English verse. Mostly unreadable. I remembered again how puzzled I was, early on, trying to read poetry, and what my own poetry first set out to do—i.e., not sound like that. Many people, drawn to the idea of poetry by a deep instinct, have been turned off by it, as I was. A thought: maybe it was opium (TB medication?) that opened Keats up for his occasional great poems?

My poems don't seem to belong with the New York School, but in a basic way they demonstrate an idea of Frank O'Hara's, which I learned from him at a difficult time in my life: that you don't have to take a stance to write a poem—you just start from yourself, wherever you are at that moment, whatever you feel like. A kind of spontaneous writing, but the poem didn't have to be "exalted" (like a Beat poem, say), or work up to anything, unless you were in that kind of state—or be a formal utterance, like the academic poetry of the time. It can just be what you have to tell a friend over the phone. Or if you are writing a poem and the telephone rings, that might be the end of the poem, wherever it breaks off. Thanks to Frank, I was able to get through my block, caused by my insistence that my poems should be something that I could no longer make them, be something other than I could do, and get writing again, because I finally stopped making demands that my poetry be anything other than what came out. And Frank could see the relationship to him, which I think was why Donald Allen included some of my poems (though to my view not particularly good ones) in his anthology *The New American Poetry* with other New York poets, with whom I hardly identified myself. Still, in writing,

> some things you let happen
> and some things you make happen.

A significant question is: who is the poem addressed to? Other poets? The so-called "public"? Hip Californians? Jewish intellectuals? Leftists? The cultured rich? My poetry has mostly been addressed to "ordinary" people who are like myself (can't define this further, but am convinced on a certain level I'm ordinary, though neurotic and oddball), and, like me, not well-educated, or perhaps self-educated. The current poetry scene is addressed to specialists, meaning other poets, critics, English department elites. Of course, poetry really has an inner "elite." But who poetry is addressed to does define the difference in poetics—"our" kind as opposed to the establishment, or any other kind.

Good title for a book about poetry—"The Snobbery Factor." Poetry as cult product. How people give lip service to what's in fashion, not daring to go against awesome critics like Bloom and Vendler.

> Poets, I swear I'd throw out nine-tenths of them.
> Above all, I don't want to write like them.
> In fact, I don't want what I do
> to sound like poetry at all.

The trouble with poets, I find, is that poetry has taken over the place of love in their hearts.

> If poetry is a refuge for snobs
> any poet turning out human
> is in the nature of a miracle.

From my statement for *The Maverick Poets* (an anthology edited by Steven Kowit): "It is hard for me to understand how, for so many poets, poetry is also an exercise in snobbery, for whom poetry means being superior, to prefer their poems cool, elegant, artificial, cryptic. I automatically identify with what snobs look down on—the slobs, the misfits, the victims, for whom poetry is an act of rebellion, the secret voice speaking out, however crudely, as in my first book's title *Stand Up, Friend, With Me*."

Some of our most popular poets, like Merrill and Ashbery, write as though the world they're part of is one in which concentration camps don't/couldn't exist.

But maybe that is what modern poetry was always about, demonstrating one's superiority over the common herd, fleeing the banalities of Kansas and Idaho. Of course, there is no democracy of standards in poetry, nor should there be.

I still find poetry boring to read. Or sitting through readings by poets. Most of it seems phony to me. Affected. Pretentious. About nothing I care about. I smell the poetry scene behind it, even when it is more or less sympathetic to my own direction. All poets are ambitious, out to make it, and there's nothing wrong with that, I tell myself, but I feel uncomfortable.

The problem I've had from the beginning was that I wrote for people like myself, assuming they were there, but the poetry world says you must write for *us*.

> While shaving my face I answer my critics,
> marshalling rebuttals, and arguing

> my right to write as I do:
> Who are you to tell me what to do? You bastards
> don't have the least idea what poetry's about,
> etcetera. . . .

> and going over and over where the chin
> makes its difficult transition to the neck:
> Why can't you let a clown cry real tears?

> Oh, I say, waving the shaver at myself,
> you pompous ass.

Anyway, I was always uncomfortable with success, and did my best to derail it. I'm more comfortable with failure, being an outsider. Why do I keep feeling that the only moral position for a poet is outside?

My first *Geography of Poets* (Bantam, 1979) was a view of America from San Francisco and New York. *A New Geography of Poets* (forthcoming from the University of Arkansas Press) will be a view of America from Long Beach/L.A. and New York. From my introduction: "While no one has been looking, an American poetry has been springing up all over the country, a kind of poetry that is completely indigenous, growing out of a populist spirit (as opposed to the elitism of mainstream poetry), reflecting, even celebrating, the limited education that is available to ordinary Americans, not to speak of the wisdom of the streets, and letting into poetry like air the independent views, humor, quirkiness, vulgarity, in short the sassiness that Americans have always had, and that Mark Twain celebrated. Beat poetry is one arm of the movement, connected to poetry as incantation, chant, preaching, prophetizing. But the 'New Sass' or 'Neo Pop' (no label quite defines it) is more akin to conversations across bar stools, dirty jokes, stand-up comedy, a finger to the powers that be. It reflects the sleaze in American life, and it is no accident that its center should be Long Beach/Los Angeles. It is influenced by the sentimentality and tough-guy corniness of old movies. Again, no accident that it is arising from the proximity of Hollywood. And Charles Bukowski is the presiding spirit. What is really happening in poetry today, the new, has still not been recognized, defined, and the critics are not even interested!"

My poetry is searching for a way of dealing with the ordinary, the banal that is out to crush me. Bukowski's solution is to incorporate the banal and survive. My Long Beach friends say that Bukowski and I are the "fathers" of Long Beach poetry.

> "Everything that comes within the Modernist movement employs modes of discourse and sequences of images that are oblique; such poetry is on the whole inaccessible to many readers and perhaps to all readers unprovided with some kind of commentary"—J. M. Cameron (*New York Review*, January 18, 1990).

This is the academic view of what happened in the great modernist revolution early this century. It is true that the rallying cry of the new poetry was Obscurity, to reject the debased popular culture the poets fled from. But there is little recognition today that the modern revolution reached for the living language, new concerns opened up, and technique became more self-conscious, meaning greater demands on the poet's attention while writing. There has now been, in official circles, again a turning away from the spoken language to a literary self-conscious language. Some see the divergence as having been engineered by T. S. Eliot, though the Beats brought modernism back again, via William Carlos Williams, to its original impulse. For the moment time seems to have passed the Beats by, though out there in the country, poetry looks different from here in New York and the elite universities.

David Trinidad says that Frank O'Hara and I were the first to start using what he calls pop material. I imagine he means my movie poems, poems like "Graffiti." Of course, when I started writing, not many poets (Auden the great exception) dared to be funny—that was considered "light verse."

My poetry denies that there is anything too intimate to be written about. Very different from the later so-called confessional poets, with their emotional outpourings embalmed in a high-literary manner.

I don't aim for a scruffy beatnik sound, though I like to be raunchy, too. I prefer the tender/gentle voice of Cavafy, unpretentious, natural sounding, though sophisticated. Allowing the quiet feelings. Not interested in celebrating my highs with jazzy improvisations. Maybe it's because I don't have that kind of highs.

After Cavafy

An old man in tears before the Muse:
In my whole life, I have only written
a few slim books of poetry,
and gotten little attention for them.
Perhaps they were too slim.

So why didn't I do more?
I see the question in your eyes.
Really, I don't know how to explain.
I didn't try hard enough, perhaps.
Tell me, have I wasted my talents,
as well as my life?

Old man, says the Muse gently,
wipe your tears. You have taken
a step on the ladder of poetry,
and getting even to the first rung
is an accomplishment the Gods
rejoice in. Sticking with it
for a lifetime is perhaps
even more difficult.
So feel good about that,
for on this path you have not failed.

Jonathan Holden
Contemporary Verse Story-telling

Excerpted from a forthcoming article in the Southern Review.

The most fundamental convention of verse has always been that it must maintain a conspicuous verbal surface. When accentual-syllabic prosody was the prevailing form of this convention—its normal form—poets could automatically fulfill the requirement. They could write about almost anything, and assume that their text would be recognizable as "poetry." Meter, by foregrounding each discrete syllable within the context of the "foot," enabled a poet to draw attention to the verbal surface of his poem without resorting to conspicuous or forced figurative language. Reading Yeats, for example, we savor the sonic textures of his verses for their own sake; they usually have little if anything to do with a poem's referential "content."

Because the convention requiring of verse a conspicuous verbal surface is such a powerful one, it is inevitable that any general decline in the use of accentual-syllabic prosody will be accompanied by a corresponding increase in some other means of foregrounding verbal surfaces. And this is, in fact, what has happened in the free-verse lyric. There are two main ways of attracting a reader's attention to language in a poem: by means of sound, by means of sense. When the traditional, metrical, sonic means of foregrounding the verbal surface of verse is not available, a poet will turn, instinctively almost, to semantic means: stocking lines with metaphors and similes, as if to compensate in the domain of "sense" what he has given up in the domain of sound. Whereas in the poems of Yeats we hardly ever encounter local tropes such as similes, in the contemporary American free-verse lyric the relatively high metaphoric density springs from the continuing anxiety by poets to fulfill the requirement to produce a conspicuous verbal surface—as if without it they would worry whether or not they were writing "poetry" at all.

This prosodic "law" of compensation, while fairly tidy when applied to the lyric, obtains more stringently when applied to narrative verse. As Timothy Steele has reminded us, the marriage of meter and narrative is as old as poetry itself. The heralded alliance of the so-called "new formalists" with something that bills itself as "The New Narrative" is either a publicity stunt or it is naive. The attachment of the prefix *new* to contemporary narrative poetry is ludicrous. . . .

Three conditions are placed on narrative verse. The first has to do with subject matter—the exigencies of exposition, characterization, and plot. (In the modern poetic milieu, none of these elements is regarded as inherently "poetical.") The second has to do with modern poetic structure, which, as we see in C. K. Williams's "The Gas Station," is predominantly the structure of the lyric: some material is presented, the poem develops this material, then makes its "turn," and the original material is *re*-presented in a sort of *reprise*, its meaning deepened, transformed by an accumulated context. In the genre of the short story, this technique is called "foreshadowing."

The third condition—the trade-offs between sound and sense necessary to maintain a conspicuous verbal surface—explains why most narrative verse, whether by William Wordsworth, Robert Browning, Robert Penn Warren, or Sydney Lea, rarely employs free verse. Because the subject matter of storytelling does not consist primarily of tropes, the prosody of even a contemporary narrative poem is apt to be traditional and formalistic—both to make the poem's language handsome and memorable, and to reassure both poet and reader that what he is reading is "poetry."

Judson Jerome
Reflections: After a Tornado

Excerpted from an unpublished article written in 1989.

Before I started school, I loved poetry. I had memorized many poems. My aunts and my grandmother read poetry aloud to me. My grandfather (who had less than five grades of schooling) and my father (who never finished high school) wrote poetry. I knew that poetry was an important part of life, that writing poetry was something men and women do.

Then, in school, I learned that poetry was also something to be studied. Very gradually in elementary school, more quickly in high school, and very rapidly in college I learned that I had the wrong understanding of poetry altogether. I had been naive as I lapped up delicious melodies and stories and moving thoughts. I wasn't even reading the poems right. You had to "interpret" poems. I thought "Stopping by Woods on a Snowy Evening" was about stopping by woods on a snowy evening. In school I learned that it was about death, which wasn't even mentioned in the poem. I thought stories and poems were supposed to have what we then called "morals," like Aesop's fables (albeit not so blatantly stated). Some of the morals weren't very moral. One of my favorites, Eugene Field's "Jes' before Christmas," taught that if a boy wanted to get a lot of presents for Christmas he'd better clean up his act. But they had some point, some relevance to life. That's why you read them: to learn something about life.

In graduate school I read such things as Sir Philip Sidney's *Defence of Poetry* that explained the ancient function of poetry was to instruct and delight. ("A little bit of sugar makes the medicine go down.") That made sense to me, but the professors didn't seem to me to be much concerned with either its instruction or its delight. Nor were they concerned with another aspect of poetry that fascinated me as a child: its craft. I loved to watch stage magicians. I knew there was no such thing as magic, that the job of the showman was to create illusion through technique. And it seemed to me that there was a lot of such technique in poetry. But the professors seemed to read great writers to try to fathom their visions of life and to see those visions in the limitations of their historical, social, and cultural contexts. They wrote books about the writers. It wasn't enough to know Milton; one must know C. S. Lewis' "reading" of Milton, and the "reading" of Milton by a dozen other critics. In fact, it was not necessary actually to read Milton at all. What mattered were the books about the writer, and the books about the books about him.

I went on to become a professor in the mold of the professors who had taught me until, in the hectic and heady era of the late 1960s and early 1970s, having become a widely published poet and highly successful radical educator, I realized that my profession was taking me farther and farther from the values that drew me to it in the first place. I was reading poetry to "keep up," to know what my peers were doing. As a poetry editor (of the *Antioch Review*) I was subconsciously responding to what I thought my professional colleagues would respond to. I was not reading submissions to be delighted or instructed by poems. I was reading to find examples of what would appeal to the taste of the literary world.

I am, of course, exaggerating somewhat, but I think this account of my experience defines a tendency many will recognize. What I did about it was "drop out," as the lingo of the times described it. I started a commune and moved there with my family. For some fifteen years I tried to ignore what was going on in the literary world I had left behind. Upon my reentry to "straight" society in 1984 I discovered that things hadn't much changed. Most of the poetry being published in the literary magazines was unreadable. It neither instructed nor delighted. Most of the time I couldn't guess why it was published or for whom it was written. Certainly not for *me*.

Today a number of poets and critics have begun looking around and discovering that the auditorium is empty. Ironically, there are now more people writing and publishing poetry than there are *reading* it, and almost no one reads it who doesn't write it and hope to publish it in the plethora of pathetic (and subsidized) literary magazines. As Dana Gioia, one of the better of our current poets, put it in a recent letter to me:

> Once writers stop writing for pleasure and readers stop searching out books for pleasure there is really nothing reliable left to base the judgment of the arts on. Contemporary criticism has replaced pleasure with ideological correctness. The ideologies may change from aesthetic to political, but the puritanical impulse to separate art from delight stays the same.

Puritanism, snobbism, elitism, academicism—whatever it is, something separated poetry from the public. By public I mean the kind of people who read and enjoy magazines such as *Time* and *Newsweek*, the *New Yorker*, the *Atlantic*, *Harper's*, *PC World*, *Lear's*, *McCall's*, most of the magazines on the stands. I mean what used to be called "the common reader," a phrase introduced by Samuel Johnson in the eighteenth century, meaning, according to Irving Howe in the *New Republic*, a reader who is not an academic, not part of the literary world, but who finds reading a vital part of his or her life. Howe says: "It sometimes seems almost as if that figure has been banished, at least in the academic literary world, as an irritant or intruder, the kind of obsolete person who still enjoys stories and still supposes that characters bear some resemblance to human beings." Now the poets seem to be waking up to the fact that without a public, without common readers, their art is meaningless.

The popularity of the film *Dead Poet's Society* reminds us that it is still possible to appeal to the public with poetry if we focus clearly upon what the public expects of it. Tom Schulman, author of the story and screenplay, reminds us in an interview of what that appeal is, at least for him: "When I read some lines in poetry, I think, God! This makes me feel so inspired! It makes me feel like going out and doing something great, whether I'm capable of it or not: trying. And I thought, 'This is bound to have that effect on others.' "

Unfortunately, the issue has been politicized as form vs. free verse, but form is beside the point. *The Pocket Book of Verse: Great English and American Poems* (1940) reminds me of what I was looking for in poetry and not finding. That was the book I cut my poetic teeth on as a teenager. A replacement sent unexpectedly by a friend for

the battered copy I lost in years long past, this copy is from the third printing, October 1940. Pocketbooks cost a quarter apiece in those days. I don't know how many printings there were in subsequent years, but I would guess a lot. I had it with me on Okinawa in an Armed Services edition. Think of the millions upon millions who had their major saturation in poetry with that book.

I began, for the first time in nearly fifty years, poring through that book, reading to remind myself of what it was that moved me so much as a young man, what poetry was like that truly spoke to the public. I found myself gasping as I turned the pages. With this blueprint, I thought, one could build a civilization: Chaucer (a poor selection), Shakespeare (songs and sonnets only), Donne, the Bible (delicious excerpts, including "The Song of Songs" presented as drama), Milton, Pope (no Dryden!), Blake, Wordsworth, Byron, Shelley, Keats, Tennyson, the Brownings, Whitman, Dickinson, Housman, Yeats, Robinson, Frost. . . . The most recent poets represented are Padraic Colum, Joyce Kilmer, Rupert Brooke, Orrick Johns, Elinor Wylie, and Stephen Vincent Benét.

Then a tornado touched down in our neighborhood. Lines down. Trees uprooted or broken. But no great damage. Living without electricity for forty-eight hours just gave me all that much more time to read (at night by kerosene lamp). But as I dragged limbs from the yard the next morning, the air humming with chainsaws, the streets littered as in a war zone, I was thinking of *The Pocket Book of Verse*. I thought of photographs of a city after a bombing. I was thinking of the present devastation wrought by modernism. All that reconstruction to be done!

And I remembered what qualities I responded to in these poems in my teens. For one thing, reckless sexuality, as in Suckling's "I have loved / Three whole days together! / And am like to love three more, / If it prove fair weather." Majestic thought, as in Gray's "Elegy Written in a Country Churchyard": "Some mute inglorious Milton here may rest." The rich sentiment of Goldsmith's "The Deserted Village." The lusty joy of song: "Here's to the maiden of bashful fifteen; / Here's to the widow of fifty; / Here's to the flaunting extravagant queen, / And here's to the housewife that's thrifty" (Sheridan). Terror and wonder, as in Blake's "The Tiger": "what immortal hand or eye / Dare frame thy fearful symmetry!" Democratic faith, as in Burns: "That man to man the world o'er / Shall brithers be for a' that." Poignant humor, as in Leigh Hunt's "Jenny kiss'd me when we met, / Jumping from the chair she sat in." Here's one I memorized because it made me weep, Thomas Hood's "The Song of the Shirt," beginning: "With fingers weary and worn, / With eyelids heavy and red, / A woman sat, in unwomanly rags, / Plying her needle and thread." How I was stirred by Emerson's "Here once the embattled farmers stood, / And fired the shot heard round the world"! I began to understand love "to the depth and breadth and height / My soul can reach," as described by Elizabeth Barrett Browning. I identified with Longfellow's lilting "A boy's will is the wind's will, / And the thoughts of youth are long, long thoughts."

Professors later taught me to sneer at poems that meant a great deal to me as an uninstructed reader. Kipling's "If" helped define manhood for me: "If you can trust yourself when all men doubt you, / But make allowance for their doubting, too." The professors used Kilmer's "Trees" as the paradigm of a bad poem. Little did I realize that I was attracted to it by its sexiness. In those days we didn't often encounter mention in print of hungry mouths being pressed against sweet flowing breasts or bosoms upon whom "snow has lain; / Who intimately live with rain." How I thrilled to the rhythms of Alfred Noyes's "The Highwayman," of Masefield's "I must go down to the sea again, to the lonely sea and the sky, / And all I ask is a tall ship and a star to steer her by." Children's poems such as Eugene Field's "Little Boy Blue" (another one I memorized because it made me weep) are in there cheek-by-jowl with Edwin Markham's "The Man with the Hoe," probably the poem that politically radicalized me in my youth. I learned from

Oscar Wilde's "The Ballad of Reading Gaol" that "each man kills the thing he loves," and, though not yet a man, I sighed, "How true! How true!"

And I began to realize that the professors had misled me in several fundamental ways, and that we, as a public, as some kind of a community with some shared values, in spite of the fragmentation of our times, would have to rediscover much more than musicality and accessibility if we were to recapture poetry from the professors. To put it bluntly: morals. The first thing we learned in college (for me: 1943; I was sixteen) was that it was vulgar to look for morals in literature. And as I reread those old poems I realized that morals were one of the things that drew me to literature, and, I venture, would draw readers today.

I don't mean preachiness. And the "morals" could be as saucy as Suckling's flaunted infidelity. They weren't necessarily conventional. But they had an application to life. As I read I knew that the poet was entertaining me, amusing me, engaging me with his or her characters, drawing me into stories, delighting my ear with music, but *with some point*. And I realized that my dissatisfaction with much of the modern poetry I was reading was that it seems to lack a point. I am left wondering why I read it. What use is it in my life? Poets have become too self-absorbed. Even when they seem to be talking about subjects other than themselves, their poems give a reader, above all, the impression that the poet is making a display of his or her sensitivity and intelligence, not truly speaking to a public but only to those who admire a particular kind of literary refinement.

These are heretical thoughts, I realized as the chainsaw ripped through our fallen redbud tree. They need to be tested.

Walter McDonald
Getting Started: Accepting the Regions
You Own—or Which Own You

An article first published in the Roundup Quarterly, *2, no. 3 (1990): 29-34.*

I think a writer finds at least one region to keep coming back to. It may be a place—Robert Frost's New England, for example, or Eudora Welty's Mississippi, or for some of us, Texas. A poet keeps prowling a certain region until he or she begins to settle it, homestead and live on it, and eventually own it.

If we read two hundred poems by a writer, we can't avoid the markings, the territorial claims—those obsessive words and images by which we're able to speak of a Robert Frost poem, or a James Wright poem—not in any way to reduce the poem or the poet—but on the contrary, to feel comfortable in that world, to be invited out to "the pasture" by Frost, or to share the blossoms and horses in the poetry of Wright.

In "The Pasture," his first poem in his first book, Frost invites us to come with him out to his pasture. Writing is like saying "welcome to my world." Every poem says that, to every reader.

Of course, not every writer's region is one of *geography*: some take an attitude, or a posture toward all events as their region. By "region" I don't mean simply *geography*—but regions of the mind, a cluster of images or obsessions which a writer draws on over and over, for poems.

Sometimes I'm asked, how *do* poets get started? How do they *find* those things they write about? When writers accept their regions, they can discover a mother lode of images. Accepting Texas into my poems has been the best thing for me, as a writer.

I came to poetry late, as an Air Force pilot. After some of my friends went off to Vietnam, and one was shot down, then another, I felt a need to say something to them, or about them. I turned to poems when nothing else worked; my first stumbling attempts were like letters to the dead, or to someone unable to hear.

Years later, when I turned to poems more than to stories, I spent a great deal of time and sheer wonderment asking, "How do other poets write?" I saw perfectly splendid poems, but how did they *find* those things to say?

This way of getting started, of finding a poem, is simply to start; if we believe in the possibilities of the imagination and take "delight in discovery" as we follow the hint of a few words, it's amazing where a first line may lead.

As the years went by, I wondered if the way I was increasingly able to write was my own uncomfortable secret—and perhaps revealed a flaw, a lack of some secret magic or muse. But it was a way of writing that worked for me, and so I rode it the way I would ride an only, ugly horse—as far as it would take me.

As the years went by, I began hearing friends say they write this way, too—and I read bold statements by other poets which made me realize that I was not alone, but that many others had discovered this way, at least some of the time. There's nothing new here, of course. This is the same way of getting started we've all used—the techniques of free association, or impromptu writing. We've all written in-class essays, or essay exams, or made phone calls, or jotted impromptu letters home. We compose this way even in ordinary conversations.

I'm not talking about finished poems, of course, but first drafts. The actual joy of rewriting comes later, the thrill and hard work of trying to make words jump through hoops. What I'm talking about is coming up with first drafts we're glad to have, wrapping our minds around something *worth* rewriting.

Robert Frost understood this act of discovery. Frost said it's a false poem, it's no poem at all if it knows the ending before it starts; he said a poem is like a piece of ice on a hot stove—it proceeds on its own melting.

I write for the pleasure of playing with words and finding stories in poems. For me, a poem starts like a spider racing from behind me on the floor to there, in sight, at my feet. It wasn't, and then it was. Where from? For what purpose? I write to discover, to follow the spider/image and see what sort of lyric-story I can spin from it, what tale develops.

To try this way of writing, I have to be willing to fail—for not all starts lead to poems. A poem called "Witching on Canvas" began as many of my poems do, with a willingness to give up some things in hopes of tracking down a first draft interesting enough to rewrite. There's never a lack of images, if I'm willing to give up enough time and energy and sit there working. Usually I don't know what I'll find today, and that's the key that keeps me going back to the blank screen—the curiosity, the thrill of the hunt, the delight I know I'll get when I discover something fun to write.

"I've watched amazed," I typed one morning, and realized this could go thousands of ways. Suddenly I began writing again about my familiar West Texas land, but in a way I'd never tried: "I've watched amazed the same burnt sienna land / we live on begin to glow under her brush."

After that start, as Frost promised, the poem's first draft rode "on its own melting," one detail after another, like watching my artist-wife at work. I found the poem by imagining what she does and what she would do if she had more time; I invented whatever would support the line—although it was more like discovery than creation.

By writing, I found that the poem was going to be about one of my territories, after all. It was suddenly there, available. Then it was simply a matter of taking the poem to its logical extreme.

Witching on Canvas

I've watched amazed the burnt sienna land
we live on begin to glow under her brush,
patches of ocher sand and flint glinting
light she invents from nothing but tubes

and bristles. With horsehairs dipped in oils
she scatters our lean cattle deep
into pebbles of canvas, witches mesquite
and cactus from hardpan white as caliche.

I've watched oil borders dry
like hardscrabble soil while she draws
babies' baths and irons real clothes in summer.
In times of fever she goes without sleep,

without a brush in her hand for weeks,
and then like cracks in the crust of each
year's drought, she drags dried borders

like plows and makes them fit, giving up

on nothing she's started, taking years
and three children to finish this scene
in the desert where we live, only dirt
and sky and in between, all that matters.

—*Crosscurrents*, 7, no. 2 (1987)

I like a poem that holds together, that has a tone consistent with its sounds and images and seems wholly thought out, but really wasn't, in first draft.

I called an early book of my poems *One Thing Leads to Another*. For me, that sums up the secret of composition, which keeps me giving up some things of this world in order to write. Frost said it, and said it better: a poem "begins in delight and ends in wisdom. . . . It finds its own name as it goes and discovers the best waiting for it in some final phrase at once wise and sad" ("The Figure a Poem Makes").

What do we find when we explore, or develop, or unwind a first line—that swatch of language which intrigues us, for whatever reason? From my own experience and the testimony of others, I suggest that what we find is possibly what we *want* to say. In this act of exciting discovery, I discover poems from the regions I own—or which own me.

When my first book was published—mainly those early poems about Vietnam—a friend asked, "Where's Texas in your poems, Walt?" I didn't know; I had never thought about it. But I started looking around and, sure enough, I began to feel the call of that wild, semi-arid West Texas which I knew better than I knew Iowa, better than Colorado, better than Vietnam.

My mother used to say that she was a little girl of five or six when her parents moved to the new town of Lubbock. She said that when the wagon rattled up on top of the caprock onto the wide flat plains—nothing but sky and miles and miles of waving native grass—she sighed, took a deep breath, and felt at home. I've never known anyone who felt so happy to live on the flat plains as my mother. I never understood that—until a friend made me glad I was alive and living in Texas. He opened my eyes to all I'll likely ever have of God's plenty, on this earth.

I discovered that it's okay to write about native soil—or anything else I wanted to; poems could be more than what I felt I *needed* to say. For years, I had not considered this world to be my home. But when I let down my bucket in a plains region doomed to dry up, I found all sorts of water, all sorts of poems, even if I could live to write for forty years in this suddenly fabulous desert.

Trying to explain how poems develop and why anyone would give up good time to try to make simple words explode, I think back to my earliest memories of language, my earliest thrills over words. I must have been three or four, no more than five: I was allowed to visit my Grandmother—Granny, we called her—no more than once a day. She lay in bed, propped up, and read to me from a big book the most amazing stories: Samson; Daniel in the lions' den; and a boy named David who grew up to be king. And I was hooked on language a year before I knew she was lying there dying of cancer.

I think back also to the first grade, when the teacher brought a man to class—a man in buckskin, in moccasins without socks, a huge feather headdress that fell all the way to the floor. That man began telling stories, and I had never heard such things. Magic! Like all the others in that winter classroom, I sat there hearing the most amazing tales, thrilled out of my mind, believing every word.

I don't even know his name. But I'll never forget the splendor of it all.

It seems a short time since I propped on my elbows and listened to my Granny reading verses like magic, in words I barely understood. It seems only a few days since I sat spellbound and heard a man tell stories so exciting that my classmates and I screamed and clapped until our hands stung.

I feel lucky that for a little while, before the golden bowl breaks and the silver cord snaps, I get to hang around words and see what happens—through my students' and other writers' words, and words that spin off my own fingertips. What writer doesn't want to move us to tears or chills or hugs or laughter? Who doesn't want to pass along a thrill like that?

Richard Moore
The No Self, the Little Self, and the Poets

Excerpted from the Hudson Review, *34 (Winter 1981-1982): 489-508.*

Who am I? What is this self I aggrandize and agonize over? Can it be that I am nobody, as Emily Dickinson suggests in that frog poem? She might have liked the idea of the No Self: the idea that our idea of the Self may be just that: only an idea. Something arbitrary, artificial, and therefore dispensable. The Yogis and the Buddhists have been telling us this for years now, and it seems to have sunk in. I think they have only helped us to a discovery that we were ripe to make for ourselves. Otherwise we would have refused to understand them.

Let us think of the various ways that a self can be defined: bodily pains and pleasures (I have good evidence that this was how Homer thought of the self); thoughts (*cogito ergo sum,* said Descartes; this intellectual being, those thoughts that wander through Eternity, said Milton's devil, Belial); actions (character isolated by deed, said Yeats). . . . There may be no end to such possible definitions. They may be as numberless as the numbers. So then, faced with this dubious variety, I accept the additional notion of the self as not there at all, the self as nothing—just as zero came to be regarded as a number in mathematics—and sit on the floor and cross my legs as snugly as they will comfortably go—like a Yogi. Why not? It was in India, after all, that zero was first accepted as a number. Sitting there in the silence of the night, I do nothing and, insofar as I am able, I think nothing. It's a good position to use once one gets used to it because the body can grow relaxed, forget its pains and pleasures for a while, and yet experience stays vivid. (The only other thoroughly relaxed and stable position is lying down, but with deep concentration this position tends toward drowsiness and blunted awareness.) To encourage the silence and the absence of thoughts, it helps to breathe very slowly, deeply and quietly and to count one's breaths, one to ten, one to ten. . . . In this state one stands a pretty good chance of directly experiencing that self which is no self, that nothing at all which remains when all the querulous somethings have ceased. As they say, it is all empty. Sometimes it is almost terrifying in its beauty.

Then, as when zero is accepted as a number in mathematics, all sorts of operations and representations become clear and possible that were impossible before. A relaxation and sureness come into life. A vividness enters the things we see, hear, and touch. Our skills increase. These effects have become commonplace—witness the vast success of the Maharishi Yogi's "Transcendental Meditation"—TM. A whole town in Vermont has taken up TM in the hope of decreasing its crime rate (or perhaps only in the hope of making the TV evening news); and a major league baseball team is trying to mix it in with batting practice. (O my Country, what is becoming of you?)

Even when the non-self does not directly appear in the quietness, it gains strength with the stilling of conventional self-concepts and exerts its beneficent influence. The result is curious: any task to be performed not only becomes easier, but also less important. We are able to solve the problem at precisely that moment when we have ceased to care whether we solve it or not. It must be that our difficulties with it resulted from our own desire. We were, in fact, not thinking about the problem but about our longing to solve it. That is, we were thinking about ourselves. In the meditation the self tends to vanish and with it the desire for a solution; and this frees us to lose ourselves in the problem without distraction.

But this non-self I have accepted will not do as a self in any ordinary way. It won't, for example, fit very well into the sentences I use, and the sentences, of course, are absolutely necessary because my experience is largely verbal—and social. What is man without society? A noble savage? A savage monster? Centuries of asking have produced a reasonably clear answer to this question. Such a man is impossible. He would be nothing at all. Just so. I have an inkling how marvelous it is to be nothing. But I am not ready for the jungle or the mountaintop. I sense that it would never work. Unlike the Buddha, I'd worry about what became of my wife and children. I'd wonder who, if anybody, was reading my poems. . . . So I have to be somebody with everybody else. There is no escape from it.

How is one to resolve such a conflict? Is there any way that the absence of the self—or perhaps some deft minimizing of the self—can be made to exist and function in ordinary social life? Is it not the ordinary life of our time, the crumbling of our civilized Cartesian world of "me" and "it," that has thrust such a need upon us? . . .

* * *

The only thing I have against progress is that it is so one-sided. In this marvelous accumulating process, things are forever being added; nothing ever seems to be taken away; or at least nothing, until recently, was ever said about it. But how are the historians to record what has been forgotten? This should present no problem. What psychoanalyst has any difficulty talking about the Unconscious Mind, which, being unconscious by definition, cannot possibly be known? Such a concept must always be a hypothesis, a myth, a way of reconciling discrepancies in our experience. History is mythical by its very nature. It is the imagined picture of a past life which explains the present experience of ancient ruins, documents, anomalies in our present habits, etc. Facts are never enough. If the result is to be in any way memorable, there has to be an imaginative matrix which holds the facts together in a coherent pattern and gives us the illusion that we understand the people of the past. And to be credible as people, they have to know things of which we are ignorant, do they not? Why bother to know them at all unless they can teach us something? But there is a school of thought, very powerful in Victorian times and still of considerable strength, which wants to learn nothing at all from *them*. Hence the myth—the shallowest myth of all—that in history things are being continually learned and nothing forgotten. The myth of progress. Technology is their prime example, and with any credibility at all, their only example.

I am at the border of a very large subject. Let me pay my respects to the customs official with a brief anecdote and be on my way, leaving

the country of technology and the shrine of progress for later visits.

A woman who spent several months living with the hunting and gathering Bushmen of the Kalahari Desert noted in her book that there were two types of insect grub important in Bushman technology. The first was inedible and deadly and provided the poison with which the hunters tipped their arrows; the second was a rare delicacy that the Bushmen loved to eat. The two types were found in the same places, and she examined them carefully to distinguish them. She went on examining them for the three months of her stay but always had to conclude that the grubs were identical. Yet the natives could tell them apart without difficulty. It seems strange that her hosts couldn't explain to her what they noticed that escaped her, but there were doubtless linguistic difficulties involved.

One would be inclined to discount a story like this if it did not agree so well with other accounts, testifying to a sensitivity and quickness of perception possessed by hunting and gathering peoples that to the civilized observer seems uncanny. Surely this has to rate as an item of technology which has been forgotten among us. We have telescopes and microscopes, but we have paid for them, apparently, with the sharpness of our naked eyes. It isn't surprising. We live in a world of labels and abstractions, particularly so as we climb our social ladders and become managers, executives, experts; and lacking the nourishment from sensory perception that our underlying egoless beings require, our senses decay; and seeking their rejuvenation, we flee on weekends to the country, where, if our equipment were taken from us, we would perish in a matter of days.

But our loss since the stability of the Stone Age has not been technological; it has been of sweetness and light. This is another large subject. Much has been written about the isolated tribes around the earth which have survived into our time at this cultural level: the Bushmen, the Pygmies in the African rain forest, the Australian aborigines, the Eskimos, various tribes in the Philippines, among which the recently discovered and publicized Tasaday on Mindanao; and I can only summarize from much fascinated, casual reading. The theory that Stone Age man was violent, aggressive, and in a constant state of war over territorial rights with neighboring tribes gets no support whatever. War among tribes at this level is either completely unknown or, as with the African Pygmies, a kind of joke which results in no harm and may well be a mocking imitation of the surrounding agricultural tribes. Observer after observer has been amazed at the gentleness, gaiety, and lack of ambition of these peoples. No demon religions, no problems of social rank and rebellious behavior seem to beset these simple classless societies, which are virtually lawless because no laws are needed. One hesitates even to describe them for fear of seeming to echo nineteenth-century sentimentality about the "noble savage."

One can only conclude that the cost of our progress from the Stone Age has been great. But to gain some insight into the manner of this loss, we shall have to explain how human beings, in every way as perceptive and intelligent as we, can be so content with so little. Why aren't *they* plagued by that "noir ambition," as Racine called it, observing it in himself, that lust for conquest, that itch for grandeur? The answer has to lie in a different conception of self. . . . Many observers have said that these people are gay and at ease because they are at one with their environment. But how is that possible? It is certainly not possible for me—or else I would not be writing this. But if we suppose that man's first, Stone Age assumption about images in the mind was . . . that they do not emanate from the picturing self but from the things they depict, then we can grasp immediately how such a man can be without ambition and completely at one with his environment. Quite literally his environment possesses him in every waking and sleeping moment, and it is difficult for him to imagine doing other things beyond his present occupation.

If we assume this, we can also understand why there was no progress, and why life in the Old Stone Age went on substantially unchanged for at least 100,000 years. For the next great "step forward," the fundamental event which made possible the accelerating development of the human species in the last 10,000 years, was the discovery of agriculture—and the parallel event in the steppe lands of Asia, the domestication of animals. Both of these achievements would clearly have been impossible for the Stone Age mind that we have described; for both involve standing aside and taking control of the forces of nature in a new and radical way. Before the kill the hunter has no control over his quarry. Rather the opposite: to hunt successfully with the weak implements he has, he must submit himself to the ways of the animal. He imitates the animal in his dances, he draws its pic-

ture on the wall of his cave, and it comes to him in dreams. In all these events, it is the animal calling out to him, drawing him after it in a hunt that may last for days. (The purely physical aspect in which man is superior to all the other animals is his endurance: he can wear out any animal he can track.) Then finally there is the kill. The Pygmies laugh at the death throes of the animals they have wounded—a sign that they are uncomfortable about the process—but also a sign that they see the animal's death as a dance. Killing for the true hunter is an act of identification and love. (This sounds shocking to me as I write it, but I see no escape from such conclusions. According to Denis de Rougement, even war can be thought of as an act of love between one nation and another.)

Thus, in primitive hunting the identification between the hunter and the hunted is complete, and essentially the same observations hold for the gathering of wild vegetable food. But to plant a seed, tend its growth, and harvest it clearly implies deliberate control. The image of the crop in the mind must belong to the mind, for the mind has organized the whole process. One can't practice agriculture without feeling superior to what one grows; one must be the master—though both the master and his field remain at the mercy of countless unpredictable forces. In short, the discovery of agriculture either necessitated or was made possible by a fundamental revolution of man's concept of the self.

But in the revolutionary changes since the invention of agriculture . . . there is one kind of person who, at least in certain moments, has retained the ancient self of the primitive hunter. I refer to the artists, and in particular, to the poets. I single out the poets because the other arts seem more susceptible to the changing moods of urban culture—though, of course, poetry has also been greatly influenced, particularly in the "large forms" of epic and drama. But it was the poets and not the painters and musicians whom Plato expelled from his perfect urban republic that was to be ruled by systematic philosophy. Those witty, irresponsible, charming, and passionate imitators best represented that stubborn human core of whimsicality that could not be permitted in a well-ordered state. But what I have to say about them applies also to the other arts.

The poet has exactly the same relationship to his subject that the Pygmy has to his whole environment. When a poet writes a genuine poem about something, the most succinct and direct way to describe the process is to say that the subject of the poem, whatever it is, invades, haunts, and possesses the poet and insists on being written about. In the best poems, there is no poet at all, but a thing, a personality—anything at all—which occupied the poet completely and determined every aspect of the poem: its story, tone, rhythm, images—everything. I do not by any means imply that composing poetry is an irrational or thoughtless process; I only say that the poet in action has no self because that self is now completely occupied by the subject of the poem, and further, that the inception of the poem is not in the poet but is most accurately described by saying, The thing wanted to be written about. The animal says to the Pygmy, Hunt me! and just so, the animal on the cave wall in Lascaux appeared to a man 20,000 years ago and said, Paint me! All three of the basic arts exist at the hunting and gathering stage, are a product of that mentality, and to this day require a return to that mentality for their proper practice.

Let me illustrate with a small anecdote. The time is near the end of my first marriage. I have acquired the habit of walking around the city with index cards stuffed in a pocket in case I should see something good to write about—for I was looking for greater freshness in my poems. I saw a line of trees in front of a hospital along a street which ran westward into the sunset. Something about the scene intrigued me, so out came the cards. The lines pleased me the way they went, the new details that kept coming out of the scene as I went on. It all seemed vivid and unfamiliar in words—a good sign. When I got home, I still liked the lines, but although they were all description, it did not seem to be just a descriptive poem. The images were implying something else which wasn't there, but I had no idea what.

Around this time I seldom read my writings to my wife, for we were becoming strangers; but this once I did—and could hardly finish. Midway through, I realized that all the images had to do with the fact that our marriage was coming to an end, which I had not yet admitted very clearly to myself, let alone to her, though she sensed it. But I had to finish reading. If I broke off, it would be worse—even more painfully obvious. Did she know? Did the bare images say to her what they said to me? It wasn't the sort of thing I could have asked about. But in any case, I knew how to finish the poem.

At this point my friend, the psychoanalyst, will say to me in gentle, indulgent tones that those trees didn't speak to me at all and that all these events can be given a perfectly rational explanation in terms of my dualistic self. Subconsciously I knew that my relationship with my first wife had become impossible. Then when I saw the trees, street, and sun, I projected this unconscious awareness into them, and that is why they interested me. Then when I read the lines to my wife, I realized the game I had been playing on myself. . . .

Fine, fine, yes, I understand. But there's only one problem. That's not what happened. That's not what I experienced. Like good scientists, don't we have to choose the simplest hypothesis that will account for the observations? (For science is also governed by principles of aesthetics.) In your explanation I have to say, "I projected my thoughts onto the trees, even though I was totally unaware of the fact, and was actually experiencing the trees, as with wills of their own, drawing my interest to them." That's getting pretty complicated, and I rejoin with triumphant simplicity: "The trees spoke to me."

But there is a better way for us to decide which of us has the better explanation. We can ask the poem. To do this properly, we have to be wide and strong readers of poems in English, so that we know good ones from poor ones. Then the answer is simple. If it is a good poem, there is something magical about it, the scene actually speaks in a moving and awesome way, and I am right about what happened; and if it is a poor poem with no compelling relation between the scene and the realization, so that the reader suspects that the poet is only playing some kind of psychological game with himself, then the analyst is quite correct.

But what if a poet writes a good poem, a powerful and magical poem, and then accepts the analyst's explanation of its inception? Why then, with the dualistic self he must acquire in order to agree with the analyst, he is deluding himself about the nature of his art. For the nature of his art is not analytical, but magical, and his poem belies his explanation of it. Poets, like the rest of us, have to live in a civilization founded on a dualistic self, so it is very likely, when they discuss their poems in the manner of conventional civilized discourse, that they will find it convenient to ignore or deny the poem's origin in the primitive selflessness.

"This is all mere assertion. Even among the poets, who would agree with you?"

Will Keats do? There is that famous passage from one of his letters: "Several things dovetailed in my mind, and at once it struck me what quality went to form a Man of Achievement, especially in Literature, and which Shakespeare possessed so enormously—I mean *Negative Capability*, that is, when a man is capable of being in uncertainties, mysteries, doubts, without any irritable reaching after fact and reason—Coleridge, for instance, would let go by a fine isolated verisimilitude caught from the Penetralium of mystery, from being incapable of remaining content with half-knowledge. This pursued through volumes would perhaps take us no further than this, that with a great poet the sense of Beauty overcomes every other consideration, or rather obliterates all consideration."

This can be interpreted many ways, but in the terms we are using, it means that the poet must renounce the demand (of the independent self) for "fact and reason," that is, for conventional order. This amounts to saying that the poet must renounce his independent self; and that is why Keats calls his capacity to do this Negative Capability. Shakespeare is the best instance because it is so utterly impossible to locate Shakespeare, the man, in his plays or even in his "personal" poems. We have characters acting and talking, and what they say is always very interesting, provocative, and sometimes even philosophical; but it is always *their* ideas, never *his*. The more Shakespeare we read, the more we realize this; for there is no consistent view. One character contradicts another, and there is never any attempt to resolve the differences in a philosophical way. One even finds whole plays contradicting one another: it's hard to imagine, for example, how the gloom, disgust, and haunting sense of sin in *Othello* and the gay relish for life and sex in *Anthony and Cleopatra* could have been products of the same mind. Only the style assures us that the same man authored both. The only possible resolution is that Shakespeare, when he wrote plays, became selfless, so that these two sets of characters and actions could possess him and reach their own form unimpeded by what he himself willed or thought.

"No, Keats will not do. Keats was a Romantic. Naturally you would be able to find passages of his that endorse your own absurdly romantic theory of art. What endorsement can you find from the neoclassic artists who felt that art must adhere to rules and be made by the conscious calculating self ?"

How about Pope, then—our quintessence of English neoclassicism? Keats detested him and his works. That ought to be credential enough. Keats liked to thumb his nose at Pope, praising Chapman's Homer at a time when Pope's was virtually the official translation, and even rewriting him from time to time. To Pope's couplet,

> True ease in writing comes from art, not chance;
> As those move easiest who have learned to dance.

Keats replies,

> When I behold, upon the night's starr'd face,
> Huge cloudy symbols of a high romance,
> And think that I may never live to trace
> Their shadows, with the magic hand of chance. . . .

Pope's word "art" in his day meant "conscious intention." Learning your trade, in poetry as in other things, is what matters, he seems to be saying. It's not luck or chance or anything mysterious like that. Nonsense! Keats retorts. Chance is exactly what it is, and it's magical, too.

But Pope isn't talking about poetic inspiration, only "ease in writing." A poet, he says, must master the techniques of his art. There is plenty of room for inspiration in this view. A poet, in developing technique, is like the worshiper laboriously purifying himself, making himself a fit vehicle for the spirit when it chooses to come. And when the spirit does come, technique is forgotten because it has become innate. The second line of Pope's couplet makes this clear. The person who is graceful in his movements because he has learned to dance isn't remembering his dancing lessons when he walks: the lessons have become part of him.

Any doubts about Pope's meaning are dispelled by earlier lines in the same poem ("An Essay on Criticism"). In writing poetry, he says, "there's a happiness as well as care"—or as we would say, there's luck as well as diligence.

> Music resembles Poetry, in each
> Are nameless graces which no methods teach,
> And which a master hand alone can reach.
> . . . .
> Thus Pegasus a nearer way may take,
> May boldly deviate from the common track,
> From vulgar bounds with brave disorder part,
> And snatch a grace beyond the reach of art.

Note that is isn't the poet who takes the "nearer way," but Pegasus, the flying horse, meaning the poem itself with its own will and brute force, taking its own path in the selfless poet.

Even Aristotle, that ancient grandfather of cold classical analysis, agrees: "The poet should work out his play, to the best of his power, with appropriate gestures." In other words, the poet must stop being himself and become the character he portrays. Surely that "power" the poet needs in order to do this is Keats's negative capability. "Hence poetry implies either a happy gift of nature or a strain of madness. In the one case a man can take the mould of any character; in the other, he is lifted out of his proper self." Note that the alternative is not whether the poet while composing does or doesn't cease to be his "proper self"—that is, his civilized dualistic self—but whether he does so willingly and thoughtfully or passively in a state of possession.

Two observations are in order at this point. First: "So you have made it seem likely that poets and other artists are survivals of that primitive selflessness in which, you say, humanity lived in happy stability for 100,000 years. What does that do for the rest of us, caught in the dilemmas of civilization? Even the poets, as you describe them, have ceased to exist; for the poets nowadays are a sorry lot, as caught up in empty fads as the silliest TV producer."

The second in some measure answers the first: "What you describe about the nature of poetry is so thoroughly ordinary that I wonder why you have gone to the trouble. Every one of us, insofar as we have any life in us at all, are inspired in this way throughout our years. Day after day we discover things: in a flash we see a way to do something, how the peg will fit into the hole, what the answer is to the problem; we find something we have lost; we become suddenly aware of someone or something we love or hate; and in all those discoveries, those inspirations, we lose our sense of self and, simply because we have become intensely aware of something other than ourselves, have become selfless."

Precisely. As Gerard Manley Hopkins said, poets when they are inspired write poems, and other people when they are inspired do other things. But you perhaps see the process more clearly in the poets. Other activities—though this is also true of poetry—are continually getting mixed up with civilized self-aggrandizements. The composer needs a symphony orchestra, press agents, a civic establishment, to do his work. The mechanic needs an elaborate shop. Housewives need washing machines and electronic ovens. All a poet needs are a few odd bits of paper, an old pencil stub, and perhaps a pair of good walking shoes. And the process that he represents, the survival of the selflessness—the childishness, if you will—of the Stone Age, is crucial to the survival of us all. The idea is a little strange to us, whose imaginations are enmeshed so inextricably with the things we can manufacture, sell, and own; but the Chinese have had it for a long time, this deep respect for the primitive, childlike response to things which underlies all our civilized systems. So let me conclude with a bit from one of their old books:

"Chuang Tzu and Hui Tzu were strolling one day on the bridge over the river Hao. Chuang Tzu said, 'Look how the minnows dart hither and thither where they will. Such is the pleasure that fish enjoy.' Hui Tzu said, 'You are not a fish. How do you know what gives pleasure to fish?' Chuang Tzu said, 'You are not I. How do you know that I do not know what gives pleasure to fish?' Hui Tzu said, 'If because I am not you, I cannot know whether you know, then equally because you are not a fish, you cannot know what gives pleasure to fish. My argument still holds.'" Chuang Tzu said, 'Let us go back to where we started. You asked me how I know what gives pleasure to fish. But you already knew how I knew when you asked me. You knew that I knew it by standing here on the bridge at Hao.'"

Robert Peters
Foreword to *Ludwig of Bavaria*

Excerpted from the revised edition (Cherry Valley, N.Y.: Cherry Valley Editions, 1987).

This is a book about beauty, friendship, art, and disease, centered around one driven soul who happened to be a king. With considerable flair, Ludwig II cultivated the esthetic experience and the dream world, and immersed them unabashedly in a nineteenth-century ambience. It is difficult to conceive of him without Novalis, Goethe, Schopenhauer, Schiller, Nietzsche, Byron, and Shelley in the background. Ludwig's world was a baroque stage where he was the leading actor, as well as director, designer, and producer. One might even say that at moments he fancied himself as the entire audience as well. His supporting cast, chosen carefully by him, were led by Richard Wagner and, in the later years, by Josef Kainz. His only real female confidante was his cousin the Empress Elisabeth of Austria, mother of the Crown-Prince who died at Mayerling. Ludwig saw his own mother as a villainess—he called her "Prose." All of these persons were larger than life. Critics agree that without Ludwig's material support, Wagner would never have written *The Ring;* and, stimulated by their turbulent friendship, Kainz became a major European actor.

Much of his personal behavior he modelled after his namesake Louis XIV of France, the Sun King. In homage, Ludwig saw himself as the Moon King, often exchanging his days for nights, and frequently dressing up as the French monarch. Ludwig's last palace, Herrenchiemsee, unfinished at his death, was a version of Versailles; Ludwig's Hall of Mirrors was even more splendid than its prototype in France.

Ludwig was homosexual, and agonizingly so. I place his sexuality at the core of his nature, explaining much of his behavior by it. His agonizing was unrelenting, and assumed the classic pattern of the guilt-ridden man who succumbs to his predilections, enjoys them and then loathes and berates himself afterwards, calling upon God, or whatever forces of strength he can summon to keep from falling again. Though they exist only in mutilated transcripts, doctored apparently by the men who dethroned him, his journals are reportedly filled with evidence of a struggle that would have driven lesser mortals to suicide. I see Ludwig as an eccentric genius whose ideas were ahead of his time. What nineteenth-century monarch so resisted war and the greed and bloodshed spawned by it? Or what monarch had the vision and the intelligence to try to realize, via his fantastic palaces and castles, ideas for a society of the future, ideas he explored with Wagner?

Poetry as biography and history is a specialty of mine. My first use of the mode was in two books on the life of Ann Lee, the English "female Christ" who founded the Shaker religion in America: *The Gift to be Simple: A Garland for Ann Lee* (Liveright, 1975) and *Shaker Light*, published in 1987 by the Unicorn Press. Other "voice" books include: *Hawker* (Unicorn, 1984), over a hundred poems in the voice of the eccentric Cornish vicar Robert Stephen Hawker, who was obsessed with dredging drowned sailors from the sea and burying them in his churchyard. He was also a poet, loved having animals attend his services, and played mermaid for his parishioners. *Kane* (Unicorn, 1985), a voice portrait of the American explorer Elisha Kent Kane who reached the Arctic in 1853. His ship froze fast in the ice off Greenland and never thawed free. Based on the explorer's journals, *Kane* delineates the experiences of that harrowing year and the return of the survivors down the Greenland coast. *The Blood Countess*, published so far as a "Gothic Horror Play for Single Performer," recreates the life and psyche of the notorious Hungarian mass murderer Elisabeth Bathory. She killed over 700 virgins and bathed in their blood, as a way, she believed, of maintaining her youth. She was thwarted in her grisly pursuits when she was walled up in her castle in 1609. Large sections of *Countess* have appeared in *Sulfur* and *Bluefish*.

311

Earlier works of mine anticipated these recent efforts: *Connections: In the English Lake District* (Anvil Press, London, 1972), never published in America, is made up of collage poems, lyrics, and narrative pieces juxtaposing some of Wordsworth's experiences in the Lake District with my own. *Byron Exhumed* (included in *The Poet as Ice-Skater*, Manroot Books, 1976) employs parody and satire in monologues by persons who have just heard of Byron's death. The title poem for my *Gauguin's Chair* (Crossing Press, 1977) depicts van Gogh's agony over the rupture of his friendship with Gauguin.

As so often happens, serendipity determines our directions, both personal and professional. In 1974, I stayed overnight with George Hitchcock and Marjorie Simon, in Santa Cruz, California. As I was on my way to bed, George handed me a copy of Wilfrid Blunt's *The Dream King*. Those readers who know this book, published by Penguin, will appreciate the superb quality of its numerous plates. Visconti's much mutilated film *Ludwig* had not yet appeared, nor had the Syberberg film. I had just written my Shaker books and was seeking a new subject, one that would present esthetic challenges different from those occasioned by Ann Lee. I was immediately intrigued by Ludwig, who struck me as an archetypal esthete and pacifist, one connected with other interests of mine. A good part of my early professional life I spent writing on Oscar Wilde, A. C. Swinburne, James McNeill Whistler, John Addington Symonds, and Walter Pater. I have always been interested in the several arts, an interest encouraged by my mentor at the University of Wisconsin, Jerome Buckley.

As the idea for a long work on Ludwig grew, I decided not to worry about writing the usual poetry book. The subject matter would determine the length. Needless to say, Blunt's biography was indispensable; my debt to it is enormous. Also important were Ernest Newman's *The Life of Richard Wagner* and Richard Gutman's *Richard Wagner: The Man, his Mind and his Music*. The story of Kainz's ring was told to me by Harold Clurman, one summer at Yaddo. I also owe much to my longtime friend and fellow-poet Paul Trachtenberg, to whom this work is partially dedicated, for his continuing presence and affection.

An earlier version of *Ludwig*, called *The Picnic in the Snow: Ludwig of Bavaria*, was published by Bill Truesdale, the New Rivers Press, in 1982, and is now out of print. Bill's enthusiasm and support were crucial at a difficult time in the book's history. The major events of *Ludwig* are based on fact; other events occurred to me as I sought to sense Ludwig and make him my own person. People in the book all figured in Ludwig's life, more or less in the roles I assign them. "Bath" is adapted from Ronald Firbank's *The Flower Beneath the Foot*, which Ludwig would have loved. I have also adapted passages from Plato and Schopenhauer, and have assembled passages from Ludwig's letters.

Robert Phillips
Finding, Losing, Reclaiming: A Note on My Poems

A previously unpublished article written in 1987.

W. H. Auden was wrong: a poem *can* make something happen. The first poem I published appeared in a national magazine when I was a high-school senior in Delaware. It was submitted by a friend without my knowledge. The poem was read by another high-school senior—a girl in upstate New York. That September we enrolled at the same university and shared some of the same classes. Remembering the name of the "poet," she inquired if that were my poem. I reluctantly admitted it was. Six years later, we married one another. Even a bad poem can make good things happen.

Why was I writing poetry as a teenager? The act was not encouraged by teachers. Not one suggested that a student could or should attempt to write a poem. A poet was a gray-bearded, historical personage. At school we spent weeks reading *Evangeline* line by line. That behind us, we attacked *Hiawatha*. How the rhythms rolled and thumped! They're in my ear yet: "By the shore of Gitche Gumee, / By the shining Big-Sea-Water. . . ." Longfellow seemed the poetry kingpin: on we plodded through "The Village Blacksmith" and "The Courtship of Miles Standish."

No, I was not writing poetry as part of an education. I was writing it to "find myself." I'd tried painting, the piano, the trumpet, even the tuba, but writing was what interested me most. It was also what set me apart. I was the class "writer"—as opposed to all those jocks, motorcyclists, and toughs. It didn't make me any more popular, but it gave me an identity.

I attempted poetry rather than fiction or journalism because poetry seemed the highest art, the greatest aspiration. It still does. As Paul Valéry said, "Prose is to poetry as walking is to dancing."

On the shelves at home I found volumes of poetry, largely inherited from my mother's Virginia family. There was Wordsworth, Tennyson, Jean Ingelow(!), and the Brownings. There was even a first edition of William Cullen Bryant's 1876 anthology, *A Library of Poetry and Song*, which I possess today. I read these with an absorption I never gave my schoolwork. So much so, I later discovered myself incorporating Wordsworth's images and even whole lines into my own poems. These I carefully expunged. But in reading and writing poetry, I found an activity which transported me beyond the sandy flats of Delaware. In attempting to write a poem, I felt I was attempting something worthwhile, something which made me worthwhile.

When I entered Syracuse University, the poets that most excited me in class were T. S. Eliot and John Crowe Ransom. Their reserve, detachment, and irony intrigued me. Here was poetry different from the Victorian effusions and sentimental outbursts I'd found on my parents' shelves. Even my beloved Wordsworth came to seem overwrought. Why were those daffodils described as both "a crowd" and "a host"? Shouldn't they be one or the other? And why did his stars both "twinkle" and "shine"? Wretched excess.

Taking my cue from the cool of Eliot and Ransom, I began to write poems which projected personae—a practice I rarely engage in today. My undergraduate poems followed Eliot's dicta of poetic impersonality and aesthetic detachment. I turned from writing poems to find myself and began writing poems to lose myself. To extinguish my personality. The Ransom influence was especially tough to shake. I'm sorry to say that my first book contains the verb *thole*, a word which only Mr. Ransom could get away with, and then only barely.

Another influence at the time were the Imagists—H. D., T. E. Hulme, Amy Lowell, and early Pound. Consequently, the problem with most of my poems was that they lacked ambition. I thought it sufficient to pile word-picture upon word-picture, so long as the images were fresh or startling. This practice ended abruptly when my writing-workshop professor, the late Donald A. Dike, wrote across a sheaf of my poems, "It is time to start writing a poetry of *statement*." From

313

then on, I attempted to write poems which not only created images, but which also said something. At last I was writing not to find or lose, but to express myself.

This realization seems simplistic in the extreme: isn't it every writer's goal to express himself, as well and as clearly as possible? Yet somehow I was a long time coming to that goal. I'm certain that in no way did I begin writing "a poetry of ideas." Issues and politics have rarely found their way into my work. In the 1980s, when asked to contribute to an anthology devoted to the major events of the 1960s, I turned in a little poem on the death of Janis Joplin! It may be, as a close friend of mine suspects, that—like Henry James—I have a mind so fine, no single idea can violate it.

Then what *is* it I wish to express? The answer to that is, I suppose, best left to readers. I will only say that every poet I care about today has a controlling passion, rather than a ruling idea. For, say, Richard Wilbur, it is a passion to celebrate. Wilbur celebrates both the things of this world and the things of the spirit. That has not been my concern, alas. While certain of my poems are celebratory, I have been more concerned with gathering losses than gains or blessings. My poems from *The Pregnant Man* seem to attempt to recapture lost wholeness—lost integrity of the mind and the body—and to reassemble lost relationships and lost trust. Poems from *Running on Empty* attempt to recapture lost childhood and innocence. My newest poems, from *Personal Accounts*, explore careers of those whose lives or works have touched mine, but which now are lost—there's that word again—except in memory.

Two impulses I recognize behind all my poems are to reclaim and to survive. Like my stone crab who gamely sprouts another leg, my flatworm who grows another head, my suburban father who sings in the shower, my goal is recapitulation in face of adversity. My hope is that the poems go beyond what happened to Phillips, to where the happening means something to the reader.

The reason I continue to write poems, I suppose, is that it is exciting. An ordinary day becomes an extraordinary one once the itch and the rub of a new poem begins. It's exciting because I never know what is going to come next. It's like turning corners in a strange city: you never know what is going to be around the corner until you've made the turn.

Charles Simic
Images and "Images"

From The Uncertain Certainty (*Ann Arbor: University of Michigan Press, 1985), pp. 105-107; first published in* Field, *no. 23 (Fall 1980).*

"Madame X is installing a piano in the Alps."
—Rimbaud

"The more impossible the problem,
the more poetical the possibilities.
An ideal situation."
—Carl Rakosi

Image: to make visible . . . What?

To reenact the act of attention.
The duration of the act itself as the frame (the field) of the image.
The intensity of the act as the source of "Illumination."

In imagism, the faith that this complex event can be transcribed to the page without appreciable loss.

Something as simple and as difficult as a pebble in a stream. The instant when it ceases to be anonymous and becomes an "object of love." A longing to catch *that* in its difference and kind. . . . A glimpse of the world untainted by subjectivity.

In such a "frame" analogies would be an interference, a distortion.
One wants the object looked *at*, not *through*.
A pebble stripped of its figurative and symbolic dimensions.
An homage to the pleasures of clear sight.

Nevertheless—the "image." The hunch that there's more here than meets the eye. The nagging sense that the object is "concealed" by its appearance. The possibility that I am participating in a meaning to which this act is only a clue. In short, is one an impartial witness, or is the object a mirror in which one occasionally catches sight of oneself imagining that impartiality?

To be conscious is to experience a distancing. One is neither World, nor Language, nor Self. One *is*, and one *is not*. It seems incredible that any of these could be accurately rendered by merely listing the attributes. "Listing" implies order, linearity, time. . . . The experience is that of everything occurring simultaneously.

This is not something of which one can form an image by imagist means. However, since one needs to talk even about the incommunicable, one says, it is *like*. . . . With that little word, of course, one has already changed the manner in which one proposes to represent the world.

If the source of light for the imagist image is the act of attention, in the universe of radical metaphor, the cause is the faith in the ultimate resemblance (identity) of everything existing and everything imagined.

The "image" is the glimpse of the "Demon of Analogy" at work. He works in the dark, as the alchemists knew.

To assert that A is B involves a risk—especially, if one admits the extent to which the act is involuntary. One cannot anticipate figures of speech. They occur—out of a semantic need. The true risk, however, is in the critique the "image" performs on Language as the shrine of all the habitual ways of representing reality.

This is its famous "Logic." The "image" never generalizes. In each entity, it detects a unique (local) logic. (A pebble does not think as a man or a stream does. It "thinks" as a pebble.) Michaux and Edson are masters of such dialectic.

It all depends on how seriously one takes the consequences of one's poetics.

The secret ambition of "image"—making is gnosis—an irreverence which is the result of the most exalted seriousness. One transgresses as one recognizes the rules by which one lives.

The "image" might come to one in a strange and mysterious way, but it's no longer possible to offer it to the world in that spirit. To know history, even literary history, is to lose innocence and begin to ponder what the "images" are saying.

"Resemble assemble reply," says Gertrude Stein. Today to make an "image" is to make a theatre. On its stage, the old goat-faced Socrates, the philosophic clown, is taking a bow.

Thus, it's not so much *what* the "image" says, but *how* it works that is interesting. Its geometry, astronomy, zoology, psychology, etc. . . .

Poets can be classified by how much faith they have in truth via "images." It's for the sake of Truth that one makes one's grandmother ride a giraffe—or one does not.

Besides, any day now, "images" will attack poets and demand that they fulfill their promises.

I am not the first one to have said this.

—1980

Gerald Stern
Living in Ruin

From the Gerald Stern issue of Poetry East, *26 (Fall 1988): 21-31.*

I have written one poem after another about living in ruins, and I am only now beginning to ask myself in a serious way what it is I'm doing and why I'm doing it. There certainly is a grand tradition both among the romantics and the high moderns, but I think the issue is too personal with me; I am too possessed, too comfortable even, for it to be a mere literary activity. And I am amazed that I never grow bored with it, that I never exhaust the mine.

I remember in the early 1970s my wife had passed by a burnt-out barracks in old Camp Kilmer, New Jersey, on one of her morning jaunts, and she greeted me with news of her find as if she were some geologist's wife who had discovered a glittering mica bed, or a botanist's wife who had tripped over some rare copulating butterflies. My passion had become public, even domestic. I of course have no shame in these matters and rushed over to size the barracks up before it got suddenly redeemed or razed, and was de-

lighted to see my poem there in the charred doors and the broken glass. I think that was my ruin of ruins for months, for years, and I never grew tired of marvelling at the great gift I was given. I was, in my way, crazier, more obsessive maybe, than that plodding geologist or that greedy botanist. The poem itself is Whitmanian in its anaphora and almost completely literal in its description. The speaker—me, whoever he is—stands in the middle of those ruins as if he were a joyful swimmer standing in the surf, splashing his body with the cold salt. His posture is cosmic, fundamental.

On the Far Edge of Kilmer

I am sitting again on the steps of the burned out
  barrack.
I come here, like Proust or Adam Kadmon, every
  night to watch the sun leave.
I like the broken cinder blocks and the bicycle tires.
I like the exposed fuse system.
I like the color the char takes in the clear light.
I climb over everything and stop before every gro-

tesque relic.
I walk through the tar paper and glass.
I lean against the lilacs.
In my left hand is a bottle of Tango.
In my right hand are the old weeds and power
    lines.
I am watching the glory go down.
I am taking the thing seriously.
I am standing between the wall and the white sky.
I am holding open the burnt door.

I guess it's a kind of "twisted in" sonnet, eight, then six, but the variation, the *breakaway*, not in the last two but the ninth and tenth, although the thirteenth and fourteenth are a conventional summary and generalization.

I loved that barracks, and I loved coming there in the warm evening—it had to be late April or May when I discovered it, when my wife discovered it. I remember the lilacs were almost gone. I think the feelings I had, at the site, were an odd combination of isolation and power. It may be that ruin, that fiery ruin in particular, produces those feelings. The isolation was caused by the remoteness of the barracks, by the peculiar situation of an old army camp being located in the very middle of a fast-growing suburban housing, industrial, and university complex, and most of all, by the total absence of other life and culture. Except detritus. The power—which was connected with the isolation—was caused, I am sure, by that wonderful feeling of survival in the midst of desolation. It must be the feeling a nosy intruder gets the day after a terrible battle or a great natural catastrophe, or the feeling the living get at the grave of an unfortunate. There is a mixture of sadness, wonder, pity, and relief. There was also a certain finality about it, and there was peace, even if there was regret. Those windows would never have to be cleaned again, or that floor swept, or that leaky roof fixed. Most of all, there was a certain joy, a joy at the lucky discovery, a joy at contemplating the beauty, for it was beautiful, a joy in the knowledge and understanding, a joy in the "grand confrontation," a joy in the salvation. And what I delighted in, as much as anything else, was that it was a multiple— at least a double—ruin. The building—I am sure— had been empty a long time before it burned down. As in most such cases, it probably burned *because* it was empty, and neglected. And other visitors had come there before me to write their stories on the wall, to break a few windows, to get drunk, to sleep in the shadows.

When we came back to Pennsylvania, in 1969, we moved into a house that had been empty, my guess is, since the flood of 1955. There was the smell of piss, of dog and cat, of burned wood. The huge porch roof was gone, the walls were shredded, the floors were rotted. My daughter, who was eleven at the time, refused to go beyond the door. And across the road—our property spanned the old highway— was a three car garage with an open grease pit inside, and strips of tar paper on the outside, and a roof that was half gone. Maple was growing in the cellar, poison ivy was everywhere, the grass hadn't been cut, and the trees hadn't been pruned, in years. It was more a wilderness than a ruin, and my friends who came to look at it thought we had gone mad. My poor wife—she went along with my obsession. For all I know it was hers, too: I don't know, we never discussed it. At any rate, it was a true ruin we had moved into; it was as if I was living in my own metaphor. The house was on the Delaware river. It was a crazy neglected pocket of abandoned older homes cheek by jowl with jerry-built newer cottages. The road was two or three city blocks long. Route 611, the highway from Philadelphia to Easton, had been shortened, modernized, widened, thirty, forty years earlier and had bypassed my road. There were four ancient buildings on the three-block stretch, three of them built about 1800, during the canal flowering. One was an old hotel, empty for years, one was our house, and one was a literal ruin, the roof, the floors all gone, two great fireplaces facing each other at opposite ends, strangely unsupported, floating in the air almost, a little woods growing in the former cellar, the pump, the outhouses, whatever else, gone. All three buildings were made of stone, and there was, in addition, a stone powerhouse situated at the lower end of the road between the lock and the river, which forty and fifty years earlier had provided electric energy for the trolley cars that moved through the woods thirty feet above the highway between Easton and all the nearby cities, including Allentown and Stroudsburg and Doylestown and Philadelphia itself. The hotel had been a bar for a while, and before that a whorehouse. I was assured of it by the carpenter and his helper, who remembered everything that happened for a hundred years back, and who remembered it every Saturday.

Almost all the poems I wrote at this time make references to the road and the river and the woods and the half-buried houses. It was either great luck or a great curse—I still don't know which—that I had moved to such a place. It was as if I were no longer inventing my own poems but they were being created for me. I just had to reach out. I still don't know if it was because my life, my psychic life, had arrived at a certain point and I was now ready to write in a new way, or whether I was able to discover this way because of my life. I think I moved to Pennsylvania to a flood-ruined, fire-damaged eighteenth-century stone house because I wanted to try out some new notes, to sing a few odd songs.

There is a poem I wrote in 1970 or 1971 that encapsulates what it is I'm talking about. It's called "Delaware West." I remember that what moved me to write the poem was discovering a collection of soft-porn magazines across the road in my old garage. If that was once an actual commercial garage, or some version of it, and the grease pit was in serious use, the mechanics amused—and thrilled—themselves over lunch by turning the pages of those old issues and making their amazing discoveries over their beer or coffee. I wish I had kept those magazines; they dated from the late forties and early fifties. My God, what treasures they were! Here is the poem:

Delaware West

I walk now along the mule path between the first
    and second locks
and come to rest in my own front yard on the Dela-
    ware River.
I am tearing one world apart and building another.
I have left the Swedes to their own dark spittle and
    the Poles to theirs.
I have discovered tires and bedsprings richer than
    anything in Bjornstrom or Polanski.
I lift one finger to store the crazy ruins of four life
    times
and one foot to the accumulated ash of half a cen-
    tury.
Under the stove, beside the broken window,
I have found the complete collection of *Orgy*.
While the light dies and the river rises
I will push the wasps aside and live in the dark
with the pregnant grandmothers, the rampant dogs
and the paralyzed strippers—
in tearful brotherhood with the grim sots
and the noisy oracles—
two long hours away from the downtown freaks
and the uptown rabbis.

Actually, as I recall, there wasn't a stove beside the broken window. But there was a broken window. Maybe three or four. The magazines were *not* called *Orgy*. Why there has not been a magazine by that name I don't know. Maybe it's too obvious. There were of course wasps, real ones; there always are. I think there *were* pregnant grandmothers and paralyzed strippers. "Rampant dogs" is a minor piece of bestiality I added myself. The "grim sots" and "noisy oracles" were my brothers on the river, the grease monkeys and their friends, making political, sexual, and religious observations. The "downtown freaks" were my friends in Soho; the "uptown rabbis" were my friends at Columbia University. My property extended to the middle of the mule path, the elevated walkway along the canal. At least I was responsible for the mowing. Of course mules were used to pull the barges—full of coal—down to Bristol, Pennsylvania, just north of Philadelphia. That poem gives me great pleasure when I read it now, or maybe it's grief—I sometimes can't tell them apart.

I think I was fascinated with ruin by the time I was nineteen or twenty, maybe earlier. I don't know if I was moved by the same things as the graveyard poets of England and America—I don't know if those things maybe get into the blood—or whether it was something else that had hold of me. Ancient ruins, as such, destroyed cities, pyramids, Buddha gods of the jungle—I have not been as touched by those things as I have by more recent decay and destruction, a ruined coal town in central Pennsylvania, an empty mansion from the 1880s; I want to be able to imagine, I guess, that I could have been there personally, that I could have participated in the life; or maybe it's *official* ruins that don't move me, whether it's Persepolis or Pompeii, and if I could discover my own city of ashes, something Babylonian or southern French or West Virginian, I would be better overcome.

I wrote a poem in the mid 1970s that compared an abandoned house in New Brunswick, New Jersey, and all its accumulated cultural debris, to the ruins of Greece, particularly those of Crete, which I had just returned from. It may be that it was so moving and sad for me because I was a witness—a living witness—to the destruction. I was personally touched. I think the house was built in 1880 or thereabouts and torn down in 1976 as a part of the "rebuilding" of New Brunswick, New Jersey, as a corporate headquarters for Johnson and Johnson and as a satellite city to New York.

If You Forget the Germans

If you forget the Germans climbing up and down
the Acropolis,
then I will forget the poet falling through his rotten floor in New Brunswick;
and if you stop telling me about your civilization in
1400 B.C.,
then I will stop telling you about mine in 1750 and
1820 and 1935;
and if you stop throwing your old walls and your
stone stairs at me,
then I will drop my overstuffed chairs and my rusty
scooters.
—Here is an old leather shoe to look at;
give me anything, a pebble from the Agora, a tile
from Phaistos;
and here is a perfectly intact bottle of Bollo;
give me a delicate red poppy or a purple thistle
growing beside the Parthenon.
Here are the photographs, myself crawling out on
the charred beam,
a carton of Salems, a crib with mattress, a pigeon
feather,
a plywood door, a piece of the blue sky,
a bottle of Smirnoff's, a bottle of Seagram's,
a bottle of Night Train Express.
Show me yours, the oldest theater in Europe,
a woman playing the harp, a marble foot,
a bronze frying pan, a fish swimming in crystal,
a boar's tusk helmet, a god screaming, a painted
eyelid.
Here are the thoughts I have had;
here are the people I have talked to and worn out;
here are the stops in my throat;
here is the ocean throwing up dead crabs and card tables.
—If you go by bus, take the Suburban Transit
and get off if you can before the Highland Park
Bridge.
If you go by car, take route 18 east
past the Riverview Bar and try to park
on either Peace or Church.
If you walk, go north on Church past the old Gra-
mercy
and the health food store and God's Deliverance
Center
to the mound of dirt and the broken telephone
booth.
Do not bury yourself outright in the litter;
walk gently over the broken glass;
admire the pictures on the upstairs rear wall.
Sing and cry and kiss in the ruined dining room
in front of the mirror, in the plush car seat,
a 1949 or '50, still clean and perfect
under the black dust and the newspapers,
as it was when we cruised back and forth all night
looking for happiness;
as it was when we lay down and loved in the old
darkness.

The poem is a kind of mock cataloguing of hopeless objects which have become not only memorials but icons and, if the poem works, assume an almost religious, or magical, value, even as the tone is desperately mocking and ironic. And the poem ends with mock—though precise—directions to the "site" and a sudden explanation of the holiness in the last two lines. The icons were plywood doors and empty bottles of whiskey and old photographs; these I compared to statues and stone stairs and ancient theaters, and though it sounds, as I describe it, almost stupidly provincial and even foolishly patriotic I don't think it comes off that way. I think it expressed the desperation, and sadness, we have all felt as we watched our world being destroyed around us—sometimes maliciously—and it expressed for me, and I hope for others, the personal loss that is the inevitable result of mutability itself and that, in America, perhaps now the world, has been exacerbated almost to a degree of madness. As far as New Brunswick, that poor city, I hate to think what a ghost from 1910 or 1930 would see and would not see if he came back to its clean streets and its heartless buildings.

I ask myself if I'm in any way like the other poets of ruin. I don't have a death's head sitting on my table; I don't have a copy of *Childe Harold* propped open to the solemn visit to Rome, or a copy of King James propped open to Jeremiah's Lament; I am not obsessed with Heliopolis and Crete; or Lisbon and Managua; I am not melancholic—or not excessively so; I don't see history—and life itself—as an exemplar of ruin; I am not always in mourning; I don't overly lament the lost Eden; I am not angry with time; I am not gloomy; I don't have a truly eschatological vision. But my subject is loss; and I am overwhelmed by separation; and I'm obsessed with the past.

There were little woven nests under the eaves and over the pillars of my house in Raubsville, and I used to sit there in my metal chair watching the swallows fly in and out. It was pure ruin, the white walls of my house, the beautiful nests, the shadows. Swallows—they are our souls going back and forth—they are as sure as bats, as swift as eagles, and they are the most graceful and most simple of all birds. Some of those nests were duplexes and the dear mothers and fathers flew in low under the rain spouts with bits of food for their babies. The fragility was overwhelming, the pathos—the delicacy, the vulnerability, the bravery—was unbearable. For whatever reason, my loss was there in those ruins; for whatever reason, my whole life was in those eaves.

My Swallow

For hours I sit here facing the white wall
and the dirty swallows. If I move too much,
I will lose everything, if I even breathe,
I'll lose the round chest and the forked tail and the
nest above the window, under the ceiling.

As far as shame, I think I have lived too long
with only the moonlight coming in to worry
too much about what it looks like. I have given
a part of my mind away, for what it's worth
I have traded half of what I have—

I'll call it half—so I can see these smudges
in the right light. I think I live in ruins
like no one else, I see myself as endlessly
staring at what I lost, I see me mourning
for hours, either worn away with grief

or touched with simple regret, but free this time
to give myself up to loss alone. I mourn
for the clumsy nest and I mourn for the two small
  birds
sitting up there above the curtains watching—
as long as I am there—and I mourn for the sky

that makes it clear and I mourn for my two eyes
that drag me over, that make me sit there singing,
or mumbling or murmuring, at the cost
of almost everything else, my two green eyes,
my brown—my hazel, flecked with green and
  brown—

and this is what I'll do for twenty more years,
if I am lucky—even if I'm not—I'll live
with the swallows and dip through the white shadows
and rest on the eaves and sail above the window.
This is the way I *have* lived, making a life

for more than twenty years—for more than forty—
out of this darkness; it was almost a joy,
almost a pleasure, not to be foolish or maudlin,
sitting against my wall, closing my eyes,
singing my dirges.

If I had to guess, I would say it was the loss of my poor mother—her dislocation and spiritual removal—that gave me my own sense of ruin; and I would say it was the death of my sister when she was nine and I was eight; and I would say it was the destruction of my brothers and sisters in Europe; and I would say it was the crude loss of our culture and religion in the hopeless rush to this dear country; and I would say it was the dropping of the bombs and the vision of annihilation that that generated; and I would say it was the brutality of power that I both witnessed and was permitted to recollect. It was a kind of slaughter, and it was the loss of innocence and trust and hope—of belief itself—in the face of that slaughter. Simple wisdom tells me of other losses as great as ours and of ruin more overwhelming, but this is our time, and it is my disaster, and my portion.

Ruin you carry with you. You don't need a wall—though I love a wall—or some falling birds to bring it on. I am free of my river now and the house we labored over, and the pleasure I had there. Over and over again I have lost everything. What else is there to expect? I live in ruin now as I never have before. It is my own internal exile—though that sounds like self-pity, doesn't it—? Let me just call it—separation. Rage has been my downfall. So has hope. There is nothing to forgive. I live there, with my good demon. Somewhere, on another wall, flowers are blooming and a man is living—he is working—in peace, in harmony. It is a victory.

Orange Roses

I am letting two old roses stand for everything I believe in.
I am restricting the size of the world, keeping it in
  side that plastic pot.
This is like Greece, the roses sitting in the hot sun,
the leaves exhausted,
the blue sky surrounding them.

I reach my fingers inside the dirt
and slowly scrape the sides.
One more flower will bloom the rest of this month,
probably symbolizing the last breath left
after a lifetime of tearful singing.

The wall in back of me is no part of this.
It shows only a large shadow overcome with
  thought.
It shows him in ruins,
his body spread out in all directions,
his pencil uprooted, his own orange roses dark and
  hidden.

Dabney Stuart
Knots into Webs: Some Autobiographical Sources

An article first published in Poets in the South, *2, no. 2 (1980-1984): 5-7.*

I was conceived early in 1937, a gamble more hopeful than it usually is, since neither of my parents was among the few who foresaw the wartime economy that would end the Great Depression. My brother performed his dethroning appearance three years later.

Many random memories from my first seven or eight years—through the end of World War II—remain bright and assertive even now. Walking down the cement sidewalks which the roots of the great oaks arching over Seminary Avenue had heaved into crumbling planes of awkwardness, we chanted, "Step on a crack, break Hitler's back," a change in the old refrain that saved our mothers a lot of discomfort. Tojo was a baldheaded arch-villain whom I had little trouble separating from my maternal grandfather—when I was awake. The drink of the period was "green beer," a concoction of fizz water and a wretchedly sweet green syrup blended by one of the soda jerks at Willey's Drug Store. The innumerable family dinners—fried chicken, mashed potatoes and gravy, peas, fluffy rolls, and in summer, watermelon in the back yard for dessert—at my paternal grandparents' have all smudged into one hodge-podge of parents and aunts on the one hand pressing me into a neat, ironed, well-mannered puppet, and on the other, cousins and friends pulling me into various games where subversive items like dirt and weird language suggested experience might be more complicated and interesting (and fearful) than the alleged grown-ups let on.

Other memories are more complicated. Our street was on the north end of Richmond, Virginia, two-and-a-half blocks from the city limits. The house my father had built—brick, two-story, three compact bedrooms—was one of the first in Ginter Park, which would now be called a "subdivision" or "development," so the neighborhood was still essentially country. Elms and oaks lined the sidewalks, their leaves a real nuisance in the fall. My father, and later our neighbors, would rake them into wide piles at the edge of the street (curbs, gutters, and uniform pavements came later) and burn them in the late afternoons.

I can still see the ash spreading like a stain on the swollen surface of the leaves, the widening ring of flame seeming to go out when it reached the edges. After a minute thick white smoke billowed from air gaps in the piles, and then from the depths the flames would suddenly burst out again. I can hear the acorns popping, their sound thicker than I expected because they had settled deeply in the leaves. Sometimes one would hiss, or whistle. The smoke climbed into the bare limbs of the trees, thinning, becoming the gathering dark.

When I was five years old, the summer before I entered public school, I almost drowned. All the stories I've heard since then present the incident as accidental. I remember sitting on a dock of weathered gray boards at my maternal grandparents' place on Hampton Creek in Hampton, Virginia. My grandfather is in the bowels of his boat curing the engine of some ailment. I push the bow of the boat away from the dock with my toes. It eases away from me, reaches the end of the line, groans, swings back. I push it again. Over and over, a ritual. My grandfather's bald head appears above the raised floor flaps of the engine box. A tool rattles against something. He curses God, questions the tool's ancestry, bends down, disappears. I push again, but this time the momentum carries my little body off the edge of the dock into the water. I can't swim.

But I can still see my arms breaststroking through the thick green water, feel my legs frogging behind. Like I was born there. My breath spills out of my mouth and nose in a chain of endless bright bubbles. I am aiming at a barnacled support post of the dock.

I never try to surface.

My grandfather pulled me out, though I don't recall that part at all. On the other side of that gap I see myself flailing in his arms, pounding his chest with my fists, for all the world as if I want to fall in again.

And one other. My father's wholesale hardware office on 14th Street near the James River adjoined a warehouse which to my small perspective seemed huge, an indecipherable warren of enormous storage rooms and tiny cubbies, connected by mysterious passageways. Though the building looked from the outside like it rose only three or four stories, there were at least seven levels inside. From the top level a metal chute spiralled down, polished to a high gloss by the boxes that slid on it to the loading dock on East Cary Street.

To get to the beginning of that chute and slide down it myself—a favorite Saturday morning pastime—meant either climbing endless lonely stairs, or going up on the freight elevator, which was also scary. It was a wooden elevator, open on two sides, with a heavy steel bar arching over the top, also open. As the elevator rose the bar pushed aside the wooden safety flaps at each level, parting them slowly upward until they lay flush against the sides of the shaft as we passed. To say the ride was rickety is like saying water is wet.

The dim lightbulbs at each level kept a perpetual twilight. It was impossible not to be intimate with the mechanical parts, too; you pulled ropes to start and stop the thing, and the drive belt looped lazily past in the shaft as you ascended. The only reason I rode the elevator instead of climbing the stairs was that one of the warehouse men had to operate it. I wasn't all by myself.

There are, of course, other such memories, some of which I haven't begun to explore, but these will do to suggest the sources of poetry for me. Knots of memory wound tightly into the dark, knots which through (and sometimes in spite of) language I try not to untie but to lighten and spread, as if into webs, so that what once was hidden and undifferentiated might become more open, its reticulate complexity more accessible, its truth touching and useful to myself and, I hope, to others as well. It's not that responsibilities begin in dreams so much as in these knots of memory to which our dreams may sometimes give access.

Much has happened to me since childhood, but I doubt I would have written poetry about any of it were it not for these radiant, determinant experiences. My responses to my own children—a daughter and two sons—my difficulties with marriage and family life, my belated consciousness that Adam's curse is mine, too, and so on, echo the experience of millions, and are unremarkable. Though they are fit material for poems, as is so much other, less personal material I have used (and use), none of it seems necessarily connected to the mysterious, primary activities from which the impulse toward poetry derives. But the spreading ash on those leaves, the smoke thinning into the night, that chain of bubbles, the dim steel arc parting the flaps as the elevator rose, do.

Although the psychic processes I understand to be the sources of poetry may sometimes result in release and balance in the actual writing of a poem, writing poems and psychotherapy are obviously not the same. Under the best circumstances a poem's inception and associative growth will be inseparably woven with formal, aesthetic choices; the two halves of the brain pedal out their stitching and unstitching as one organ, the way they're supposed to. The formal qualities of a poem, however, are perceptible to eye and ear and, in an essay like this, it seems more appropriate to note the less easily discernible configurations.

Checklist of Further Resources

Allen, Donald M., ed. *The New American Poetry: 1945-1960*. New York: Grove, 1960.

Allen and Warren Tallman, eds. *Poetics of the New American Poetry*. New York: Grove, 1974.

Altieri, Charles. *Enlarging the Temple: New Directions in American Poetry During the 1960s*. Lewisburg, Pa.: Bucknell University Presses / London: Associated University Presses, 1979.

Altieri. *Self and Sensibility in Contemporary American Poetry*. New York: Cambridge University Press, 1984.

Ashbery, John, ed. *The Best American Poetry 1988*. New York: Scribners, 1988.

Bawer, Bruce. *The Middle Generation: The Lives and Poetry of Delmore Schwartz, Randall Jarrell, John Berryman, and Robert Lowell*. Hamden, Conn.: Archon, 1986.

Bell, Marvin. *Old Snow Just Melting*. Ann Arbor: University of Michigan Press, 1983.

Berg, Stephen, and Robert Mezey, eds. *Naked Poetry: Recent American Poetry in Open Forms*. Indianapolis: Bobbs-Merrill, 1969.

Berg and Mezey, eds. *The New Naked Poetry: Recent American Poetry in Open Forms*. Indianapolis: Bobbs-Merrill, 1976.

Berke, Roberta Elzey. *Bounds Out of Bounds: A Compass for Recent American and British Poetry*. New York: Oxford University Press, 1981.

Biggs, Mary. *A Gift that Cannot Be Refused: The Writing and Publishing of Contemporary American Poetry*. New York: Greenwood Press, 1990.

Bigsby, C. W. E., ed. *The Black American Writer*. De Land, Fla.: Everett/Edwards, 1969.

Bloom, Harold. *Figures of Capable Imagination*. New York: Seabury Press, 1976.

Bloom, ed. *American Poetry 1915-1945*. New York: Chelsea House, 1987.

Bloom, ed. *American Poetry 1946-1965*. New York: Chelsea House, 1987.

Bloom, ed. *Contemporary Poets*. New York: Chelsea House, 1987.

Bly, Robert. *Talking All Morning*. Ann Arbor: University of Michigan Press, 1980.

Boyars, Robert, ed. *Contemporary Poetry in America*. New York: Schocken Books, 1974.

Breslin, James E. B. *From Modern to Contemporary: American Poetry: 1945-1965*. Chicago & London: University of Chicago Press, 1984.

Cambon, Glauco. *Recent American Poetry*. Minneapolis: University of Minnesota Press, 1962.

Cargas, Harry J. *Daniel Berrigan and Contemporary Protest Poetry*. New Haven, Conn.: College & University Press, 1972.

Carr, John, ed. *Kite-Flying and Other Irrational Acts: Conversations with Twelve Southern Writers*. Baton Rouge: Louisiana State University Press, 1972.

Carruth, Hayden. *Effluences from the Sacred Caves*. Ann Arbor: University of Michigan Press, 1983.

Charters, Samuel. *Some Poems/Poets: Studies in American Underground Poetry Since 1945*. Berkeley: Oyez, 1971.

Clark, Tom. *The Poetry Beat*. Ann Arbor: University of Michigan Press, 1990.

Conversations with Writers, 2 volumes. Detroit: Bruccoli Clark/Gale Research, 1977, 1978.

Cooke, Bruce. *The Beat Generation*. New York: Scribners, 1971.

Dacey, Philip, and David Jauss, eds. *Strong Measures: Contemporary American Poetry in Traditional Forms*. New York: Harper & Row, 1986.

David, Lloyd, and Robert Irwin, eds. *Contemporary American Poetry: A Checklist*. Metuchen, N.J.: Scarecrow, 1975.

Deodene, Frank, and William P. French, eds. *Black American Poetry Since 1944: A Preliminary Checklist*. Chatham, N.J.: Chatham Bookseller, 1971.

Dickey, James. *Babel to Byzantium: Poets & Poetry Now*. New York: Farrar, Straus & Giroux, 1968.

Dickey. *Spinning the Crystal Ball: Some Guesses at the Future of American Poetry*. Washington, D.C.: Library of Congress, 1967.

Dickey. *The Suspect in Poetry*. Madison, Minn.: Sixties Press, 1964.

DiYanni, Robert, ed. *Modern American Poets: Their Voices and Visions*. New York: Random House, 1987.

Dodsworth, Martin, ed. *The Survival of Poetry: A Contemporary Survey*. London: Faber & Faber, 1970.

Duberman, Martin. *Black Mountain: An Exploration in Community*. New York: Dutton, 1972.

Ellmann, Richard, and Robert O'Clair, eds. *The Norton Anthology of Modern Poetry*. Second edition. New York: Norton, 1988.

Ehrhart, W. D., ed. *Carrying the Darkness: The Poetry of the Vietnam War*. Lubbock: Texas Tech University Press, 1989.

Ehrhart, ed. *Unaccustomed Mercy: Soldier-Poets of the Vietnam War*. Lubbock: Texas Tech University Press, 1989.

Feirstein, Frederick, ed. *Expansive Poetry: Essays on the New Narrative & the New Formalism*. Santa Cruz: Story Line Press, 1989.

Feldman, Gene, and Max Gartenberg, eds. *The Beat Generation and the Angry Young Men*. New York: Citadel, 1958.

Fifty Years of American Poetry: Anniversary Volume for the Academy of American Poets. New York: Abrams, 1984.

First Printings of American Authors, 4 vols. Detroit: Bruccoli Clark/Gale Research, 1977-1979.

Fox, Hugh, ed. *The Living Underground: An Anthology of Contemporary American Poets*. New York: Whitsun, 1973.

Francis, Robert. *Pot Shots at Poetry*. Ann Arbor: University of Michigan Press, 1980.

French, Warren, ed. *The Fifties: Fiction, Poetry, Drama*. De Land, Fla.: Everett/Edwards, 1970.

Gallagher, Tess. *A Concert of Tenses*. Ann Arbor: University of Michigan Press, 1986.

Gayle, Addison, Jr., ed. *Black Expression: Essays by and about Black Americans in the Creative Arts*. New York: Weybright & Talley, 1969.

Gershator, Phillis, ed. *A Bibliographic Guide to the Literature of Contemporary American Poetry, 1970-1975*. Metuchen, N.J.: Scarecrow, 1976.

Glicksberg, Charles I. *The Sexual Revolution in Modern American Literature*. New York: Humanities Press, 1972.

Gould, Joan. *Modern American Women Poets*. New York: Dodd, Mead, 1984.

Graham, Jorie, ed. *The Best American Poetry 1990*. New York: Scribners, 1990.

Guttman, Allen. *The Jewish Writer in America: Assimilation and the Crisis of Identity*. New York: Oxford University Press, 1971.

Haines, John. *Living Off the Country*. Ann Arbor: University of Michigan Press, 1981.

Hall, Donald. *Goatfoot Milktongue Twinbird*. Ann Arbor: University of Michigan Press, 1978.

Hall. *Poetry and Ambition*. Ann Arbor: University of Michigan Press, 1988.

Hall. *The Weather for Poetry*. Ann Arbor: University of Michigan Press, 1982.

Hall, ed. *The Best American Poetry 1989*. New York: Scribners, 1989.

Hall, ed. *Contemporary American Poetry*. Baltimore: Penguin, 1962.

Halpern, Daniel, ed. *The American Poetry Anthology*. New York: Avon, 1975.

Hamilton, Ian. *A Poetry Chronicle*. New York: Barnes & Noble, 1973.

Harris, Marie, and Kathleen Aguero, eds. *An Ear to the Ground: An Anthology of Contemporary American Poetry*. Athens: University of Georgia Press, 1989.

Hassan, Ihab. *Contemporary American Literature, 1945-1972: An Introduction*. New York: Ungar, 1973.

Hayden, Robert. *Collected Prose*. Ann Arbor: University of Michigan Press, 1984.

Henderson, Stephen, ed. *Understanding the New Black Poetry*. New York: Morrow, 1973.

Heyen, William, ed. *American Poets in 1976*. Indianapolis: Bobbs-Merrill, 1976.

Hill, Herbert, ed. *Anger and Beyond: The Negro Writer in the United States*. New York: Harper & Row, 1966.

Hine, Daryl, and Joseph Parisi, eds. *The "Poetry" Anthology 1912-1977*. Boston: Houghton Mifflin, 1978.

Hoffman, Daniel, ed. *American Poetry and Poetics*. Garden City, N.Y.: Doubleday, 1962.

Hoffman, ed. *Harvard Guide to Contemporary American Writing*. Cambridge & London: Belknap Press of Harvard University Press, 1979.

Hoffman, ed. *New Poets 1970*. Philadelphia: Department of English, University of Pennsylvania, 1970.

Hollander, John, ed. *Modern Poetry: Essays in Criticism*. London, Oxford & New York: Oxford University Press, 1968.

Howard, Richard. *Alone with America: Essays on the Art of Poetry in the United States since 1950*. Enlarged edition. New York: Atheneum, 1980.

Howard, ed. *Preferences: 51 American Poets Choose Poems From Their Own Work and From the Past*. New York: Viking, 1974.

Ignatow, David. *Open Between Us*. Ann Arbor: University of Michigan Press, 1980.

Ignatow, ed. *Political Poetry*. New York: Chelsea, 1960.

Juhasz, Suzanne. *Naked and Fiery Forms: Modern American Poetry by Women, A New Tradition*. New York: Harper & Row, 1976.

Justice, Donald. *Platonic Scripts*. Ann Arbor: University of Michigan Press, 1984.

Kalstone, David. *Five Temperaments*. New York: Oxford University Press, 1977.

Kazin, Alfred. *Contemporaries*. Boston: Little, Brown, 1962.

Keller, Lynn. *Remaking It New: Contemporary American Poetry and the Modern Tradition*. New York: Cambridge University Press, 1987.

Kinnell, Galway. *Walking Down the Stairs*. Ann Arbor: University of Michigan Press, 1978.

Kostelanetz, Richard. *The Old Poetries and the New*. Ann Arbor: University of Michigan Press, 1981.

Kostelanetz, ed. *The Young American Writers: Fiction, Poetry, Drama, and Criticism*. New York: Funk & Wagnalls, 1967.

Kumin, Maxine. *To Make a Prairie*. Ann Arbor: University of Michigan Press, 1979.

Lacey Paul A. *The Inner War: Forms and Themes in Recent American Poetry*. Philadelphia: Fortress Press, 1972.

Leary, Paris, and Robert Kelly, eds. *A Controversy of Poets*. Garden City, N.Y.: Anchor, 1965.

Lee, Al, ed. *The Major Young Poets*. New York: Meridian, 1971.

Lehman, David, ed. *Ecstatic Occasions, Expedient Forms: 65 Leading Contemporary Poets Select and Comment on Their Poems*. New York: Collier, 1987.

Lensing, George S., and Ronald Moran. *Four Poets and the Emotive Imagination: Robert Bly, James Wright, Louis Simpson, and William Stafford*. Baton Rouge: Louisiana State University Press, 1976.

Lepper, Gary M. *A Bibliographical Introduction to Seventy-Five Modern American Authors*. Berkeley: Serendipity Books, 1976.

Levertov, Denise. *The Poet in the World*. New York: New Directions, 1973.

Levine, Philip. *Don't Ask*. Ann Arbor: University of Michigan Press, 1981.

Libby, Anthony. *Mythologies of Nothing: Mystical Death in American Poetry 1940-1970*. Urbana & Chicago: University of Illinois Press, 1984.

Lieberman, Laurence. *Unassigned Frequencies*. Urbana: University of Illinois Press, 1977.

Logan, John. *A Ballet for the Ear*. Ann Arbor: University of Michigan Press, 1983.

Malkoff, Karl. *Crowell's Handbook of Contemporary American Poetry*. New York: Crowell, 1973.

Malkoff. *Escape from the Self: A Study in Contemporary American Poetry and Poetics*. New York: Columbia University Press, 1977.

Margolies, Edward. *Native Sons: A Critical Study of Twentieth-Century Negro American Authors*. Philadelphia & New York: Lippincott, 1968.

Martin, Robert K. *The Homosexual Tradition in American Poetry*. Austin: University of Texas Press, 1979.

Martz, William J., ed. *The Distinctive Voice*. Glenview, Ill.: Scott, Foresman, 1966.

Matthews, William. *Curiosities*. Ann Arbor: University of Michigan Press, 1989.

Mazzaro, Jerome. *Postmodern American Poetry*. Urbana & Chicago: University of Illinois Press, 1980.

Mazzaro, ed. *Modern American Poets*. New York: McKay, 1970.

McCorkle, James. *The Still Performance: Writing, Self, and Interconnection in Five Postmodern American Poets*. Charlottesville: University Press of Virginia, 1989.

McDowell, Robert, ed. *Poetry After Modernism*. Brownsville, Oreg: Story Line Press, 1990.

Mersmann, James F. *Out of the Vietnam Vortex: A Study of Poets and Poetry Against the War*. Lawrence: University Press of Kansas, 1974.

Mills, Ralph J., Jr. *Cry of the Human: Essays on Contemporary American Poetry*. Urbana & Chicago: University of Illinois Press, 1975.

Molesworth, Charles. *The Fierce Embrace: A Study of Contemporary American Poetry*. Columbia & London: University of Missouri Press, 1979.

Morse, Carl, and Joan Larkin, eds. *Gay and Lesbian Poetry in Our Time*. New York: St. Martin's Press, 1988.

Moss, Howard, ed. *The Poet's Story*. New York: Macmillan, 1973.

Myers, Carol Fairbanks. *Women in Literature: Criticism of the Seventies*. Metuchen, N.J.: Scarecrow, 1976.

Myers, Jack, and Michael Sims. *The Longman Dictionary of Poetic Terms*. New York: Longman, 1989.

Nielsen, Aldon Lynn. *Reading Race: White American Poets and the Racial Discourse in the 20th Century*. Athens: University of Georgia Press, 1988.

Nims, John Frederick. *A Local Habitation*. Ann Arbor: University of Michigan Press, 1985.

Oberg, Arthur. *Modern American Lyric*. New Brunswick: Rutgers University Press, 1977.

O'Brien, John, ed. *Interviews with Black Writers*. New York: Liveright, 1973.

Ostriker, Alicia. *Stealing the Language: The Emergence of Women's Poetry in America*. Boston: Beacon, 1986.

Ostriker. *Writing Like a Woman*. Ann Arbor: University of Michigan Press, 1983.

Packard, William, ed. *The Craft of Poetry: Interviews from the New York Quarterly*. Garden City, N.Y.: Doubleday, 1974.

Padgett, Ron, and David Shapiro, eds. *An Anthology of New York Poets*. New York: Vintage, 1970.

Paolucci, Anne, ed. *Dante's Influence on American Writers, 1776-1976*. New York: Griffon House for the Dante Society of America, 1977.

Parkinson, Thomas, ed. *A Casebook on The Beats*. New York: Crowell, 1961.

Paul, Sherman. *In Search of the Primitive: Rereading David Antin, Jerome Rothenberg, and Gary Snyder*. Baton Rouge: Louisiana State University Press, 1986.

Perkins, David. *A History of Modern Poetry*, 2 volumes. Cambridge: Belknap Press of Harvard University Press, 1987.

Perloff, Marjorie. *Frank O'Hara: Poet among Painters*. New York: Braziller, 1977.

Perloff. *The Poetics of Indeterminacy: Rimbaud to Cage*. Princeton: Princeton University Press, 1981.

Peters, Robert. *Hunting the Snark: A Compendium of New Poetic Terminology*. New York: Paragon House, 1989.

Phillips, Robert. *The Confessional Poets*. Carbondale: Southern Illinois University Press, 1973.

Piercy, Marge. *Parti-Colored Blocks for a Quilt*. Ann Arbor: University of Michigan Press, 1982.

Pinsky, Robert. *The Situation in Poetry: Contemporary Poetry and Its Tradition*. Princeton: Princeton University Press, 1976.

Pope, Deborah. *A Separate Vision: Isolation in American Women Poets*. Baton Rouge: Louisiana State University Press, 1984.

Poulin, A., Jr., ed. *Contemporary American Poetry*. Fourth edition. Boston: Houghton Mifflin, 1985.

"Power of the Word" [television series], Bill Moyers, host. PBS, 15 September - 20 October 1989 [available on videocassette from PBS, P.O. Box 68618, Indianapolis, Ind. 46286].

Prunty, Wyatt. *"Fallen from the Symboled World": Precedents for the New Formalism*. New York: Oxford University Press, 1990.

Ramsey, Paul, ed. *Contemporary Religious Poetry*. Mahwah, N.J.: Paulist Press, 1987.

Ransom, John Crowe, Delmore Schwartz, and John Hall Wheelock. *American Poetry at Mid-Century*. Washington, D.C.: Library of Congress, 1958.

Rexroth, Kenneth. *American Poetry in the Twentieth Century*. New York: Herder & Herder, 1971.

Richman, Robert. *The Direction of Poetry: An Anthology of Rhymed and Metered Verse Written in the English Language Since 1975*. Boston: Houghton Mifflin, 1988.

Rosenthal, M. L. *The Modern Poets: A Critical Introduction*. London, Oxford & New York: Oxford University Press, 1960.

Sexton, Anne. *No Evil Star*. Ann Arbor: University of Michigan Press, 1985.

Shaw, Robert B., ed. *American Poets Since 1960: Some Critical Perspectives*. Cheadle, England: Carcanet Press, 1973.

Simic, Charles. *The Uncertain Certainty*. Ann Arbor: University of Michigan Press, 1985.

Simic. *Wonderful Words, Silent Truth*. Ann Arbor: University of Michigan Press, 1990.

Simpson, Louis. *The Character of the Poet*. Ann Arbor: University of Michigan Press, 1986.

Simpson, *Collected Prose*. New York: Paragon House, 1989.

Simpson. *A Company of Poets*. Ann Arbor: University of Michigan Press, 1981.

Slesinger, Warren, ed. *Spreading the Word: Editors on Poetry*. Columbia, S.C.: Bench Press, 1990.

Smith, Dave, and David Bottoms, eds. *The Morrow Anthology of Younger American Poets*. New York: Quill, 1985.

Spears, Monroe K. *Dionysus and the City: Modernism in Twentieth Century Poetry*. New York: Oxford University Press, 1970.

Stafford, William. *Writing the Australian Crawl*. Ann Arbor: University of Michigan Press, 1986.

Stafford. *You Must Revise Your Life*. Ann Arbor: University of Michigan Press, 1978.

Steele, Timothy. *Missing Measures: Modern Poetry and the Revolt Against Meter.* Fayetteville: University of Arkansas Press, 1990.

Steinman, Lisa Malinowski. *Made in America: Science, Technology, and American Modern Poets.* New Haven: Yale University Press, 1987.

Stepanchev, Stephen. *American Poetry Since 1945: A Critical Survey.* New York: Harper & Row, 1965.

Stokesbury, Leon, ed. *Articles of War: A Collection of American Poetry About World War II.* Fayetteville: University of Arkansas Press, 1990.

Stokesbury, ed. *The Made Thing: An Anthology of Contemporary Southern Poetry.* Fayetteville: University of Arkansas Press, 1987.

Strand, Mark, ed. *The Contemporary American Poets: American Poetry Since 1940.* New York: World, 1969.

Turco, Lewis Putnam. *The New Book of Forms: A Handbook of Poetics.* Hanover, N.H.: University Presses of New England, 1986.

Turco. *Visions and Revisions of American Poetry.* Fayetteville: University of Arkansas Press, 1986.

Turner, Alberta, ed. *50 Contemporary Poets: The Creative Process.* New York: Longman, 1977.

Turner, ed. *45 Contemporary Poets: The Creative Process.* New York: Longman, 1985.

Turner, Darwin T. *Afro-American Writers.* New York: Appleton-Century-Crofts. 1970.

Turner, Frederick. *Natural Classicism: Essays on Literature and Science.* New York: Paragon House, 1985.

Tytell, John. *Naked Angels: The Lives and Literature of the Beat Generation.* New York: McGraw-Hill, 1976.

Vendler, Helen. *Part of Nature, Part of Us: Modern American Poets.* Cambridge: Harvard University Press, 1980.

Vendler, ed. *The Harvard Book of Contemporary Poetry.* Cambridge: Belknap Press of Harvard University Press, 1985.

Vendler, ed. *Voices & Visions: The Poet in America.* New York: Random House, 1987.

Vinson, James, and D. L. Kirkpatrick, eds. *Contemporary Poets.* Third edition. New York: St. Martin's, 1985.

Von Hallberg, Robert. *American Poetry and Culture 1945-1980.* Cambridge: Harvard University Press, 1985.

Waggoner, Hyatt H. *American Poets: From the Puritans to the Present.* Revised edition. Baton Rouge: Louisiana State University Press, 1984.

Wakoski, Diane. *Creating a Personal Mythology.* Los Angeles: Black Sparrow Press, 1975.

Wakoski. *Toward a New Poetry.* Ann Arbor: University of Michigan Press, 1980.

Wallace, Ronald, ed. *Vital Signs: Contemporary American Poetry from the University Presses*. Madison: University of Wisconsin Press, 1989.

Williamson, Alan. *Introspection and Contemporary Poetry*. Cambridge: Harvard University Press, 1984.

Wright, Charles. *Halflife*. Ann Arbor: University of Michigan Press, 1988.

Wright, James. *Collected Prose*. Ann Arbor: University of Michigan Press, 1982.

Writers at Work: The "Paris Review" Interviews, 8 volumes. New York: Viking, 1958-1988.

"Writers' Workshop" [television series], William Price Fox, host. PBS/SCETV, 1982 [available on videocassette from SCETV, 2712 Millwood Avenue, Columbia, S.C. 29205-1221].

Zaranka, William, ed. *The Brand-X Anthology of Poetry*. Cambridge: Apple-Wood Books, 1981.

Contributors

Wendy Barker ....*University of Texas at San Antonio*
David Bergman...*Towson State University*
Patrick Bizzaro...*East Carolina University*
Matthew C. Brennan ....*Indiana State University*
John W. Crawford...*Henderson State University*
Robert Darling ....*Keuka College*
Chard deNiord...*Putney School*
Thomas F. Dillingham ....*Stephens College*
SuAnne Doak...*Cisco Junior College*
Barbara Drake ....*Linfield College*
Marsha Engelbrecht..*Bakersfield, California*
Richard Flynn ....*Georgia Southern University*
Forrest Gander ....*Providence College*
Jane Greer ....*Plains Poetry Journal*
R. S. Gwynn ....*Lamar University*
Charles Hood...*Antelope Valley College*
Jane Hoogestraat.....................................*Southwest Missouri State University*
Robert E. Hosmer, Jr. ....*Smith College*
James T. Jones ....*Southwest Missouri State University*
David Kirby..*Florida State University*
Judith Kitchen...........................*State University of New York College at Brockport*
John Lang..*Emory & Henry College*
Robert McPhillips...*Iona College*
Richard B. Sale ....*University of North Texas*
Leon Stokesbury ....*Georgia State University*
James T. F. Tanner...*University of North Texas*
David Bergman...*Towson State University*
Keith Tuma ....*Miami University*
Steven Wilson..*Southwest Texas State University*
Charlotte M. Wright ....*University of North Texas*

Cumulative Index

Dictionary of Literary Biography, Volumes 1-105
Dictionary of Literary Biography Yearbook, 1980-1989
Dictionary of Literary Biography Documentary Series, Volumes 1-8

Cumulative Index

DLB before number: *Dictionary of Literary Biography*, Volumes 1-105
Y before number: *Dictionary of Literary Biography Yearbook*, 1980-1989
DS before number: *Dictionary of Literary Biography Documentary Series*, Volumes 1-8

A

B

C

D

F

G

L

N

O

Q

R

S

T

(Continued from front endsheets)

80: *Restoration and Eighteenth-Century Dramatists,* First Series, edited by Paula R. Backscheider (1989)

81: *Austrian Fiction Writers, 1875-1913,* edited by James Hardin and Donald G. Daviau (1989)

82: *Chicano Writers,* First Series, edited by Francisco A. Lomelí and Carl R. Shirley (1989)

83: *French Novelists Since 1960,* edited by Catharine Savage Brosman (1989)

84: *Restoration and Eighteenth-Century Dramatists,* Second Series, edited by Paula R. Backscheider (1989)

85: *Austrian Fiction Writers After 1914,* edited by James Hardin and Donald G. Daviau (1989)

86: *American Short-Story Writers, 1910-1945,* First Series, edited by Bobby Ellen Kimbel (1989)

87: *British Mystery and Thriller Writers Since 1940,* First Series, edited by Bernard Benstock and Thomas F. Staley (1989)

88: *Canadian Writers, 1920-1959,* Second Series, edited by W. H. New (1989)

89: *Restoration and Eighteenth-Century Dramatists,* Third Series, edited by Paula R. Backscheider (1989)

90: *German Writers in the Age of Goethe, 1789-1832,* edited by James Hardin and Christoph E. Schweitzer (1989)

91: *American Magazine Journalists, 1900-1960,* First Series, edited by Sam G. Riley (1990)

92: *Canadian Writers, 1890-1920,* edited by W. H. New (1990)

93: *British Romantic Poets, 1789-1832,* First Series, edited by John R. Greenfield (1990)

94: *German Writers in the Age of Goethe: Sturm und Drang to Classicism,* edited by James Hardin and Christoph E. Schweitzer (1990)

95: *Eighteenth-Century British Poets,* First Series, edited by John Sitter (1990)

96: *British Romantic Poets, 1789-1832,* Second Series, edited by John R. Greenfield (1990)

97: *German Writers from the Enlightenment to Sturm und Drang, 1720-1764,* edited by James Hardin and Christoph E. Schweitzer (1990)

98: *Modern British Essayists,* First Series, edited by Robert Beum (1990)

99: *Canadian Writers Before 1890,* edited by W. H. New (1990)

100: *Modern British Essayists,* Second Series, edited by Robert Beum (1990)

101: *British Prose Writers, 1660-1800,* First Series, edited by Donald T. Siebert (1991)

102: *American Short-Story Writers, 1910-1945,* Second Series, edited by Bobby Ellen Kimbel (1991)

103: *American Literary Biographers,* First Series, edited by Steven Serafin (1991)

104: *British Prose Writers, 1660-1800,* Second Series, edited by Donald T. Siebert (1991)

105: *American Poets Since World War II,* Second Series, edited by R. S. Gwynn (1991)

Documentary Series

1: *Sherwood Anderson, Willa Cather, John Dos Passos, Theodore Dreiser, F. Scott Fitzgerald, Ernest Hemingway, Sinclair Lewis,* edited by Margaret A. Van Antwerp (1982)

2: *James Gould Cozzens, James T. Farrell, William Faulkner, John O'Hara, John Steinbeck, Thomas Wolfe, Richard Wright,* edited by Margaret A. Van Antwerp (1982)

3: *Saul Bellow, Jack Kerouac, Norman Mailer, Vladimir Nabokov, John Updike, Kurt Vonnegut,* edited by Mary Bruccoli (1983)

4: *Tennessee Williams,* edited by Margaret A. Van Antwerp and Sally Johns (1984)

5: *American Transcendentalists,* edited by Joel Myerson (1988)

6: *Hardboiled Mystery Writers,* edited by Matthew J. Bruccoli and Richard Layman (1989)

7: *Modern American Poets,* edited by Karen L. Rood (1989)

8: *The Black Aesthetic Movement,* edited by Jeffrey Louis Decker (1991)

Yearbooks

1980, edited by Karen L. Rood, Jean W. Ross, and Richard Ziegfeld (1981)